A Commentary on the Order of Mass of *The Roman Missal*

A Commentary on the Order of Mass of *The Roman Missal*

A New English Translation

Developed under the Auspices of the Catholic Academy of Liturgy

General Editor

Edward Foley

Associate Editors

John F. Baldovin
Mary Collins
Joanne M. Pierce

Foreword by

His Eminence Cardinal Roger Mahony
Archbishop Emeritus of Los Angeles

A PUEBLO BOOK

Liturgical Press
www.litpress.org

Collegeville, Minnesota

A Pueblo Book published by Liturgical Press

Cover design by David Manahan, OSB. Illustrations by Frank Kacmarcik, OblSB.

1 2 3 4 5 6 7 8 9

Library of Congress Cataloging-in-Publication Data

A commentary on the order of Mass of the Roman missal : a new English translation developed under the auspices of the Catholic Academy of Liturgy ; general editor, Edward Foley ; associate editors, John F. Baldovin, Mary Collins, Joanne M. Pierce ; foreword by Roger Mahony.

p. cm.

"A Pueblo book."

Includes index.

ISBN 978-0-8146-6247-2 — ISBN 978-0-8146-6256-4 (e-book)

1. Catholic Church. Missale Romanum (1970) 2. Catholic Church—Liturgy—Texts—History and criticism. 3. Missals—Texts. 4. Lord's Supper—Catholic Church—Liturgy—Texts. 5. Mass—Celebration. I. Foley, Edward. II. Baldovin, John F. (John Francis), 1947– III. Collins, Mary, 1935– IV. Pierce, Joanne M. V. Catholic Academy of Liturgy.

BX2015.C58 2011
264'.02036—dc23

2011034410

Contents

Eucharistic Prayers for Reconciliation

Eucharistic Prayer for Use in Masses for Various Needs

The Communion Rite

The Concluding Rites

Foreword

His Eminence
Cardinal Roger Mahony
Archbishop Emeritus of Los Angeles

The publication of *A Commentary on the Order of Mass of the Roman Missal* coincides with the introduction of the new English translation of the Roman Missal in the life of our worshiping communities in English-speaking North America. This volume is intended as a companion to *A Commentary on the General Instruction of the Roman Missal* (Liturgical Press, 2007), which was quickly recognized as an indispensable resource for those charged with understanding and implementing the principles and spirit of the *GIRM*. Taken together, these two commentaries are illustrative of the very best of liturgical scholarship in the English-speaking world at the service of the Church.

The present *Commentary* is in some ways reminiscent of the *New Commentary on the Code of Canon Law* (Paulist Press, 2000). Following the promulgation of the 1983 *Code of Canon Law*, priests, theologians, seminarians, pastoral leaders, bishops and canonists who were faced with thorny canonical questions of interpretation and implementation turned to the pages of the *Commentary* to seek counsel from reliable scholars such as Ladislas Orsy, SJ, and Frederick McManus. Few, if any, were disappointed.

This *Commentary* is the fruit of years of collaboration on the part of a wondrous array of scholars under the guidance and direction of general editor Edward Foley, Capuchin, and his associate editors John Baldovin, SJ, Mary Collins, OSB, and Joanne Pierce. The *Commentary*'s distinguished contributors include David Power, OMI, Catherine Vincie, RSHM, and Michael Witczak. The volume includes both the Latin text and the new English translation of the *Ordo Missae*, with historical, theological, linguistic and mystagogical reflections on every major section of the *Ordo*, excepting the prefaces. The purpose of the volume is to provide a scholarly commentary for bishops, teachers, pastors and students, examining the foundations and principles of the *Order of Mass*. It is both encyclopedic and concise, gathering an immense amount of complex material into an accessible, albeit hefty, volume accompanied by extensive indices, with the English and Latin texts of the *Ordo Missae* at the very heart of the book. This is a constructive work commending the fine work that has been accomplished thus far, and recommending how the ongoing work of translation and liturgical reform can continue to move forward.

Each and every one of the scholars involved in this project shares a deep commitment to ongoing liturgical reform in accord with the principles of the Second Vatican Council's Constitution on the Sacred Liturgy, *Sacrosanctum Concilium*. Thus, the sympathetic presentation of the *Order of Mass* in this volume is not uncritical but, rather, highlights in careful and insightful ways those questions and concerns requiring further reflection and discussion. It is a singular delight for me to offer my heartfelt affirmation and deep appreciation of the work of these scholars in their service of the liturgical life of the Church.

Introduction

As we approach the fiftieth anniversary of the convening of the Second Vatican Council, one can only marvel at the many changes that have taken place in the liturgy over these past five decades. Vernacular celebrations have come to characterize Roman Catholic liturgy around the world, virtually every official ritual in our collective repertoire has been revised—some more than once—and the council's image of full, conscious, and active participation has been realized in many places and in wondrous ways.

At the same time, as historians remind us, the aftermath of any ecumenical council unfolds slowly. For example, the liturgical books that emerged after the Council of Trent (1545–63) sometimes took decades to appear and their full implementation took centuries. Thus, it should be no surprise to contemporary Roman Catholics that the liturgical reforms envisioned by Vatican II continue—and not simply in a clear trajectory from point A to point B, but more as a swinging pendulum through succeeding pontificates, curial directives, and episcopal leadership—as varying interpretations of Vatican II and the direction of its liturgical reforms unfold.

While the promulgation of a new English translation of the Roman Missal (ICEL2010)—the first in almost forty years—is undoubtedly a significant moment for English-speaking Roman Catholics around the world, it may be best to understand it as a midpoint in the current pendulum swing rather than an end point of liturgical reform. Arriving at this translation is the result of an arduous and sometimes contentious process. The twists and turns of this translation process have been so complex that the editors of this volume found it necessary to map out a time line (see xxiii–xxvii below) of the many events that marked this translation process, both for the sake of our readers as well as for our own shared understanding.

The development and writing of this commentary was guided by three primary goals. First, because of the previously noted complexity of this translation process, editors and contributors thought it valuable and necessary to situate ICEL2010 historically and theologically. To that end, we have provided extended essays on the history of vernacular translation as well as an overview of the historical development of the *Ordo Missae* (*OM*) at the beginning of the volume. Furthermore, we have included both historical and theological introductions to each unit of the *OM* examined in this volume. Our intent is to offer an accessible and up-to-date historical introduction to the current Order of Mass. The theological analyses that parallel the historical reflections are designed to provide both systematic examinations of the texts and rites of the *OM* as well as overviews of some of the theological developments that gave rise to them.

A second concern of the editors and authors was to contribute to the pastoral implementation of these texts and rites. To that end, we have provided a general introductory article on mystagogy at the beginning of the volume as well as mystagogical reflections on each of the liturgical units of the *OM* addressed throughout this volume. Furthermore, many of our commentaries on the English translation (ICEL2010) note some of the pastoral challenges that may arise in the presider's proclamation of these texts, offer guidelines on how such texts might be interpreted for intelligible proclamation, and underscore where catechesis will be essential for the proper pastoral reception of such texts.

Finally, recognizing that ICEL2010 is neither the first English translation of the *OM* nor the last, the editors and authors of this volume are committed to the ongoing development of vernacular worship for English-speaking Roman Catholics. Every vernacular translation is an experiment as well as a compromise, both a pastoral gift and a pastoral challenge. Multiple times throughout this volume contributors have recognized that translation is more art than science and thus a most demanding ministry in service of the church's liturgy. Our hope is to contribute to the ongoing development of this ministry by offering an informed and critical analysis of ICEL2010.

Like our previous *A Commentary on the General Instruction of the Roman Missal*, this project was prepared primarily for those in positions of leadership in the church. We hope that bishops, teachers of liturgy and sacramental theology, pastors, directors of liturgy at every level, and those who exercise other forms of liturgical leadership will find this book helpful in their work. At the same time, we have tried to make this commentary accessible to a wide variety of others interested in learning more about the eucharistic liturgy and its current English translation, especially graduate students of the liturgy and those preparing for pastoral ministry.

Mirroring the eucharistic liturgy that stands at the heart of this project, our endeavor has been a collegial one from the outset. Conceived in the context of the Catholic Academy of Liturgy (CAL)—an association of Roman Catholic specialists in liturgy and its allied arts, connected with the North American Academy of Liturgy—this project was shaped through a series of conversations that included many of the nineteen authors who eventually contributed to this commentary. The editorial board was rich in colleagueship, and I am grateful to associate editors John Baldovin, Mary Collins, and Joanne Pierce for their expertise and friendship. We are also grateful to the leadership of CAL for their cosponsorship of this venture. Special thanks to Justin Huyck for his fine work on the indices that accompany this volume, and to Edward Hagman, OFM Cap, for his careful proofreading. Finally, we express our enduring gratitude to Liturgical Press, which has been a strong and constant partner throughout this project. Special thanks are due to Peter Dwyer who has demonstrated unwavering support of CAL and this work accomplished with their sponsorship, and to Hans Christoffersen for his gracious editorial leadership and unabated encouragement in this project. Gratitude is also due to Lauren L. Murphy for her painstaking editorial work and Colleen Stiller who is unflappable as editorial moves to production. This great team from Liturgical Press sets the bar for collaboration. At the same time, any errors in this volume are not to be laid at their doorstep but at mine. I revel in their colleagueship, but take responsibility for this content in all its graces and errors.

In the preface of form II of the Mass for Various Needs and Occasions (see 520–21 below), we acknowledge that being church requires pilgrimaging together through this world. At the same time we praise God during that prayer for accompanying us on this journey and profess faith that God's own Spirit is leading us on this path. Whatever the twists and turns of emerging vernacular liturgy in the Roman Catholic Church, we believe deeply that God's own Spirit is with us on this trek as well, as we pilgrimage toward full, conscious, and active participation for the glory of God and in service to the church and the world.

Edward Foley, Capuchin
Holy Thursday, 2011

Abbreviations, Acronyms, and Identifications

AAS	*Acta Apostolicae Sedis* (Rome: 1909 to present)
ADA	*Acta et Documenta Concilio Oecumenico Vaticano II Apparando, series prima (antepraeparatoria),* 5 vols. (Vatican: Typis Polyglottis Vaticanis, 1960–1961)
ADP	*Acta et Documenta Concilio Oecumenico Vaticano II Apparando, series secunda (praeparatoria),* 3 vols. (Vatican: Typis Polyglottis Vaticanis, 1964–1969)
Andrieu	Michel Andrieu, ed., *Les Ordines Romani du haut moyen-âge*, 5 vols., Spicilegium Sacrum Lovaniense 11, 23, 24, 28, 29 (Louvain, 1931–1961)
ApTrad	Apostolic Tradition
ASSCO	*Acta Synodalia Sacrosancti Concilii Oecumenici Vaticani II*, 4 vols. (Vatican: Typis Polyglottis Vaticanis, 1970–1978, 1980)
Bugnini	Annibale Bugnini, *The Reform of the Liturgy 1948–1975*, trans. Matthew J. O'Connell (Collegeville, MN: Liturgical Press, 1990)
ca.	*circa*
CCL	*Corpus Christianorum, Series Latina* (Turnhout: Brepols, 1954ff.)
CDF	Congregation for the Doctrine of the Faith
CDW	Congregation for Divine Worship
CDWDS	Congregation for Divine Worship and the Discipline of the Sacraments
CE	Common Era
CCC	Catechism of the Catholic Church
CaerEp	*Caeremoniale Episcoporum*, editio typica (Vatican City: Typis Polyglottis Vaticanis, 1985); English trans. ICEL, *Ceremonial of Bishops* (Collegeville, MN: Liturgical Press, 1989)
chap., chaps.	chapter, chapters
CLP	*Comme le prévoit.* Instruction on the translation of liturgical texts for celebrations with a congregation, 25 January 1969. Issued simultaneously in six languages. See "*Comme le prévoit,*" *Notitiae* 5 (1969): 3–12. English version in DOL 838–880.

CSDW	Congregation for Sacraments and Divine Worship
d.	died
DOL	International Commission on English in the Liturgy, *Documents on the Liturgy 1963–1979: Conciliar, Papal, and Curial Texts* (Collegeville, MN: Liturgical Press, 1982). All numbers in this volume refer to the marginal numbers running sequentially throughout DOL.
editio typica	The official Latin text promulgated by the Holy See
ELLC	English Language Liturgical Consultation
EP(s)	eucharistic prayer(s)
EP I	Eucharistic Prayer I
EP II	Eucharistic Prayer II
EP III	Eucharistic Prayer III
EP IV	Eucharistic Prayer IV
EP RI	Eucharistic Prayer for Reconciliation I
EP RII	Eucharistic Prayer for Reconciliation II
EP MVN	Eucharistic Prayer for Use in Masses for Various Needs
EuchPar	*Eucharistiae Participationem*, Circular letter from CDW, *Notitiae* 9 (1973): 193–201, with a short commentary following, 202–8. English trans. in DOL 1975–1993.
Gelasianum	Leo Cunibert Mohlberg, ed., *Liber Sacramentorum Romanae Aeclesiae Ordinis Anni Circuli* (Vat. Reg. lat. 316), *Rerum Ecclesiasticarum Documenta, Series Maior, Fontes* IV (Rome: Herder, 1960)
GIRM1970	ICEL translation of *IGMR1970*
GIRM1975	ICEL translation of *IGMR1975*
GIRM2003	ICEL translation of *IGMR2002*, incorporating adaptations approved for dioceses of the United States
gray book	term introduced in 2003 ICEL Statutes to replace "white book," i.e., indicating that this was a final text for voting by bishops' conferences
green book	the provisional English translation of the Latin text submitted to the various English-speaking bishops' conferences around the world
GS	*Gaudium et spes*, Vatican II "Pastoral Constitution on the Church in the Modern World," 1965
Hadrianum	Jean Deshusses, ed., *Le Sacramentaire Grégorien d'après ses principaux manuscrits*, 2nd ed., Spicilegium Friburgense 16 (Fribourg: Éditions Universitaires, 1979)

ICEL	International Commission on English in the Liturgy
ICEL1973	Original English translation of *Missale Romanum, editio typica* by ICEL, proposed for a five-year period of use *ad experimentum*
ICEL1995	New draft translation of *MR1975*, submitted as a green book to the eleven English-speaking bishops' conferences
ICEL1998	Unpublished ICEL translation of *MR1975*, approved by eleven English-speaking bishops' conferences but never confirmed by Rome
ICEL2003	New draft translation of *MR2002*, submitted as a green book to the eleven English-speaking bishops' conferences
ICEL2006	ICEL translation of *MR2002*, submitted as a gray book, approved by the eleven English-speaking bishops' conferences with multiple corrections
ICEL2008	ICEL translation of the *Ordo Missae* from *MR2002*, submitted by the English-speaking bishops' conferences, and given the *recognitio* by Rome
ICEL2010	ICEL translation of *MR2002* with the 2008 emendations, given the *recognitio* by Rome
ICET	The International Consultation on English Texts
IGMR	*Institutio Generalis Missalis Romani*
IGMR1969	The first version of *IGMR*, associated with *OM1969*
IGMR1970	The second version of *IGMR*, associated with *MR1970*, officially considered the first edition of the *IGMR*
IGMR1972	The third version of *IGMR*, issued in light of Paul VI's *Ministeria quædam* (1972) on first tonsure, minor orders, and the subdiaconate
IGMR1975	The fourth version of *IGMR*, associated with *MR1975*, officially considered the second edition of the *IGMR*
IGMR1983	The fifth version of *IGMR*, issued in light of the 1983 Code of Canon Law
IGMR2000	A preliminary sixth version of the *IGMR*, intended to accompany the *MR editio typica tertia*
IGMR2002	The seventh version of *IGMR*, associated with *MR2002*, officially considered the third edition of the *IGMR*
IntOec	*Inter Oecumenici*, issued by the Sacred Congregation of Rites, 1964; English trans. in DOL 293-391
ITTOM	Introduction to the Order of Mass, issued by the Bishops' Committee on the Liturgy of the USCCB (Washington, DC: USCCB, 2003)

Jasper & Cuming	R. C. D. Jasper and G. C. Cuming, *Prayers of the Eucharist: Early and Reformed*, 3rd ed. (Collegeville, MN: Liturgical Press, 1990)
Johnson	Lawrence Johnson, *Worship in the Early Church: An Anthology of Historical Sources*, 4 vols. (Collegeville, MN: Liturgical Press, 2009)
Jungmann MRR	Josef A. Jungmann, *The Mass of the Roman Rite*, trans. Francis Brunner, 2 vols. (New York: Benziger, 1951 & 1955; reprinted Westminster, MD: Christian Classics, 1986)
Jungmann MS	Josef A. Jungmann, *Missarum sollemnia: Eine genetische Erklärung der römischen Messe*, 5th ed., 2 vols. (Vienna: Herder, 1962)
LitAuth	*Liturgiam Authenticam*, issued by CDWDS in 2001. Published with both Latin text and English trans. in *Liturgiam authenticam: Fifth Instruction on the Vernacular Translation of the Roman Liturgy* (Washington, DC: USCCB, 2001)
LG	*Lumen Gentium*, Vatican II's "Dogmatic Constitution on the Church," 1964
MR	*Missale Romanum*
MR1474	*Missalis Romani Editio Princeps Mediolani Anno 1474 Prelis Mandata*, ed. Anthony Ward and Cuthbert Johnson (Rome: C.L.V-Edizioni Liturgiche, 1996)
MR1570	*Missale Romanum*, promulgated by Pius V; for edition see Sodi-Triacca below
MR1962	*Missale Romanum*, promulgated by John XXIII; for edition, see Sodi-Toniolo below
MR1970	*Missale Romanum, editio typica*, promulgated by Paul VI as *Missale romanum ex decreto sacrosancti oecumenici concilii Vaticani II instauratum auctoritate Pauli PP VI promulgatum* (Città del Vaticano: Typis Polyglottis Vaticanis, 1970)
MR1975	*Missale Romanum, editio typica altera*, promulgated by Paul VI as *Missale romanum ex decreto sacrosancti oecumenici concilii Vaticani II instauratum auctoritate Pauli PP VI promulgatum* (Città del Vaticano: Typis Polyglottis Vaticanis, 1975)
MR2002	*Missale Romanum, editio typica tertia*, promulgated by John Paul II, as *Missale Romanum: ex decreto Sacrosancti Oecumenici Concilii Vaticani II instauratum: auctoritate Pauli PP. VI promulgatum: Ioannis Pauli PP. II cura recognitum* (Città del Vaticano: Typis Polyglottis Vaticanis, 2002), emended in 2008
n., nn.	note, notes
NABRE	New American Bible, Revised Edition

NJBC	*New Jerome Biblical Commentary*, ed. Raymond Brown, Joseph Fitzmyer, Roland Murphy (Englewood Cliffs, NJ: Prentice Hall, 1990)
no., nos.	number, numbers
Nova Vulgata	*Nova Vulgata Bibliorum Sacrorum Editio* (Città del Vaticano: Libreria Editrice Vaticana, 1986)
NRSV	New Revised Standard Version
OHCW	*The Oxford History of Christian Worship*, ed. Geoffrey Wainwright and Karen Westerfield Tucker (Oxford and New York: Oxford University Press, 2006)
OLM1969	*Ordo Lectionum Missae* (Città del Vaticano: Typis Polyglottis Vaticanis, 1969)
OLM1981-Pr	*Proemium* (Introduction) of the *Ordo Lectionum Missae, editio typica altera* (Città del Vaticano: Libreria Editrice Vaticana, 1981)
OM(s)	*Ordo (Ordines) Missae*
OM1969	*Ordo Missae* promulgated by the Sacred Congregation for Divine Worship in 1969, and incorporated into *MR1970*
OM2008	*Ordo Missae* from *MR2002*, emended edition
OR I	*Ordo Romanus Primus*; for the critical edition, see Andrieu above
PG	*Patrologia Graeca*, ed. J. P. Migne, 161 vols. (Paris: 1857–66)
PL	*Patrologia Latina*, ed. J. P. Migne, 221 vols. (Paris: 1844–64)
Prex Eucharistica 1	Anton A. Hänggi and Irmgard Pahl, eds. *Prex Eucharistica: Textus e variis liturgiis antiquioribus selecti*, Spicilegium Friburgense 12 (Fribourg: Éditions universitaires Fribourg Suisse, 1968)
Prex Eucharistica 3	A. Gerhards, H. Brakmann, and M. Klöckener, eds. *Prex Eucharistica III: Studia—Pars Prima: Ecclesia Antiqua et Occidentalis* (Fribourg: Academic Press, 2005)
RCIA	Rite of Christian Initiation of Adults, 1988
SC	*Sacrosanctum Concilium*, Vatican II's "Constitution on the Sacred Liturgy," 1963
SacCar	*Sacramentum Caritatis*, post-synodal exortation of Benedict XVI on the Eucharist, 2007; online at http://www.vatican.va/holy_father/benedict_xvi/apost_exhortations/documents/hf_ben-xvi_exh_20070222_sacramentum-caritatis_en.html
Sodi	Manlio Sodi and Alessandro Toniolo, *Concordantia et Indices Missalis Romani, editio typical tertia* (Città del Vaticano: Libreria Editrice Vaticana, 2002); online at www.liturgia.it/editiotertia.htm

Sodi-Toniolo	*Missale romanum: ex decreto ss. concilii tridentini restitutum summorum pontificum cura recognitum*, ed. Manlio Sodi and Alessandro Toniolo, Monumenta liturgica piana 1 (Città del Vaticano: Libreria Editrice Vaticana, 2007)
Sodi-Triacca	Manlio Sodi and Achille Maria Triacca, eds. *Missale Romanum: editio princeps, 1570* (Città del Vaticano: Libreria editrice vaticana, 1998)
Tanner	Norman Tanner, ed., *Decrees of the Ecumenical Councils*, 2 vols. (London and Washington, DC: Sheed & Ward and Georgetown University Press, 1990)
USCCB	United States Catholic Conference of Bishops
VarLeg	*Varietates Legitimae*, issued by CDWDS, 2004
Veronense	Leo Cunibert Mohlberg, ed., *Sacramentarium Veronense, Rerum Ecclesiasticarum Documenta, Series Maior, Fontes* I (Rome: Herder, 1966)
Vogel	Cyrille Vogel, *Medieval Liturgy: An Introduction to the Sources*, trans. and ed. William Story and Niels Krogh Rasmussen (Portland: Pastoral Press, 1986)
Vulgate	*Biblia Sacra iuxta Vulgatam versionem*, ed. Robert Weber, et al. (Stuttgart: Deutsche Bibelgesellschaft, 1983)
white book	the presumed "final" translation of the Latin text submitted to Rome by various English-speaking conferences of bishops for the *recognitio*; while the term was replaced with "gray book" in 2003 ICEL Statutes, the USCCB called its approved ICEL gray book sent to Rome for *recognitio* in June 2006 its "white book."

Time Line Leading to the New English Translation of the Roman Missal (ICEL2010)[1]

- **17 October 1963**: Bishops representing ten English episcopal conferences (Australia, Canada, England and Wales, India, Ireland, New Zealand, Pakistan, Scotland, South Africa, and the United States) gather at the Venerable English College in Rome to lay the foundation for what would become the International Commission on English in the Liturgy (ICEL)
- **4 December 1963**: *Sacrosanctum Concilium* (*SC*) is promulgated, allowing for vernacular translations of the liturgy
- **25 January 1964**: Paul VI issues *Sacram Liturgiam*, indicating that translations had to be submitted to the Vatican for an official *recognitio*
- **October 1964**: Bishops of ICEL draw up a mandate to guide the work of ICEL's advisory committee, approved by the member conferences of bishops
- **9–13 November 1965**: Concilium holds a conference in Rome with 249 participants from around the world to develop common orientations and general criteria for liturgical translation, eventually leading to the instruction *Comme le prévoit*
- **1966**: ICEL issues *English for the Mass*, the first of over thirty consultation books and study texts sent to the various English-speaking conferences for their comment, discussion, and review
- **31 January 1967**: Paul VI allows the use of the vernacular in the eucharistic prayer *ad experimentum*

[1] This timeline is compiled from official statements of various curial and episcopal leaders, news reports, the personal notes of some individuals involved in the process, the *Annual Report of the Episcopal Board of ICEL to the Member and Associate Member Conferences* (1976, 1988–89, 1990–91, 1992–95, 1996–97), unpublished versions of liturgical texts and instructions, and Peter Finn's time line published in his "ICEL: Alphabet Soup," *Today's Liturgy* (Easter 2003): 14–20.

- **1967**: The Philippines joins the other ten bishops' conferences as the eleventh member of ICEL
- **1967**: ICEL issues the first provisional draft translation, *The Roman Canon*
- **25 January 1969**: The Sacred Congregation of Rites (with Concilium) issues the instruction *Comme le prévoit* (*CLP*), on the translation of liturgical texts for celebrations with a congregation
- **3 April 1969**: Paul VI issues the apostolic constitution *Missale Romanum*, approving the new *Missale Romanum* (*MR1970*), which is to take effect on 30 November 1969 (the First Sunday of Advent)
- **6 April 1969**: The Sacred Congregation of Rites (with Concilium) issues the decree *Ordine Missae*, promulgating the *editio typica* of the *Ordo Missae* (*OM1969*) and issues *Institutio Generalis Missalis Romani* (*IGMR1969*)
- **26 March 1970**: The Sacred Congregation for Divine Worship promulgates the second version of the *Institutio Generalis Missalis Romani* (*IGMR1970*) along with the first *editio typica* of the *Missale Romanum* (*MR1970*)
- **15 May 1972**: The USCC publishes a provisional English text of the *Sacramentary for Sundays and Other Occasions* approved by the Sacred Congregation for Divine Worship on 14 January 1972
- **23 December 1972**: The Sacred Congregation for Divine Worship issues the third version of *Institutio Generalis Missalis Romani* (*IGMR1972*), in light of *Ministeria quædam* (15 August 1972) and its suppression of the subdiaconate
- **1973**: ICEL produces the first translation of *MR1970* (ICEL1973)
- **26 October 1974**: Paul VI issues the decree *Postquam de Precibus*, authorizing the use of Eucharistic Prayers for Reconciliation I and II
- **27 March 1975**: The Sacred Congregation for Divine Worship issues the fourth version of *Institutio Generalis Missalis Romani* (*IGMR1975*), as well as the decree *Cum Missale Romanum* promulgating the *Missale Romanum, editio altera* (*MR1975*)
- **1976:** ICEL forms an ad hoc committee to study the question of inclusive language
- **1976:** ICEL reorganizes to prepare for revising all first-generation translations in light of pastoral experience; three standing subcommittees (on

translation and revision of liturgical texts, original texts, and presentation of texts) are added to the already existing subcommittee on music

- **9 November 1977**: Episcopal board of ICEL announces that it will begin a comprehensive program of revision
- **1980**: ICEL issues the green book *Eucharistic Prayers*, containing interim revisions of the eucharistic prayers introducing more inclusive language
- **1982**: ICEL issues a workbook on the "Revision [of] the Roman Missal—Presidential Prayers"
- **1983**: Revisions are made to the fifth version of the *Institutio Generalis Missalis Romani* (*IGMR1975*) in order to bring it into conformity with the newly revised Code of Canon Law (1983)
- **March 1986**: ICEL issues a workbook to the bishops and consultants of the various English-speaking conferences on the "Revision [of] the Roman Missal Order of Mass"
- **1988**: ICEL issues the first of three progress reports (the others in 1990 and 1992) on the revision of the Roman Missal
- **1992:** Vatican gives permission to employ the New Revised Standard Version of the Bible for liturgical use
- **1993–1996:** The revised Sacramentary in two volumes is issued to English-speaking bishops' conferences in eight parts for their discussion and vote
    - **September 1993**: Segment one—Ordinary Time
    - **April 1994**: Segment two—Proper of Seasons
    - **August 1994**: Segment three—Order of Mass and EPs
    - **February 1995**: Segment four—prefaces, solemn blessings, prayers over the people
    - **May 1995**: Segment five—Proper of Saints
    - **August 1995**: Segment six—Holy Week and Antiphonal for Volume I
    - **February 1996**: Segment seven—Common of Saints, Ritual Masses, Votive Masses, Masses for the Dead
    - **August 1996**: Segment eight—Mass for Various Needs and Occasions, Antiphonal for Volume II

- **1994**: Vatican objects to the Canadian publication of a New Revised Standard Version lectionary
- **April 1996**: The Congregation for the Doctrine of the Faith instructs the president of the NCCB to withdraw the *imprimatur*, granted by the USCC in January 1995, for the *Liturgical Psalter* prepared by ICEL
- **1997**: All eleven English-speaking conferences of bishops approve the new Sacramentary based on the eight segments previously submitted to them
- **September 1997**: English translation of the Ordination Rite, approved by all English-speaking conferences of bishops, is rejected by the Vatican
- **1998**: Each of the eleven English-speaking bishops' conferences of ICEL submits the new Sacramentary, based on multiple revisions of the eight segments of the Sacramentary in two volumes, to Rome for approval
- **October 1999**: Cardinal Medina, prefect of the Congregation for Divine Worship and the Discipline of the Sacraments, demands widespread changes in ICEL's mandate, structures, and personnel
- **20 April 2000**: John Paul II authorizes a new edition of the *Missale Romanum*
- **15 July 2000**: The NCCB Secretariat for the Liturgy issues "An English Language Study Translation of the *Institutio Generalis Missalis Romani*" (*IGMR2000*)
- **28 March 2001**: The Congregation for Divine Worship and the Discipline of the Sacraments issues *Liturgiam Authenticam*, the fifth instruction "for the right application of the Constitution on the Sacred Liturgy," changing the rules for vernacular translation of the Latin liturgy
- **16 March 2002**: The Sacred Congregation for Divine Worship and the Discipline of the Sacraments rejects the proposed English translation of the Roman Missal
- **18 March 2002**: *Missale Romanum editio typica tertia* (*MR2002*) and the seventh version of the *Institutio Generalis Missalis Romani* (*IGMR2002*), previously promulgated by John Paul II, are published by the Congregation for Divine Worship and the Discipline of the Sacraments
- **20 April 2002**: John Paul II establishes the *Vox Clara* committee to oversee the English translation of liturgical texts

- **July 2002**: The Vatican releases a preliminary sixth version of the *Institutio Generalis Missalis Romani* (*IGMR2000*), intended to accompany the *Missale Romanum, editio typica tertia*
- **17 March 2003**: The USCCB issues the approved English translation of *IGMR2002* (GIRM2003)
- **15 September 2003**: Cardinal Arinze issues a formal decree establishing ICEL as a mixed commission, with new statutes governing its operation
- **2 February 2004**: ICEL sends a newly drafted English translation of the Order of Mass (green book), made in accordance with *Liturgiam Authenticam* (as are all subsequent translations), to the English-speaking bishops' conferences of the world (ICEL2003/2004)
- **1 June 2005**: Because of so many substantive comments (e.g., regarding length of sentences, archaic language, etc.) on the first green book (2 February 2004), ICEL issues a second draft green book translation of the Order of Mass
- **17 February 2006**: ICEL issues its final draft gray book translation of the Order of Mass to the English-speaking bishops' conferences for their approval (ICEL2006)
- **2006**: The 2006 gray book of the Order of Mass from ICEL is approved by various English-speaking bishops' conferences
- **September 2007**: Vatican gives *recognitio* to Canadian bishops for using a "corrected" NRSV translation in their new lectionary
- **23 June 2008**: Vatican gives *recognitio* for the English translation of the Order of Mass submitted by English-speaking bishops' conferences (ICEL2008), which contained revisions of the 2006 gray book
- **2008**: Rome publishes a *Missale Romanum, editio typica tertia emendata*
- **November 2009**: US bishops and other English-speaking conferences submit an English translation of the Roman Missal to Rome (ICEL2008)
- **26 March 2010**: The Vatican's *recognitio* is given to the English translation of the Roman Missal (ICEL2010)
- **28 April 2010**: The *recognitio* is announced at meeting of *Vox Clara* with Benedict XVI
- **24 July 2010**: The *recognitio* of the adaptations for the Roman Missal in the United States is granted

- **20 August 2010**: English translation of the Order of Mass is made public, with over one hundred changes to what had been established by the text of 2008, which had received the *recognitio* in March of 2010
- **November 2010:** English translations of the Masses for Reconciliation and Masses for Various Needs and Occasions are made public
- **31 December 2010**: Text and music files of ICEL2010 are transmitted to seven US publishers approved for releasing ritual editions of the *Roman Missal*; they encompass an estimated ten thousand changes in what was originally sent to Rome as the gray book of the Roman Missal approved by eleven English-speaking episcopal conferences

Introductory Essays

The *Ordo Missae* of the Roman Rite

Historical Background

Joanne M. Pierce and John F. Romano

The structure or "order" of the Mass of the Roman Rite can best be understood when viewed through a number of different lenses. The task of this essay is to provide one such view through the lens of its historical development over the centuries. Such a task is not as straightforward as it sounds, for liturgical history is as much a matter of interpretation of sources as it is an attempt to collect and analyze the data provided by these sources.

Interpretation

As liturgical scholar Robert Taft has noted, "Only the unhistorical mind thinks history is the past. History is a view of the past, and as such is the product of the historian's mind."[1] History is thus always a construct, an interpretation, and this is true of liturgical history as well. Every analyst brings their presuppositions to the study of liturgical sources from various historical periods, e.g., in defense of an accepted "orthodox" interpretation or to support a "revisionist" challenge to that interpretation, "otherwise it [history] is mere repetition of what has already been written."[2]

In the sixteenth century, for example, some prominent Lutheran theologians attempted to justify elements of their Mass reforms by appealing to liturgical texts that they identified as dating back to the earliest decades of Christianity. In particular, the Lutheran historian Matthias Flacius Illyricus (d. 1575) engaged in a lengthy study of liturgical manuscripts in his search for such evidence. In 1557, he edited and published an elaborate *ordo missae* (*OM*), claiming that the manuscript text was a solid witness to early Christian eucharistic practice, particularly in support of the practice of lay communion from the cup. Late nineteenth- and twentieth-century research,

[1] Robert F. Taft, review of Paul Bradshaw, *The Search for the Origins of Christian Worship: Sources and Methods for the Study of Early Liturgy*, in *The Catholic Historical Review* 80 (1994) 556–58; on history as interpretation, cf. Collins and Foley, 82 below.

[2] John Baldovin, *Reforming the Liturgy: A Response to the Critics* (Collegeville, MN: Liturgical Press, 2008), 160.

however, proved that the manuscript dated from the early eleventh century and thus was not a witness to ancient Christian practice. Furthermore, the rubric accompanying the distribution of Communion to the laity made no reference in the original hand to "the Blood of Christ"; the phrase *et sanguis* had been added in pencil (likely centuries later) over the rubric's mention of the "Body of Christ."[3] Illyricus' interpretation had been shaped by the motives underlying his research agenda.

The great Roman Catholic liturgical scholars of the mid-twentieth century also interpreted the sources according to what they understood to be the needs of the church at their own time. The most important analysis of the development of the Roman Mass was first published by the Austrian Jesuit Josef Jungmann in 1948. His monumental two-volume study, titled *Missarum Sollemnia*, went through five editions, the last published in 1962 just as Vatican II began. The second edition (1949) was the only one translated into English; it was published in the United States in 1951 as *The Mass of the Roman Rite.*[4] While Jungmann does borrow ideas from interpretive frameworks considered "orthodox" in his time—e.g., he does not hesitate to describe the Last Supper as "the first Holy Mass"[5]—his main concern in his massive study is to distill the essential structure of the Mass from multiple later accretions: "Jungmann . . . [was] convinced that the Middle Ages saw a considerable decline in the fortunes of Christian liturgical celebration. . . . The clear implication is that at a certain point liturgical development ceased, i.e., it died."[6] As Jungmann notes in his introduction, "It is the task of the history of the liturgy to bring to light these ideal patterns of past phases of development which has been hidden in darkness and whose shapes are all awry."[7]

This task was not simply an academic exercise for Jungmann: The impetus for his study of the Mass was shaped, in part, by his desire for reform and renewal of the liturgy that had already found expression in various ways earlier in the twentieth century. In his view, the external "forms" of the eucharistic liturgy could and should be clarified ("a purity and clarity such as it possessed in the time of the Fathers") so that all of the faithful could participate with "an entirely new understanding" of its structure and

[3] Ironically, this early medieval manuscript is still an important element in studying the history of the *OM* in the West but for an entirely different reason than Flacius Illyricus had imagined (see 22, n. 108 below).

[4] See Jungmann in the list of abbreviations above (xx) for publishing information.

[5] Jungmann MRR, 1:7.

[6] Baldovin, *Reforming the Liturgy*, 160.

[7] Jungmann MRR, 1:5.

meaning and thus realize even more fully "that they are the Church" united together in Christ as his Body.[8] To this end, uncovering the more pristine liturgy "of the Fathers" was his goal.

Diverging from the previously held academic assumption that such documents are a relatively simple description of reality, contemporary scholars of the liturgy tend to approach liturgical sources with hermeneutical methods similar to those that have come to prominence in biblical studies. Thus scholars have engaged in careful source criticism of liturgical sources, questioned how to read silences in such documents, and demonstrated increased skepticism about how much information authoritative sources provide about real practice or how much stock one can place in explanations for the origins of specific customs.[9] Such methods call into question long-standing assumptions that underlie previous studies of the liturgy. Contemporary liturgical scholars, like those in other areas of historical theology, thus tend to reject the notion of any earlier historical period as a so-called golden age of Christian life and practice and approach the sources from a different perspective:

> This is not to say that the third century—or the second or the first—represents a golden age of Christian worship. There is no period to go back to and imitate: not fourth-century Jerusalem, or seventh-century Rome, or tenth-century Constantinople, or fourteenth-century Salisbury or sixteenth-century Geneva, for that matter.[10]

Dispelling the notion of a golden age is only one of the important shifts in ways that researchers have approached, read, and interpreted liturgical texts over the past fifty years.

While this is not the place for a lengthy discussion of the history of hermeneutics,[11] there are a few important elements that should be noted here. In addition to the methods used in biblical study (e.g., source, redaction, historical, and form criticism), other "postcritical" and "postcolonial" methods stemming from more contemporary literary, linguistic, philosophical, and contextual studies are also used in the analysis of liturgical sources, including texts.

[8] Ibid., 1:164–65.

[9] Paul Bradshaw, *The Search for the Origins of Christian Worship: Sources and Methods for the Study of Early Liturgy*, 2nd ed. (Oxford and New York: Oxford University Press, 2002), 14–20.

[10] Baldovin, *Reforming the Liturgy*, 163.

[11] For a fine overview of this topic, see Maurizio Ferraris, *History of Hermeneutics*, trans. Luca Somigli, Contemporary Studies in Philosophy and the Human Sciences (Atlantic Highlands, NJ: Humanities Press, 1996).

Here, the interpretive focus shifts away from determining "the authorial intention, history, and context"[12] of a liturgical text. Instead, the starting point is a familiarity with the texts themselves, including an analysis of their literary genre or form, moving next to an evaluation of the "interplay of different elements" in the actual liturgical celebration.[13] In contemporary discussion, most scholars base their analytical work on several key points: critique of historical/theoretical foundations; attention to culture and context; openness to the plurality of traditions around the "common memory of the one foundational event, which is the story of Jesus of Nazareth and his crucifixion"; attention to language itself (including the variations of genre and usage); and finally, recognition of the importance of taking seriously the "actuality of event," that is, the "originating event of Christian faith," without which none of the language of revelation (and thus the written texts through which it is transmitted) makes sense or has any meaning.[14]

Interpretive methods have expanded to take into account the complexity of the context of the liturgical sources (societal, cultural, literary) as well as the specific nature and use of both verbal and nonverbal sources and the ways the text has been and is read and received by specific individuals (and groups) across time and place. Some scholars have begun to move beyond the text and consider the inextricable relationship between text and liturgical performance: For them, acting out the words of the text is an essential part of understanding and experiencing worship.[15] Indeed, contemporary hermeneutics raise major questions about the very "text"-centered nature of much of contemporary liturgical scholarship.

The *OM* as a Liturgical Document

While at first glance the *OM* seems to be a relatively straightforward, step-by-step description of the actions of the eucharistic liturgy, it is clear that understanding it—especially in the midst of previously noted historical trends—is increasingly challenging for scholars. It is important first to define the meaning of the term *ordo missae.* The Latin word *ordo* is translated

[12] Joyce Ann Zimmerman, *Liturgy and Hermeneutics* (Collegeville, MN: Liturgical Press, 1999), 12.

[13] David Power, *Sacrament: The Language of God's Giving* (New York: Crossroad, 1999), 41–42.

[14] Ibid., 47–48.

[15] See, for example, Paul Connerton, *How Societies Remember* (Cambridge and New York: Cambridge University Press, 1989), 41–71.

most simply as "order" or "arrangement."[16] This noun is found frequently in the Vulgate, often referring to the proper arrangement of the cult or its ministers.[17] More broadly, it can also refer to the correct and harmonious arrangement of people in society.[18] Order was a particular concern for liturgical celebration. Often throughout Christian history it was thought important to achieve and maintain a sense of order in the liturgy, sometimes thought to mirror the more exalted order of heavenly worship.[19] Although we only have a small number of extant liturgical documents, those that remain can help us to reconstruct how this order was achieved in practical terms. An *ordo* (plural *ordines*) is a liturgical script, a description of the action of a celebration of the public worship of the church.[20] *Libri ordinarii* or ordinaries were reference books designed and used for a specific cathedral or community, which contained information on the texts to be read, chanted, or sung in the Eucharist or Divine Office.[21] The *OM* is a subset of the larger class of *ordines*, intended specifically to outline eucharistic worship, providing rubrics, prayer texts, and music that facilitate the performance of the Mass, originally intended for the priest alone.[22]

Eucharistic practice in the early centuries of Christianity was a local affair, and it is improbable to claim that any single document represents a form of worship that held sway throughout the Roman Empire. The majority of early forms of eucharistic celebrations were not preserved in any kind of written form. Early presiders improvised the prayers of the Mass, even

[16] Ursula Keudel, "*Ordo* nel 'Thesaurus linguae latinae,'" in *Ordo: Atti del II colloquio internazionale. Roma, 7–9 gennaio 1977*, ed. Marta Fattori and Massimo Bianchi, Lessico intellettuale europeo 20 (Rome: Edizioni dell'Ateneo & Bizarri, 1979), 13–22.

[17] For example, Exod 28:17; 28:20; 39:10; 39:13; 40:21; 40:23; Lev 17:15; Num 7:5; Deut 15:2; Ps 109:4; Luke 1:8; 1 Cor 14:40; 15:23; Col 2:5.

[18] Otto Gerhard Oexle, "Ordo, Ordines I," *Lexikon des Mittelalters*, ed. Robert Auty et al., 10 vols. (Munich and Zurich: Artemis Verlag, 1977–99), 6:1436–37.

[19] Eric Peterson, *The Angels and the Liturgy: The Status and Significance of the Holy Angels in Worship*, trans. Robert Walls (London: Darton, 1964).

[20] For *ordines*, see especially Aimé Georges Martimort, *Les Ordines, les ordinaires et les cérémoniaux*, Typologie des sources du moyen âge occidental 56 (Turnhout: Brepols, 1991), 20–50; Eric Palazzo, *A History of Liturgical Books from the Beginning to the Thirteenth Century*, trans. Madeleine Beaumont (Collegeville, MN: Liturgical Press, 1993), 175–85; Cyrille Vogel, *Medieval Liturgy: An Introduction to the Sources*, trans. and rev. William G. Storey and Niels Krogh Rasmussen (Washington, DC: Pastoral Press, 1986),135–224.

[21] Edward Foley, "'Libri ordinarii': An Introduction," *Ephemerides liturgicae* 102 (1988): 129–37.

[22] For brief description of the *OM*, see Andrew Hughes, *Medieval Manuscripts for Mass and Office: A Guide to Their Organization and Terminology* (Toronto and Buffalo: University of Toronto Press, 1982), 148–53; John Harper, *The Forms and Orders of Western Liturgy from the Tenth to the Eighteenth Century: A Historical Introduction and Guide for Students and Musicians* (New York: Oxford University Press, 1991), 62–63, 66, 195, 308.

EPs.[23] Only gradually did guidelines emerge that helped to shape the content of these prayers, and not until the third and fourth century did written EPs become widespread and begin to supplant extemporaneous prayer. No *ordines* from this period have survived. As documents of practice envisioned as appropriate for only a limited time, they might have been written down on papyrus and perished after their initial period of use. In fact, we do not possess any *ordines* earlier than the seventh century, and only in the ninth century does the *OM* appear as a separate text, either as a small booklet (or *libellus*) or as a separate section in larger liturgical books.[24] There are many earlier sources, however, that offer important information about the structure of the eucharistic celebration in antiquity and the early medieval period.

Early Sources

Recent scholarship has largely abandoned the notion that there was one unified apostolic tradition of liturgy handed down by Jesus and then transmitted in attenuated form through the apostles and the later churches. When viewed broadly, the history of the eucharistic liturgy before modernity must be seen as one marked more by diversity rather than uniformity,[25] and any further work on the history of its development must take this diversity into account: "Multiple accounts of Eucharistic origins and development, involving 'thicker' description of particular settings and practices, may therefore be necessary before there can be a more adequate single historical picture."[26] This is particularly true in studying the historical development of the *OM*; scholars are careful not to interpret this development as more marked by uniformity on the one hand, or diversity on the other hand, beyond what the sources themselves might indicate.

[23] Allan Bouley, *From Freedom to Formula: The Evolution of the Eucharistic Prayer from Oral Improvisation to Written Texts* (Washington, DC: Catholic University of America Press, 1981).

[24] For example, in some manuscripts of the Gregorian Sacramentary; see Vogel, *Medieval Liturgy*, 82–83 (early ninth-century Sacramentary of Hildoard, an "uncorrected" text of the *Hadrianum*) and 98–100 (early- to mid-ninth-century Sacramentary of Trent, a more complex composition).

[25] Bradshaw, *The Search*, and in particular his discussion of the evolution of eucharistic liturgy, 118–43. Bradshaw's theories have come under intense discussion. He has, for instance, been criticized for being too much of a "splitter" as opposed to a "lumper," an approach that makes it difficult to make general statements about past liturgical practice. See the review by Taft in *The Catholic Historical Review*, cited in n. 1 above.

[26] Andrew McGowan, "Rethinking Agape and Eucharist in Early North African Christianity," *Studia liturgica* 34 (2004): 165–76; here 167.

Scriptural Texts

In the NT there are several references to what took place during the "breaking of the bread," although these are not provided as outlines for an order of service. Rather than assume that the NT contains literal renderings of past liturgical practice, recent scholarship has introduced new ways of examining these texts. For example, some twentieth-century scholarship on the scriptural texts of the words of Jesus over the elements (referred to as the institution narratives) has begun to question "the relatively common assumption among NT scholars regarding the liturgical character of these traditions . . . [that is, that they] . . . are texts for liturgical recitation over bread and cup at the Eucharistic meal."[27] Furthermore, attention has shifted from uncovering the actual "historical core" of the Last Supper to locating "the source of the Eucharist more broadly within the context of other meals in Jesus' life . . . and to take seriously various layers of meaning that can be discerned within the New Testament."[28] The variety of "meal accounts," both in the narratives of Jesus' life and ministry as well as in others describing immediate "apostolic" practice, provide a rich pattern of eucharistic "meaning," the real focus for contemporary interpreters, as opposed to what might be called "the quest for the historical Last Supper." Finally, scholars have begun to question if the biblical accounts of the Last Supper were shaped less by a concern for historical accuracy and more by the interests and liturgical practices of the communities that produced them; instead of mirroring the actions of Jesus, they may instead address some of the more significant or controversial elements of their diverse eucharistic celebrations.[29]

The Synoptic Gospels offer related perspectives on the actions of the Last Supper as well as reflect the liturgical practice of their own communities. Nevertheless, contemporary liturgical researchers warn against interpreting the structure and wording of these narratives as actual liturgical texts in and of themselves: "The most that we can say is that, because the narratives were passed on within Christian communities which celebrated the Eucharist, their liturgical experience appears, not surprisingly, to have had some effect on the way in which they told the story of the Last Supper."[30] For

[27] Andrew McGowan, "'Is There a Liturgical Text in This Gospel?': The Institution Narratives and Their Early Interpretative Communities," *Journal of Biblical Literature* 118 (1999): 73–87; here, 73.

[28] Paul Bradshaw, *Eucharistic Origins* (London: SPCK, 2004), 2.

[29] Eugene LaVerdiere, *The Eucharist in the New Testament and the Early Church* (Collegeville, MN: Liturgical Press, 1996), esp. 12–26.

[30] Bradshaw, *The Search*, 48.

example, the earliest gospel, Mark, was probably composed at Rome in about 70 CE.[31] In Mark and the other Synoptic Gospels the Last Supper is a Passover meal; however, scholars urge caution in making too much of this, "since Mark's church is unlikely to have been concerned with the observance of the external details of the Jewish Passover ritual . . . [since] the entire focus of the meal is on Jesus' death."[32] Contemporary liturgical interpretation is much less concerned with arriving at a description of the actual "order of service" for the Last Supper, and some are moving away from attempts to discern within these institution narratives the local eucharistic practice of the communities within which these gospels were redacted:

> Thus, the institution narratives were neither liturgical texts to be recited at the celebration nor liturgical instructions to regulate it, but instead catechesis of a liturgical kind. It was their regular repetition for catechetical purposes within some—but apparently not all—early Christian communities that gave them their particular literary style and character, and that in turn has misled New Testament scholars into imagining that they must therefore have been read as part of every celebration.[33]

The earliest account of an "institution narrative" is found in 1 Corinthians, dating from about 54 CE, written by Paul in response to a letter from the Christians at Corinth raising several questions about various problems the group was facing.[34] After discussing issues involved with social interactions with pagans, Paul offers his opinion on a number of questions raised in connection with behavior at "liturgical assemblies" (chaps. 11–14).[35] His initial comments address one of the major issues: when the group comes together, the factions and divisions within the community are clearly expressed in their behavior at the Lord's supper. Paul's references to some "becoming drunk" while others "go hungry" clearly indicate the setting in the context of a full meal at which some (probably because of lower socioeconomic status) might arrive late or even be shunted off into another room while the more privileged arrive earlier and partake of better food and more

[31] Pheme Perkins, "The Gospel of Mark," in *New Interpreter's Bible* (Nashville: Abingdon Press, 1995), 8:517.

[32] Ibid., 703.

[33] Bradshaw, *Eucharistic Origins*, 14.

[34] See J. Paul Sampley, "The First Letter to the Corinthians," in *New Interpreter's Bible*, ed. Leander Keck (Nashville: Abingdon Press, 2000), 10:777; also, Jerome Murphy-O'Connor, "The First Letter to the Corinthians," NJBC, 49:8.

[35] Murphy-O'Connor, "The First Letter to the Corinthians," 49:51–64.

wine.[36] As Paul writes, "When you meet in one place, then, it is not to eat the Lord's supper" (1 Cor 11:20), language "designed to shock" in a culture so strongly "ordered around shame and honor."[37] This misbehavior signals to Paul that they have "lost any sense that love as the right relation to others is the . . . necessary expression of their faith as the right relation to God."[38] Because of this "lack of love . . . in reality there was no Eucharist."[39]

It is in this context that Paul offers to the Corinthian readers his own witness and memory of the eucharistic tradition "handed on" from the Lord. First, Jesus takes bread, gives thanks, and breaks it with the words, "This is my body that is for you. Do this in remembrance of me" (1 Cor 11:24). Next, "after supper," Jesus acts "in the same way" with the cup, saying, "This cup is the new covenant in my blood. Do this, as often as you drink it, in remembrance of me"[40] (1 Cor 11:25). In the light of the context, however, this text "is not functioning as an *ordo* or script: Paul quotes it in order to remind the Corinthians of the meaning that he attaches to their celebration of the Lord's Supper,"[41] adding force and urgency to his judgments about the morality of their conduct.

Contemporary researchers have studied the meal practices in the wider Greco-Roman culture of the first century in order to uncover other influences that might have shaped the earliest Christian eucharistic practice.[42] Some of these elements may indeed have been structural (and influential for Jewish as well as Christian practice). For example, the structure of the Greek *symposium* (or Latin *convivium*) suggests the possibility that some early Christian Eucharists began with the meal (what we might understand to be the Liturgy of the Eucharist) and ended with readings and discussion (suggestive of the Liturgy of the Word).[43] In addition, the wider societal

[36] Sampley, "The First Letter to the Corinthians," 10:777 and 934; also, Murphy-O'Connor, "The First Letter to the Corinthians," 49:56.

[37] Sampley, "The First Letter to the Corinthians," 10:928 and 934.

[38] Sampley, "The First Letter to the Corinthians," 10:934.

[39] Murphy-O'Connor, "The First Letter to the Corinthians," 49:56.

[40] The anamnetic phrase for the cup ("Do this . . .") may have originated with Paul himself; see Murphy-O'Connor, "The First Letter to the Corinthians," 49:56.

[41] Bradshaw, *Eucharistic Origins*, 13.

[42] See, for example, Dennis Smith, *From Symposium to Eucharist: The Banquet in the Early Christian World* (Minneapolis: Fortress Press, 2003); Jan Michael Joncas, "Tasting the Kingdom of God: The Meal Ministry of Jesus and Its Implications for Contemporary Ministry and Life," *Worship* 74 (2000): 329–65; Blake Leyerle, "Meal Customs in the Graeco-Roman World," in *Passover and Easter: The Liturgical Structuring of a Sacred Season*, ed. Paul Bradshaw and Lawrence Hoffmann, Two Liturgical Traditions 5 (Notre Dame, IN: University of Notre Dame Press, 1999), 29–61; Andrew McGowan, *Ascetic Eucharists: Food and Drink in Early Christian Ritual Meals* (Oxford: Clarendon Press, 1999).

[43] Joncas, "Tasting the Kingdom of God," 363.

expectations for forms of meals and meal-sharing may also have shaped emerging understandings of church, Eucharist, and worship practices. Patterns of inclusion and exclusion, for example, offer insights into the powerful countercultural, ethical, and eschatological suppositions of early Christian communities.[44]

Other Early Sources

Noncanonical sources are also "read" differently in contemporary scholarship. Here too scholars approach these through the lenses of contemporary hermeneutics; Christian tradition is understood to be pluriform in its traditions, in the unfolding of historical practice and interpretation.[45] For example, the use of water instead of wine seems to have been a fairly widespread practice by certain ascetic Christian communities, best understood in the wider context of all of their communal meals, where the concern for avoiding the product of pagan sacrifice, "the sacrificial elements of meat and wine,"[46] influenced early dining patterns more generally. Meat consumed at meals was usually made available, directly or indirectly, from animals killed in ritual sacrifices, and the drinking of wine at meals was prefaced by the practice of libation, a ritual "pouring out" of a small splash of wine directly onto the ground, in honor of the gods. So, strict, ascetic Christian groups consumed food that was understood to be culturally more ordinary, not sacral: bread (the "opposite" of meat) and water (the "opposite" of wine).[47]

Other early sources also offer some insight into the structure of the early eucharistic celebration. For example, the writings of early Christian apologists and bishops can offer some fragmentary glimpses into the structure of the eucharistic celebrations of their home communities. One key example is the *First Apology* of Justin Martyr (Rome), from *ca.* 150 CE and addressed to the emperor, containing two brief descriptions of Christian eucharistic practice. One is part of a longer description of baptism, and the second appears to be "an outline of a normal Sunday gathering."[48] This might well be a description of the Eucharist as celebrated by the Syrian Christian community in Rome—there could have been many different "ethnic" versions

[44] Ibid., 356.

[45] See, for example, Raymond Brown, *The Churches the Apostles Left Behind* (New York: Paulist Press, 1984).

[46] McGowan, *Ascetic Eucharists*, 142.

[47] Ibid., 60–66.

[48] Bradshaw, *Eucharistic Origins*, 61; cf. *First Apology*, 65:1–5, 66:1–4, and 67:1–7 = *Prex Eucharistica*, 1:68–73.

of Christian worship practiced by different churches in the city—one not meant for Christian consumption but instead as a defense of Christian beliefs and practice to non-Christians.[49] Nonetheless, there are certain elements of note in this text, e.g., in the baptismal section, Justin explicitly refers to (1) common prayers on behalf of the newly baptized and the community, (2) the exchange of a kiss at their conclusion, (3) a prayer over bread and cups of water and wine mixed with water[50] concluded by a communal "Amen" of assent, and (4) the distribution of these elements by "deacons" to those present (as well as to those not present). Later in the text, the words of Jesus over the bread and cup are also cited.

The second description of a Eucharist describes an "assembly" on the "day called Sunday," at which readings from "the records of the apostles or writings of the prophets are read as time allows," after which the presider "in a discourse admonishes and exhorts (us) to imitate these good things." The community next offers prayers, the "bread and water and wine" are brought and the presider prays over them, after which the people "assent, saying the Amen." Then "the (elements over which) thanks have been given are distributed and everyone partakes."[51]

In the practice of Justin's Syrian-influenced Christian community, we find a number of familiar-looking elements that will be included in later *OM*s: (1) shared intercessory prayers; (2) readings from the "apostles" or the "prophets;" (3) an expository address to the community by the presider; (4) the "bringing" of the bread and cup; (5) a prayer of "blessing" and "thanksgiving" over the bread and cup, including a version of the words of Jesus from 1 Corinthians and the Synoptics; and (6) distribution of the blessed elements, with provision made for those who are absent. This is also not an *ordo*, however; it is a set of descriptions included by Justin in his defense of Christian practice against common rumor and public suspicion.

Another category of early Christian sources are texts known as church orders.[52] Unlike the *Apologies*, these documents were intended to be used within particular Christian communities as guides to structuring a number

[49] Bradshaw, *Eucharistic Origins*, 63–64.

[50] There has been occasional controversy since the late nineteenth century over whether or not the reference to wine here is an interpolation; this would imply that Justin's Eucharist involved the thanksgiving over a cup of water, not wine: "At the very least, Justin's account should be treated with some reserve on this particular point" (Bradshaw, *Eucharistic Origins*, 76–77).

[51] *Second Apology*, 67:2–5 = Jasper & Cuming, 29–30.

[52] For further discussion, see Basil Studer, "Liturgical Documents of the First Four Centuries," in *Introduction to the Liturgy*, ed. Anscar Chupungco, Handbook for Liturgical Studies 1

of elements of communal Christian practice. The *Didache* is the earliest known church order, "a rule for ecclesiastical praxis, a handbook of Church morals, ritual and discipline,"[53] most likely composed in Syria and dating from either the mid-first century or early second century.[54] It contains two sets of prayers over bread and wine: a set of blessings over cup and bread (9:1-5) and a thanksgiving prayer with three benedictions after a meal (10:1-5), which may well be considered a "eucharistic prayer."[55] The *Didache* continued to influence later church orders in the same geographical region for three more centuries:[56] the *Didascalia Apostolorum* (mid-third century)[57] and, through that text, the first books of the much longer *Apostolic Constitutions*.[58] As will be noted later, the euchology of the *Didache* also had an influence on the texts of *MR1970*.[59]

Another early church order (ApTrad) was once thought to be a description of early third-century worship of the city of Rome by the writer and "antipope" Hippolytus; a growing number of scholars now believe it represents a complex combination of different rites, from different times and places, compiled later into a single document.[60] If so, then certain elements may date from "as early as the mid-second century to as late as the mid-fourth," and some conclude that it is "unlikely that it represents the practice of any single Christian community" and further study should focus on "attempting to discern the various elements and layers that constitute it."[61]

The ApTrad contains two accounts of EPs: one after the ordination of a bishop (4:1-13) and another associated with the baptismal liturgy (21:25-

(Collegeville, MN: Liturgical Press, 1998), 200–205; also, Maxwell Johnson, "The Apostolic Tradition," OHCW, 44–60.

53 Kurt Niederwimmer, *The Didache: A Commentary, Hermeneia* series (Minneapolis: Augsburg Fortress, 1998), 2.

54 Bradshaw, *The Search*, 85–86.

55 Niederwimmer, 161.

56 For a more detailed analysis, see ibid., 13–17.

57 See Alistair Stewart-Sykes, *The Didascalia Apostolorum: An English Version with Introduction and Annotation* (Turnhout: Brepols, 2009).

58 For a helpful flow chart of these interactions, see Vogel, *Medieval Liturgy*, 399. For a more detailed presentation of the texts, in parallel columns, see Paul Bradshaw, Maxwell Johnson, and L. Edward Phillips, *The Apostolic Tradition: A Commentary*, ed. Harold W. Attridge, *Hermeneia* series (Minneapolis: Fortress Press, 2002).

59 See 205 below.

60 See especially John Baldovin, "Hippolytus and the *Apostolic Tradition*: Recent Research and Commentary," *Theological Studies* 64 (2003): 520–42; and Bradshaw et al., *The Apostolic Tradition*.

61 Bradshaw et al., *The Apostolic Tradition*, 14.

38),[62] during which three cups are distributed, with clear reference to the newly baptized (one of water, one of mixed milk and honey, and one of wine). Brief prayers to accompany the offering of oil and cheese follow (5:1-2 and 6:1-4). A third prayer of thanksgiving at an evening meal (29C) seems not to have been a eucharistic celebration. It is important to note again, however, that early Christian meal and Eucharist are not "so sharply and simply differentiated from one another in the very early period of the Church's history."[63]

Regardless of its actual date and composition, the ApTrad has been influential in other ways in the history of the *OM*. Several other compilers of later church orders make use of the ApTrad more or less heavily in preparing their own documents: e.g., the Egyptian *Canons of Hippolytus* (mid-fourth century), the *Apostolic Constitutions* (where it forms much of Book VIII, and is also known as the *Epitome*), and the fifth-century *Testamentum Domini* (probably also from Syria).[64] Like the texts of the *Didache*, the EP section of the ApTrad had a significant influence on the liturgical reforms of the later twentieth century, including the composition of EP II of *MR1970*.[65]

Beyond the early church orders, other sources offer additional information about important phases in the development of liturgical forms during the late patristic period.[66] Especially important for the development of the *OM* are the changes made to the way liturgy was celebrated in Rome by the popes, the heads of the public cult. In the city of Rome, the most central change was the translation of the liturgy from Greek to Latin in the fourth century, likely during the pontificate of Damasus I (366–84).[67] It has been argued that this transition was intended to exalt traditional Roman values

[62] Numberings according to the edition of Bradshaw et al., *The Apostolic Tradition*.

[63] Bradshaw et al., *The Apostolic Tradition*, 160.

[64] Robert Beylot, ed., *Testamentum Domini Ethiopien* (Louvain: Peeters, 1984); also, Bradshaw, *The Search*, 84–96; Vogel, *Medieval Liturgy*, 399.

[65] See 311–15 below.

[66] See, for example, Martin Klöckener, "Das eucharistische Hochgebet in der nordafrikanischen Liturgie der christlichen Spätantike," *Prex Eucharistica*, 3:43–128, esp. the comparative table, 124–25.

[67] Theodor Klauser, "Der Übergang der römischen Kirche von der griechischen zur lateinischen Liturgiesprache," *Miscellanea Giovanni Mercati*, Studi e Testi 121 (Vatican City: Biblioteca Apostolica Vaticana, 1946), 1:467–82; Massey H. Shepherd, "The Liturgical Reform of Damasus I," in *Kyriakon: Festschrift Johannes Quasten*, ed. Patrick Granfield and Josef A. Jungmann (Münster: Aschendorff, 1970), 2: 847–63; cf. Pecklers and Ostdiek, 37 below.

and assert Damasus' power.[68] The responsorial psalm was likely introduced into the Roman liturgy by Pope Celestine I (422–32).[69] Certain fifth- and sixth-century popes were responsible for the composition of EPs, some in response to contemporary issues.[70] Pope Gregory I (590–604) altered the wording of the Canon of the Mass.[71] Sergius I (687–701) introduced the *Agnus Dei* to the eucharistic celebration in Rome.[72]

The Early Medieval Period (to 1200)[73]

While early church orders and descriptions of papal changes to the liturgy offer scholars some access to understanding the contexts, texts, and practices of the Eucharist in late antiquity, technically speaking, we do not possess any *ordines* until the seventh century. The first extant *ordo* for the Mass is the celebrated witness to the papal high Mass during Easter Week, *OR I*.[74] Like many other Roman *ordines*, it survived due to its popularity among the Christians north of the Alps, who would copy and carry back descriptions of the Mass to their homes after pilgrimages. An examination of its contents reveals that *OR I* was intended to regulate the complicated interactions of the numerous members of the papal court and preserve a clear idea of who was responsible for costly liturgical furnishings. This

[68] Maura K. Lafferty, "Translating Faith from Greek to Latin: *Romanitas* and *Christianitas* in Late Fourth Century Rome and Milan," *Journal of Early Christian Studies* 11, no. 1 (2003): 21–62.

[69] Peter Jeffery, "The Introduction of Psalmody into the Roman Mass by Pope Celestine I (422–432): Reinterpreting a Passage in the Liber Pontificalis," *Archiv für Liturgiewissenschaft* 26 (1984): 147–55.

[70] See, for example, Antoine Chavasse, "Messes du pape Vigile (537–555) dans le sacramentaire léonien," *Ephemerides liturgicae* 64 (1950): 161–213; and 66 (1952): 145–219; Charles Coebergh, "Le pape saint Gélase Ier auteur de plusieurs messes et préfaces du soi-disant sacramentaire léonien," *Sacris erudiri* 4 (1952): 46–102; Henry Ashworth, "The Influence of the Lombard Invasions on the Gregorian Sacramentary," *Bulletin of the John Rylands Library* 36 (1953–54): 305–27; Arthur P. Lang, *Leo der Grosse und die Texte des Altgelasianums: mit Berücksichtigung des Sacramentarium Leonianum und des Sacramentarium Gregorianum* (Steyler: Verlagsbuchhandlung, 1957); and, most recently, Bryan D. Spinks, "The Roman Canon Missae," *Prex Eucharistica*, 3:129–43.

[71] *Gestorum pontificum Romanorum volumen I. Libri pontificalis pars prior*, ed. Theodor Mommsen (Berlin: Weidmannos, 1898), 161; *The Letters of Gregory the Great*, ed. John R. C. Martyn, Mediaeval Sources in Translation 40 (Toronto: Pontifical Institute of Mediaeval Studies, 2004), 2:561–63; Andreas Heinz, "Papst Gregor der Grosse und die römische Liturgie," *Liturgisches Jahrbuch* 54 (2004): 69–84.

[72] Mommsen, *Gestorum pontificum Romanorum*, 215.

[73] For a helpful chart illustrating some of this development, see John Baldovin, "The Empire Baptized," OHCW, 97.

[74] John F. Romano, "The Fates of Liturgies: Towards a History of the First Roman Ordo," *Antiphon* 11 (2007): 43–77.

influential text focused almost exclusively on the actions of the Mass, excluding most spoken parts of the Mass or explanation of its meaning. Roman liturgical documents like it were held up as an ideal and flourished in the Frankish Empire in the eighth and ninth centuries; they fostered imitation of Roman practices, even if it is unclear to what extent the liturgy north of the Alps was Romanized.[75]

Early *ordines* like *OR I* were one of many liturgical books employed to regulate early medieval Roman worship. The numerous ministers needed separate books for prayers, readings, and rubrics. One of these volumes was the Sacramentary, the most significant book employed by the presider for celebrating the Mass,[76] which (in various arrangements) would include a calendar, prayers for individual celebrations, and an *OM*.[77] In the late seventh-century papal Gregorian Sacramentary, an abbreviated *OM* that outlines the basic parts of the Mass and some of the major prayers appears.[78] Often, particularly between the ninth and twelfth centuries, the *OM* circulated not as part of a prayer book but in its own independent booklet,[79] which could be used in conjunction with other books to celebrate the Eucharist. The system of having several different service books gradually became impractical, at least in part because of the growing practice of private Masses for votive purposes with only one priest. The *OM* eventually became part of the "full" missal (*missalis plenarius*), intended to bring together all of the parts of the Mass in one place.[80] Missals started appearing in the ninth century, and by the twelfth century they had already achieved ascendancy over older sacramentaries.[81]

[75] Yitzhak Hen, "Liturgische hervormingen onder Pepijn de Korte en Karel de Grote: de illusie van romanisering," *Millennium* 15 (2001): 97–113; also, his *The Royal Patronage of Liturgy in Frankish Gaul*, Henry Bradshaw Society Subsidia 3 (London: Boydell Press, 2001).

[76] Palazzo, *A History of Liturgical Books*, 21.

[77] Daniel Sheerin, "The Liturgy," in *Medieval Latin: An Introduction and Bibliographical Guide*, ed. Frank Anthony Carl Mantello and A. G. Rigg (Washington, DC: Catholic University of America Press, 1996), 157–82; here 171.

[78] *Hadrianum*, 85–92.

[79] Harper, *The Forms*, 62–63. The earliest separate *OM* is the ninth-century *OM* found in the Sacramentary of Amiens; see Victor Leroquais, "L'*ordo missae* du sacramentaire d'Amiens, B.N. lat. 9432," *Ephemerides liturgicae* 41 (1927): 435–45.

[80] Hughes, *Medieval Manuscripts*, 119; Andreas Odenthal, "Zwei Formulare des Apologientyps der Messe vor dem Jahre 1000: Zu Codex 88 und 137 der Kölner Dombibliothek," *Archiv für Liturgiewissenschaft* 37 (1995): 25–44; here 42–43.

[81] Vogel, *Medieval Liturgy*, 105; for a helpful summary of the history, content, and structure of early medieval sacramentaries see Palazzo, *A History of Liturgical Books*, 21–61.

Despite being classified in the same genre, there is a bewildering variety in the specific contents of the *OM*.[82] While this kind of variety is foreign to modern Roman Catholic liturgical books, it is in fact typical of medieval liturgy,[83] making it impossible to reduce the wide variety of eucharistic practice across the Middle Ages to one uniform pattern.[84] This kind of plurality was viewed not with opprobrium but with acceptance and even interest by ancient and early medieval Christians.[85]

An examination of the various *OM* manuscripts gives us a more concrete sense of how their contents diverge.[86] They do not all have equal numbers of prayer texts or other liturgical "units" in them and, as a result, are often different lengths. Depending on the individual manuscript, the *OM* might contain a wide variety of prayer texts.[87] Some include only the *incipit*s or opening phrases of certain prayers, while others contain the prayer texts in more complete forms. The number and detail of rubrics for individual ritual elements can differ. Graphically, the *OM*s are also presented in various ways. Many manuscripts use rubricated or larger letters to call attention to the most significant prayers; this is especially true of the Canon. Some use musical notation to show how to sing the chants provided, even if music was not provided in the rest of the *OM* or Missal. Some provide illuminations, especially full page pictures before the Canon. In addition, the *OM* itself is located at different points in different missals. Sometimes it is at the beginning or end,[88] but more usually the *OM* is placed before Easter Sunday.

In spite of the internal differences among *OM*s, certain commonalities bind these texts together. At heart, they are flowcharts that demonstrate for the priest how to perform the Mass and, as a result, must include the items

[82] Joanne Pierce, "New Research Directions in Medieval Liturgy: The Liturgical Books of Sigebert of Minden (1022–1036)," in *Fountain of Life*, ed. Gerard Austin (Collegeville, MN: Liturgical Press, 1986), 51–67; here 52.

[83] Jungmann MRR, 1:97–98; Hans Bernhard Meyer, *Eucharistie: Geschichte, Theologie, Pastoral*, ed. Hans Bernhard Meyer et al., Gottesdienst der Kirche: Handbuch der Liturgiewissenschaft 4 (Regensburg: F. Pustet, 1989), 207–8.

[84] Edward Foley, "A Tale of Two Sanctuaries: Late Medieval Eucharist and the Analogous," in *Companion to the Medieval Eucharist*, eds. Ian Levy, Gary Macy, and Kristen Van Ausdall (Leiden: Brill, 2011), 327–63.

[85] Victor Saxer, *Les rites de l'initiation chrétienne du IIe au VIe siècle. Esquisse historique et signification d'après leurs principaux témoins* (Spoleto: Centro Italiano di studi sull'alto Medioevo, 1988), esp. 663–64.

[86] For a detailed description of the form of an *OM*, see Hughes, *Medieval Manuscripts*, 151–53.

[87] Palazzo, *A History of Liturgical Books*, 24.

[88] Ibid.

that will assist him in this task: prayer texts that provide which words to pronounce at certain points in the service, rubrics to direct him how to act, and musical texts that designate what to sing. Frequently, these texts provide direction that would not be clear from the prayers and music included in sacramentaries or missals, rubrics that must be listed in sequential order for the priest to follow. Although there is no one standard table of contents, stress is often placed on specific "moments" in the eucharistic celebration. Important points include: (1) the vesting ceremony, (2) the *Confiteor*, (3) the *Gloria in excelsis Deo*, (4) the creed, (5) offertory prayers, (6) the preface, (7) the Canon, (8) communion prayers, and (9) readings and chants said at the end of Mass. In addition, many of the prayer texts interlaced within these sections of the *OM* belong to the genre known as apologies (*apologiae*), private prayers of the presider expressing his sinfulness or unworthiness.[89]

Because of the variability in the content of the *OM* before the advent of printing, much of the work of recent scholars has centered on simply recovering the different forms of this text and editing them,[90] yet a good deal of work remains on this front. Many examples of *OM*s remain unedited, which impedes a broader understanding of their contents and the historical evolution of this genre.[91] Some older editions of *OM* are now outdated and need to be reedited if they are to be used effectively in critical modern studies.[92] Only by editing and publishing the contents of as many manuscripts as possible and comparing all of these examples of the *OM* can we understand more deeply its history and development.

While many of the ceremonies and prayers of the *OM*, if not individual examples of *OM*s, received attention from scholars, few attempted to

[89] Joanne M. Pierce, "The Evolution of the *Ordo Missae* in the Early Middle Ages," in *Medieval Liturgy: A Book of Essays*, ed. Lizette Larson-Miller (New York and London: Garland Publishing, 1997), 8.

[90] See, for example, the list of edited *OM*s in ibid., 3–24; here 6–8. For recent editions to be added to her list, see especially Andreas Odenthal, "Ein Formular des 'rheinischen Messordo' aus St. Aposteln in Köln," *Archiv für Liturgiewissenschaft* 34 (1992): 333–44; Odenthal, "Zwei Formulare"; Michael G. Witczak, "St. Gall Mass Orders (I): MS. Sangallensis 338: Searching for the Origins of the 'Rheinish Mass Order,'" *Ecclesia orans* 16 (1999): 393–410; Witczak, "St. Gall Mass Orders (II): MS. Sangallensis 339," *Ecclesia orans* 22 (2005): 47–62; and Witczak, "St. Gall Mass Orders (III): MS. Sangallensis 340," *Ecclesia orans* 24 (2007): 243–61.

[91] Odenthal, "Zwei Formulare," 26; Pierce, "Evolution," 13; Niels Krogh Rasmussen, "An Early 'ordo missae' with a 'litania abecedaria' addressed to Christ (Rome, Bibl. Vallicelliana, Cod. B. 141, XI. Cent.)," *Ephemerides liturgicae* 86 (1972); 198–211; here 199–200; Witczak, "St. Gall Mass Orders (I)," 396.

[92] This especially holds for texts edited in the eighteenth century by Edmond Martène; see Pierce, "The Evolution," 6–8.

construct a paradigm of how the genre of the *OM* emerged as a complete unit and how it changed over time.[93] The twentieth-century scholar primarily responsible for developing the first typology of the *OM* was Boniface (Bonifaas) Luykx.[94] His theory was intended to articulate some kind of progressive classification system for these diverse texts. He distinguished three levels or stages in the development of the *OM*:

1) *The Apology type*: Apologies are private prayers said by the priest in which he accuses himself of sins and asks God for pardon and purification in order to be worthy to celebrate Mass. These *OM*s included chains of these prayers said at the beginning of Mass at the foot of altar, at the offertory, and at Communion. Apology type *OM*s first appeared in the ninth century and flourished in the tenth century.

2) *The Frankish type*: In addition to sacerdotal apologies, these *OM*s included additional, private prayers by the priest or presider that accompanied and often articulated different levels of spiritual meaning for various ritual actions. Prayers and psalms were added to the Mass at several different points, including vesting prayers, the entrance procession, the censing of the altar, before and after the gospel, the offertory prayers, the *Sanctus*, the mixing the of the bread and wine, and at end of Mass. This type also featured a novel concentration of gestures (like signs of the cross and bows) by the priest and new rubrics. This form would eventually replace the earlier Apology type *OM*. It flourished in the eleventh century, especially in the Frankish Empire.

3) *The Rheinish OM*: *Ordines* of this type were expanded by a further increase in the number of prayers and psalms, to the extent that nearly every liturgical action was connected with a private sacerdotal prayer and preceded by rubrics. The end result was a Mass that was almost entirely the personal experience of a priest, rather than a communal one. Several different elements were added or elaborated, including the vesting and preparation before Mass, the entrance rite, the *Confiteor*,

93 Pierce, "The Evolution," 3–4.

94 Bonifaas Luykx, *De oorsprong van het gewone der Mis*, De Eredienst der kerk 3 (Utrecht and Antwerp: Spectrum, 1955), and its German translation, "Der Ursprung der gleichbleibenden Teile der heiligen Messe (*Ordinarium Missae*)," *Liturgie und Mönchtum* 29 (1961): 72–119. For a summary and discussion of the classification, see Pierce, "The Evolution," 10–13. A useful Italian summary and discussion is found in Bonifacio Baroffio and Ferdinando dell'Oro, "L''ordo missae' di Warmondo d'Ivrea," *Studi medievali* ser. 3, 16 (1975): 795–821; here 801–6. For a comparative chart of Luykx's three types, see Odenthal, "Zwei Formulare," 26.

> the treatment of gospel books, the kiss of peace, communion prayers, kissing of the altar, and thanksgiving prayers after Mass. The offertory would henceforth become more clericalized, including the blessing of offerings and washing of the priest's hands and increasingly excluding the laity. While this form was initially intended for use by a bishop, it would eventually become the standard for all priests. The Rheinish *OM* would soon supplant both other forms. It emerged at the beginning of the eleventh century, originating most likely in the Swiss monastery of St. Gall. From there, it was adopted by the German cities of Reichenau and Mainz, then radiated further from all three centers.

The overall effect of incorporating the elements contained within these three types of *OM*s (especially the Rheinish *OM*) on the Mass was considerable.[95] The Roman Mass before this point was known for its soberness, simplicity, and straightforwardness.[96] These *OM*s filled out the framework of the Roman Rite with new prayers, psalms, and gestures, elaborating the "soft spots" of the liturgy[97] that had not previously received full elaboration, especially actions that occur without words. They imbued the Roman eucharistic liturgy with new embellishment, drama, and allegorical symbolism.[98]

The theories of Luykx on the development of the Mass order have been generally accepted. His work is cited with approval in standard studies of the history of the liturgy or the Mass, such as S. J. P. Van Dijk and Joan Hazelden Walker,[99] Josef A. Jungmann,[100] Burkhard Neunheuser,[101] Hans Bernhard Meyer,[102] and Eric Palazzo.[103] This is especially striking in Jungmann's

[95] Jungmann MS, 1:124–30.

[96] See the classic formulation of Edmund Bishop, "The Genius of the Roman Rite," in *Liturgica Historica: Papers on the Liturgy and Religious Life of the Western Church* (Oxford: Clarendon Press, 1918), 1–19; for a different perspective see the discussion of the work of Burkhard Neunheuser and the comments of Power below, 259, esp. n. 3; also 414.

[97] On Robert Taft's use of this term, see Baldovin 115 below; also Witczak 201; Pierce uses this concept to describe the incorporation of elements of the *OM* into the Mass in "The Evolution," 10–11.

[98] Anscar Chupungco, "History of the Liturgy until the Fifteenth Century," in Chupungco, *Introduction to the Liturgy*, 131–52; here 145.

[99] S. J. P. Van Dijk and Joan Hazelden Walker, *The Origins of the Modern Roman Liturgy: The Liturgy of the Papal Court and the Franciscan Order in the Thirteenth Century* (Westminster, MD: Newman Press, 1960), 49–51. The authors refer to the Rheinish *OM* as the "Lotharingian type."

[100] Jungmann MS, 1:123–29.

[101] Burkhard Neunheuser, *Storia della liturgia attraverso le epoche culturali* (Rome: Edizioni Liturgiche, 1977), 88–89.

[102] Meyer, *Eucharistie*, 204–8.

[103] Palazzo, *A History of Liturgical Books*, 24.

influential study of the Mass, which only in its fifth and last edition (1962) fully incorporated Luykx's results.

Some scholars have begun not only to recapitulate but also to build upon his scheme,[104] although not every scholar remains fully convinced that Luykx has definitively solved the problem of the origins of the *OM*.[105] Recent studies concur that Luykx's ideas are best characterized as a hypothesis that was never fully tested and cannot be until more examples see the light of publication.[106] Even scholars who agree with his overall structure anticipate that it will need further refinement,[107] especially in the case of texts that do not easily fit into Luykx's typology.[108] Some of these important areas for further study include the variety and malleability of apologies and the new spiritual character of these elements of the *OM* (as compared to the older Roman Mass), which introduced a much more individualistic, devotional series of prayers often stressing personal penitence.[109] Scholars have also begun asking not only what is in the *OM*, but also how these texts were used by priests; e.g., some of the long lists of apologies in certain of these *OM*s—like the Minden *OM*—might have been menus from which the priest chose, rather than all individually pronounced during any given celebration of the Mass.[110] This suggestion may hold in other cases as well and is in line with the new focus on performance, which examines how texts were used during the actual experience of worship.[111] Other studies have explored these *OM*s for what they have to tell us about the mentalities and piety of those who crafted and used them. The apologies, for instance, are seen as representative of a brand of spirituality that particularly stresses sinfulness,

[104] For example, Joseph Lemarié was able to define more precisely the new additions in the Rheinish *OM* by comparing it with other known *OM*s; see Joseph Lemarié, "A propos de l'Ordo Missae du Pontifical d'Hugues de Salins," *Didaskalia* 9 (1979): 3–9. For an English summary and discussion, see Pierce, "The Evolution," 12–13.

[105] See especially Theodor Klauser, *A Short History of the Western Liturgy: An Account and Some Reflections*, trans. John Halliburton (London: Oxford University Press, 1969), 104–5.

[106] Pierce, "The Evolution," 14; also, Witzcak, "St. Gall Mass Orders (I)," 396.

[107] Cf. Rasmussen, "An Early 'ordo missae,'" 200.

[108] For example, the Salins *OM*; see Lemarié, "A propos de l'Ordo Missae," esp. 8–9. Another elaborate, and perhaps influential, *OM* of the Rheinish type is the Minden *OM*, prepared for the eleventh-century German bishop Sigebert of Minden (first published as the *Missa Illyrica* by Flacius Illyricus; see 3–4 above). See Joanne M. Pierce, "Sacerdotal Spirituality at Mass: Text and Study of the Prayerbook of Sigebert of Minden," (PhD diss., University of Notre Dame, 1988). The main results of this study were published in her "New Research Directions."

[109] Pierce, "New Research Directions," 61–62.

[110] Lemarié, "A propos de l'Ordo Missae," 6.

[111] Eric Palazzo, "Performing the Liturgy," in *Early Medieval Christianities*, ed. Thomas F. X. Noble and Julia M. H. Smith, Cambridge History of Christianity 3 (Cambridge and New York: Cambridge University Press, 2008), 472–88.

unworthiness, and the necessity for purification.[112] Vesting prayers reveal that the allegorical method of interpretation popularly applied to the Bible also attached a deeper moral purpose to ritual actions.[113]

The impact of these *OM*s would not be limited to the area of personal spirituality, but would in fact shape the form of the Western Mass, even after the liturgical reforms of Pope Gregory VII (1073–85), ironically enacted in an "attempt at 'restoring' the integrity of the Roman liturgy and purifying it of 'Germanic' influences."[114] The developmental stages of the *OM* were one of the main elements in the broader story in the history of the liturgy. Between the eighth and tenth centuries, the Mass would transform itself in Frankish and Germanic lands, mixing together the imported Roman liturgy with local patterns of worship. The resulting Romano-Frankish Mass would not remain north of the Alps but in the tenth century would travel back to Rome and profoundly influence the worship of the eternal city. The Rheinish *OM*, along with the Romano-Germanic Pontifical, was one of the main documents that contributed fundamentally to this process[115] and changed the standard for what was considered the "Roman" Mass.

The Late Medieval Period (1200–1500)

The story of the *OM* did not end in the city of Rome at the end of the twelfth century. Important political and liturgical changes were made in the thirteenth century that would again influence the whole of Western Europe. Increasingly powerful popes began to impose the model of worship of the papal Curia more widely.[116]

[112] See Pierce, "The Evolution," 8–9. For one significant case study, see Joaquim O. Bragança, "A apologia 'Suscipe confessionem meam,'" *Didaskalia* 1 (1971): 319–34. Apologies were particularly significant in the early eleventh-century *OM* prepared for Sigebert of Minden.

[113] Joanne M. Pierce, "Early Medieval Vesting Prayers in the *Ordo Missae* of Sigebert of Minden (1022–1036)," in *Rule of Prayer, Rule of Faith: Essays in Honor of Aidan Kavanagh, O.S.B.*, ed. Nathan Mitchell and John Baldovin (Collegeville, MN: Liturgical Press, 1996), 80–105.

[114] Timothy Thibodeau, "Western Christendom," OHCW, 225; also, Vogel, *Medieval Liturgy*, 105–6. For other historical summaries, see especially Jungmann MRR, 1:74–92; also, Theodor Klauser, "Die liturgischen Austauschbeziehungen zwischen der römischen und der fränkischen-deutschen Kirche vom achten bis zum elften Jahrhundert," *Historisches Jahrbuch* 53 (1933): 169–89.

[115] Neunheuser, *Storia*, 89.

[116] The liturgical situation in Rome at the time was complex. Note that "by the year 1275, the city of Rome knew four liturgical customs: the papal court, St. Peter's in the Vatican, the reform of Cardinal Orsini (later Pope Nicholas III), and the Lateran Basilica" (Cassian Folsom, "The Liturgical Books of the Roman Rite," in Chupungco, *Introduction to the Liturgy*, 245–314; here 265).

The main movers in this process were Franciscan friars who in 1230 had "adopted" for the use of their order a Roman curial missal known as the "missal of Honorius," after Pope Honorius III (d. 1227).[117] In accordance with their mendicant style of life, they then traveled throughout Europe with these *Regula* missals, stamped with the Roman Curia's method of celebrating Mass.[118] Revisions were made to this missal by the English Franciscan Haymo of Faversham in 1243–44, with a second edition published in the following decade.[119] The *OM* of Haymo's missal is often referenced by the first two words of its opening rubric, *Indutus planeta*, describing the initial actions of the priest when beginning Mass.[120]

Although more work needs to be done on missals of this period, it is clear that the need for a travel-adapted *OM* was felt beyond the Franciscan orbit. One example comes from southwestern Germany. The fourteenth-century archbishop of Trier, Balduin of Luxemburg (d. 1354) seems to have traveled with a portable breviary containing a brief *OM*[121] titled *Officium sacerdotis quando se preparat ad missam*. The preparation rites before Mass seem to have been heavily influenced by the Rheinish type *OM*, and sections of the *OM* differ in several ways from that found in the *MR1570*.[122]

The introduction of the printing press in the mid-fifteenth century expanded the degree of influence that the Franciscan curial liturgy achieved. With printing, the exact words of this *OM* could be easily disseminated and promoted throughout Europe. The second edition of Haymo's missal was reestablished in Rome early in the next century. It was "approved by Clement V (1305–14) and adopted by the papal chapel . . . [this *Missale secundum consuetudinem Romanae Curiae* later forming] . . . the basis for the

[117] Ibid., 265–66.

[118] See Van Dijk and Walker, *The Origins of the Modern Roman Liturgy*. Earlier work on this liturgical development was done by Vincent L. Kennedy, "The Franciscan Ordo Missae in the Thirteenth Century," *Mediaeval Studies* 2 (1940): 204–22.

[119] For the edition, see *Sources of the Modern Roman Liturgy: The Ordinals by Haymo of Faversham and Related Documents (1243–1307)*, ed. S. J. P. Van Dijk, 2 vols. (Leiden: Brill, 1963), 2:3–14; also Folsom, "The Liturgical Books," 266.

[120] *Indutus planeta sacerdos stet ante gradum altaris*. See Edward Foley, "Franciscan Liturgical Prayer," in *Franciscan Prayer*, ed. Timothy Johnson (Leiden: Brill, 2007), 385–412; here 393–97; also, Nathan Mitchell and John Baldovin, "*Institutio Generalis Missalis Romani* and the Class of Liturgical Documents to Which It Belongs," in *A Commentary on the General Instruction of the Roman Missal*, ed. Edward Foley, Nathan Mitchell, Joanne Pierce (Collegeville, MN: Liturgical Press, 2007), 18–19.

[121] Described by Andreas Heinz, "Der Ordo Missae im 'Reisemissale' des Trierer Erzbischofs Balduin von Luxemburg (1308–1354)," in *Ars et Ecclesia. Festschrift für Franz J. Ronig zum 60. Geburtstag*, ed. Hans-Walter Stork, Christoph Gerhardt, and Alois Thomas (Trier: Paulinus-Verlag, 1989), 217–33.

[122] Ibid., 220–33.

first printed missal,"[123] i.e., *MR1474*. Its *OM*, which begins *Paratus sacerdos*, however, is somewhat less detailed that its model, *Indutus planeta*, and appears to follow a late twelfth-century *OM* used by the papal Curia.[124] Through the work of the Franciscans and the new printed missals, the *ordo* of the papal Curia achieved a certain level of popularity in Europe in the century and a half before the Council of Trent (1545–63).[125]

These would not be the only influences on the *OM* or the *MR1570*. The latter was also prepared with reference to the already widespread late fifteenth-century *OM* of the papal master of ceremonies John Burckard of Strasbourg, published in 1501. This *OM* also represented curial practice,[126] and combined mostly medieval elements and some new modifications when it was crafted.[127] The editorial process was conservative, involving pruning certain formulae and changing the wording of others.[128] This is an elaborate text, which "in its length, precision, scope, and rubrical detail . . . goes well beyond medieval precedents, such as *Indutus planeta* and *Paratus* . . . that are relatively brief by comparison," as is the *OM* of *MR1474*.[129]

The Council of Trent called for a revision of the Roman liturgical books and left this task in the hands of the papacy. The work of a commission supervised by Pius IV and Pius V, *MR1570* would be the second of these new liturgical books to appear after the council—the first being the breviary of 1568. The Missal's prefatory directions—the *ritus servandus*, forerunner of the contemporary *IGMR*—depended heavily on Burckard's text, while its edition of the *OM* was based largely on that of the *MR1474*.[130] Through both of these key elements, *MR1570* would ultimately set the standard for the celebration of Mass for centuries both in traditionally Roman Catholic lands and new missionary territory throughout the world.

[123] Folsom, "The Liturgical Books," 266.

[124] This *OM* is known as *Paratus*; see Foley, "Franciscan Liturgical Prayer," 397; also, Mitchell and Baldovin, "*Institutio Generalis*," 19–20, and n. 88. The ceremonial of the Franciscan missal can be found in *Ordines of Haymo of Faversham*, Henry Bradshaw Society 85 (London: Boydell Press, 1853).

[125] Nathan Mitchell, "Reforms, Protestant and Catholic," OHCW, 307–50; here 337.

[126] Jungmann MRR, 1:135; for an edition, see *Tracts on the Mass*, ed. J. Wickham Legg, Henry Bradshaw Society 27 (London: Harrison and Sons, 1904), 121–71.

[127] For a more complete description, see Mitchell and Baldovin, "*Institutio Generalis*," 20–22.

[128] Jungmann MRR, 1:127–35.

[129] Mitchell and Baldovin, "*Institutio Generalis*," 21.

[130] See Jungmann MRR, 1:135–37, as well as Mitchell and Baldovin, "*Institutio Generalis*," 21–22.

From Reformation to 1962

After the promulgation of the *MR1570*, the *OM* would retain virtually the same form for nearly four hundred years.[131] Two very slight revisions were made to *MR1570* in 1604 and 1634.[132] Nevertheless, there was significant variation in the *OM* even during this period. When Pius V promulgated *MR1570*, the papal bull *Qui Primum* noted that other eucharistic rites[133] could be retained if they were more than two hundred years old (either by papal institution or by custom). Some religious orders retained their earlier usages (e.g., Carthusians, Dominicans, and Premonstratensians), as did some cities or regions. In Spain and Italy, for example, the Old Spanish rite in Toledo[134] and the Ambrosian rite in Milan[135] continued to be celebrated.[136]

However, most (Roman rite) dioceses throughout Europe willingly adopted *MR1570* regardless of the antiquity of their own traditions, with the exception of France; there, many bishops chose to retain their diocesan missals, "correcting" them with Tridentine texts.[137]

Later religious and political influences in France during the mid-seventeenth century led to the development of what have been called "neo-Gallican" liturgies, as "a number of dioceses in France published a series of service books with rubrics printed in French and with variations in

[131] For the 1570 *OM*, see Robert Cabié, *The Eucharist*, ed. Aimé Georges Martimort, trans. Matthew O'Connell, The Church at Prayer 2 (Collegeville, MN: Liturgical Press, 1986), 149–71. For a modern reproduction of this missal, see Sodi-Triacca, 279–352. For a discussion of the process of this reform, see Mitchell, "Reforms, Protestant and Catholic," 337–39.

[132] These changes included clarification of rubrics, adjustment of the wording of some scriptural texts, editing of the priest's prayers at the beginning of Mass, and revision of the final blessing at the end of Mass; see Jungmann MRR, 1:140; also Folsom, "Liturgical Books of the Roman Rite," in Chupungco, *Introduction to the Liturgy*, 267.

[133] On the very definition of a "rite," and whether many of these continuing practices actually constituted a rite (with special attention to the so-called Norbertine rite), see Andrew Ciferni, "The Post–Vatican II Discussion of the So-Called Praemonstratensian Rite: A Question of Liturgical Pluriformity," (PhD diss., University of Notre Dame, 1978), esp. 1–34.

[134] An accessible overview of the history and contemporary restoration of this rite can be found in Raul Gomez, *Mozarabs, Hispanics, and the Cross* (Maryknoll, NY: Orbis, 2007).

[135] A recent dictionary on this rite was published by Marco Navoni, ed., *Dizionario di liturgia ambrosiana* (Milan: Nuove Edizione Duomo, 1996). Introductions to many liturgical books employed in the contemporary Ambrosian Liturgy are posted by the Pontificio Istituto Ambrosiano di Musica Sacra at http://www.unipiams.org/?id=32 (accessed 19 January 2009).

[136] Cabié, *The Eucharist*, 149; in 1948 Jungmann noted that other dioceses retaining their own rites included "Trier, Cologne, Liége, Braga and Lyons, of which only the last two have kept their own rite until now" (MRR, 1:138).

[137] Pierre Jounel, "Les liturgies diocésaines de France de 1685 à 1875," in *Liturgie aux multiples visages: mélanges*, Bibliotheca 'Ephemerides liturgicae' Subsidia 68 (Rome: C.L.V. Edizioni Liturgiche, 1993), 201–9; here, 201.

content from diocese to diocese."[138] A "unique phenomenon in liturgical history,"[139] these neo-Gallican books reflected the Jansenist morality and Gallican ecclesiology[140] of the time (the latter especially supported by the Bourbon kings). Their compilers and composers were also influenced by the "biblical and patristic revival taking place in France and throughout Europe [which] gave added incentive to return to the sources."[141] In fact, a number of Catholic scholars in the seventeenth and eighteenth centuries undertook the massive task of collecting "ancient" liturgical texts, and many of these early modern editions are still in use.[142]

Many French bishops and abbots chose to use one of two influential diocesan missals as models in preparing their own missals: the Missal of Paris (1738) and the Missal of Troyes (1736).[143] Their use continued in France through the French revolution into the nineteenth century. The number, texts, and "themes" of Mass formularies in these missals varied—sometimes widely—from those of *MR1570*; however, the structure of the *OM* itself remained unchanged. Because of the revolutionary social and political turmoil and increasing pressure from Ultramontanist critics urging the adoption of the Roman liturgical books (most notably Dom Prosper

[138] Keith Pecklers, "History of the Roman Liturgy from the Sixteenth until the Twentieth Centuries," in Chupungco, *Introduction to the Liturgy*, 163; also F. Ellen Weaver, "The Neo-Gallican Liturgies Revisited," *Studia liturgica* 16 (1986–87): 54–72. These sets of diocesan liturgical books included missals, breviaries, and rituals. For more on the missals, see Franco Brovelli, "Per uno studio dei messali francesi del XVIII secolo. Saggi di analisi" *Ephemerides liturgicae* 96 (1982): 279–406 and *Ephemerides liturgicae* 97 (1983): 482–549; also, Pierre Jounel, "Les missels diocésains français du 18e siècle," *La Maison-Dieu* 141 (1980): 91–96; and Jounel, "Presentation des missels diocésains français du XVIIe au XIXe siècle," *La Maison-Dieu* 141 (1980): 97–166.

[139] Jounel, "Les liturgies diocésaines," 201 (translation by Pierce).

[140] See, for example, Joanne Pierce, "A Study of the Ecclesiology of the Missal of Troyes (1736)," *Ecclesia orans* 6 (1989): 33–68. The catechetical dimension of many of these missals is also important to note; see C. van der Plancke, "Un conscience d'Eglise à travers la catéchèse janséniste du XVIIIe s.," *Revue d'histoire ecclésiastique* 72 (1977): 5–39.

[141] "Liturgical innovations continued to the extent that by the eighteenth century, 90 of the 139 dioceses in France had its own liturgy" (Pecklers, "History of the Roman Liturgy," in Chupungco, *Introduction to the Liturgy*, 164). Ripples of similar efforts were felt elsewhere during the eighteenth century; the Italian Synod of Pistoia (1786), in an effort to "return to the pristine liturgy of the early Church," called for missals with Latin texts accompanied by vernacular translations, as well as a reduction in the number of altars to one in each church, although in 1794 these and other recommendations of the synod were condemned; see Pecklers, "History of the Roman Liturgy," 165; also Jungmann MRR, 1:153, n. 62.

[142] Jungmann MRR, 1:153, n. 62. Among these researchers are Cardinal Giuseppe Tommasi (d. 1713), Antonio Vezzosi (d. 1783), Jean Mabillon (d. 1707), Edmond Martène (d. 1739), and later (and much more extensively) J.-P. Migne (d. 1875).

[143] Jounel, "Les liturgies diocésaines," 205.

Guéranger[144]), these neo-Gallican missals were eventually replaced in French dioceses by *MR1570*; the diocese of Orléans would be the last to give up its liturgical books in 1875.[145]

Later developments had important effects, not on the structure of the *OM*, but on lay participation in the Mass itself. Through the efforts of Guéranger, the monks at his abbey of Solesmes researched and revived Gregorian chant during the nineteenth century, and their liturgical example assisted "in bringing about ecclesial unity and uniformity in France."[146] Through his books on liturgy, Guéranger "educated many of the French clergy and laity,"[147] and influenced other liturgical scholars. These leaders would, in turn, move beyond the nineteenth-century Ultramontanist goal of restoring the uniformity of the Roman Rite to form the liturgical movement of the twentieth century, with its own governing principle: "full and active participation" of the laity in the liturgy.[148]

The work of the leaders of the twentieth-century liturgical movement in promoting this goal was aided by other developments. For example, Pius X "coined the phrase 'active participation' in his 1903 *motu proprio* on sacred music."[149] His decree *Quam singulari* (1910) set the age of seven (the "age of reason") for First Communion, and his encyclical *Divino afflatus* (1911) "led to changes in the Roman Missal published by Benedict XV in 1920."[150] The publication of bilingual missals (some appearing as early as the late nineteenth century)[151] for the use of the laity, with the Latin texts and their vernacular translation on alternating pages or in parallel columns, had an important effect on making the liturgy more comprehensible to laypeople;

[144] See R. William Franklin, "The People's Work: Anti-Jansenist Prejudice in the Benedictine Movement for Popular Participation in the Nineteenth Century," *Studia liturgica* 19 (1989): 60–77. See also André Haquin, "The Liturgical Movement and Catholic Ritual Revision," OHCW, 697–98.

[145] Jounel, "Les liturgies diocésaines," 201 and 209.

[146] Pecklers, "History of the Roman Liturgy," in Chupungco, *Introduction to the Liturgy*, 166.

[147] Ibid.

[148] As articulated first in 1909 by Dom Lambert Beauduin of the monastery of Mont César in Belgium; see ibid., 167.

[149] Michael Witczak, "The Sacramentary of Paul VI," in *The Eucharist*, ed. Anscar Chupungco, *Handbook for Liturgical Studies* 3 (Collegeville, MN: Liturgical Press, 1999), 133–75; here, 133.

[150] Ibid.

[151] "In the revision of the *Index of Forbidden Books*, issued under Leo XIII in 1897, the prohibition [against translating the OM into vernacular languages] was no longer mentioned," and it seems not to have been "seriously" enforced for several decades earlier (Jungmann MRR, 1:161).

later came the promotion of various forms of Mass celebration with a more active role assumed by the laity.[152]

During this period, other editions of the *MR* were issued (1884, 1920, 1955), largely encompassing minor changes or corrections in the calendar, rubrics, or texts of readings.[153] However, *MR1920* also included new prefaces "for the first time in a thousand years."[154] New Mass formularies were included for new feasts (for example, the feast of St. Joseph the Worker on May 1 was added by Pius XII [d. 1958] in 1955) as well as rubrical instructions detailing differences in ceremonial among the pontifical, solemn, and private forms of the Mass.[155] During the 1950s more explicit revision and renewal of the liturgy quietly began to take place under the leadership of Pius XII. After his 1947 encyclical *Mediator Dei*, the papal "Pian Commission" oversaw a number of liturgical reforms, including the revision of the Easter Vigil (1951) and the rites for Holy Week (1955).[156] A final edition of the Tridentine *MR* appeared in 1962, when John XXIII (d. 1963) inserted the name of St. Joseph into the Roman Canon. By this time, however, more sweeping changes were coming: "John XXIII had also called a council in 1959, and it was clear that the reform of the liturgy would be a part of its agenda."[157]

Vatican II and Its Aftermath

The last major revision of the *OM* occurred in the aftermath of Vatican II (1962–65).[158] A new *OM* was issued in 1969 followed by *MR1970* and *MR1975* and now *MR2002*.[159] The overriding aim of the postconciliar reforms was to increase the participation of the laity in the Mass, which was to have a corresponding effect on the shape of the *OM*. The commission of

[152] For example, the *missa recitata* and the "dialogue Mass," in which the laity would actually recite the responses of the *OM*, and in Germany, the *Deutsches Hochamt* ("Sung Mass") with the use of vernacular hymnody; see ibid, 1:162–63.

[153] Pecklers, "History of the Roman Liturgy," in Chupungco, *Introduction to the Liturgy*, 161.

[154] Jungmann MRR, 1:167.

[155] Marcel Metzger, "The History of the Eucharistic Liturgy in Rome," in Chupungco, *The Eucharist*, 130.

[156] Keith F. Pecklers, *The Genius of the Roman Rite: On the Reception and Implementation of the New Missal* (Collegeville, MN: Liturgical Press / Pueblo, 2009), 25.

[157] Witczak, "The Sacramentary of Paul VI," in Chupungco, *The Eucharist*, 133.

[158] For a detailed account of the liturgical changes after Vatican II, see Cabié, *The Eucharist*, 189–230; for a detailed account of the process by which the *OM* was reformed, see Bugnini, 337–92.

[159] Jan Michael Joncas, "The *Ordo Missae* in the *Missale Romanum 2002*," *Worship* 76 (2002): 521–36.

experts charged with the task of revising the liturgical books, the Consilium,[160] was divided into several working groups, each assigned to a particular component of liturgical reform; Group 10 was the study group responsible for the *OM*. The initial parameters of its work on the *OM*, as called for in *SC*, no. 50, were outlined in *IntOec*.[161] Group 10 actually began meeting in April 1964 before *IntOec* was promulgated; these meetings concluded in May 1968.[162] Study Group 10 included some of the foremost liturgical scholars of the time, including Josef Jungmann, Pierre Jounel, Pierre-Marie Gy, and Cipriano Vagaggini. Later additions included Joseph Gelineau, Louis Bouyer, and, as an advisor, the secretary of the national liturgical commission in the United States, Frederick McManus.[163]

Over the course of these four years, the work of Group 10 would continue steadily in a series of careful steps, including meeting together as a working group and reporting back periodically to the wider Consilium. In all, seven schemata of the *OM* were drawn up before the final *OM* was promulgated.[164] One important component of the revision process was the "testing" of proposed schemata (with variations) of the *OM* through "experimental celebrations" with special invitees as the congregation; in 1967 the congregation was composed of members of the assembled synod of bishops.[165] Feedback was solicited in some detail, and in early 1968 Paul VI himself requested a short series of changes, including the sign of the cross at the beginning of Mass,[166] a review of the offertory formulas, and a reordering of the "rites for the greeting of peace."[167]

Paul VI issued the apostolic constitution *Missale Romanum* on 3 April 1969,[168] promulgating the new Roman Missal (effective the First Sunday of Advent 1969). In this brief document he notes the basic principles from *SC*

[160] See Pecklers and Ostdiek 57 below.

[161] DOL nos. 293ff; on the *OM*, nos. 340–51.

[162] Piero Marini, "Elenco degli 'Schemata' del 'Consilium' e della Congregazione per il Culto Divino," *Notitiae* 18 (1982): 455–772; here one can find a complete list of Group 10's meeting dates and agendas.

[163] Bugnini, 337.

[164] For a helpful summary, see Frederick McManus, "The Roman Order of Mass from 1964 to 1969: The Preparation of the Gifts," in *Shaping English Liturgy: Studies in Honor of Archbishop Denis Hurley*, ed. Peter Finn and James Schellman (Washington, DC: The Pastoral Press, 1990), 109–10.

[165] Bugnini, 342–50.

[166] For a more detailed examination of the various schemata of the opening and closing rites, not only in terms of textual changes but also in the light of semiotics theory, see Mark Searle, "*Semper Reformanda*: The Opening and Closing Rites of the Mass," in *Shaping English Liturgy*, ed. Finn and Schellman, 53–92.

[167] Ibid., 369–70.

[168] DOL 1357ff.; also Mitchell and Baldovin, "*Institutio Generalis*," 24–27.

on which the revision was based: clarity, simplicity of structure, participation of the laity, expansion of biblical readings, and provisions for concelebration. The standard phrasing of the words of institution in every EP is described as "the chief innovation"[169] in the new *OM*. Three days later the new *OM* was promulgated through the decree *Ordine Missae*.[170] On 26 March 1970, *MR1970* was promulgated by the decree *Celebrationes eucharisticae*.[171]

The new *OM* was not simply a result of "pruning" the *OM* found in *MR1570* of elaborations and accretions. In some cases, the group did eliminate elements considered to be repetitive or disadvantageous to the faithful but, in other cases, added parts that had been removed over the centuries to the detriment of the rite. Among the many changes in the rite, a few significant ones included the following: the music for the entrance procession, preparation of the gifts, and Communion are freely chosen rather than singing fixed antiphons; the priest and people sign themselves at the beginning of the Mass; a new reading from the OT was introduced; the prayer of the faithful, which had dropped out of use, was restored; the preparation of gifts (no longer an offertory) uses new prayers and encourages people to bring up gifts; there are new options for the EP; there is a doxology after the Our Father; the faithful exchange a sign of peace; during Communion, the faithful may receive Communion in the hand and drink from the chalice; finally, there is a blessing by the priest at the end of the Mass. In some cases, older items were retained but their meaning or referent was altered. For instance, the *Confiteor* was originally a priest's private prayer, but after the reform it was to be said by all of the faithful in order to "cleanse" the entire community before Mass.[172] As a whole, this kind of editing was meant to reveal the significance of parts of the Mass and the relationship among them.[173]

The alterations made to the *OM* after Vatican II often aimed at the elimination or modification of early medieval elements originally added to the Mass in France and Germany and only later incorporated into eucharistic celebration at Rome.[174] This especially involved private sacerdotal prayers and devotional gestures. The revisers of the *OM* after Vatican II were aware

[169] DOL 1360.

[170] DOL 1367.

[171] DOL 1765.

[172] Cabié, *The Eucharist*, 195–96.

[173] For an early analysis, see Adrien Nocent, "The Parts of the Mass," in *The Liturgy of Vatican II: A Symposium in Two Volumes*, ed. William Baraúna, English ed. Jovian Lang (Chicago: Franciscan Herald Press, 1966), 2:27–61.

[174] Anscar Chupungco, *Liturgies of the Future: The Process and Methods of Inculturation* (New York: Paulist Press, 1989), 56–71.

of the scholarship on the liturgy and made a conscious attempt to achieve a brand of classical Roman simplicity, especially as epitomized by *OR I*.[175] This clarification process was one of the key elements guiding Jungmann's massive study of the Mass in the mid-twentieth century. Some contemporary critics of the postconciliar liturgical reforms, however, based on their reading of history, charged that the 1970 *Novus ordo* represented either an entirely new rite without a basis in the past or, at the very least, an overreaching reform that did not flow "organically" from Catholic liturgical tradition.[176] In spite of this criticism, there has been widespread satisfaction with the new *OM*, although some would like to see a reduction of certain long-standing but now arguably esoteric elements of Mass and a greater flexibility in celebration than the current *OM* would allow.[177]

Conclusion

The history of the *OM* should not be viewed as a distant event that is over and done with; rather, the process by which it was formed and reformed continues to resonate in the church to this day. Contemporary research offers some helpful insights. It seems clear that the history of the development of the *OM* is a prime example of the changes undergone by Western Christian and Roman Catholic liturgy in new cultural settings. Further study of the stages of this development could be helpful in discussions regarding the adaptation of liturgical rites into different cultures and contexts. In addition, the prayer texts and gestures of the *OM*s tell us much about the spiritual concerns of the people who shaped and used them, providing useful frameworks for evaluating the suitability of certain prayers or gestures for our own historical context. In the vast diversity that marks twenty-first-century Roman Catholicism, certain traditional elements might not always resonate with contemporary spiritual needs, pieties, or customs. The evolution of the *OM* also provides us with one source of evidence about a liturgical world in which neither complete local diversity nor Roman-centered uniformity reigned supreme but rather both tendencies interacted

[175] Anscar Chupungco, "History of the Liturgy until the Fifteenth Century," in Chupungco, *Introduction to the Liturgy*, 141.

[176] Baldovin, *Reforming the Liturgy*, 37–64. For a critique of the work done on the *OM* after the council, see, for instance, Alcuin Reid, "*Sacrosanctum concilium* and the Reform of the *Ordo Missae*," *Antiphon* 10 (2006): 277–95.

[177] Charles W. Gusmer, "Reviewing the Order of Mass," *Worship* 57 (1983): 345–48.

in creative tension. This could serve as a basis for modern discussions of how to strike such a balance in our own historical and cultural settings.[178]

Further study of the *OM*, combined with a more general consideration of the current state of worship, will continue to generate useful lessons in shaping contemporary and future eucharistic liturgy. Any such inquiries must take seriously our long and rich tradition of worship. If our study of the past is any guide, however, dynamic development in liturgical practice is not a measure of weakness or inauthenticity in worship. We may read these texts and interpret this process instead as evidence of a living, vibrant tradition that continues to change, and indeed must change, as the context of its living participants across the globe changes "from age to age."

[178] See *Continuity and Change in Christian Worship*, ed. R. N. Swanson (Woodbridge, Suffolk; Rochester: Boydell Press, 1999).

The History of Vernaculars and Role of Translation

Keith Pecklers and Gilbert Ostdiek

This article begins by considering the historical period from the birth of Christianity to Vatican II (1962–65). A second section considers the developments from Vatican II until the promulgation of *LitAuth*. The closing section reviews developments since *LitAuth*.

Before Vatican II

Liturgical Language in the Early Church

It is probable that the first followers of Jesus in Jerusalem celebrated the liturgy in the language that Jesus himself employed in his preaching—Aramaic—while Hebrew was used for proclaiming any biblical readings from the OT.[1] As the church spread throughout Asia Minor and into other Greek-speaking parts of the Roman Empire, including Rome itself, the church's liturgical language shifted to *Koiné* Greek—used in the empire's major cities—while local languages continued to be employed in the countryside. *Koiné* Greek emerged in postclassic antiquity in the third century BCE as the first supraregional Greek dialect to serve as a *lingua franca* for the eastern Mediterranean and Near East during the Roman period. Given the cosmopolitan nature of first-century CE Rome, it was not surprising that both Jewish and Christian communities spoke this form of Greek there. During the first two centuries of the Common Era, as many as ten bishops of Rome were Greek-speaking. The use of *Koiné* Greek could have spread as far as southern Gaul.

In other parts of the world where Greek was not common, the vernacular or local language was employed in worship on the basis of intelligibility and comprehension. In the region around Antioch, for example, Syriac became the normative liturgical language. The fourth-century Spanish

[1] Aimé Georges Martimort, "Essai historique sur les traductions liturgiques," *La Maison-Dieu* 86 (1966): 75–105.

pilgrim Egeria notes that in the Jerusalem liturgy, the bishop who spoke to worshipers in Greek was translated into Syriac; for the Latins present who knew neither Greek nor Syriac, a translation was provided:

> Even though the bishop may know Syriac, he always speaks Greek and never Syriac; and, therefore, there is always present a priest who, while the bishop speaks in Greek, translates into Syriac so that all may understand what is being explained. Since whatever scriptural texts are read must be read in Greek, there is always someone present who can translate the readings into Syriac for the people. . . . So that those here who are Latins, those consequently knowing neither Greek nor Syriac, will not be bored, everything is explained to them, for there are brothers and sisters who are bilingual in Greek and Latin and who explain everything to them in Latin.[2]

Gradually, Scripture readings were translated into Syriac and Latin for those who did not know Greek. In Egypt, although Greek was first spoken at Alexandria, Coptic was introduced into the liturgy in the sixth and seventh centuries to distinguish Egypt from other churches and regions.[3] In emerging pastoral provisions for vernacular usage the operative principle was one firmly established by St. Paul: liturgical prayer should be intelligible to the assembly so that those gathered might properly participate and be edified by what they celebrate, offering their assent with a great "Amen." This was an antidote to the charismatics of the Corinthian community who spoke in a language that nobody could understand (1 Cor 14:13-18).

Clearly a fundamental desire of early church leaders was to foster comprehensibility within worship, both to assist liturgical participation and to contribute to the edification and upbuilding of the community. This was particularly evident in early developments of the Roman Rite, offering a primitive example of what would later be called liturgical inculturation: contextualizing worship within a particular culture so that the liturgy more properly reflects the genius and ethos of that particular celebrating community.

[2] *Egeria: Diary of a Pilgrimage*, trans. George E. Gingras, Ancient Christian Writers 38 (New York: Newman Press, 1970), chap. 47 = 125–26.

[3] Anscar Chupungco, "The Translation of Liturgical Texts," in *Introduction to the Liturgy*, ed. Anscar Chupungco, Handbook for Liturgical Studies 1 (Collegeville, MN: Liturgical Press, 1998), 383.

The Diffusion of Latin and the Primacy of Rome

With the third-century invasion of the "barbarians" who wrote their laws in Latin, that language grew increasingly common in North Africa and gradually spread to Rome and throughout the West. North African writers contributing to that process included Tertullian (d. after 220), Cyprian of Carthage (d. 258), Arnobius (d. after 305), Lactantius (d. *ca.* 325), and Augustine (d. 430). Tertullian was educated in Rome and could both read and write Greek. Yet by *ca.* 230, an educated Carthaginian such as Cyprian was unable to read or speak Greek. By then much of the Greek version of the Hebrew Scriptures (*Septuagint*) had been translated into Latin along with the Greek NT. It's plausible that the *Septuagint* had actually been translated by Jews who, like their Christian contemporaries in North Africa, were similarly linguistically disadvantaged.

As North Africa took the lead in this gradual Latinization of the liturgy, it is not surprising that Carthage predates Rome in the use of Latin biblical texts; the first recognized Latin version of the Bible for liturgical use appeared there around 250 CE. Borrowing from secular and military vocabulary of the day, North African theologians played a significant role in creating juridical and liturgical terminology that would eventually be utilized throughout the Christian West, introducing, e.g., *sacramentum*, *ordo*, *plebs*, *disciplina*, and *institutio*. Attempts to introduce Latin into the liturgy already occurred during the pontificate of the North African Victor I (d. 203). In the third century, as the number of Oriental immigrants waned and North Africans increased, the growth of Latin usage increased substantially. This made the introduction of Latin into the Roman liturgy much easier, all the more so since a Latin version of the Bible had found its way to Rome by this time. Bishops of Rome first opted for a bilingual liturgy: Latin for the readings and Greek for the EP. This period of linguistic transition, necessitated by the coexistence of two distinct linguistic groups, lasted until the late fourth century, when Damasus I (d. 384) established Latin—the current vernacular of the Roman Church—as the normative liturgical language.[4] This shift spurred the growth of new liturgical compositions that would better reflect the Latin and Roman genius rather than mere translations from Greek liturgical texts.

Latin translations of the third century exhibit certain inconsistencies. On the one hand, translations tended to be quite literal and slavish, even to the extent that Greek word order was reproduced along with the use of particles like *men* and *de*. On the other hand, the same Latin word was not

[4] See Pierce and Romano, 15 above.

always used to translate a Greek term. Thus, the Greek word *doxa* was alternately rendered as *gloria*, *claritas*, and *maiestas*. Since the third century lacked any universally fixed liturgical texts, it is probable that the progressive shift from Greek to Latin produced a variety of intermediary formulas with significant variations even within the EP. As Jungmann has noted, the oldest form of the Roman liturgy further exhibited a penchant for duplication with a regular tripling or even quadrupling of orations resulting in a repetitive style designed for a more cumulative effect:[5] anything but the classic brevity and precision that was later thought to characterize the Roman Rite.

In 360 the Roman rhetorician Marius Victorinus cited a part of the EP in his Latin text *Adversus Arium*. When he arrives at the anaphora his text shifts into Greek without explanation and, after the anaphora, back to Latin. This suggests that in this period Greek was still the language for the EP and other liturgical prayers. That situation would soon change. Only twenty years later (374–82), the anonymous writer Ambrosiaster also quoted a fragment of the EP—this time in Latin. That coincided with the papacy of Damasus I when Latin had become established as the liturgical language of the Roman Church. Damasus paved the way for future bishops of Rome[6] by authoring several Latin formularies that are preserved in the *Veronense*.

Ambrose of Milan's *De Sacramentis* (*ca.* 387–91) contains a fragment of a Latin EP that closely resembles the medieval Roman Canon, leading some scholars to argue that the Latinizing of the Roman liturgy occurred earlier in the fourth century than originally suggested.[7] Nonetheless, the use of Latin continued to develop and spread throughout central and Western Europe between the fourth and sixth centuries, as did the Latinization of the Roman Rite. New Latin compositions of collects and EPs were generated by Innocent I (d. 417), Leo the Great (d. 461), Gelasius I (d. 496), Vigilius (d. 555), and Gregory the Great (d. 604).

It is naïve to think, however, that the same type of Latin consistently appeared. Early Latin existed on several levels with various strata: (1) ordinary vernacular Latin spoken on the streets; (2) more elevated (literary) Latin employed by the elite; and (3) more sacral, liturgical Latin, which

[5] Jungmann MRR, 1:57.

[6] Theodor Klauser, *A Short History of the Roman Liturgy* (London: Oxford University Press, 1969), 18–19.

[7] Cyrille Vogel, *Medieval Liturgy: An Introduction to the Sources*, rev. and trans. William Storey and Niels Rasmussen (Washington, DC: Pastoral Press, 1986), 295–96.

tended to be archaic and hieratic, used in early Mediterranean religions.[8] This historical period reveals distinctive opinions concerning the type of Latin most appropriate for worship. Hilary of Poitiers (d. 367) argued for classical or "elevated" Latin in the composition of liturgical prayers and hymns. Ambrosiaster had a very different approach. Following the previously noted Pauline principle of intelligibility, he encouraged the use of Latin during the Eucharist so that the community might make the prayer its own and be edified.[9] Consequently, it was preferable to use a brief prayer intelligible to the assembly rather than a lengthy prayer in elevated style that was incomprehensible to the masses. This position was shared by Ambrose who—despite the fact that he came from a bilingual aristocratic background and was trained in rhetoric—argued in favor of a liturgical Latin accessible to the assembly. Despite his principles, however, Ambrose's own liturgical compositions appear to reflect a *via media* between the elevated Latin preferred by Hillary of Poitiers and the more pastorally accessible Latin encouraged by Ambrosiaster.[10]

As the Roman Rite evolved, liturgical Latin was increasingly hieratic and juridical,[11] influenced by the language of the imperial court. It reflected Roman rhetorical style with rhythmic and well-balanced verses evoking the eternal majesty of God. These prayers tended to appeal more to intellect than heart and were of such sophisticated construction that the average Christian in fourth- to sixth-century Rome would have had difficulty in grasping their meaning. Ambrose, like his North African student Augustine, employed biblical imagery in his liturgical compositions that supported the catechetical and pastoral dimensions of his worship. Scripturally inspired, these compositions engaged the imagination of the liturgical assembly at the level of the heart. This was not the case with the Roman collects and was only occasionally evident in other Roman liturgical texts. Indeed, the brevity and formality of Roman prayers made the interpretive task all the more difficult.[12]

[8] Robert Taft, "Translating Liturgically," *Logos: A Journal of Eastern Christian Studies* 39, nos. 2–4 (1998): 165; on the sacrality and hierarchic nature of liturgical Latin, see Christine Mohrmann, *Liturgical Latin: Its Origins and Character* (Washington, DC: The Catholic University of America Press, 1957), esp. chap. 3, "General Characteristics of Liturgical Latin," 60–90.

[9] Klauser, *A Short History*, 22.

[10] Enrico Cattaneo, *Il Culto Cristiano in Occidente* (Roma: Centro Liturgico Vincenziano, 1992), 88.

[11] For a further discussion of liturgical Latin in Rome, see Power, 255–58 below; also Mohrmann, *Liturgical Latin*, 62 *et passim*.

[12] Klauser, *A Short History*, 41–42.

Seventh-century Rome witnessed the arrival of a new wave of Oriental immigrants; subsequently the Roman liturgy became bilingual once again, with biblical readings again proclaimed in Greek along with some rites of the catechumenate. From 638 until 772, nine of the twenty-five popes came from the East, highlighting the continuing cosmopolitan nature of the Roman Church. With strong Frankish intervention in liturgical matters, however, that cultural accommodation would be short-lived, and Latin would hold sway as the normative liturgical language in the Christian West.[13]

By contrast, the East was far more successful in maintaining local traditions, including its varied liturgical languages. Armenian, Coptic, and Syriac languages were already well established when Christianity grew in those regions, and the first task of missionaries arriving there was to translate the Bible into the vernacular. The Bible was translated into Syriac as early as the second century, Armenian in the third, and Coptic in the fourth. The development of Eastern liturgies with their particular languages was closely linked to the development of patriarchal sees—primarily Alexandria, Antioch, Jerusalem, and Constantinople. One should not presume, however, that linguistic developments were clearly defined across the Oriental churches. In Egypt, for example, the Coptic Rite was celebrated in Greek in Hellenized cities while Coptic was used in rural areas as early as the fourth century. Unlike the West, which would gradually succumb to pressure for a uniform Roman Rite with a universal language—with notable exceptions such as the Ambrosian Rite—the Christian East held firm to its ecclesiological principles reflected not only in its liturgical language and worship but also in its synodal structures of leadership.

Medieval Developments

The classic Roman Rite grew between the fifth and eighth centuries. Bishops of Rome like Gregory the Great were aware of the liturgical diversity that existed in different regions and cultures but did not find this a threat to the church's unity or Rome's primacy. The expansion of the Roman Rite and its use of Latin were already assisted by abbots and bishops as early as the seventh century when they came to Rome as pilgrims. Returning home, they desired to implement the Roman way of doing things, having witnessed certain unique liturgical practices during their Roman sojourn. Apart from the novelty of introducing Roman liturgical traditions,

[13] Vogel, *Medieval Liturgy*, 296.

there was also a deeper spiritual reason for doing so: Rome was the city of Peter and Paul, the city of martyrs, and the See of the Bishop of Rome.

What began informally through Frankish abbots and bishops as they crossed the Alps to return to their monasteries and dioceses became much more systematic with the Carolingian reforms; local rites were suppressed in favor of a unified Roman Rite with a common language. Even as the romance languages emerged in those regions where Latin had been spoken, and despite the fact that Latin was no longer known or understood, Latin continued to hold sway in the church's worship. As Latin became less accessible to the liturgical assembly, the distance between the *presbyterium* and the nave grew ever wider with an increasingly clericalized liturgy. Lay popular devotions gradually emerged as a substitute for the participation that the continued use of Latin had denied them. Latin usage came to be equated with being Catholic—a position especially offensive to Eastern Catholics whose local languages remained intact despite the efforts at liturgical uniformity in the West.[14]

By the ninth century, the Roman Rite was no longer pure and classical as it now included various non-Roman elements through contact with other rites. As this hybrid rite spread throughout the West thanks to the efforts of Pepin (d. 768) and Charlemagne (d. 814), a very different dynamic was occurring across the Adriatic Sea in Moravia and Pannonia. Thanks to the missionary activity of the brothers Cyril (d. 869) and Methodius (d. 885), the Byzantine Rite spread throughout the Balkan Peninsula, helped by its translation into Old Slavonic. When they began their work around the year 864, these two "Apostles to the Slavs" first translated the gospels then subsequently other liturgical texts. Cyril also composed the Glagolithic alphabet, which articulated the particular sounds spoken by the Moravians. This important work recognized the significance of vernacular usage as a key tool in the process of evangelization.[15]

Cyril and Methodius, however, were not without their detractors. Their arrival in Moravia had been preceded by German missionaries who took a dim view of such cultural concessions since Boniface (d. 754), the "Apostle to the Germans," had forged a strong relationship between German tribes and Rome. Thus, German clerics saw such vernacular innovations as a potential threat to unity with the See of Peter, as well as theatening the church's deposit of faith. These views were sympathetic with those of a

[14] Keith F. Pecklers, *Dynamic Equivalence: The Living Language of Christian Worship* (Collegeville, MN: Liturgical Press, 2003), 3–4.

[15] Ibid., 4–5.

group known as the "trilinguists"—German clergy of the eighth century who argued that the only liturgical languages worthy of usage were the three inscribed on the cross: Latin, Greek, and Hebrew. Despite the fact that the Council of Frankfurt (794) had condemned the "trilinguists," a number of their supporters were still in evidence one century later, and these did their best to impede the missionary activity of Cyril and Methodius, not only in Moravia, but also in Rome itself where they were denounced to the pope. Undaunted by such tensions, however, the two brothers pressed on and their efforts gradually bore fruit. Indeed, when they were received in Rome by Pope Hadrian II (d. 872), they were granted full permission for the use of Old Slavonic in the liturgy. Much to the disappointment of the "trilinguist" sympathizers, Cyril and Methodius celebrated their vernacular liturgy in the pope's presence as he ordained a number of Moravian presbyters and deacons. Cyril died in Rome during that visit.

With the election of a new pope in 872, the Moravian privilege for vernacular worship was again called into question. Only one year after taking office, John VIII forbade the use of Old Slavonic in the liturgy; the pope himself had been influenced by the position of the "trilinguists." John was eventually won over to the vernacular position, however, and went so far as to place a copy of Cyril and Methodius' Old Slavonic translation of gospels on the altar in Saint Peter's. He then rescinded the prohibition against the use of Old Slavonic in the liturgy, assisted at that vernacular liturgy himself, and declared that opponents to the liturgical use of Old Slavonic were to be "cut off from the Church."[16] Methodius died the same year in which Stephen V (d. 891) was elected. Stephen restructured the Moravian Church according to the more traditional and anti-vernacular German plan, to the great disadvantage of the Western Church in Eastern Europe. Unable to feel at home in such a repressive environment, Methodius' disciples moved to Bulgaria where they were again able to worship in Old Slavonic. That vernacular worship then also spread to Romania and later to Russia, becoming increasingly distant from Roman centralization of papal authority and closer to Orthodoxy.[17]

In tenth-century Dalmatia, the issue was revisited. A council at Split had forbidden the ordination of priests who only knew Slavonic, but Bishop Gregory of Nin who was a strong defender of the vernacular appealed to Pope John X (d. 928) and the use of Old Slavonic was resumed in their

[16] Cyril Korolevsky, *Living Languages in Catholic Worship: An Historical Inquiry* (Wesminster, MD: Newman Press, 1957), 76–77.

[17] Ibid., 83–84.

cathedral. In the eleventh century, consistent with his efforts at supplanting the Hispanic Rite in favor of the universal Roman Rite, Pope Alexander II (d. 1073) again forbade usage of Old Slavonic, as well. An official pronouncement in favor of Old Slavonic would be issued only in 1248 by Pope Innocent IV (d. 1254), whose authorization of Slavonic closely resembled that of John VIII. That permission would only be made definitive by Pope Urban VIII (d. 1644) in the year 1631. There are those who contend that Old Slavonic has been in continuous usage at the Cathedral of Split since the tenth century, but this becomes difficult to document, especially in light of Alexander II's prohibition in the late eleventh century. Nonetheless, we can affirm that the liturgy has been celebrated there in the vernacular for a very long time—at least several centuries prior to the Council of Trent (1545–63) and through to Vatican II.

Even as Latin remained the *lingua franca* of the Western Church, vernacular concessions continued to be granted on the local level. When the Benedictine monastery of Emmaus at Prague was founded in 1346, for example, the liturgical hours were celebrated primarily in Slavonic. This development must be seen in light of the wider liturgical movement that grew in Bohemia during the fourteenth century. Milíč of Kroměříž, a pioneer priest who founded a community of clergy and laity to promote his reform, encouraged a renewal of the church's worship that included daily celebration of the Eucharist with vernacular preaching and reception of communion at Mass. Through such efforts, Czech became a valid religious language alongside Latin. The production of biblical translations led to experimentation with translations for liturgical proclamation. That, in turn, led to various efforts at translating the entire Roman Mass and Divine Office into Czech, which took hold in the early fifteenth century with the incorporation of vernacular hymnody as well.[18] In sixteenth-century Dubrovnik, there existed a complete Roman Missal in Croatian that was clearly intended for liturgical use by the way it was printed and bound.[19]

Regarding the Byzantine liturgy, at the end of the twelfth century the Greek Patriarch of Antioch, Balsamon, declared that those who did not understand Greek were to celebrate the liturgy in their own language, faithfully translating the texts directly from the Greek original. Balsamon's principle continued to be applied for centuries, especially as the Byzantine tradition found its way into Asian countries like China and Japan.[20] In that

[18] David R. Holeton, "The Bohemian Brethren," OHCW, 312–14.

[19] Korolevsky, *Living Languages*, 86, 88.

[20] Josef A. Jungmann, *Pastoral Liturgy* (London: George Berridge & Co. Ltd., 1962), 96–97.

same period, vernacular preaching emerged in Western Europe. As bishop of Paris, for example, Maurice de Sully (d. 1196) provided sixty-four sermons in French as a model for his clergy; Abbot Samson (d. 1212) preached both in French and in the local dialect of Suffolk.[21] There were also lay vernacular missals in the late Middle Ages that both contained and omitted the Latin Canon depending on the missal. For example, the *Messen singen oder lesen* (1480) included the full Canon whereas later editions of that text included the Canon but omitted the words of consecration. A French translation of the Missal was available as early as 1370 and then subsequently in 1587, 1607, 1618, and 1651.[22]

Vernacular Privileges as Tools of Evangelization

Newly founded missionary orders also recognized the importance of the vernacular for their efforts at evangelization and consequently requested various vernacular privileges. When Pope Clement V (d. 1314) named Franciscan missionary John of Montecorvino (d. 1328) the first bishop of Peking, he was granted permission for the use of Mandarin Chinese in the liturgy; the bishop also provided his own translations of the psalms and NT. Some years later, Dominican missionaries in Greece received permission from Pope Boniface IX (d. 1404) to celebrate Mass in Greek. In Armenia, permission was granted to the Friars of Union (affiliated with the Dominicans) for the celebration of the entire Dominican liturgy in Armenian from the 1330s to 1794—the entire period of their existence.[23]

In 1492, archbishop of Granada Hernando de Talavera provided prayers and other liturgical resources in Arabic as a pastoral concession in assisting the numerous converts who had come into the Spanish Church from Judaism and Islam.[24] He also published Arabic catechisms and required his clergy to learn Arabic for their pastoral ministry with converts. Elsewhere in Spain, the Franciscan Cardinal Ximénez de Cisneros (d. 1517) made his own contribution to liturgical reforms in the vernacular and was a strong defender of the Old Spanish Rite.[25] Augustinians, Dominicans, and Franciscans carried vernacular efforts from Spain to the New World. The *Manual*

[21] Sophia Menache, *The Vox Dei: Communication in the Middle Ages* (Oxford: Oxford University Press, 1990), 22–23.

[22] Jungmann MRR, 1:143–44.

[23] Korolevsky, *Living Languages*, 94.

[24] Jaime Lara, "The Liturgical Roots of Hispanic Popular Religiosity," in *Misa, Mesa, y Musa: Liturgy in the U.S. Hispanic Church*, ed. Kenneth David (Schiller Park, IL: World Library Publications, 1997), 27.

[25] Jaime Lara, "'Precious Green Jade Water:' A Sixteenth-Century Adult Catechumenate in the New World," *Worship* 71 (1997): 416, n. 5.

de Adultos was published in Mexico (1540) specifically for the baptism and marriage of Aztec and Mayan adults. That text, however, was short-lived. The reforms of the Council of Trent replaced it with the Latin *Manuale Sacramentorum secundum ecclesiae Mexicanae* (1560).[26]

The Vernacular and the Sixteenth-Century Reformation

A key theme of the sixteenth-century Reformation was its insistence on the vernacular within worship to ensure maximum comprehension by the baptized.[27] A fundamental shift for Martin Luther (d. 1546) came in 1520 when he decided to leave his position as an academic arguing in Latin with the university elite in favor of a new role as pastoral reformer, utilizing his native German language as the most effective tool to reach the wider public. Luther, of course, was not alone. In 1524, Diobald Schwartz prepared a fairly conservative German translation of the Latin Mass followed by Martin Bucer's (d. 1551) Strasbourg liturgy in 1525. Bucer's text underwent eighteen revisions until it became the definitive Strasbourg German Mass in 1539. It is probable that Bucer's own reforms had some influence on Luther, who tended to move slowly, advising caution in preparing liturgical texts lest they be translated in haste. Well ahead of his time, Luther realized that producing good liturgical texts was a lengthy and painstaking process that required more than a literal translation from Latin into German. He began using German hymns in the Eucharist in 1523 and composed twenty-four himself that year and more the next, totaling at least thirty-seven in all. He published his vernacular version of the Mass, *Deutsche Messe*, in 1526. Ulrich Zwingli (d. 1531) introduced his own vernacular liturgy in 1523, and John Calvin (d. 1564) introduced a French version of Bucer's German Strasbourg liturgy in 1540, which he revised in 1542 when he returned to Geneva.[28]

In the English-speaking world, the Anglican *Book of Common Prayer* offers a most eloquent example of a sixteenth-century vernacular liturgical book. The foundations of the book are fundamentally Catholic—drawn from the Old Spanish Rite, medieval missals, and pontificals—and the liturgical texts were rendered elegantly. Archbishop Thomas Cranmer (d. 1556) who crafted that text employed solid liturgical principles such as full participation by the liturgical assembly assisted by use of the vernacular. Like Luther, Cranmer's liturgical innovations were gradual. Work on his 1552 Communion Service,

[26] Ibid., 418–24.

[27] For an excellent treatment on the importance of vernacular worship within the Reformation, see Herman Schmidt, *Liturgie et langue vulgaire: Le Problème de la langue liturgique chez les premiers Réformateurs et au Concile de Trent* (Rome: Analecta Gregoriana, 1950).

[28] See Pecklers, *Dynamic Equivalence*, 127–29.

for example, was actually begun five years earlier in 1547 when he first introduced English into the Latin Mass. The *First and Second Prayerbooks of Edward VI* (1549 and 1551)—eventually known as the *Book of Common Prayer*—were reissued in 1559, 1604, and 1662 with only minor revisions.[29]

The Council of Trent needed to respond in some way to the extensive promotion of the vernacular by the Reformers; not surprisingly, this subject found its way into the council's agenda. What is surprising, however, is the level of support the subject garnered among the bishops participating in the various sessions over the council's eighteen-year span. Precedence for supporting use of the vernacular arose thirty years prior to the council's opening. Camaldolese monks Paolo Giustiniani and Pietro Quirini presented a *libellus* to Pope Leo X (d. 1521) that recalled the vernacular worship of the early church and questioned why in their own day the church insisted on using a liturgical language that the majority of the laity did not comprehend.[30] A number of bishops at Trent held similar positions while others—generally bishops coming from Protestant areas—argued that Latin should be retained because of its association both with mystery and Catholic dogma. One bishop actually argued that Jesus spoke Latin at the Last Supper and, therefore, the church should continue the practice! Nonetheless, when the council discussed a proposed document on liturgical language in August of 1562, four out of five bishops were in favor of the vernacular.

On 5 September 1562 a compromise document was presented to the bishops and approved. It stated that out of pastoral concern for the faithful, it was not the proper moment to shift from Latin to the vernacular; more time for catechesis would be needed. Those same bishops encouraged some use of the vernacular during Mass, however, especially on Sundays and feasts when preaching in the vernacular was recommended. This led to an increase in vernacular worship after the council. In Bavaria, the practice of vernacular hymnody was fairly well established by the fifteenth century, and it became even more widespread throughout Germany after Trent. The 1582 Synod of Breslau declared that vernacular hymns should be sung at the gradual as a type of gospel hymn (still sung today in Anglican churches) and also within the EP after the consecration at low Masses, when there was not a choir singing the Mass in Latin. In 1605, the *Cantual of Mainz* included a number of possibilities for vernacular singing during Mass.

[29] See Geoffrey J. Cuming, *A History of Anglican Liturgy* (London: The Macmillan Press, Ltd., 1982), 33–35, 47–52.

[30] Cattaneo, *Il Culto Cristiano*, 282–85.

Post-Tridentine Vernacular Advances

Subsequent centuries witnessed further vernacular advances regarding not only hymnody and preaching but also the liturgical texts themselves. In 1615 Pope Paul V (d. 1621) gave permission for the use of Mandarin Chinese in the celebration of Mass and the Divine Office at the Jesuit Mission in Peking along with the translation of the Bible, responding to a request made by Jesuit Cardinal Robert Bellarmine. In 1631 full vernacular privileges were granted to missionaries in Georgia for the celebration of Mass either in Georgian or Armenian. Already in the sixteenth century lay missals had become popular among wealthier Catholics in Germany, France, Belgium, and England. By the year 1660 an elaborate, four-volume French-Latin missal was published, calling significant attention to the vernacular in the midst of the Catholic-Jansenist debate. It was produced by Joseph de Voisin, a Parisian priest, and carried the imprimatur of the cardinal archbishop of Paris. Nonetheless, the missal was condemned by an assembly of French clergy the very year it was published and condemned the following year by Pope Alexander VII (d. 1667); it was also placed on the *Index of Forbidden Books* where it remained until 1897. The missal continued to be available in Parisian bookshops, however, and the cardinal continued to support both Voisin and the text, arguing that it helped the laity in better preparing for Sunday Mass.[31]

Despite Roman prohibitions, vernacular missals continued to be published throughout Europe (including France), and no further Roman intervention was registered. By 1830 only twelve dioceses in France were still using the 1570 Latin Missal of Pius V. A similar promotion of the vernacular was unfolding in England led by Catholic priests James Dymock and John Goter (a former Presbyterian). In 1676 Dymock published *The Great Sacrifice of the New Law expounded by the figures of the Old*, providing a complete English translation of the Ordinary of the Mass including the Canon, along with the Proper for Trinity Sunday and a Mass for the Dead. This was probably the first time that the Canon was translated into English. In 1718, Goter published the entire Mass in English: *The Holy Mass in Latin and English* (later editions were called *The Roman Missal in Latin and English*). Goter's work became a model for subsequent vernacular missals published between 1780 and 1850 during the English Catholic Enlightenment.[32]

[31] Gerald Ellard, *The Mass of the Future* (Milwaukee: Bruce Publishing Co., 1948), 127.

[32] James D. Crichton, *Lights in the Darkness: Fore-Runners of the Liturgical Movement* (Blackrock, Co. Dublin: The Columba Press, 1996), 65–71.

Eighteenth-century Italy engaged in its own vernacular promotion largely through the pastoral efforts of Sicilian Theatine Cardinal Giuseppe Maria Tommasi (d. 1713) and Lodovico Antonio Muratori (d. 1750) of Milan, who translated the entire Ordinary of the Mass into Italian. The Jansenist Synod of Pistoia (1786) relied heavily on Muratori's research, calling for the restoration of a vernacular liturgy where clergy and lay faithful sang the Mass parts together.[33]

In North America Jesuit missionaries had already received permission from Rome for use of the Iroquois language in the liturgy in a region centered around modern-day Montreal. Of even greater significance was the vernacular leadership offered by John Carroll (d. 1815), the first bishop of Baltimore as well as the first bishop in the United States. Carroll argued for vernacular worship on the grounds of intelligibility since Latin impeded the work of evangelization. During the first diocesan synod (November 1791), some use of English was allowed in liturgical celebrations. The gospel was to be read in English on Sundays and feast days; Benediction of the Blessed Sacrament with Sunday Vespers should have been followed by a catechetical instruction in English; vernacular hymns and prayers were recommended throughout various services. In subsequent years, attempts at unapproved liturgical translations abounded, leading Carroll to call another synod (November 1810) in which he attempted to correct the problem and offer clear directives on when vernacular usage was permitted and only with approved texts.[34] In 1822 Bishop John England of Charleston edited the first American edition of the Roman Missal in English. Published in New York, the missal borrowed much material from a text that was already being used in England with full support of the English hierarchy.[35] Vernacular hymnody and prayers became standard fare in national parishes founded in Canada and the United States in the late nineteenth and early twentieth centuries, responding to the pastoral need of the new wave of immigrants.

Twentieth-Century Developments

Vernacular advances around the world continued in the twentieth century. In 1906 Pius X (d. 1914) gave permission for certain regions of Yugoslavia to use the classic Paleoslav language in liturgical celebrations. Fourteen

[33] Cattaneo, *Il Culto Cristiano*, 373–74.

[34] John Tracy Ellis, "Archbishop Carroll and the Liturgy in the Vernacular," in *Perspectives in American Catholicism* (Baltimore: Helicon Press, 1963), 127–33.

[35] John England, ed., *The Roman Missal Translated into the English Language for the Use of the Laity* (New York: William H. Creagh, 1822), iii.

years later Benedict XV (d. 1922) granted similar permission for the use of Croatian and Slovenian and the vernacular singing of the epistle and gospel in solemn Masses; he also allowed the use of Czech in those parts of Bohemia where it had been customary since the fifteenth century as noted above. A bilingual ritual was approved for Bavaria in 1929 and a Vienna edition in 1935 used throughout Austria. In North America, an unsuccessful petition for an English ritual was launched in 1910; the US bishops did not respond to the request and the subject was dropped. The church in the United States had to wait until 1954 for an approved bilingual ritual—significantly later than many other parts of the world. Bilingual missals continued to be printed around the world; one of the most celebrated was *My Sunday Missal* (1938), published by Brooklyn priest Joseph Stedman. Known as the "if you can count to fifteen you can't get lost Missal," its appeal was due largely to its easy layout, large print, and popular style. Translated into Chinese, French, German, Italian, Polish, and Oticipwe Native American, the book sold more than fifteen million copies. In 1941 and 1942, permission was granted to create bilingual editions of the Roman Ritual in Africa, China, India, Indo-China, Indonesia, Japan, and New Guinea. Such translations were of great help in the task of evangelization in those places. In 1948 a bilingual ritual was approved in France for the celebrations of baptism, marriage, and anointing of the sick. The following year a translation of the *MR1570* into Mandarin Chinese was approved with the exception of the Canon, which remained in Latin. In those parts of India where Hindi was spoken, permission was granted in 1950 for the use of that vernacular in celebrating the sacraments. A German-Latin edition of the *Collectio Rituum I* was published in 1951, containing even more vernacular than had been produced in France.[36]

Such vernacular concessions did not come about by accident. Rather, it was the painstaking efforts of vernacular lobbyists—sometimes bishops themselves—who made it their aim to restore a participative liturgy accessible to the masses, using the Pauline principle of intelligibility as their guide. Such efforts were well represented in the International Vernacular Society founded in 1945 by the German liturgical pioneer Hans Anscar Reinhold[37] and then led soon after by the eccentric Scottish–New Zealander

[36] Ellard, *The Mass of the Future*, 152–54.

[37] For an excellent treatment of Reinhold's life and work, see Julia A. Upton, *Worship in Spirit and Truth: The Life and Legacy of H. A. Reinhold* (Collegeville, MN: Liturgical Press / Pueblo, 2009).

Colonel John Kimbell Ross-Duggan.[38] The Vernacular Society's membership of ten thousand stretched far beyond the English-speaking world, largely because of the Society's review *Amen*, which had international circulation. Members were a mixed group of Catholic clergy and laity, some of whom had been steeped in the Anglican tradition so attentive to the beauty and power of well-crafted English liturgical texts. One vernacularist actually proposed using the *Book of Common Prayer* as the *editio typica* or base text for an English translation of the Missal, stating, "It's Catholic—Let's Claim It!"[39]

Despite their good intentions, however, many preconciliar vernacularists were not the most diplomatic of individuals. Indeed, many bishops and some pioneers in the liturgical movement were afraid to be listed as members of the Vernacular Society lest their association with the group jeopardize their own efforts at liturgical renewal. To this end, it is difficult to ascertain the extent to which the vernacular concessions granted at Vatican II were the fruit of the Vernacular Society's efforts. That organization certainly played some role and influenced several bishops, including some in the Roman Curia. The most significant influence, however, appears to have come from the great vernacularist Archbishop Paul Hallinan of Atlanta and the two US liturgical pioneers Godfrey Diekmann, OSB, and Monsignor Frederick McManus of Boston—both of whom were *periti* at the council.

One significant preconciliar event was the International Liturgical Congress at Assisi in September 1956. Organized by the Vatican's Sacred Congregation for Rites, the invitation-only event drew more than 1,400 participants from every corner of the globe—a fair number of bishops and several cardinals. The host was Cardinal Gaetano Cicognani, prefect of the Congregation, who made it clear that while the subject was to be pastoral liturgy, the only item not to be discussed was worship in the vernacular. Nonetheless, beginning with Jesuits Josef Jungmann and Augustin Bea who gave the two major introductory addresses at the congress, every speaker advocated the vernacular directly or indirectly. As the group prepared to travel to Rome at the end of the week for an audience with Pope Pius XII, there was some hope that the pope would use the occasion to announce certain vernacular concessions. To their disappointment, he stated just the opposite: it is the "unconditional obligation" of those celebrating in the Latin Rite to use Latin; he also insisted that Gregorian chant should not be

[38] For a full chronicle of the Vernacular Society's history, see Pecklers, *Dynamic Equivalence*, 42–216.

[39] Ibid., 151–52.

translated into the vernacular.[40] Nonetheless, the council's Preparatory Liturgical Commission was drawn from the list of participants at Assisi, and it was the pastoral vision exhibited at Assisi that influenced the shaping of the council's liturgical agenda.

From Vatican II to *LitAuth*[41]

Vatican II and the Vernacular

Preparation for Vatican II[42] began in 1959 under the direction of the Antepreparatory Commission. A consultation of 2,594 future council fathers—bishops, prelates, and religious superiors—elicited 1,998 responses. Later supplementary consultations (e.g., of Catholic faculties of theology, curial bodies, etc.) brought the totals to 2,812 consultations, with 2,150 replies.[43] The responses were collated and synthesized into proposals to be sent to the Central Preparatory Commission, which succeeded the Antepreparatory Commission.[44]

The vernacular question, so prominent at the Assisi Conference (1956), was raised frequently in the responses of the bishops and prelates.[45] Of those who addressed the question, only a small minority proposed total

[40] Ibid., 78–83.

[41] Historical documentation for this section is extensive. Complete reports of the preparation for and proceedings of Vatican II are in *ADA* and *ADP*, respectively, and *ASSCO*. For a concise overview of historical accounts and commentary for the council and the subsequent implementation of the council's liturgical reform, see Keith F. Pecklers, *The Genius of the Roman Rite: On the Reception and Implementation of the New Missal* (Collegeville, MN: Liturgical Press, 2009), 47–68. For an account focusing on the vernacular, see Pecklers, *Dynamic Equivalence*, 173–98.

[42] On the preparatory phase, see: Bugnini, 14–28; Carlo Braga, "La 'Sacrosanctum Concilium' nei Lavori della Commissione Preparatoria," *Notitiae* 20, no. 1 (1984): 87–134; Joseph A. Komonchak, "The Struggle for the Council during the Preparation of Vatican II (1960–1962)," in *History of Vatican II*, ed. Giuseppe Alberigo, English ed. Joseph A. Komonchak (Maryknoll, NY: Orbis, 1995), 1:206–26; Aimé Georges Martimort, "La Constitution sur la Liturgie de Vatican II: Esquisse Historique," *La Maison-Dieu* 158 (1984): 33–52; Herman Schmidt, *La Costituzione sulla Sacra Liturgia: Testo—Genesi—Commenta—Documentazione* (Roma: Casa Editrice Herder, 1966), 96–123.

[43] Étienne Fouilloux, "The Antepreparatory Phase: The Slow Emergence from Inertia (January, 1959–October, 1962)," in *History of Vatican II*, ed. Alberigo, 55–166; here at 98–99. He notes (93) that Pope John XXIII insisted on an open-ended invitation rather than the specific questions of the proposed questionnaire.

[44] The *Analyticus conspectus*, more than fifteen hundred pages, is recorded in *ADA* 2:9–10, appendices I–II. A much shorter final synthesis was prepared but remained unpublished, and it may not have impacted the work of the preparatory commissions. For a critical analysis of the process used to synthesize the proposals, see Fouilloux, "Antepreparatory Phase," 140–49.

[45] Braga, "La 'Sacrosanctum Concilium,'" 88, notes that of the 9,348 proposals in the *Analyticus conspectus*, 1,885 (20 percent) dealt with liturgy directly or indirectly.

retention of Latin; the vast majority favored some use of the vernacular.[46] Such a widespread call for extended use of the vernacular ensured that it would receive serious consideration at the council; it would also prove to be very controversial.[47]

The Central Preparatory Commission established sixteen preparatory commissions to prepare materials for the council. One of these, the Liturgical Commission, received eight official *Quaestiones*, including one about retaining Latin in the liturgy and admitting the vernacular.[48] The Liturgical Commission's work, in turn, was distributed to subcommissions.[49] The question about the language of liturgy was assigned to the subcommission on Latin Language.

The Central Preparatory Commission posed several questions for the subcommission on Latin: (1) whether Latin was to be retained in full force in the liturgy of the Latin Church; (2) whether some part was to be opened to vernacular languages and, if so, which parts and to what extent—in the Mass, the sacraments and sacramentals, and the Divine Office; and (3) how young clerics could be adequately prepared to celebrate in Latin.[50]

That last question highlights an intriguing bit of history in the ongoing disagreement about the use of Latin involving several commissions of the Curia.[51] In the midst of that tug-of-war, John XXIII issued the apostolic constitution *Veterum Sapientia* on 22 February 1962,[52] which called for intensifying the study of Latin by seminarians. Debate followed on whether

[46] Komonchak, "The Struggle," 215–16, n. 194, gives the following figures for the 1,998 responses of the bishops and prelates: about 60 respondents urged that Latin be preserved; 354 asked for greater use of the vernacular in the Mass, at least in the "catechetical" parts; and 305 called for vernacular in the sacraments, except for the form (a ratio of 10 to 1 favoring some use of the vernacular). The summary of all 2,150 responses in the *Analyticus conspectus*, *ADA* 2:10, appendix II, 387–429, lists 31 proposals (70 responses cited) in favor of sole use of Latin, and 245 proposals (1,384 responses cited) in favor of some use of the vernacular (a ratio of citations almost 20 to 1 supporting the vernacular).

[47] Komonchak, "The Struggle," 214.

[48] *De lingua liturgica latina et de linguis vernaculis in celebranda liturgia admittendis* (Braga, "La 'Sacrosanctum Concilium,'" 89).

[49] Initially, seven were approved for the Central Preparatory Commission by Pope John XXIII on 2 July 1960, with the provision that the commissions could add others (*ADP* 2:1, 408, 412). The liturgy questions eventually increased to thirteen. See Braga, "La 'Sacrosanctum Concilium,'" 93–94, 108–10; Bugnini, 15–16.

[50] Braga, "La 'Sacrosanctum Concilium,'" 115–16. The last question ended up on the agenda of another preparatory commission.

[51] The Commission for Studies and Seminaries, the Commission on the Missions, and the Secretariat for Christian Unity. For a full account of this somewhat puzzling episode, see Komonchak, "The Struggle," 211–26.

[52] John XXIII, "Constitutio Apostolica: De Latinitatis studio provehendo," *AAS* 54 (1962), 129–35. Co-author Gilbert Ostdiek chanced to be at St. Peter's when John XXIII, flanked by a

or not this document applied to use of the vernacular in the liturgy.[53] The debate had the effect of leading Annibale Bugnini and the Liturgical Commission to insist strongly that the final preconciliar draft of the schema on the liturgy should provide for the retention of at least some Latin in the liturgy. That draft, which the Central Preparatory Commission presented for conciliar debate, addressed the question of liturgical language in eight places.[54]

Materials brought to the council floor for debate[55] went through a series of steps: discussion, proposals for amendment, vote on the amendments, further modification, and final vote. The results of these debates were forwarded to ten conciliar commissions to be amended or modified as needed and then returned to the floor for further conciliar discussion and vote.[56] One such commission, the Conciliar Commission on the Liturgy, continued to meet both while the council was in session and during the recess between sessions. Its work was assigned to fifteen subcommissions.[57]

The schema on the sacred liturgy, the first to be taken up by the council, was discussed in fifteen general assemblies from 22 October through 13 November 1962. There were 328 oral and 297 written interventions.[58] The issue of Latin and vernacular was one of the major topics.[59] Intertwined with it were issues of liturgical adaptation and the authority of bishops' conferences to oversee and regulate the liturgy in their territories, a far more tendentious issue that involved reversing centuries of curial centralization.[60]

---

frowning Bishop Baggio (the long-time curial Latinist), read the constitution from the papal altar. A little smile played on John's face as he read it—in Italian!

[53] For commentary, see: Komonchak, "The Struggle," 223–26; Frederick R. McManus, "*Veterum Sapientia*," *Worship* 36 (1962): 408; Pecklers, *Dynamic Equivalence*, 117–20.

[54] The entire schema can be found in *ASSCO* 1:1, 262–303. Liturgical language is addressed specifically in nos. 24 [36], 21 [39], 41 [54], 48 [63], 63 [76], 65 [78], 79 [101], and 93 [113]—with the bracketed numbers being those of *SC*. Rather than treat the question of liturgical language as a stand-alone topic at the risk of strong opposition from curial officials, the subcommission on Latin had decided to address it in the context of pertinent topics throughout the schema (see Martimort, "La constitution," 39).

[55] On the conciliar debates about the liturgical schema, see Bugnini, 29–38; Reiner Kaczynski, "Toward the Reform of the Liturgy," in *History of Vatican II*, ed. Alberigo, 3:189–219; Mathus Lamberigts, "The Liturgy Debate," in *History of Vatican II*, ed. Alberigo, 2:107–66; Martimort, "La Constitution," 33–52; Schmidt, *La Costituzione*, 124–208.

[56] Votes were cast either as "yes" (*placet*), "no" (*non placet*), or "yes with reservations" (*placet juxta modum*). The Conciliar Commission on the Liturgy considered all reservations (*modi*) and proposed modifications for conciliar discussion and vote.

[57] For an overview see Bugnini, 30–33.

[58] Lamberigts, "The Liturgy Debate," 110.

[59] Ibid., 112.

[60] Ibid., 117–18.

The interwoven issues of liturgical language and episcopal authority surfaced especially in discussion of no. 24 of the schema (*SC*, no. 36), which garnered some eighty interventions. The debate on language turned on issues such as ecclesial unity, theological fidelity, pastoral concern for active participation, and respect for the cultures of peoples.[61] The debate on episcopal authority in matters of liturgical language wrestled with the bishops' role in relation to Rome. Traces of the struggle can still be found in successive versions of the liturgical schema. The preparatory schema provided that each episcopal conference was to decree or enact (*statuere*) the use and limits of the vernacular, and its decisions were to receive the *recognitio* of Rome (*actis a Sancta Sede recognitis*[62]). The schema reached the council floor in an altered version[63] in which the episcopal conference was to propose (*proponere*) the use and limits of the vernacular for Rome's decision. Vigorous conciliar debate led to a restoration of the language of *statuere* for episcopal authority in the third version of the schema, but the technical term *recognitio* was replaced by "approval or confirmation" (*actis ab Apostolica Sede probatis seu confirmatis*).[64] The fourth and final version of the schema retained the language of the third.

The meaning of the term *recognitio* in Roman documents is not completely clear, and modern translations normally leave it in Latin. It literally means to review or examine, with the implication that Rome could amend an act of local bishops without overriding their authority with its own.[65]

[61] For a summary of the arguments for and against an exclusive retention of Latin, ibid., 120–23.

[62] Here the text cites can. 291 of the 1917 *Code of Canon Law* concerning the acts of provincial plenary councils. The 1983 *Code of Canon Law*, no. 657, §1, applies the *recognitio* to translation of liturgical books.

[63] Who made the change is unclear. See Bugnini, 26–27; Komonchak, "The Struggle," 313–14.

[64] In his *relatio* presenting this amendment on the council floor, Bishop Karel Calewaert explained that *confirmatis* explains the more generic *probatis* and that Rome's action "adds a new juridical force" to the law established by the lower authority (*ASSCO* I:4, 288). See Frederick R. McManus, "The Constitution on the Sacred Liturgy: Commentary," *Worship* 38 (1963–64): 354–56. Despite its being abandoned in later revisions of no. 24 of the schema, *recognitio* survived in no. 48 (SC, no. 63b), which deals with revision of the *Roman Ritual*.

[65] A recent response from the Pontifical Council for Legislative Texts ("Nota: La 'Recognitio' nei documenti della Santa Sede," *Communicationes* 38, no. 1 [2006]: 10–17) states explicitly that the term is ambiguous; it means a thorough review, not authorization, and is better stated as *approbatio* or *confirmatio*. This fine distinction in the matter of the authority of episcopal conferences to approve liturgical translations may now be moot in light of *LitAuth*, no. 104, where Rome reserves to itself the right to prepare and approve translations. *LitAuth* states that the "*recognitio* is not a mere formality, but rather is an exercise of the power of governance" (no. 82).

The purpose of the *recognitio* is to safeguard doctrine and discipline and to give bishops' acts the added status of Rome's "blessing."

Other areas evoking strong debate in the council hall were the limits to the use of the vernacular in the Mass and the Divine Office. The process of debating and amending the schema on the liturgy continued in the second period of the council (autumn 1963), resulting in a great number of changes in the text.[66] The council fathers voted on the final text of the schema on 20 and 22 November 1963, and it was promulgated on 4 December of that year.

In the matter of liturgical language, *SC* adopted a *via media*. Latin was to be preserved, but use of the vernacular was also to be allowed. *SC* specified particular places for introduction of the vernacular, but it was careful to leave the extent of the vernacular open for episcopal conferences to determine in light of the needs of their people and cultures. The specific provisions that *SC* made for the use of the vernacular were as follows:[67]

- no. 36.1: Latin is to be preserved
- no. 36.3: the competent territorial ecclesiastical authority[68] is to decide, with the approval or confirmation of Rome, whether and to what extent the vernacular is to be used
- no. 36.4: translations into the mother tongue must be approved by the competent territorial ecclesiastical authority[69]
- no. 39: that same territorial authority is to specify adaptations, including liturgical language
- no. 54: suitable place may be allotted to the mother tongue in celebration of the Eucharist, in the first place[70] to the readings, prayer of the

[66] Bugnini, 33–37, lists the principal amendments.

[67] These concessions seem modest in hindsight, but at the time, after fifteen centuries of Latin, they were remarkably bold. For an extended three-part commentary on these provisions of *SC* written shortly after its promulgation, see McManus, "The Constitution," 314–74, 450–98, 515–65, *passim*. A specialist in liturgical law, McManus knew the development and intent of these provisions in great detail, having served as a consultor on the Preparatory Conciliar Commission and as a *peritus* on the Conciliar Commission on the Liturgy.

[68] The language of "episcopal conference" (*Conferentiae Episcopalis*) used in the first two versions of the schema was replaced in the last two versions by the phrase, "competent territorial ecclesiastical authority" (*competentis auctoritatis ecclesiasticae territorialis*). The earlier wording became common after the council.

[69] Note that at this point the *SC* does not speak about the approval or confirmation by Rome.

[70] The Latin has *praesertim* (especially), so this list is meant to be illustrative rather than restrictive. In his *relatio* presenting emendations to *SC*, no. 54, Bishop Jesús Enciso Viana

faithful, and parts which pertain to the people; for a more extended use of the mother tongue the norms governing adaptation (no. 40) apply

- no. 63: use of the mother tongue is to be extended in administration of the sacraments and sacramentals
- no. 63.a: use of the vernacular follows the norm of no. 36
- no. 63.b: the competent territorial authority is to prepare adaptations of the new edition of the Roman Ritual, including the language employed, with the approval of Rome[71]
- no. 75: the address given by the bishop in the rites of ordination may be in the mother tongue
- no. 78: in the celebration of marriage the nuptial blessing may be said in the mother tongue
- no. 101.1: Latin is to be retained in the Divine Office, but the ordinary can grant use of the vernacular
- no. 101.2: the competent [religious] superior can grant the use of the vernacular
- no. 101.3: clerics who pray the Divine Office in the vernacular with a group of the faithful satisfy their obligation
- no. 113: as regards the language used in songs for the Mass, the sacraments, and the Divine Office, the provisions of no. 36 are to be observed

Provisions for the Vernacular in the Implementation of the Reform

Implementation of the liturgical renewal laid out in *SC* started without delay.[72] On 13 January 1964, Paul VI appointed Annibale Bugnini to lead a

---

explicitly noted that no part of the Mass was expressly excluded from the possible use of the vernacular (*ASSCO* 2:2, 291). He also noted that *SC*, no. 36 was worded in a *via media* between those who wanted the Mass to be totally in Latin or totally in the vernacular (ibid., 290); for that same reason, *tribuatur* in the first two redactions of the schema had been changed to *tribui possit* ("a suitable place for vernacular may be allotted to the mother tongue"; ibid., 302), just as in *SC*, no. 36 the original text had used the gerundive form to say that "Latin is to be preserved" (*servandus est*), whereas the final version substitutes the softer subjunctive form (*servetur*).

[71] As noted above, *recognitio* is retained here.

[72] On the early stages of the implementation, see: Kaczynski, "Toward the Reform," 234–56; Bugnini, 49–95; Piero Marini, *A Challenging Reform: Realizing the Vision of Liturgical Renewal*, ed. Mark R. Francis, John R. Page, Keith F. Pecklers (Collegeville, MN: Liturgical Press, 2007).

council for implementing the liturgical reform, known by the first word of its Latin title, *Consilium ad exsequendam Constitutionem de sacra Liturgia*. The Consilium was publicly announced on 25 January 1964, by Paul VI in his motu proprio, *Sacram Liturgiam*. That document also established several general norms for implementing *SC* in advance of the more thorough revisions of the rites that would follow later. Regarding the vernacular, the last sentence of article IX, unlike *SC*, no. 36.4, specified that all translations of Latin liturgical texts required the approval or confirmation by the Holy See.[73] This raised once again the question of the authority of episcopal conferences and reopened the struggle between the Sacred Congregation of Rites and the Consilium about final authority to guide the implementation. The issue was settled when the Consilium was established as a separate body with full authority.

Several statements of the Consilium followed regarding the vernacular. Chief among these were the following:

- *IntOec*, instruction on the orderly implementation of *SC*, 26 September 1964 (on the vernacular, see nos. 30, 37, 40–43, 48g, 51, 57–59, 61, 74a-b, 82–83, 86, 89 = DOL 322, 329, 332–35, 340, 343, 340–49, 353, 366, 374–75, 378, 361)
- *Consilium ad exsequendam*, 16 October 1964, letter to the conferences of bishops calling for deliberateness and prudence in the translation of liturgical texts[74] and for a uniform translation in the major modern languages (DOL 764)
- *In edicendis normis*, 23 November 1965, instruction on the use of the vernacular in the Liturgy of the Hours and the conventual or community Mass (DOL 791–811)
- *Tres abhinc annos*, 4 May 1967, instruction on the orderly implementation of the Constitution on the Liturgy (on the vernacular, see nos. 2, 28 = DOL 448, 474)
- *Aussitôt après*, 10 August 1967, communication to the presidents of episcopal conferences on the translation of the Roman Canon (DOL 820–25)

[73] Paul VI, "Motu Proprio, *Sacram Liturgiam*," art. 9 = DOL 287. For commentary, see Kaczynski, "Toward the Reform," 248–56; Bugnini, 54–59; Marini, *A Challenging Reform*, 15–33; McManus, "The Constitution," 358.

[74] The principle of proceeding gradually had already been voiced by the Consilium, "Letter *Le sarei grato*," no. 3, 25 March 1964, to the papal nuncios and apostolic delegates for them to communicate to the conferences of bishops = DOL 618.

- *Circa Instructionem*, March 1969, declaration on interim translations of liturgical texts (DOL 881–83)

Other congregations also issued statements concerning the vernacular and translation, e.g.:

- Sacred Congregation on Divine Worship, *Dum toto terrarum*, 25 October 1973, circular letter to presidents of episcopal conferences on the translation of sacramental forms (DOL 904–8)
- Sacred Congregation on the Doctrine of the Faith, *Instauratio liturgica*, 25 January 1974, declaration on the translation of sacramental forms (DOL 909)
- Sacred Congregation on Sacraments and Divine Worship, *Decem iam annos*, 5 June 1976, letter to presidents of episcopal conferences on the use of the vernacular (DOL 911–17)

In keeping with the open-ended, nonrestrictive character of *SC*, no. 36.2 noted above, requests for and authorization of extended use of the vernacular grew rapidly. From the readings, prayers of the faithful, and people's parts (*SC*, no. 54), the vernacular was extended to the antiphons, chants, acclamations, dialogues, Our Father and embolism, the formula for communion of the faithful, the collects,[75] the preface,[76] and the Canon of the Mass.[77] In the case of the sacraments, the second conciliar version of the schema on the liturgy had been amended to allow the use of the vernacular; however, the sacramental form was to be kept in Latin, except for marriage.[78] That restriction was removed in the final text of *SC* (no. 63a). By 1973 translation of the sacramental forms was possible, with approval reserved to the pope. As noted above, the 1965 letter *In edicendis normis* had opened up the possibility of using the vernacular in the Divine Office. In sum, within a decade after the council people could participate in liturgical celebrations entirely in their own tongue.[79]

[75] *Notitiae* 1 (1969): 9.

[76] Secretary of State, "Letter *Ho l'onore*," 27 April 1965 = DOL 766. If the preface dialogue and the Holy Holy were in the vernacular, the reasoning went, it made no sense to keep the preface in Latin.

[77] Paul VI, "Concession," 31 January 1967, allowing use of the vernacular in the Canon, *ad experimentum* = DOL 816–17; see also 486.

[78] *ASSCO* 2:2, 551. Numerous petitions for vernacular in the EP had been submitted by the conferences.

[79] The task of vernacularization to be overseen by the Consilium was monumental and presented some unique difficulties. First was the scale of the project. The texts of the *MR* alone

Translation into the Vernacular

In addition to offering episcopal conferences guidance about the extent of the use of the vernacular, the Consilium also worked to provide principles and procedures for the process of translation. One of its early actions was to gather some 249 conference representatives and experts already working on translations around the world for a conference on translation in Rome, 9–13 November 1965.[80] The stated goals of the conference were to learn from the actual experience of translators and to develop common orientations and general criteria for them. The agenda included seventeen major presentations and language conscription break-outs.[81] Presenters included such notables as Carlo Braga, Joseph Gelineau, Salvatore Marsili, Aimé Georges Martimort, Frederick McManus, A.-M. Roguet, and Herman Schmidt. Though many presenters drew contrasts between approaches to translation now generally characterized as "literal" and "dynamic" equivalence, with preference for the latter, there were very few references to scholarly theories of translation then making their appearance.[82] In an address to those gathered, Paul VI noted in support that "liturgical translations have become . . . the voice of the Church" rather than mere "aids" to understand the Latin Mass. He acknowledged the difficulty of the translators' task in the words of St. Jerome: "If I translate word for word, it sounds absurd; if I am forced to change something in the word order or style, I seem to have stopped being a translator."[83]

---

numbered some 2,500. Second, the vernacular texts were initially all to be translations. When Latin was first being introduced into the Roman liturgy (see 37ff. above), there were few fixed texts needing translation; prayers were extemporized, albeit according to known patterns, style, and kind of vocabulary. Earliest to be fixed in Latin were portions of the Canon, with the vast corpus of ancient collects dating later, to the fifth and sixth centuries. In guiding the translation of liturgical texts, the Consilium faced, in effect, a huge task for which the Church had not had extensive or recent experience.

[80] For a brief account, see "Conventus de Popularibus Interpretationibus Textuum Liturgicorum," *Notitiae* 1 (1965): 393–98.

[81] The acts of the conference were published as *Le Traduzioni dei Libri Liturgici: Atti del Congresso tenuto a Roma il 9–13 novembre 1965* (Città del Vaticano: Libreria Editrice Vaticana, 1966).

[82] Herman Schmidt, "Relazione bibliografica commentata," in *Le Traduzioni dei Libri Liturgici*, 43–56, was a notable exception. He was well versed in the area of contemporary theories of language.

[83] Quoted in DOL 786. Italians have captured the latter half of this quandary in a pithy play on words: *traduttore traditore* ("translator traitor"). On the phenomenon of translators often facing moral attacks and accusations of infidelity and treason, see Robert Wechsler, *Performing without a Stage: The Art of Literary Translation* (North Haven, CT: Catbird Press, 1998), 58–94.

In the aftermath of the conference, in 1967 the Consilium activated a special group (*coetus 32bis*) to begin preparing an instruction on translation.[84] A draft was prepared in French and sent to the "mixed" (i.e., international) commissions for translation and amplification with illustrations and concerns specific to their languages. An interim Latin text was prepared by the Consilium, but it was never finalized into an *editio typica* or published.[85] The Consilium then amended the texts it received from the "mixed" commissions. The Italian version was submitted to Paul VI for review, and he annotated it copiously. His amendments were incorporated into the other major language versions, and all six were issued in 1969 under the same protocol number using the title of the original French draft (*CLP*).[86]

CLP presents itself not as a theoretical discussion of translation, but as a practical guide for the process and procedures of translation.[87] It deliberately avoids technical language. Though its approach to translation can generally be described as dynamic equivalence, that is, translation of meaning-for-meaning[88] rather than word-for-word, it also states that the latter approach may at time suffice (*CLP*, nos. 21–22, 24). The main body of the section on general principles is framed—as indicated by the subdivisions in the preliminary Latin text—around concern for a threefold fidelity: to the message, to the intended audience, and to the manner in which the message is communicated to them in their language (*CLP*, nos. 19 and 29).[89] It envisioned a three-stage process: first translation, then revision of the translations after sufficient pastoral experience (*CLP*, no. 1), and eventually creation of original texts more suited to the cultures and pastoral situations of peoples (*CLP*, no. 43).[90]

[84] For an overview of the development and content of the instruction, see Bugnini, 236–40.

[85] The CDWDS would later claim that *CLP* was never official, though it was issued under Consilium's authority.

[86] This was a remarkable example of worldwide consultation and collegiality at work; in DOL 838–80.

[87] For commentary, see Joseph Gelineau, "Quelques remarques en marge de l'Instruction sur le traduction des textes liturgiques," *La Maison-Dieu* 98 (1960): 156–62; Gilbert Ostdiek, "Instruction on the Translation of Liturgical Texts: A Commentary," *FDLC Newsletter* 21, no. 2 (March–April 1994): 9–14, 15, 16.

[88] *CLP*, no. 12 = DOL 848: "The translator must keep in mind that the 'unit of meaning' is not the individual word but the whole passage."

[89] *CLP* gives high priority to fidelity to the needs of communication: "if any particular kind of quality is regarded as essential to a literary genre (for example, the intelligibility of prayers when said aloud), this may take precedence over another quality less significant for communication (for example, verbal fidelity)" (no. 29 = DOL 866).

[90] Bugnini calls this paragraph "an extraordinary expression of openness" (238).

Translation of the Reformed Liturgy into English

The beginnings of ICEL date to informal conversations in the fall of 1962, during the first period of Vatican II.[91] By that point in the conciliar debate it was clear that the use of the vernacular would be allowed and entrusted to decisions of the episcopal conferences. Those conversations about the need to plan collaboratively for translations to be used in the English-speaking world led to a more formal organizational meeting in mid-October 1963. As the meetings continued over the next months, plans were drawn up for the future ICEL, its organizational structure, procedures for translations, and other practical matters. In 1964 the committee prepared a formal mandate establishing an International Advisory Committee for the purpose of "achieving an English version of liturgical texts acceptable in English-speaking countries."[92] The mandate placed translation at the center of the work, but it also foresaw the need for original texts, in anticipation of the 1969 Instruction from the Consilium (*CLP*, no. 43). Ten conferences quickly adopted this mandate, to be joined later by an eleventh, and ICEL's task was underway.

In January 1965 the Advisory Committee laid out some first principles to guide the liturgical translations.[93] After 1969, ICEL was able to use *CLP*'s fuller set of official principles. Within a remarkably short period, ICEL produced the first generation of English texts, principally: the Rite of Baptism for Children (1969), the Rite of Marriage (1969), the Rites of Ordinations of Deacons, Presbyters, and Bishops (1969), the Rite of Funerals (1970), the Rite of Confirmation (1971), the Rite of Anointing and Pastoral Care of the Sick (1973), the Rite of Christian Initiation of Adults (1974), the Sacramentary (1973), the Rite of Penance (1974), and the Liturgy of the Hours (1974).

Next to the four-volume Liturgy of the Hours, the Sacramentary was the most massive project. Although the *editio typica* of the *MR* was not ready until 1970, ICEL worked in advance from earlier drafts. Most problematic for translators were the succinct Roman collects. Despite several consultations and experimental use, there was no clear unanimity on what approach

[91] For a complete history of ICEL, see Frederick R. McManus, "ICEL: The First Years," in *Shaping English Liturgy: Studies in Honor of Archbishop Denis Hurley*, ed. Peter Finn and James Schellman (Washington, DC: The Pastoral Press, 1990), 433–59; John R. Page, "ICEL, 1969–1989: Weaving the Words of Our Common Christian Prayer," in ibid., 473–89. McManus was a participant in the founding events of ICEL.

[92] For the text of the mandate, see McManus, "ICEL," 447–48.

[93] For a sample of these principles—which resonate well with the later *CLP* principles—see ibid., 454.

to use. Opinions ranged from word-for-word translations, to paraphrases only, to expansions of the Latin texts. The final decision was to provide both translations and, for the opening prayers, alternative prayers that were based on the Latin but were fuller and freer.[94]

In keeping with *CLP*, no. 1, which foresaw revision of the translations after a period of pastoral experience, in the early 1980s ICEL undertook a revision process to produce second-generation texts. Principal among these were the Pastoral Care of the Sick and Dying (1983), the Rite of Christian Initiation of Adults (1988), the Order of Christian Funerals (1989), and the Sacramentary (1982–98). The Sacramentary project[95] began with two worldwide consultations, on the presidential prayers (1982) and the Order of Mass (1984), to assess their pastoral effectiveness. In light of the results, ICEL decided to leave the now familiar texts of the Order of Mass untouched unless there were serious theological problems. The collects, however, would be translated anew. As the work on the Sacramentary progressed, an open process was maintained and ICEL issued three progress reports to invite assessment and feedback from the conferences and their national liturgical commissions and consultors.[96]

The primary principles for the retranslations were those of *CLP*. In addition, ICEL adopted further working guidelines based on the favorable reaction of the conferences to the style of language it had used for the Dedication of a Church and an Altar (1978). These included fidelity to and fuller translation of the Latin, attention to latent biblical allusions, a heightened register like that of formal public speech, and greater attention to the requirements of oral proclamation (speech stresses, cadences, rhythms).[97] To

[94] Page, "ICEL," 475–76. The three members of the editorial committee all received their early schooling in English style in the British Isles, where they were taught to use short, crisp sentences and to choose words with Anglo-Saxon roots rather than Latin roots. This accounts in great part for the style of the 1973 collects, which have often been criticized as staccato, incomplete translations, and even paraphrases of the Latin.

[95] John R. Page, "The Process of Revision of the Sacramentary," in *Liturgy for the New Millennium: A Commentary on the Revised Sacramentary*, ed. Mark R. Francis and Keith F. Pecklers (Collegeville, MN: Liturgical Press / Pueblo, 2000), 1–16.

[96] *Progress Report on the Revision of the Roman Missal* I–III (Washington, DC: ICEL, 1988, 1990, 1992).

[97] For commentary, see Gilbert Ostdiek, "Principles of Translation in the Revised Sacramentary," in *Liturgy for the New Millennium*, ed. Francis and Pecklers, 17–34. The two principal translator-editors with whom Ostdiek worked on the Subcommittee for the Translation and Revision of Texts brought special concern for this last guideline. Educated in the classical seminary program of humanities, philosophy, and theology and well-versed in Latin, both had done doctoral degrees in English literature, specializing in the Elizabethan period. At that time, when 95 percent of the people in England were said to be functionally illiterate, works such as the *King James Bible*, Cranmer's *Book of Common Prayer*, and the works of Shakespeare

aid their work, ICEL provided translators with a 415-page lexicon of terms[98] and a "face-sheet" for each prayer with the Latin text and current translations in all the major modern languages. A record was also kept of every stage in the revision of each prayer for review of the translations.

From *LitAuth* to the Present

Growing Tensions over the English Translation

The Sacramentary project was completed in 1998. Despite approval by all the member conferences of ICEL, Rome withheld the *recognitio*[99] and the revised Sacramentary, sixteen years in preparation, was shelved. This was a culmination of increasingly difficult relations between Rome and ICEL, principally over ICEL's relations to the conferences and to Rome and over questions of the approach to translation. In the late 1980s, Rome had begun to take a more active role in critiquing and amending the texts submitted for *recognitio*. This was true of the Rite of Christian Initiation of Adults and especially of the Order of Christian Funerals, which garnered extensive comments and calls for revision. By the mid-1990s, Rome's attitude toward translation had taken an even sharper turn toward literal equivalence.[100] A revision of the Rites of Ordination (1994) was rejected by Rome, the first such case.[101] By 2000, it was clear that new principles would soon be issued calling for word-for-word translation and that ICEL would be significantly restructured to bring it under tighter control and to reduce its task to translation only according to new guidelines under the strict supervision and control of Rome.[102]

---

were written not to be read but to be heard. The two translator-editors sought to apply the oral quality of that literature to ICEL's translations, and this was assiduously tested at all ICEL meetings by proclaiming every text aloud before discussing it.

[98] *A Lexicon of Terms in the Missale Romanum*, compiled and edited by Thomas C. O'Brien, recorded all occurrences and variations in meaning for all the major terms used in the *MR*.

[99] The text of the CDWDS letter to the conferences can be found online at http://www.adoremus.org/CDW-ICELtrans.html (accessed July 2010).

[100] ICEL had received several oral assurances from Rome that its work on the revision of the Sacramentary would still be judged on the basis of *CLP*.

[101] This was actually meant to be a simple touch-up and not a complete retranslation, given the massive effort being devoted to the revision of the Sacramentary.

[102] For a summary chronicle of what the media labeled the "liturgy wars," see Tom Elich, "Liturgical Translation at a Crossroads," *COMPASS: A Review of Topical Theology* 36, no. 4 (Summer 2002), online at http://www.compassreview.org/summero2/6.html (accessed July 2010). For an account of the denouement of the conflict, see John Wilkins, "Lost in Translation: The Bishops, the Vatican, and the English Liturgy," *Commonweal* 132, no. 21 (2 December 2005): 12, 14–16, 18–20; Maurice Taylor, *It's the Eucharist, Thank God* (Brandon, Suffolk, UK: Decani Books, 2009), 47–74. Bishop Taylor chaired the Episcopal Board of ICEL during this time of

LitAuth *and the Principles of Translation*

On 28 March 2001, the CDWDS published the new guidelines, *LitAuth*.[103] *LitAuth* acknowledges the positive results of the liturgical renewal to date (no. 3). It immediately goes on, however, to express an overarching concern for future development of the renewal, namely, that

> the greatest prudence and care is required in the preparation of liturgical books marked by sound doctrine, which are exact in wording, free from all ideological influence, and otherwise endowed with those qualities by which the sacred mysteries of salvation and the indefectible faith of the Church are efficaciously transmitted by means of human language into prayer, and worthy worship is offered to God the Most High. (no. 3)

These words seem to imply that such prudence and care have not yet been fully achieved. Similarly, *LitAuth* notes that translation into the vernacular is a part of inculturation but that care must be taken "to maintain the identity and unitary expression of the Roman Rite" without opening up "an avenue for the creation of new varieties or families of rites" (no. 5). In that light, *LitAuth* judges that omissions and errors in some existing translations have "impeded the progress of inculturation that actually should have taken place" (no. 6). Other underlying concerns of *LitAuth* are intimated in the principles it then sets down for future translations. Of particular interest here are sections 2 and 3: "On the Translation of Liturgical Texts into Vernacular Languages" (nos. 19–69) and "On the Preparation of Translations and the Establishment of Commissions" (nos. 70–108).

Some of *LitAuth*'s general principles for future translations are similar to those of *CLP*, e.g.:

- a flowing text, easily understood but marked by dignity and beauty (nos. 20, 25)

---

turmoil and transition. By the turn of the millennium, a growing voice of discontent over the implementation of the liturgical renewal, especially the translations, had spread in the public media. It eventually led to a call for a "reform of the reform." These sentiments had apparently found a favorable hearing in Rome. For an account and commentary, see Rita Ferrone, *Liturgy: Sacrosanctum Concilium* (New York: Paulist Press, 2007), 81–87; John Baldovin, *Reforming the Liturgy: A Response to the Critics* (Collegeville, MN: The Liturgical Press, 2008).

[103] In May of 2001 CDWDS issued a lengthy press release summarizing the context and content of the instruction (reprinted in the USCCB edition of *LitAuth*, appendix A, 171–86). In addition to Rome's dissatisfaction with ICEL's work, an additional rationale given for *LitAuth* was that a third typical edition of the *MR* (*MR2002*), would require a completely new translation because of significant revisions and added materials.

- promoting full participation of the whole person through texts in the context of the ritual actions (no. 28)
- accompanied by catechetical interpretation that excludes prejudice or unjust discrimination (no. 29)

Other *LitAuth* principles place significant restrictions:

- texts are intended to express transcendent truths rather than mirror inner dispositions of the faithful (no. 19)
- exact translations are required without omission, addition, paraphrase, or gloss (nos. 20, 21, 45c, 55, 56)
- no adaptations or original texts are allowed without prior consent of Rome (nos. 20, 22)
- translations are to be only from the Latin *editio typica*, not from other modern languages (nos. 23–24)[104]
- no alteration of gendered language is allowed (nos. 30–31)
- no reliance on academic manuals of style is allowed (no. 32)
- a sacred style of speech is sought, free of overly servile adherence to prevailing modes of expression (no. 27)
- a sacral language that may sound odd or obsolete will develop (nos. 43, 47)

LitAuth then offers more specific norms, giving attention to biblical texts (one uniform text, based on the New Vulgate) and other specific kinds of liturgical texts.

From the tenor of these and other principles, it is clear that *LitAuth* adopted the approach to translation that is called literal or formal equivalence,[105] often characterized as word-for-word translation. It strives to retain from the source text as much as possible of the syntax (e.g., relative

[104] One of Rome's concerns has been the use of ICEL translations as the basis for other translations. See Pecklers, *The Genius of the Roman Rite*, 61. Also intimated here is Rome's current aversion to original texts.

[105] This is in contrast to dynamic equivalence (meaning-for-meaning), which underlies much of *CLP*. In actual fact, the second generation of ICEL texts used what some have called functional equivalence, i.e., an approach midway on the spectrum between formal and dynamic equivalence that draws on both sides of the spectrum as appropriate for a given text.

and subordinate clauses), word order, vocabulary, and even capitalization.[106] This goal is more readily realized in those modern languages derived from Latin. It is less attainable in modern languages with Anglo-Saxon roots, and it is extremely difficult in languages with a totally different syntactic and semantic structure such as those of Asian cultures.

As could be expected, the appearance of *LitAuth* occasioned a wide range of reactions, both negative and positive. One of the most telling critiques is that of Peter Jeffery, a chant historian who places himself on the conservative side of the Roman Catholic spectrum. Perhaps his most trenchant critique concerns the document's unfounded assumptions about the totally unvaried and uniform character of the liturgical tradition of the Latin Church.[107] Others have critiqued the document's stance on the requirements for scriptural translations,[108] its principles of translation,[109] its understanding of liturgical language in light of a rereading of *SC*,[110] its approach to inculturation,[111] and its negative impact on ecumenical relations in matters liturgical.[112] Others, such as the prefects of CDWDS, have come stoutly to its defense.[113]

[106] This is based on the often expressed conviction that every part of speech and grammatical construction has specific deeper theological meaning and must therefore be retained intact in the translations.

[107] Peter Jeffery, *Translating the Tradition: A Chant Historian Reads Liturgiam Authenticam* (Collegeville, MN: Liturgical Press, 2005). He characterizes *LitAuth* as "remarkably uninformed about the history of the Roman and Latin liturgical tradition," manifesting "a nearly fundamentalist view of the liturgical texts currently in force" (52, 53). He frequently quotes a theological dictum to describe the fact that varying positions are found in tradition: *diversa, sed non adversa*. What Jeffery finds most worrisome about *LitAuth* "is that what it lacks in factuality it makes up with naked aggression. It speaks words of power and control rather than cooperation and consultation, much less charity" (97). He concludes that *LitAuth* "should be summarily withdrawn" (110).

[108] Catholic Biblical Association Board, "Letter and Critique on *Liturgiam authenticam*" (2001 Catholic News Service / U.S. Conference of Catholic Bishops), online at http://www.catholicculture.org/culture/library/view.cfm?recnum=3958 (accessed August 2010); Joseph Jensen, "*Liturgiam authenticam* and the New Vulgate," *America* 185, no. 4 (13–20 August 2001): 11–13.

[109] E.g., John Baldovin, "Translating the Liturgy," *America* 195, no. 8 (25 September 2006): 26–27; Donald Trautman, "The Quest for Authentic Liturgy," *America* 185, no. 12 (22 October 2001): 7–11.

[110] See Nathan D. Mitchell's ongoing commentary on liturgical language in his "Amen Corner," esp. *Worship* 73 (2003): 356–69; 77 (2003): 56–69, 171–81, 250–63; 81 (2007): 69–83, 170–84, 268–82, 329–43, 448–60; 82 (2008): 543–55.

[111] Anscar Chupungco, "Reviews and Reflections: *Liturgiam Authenticam* and Inculturation," online at http://eapi.admu.edu.ph/eapr002./anscar.htm (accessed August 2010).

[112] E.g., Maxwell E. Johnson, "The Loss of a Common Language: The End of Ecumenical-Liturgical Convergence?" *Studia liturgica* 37, no. 1 (2007): 55–72.

[113] Cardinal Jorge A. Medina Estévez, "Translations and Consultation of the Nova Vulgata of the Latin Church," online at http://www.bible-researcher.com/liturgiam-authenticam3

Ratio Translationis

LitAuth included the provision that CDWDS, after consulting the bishops, would prepare a *ratio translationis* "in which the principles of translation found in this Instruction will be applied in closer detail to a given language" (no. 9).

Early development of the *ratio* took place under the auspices of *Vox Clara*, a committee appointed by CDWDS to oversee the work of ICEL. After consulting the bishops' conferences of the English-speaking world, *Vox Clara* refined the document and presented it to CDWDS for approval. The English-speaking conferences received a preliminary version of the *ratio* for response in June 2005, and the final version was issued in 2007 under the title *Ratio Translationis for the English Language*.[114] This is intended to be an illustrative document whose purpose is to flesh out the practical applications of *LitAuth*'s principles to the English language. It is divided into three parts: presuppositions, principles, and application of the principles.[115]

LitAuth *and the Reconstitution of ICEL*

The third section of *LitAuth* (nos. 70–108) laid out new norms for the structures and procedures for translating liturgical texts. The restructuring of ICEL required by *LitAuth* was far-reaching: CDWDS erects "mixed commissions" if requested by conferences of bishops,[116] and these commissions are to be governed by statutes approved by Rome (nos. 93 and 103).[117] Draft

.html (accessed August 2010); Cardinal Francis Arinze, "Language in the Roman Rite Liturgy: Latin and Vernacular," Keynote Address at the Gateway Liturgical Conference, St. Louis, Missouri, 11 November 2006, online at http://www.adoremus.org/Arinze_StLouis06.html (accessed August 2010).

[114] The *ratio* was considered confidential, for the use of translators, ICEL, and *Vox Clara*. The USCCB has not made it available to the general public. Thus not only the identity of the translators (*LitAuth*, no. 75) but also the detailed guidelines by which they are to work, as well as the translations they produce, have not been open to public scrutiny or review. This seems out of sync with *LitAuth*, nos. 72 and 75, which state that translations should not be the work of a small group and that readiness to have their work reviewed and revised by others is an essential trait for translators.

[115] For fuller details, see http://www.nccbuscc.org/liturgy/innews/0705.pdf (accessed August 2010).

[116] ICEL was originally established by the authority and mandate of the English-speaking conferences.

[117] The founding constitution of ICEL written by the conferences was thus to be replaced by statutes formulated under the direct oversight of Rome. In a letter to the Episcopal Board of ICEL on 26 October 1999, the cardinal prefect of CDWDS, Jorge Medina Estévez, had already set down the conditions that the new statutes would have to meet, online at http://www.adoremus.org/2-00-medinaletter.html (accessed August 2010).

statutes submitted by ICEL in 2002 were judged deficient in certain aspects and were returned for revision.[118] The revised statutes, resubmitted on 1 June 2003, received Rome's approval on 15 September 2003, which formally established ICEL as a "mixed commission."

There have been a number of significant changes in the internal structures and procedures of the new ICEL. Rome now requires its *nihil obstat* for all principal collaborators who are not bishops, total confidentiality in all ICEL work, and term limits for commission members, collaborators, and experts (*LitAuth*, nos. 100–102). Standing committees have been replaced by ad hoc working groups, and there are more stringent procedures for preparing and submitting materials to Rome for approval and for proposing adaptations (*LitAuth*, nos.70 and 80). Although the technical term *recognitio* is used throughout *LitAuth* (e.g., nos. 15, 18, 22), it is clear that Rome's authority to approve translations has superseded that of the episcopal conferences. For example, the CDWDS "will be involved more immediately and directly in the preparation of translations" into the major languages (*LitAuth*, no. 76), and Rome has reserved to itself the authority to prepare and approve for liturgical use its own translations (*LitAuth*, no. 104).[119]

To assist the CDWDS in exercising its oversight and authority, another level above ICEL has been inserted into the process. As noted above, CDWDS appointed *Vox Clara* to monitor the English translation of the *MR* and to review and edit the materials ICEL submits to CDWDS for approval. *Vox Clara* is composed of twelve senior prelates from the English-speaking world, assisted by several consultors, and it has met once or twice each year to carry out its work.[120]

Regarding the process of translations, its confidential nature makes it difficult to give a complete picture.[121] The work has been done in strict confidentiality, and the translations have only been reviewed internally within ICEL, *Vox Clara*, and the CDWDS. The translators have been directed to work directly and primarily from the Latin texts of the *MR2002*, although

[118] See the letter of Cardinal Arinze, the new prefect of CDWDS, to the conference presidents dated 23 October 2002, online at http://www.adoremus.org/1202Arinze-ICEL.html (accessed August 2010).

[119] There is a rather curious sequence here: Rome prepares and approves a translation for liturgical use, a conference then approves it for use in its territory and subsequently submits it back to Rome for the *recognitio*.

[120] *Vox Clara* reports can be accessed on the web. These reports regularly list the membership, as is not the case with the membership of ICEL and its translators.

[121] Pecklers, *The Genius of the Roman Rite*, 93–104, gathers some of the more important available details.

they have had access to the previous ICEL translations (e.g., ICEL1973 and ICEL1998) and to current translations of the major modern languages. The quality of the English translations will be able to be assessed fully only when the revised *MR* will have been in actual use long enough to judge their pastoral effectiveness.

Conclusion: Lessons and Questions

The Vernacular and Inculturation

By way of conclusion, three lessons from history merit reflection. The first concerns the vernacular and inculturation. The question of the vernacular is not uniquely modern. The first part of this essay has shown that this issue is not new; history witnesses to the church's recurring efforts to announce and celebrate the good news of salvation for people of every time, place, and culture. That history is a story of successive inculturations. Central to that process has been the use of local languages. Past vernacularizations have not always been accomplished with unanimity. *Diversa sed non adversa* is a healthy lesson to take to heart in this time of tension and change.

What is different now is that we have a full record of what the process has entailed—the painful decision to allow modern forms of the vernacular to replace Latin,[122] the development of procedures and principles to carry out the process, and the long struggle over whose responsibility that is. *LitAuth*, no. 8 directs us to read its norms in conjunction with the 1994 instruction on inculturation, *VarLeg*. *VarLeg*, no. 35 notes that inculturation must balance both restoration and adaptation of the tradition. A preliminary condition for inculturation of the liturgy itself is translation of the gospel into the local language, since it is "by the mother language, which conveys the mentality and the culture of a people, that one can reach the soul, mold it in the Christian spirit, and allow [them] to share more deeply in the prayer of the Church" (*VarLeg*, no. 28). Biblical translations should enable hearers to recognize themselves and their lives proclaimed in the texts (*LitAuth*, no. 42). Should this not hold for liturgical texts as well?

The Role of Translation

Another difference in contemporary inculturation of the Latin liturgy is that all texts are now to be translations of Latin originals. Translation thus

[122] In a noonday message to the people in St. Peter's Square on 7 March 1965, Paul VI acknowledged this pain, saying, "The Church has made this sacrifice of an age-old tradition [Latin] and above all of unity in language among diverse peoples to bow to a higher universality, an outreach to all peoples" (DOL 399).

plays a central role in bringing the vernacular into the Vatican II liturgy. Furthermore, the church did not have recent or extensive experience in doing this, and the learning curve has been steep. Inevitably, there have been fits and starts in the earlier ICEL process, as well as strengths and weaknesses in the translations.

Translation of the Vatican II liturgy has been beset by a number of issues. What approach is to be taken: Formal equivalence? Dynamic equivalence? Functional equivalence? Can the structures of Latin, such as syntax, word order, and all the denotations and connotations of the vocabulary be carried over intact into every modern receptor language (*LitAuth*, no. 52)? Are the differences between inscribed text and utterance or oral speech important considerations for prayer texts proclaimed and heard in the assembly?[123] What is the appropriate style and register of liturgical prayer: Ordinary speech? Elevated public speech? Speech that sounds odd and obsolete (*LitAuth*, nos. 27 and 43)? What are the differences between ritual language, sacral language, and hieratic language,[124] and which is most appropriate for liturgy? Is there, in fact, one consistent style of liturgical Latin throughout history, or have cultural influences led to significant linguistic differences across time?[125] These issues will likely continue to need thoughtful research and measured discussion in the future.

The first, massive generation of ICEL texts, crafted hurriedly within ten years after the promulgation of *SC*, was not without flaws. For that reason, preparation of a second generation of texts was undertaken to revise and improve these texts in light of a decade of pastoral experience.[126] Might not

[123] See Gilbert Ostdiek, "Liturgical Translations: Some Reflections," in *The Voice of the Church: A Forum on Liturgical Translation*, 20–32 (Washington, DC: United States Catholic Conference, 2001), drawing on Walter Ong, *Orality and Literacy: The Technologizing of the Word* (New York: Methuen, 1982), esp. chap. 3.

[124] *LitAuth* calls for a sacral language (nos. 27 and 47). Christine Mohrmann developed what has become for many the classic position, that the patristic Church developed a sacred Latin. See her *Liturgical Latin*, 60–90; also, Uwe Michael Lang, "Rhetoric of Salvation: The Origins of Latin as the Language of the Roman Liturgy," in *The Genius of the Roman Rite: Historical, Theological, and Pastoral Perspectives on Catholic Liturgy*, ed. Uwe Michael Lang (Chicago: Liturgy Training Publications, 2010), 22–44. Anscar Chupungco holds that the highly cultivated liturgical Latin was not a sacred language but a kind of ritual language required for solemn basilican liturgies ("Ritual Language and Liturgy," in *Finding Voice to Give God Praise: Essays in the Many Languages of the Liturgy*, ed. Kathleen Hughes [Collegeville, MN: Liturgical Press, 1998], 87–99; here 91). See also Taft, "Translating Liturgically," 160–65, who holds a similar position. For more extended commentary, see Nathan D. Mitchell, "Christine Mohrmann (1903–1988): The Science of Liturgical Language," *Liturgy Digest* 1, no. 2 (Winter 1994): 4–43.

[125] E.g., between the classical Latin liturgical texts of the fourth to fifth centuries and later texts such as the *Missale Parisiense* (1481), which is notoriously difficult to translate.

[126] This follows the steps laid down in *CLP*, no. 1 = DOL 838.

the present retranslation of *MR2002*, based on a very different set of principles, also need revision in the light of pastoral experience in the years to come? This two-step process could fittingly serve as the best "school and discipline" for learning anew the art of composing original texts[127] at some future time when the restrictions now in place[128] might be relaxed in light of new pastoral needs.

The Ecclesial Context

Finally, translation of the prayers of the liturgy into the vernacular does not take place in a vacuum; it cannot be isolated from the ecclesial context in which it takes place.

On the level of ecclesiology, the story of the Vatican II reform of the liturgy and its implementation (section 2 above) reveals a striking double reversal. The Vatican II debate over the vernacular led to a dramatic shift in how authority is exercised. The long hegemony of Rome and its curial offices in matters liturgical was reversed by the council because bishops from around the world insisted on vernacular liturgy for the pastoral good of their people. New structures of local authority and collaboration were put in place by the council. Since then, the pendulum has reversed and slowly swung back toward the preconciliar status, as evidenced in the principles and procedures laid down in *LitAuth*. Another reversal does not seem likely now, yet one can hope that serious theological reflection will continue to address the question of how the church can best carry out its mission of pastoring the People of God gathered for liturgy.

On the level of pastoral practice, there are ways to facilitate a peaceful reception of ICEL2010. One way is to address the present climate of division over the liturgy.[129] Why are there "liturgy wars" and what can be done about it? Peter Jeffery offers an analysis worth considering.[130] To promote full participation in the liturgy (*SC*, no. 14), Vatican II approved a simplification of the rites and the introduction of the vernacular (*SC*, nos. 34, 36, 63). The combined effect of these two provisions has been to place primary focus on the words of the liturgy and their intelligibility. Hence the recent war over words.[131] Jeffery has several suggestions: (1) listen to both sides to

[127] Ibid, no. 43, for this image = DOL 880.

[128] See *LitAuth*, no. 22 on adaptations.

[129] Postings on the web over the past years reveal how adamant, judgmental, and even uncharitable people have become, and that is likely to continue. *LitAuth* has allayed the deep dissatisfaction felt by those who firmly opposed the reform; that same dissatisfaction is now being felt by those who worked tirelessly to promote it.

[130] Jeffery, *Translating Tradition*, 88–120.

[131] See the two liturgical ideals described by Jeffery, *Translating the Tradition*, 106–9.

understand the diversity present both in the tradition and today; (2) work for a fuller balance and reintegration of both verbal and nonverbal languages, full and robust, allowed to speak for themselves (*LitAuth*, no. 135); and (3) care for these languages and through them allow people to honor both the need for transcendence and mystery and the need for community and a liturgy that sends us into service. Empathetic pastoral care is urgently needed if God's people gathered in prayer are to be brought together into one, to manifest by action and attitude "the mystery of Christ and the real nature of the true Church" (*SC*, no. 2).

There is another, more focused effort that can be made on the pastoral level to ensure that the revised Missal will serve the church well. *LitAuth* frequently calls attention to the need for effective homilies and catechesis (e.g., no. 29). Simple instruction about the changes is not enough. What people now hunger for is a true mystagogy, a liturgical spirituality that will enable them to name what they have already experienced on a deeper level in years of celebrating the renewed liturgy.[132]

[132] E.g., a mystagogy of Eucharist: on the "spiritual significance" of the presentation of the gifts (GIRM no. 73) as a presentation of our lives and ourselves for the offering; on that act of offering ourselves along with Christ's self-offering in the anamnesis after the words of institution (*SC*, no. 48, GIRM no. 79.f); and on the meaning of the dismissal as a sending forth on mission and the lens through which liturgy and life are to be understood (John Paul II, *Mane nobiscum Domine*, no. 24, and Benedict XVI, *SacCar*, no. 51, online, respectively, at http://www.vatican.va/holy_father/john_paul_ii/apost_letters/documents/hf_jp-ii_apl_20041008_mane-nobiscum-domine_en.html; and http://www.vatican.va/holy_father/benedict_xvi/apost_exhortations/documents/hf_ben-xvi_exh_20070222_sacramentum-caritatis_en.html (accessed August 2010).

Mystagogy
Discerning the Mystery of Faith

Mary Collins and Edward Foley

Reflections on the Mystery

Why Mystagogy[1] Concerns Us

Many recent reflections on Roman Catholic liturgy—whether pastoral or scholarly in orientation—seem to agree that something essential has gone missing in the course of Vatican II's liturgical reform. This sense of vital absence lies behind the current impetus for the "reform of the reform," particularly but not exclusively in the celebration of the eucharistic liturgy. Critics' viewpoints differ on what is lacking.[2] Is it awareness of the sacred? Attentiveness to the Mystery? Aesthetic sensibility? Sufficient knowledge of Catholic doctrine? Consensus in assessing the contemporary role of the church in the world? Something—or much—appears to have gone wrong.

Bishops, theologians, pastoral liturgists, and critics from many quarters have proposed various reasons for Roman Catholic worshipers' perceived unease. A quest for recovery of what is "missing" has sent seekers in multiple directions and spawned proposals for various remedies. Benedict XVI has discussed at length his conviction that the root of widespread malaise in the liturgy lies in the cultural context within which the liturgy is celebrated, i.e., the dominant Western culture of secular modernity and postmodern relativism in the church in the North Atlantic regions. Benedict has also spoken of mystagogy as an available traditional resource for countering the weight of secularism on a life of faith.[3]

[1] "Mystagogy" will be twice defined in this article: first, at the beginning of the historical section (83 below), and in a more comprehensive way at the end of the article (100 below).

[2] John Baldovin engages representative voices and provides bibliography for further reflection on the ongoing critique in his *Reforming the Liturgy: A Response to the Critics* (Collegeville, MN: Liturgical Press, 2008).

[3] Benedict XVI as Cardinal Ratzinger spoke of a "dictatorship of relativism which does not recognize anything as for certain and which has as its great goal one's own ego and one's own desires," Homily for the Day, 18 April 2005; at http://www.vatican.va/gpII/documents/homily-pro-eligendo-pontifice_20050418_en.html (accessed 2 March 2011). He has returned

From another vantage point, the eminent Italian-born German liturgist Romano Guardini (d. 1968) suggested, just after the promulgation of *SC*, that the weak link to vital liturgical renewal was "the typical nineteenth-century man" himself and by implication his twentieth- and twenty-first-century successors. In Guardini's judgment typical worshipers were no longer able to perform a liturgical act; in fact they were "unaware of its existence." What he saw as the fundamental obstacle to revitalized liturgy was the Roman Catholic world's formation in devotional piety over many generations. Private prayers recited during Mass fostered individual piety but had left both priests and laity ill-equipped to understand or engage in corporate ecclesial liturgical acts. In light of the promulgation of *SC*, Guardini wrote:

> The question is whether the wonderful opportunities now open to the liturgy will achieve their full realization; whether we shall be satisfied with just removing anomalies, taking new situations into account, giving better instruction on the meaning of ceremonies and liturgical vessels *or whether we shall relearn a forgotten way of doing things and recapture lost attitudes*.[4]

MR2002 and its English translation ICEL2010 bear witness to the magisterial concern to confront the weight of secularism through restoration of authentic Roman Catholic awareness of an abiding confidence in the sacred mystery of the world's salvation as the Mystery is celebrated in the church's eucharistic liturgy. ICEL2010 reflects an effort to revitalize Catholic liturgical worship for twenty-first-century English-language speakers in two ways. It aims first to remove perceived obstacles to discerning the saving Mystery of Christ in the Eucharist. Then it enhances the use of traditional religious symbols, gestures, postures, and hieratic language in the hope that the worshiping church might better discern the Mystery of Christ present in its eucharistic celebrations. Yet even this current effort at revising texts and rites will inevitably fall short of its goal without the church giving equal attention to mystagogy. The danger Guardini was alert to in 1964 remains a danger five decades later: "[T]hose whose task it is to teach and educate will have to ask themselves—and this is all-decisive—whether they them-

---

to this theme often. In *SacCar* he speaks of mystagogical catechesis in addressing interior participation in the Eucharist (nos. 64–65).

[4] Romano Guardini, "Open Letter to Mgr. Wagner, organizer of the Third German Liturgical Congress," *Herder Correspondence* (Special Issue, 1964): 24–26, reprinted in *Foundations in Ritual Studies*, ed. Paul Bradshaw and John Melloh (Grand Rapids: Baker Academic, 2007), 3–8; emphasis added. For an overview of nineteenth-century Catholicism, see Joseph A. Komonchak, "Modernity and the Construction of Roman Catholicism," *Christianesimo nella storia* 18 (1997): 353–85.

selves desire the liturgical act or, to put it plainly, whether they know of its existence and what exactly it consists of and that it is neither a luxury nor an oddity, but a matter of fundamental importance."[5]

This general introductory essay on mystagogy and the Roman Missal will explore the connection between the revealed Mystery of our Roman Catholic faith and the practice of mystagogy as the way the church guides believers to discern God-with-us especially in the eucharistic liturgy. The first part of the essay will briefly recall biblical, doctrinal, and theological understandings of the Mystery and its distinctive expression in liturgy. Believers aspiring to discern the Mystery within which we live need to be aware of its breadth and demands if they are to embrace it with thanksgiving. The second part of the essay will provide a more detailed historical survey of mystagogy both as concept and as practice. Finally, we provide a pastoral synthesis summarizing what we believe to be fundamental characteristics of mystagogy, then highlighting various contemporary modes of mystagogy, and finally offering a summative definition of mystagogy. This introductory essay aims to provide background for the treatment of mystagogy in each subsequent section of this commentary on *OM2008*. In these sectional studies various authors will offer mystagogical approaches to particular liturgical texts and rites along with their own elaborations of the nature and purpose of mystagogy. Our special aim in this introductory essay is to underscore the dynamic relationship between Roman Catholic doctrinal understanding of the Mystery of our faith and the expression of that Mystery in liturgy and life.

The Mystery of our Faith in NT Writings

While the primary focus of this commentary is *OM2008* and its English translation, it is both necessary and helpful to reflect briefly on the breadth of the church's understanding of the Mystery of Christ, which is at the heart of every liturgical event. The earliest Christian references to the Mystery are to be found in the writings of St. Paul, further developed in subsequent Pauline literature. Not surprisingly, the reality that Paul and the early church knew in their lives as the presence of divine Mystery eluded all their efforts to capture in words what they understood that God has done in Christ. An early Christian hymn cited in 1 Timothy 3:16 says,

> Undeniably great is the mystery of devotion,
> Who was manifested in the flesh,
> vindicated in the spirit,

[5] Guardini in Bradshaw and Melloh, *Foundations*, 5.

> seen by angels,
> proclaimed to the Gentiles,
> believed in throughout the world,
> taken up in glory.

Undeniably, the Mystery is profound! Yet what is named in the hymn fragment is still only a partial glimpse of the Mystery named and embraced in the NT canon.

In Paul's final blessing to the Romans a broad vision of a divine plan that transcends and comprehends human history is evident. He exhorts the church at Rome to glorify God for "the revelation of the mystery kept secret for long ages but now manifested through the prophetic writings and, according to the command of the eternal God, made known to all nations" (Rom 16:25b-26). Pauline letters to the Ephesians and Colossians underscore the implications of Paul's early proclamation of the Mystery revealed in Christ. The Colossians are reminded that the Mystery of Christ reaches back to the creation of the world and that although it has been hidden throughout the ages and generations, it has been revealed "to his saints" and now even to the Gentiles (Col 1:15-20, 26). The Ephesians are reminded that the "mystery of Christ" is the very reason for Paul's mission to them, for they are fellow heirs with the apostles and prophets, members of the one body and sharers in the promise of Christ Jesus (Eph 3:1-6).

In his letters to various churches he founded and visited, Paul writes of multiple manifestations of the one "Mystery of Christ." He focuses the attention of the Corinthian church specifically on the eucharistic manifestation of what God means to be doing among them for the world's salvation. According to Paul the eucharistic presence of the Mystery is inseparable from the Mystery of the Body of Christ, which is the church. Unfortunately the community's behavior says to Paul that they are not yet discerning the fullness of the Mystery of the Body, even if they are performing the ritual action (1 Cor 11:17ff.). So Paul instructs them once again in detail about what he had personally handed on to them.

He describes the ritual action of taking the bread and the cup and speaking Jesus' words of thanksgiving to his Abba as well as Jesus' injunction to his disciples to continue doing this together in his memory (1 Cor 11:23ff.). Then he explains the implications of what they are doing. The bread that is Jesus' Body given for them and the cup of the new covenant in his blood consumed by them are a sharing that makes them One Body (1 Cor 10:16-17). By their communal liturgical action the Corinthians are meant to be witnesses to the eschatological reign of God already breaking through. The old enmities of human history are passing; the new covenant is being revealed to the whole world through them, even as they await the fullness of Christ's coming in glory (1 Cor 10:26).

The contradiction Paul laments is obvious to him if not yet to the church at Corinth. They accept the gift of the sacramental Body of Christ and its promise of new life in Christ's ecclesial and eschatological Body. Yet they do not honor the very real Body that is the local church being built up through the shared eucharistic meal. They fail to recognize the church, the ecclesial Body of Christ, as itself a revelation of the Mystery. Nor can they discern the eschatological Mystery of the Body of the risen and glorified church coming to full stature in and through them. They seem stuck on the surfaces of things.

Summing up his extended discussion of Paul's broad teaching on the Mystery of Christ, Joseph Fitzmyer notes that speaking comprehensively of Christ "requires attention to the relation of the Lord to the Spirit in the Father's plan of salvation."[6] So it is not surprising that in the formulation of the NT canon, multiple inspired voices were included as witnesses to the Mystery, attesting that no single witness is able to say once and for all everything that has been revealed through the incarnation, much less the continuing cosmic presence of God among us. Francis Moloney points to the Johannine writings as a case in point. The Johannine perspective, like Paul's, begins as "the story of Jesus of Nazareth . . . yet, despite appearances, [the gospel of] John really is not a story about Jesus but a story about what God has done in Jesus."[7]

In the Johannine community a distinctive awareness emerged that there was "something more to come, *after* the ministry of Jesus" namely the guiding presence of the Paraclete, the Holy Spirit.[8] In the Paraclete passages of the Gospel of John (14:15-31; 16:4b-33),[9] the Holy Spirit plays an important role in the community as guide to the disciples "since Jesus was not able to tell his disciples everything they must know," nor were they immediately able to understand his words and actions. The Holy Spirit at work in the believing assembly can and does engage worshipers' minds, hearts, and imaginations at many points and in different ways. As the CCC affirms, "The preparation of hearts [for encountering Christ] is a joint work of the Holy Spirit and the assembly, especially its ministers" (no. 1098). If the Holy Spirit in the church is the prime mystagogue—stirring faith, hope, gratitude, and a sense of mission as the CCC proposes—homilists, catechists, ritual

[6] Joseph Fitzmyer, "Pauline Theology," NJBC, 82:61.

[7] Francis Moloney, "Johannine Theology," NJBC, 83:18.

[8] Pheme Perkins, "The Gospel According to John," NJBC, 61.

[9] Ibid., 61:198.

musicians, church architects, presiders, and all liturgical ministers and a believing community are active collaborators.

Emerging Expressions of the Mystery

Dei Verbum reaffirmed at Vatican II the church's basic doctrine—underlying all other doctrinal and creedal formulations—that Jesus Christ is the summation of divine revelation, of whom both the inspired Scripture and the living tradition speak (nos. 7–10). The continuing gift of the Holy Spirit in the church guided the postapostolic generations in their efforts both to give thanks liturgically and also to speak and act clearly and convincingly about the Mystery wherever they announced the good news of Christ.

Doctrinal and theological developments grew through the church's dialogue with contemporary cultures and contexts. By his own admission, Paul had not done well in his initial efforts to explain the Mystery of Jesus Christ to the philosophers in Athens (Acts 1:16-33). His letters too indicate that his best efforts to say what the revelation made in Jesus meant for both devout Jews and Gentile disciples eluded his aspirations. At times Paul's frustration with his own failure is evident whenever he shifts from teaching new believers to scolding them![10] Paul, like Jesus, was impassioned in his desire to help his listeners see how the presence of the Mystery could be discerned and how that Mystery could be encountered authentically. Subsequent generations of teachers did not give up the effort to articulate the belief of the church as clearly as was humanly possible. Yet neither eloquence nor philosophical clarity could overcome the reality: divine Mystery eludes human thought and speech. This is not surprising, for "the proper language for responding to Divinity is the social language of the rite,"[11] as Paul had tried to teach the Corinthian church.

Here it is important to underscore that authentic revelation of the Mystery involves practices—liturgical and ethical—in addition to the many kinds of texts, starting with the Scripture, that are the Christian community's heritage. Interestingly, little textual documentation of actual liturgical practice exists for the early centuries, even though the church's uninterrupted liturgical celebrations of baptism and the Eucharist witness to its awareness of and gratitude for the saving Mystery of Christ.

[10] "O stupid Galatians! . . ." (Gal 3:l-5) voices both exasperation and endearment. The sentiments recur in his letters to the Romans and Corinthians.

[11] Roger Grainger, *The Language of the Rite* (London: Darton, Longman & Todd, 1974), 45; also, Margaret Mary Kelleher, "Sacraments and the Ecclesial Mediation of Grace," *Louvain Studies*, 23 (Summer 1998): 180–97.

Across generations and over centuries the church's teachers and theologians produced carefully crafted creeds and doctrinal statements about particular aspects of the one Mystery of Christ Jesus, God, and the Holy Spirit. Concurrently, eucharistic faith in the living presence of Christ grew through the process of communal celebrations, pastoral instruction, and authentic discipleship. Formal systematic eucharistic theology would follow.[12] Contemporary Catholic theologians, in fact, call the active expression of the church's belief in its liturgical actions *theologia prima*; it is the basis for discursive theological reflection or *theologia secunda*.[13]

As the church of Christ expanded culturally and demographically, speaking of the ineffable Mystery (*theologia secunda*) was gradually transposed through the processes of human reasoning. Reflection on the Mystery underwent a slow transposition that culminated in reflection on distinctive "mysteries." While a theologian like Thomas Aquinas (d. 1274) still ventured to offer a comprehensive presentation of the Mystery of our faith, over time many theologians became specialists: one concentrating on the doctrine of God, another on Christology or in Christological subspecialties like the doctrine of atonement, the meaning of justification, or the sacrifice of Christ. Theological studies, ministry training, and childhood catechesis also approached the Mystery under distinct aspects. It became common to speak of the fullness of Mystery as "mysteries" in the plural. A popular expression of this manner of thinking and believing is reflected in the devotional enumeration of the mysteries of the rosary: joyful, sorrowful, glorious, and, most recently, luminous—yielding a total of twenty mysteries named, even while much that the church knows and believes still goes unnamed in this listing. Enumeration of multiple mysteries can confuse as well as clarify. Not surprisingly, a turn toward reintegration of what had become fragmented in Western theology has led to new theological initiatives. This can be seen in developments over the past century.

A Reintegrating Vision of the Enacted Mystery

The life work of the nineteenth-century German theologian Matthias Scheeben (d. 1888) culminated in his much-celebrated book on the mysteries

[12] For an overview of these developments see Edward Kilmartin, *The Eucharist in the West*, ed. Robert Daly (Collegeville, MN: Liturgical Press, 1998), 3–78; also, Gary Macy, *The Theologies of the Eucharist in the Early Scholastic Period* (Oxford: Clarendon Press, 1984); Mary Collins, "Evangelization, Catechesis, and the Beginning of Western Eucharistic Theology," *Louvain Studies*, 23 (1998): 124–44.

[13] David Fagerberg provides an extended account of the source(s) of theology in *Theologia Prima: What is Liturgical Theology?* 2nd ed. (Chicago: Liturgical Training Publications, 2004).

of Christianity. In it he aimed to conceptually reintegrate apparent multiplicity in the doctrinal tradition into nine "key mysteries."[14] Twentieth-century theologian Karl Rahner (d. 1984) also addressed the concern for theological integration in his essay "The Concept of Mystery in Catholic Theology."[15] He affirmed the doctrine of the Trinity, the paradoxical oneness of the Mystery of the Triune God, as basic to consideration of all other forms of discourse in which theologians engaged. More broadly, Rahner believed that a significant number of people in the contemporary West are impoverished by a diminished or distorted sense of the mystery of human existence. The task of illuminating and articulating the religious dimension of human experience he dubbed "transcendental mystagogy."[16]

In his later writings, Edward Kilmartin, influenced by his engagement with the Orthodox theological tradition, also argued for entering into reflection on the faith of the church through the ineffable trinitarian Mystery. In his introduction to Maronite theologian Jean Corbon's *The Wellspring of Worship*, Kilmartin wrote, "Everything that can be identified as a peculiarly Christian truth is, in one way or another, a derivative of the one central truth that humanity was created in order to live forever in personal community with the Holy Trinity."[17]

Kilmartin's essay returns us to the observation cited earlier that "the proper language for responding to Divinity is the social language of the rite."[18] The "language of the rite" at issue is embodiment, a way of saying what cannot be said in human words alone, no matter how well they are composed. Even more significantly, the Roman Catholic tradition of ritual embodiment in response to the presence of the sacred Mystery is a social language, an embodiment of relationships that are at the heart of the worshiping community's identity. This is already recognized in Paul's First Letter to the Corinthians. His lament concerning their Eucharist celebration is directed to this point. It was the actions and interactions of the assem-

[14] Matthias Scheeben, *The Mysteries of Christianity*, trans. Cyril Vollert (St. Louis: Herder, 1946). The table of contents presents his sequencing of the mysteries: the Trinity, God as Creator, sin, the divine economy, the Eucharist, the Church and the Sacraments, justification, the last things, and predestination.

[15] Karl Rahner, "The Concept of Mystery in Catholic Theology," in *Theological Investigations IV*, trans. Kevin Smith (Baltimore: Helicon, 1966), 36–73; also, see James Bacik, *Apologetics and the Eclipse of Mystery: Mystagogy according to Karl Rahner* (Notre Dame: University of Notre Dame Press, 1980), esp. chaps. 1–4.

[16] See Bacik for an overview of Rahner's thought on mystagogy, esp. 15–17 on the nature of transcendental mystagogy.

[17] Edward Kilmartin, forward to Jean Corbon, *The Wellspring of Worship*, trans. by Matthew J. O'Connell (New York: Paulist Press, 1988 [1980]).

[18] See n. 11, above.

bly—including but not limited to spoken words—that embodied or failed to embody eucharistic faith. What the assembly was affirming or denying in its embodying of relationships might confirm or counter the words they were proclaiming in Jesus' memory.

The ecclesial tradition over the centuries has developed a broad repertoire of communal rituals handed on from generation to generation for expressing and affirming what their experience told them to be true, even when they could not explain it—as with their conviction about trinitarian faith and the real presence of Christ in the Eucharist. As Roger Grainger notes, "the rite is the language of the un-thinkable. It is a way of 'living those things which do not bear thinking,' "[19] which elude every response but awe. When rational speech fails in the presence of Mystery, human expression is not resourceless. Orthodox and Roman Catholic bodies have learned how and when to bow in response to divine presence, how and when to bend the knee, how and when to join voices in unison or in harmony, how and when to move together in procession, even what to utter: "Hallelujah," "Amen," "Glory!" There is no exclusively correct form of Christian ritual language. Eastern and Western churches have distinctively ritualized bodies, and these in turn have been further influenced by the local cultures in which they have flourished.

What Romano Guardini noted as problematic for the church at worship in the middle of the twentieth century was ignorance of its own living tradition of ritual language, ignorance of how to "perform a proper liturgical act," due to a slow breakdown in the intergenerational transmission process. While many have seen the breakdown as a consequence of the implementation of the postconciliar liturgy, Guardini had seen ritual ignorance as a preexisting Western European condition that *SC* had aspired to address when it called for "full, conscious, and active part in liturgical celebrations" (no. 14). In his judgment, improving the situation began with knowing the right question to ask. "[H]ow can the act of walking become a religious act, a retinue for the Lord progressing through his land, so that an 'epiphany' may take place?"[20] transcends a more superficial question like how better to organize the procession. Embodiment and discernment of walking as a religious act can come together through the gift of the Holy Spirit alive in the worshiping community and its ministers, lay and ordained.

[19] Grainger, *The Language of the Rite*, 109.
[20] Guardini, "Open Letter," 5.

What the church aspires to embody liturgically is expressed clearly by the council fathers. They wrote, "The liturgy . . . is supremely effective in enabling the faithful to express in their lives and portray to others the mystery of Christ and the real nature of the true church" (no. 2). In short, the liturgical celebration embodies visibly the deep relationships that constitute the church and its mission in the world. The foundational relationship celebrated in the Catholic tradition of worship is the church's existence within trinitarian communion in, with, and through Christ. The paschal dimension of the Mystery—giving life by the outpouring of life—has taken on interactive symbolic expression in the eucharistic thanksgiving in memory of Jesus, whose life, death, and resurrection gave a human face to the mysterious trinitarian and paschal process. The church's traditional practice of mystagogy serves to draw worshipers from the surfaces of things to a deeper grasp of the mystery of their own lives in Christ, as the second part of this article shows.

Historical Reflections

Introduction

Contemporary philosophies of history distinguish between "records of the past" and the "interpretation of those records." This critical distinction admits that history is not so much the dispassionate reporting of some previous epoch as it is the interpretation of that epoch or one or more of its aspects.[21] Such a realization exposes the irony that it is not possible to employ history to define a concept like mystagogy without having basic presuppositions about and even a rudimentary definition of it, so that the historian not only knows what to look for in order to interpret the ancient record but even knows where to begin looking.

In his laudable venture to prove that mystagogy is "a true and proper theology: a liturgical theology,"[22] for example, Enrico Mazza locates the origins of mystagogical interpretations in the NT writings of Paul and John and argues that the main activity of mystagogy is "the use of Scripture." Consequent to this presumption is the assertion that the key "problem faced in mystagogy is how to apply the scriptures to the mystery being celebrated."[23] While Mazza recognizes that among the Greek fathers mystagogy

[21] Joyce Appleby, Lynn Hunt, and Margaret Jacob, *Telling the Truth about History* (New York and London: W. W. Norton, 1994), esp. chap. 7: "Truth and Objectivity," here 248.

[22] Enrico Mazza, *Mystagogy: A Theology of Liturgy in the Patristic Age*, trans. Matthew O'Connell (New York: Pueblo, 1989), 3.

[23] Ibid., 9.

first means the actual "performance of a sacred act" (especially baptism and Eucharist) and secondarily the "'oral or written explanation' of the mystery hidden in the scriptures and celebrated in the liturgy,"[24] he largely focuses on the second.

Reflecting upon the relationship between Scripture and sacrament, Louis-Marie Chauvet employs the work of numerous scriptural and patristic scholars to invert Mazza's framework, as it were, by asserting that the Bible (both Testaments) was "born of the liturgy."[25] In the language of Robert Taft, this admits the *Sitz im Gottesdienst*[26] of the Scriptures themselves. If assemblies of Christians in Eucharist and baptism "seem to have functioned empirically as the decisive crucible where the Christian Bible was formed,"[27] should we not look to such ritual events—rather than the texts born of this action, as Mazza does—also as the crucible of mystagogy itself? Thus, there are three presuppositions behind these historical reflections: (1) mystagogy is a form of theological reflection integral to and born of the liturgical event itself; (2) Scripture is only one (albeit important) lens for defining mystagogy; and (3) the proper origins of mystagogical interpretations are to be found in Jesus, especially his table ministry culminating in the final meal(s) with his disciples.

Jesus as Mystagogue[28]

The foundational reason that mystagogy is considered a potential theological method in Christianity must be the memory of Jesus as both a frequent and adept ritualizer, especially evident in his table ministry. Robert Karris captures this ritual propensity when noting that, in the Gospel of Luke, "Jesus is either going to a meal, at a meal, or coming from a meal." This waggish characterization supports a serious theological point: "in Luke's Gospel Jesus got himself crucified by the way he ate."[29] Besides the Gospel of Luke, Edward Schillebeeckx demonstrates that Jesus' practice of

[24] Ibid., 1.

[25] Louis-Marie Chauvet, *Symbol and Sacrament: A Sacramental Reinterpretation of Christian Existence*, trans. Patrick Madigan and Madeleine Beaumont (Collegeville, MN: Liturgical Press, 1995), 190–200; here 190.

[26] See, for example, his use of this phrase in *The Liturgy of the Hours in East and West* (Collegeville, MN: Liturgical Press, 1986), 208.

[27] Chauvet, *Symbol and Sacrament*, 197.

[28] Against this usage see Günther Bornkamm, "*mustērion*," *Theological Dictionary of the New Testament*, ed. Gerhard Kittel, trans. Geoffrey W. Bromiley (Grand Rapids: W. B. Eerdmans, 1968), 4:802–28; here 824.

[29] Robert Karris, *Luke: Artist and Theologian* (New York: Paulist Press, 1985), 47.

eating with sinners extends across the gospel landscape.[30] Joachim Jeremias realized early on that this practice was a key psychological factor in turning the Pharisees against Jesus.[31] Sallie McFague, among others, considers Jesus' eating and drinking with sinners as illustrative of the enacted parable of Jesus' own life in which he is revealed as "parable of God."[32] Beyond eating and drinking with sinners, meal-sharing is generally recognized as a key practice of the historical Jesus.[33]

In recent decades there has been significant rethinking of the nature of practice. Rather than simply the enactment of theory, the following of rules, or random human behavior, a wide range of theorists recognize patterns of practice as ways of knowing and believing. Pierre Bourdieu, for example, has written extensively about the "logic of practice" especially under the rubric of "habitus." Habitus for Bourdieu is less a conscious mental state than it is set of dispositions, or what he calls a "feel for the game."[34] He explains, "I am talking about dispositions which are *acquired through experience*, thus variable according from place to place and time to time. This 'feel for the game' (*sens du jeu*) as we call it is what enables an infinite number of moves to be made, adapted to the infinite number of possible situations which no rule, however complex, can foresee."[35] He later defines *sens du jeu* as "the practical mastery of the logic or of the immanent necessity of the game, a mastery acquired through experience of the game, and one which works outside conscious control and discourse."[36] Bourdieu's concern is "to give to practice an active, inventive intention . . . to stress the

[30] "Marcan tradition: Mk. 2:15-17, pl. Luke 15:2; Q tradition: Lk. 15:4-10, pl. Mt.; SL (source or tradition peculiar to Luke): Lk. 7:36-47; 15:11-32; 19:1-10; SM (source or tradition peculiar to Matthew): Mt. 20:1-15. See also Lk. 11:19, pl. Then too the Johannine Tradition: Jn: 4:7-42" (Edward Schillebeeckx, *Jesus: An Experiment in Christology*, trans. Hubert Hoskins [New York: Vintage Books, 1981], 688, n. 127; more recently, see Craig S. Keener, *The Historical Jesus of the Gospels* [Grand Rapids: William Eerdmans, 2009], 211–12).

[31] Joachim Jeremias, *The Eucharistic Words of Jesus*, trans. Norman Perrin (Philadelphia: Fortress, 1964), 204–5; this position has been repeated by many others including Jeremias' student and translator Norman Perrin, *Rediscovering the Teaching of Jesus* (New York: Harper & Row, 1967), 103.

[32] Sallie McFague, "Parable," in *The Westminster Dictionary of Christian Theology*, ed. Allan Richardson and John Bowden (Philadelphia: Westminster Press, 1983), 426.

[33] Schillebeeckx, *Jesus*, 218; John Dominic Crossan, *The Historical Jesus: The Life of a Mediterranean Jewish Peasant* (San Francisco: HarperSanFrancisco, 1991), 341.

[34] "Game" here is based on Wittgenstein's use of the term when explaining the operation of language. Ludwig Wittgenstein, *Philosophical Investigation*, trans. G.E.M. Anscombe (Oxford: Blackwell, 2001), cf. remarks 7, 31, 32, 43, and 83.

[35] Pierre Bourdieu, *In Other Words: Essays towards a Reflective Sociology*, trans. Matthew Adamson (Cambridge: Polity Press, 1990 [1987]), 9.

[36] Ibid., 61.

generative capacities of dispositions."[37] With specific regard to ritual, he opines "ritual action . . . is in fact a gymnastics or a dance . . . and follows a practical logic, that is, a logic that is intelligible, coherent, but only up to a point . . . and oriented toward practical ends, that is, the actualization of wishes or desires (of life or of death), etc."[38]

It is imminently reasonable to consider Jesus, in Bourdieu's language, as one who had this *sens du jeu* in his table ministry. This pivotal ritual practice, improvised across gospel landscape, could appropriately be understood as a religious strategy Jesus employed to explore, define, and explicate God's reign as an invitation to repentance and a newly envisioned eschatological banquet. Mystagogy properly understood recognizes both the "imminent necessity" and the "imminent logic" of ritual practice.[39] Since mystagogy is not merely synonymous with ritual practice, however, but intimately connected with reflection on that practice (often employing a scriptural lens) any explanation of Jesus as mystagogue must consider how his table practice was a point of reflection for Jesus himself as well as for others.

Bruce Chilton offers one example of such reflection in his analysis of the various stages of table practice and theology in the NT.[40] Chilton argues that Jesus' cleansing or "occupation" of the temple (Mark 11:15-19) indicated a turning point in his understanding of purity and sacrifice.

> That incursion is . . . the culmination of a program which had stressed forgiveness and genuine ownership of what was offered as requirements of acceptable sacrifice in the temple. Once Jesus' *halakha* [about acceptable sacrifice] is not accepted, the character of his meals with the disciples changed. Earlier, they have been enactments of the purity which was demanded within sacrifice. Now that social purity and especially the food and drink consumed *are* the sacrifice. God is better pleased with that "blood" and "body" than with that which is offered incorrectly on Mount Zion.[41]

The most explicit textual evidence of Jesus' mystagogical reflections on the changed meal was its only new characteristic after the temple incursion:

[37] Ibid., 13.

[38] Pierre Bourdieu, *Practical Reason: On the Theory of Action* (Stanford: Stanford University Press, 1998 [1994]), 132.

[39] Bourdieu, *In Other Words*, 64.

[40] Bruce Chilton, *A Feast of Meanings: Eucharistic Theologies from Jesus through Johannine Circles*, Supplements to Novum Testamentum 72 (Leiden and New York: Brill, 1994).

[41] Ibid., 69.

the institution narrative.[42] In the midst of what is remembered as his final meal, Jesus reinterpreted the event in the event: he offered his ultimate interpretation of his meal practice, so intimately touching the very Mystery of God in Christ that it remains central both to eucharistic practice and to the reflection upon that practice. It is this "mystagogy in the moment" that becomes the core of the tradition that Paul feels compelled to hand on (1 Cor 11:23-26), revealing that Jesus is both the divine Mystery and divine mystagogue.

Ancient Mysteries

While the ancient mystery cults had little apparent impact on Jesus' own "mystagogical" approach, they were influential for emerging Christian as well as contemporary interpretations of worship and thus need to be briefly summarized here. The origin of the Greek *mustērion* is disputed; common is the suggestion that it derives from *muein*, to close (the lips). "The etymology leads only to the fairly certain general conclusion that a *mustērion* is something on which silence must be kept."[43] By at least the time of Herodotus (d. *ca.* 431 BCE) *muein* meant "to initiate." Better understood as cults than religions,[44] mystery cults are pervasive in the ancient near Eastern and Western worlds, becoming more prominent after 600 BCE. Walter Burkert argues that this is because of the great event of "the discovery of the Individual," which occurs in seventh- and sixth-century Greek; the ensuing "search for private fulfillment"; and the problem of "individual death," which is not simply a fact of communal life but now a "personal problem more than before."[45]

Elements common to the ancient mystery cults, according to Burkert, were an emphasis on initiation, strong agrarian as well as sexual overtones, and accompanying myths usually of sufferings gods and usually with emphasis on secrecy[46] surrounding the cult. The assertion that the initiated

[42] Chilton considers this the only distinctive element in Jesus' meals after the temple incursion. Ibid., 66.

[43] Bornkamm, "*mustērion*," 803.

[44] "Initiation at Eleusis or worship at Isis or Mithras does not constitute adherence to a religion in the sense we are familiar with. . . . Whereas in [Judaism, Christianity, and Islam] there has been much conscious emphasis on self-definition and on demarcating one religion as against the other, in the pre-Christian epoch the various forms of worship . . . and the institution of mysteries in particular, are never exclusive" (Walter Burkert, *Ancient Mystery Cults* [Cambridge: Harvard University Press, 1987], 4).

[45] Walter Burkert, *Greek Religion: Archaic and Classical*, trans. J. Raffan (Cambridge, MA: Harvard University Press, 1985), 278.

[46] See Fritz Graf, "Mysteries," *Brill's New Paul*, ed. Hubert Cancik, et al. (Leiden and Boston: Brill, 2006), 9:434–44; here 438.

suffers the fate of the god does not generally hold true,[47] although the belief that the initiated gains the guarantee of a blessed life in another world is prominent in many mystery cults, especially as belief in the afterlife developed in later Hellenization.[48] Among the most widespread and well documented of these were the mysteries of Eleusis, celebrating the cult of the goddess Demeter.[49]

The rise of Greek philosophy exerted a significant effect on reimagining the mystery cults. While not immediately altering the practices of the mysteries, philosophy decisively alters the thinking about such mysteries now transformed into a "philosophical religion."[50] Philosophers, like the poets before them,[51] were intent on critiquing religious myths in which gods were often revealed as devious, even murderous. Yet, directly challenging such myths and accompanying cultic practices was dangerous. The solution was to treat such myths and the practice of mysteries as allegories for the true ascent of the mind. Such allegorical interpretation is already evident in Plato (d. 327 BCE) who, for example, considers the ascent of the soul in the *Phaedrus* and *Symposium* as initiation "in the language of the mysteries."[52] Philosophical mystagogy as full-fledged initiation into the contemplative life is fully developed in the Enneads of the neoplatonic philosopher Plotinus (d. 270). "Here the mysteries are not cultic actions but obscure and secret doctrines, whose hidden wisdom may be understood only by those capable of knowledge. The gradual ascent of knowledge to full vision is here the true initiation."[53]

The Scriptures: Mysteries and Mystagogy

The language of *mustérion* can be found both in the Septuagint and the NT. Some passages of the Septuagint clearly reference the ancient mystery cults (e.g., Wis 14:15); others show some influence of Greek mystagogic philosophy (e.g., Wis 6:22). New in the book of Daniel is not only an

[47] For an opposite view, see Kurt Rudolph, "Mystery Religions," *Encyclopedia of Religion*, ed. Lindsay Jones, 2nd ed. (Detroit: McMillan Reference USA, 2005), 9:6326–34; here 6327.

[48] Burkert, *Greek Religion*, 276–77.

[49] The literature is vast: besides Burkert, *Greek Religion*, 285–90, and the other sources here cited, see the revised bibliography in Rudolph, "Mystery Religions," 6333–34 and the bibliography in Graf, "Mysteries," 442–44.

[50] Burkert, *Greek Religion*, 305ff.

[51] Most famous is *Heracles* in which Euripides (d. *ca.* 406 BCE) "suggests as vividly as he can the cruelty and perhaps even the absurdity of the traditionally viewed deities who act in this world" (Michael R. Halleran, "Rhetoric, Irony, and the Ending of Euripides' 'Herakles,'" *Classical Antiquity* 5, no. 2 (1986): 171–81; here 181).

[52] Burkert, *Greek Religion*, 324.

[53] Bornkamm, "*mustérion*," 808.

eschatological dimension of the term but also teaching that God reigns over the "mysteries," a theme further developed in the Dead Sea Scroll texts.[54] The disclosure of divine secrets is a central theme of Jewish apocrypha.[55] Hellenistic Judaism reflects knowledge of the mystery cults, and Philo (d. 45–50 CE) draws upon the Greek tradition of philosophical mystagogy to explain Jewish teaching. Certain cultic practices of the Essenes are reminiscent of mystery religions.

Various forms of *mustérion* occur twenty-eight times in the NT, mostly in Paul.[56] Günther Bornkamm summarizes its central meaning in Paul as the mysterious wisdom of God, prepared before the world was, concealed from the eons, hidden in God, and fulfilled in Christ. The apostolic mission to proclaim the good news about Christ belongs to the *mustérion* event.[57] In the Synoptics, the "secret" is the parable of the sower (Mark 4:11; Matt 13:11; Luke 8:10), presented as a kind of wisdom-riddle about God's reign whose solution is revealed by Jesus to his disciples.[58] It is clear that *mustérion* in the NT designates more language event than cult,[59] sometimes marked by typological or allegorical devices.

Besides the language of *mustérion*, the NT represents emerging Christian practice as mirroring elements of the mystery cults, e.g., as a religion of salvation and personal choice that included initiatory rites and sacred meals.[60] Cautioning against simplistic conclusions about dependence, Marvin Meyer suggests that such resemblances "may be attributed to the fact that [Christianity and mystery cults] responded in a similar fashion to the religious challenges of the Greco-Roman world."[61]

[54] Daniel L. Smith-Christopher, "The Book of Daniel," *The New Interpreter's Bible*, ed. Leander Keck (Nashville: Abingdon Press, 1996), 53.

[55] Bornkamm, "*mustérion*," 815.

[56] (1) *mustéria* (4x) in Matt 13:11; Luke 8:10; 1 Cor 13:2; 1 Cor 14:2; (2) *mustérion* (17x) in Mark 4:11; Rom 11:25; 1 Cor 2:1; 15:51; Eph 1:9; 3:3; 5:32; 6:19; Col 1:26; 4:3; 2 Thess 2:7; 1 Tim 3:9; 3:16; Rev 1:20; 10:7; 17:5; 17:7; (3) *mustériou* (4x) in Rom 16:25; Eph 3:9; Col 1:27; 2:2; (4) *mustériō* (2x) in 1 Cor 2:7; Eph 3:4; (5) *mustériōn* (1x) in 1 Cor 4:1. See no. 3466 in various editions of *Strong's Exhaustive Concordance of the Bible*; for a more extended discussion of Paul's contribution, see 75–77 above.

[57] Bornkamm, "*mustérion*," 820–21.

[58] Adela Yarbro Collins, "The Influence of Daniel on the New Testament," in John F. Collins, ed., *Daniel*, *Hermeneia* Series (Minneapolis: Fortress, 1993), 90–123; here 105–6.

[59] As with the term *leitourgía*, *mustérion* is not employed in the so-called sacramental passages of the NT, e.g., in last supper narratives or John's Bread of Life discourse.

[60] This summary is reliant upon Marvin Meyer, "Mystery Religions," *The Anchor Bible Dictionary*, ed. David Noel Freedman (New York: Doubleday, 1992), 4:941–45; here 944.

[61] Ibid., 944.

The Early Church: Second to Fifth Centuries

As emerging Christianity grew ever more distinct from its sibling, Rabbinic Judaism,[62] pressure increased to distinguish itself from the many mystery cults and forms of Gnosticism with their mystagogic philosophies rampant throughout the ancient world. Apologists were in the difficult position of refuting the false claims and practices of mystery cults[63] while at the same time upholding Christianity as a type of mystery and even portraying Christ as a mystagogue.[64] Such apologetics were needed as the church's cultic life evolved, the unenlightened were barred from participating in the Eucharist, and increasingly complex forms of initiation into the Christian mysteries developed—some of which required promises of secrecy. Thus, to outsiders, Christianity could appear to be a type of the mystery cults it was so vigorously denouncing.

In the third and fourth centuries CE the word *mustérion*, contrary to the NT witness, gradually emerged as a term for baptism and Eucharist. The rejuvenation of the cultic usage of this word within Christianity appropriately links the saving acts of Christ with their ritual representation through this common term.[65] Common practice by the late fourth century, the gradual embrace of mystery language marks Christianity as increasingly dominant within the empire and less timid about borrowing from other religions. With the gradual Latinization of Christianity,[66] *sacramentum* became the Latin equivalent for *mustérion*.[67] Jerome will translate six of the twenty-eight variants of *mustérion* in the NT as *sacramentum*,[68] otherwise employing *mysterium*. The use of *sacramentum*, with its many legal connotations, will contribute to a widening gap between the cult and the Mystery of God in Christ witnessed in the Scriptures. Initially the relationship between the ritual "mysteries" and biblical "mysteries" was so vivid that there was no discontinuity between the biblical message and worship.[69] By the early Middle Ages, however, that will already begin to change.

[62] See Hayim Goren Perelmuter, *Siblings: Rabbinic Judaism and Early Christianity at Their Beginnings* (New York: Paulist, 1989).

[63] E.g., Justin Martyr's attack on Mithraists whom he charges diabolically imitate Christian eucharistic practice (*First Apology*, 66).

[64] Clement of Alexandria (d. *ca.* 215) speaks of Christ as one who "exhorts us to follow the gnostic life" and, like a mystagogue, "trains the soul" (Stromata IV.6).

[65] Bornkamm, "*mustérion*," 826.

[66] On this process see Ostiek and Pecklers, 37–39 above.

[67] First in Tertullian, *Prescriptions against the Heretics* 40.2; on this change see Ostdiek and Pecklers 37 above.

[68] Eph 1:9; 3:3; 5:32; 1 Tim 3:16; Rev 1:20; 17:7.

[69] Louis-Marie Chauvet, "Sacramentum," in *Encyclopedia of Christian Theology* (New York and London: Routledge, 2005 [1999]); 1408–15; here 1409.

The late fourth and early fifth centuries CE loom large in the history of mystagogy. Celebrated bishops produced catechesis related to the initiation of believers, significant portions of which are preserved.[70] It is with these works that Enrico Mazza's analysis is especially helpful. In the tradition of Jean Daniélou,[71] Mazza demonstrates the centrality of scriptural exegesis, generally in patristic theologies and more specifically in sacramental-liturgical theologies of the patristic era.[72] The dominant hermeneutical approach in fourth- and fifth-century mystagogy is biblical typology, i.e., reading the liturgy through the lenses of the OT and NT in order to reveal the meaning of the mystery being celebrated.

Mazza repeatedly makes clear that the purpose of this mystagogy is to "explain to the neophytes . . . the meaning and nature of the liturgical actions in which they have participated."[73] Such explanations are to provide "understanding and motivation" for living the Christian life. This "understanding" was clearly cast in a neoplatonic framework, which not only distinguishes between the world of the senses and the invisible world of ideas but also gives priority to the latter. Thus, these mystagogical explanations were not an excavation of the experiences of the community in worship or a theology "from" the liturgy but more explanations delivered to the faithful employing biblical typology to render a theology "of" the liturgy[74] that might motivate neophytes to more faithful gospel living. Ironically, the neoplatonic epistemology that imbues these mystagogical works predicates a necessary prejudice against experience or a trusting of the senses. Consequently, Ambrose could warn his hearers not to trust the "bodily eyes" in understanding the sacrament. Employing the typological image of Jesus spreading clay on the eyes of the blind man at Siloam (John

[70] Notably, Ambrose of Milan's (d. 397) *De Sacramentis* and *De Mysteriis* in Ambroise de Milan, *Des Sacraments, Des mystères*, ed. Bernard Botte, *Sources chrétiennes* 25 (Paris: Cerf, 1961); Cyril of Jerusalem's (d. 387), protocatechesis, catechetical lectures and mystagogical catechesis (although it is disputed whether the mystagogical catecheses ascribed to him are his work or that of his successor John of Jerusalem, d. 417) in Cyrille de Jerusalem, *Catéchèses mystagogiques*, ed. Auguste Piédagnel, 2nd ed., *Sources chrétiennes* 126 (Paris: Cerf, 1988); John Chrysostom's (d. 407) catechetical homilies in Jean Chrysostome, *Huit catéchèses baptismales inédites*, ed. Antoine Wenger, 2nd ed., *Sources chrétiennes* 63 (Paris: Cerf, 1970); and Theodore of Mopsuestia's (d. 428) mystagogical catechesis in Theodorus, *Les homélies catéchétiques*, trans. Raymond Tonneau and Robert Devreesse, Studi e Testi 145 (Vatican City: Biblioteca Apostolica Vaticana, 1949).

[71] Jean Daniélou's summative work here is *Bible et Liturgie: la théologie biblique des sacrements et des fêtes d'après les Pères de l'Église* (Paris: Cerf, 1951).

[72] Mazza, *Mystagogy*, 7–13.

[73] Ibid., x.

[74] Mazza consistently speaks of the fathers developing "a theology of this liturgy," e.g., *Mystagogy*, 165–66.

9:6-7), he reminds them that in confessing their sins Jesus spread mud over their eyes so that they might "see sacramental things with the eyes of your heart."[75] While contemporary pastoral and theological sources often draw heavily upon these fourth- and fifth-century sources, suggesting that current usage is a "recovery" from this period, this is at least problematic, if not inaccurate. While we have recovered the language, today's mystagogical focus is more properly on the community's experience of the rites and, thus, more a theology "from" than "of" the liturgy.

Mystagogy was not the only form of theological reflection or instruction known to the early church. Already in the NT, proclamation (*kerygma*) is distinguished from teaching (*didache*), the former ordinarily addressed to unbelievers and serving as the basis of teaching for those who believed and were baptized.[76] Clement of Alexandria (d. *ca.* 215) and Origen (d. *ca.* 254) attest to the evolution of theological instruction that moves well beyond formation for initiation to the establishment of a theological academy. Many of the fathers offered instructions, including instructions on the sacraments, that were not mystagogical (e.g., Tertullian's *De Baptismo*). Augustine (d. 430) wrote a foundational work on catechesis (*De Catechizandis Rudibus*) that was directed not toward catechumens or inquirers but toward the catechists who would lead them into initiation. Thus mystagogy was only one strand, albeit a central one, of faith formation evident in the early centuries of Christianity. By the sixth century CE, however, mystagogy was in steep decline.

The Waning of Mystagogy: The Medieval Church

The reasons for this decline are multiple. Chief among them is the growing dominance of Christianity throughout the empire, infant baptism as the normative form of initiation, and the gradual disappearance of the catechumenate. The impressive catechumenal population of late fourth- and fifth-century Christianity was, in one sense, an aberration that accompanied the marriage of Christianity and the empire. Declared the official religion of the empire in 380 under Emperor Theodosius (d. 395), Christianity was increasingly a factor of birth rather than an adult faith choice. In Rome by *ca.* 500 John the Deacon was reporting that infants were participating in all catechumenal and initiatory rites (including scrutinies), whom John notes

[75] Ambrose, *De Sacramentis* 3.11; Mazza recognizes that "the Platonism that the Fathers used sometimes casts doubt on the adequacy of their theological approach [especially] when it comes to ensuring sacramental realism" (*Mystagogy*, 170).

[76] John McKenzie, "'Proclamation' and 'Teaching' in the Primitive Church," *Living Light* 1, no. 2 (1964): 118–36; here 127.

understood nothing of what was occurring.[77] This explains why the *Gelasianum* (reflecting mid-seventh-century Roman practice) notes that scrutinies have been moved from Sunday to Monday to accommodate infants[78] and why *OR XI* (reliant upon the *Gelasianum*) forbids breastfeeding infants before they receive Communion.[79] Infant baptism had become normative.

These initiatory changes occurred in contexts of increasing social instability. Centuries of invasions by Germanic tribes decimated the Western empire. The Islamic conquest overwhelmed the great catechetical centers of North Africa and contributed to the growing isolation of the Eastern empire. The clergy of northern Europe, drawn from mostly illiterate tribal people, were clearly ill-equipped to function as catechists, much less as mystagogues. Furthermore, the growing emphasis on the sinfulness of the baptized and the rise of monasticism, with its reappropriation of initiatory rites and images, rendered the monks the new elect, novices the new catechumens, and monasteries a locus of transformed mystagogy.[80]

Despite what many describe as the "demise" of the catechumenate and mystagogy in the Middle Ages,[81] mystagogical residue is detectable across this epoch. As the responsibility for educating children in the faith increasingly fell to parents and godparents,[82] it was yet the ancient liturgies of initiation (scrutinies, *traditio*, *redditio*) that lay behind the expectations to teach children the Creed, Lord's Prayer, *Ave*, and basic Christian devotion. As such, the initiatory tradition was still "conceived as containing the minimal outline of faith and morals."[83] In some places people could not become a godparent until they had been examined on the Creed and Lord's Prayer.[84] Mystagogical strands are also detectable in some of the preaching.

[77] *Epistola Johannis Diaconi ad Senarium*, in *Analecta reginensia*, ed. André Wilmart, Studi e Testi 59 (Vatican City: Biblioteca Apostolica Vaticana, 1933), 170–79, specifically nos. 2 and 7 = 171 and 175.

[78] Leo Mohlberg, ed., *Liber Sacramentorum Romanae Aeclesiae Ordinis Anni Circuli*, Rerum Ecclesiasticarum Documenta, Series Maior, Fontes IV (Rome: Herder, 1981), no. 283 = 42.

[79] No. 103 = 446. See the rehearsal of further evidence on the prevalence of infant baptism in the seventh century in J. D. C. Fisher, *Christian Initiation: Baptism in the Medieval West*, Alcuin Club 47 (London: SPCK, 1965), esp. 3–9.

[80] See, for example, the Mystagogia of Maximus the Confessor (d. 662), Charalambos Soteropoulos, *Hē Mystagōgia tou Hagiou Maximou tou Homologētou* (Athens: n.p., 1978).

[81] Cf. Joseph Jungmann, *Handing on the Faith: A Manual of Catechetics*, trans. A. N. Fuerst (New York: Herder & Herder, 1962), 11.

[82] Joseph Lynch, *Christianizing Kinship* (Ithaca, NY: Cornell University Press, 1998), 172.

[83] Milton Gatch, "Basic Christian Education from the Decline of Catechesis to the Rise of Catechisms," in *A Faithful Church: Issues in the History of Catechesis*, ed. John H. Westerhoff and O. C. Edwards (Wilton, CT: Morehouse-Barlow Co., 1981), 79–108; here 88.

[84] Aubert Clark, "Medieval Catechetics and the First Catechisms," *Living Light* 1, no. 4 (1965), 92–107; here 97.

The Anglo-Saxon monk Ælfric of Eynsham (d. *ca.* 1010), for example, offered sermons for Rogationtide that expounded both the Lord's Prayer and the basic tenets of the Creed,[85] which were often part of the medieval vernacular *prône* inserted in the Mass.[86]

The lay prayer books, emerging first in Latin and then in the vernacular, contain devotional prayers that reflect a somewhat mystagogical approach to understanding the sacraments, especially penance[87] and Eucharist.[88] Similar were the *ars moriendi*, with their prayers for the dying and instructions for both clergy and laity about preparing the faithful for death, especially through the final sacraments.[89] Tangentially, one must admit that the many liturgical dramas and miracle plays born of the medieval liturgy were also their own kind of mystagogy, often expounding the mysteries of the liturgical seasons or feasts in cycles of plays.[90] Finally, the medieval cathedral was a type of mystagogue whose very design, iconography, stained-glass windows, and sacramental carvings and mosaics provided a visual form of theological reflection often rooted in the sacramental practices of

[85] Milton Gatch futher notes that the *sermones catholici* of Ælfric are unusual in that they announce to the congregation things about the progress of the liturgical year, e.g., the omission of the Alleluia and Gloria after Septuagesima. See his *Preaching and Theology in Anglo-Saxon England: Ælfric and Wulfstan* (Toronto: University of Toronto Press, 1977), 51.

[86] For an overview of this practice, see the summary work in Katharine Jackson Lualdi, "Change and Continuity in the Liturgy of the *Prône* from the Fifteenth to the Seventeenth Century," in *Prédication et liturgie au Moyen Âge*, ed. Nicole Bériou and Franco Morenzoni (Turnhout: Brepols, 2008), 373–89.

[87] Especially after the requirement of Lateran IV (1215) for annual communion and (ordinarily) confession, confession manuals were produced in abundance; originally designed to direct the clergy in hearing confessions, they increasingly were accessed by laity as aids to making a good confession. While often focused on the examination of conscience with their list of sins, works of mercy, etc., they were interlaced with reflections on the meaning of the various parts of the sacrament and their significance for daily living. See, for example, Gustave A. Arroyo, "Les manuels de confession en castillan dans l'Espagne médiévale" (Université de Montréal: M.A. Mémoire, 1989), esp. the overview of the genre and introduction to the literature in chap. 1 (http://www.fordham.edu/halsall/projects/arroyo/manuels.htm, accessed 26 July 2010).

[88] See, for example, the devotional prayer to be said at the ringing of the bell at the *Hanc igitur* during the Canon of the Mass in *The Lay Folks Mass Book*, ed. Thomas Simmons (London: Oxford University Press, 1879), 38.

[89] A classic introduction is Mary Catherine O'Connor, *The Art of Dying Well: The Development of the Ars Moriendi* (New York: AMS Press, 1966); more recently, see Eamon Duffy, *The Stripping of the Altars: Traditional Religion in England 1400–1580* (New Haven and London: Yale University Press, 1992), 313–27.

[90] At the origin of this genre is the *Quem quaeritis* drawn from Easter Matins, as recorded in *Regularis Concordia*, ed. Thomas Symons (London: Thomas Nelson & Sons, 1953), no. 51 = 49; more recently, see Nils Holger Petersen, "Les textes polyvalents du Quem quaeritis à Winchester au xe siècle," *Revue de musicologie* 86, no. 1 (2000): 105–18.

the day.[91] Thus, mystagogical residue can yet be identified through the medieval West, though admittedly they do not provide a dominant pattern of formation or theological reflection.

Medieval theology paid attention to the importance of entering the Mystery, but medieval "mysticism" was often much more personal and affective than analogous reflections in the patristic period and seldom was linked with worship. One exception was the liturgical meditations found in the *Exercises* of Gertrude the Great (d. *ca.* 1302). Ultimately, mystical works like *The Interior Castle* by Teresa of Avila (d. 1582) in the early Reformation period were more directed to the professional religious, and mystical experiences were the purview of a chosen few and particularly graced rather than all the baptized.

From Reformation to Liturgical Renewal

The sixteenth-century Reformation and so-called Counter-Reformation reflect a mystagogical situation as subterraneous as that of the Middle Ages. This golden age of the catechism, in which disputed doctrines required succinct and exact answers, was not disposed to forms of theological reflection intended on juxtaposing people's experience with the growing diversity of Christian rites and sacramental expressions. At the same time, mystagogical residue is not only yet detectable, but new seeds were planted in this epoch that furthered the mystagogical flourishing of the twentieth century.

Because challenges to sacramental practice and theology were pivotal to the Reformers, there was renewed catechesis and preaching about the sacraments on all sides. Luther and most Reformers offered scriptural interpretations of the sacraments, though much less allegorical than patristic sources.[92] Besides widespread preaching on the sacraments, a multitude of catechisms treated the sacraments. Some of these, including the sections of Luther's *Small Catechism* (1529) on the Our Father, Creed, baptism, Eucharist, and confession were published as posters for public display in homes,

[91] Erwin Panofsky goes even further, comparing the high gothic cathedral to a theological *summa* of the day, in its imagery seeking "to embody the whole of Christian knowledge" (*Gothic Architecture and Scholasticism* [Cleveland, OH: World Publishing Company, 1957], 44).

[92] Gerhard Ebeling held that Luther largely abandons allegorical interpretations for a more literal approach; see his "The New Hermeneutics and the Early Luther," *Theology Today* 21, no. 1 (1964): 34–46; here 44; Timothy Maschke offers a recent corrective to Ebeling's widely held thesis and suggests that Luther did not reject allegorical interpretations but developed a deeper understanding of allegory rooted in the Scriptures; see his "The Authority of Scripture: Luther's Approach to *Allegory* in Galatians," *Logia* 4, no. 2 (1995): 25–31.

schools, and churches.[93] Since a personal apprehension of the faith, and not simply right answers, was the concern of Reformers on all sides,[94] some catechisms asked what could be considered fundamental mystagogical questions. For example, the larger catechism (1528) of the Swabian Reformer Johann Brenz (d. 1570) repeatedly asks, "what is the value to you of this article [clause]" of the Creed?[95] This personal appropriation of the Creed, the Lord's Prayer, and the Lord's Supper was amplified in the age of pietism (post-1675) with its emphases on personal experience, affectivity, and a visible ethic or piety. Besides preaching and catechesis, vernacular hymnody of this era assumed a new catechetical and mystagogical role. Notable is the eucharistic hymnody of Charles Wesley (d. 1788), which, for example, reiterates an ancient *lex orandi* in affirming the eucharistic ritual as the place of encounter with the living Christ.[96] Finally, older church buildings newly whitewashed, stripped of statues and tabernacles, and new church buildings with towering pulpits dwarfing altars without reredos were powerful mystagogues, reaffirming the primacy of the Word, the problematic of sanctoral devotions, and the rejection of any eucharistic presence beyond *in usu*. The churches of the Counter-Reformation—often filled with confessionals but devoid of any prominent or sometimes even visible baptistery—were mystagogical in their own ways as well.

An explicit turn to liturgy as a locus of encounter with the sacred mysteries emerged in the work of Prosper Guéranger (d. 1875). His *L'Année Liturgique*[97] considered the liturgical year a "sacred cycle of mysteries" and a "manifestation of Jesus Christ and His mysteries" into which the faithful are initiated in order to come to know the "secrets of eternal life."[98] This new liturgical mysticism was paralleled by a new recognition of the

[93] William Haugaard, "Continental Reformation," in Westerhoff and Edwards, *A Faithful Church*, 109–73; here 122.

[94] Ibid., 110.

[95] Elbert Wills, "Johann Brenz's Larger Catechism of 1528," *Lutheran Quarterly* 7, no. 2 (1955): 114–27, here 118 and eight more times *passim*.

[96] "In the rite Though hast enjoyn'd, Let us now our Saviour Find" (no. 33 in *Hymns on the Lord's Supper* [1745]).

[97] Guéranger only finished nine of the fifteen volumes (Paris, 1841–1890) before his death; the last six were completed by Lucien Fromage (d. 1916); complete text (14th ed., Tours: Alfred Mame et fils, 1920–22) available at http://www.abbaye-saint-benoit.ch/gueranger/anneliturgique/index.htm (accessed 27 July 2010), also in various English translations. See Cuthbert Johnson, *Prosper Guéranger (1805–1875): A Liturgical Theologian: An Introduction to His Liturgical Writings and Work*, Studia Anselmiana 89 (Rome: Pontificio Ateneo S. Anselmo, 1984).

[98] *L'Année Liturgique: L'Avent*, x and xi.

significance of patristic sources for church life.[99] The pioneering work of Jacques Paul Migne (d. 1895) in collecting and publishing patristic texts would give way to the *ressourcement* movement, whose turn "back to the sources" shed new light on ancient liturgical texts and made accessible great patristic mystagogical works. Characteristic of *ressourcement* theology was a reappropriation of typological and allegorical interpretations of scripture,[100] paralleled by renewed appreciation of symbolic interpretations of worship.[101]

Odo Casel (d. 1948) relentlessly proposed a "mystery theology" in over one hundred articles, letters, and books.[102] While significant aspects of his thought are rejected (e.g., that the ancient mystery cult was a resource that the ancient church employed for her own purposes),[103] his emphasis on liturgy as a true participation in the saving Mystery of Christ's death and resurrection is widely accepted[104] and contributed to understanding the church as the Mystical Body of Christ, an understanding enshrined in the 1943 encyclical *Mystici Corporis* by Pius XII (d. 1958).[105]

On the pastoral side, catechumenal structures—some of which had been established in Africa already in the mid-nineteenth century[106]—were now appearing in Europe as well.[107] Catechetical developments were also critical

[99] Mary Charles Bryce, "Evolution of Catechesis from the Catholic Reformation to the Present," in Westerhoff and Edwards, *A Faithful Church*, 204–35; here 224.

[100] See the introduction in Jean Daniélou, *Bible et Liturgie*.

[101] A classic example is Romano Guardini's mystagogical reflections on the sacred signs of the liturgy, *Von heiligen Zeichen* (Würzburg: Werkbund Verlag, 1937); English: *Sacred Signs*, trans. Grace Branham (Wilmington, DE: Michael Glazier, 1979).

[102] Central is his *Das Christliche Kultmysterium*, 4th ed. (Regensburg: Friedrich Pustet, 1960 [1932]); English: *The Mystery of Christian Worship*, ed. Burkhard Neunheuser (London: Darton, Longman & Todd, 1962).

[103] Casel, *The Mystery of Christian Worship*, 34.

[104] Burkhard Neunheuser, "Odo Casel in Retrospect and Prospect," *Worship* 50 (1976): 489–503.

[105] Henri de Lubac's work ironically demonstrates that *corpus mysticum* originally referred to the eucharistic species, and it was only in the second half of the twelfth century that the church was identified as *corpus mysticum*. See his *Corpus Mysticum*, 2nd ed. (Paris: Aubrie, 1949), 121.

[106] Charles Lavigerie (d. 1892), founder of the Society of Missionaries of Africa, "had pursued doctoral work on the ancient Syriac church in the mid-1800s, which sparked his lifelong interest in the adult catechumenate"; as archbishop of Algiers he established a four-year catechumenate through his missionaries. Jay Carney, "Making Disciples of All Nations: Adaptation and Christian Civilization in the Missiological Thought of Charles Lavigerie," Engaging Particularities Conference Papers (Boston College, 2007); online at http://escholarship.bc.edu/cgi/viewcontent.cgi?article=1012&context=engaging_cp (accessed 27 July 2010).

[107] For example, in the Parish of Sacré Coeur in Colombes near Paris. See Gerard Sloyan, "Developments in Religious Education since 1800," *Living Light* 2, no. 4 (1965–66): 82–97; here 89.

to the recovery of mystagogy. These included Josef Jungmann's (d. 1975) seminal work on the recovery of *kerygma* at the heart of the catechetical enterprise and the essential relationship between Scripture, liturgy, and Christian living.[108] In Louvain the Jesuit faculty opened a Catechetical Documentary Centre (1935), which a decade later moved to Brussels as *Lumen Vitae*. Through their work and publications, a "four-sources" theory emerged that held that Scripture, liturgy, doctrine, and Christian life were the four elements fundamental for authentic catechesis.[109] This explicit acknowledgment of human experience as a theological source, found liturgical resonance in Pius XII's assertion that the faithful were not "objects" of the church's worship but subjects in that worship with Christ.[110]

It is out of this long recovery and renewal in liturgy, historical theology, catechetics, missiology, and dogmatics that *SC* would finally call for the restoration of the catechumenate (no. 68), and the *RCIA* would establish the official renewal of mystagogy in the liturgy and theological vocabulary of the Roman Catholic Church.

Pastoral Synthesis

The Purpose of Mystagogy

While mystagogy is addressed here within the context of a liturgical commentary, it is clear that the purpose of mystagogy is neither narrowly sacramental nor fundamentally liturgical. As St. Paul made clear, the center of the Mystery is the crucified Christ (1 Cor 1:23), not any cultic enactment about the "Christ event." The goal of mystagogy is an encounter with the Mystery, i.e., an encounter with the God of Jesus Christ. That encounter is not for the sake of individual fulfillment or even personal growth in holiness but in witness of the eschatological reign of God breaking through. Mystagogy is in service of the growing realization of God's reign here and now in the world.

As the Johannine gospel writer made clear, realizing God's reign is not simply a matter of knowing, of grasping a new revelation or achieving some elevated gnostic state. Realizing the reign of God is a matter of both flesh and spirit (John 6:63), which requires serious engagement in the strenuous

[108] Josef Jungmann, *Die Frohbotschaft und unsere Glabensverkundigung* (1936); English: *Good News Yesterday and Today*, trans. and ed. William Huesman (New York: W.H. Sadlier, 1962); for an assessment, see Daniel Ruff, "From *Kerygma* to Catechesis: Joseph A. Jungmann's Good News Yesterday and Today," *Living Light* 39, no. 1 (2002): 62–73.

[109] Bryce, "Evolution of Catechesis," 228.

[110] *Mediator Dei* (1947) no. 20.

work of creation in Christ (cf. John 1:1-14). It is engagement that is marked by an inclusive attitude (John 17:20) and a commitment to deep and humble service (John 13:1-17).

As previously noted,[111] this is precisely what was missing in the Corinthian community, which St. Paul so severely took to task. While this attitude of humble service was absent from the cultic life that Paul reviews in 1 Corinthians 11, Paul's letter is not essentially or ultimately a ritual critique of that community. It is not the ritual that had gone astray but the ethics of a community—made apparent in their ritual manifestation at Eucharist—that had gone astray. Ethical living is an unerring hallmark of our transformative engagement with the in-breaking of God's reign. It is to this ethical transformation in Christ that all authentic mystagogy is directed.

Who Is a Mystagogue?

One of the downsides of the raft of scholarship on the history of the catechumenate that surrounded the emergence of the RCIA after Vatican II has been the tendency to identify mystagogues with the great pastoral bishops of the fourth and fifth centuries, e.g., Ambrose, Cyril of Jerusalem, John Chrysostom, Theodore of Mopsuestia, and Augustine. While these were unquestionably sainted and gifted leaders, this narrow definition of a mystagogue raises two serious problems.

First, it overlooks the primary and critical role of the Holy Spirit. As noted above,[112] both the biblical witness and contemporary church teaching underscore the central role of the Holy Spirit in stirring the hearts of the faithful to engage in kingdom work. Just as *SC* notes that liturgy is first of all an act of Christ, head and members (no. 7), so is the ongoing work of *leitourgía*—broadly speaking—always at the impetus of the Holy Spirit.

Reckoning with the fundamental role of the Holy Spirit in mystagogy unveils a second problem with a primary definition of mystagogues as pastoral bishops of the "patristic" era. While it is true that bishops and saints share in the life of the Spirit, the mystagogical impetus of the Holy Spirit is not confined to them. The communion epiclesis during the EP calls for the pouring forth of the Holy Spirit on the church, i.e., on all the baptized. Consequently, the baptized are not the "objects" of authentic mystagogy—just as they are not objects in or of the liturgy. Rather, they are the primary subjects of mystagogy through the impetus of the Holy Spirit. This is a particularly salient point for the laity, who often are considered as the

[111] See 76 above.
[112] See 77 above.

objects of preaching, the recipients of sacraments, and the audience of a reformed liturgy that is somehow designed to cajole them into participation. If mystagogy is not simply about producing more active participation in the liturgy of the church but is instead directed to authentic engagement with the in-breaking of God's reign in the "liturgy of the world,"[113] then the initiative of the laity under the impetus of the Holy Spirit is central to any understanding of mystagogy. *LG* is particularly clear about the role of the laity in bringing about God's reign in the world and pointedly notes that "all lay people, through the gifts which they have received, are at once the witnesses and the living instruments of the mission of the church itself" (no. 33). Thus we conclude that the people of God, in their particular contexts and various configurations, are *de facto* mystagogical communities.

Mystagogue Defined

Officially the Roman Catholic Church seems to define mystagogy in two different ways. In the RCIA mystagogy is defined as "the period of postbaptismal catechesis" (no. 244). This period is meant to help both the community and the newly initiated to "grow in deepening their grasp of the paschal mystery and in making it part of their lives." This is achieved in three ways: "through meditation on the Gospel, sharing in the eucharist, and doing the works of charity" (no. 244). The CCC, on the other hand, seems to equate mystagogy with "liturgical catechesis." Thus it instructs: "Liturgical catechesis aims to initiate people into the mystery of Christ (It is 'mystagogy.') by proceeding from the visible to the invisible, from the sign to the thing signified, from the 'sacraments' to the 'mysteries'" (no. 1075). The CCC then goes on to note that "such catechesis is to be presented by local and regional catechisms" (no. 1075).

Both of these definitions seem anchored in a "patristic" model of initiatory catechesis—especially as found in the writings of Ambrose and Cyril of Jerusalem—that is temporally defined and whose content is traditionally an "explanation" of the rites by a pastoral bishop.[114] The RCIA does emphasize the neophytes' "experience of the sacraments" and recognizes how "this experience . . . increases as it is lived" (no. 245). At the same time,

[113] Karl Rahner's distinction between the "liturgy of the church" and "liturgy of the world" is helpful here; see his "Considerations on the Active Role of the Person in the Sacramental Event," in *Theological Investigations XIV: Ecclesiology, Questions in the Church, The Church in the World*, trans. David Bourke (New York: Seabury Press, 1976), 169–70; for a valuable study on these distinctions, see Michael Skelley, *The Liturgy of the World: Karl Rahner's Theology of Worship* (Collegeville, MN: Liturgical Press, 1991), esp. chaps. 4–6.

[114] See n. 70 above that delineates some of these classical "mystagogical catecheses."

the language of "deepening their grasp of the paschal mystery" (no. 244), "a fuller and more effective understanding of mysteries" (no. 245), and giving the first place to being "truly . . . renewed in mind" (no. 245) provides at least a bifurcated image of mystagogy that is at least as much about "knowing" as anything else.

Previously we offered a preliminary definition of mystagogy as a form of theological reflection integral to and born of the liturgical event itself. Expanding on the definition, it is clear that mystagogy is not a "when," for it can be done before a liturgy (e.g., sacramental preparation grounded in the rites), during a liturgy (e.g., mystagogical preaching), or after a liturgy (e.g., post-ritual reflection such as envisioned in the RCIA).[115] From our perspective it is also not primarily catechesis, especially as that is conceived as the input—as insightful as that might be—by some leader in the community. As noted above, this is one of the difficulties with the way that Ambrose's "mystagogical catechesis" is offered by some as a mystagogical model.[116] While Ambrose had enormous insight, he was not mining the experience of the neophytes but instructing them through scriptural explanations. This does not seem to take into account the role of the baptized as subjects in the mystagogical process.

Thus, we propose that mystagogy is:

> *an imaginative form of theological reflection, prompted by the Holy Spirit, contextualized in a particular faith community, integral to and born of the liturgical event itself, more poetic than discursive, that respects the affective as well as cognitive gifts of the assembly, for the sake of encountering the mystery of God in Christ, which leads to personal and ecclesial transformation in service of the in-breaking of God's reign of justice and peace into the world.*

Many of the elements drawn together in this definition have been referenced above. We have already noted that mystagogy is prompted by the *Holy Spirit*, meant to facilitate an *encounter with the God of Jesus Christ*, and tuned to collaborating with the *in-breaking of God's reign* in the world. While it involves the individual baptized, like liturgy itself, mystagogy is an *ecclesial* act done by Christ, head and members. What distinguishes it from other forms of theological reflection is its grounding in the *liturgical event* itself, i.e., not only its texts but also its assembly, ministers, movements, singing, artifacts, setting, music, silence, etc. Since this is event-centered theological

[115] See Edward Foley, "Musical Mystagogy," in *Finding Voice to Give God Praise*, ed. Kathleen Hughes (Collegeville, MN: Liturgical Press, 1998), 276–87.

[116] See 90–91 above.

reflection, the *context* of that event in all of its richness is essential to the reflection.[117] Because it is about transformation, by necessity mystagogy is an *imaginative* act since it requires a community to believe and live itself into a reality that is not yet completely realized. Finally, the *ethical presumptions*, so foundational to Paul's response to the Corinthians, resonate with a eucharistic liturgy that announces both that it is "just" to give God thanks and "peace" in the midst of its communion action.

Summary

This theological summary, historical excursus, and pastoral synthesis on mystagogy had as its intent to provide a general introduction to the mystagogical reflections that will punctuate this volume, as well as to underscore the dynamic relationship between Roman Catholic doctrinal understanding of the Mystery of our faith and the expression of that Mystery in liturgy and life. In reality, these reflections are more "about mystagogy" than actually mystagogical reflections. Even the imaginative mystagogical reflections that follow throughout this volume have to be seen more as models or stimuli than as substitutes for the kind of mystagogical reflection living communities of faith need to undertake. There is no such thing as a "universal" mystagogy, just like there is no such thing as "generic Eucharist" or "generic baptism." Speaking of the latter, Kenan Osborne notes:

> Baptism is not a replication, a verbal phrase emphasizing an action, nor is a baptism a replicated clone, a substantive phrase emphasizing a thing. Each baptism is not a duplication of a rote activity, nor is each baptism the enfleshing of a duplicative reality. Rather, each baptism is an existential event, an existential action, an existential *Ereignis*. Each baptism is an individualized, historically discreet, temporally unrepeatable moment in the life of an individual, of a particular community of Christians, and of the temporal-historical presence of an active God. There is no such thing as generic baptism.[118]

[117] Stephen Bevans has effectively argued that all theology that claims the contextual name must take into account four things: (1) the experiences of a person's or group's personal life—the experiences of success, failure, births, deaths, and relationship that affect the way we experience God; (2) the dynamics of culture; (3) the particularities of one's social location shaped by factors such as gender, education, wealth, and access; and (4) the local and global powers of social change symbolized, for example, by contemporary communications and commerce. See his *Models of Contextual Theology*, rev. ed. (Maryknoll NY: Orbis, 2002), 5–6.

[118] Kenan Osborne, *Christian Sacraments in a Postmodern World: A Theology for the Third Millennium* (Mahwah, NJ: Paulist Press, 1999), 58.

It is our hope that these ideas and reflections, frameworks and histories, will enhance our shared invitation to encounter the Mystery as we and the world are transformed in that Mystery in Christ.

The Introductory Rites

The Latin Text

Ritus initiales

1. Populo congregato, sacerdos cum ministris ad altare accedit, dum cantus ad introitum peragitur.

Cum ad altare pervenerit, facta cum ministris profunda inclinatione, osculo altare veneratur et, pro opportunitate, crucem et altare incensat. Postea cum ministris sedem petit.

Cantu ad introitum absoluto, sacerdos et fideles, stantes, signant se signo crucis, dum sacerdos, ad populum conversus, dicit:

In nómine Patris, et Fílii, et Spíritus Sancti.

Populus respondet:

Amen.

2. Deinde sacerdos, manus extendens, populum salutat, dicens:

Grátia Dómini nostri Iesu Christi, et cáritas Dei, et communicátio Sancti Spíritus sit cum ómnibus vobis.

Vel:

Grátia vobis et pax a Deo Patre nostro et Dómino Iesu Christo.

Vel:

Dóminus vobíscum.

Populus respondet:

Et cum spíritu tuo.

Episcopus, loco Dóminus vobíscum, in hac prima salutatione dicit:

Pax vobis.

---

3. Sacerdos, vel diaconus vel alius minister, potest brevissimis verbis introducere fideles in Missam diei.

The English Text

The Introductory Rites

1. When the people are gathered, the Priest approaches the altar with the ministers while the Entrance Chant is sung.

When he has arrived at the altar, after making a profound bow with the ministers, the Priest venerates the altar with a kiss and, if appropriate, incenses the cross and the altar. Then, with the ministers, he goes to the chair.

When the Entrance Chant is concluded, the Priest and the faithful, standing, sign themselves with the Sign of the Cross, while the Priest, facing the people, says:

In the name of the Father, and of the Son, and of the Holy Spirit.

The people reply:

Amen.

2. Then the Priest, extending his hands, greets the people, saying:

The grace of our Lord Jesus Christ,
and the love of God,
and the communion of the Holy Spirit
be with you all.

Or:

Grace to you and peace from God our Father
and the Lord Jesus Christ.

Or:

The Lord be with you.

The people reply:

And with your spirit.

In this first greeting a Bishop, instead of The Lord be with you, says:

Peace be with you.

---

3. The Priest, or a Deacon, or another minister, may very briefly introduce the faithful to the Mass of the day.

Actus paenitentialis[*]

4. Deinde sequitur actus paenitentialis ad quem sacerdos fideles invitat, dicens:

Fratres, agnoscámus peccáta nostra,
ut apti simus ad sacra mystéria celebránda.

Fit brevis pausa silentii. Postea omnes simul formulam confessionis generalis perficiunt:

Confíteor Deo omnipoténti et vobis, fratres,
quia peccávi nimis
cogitatióne, verbo, ópere et omissióne:

et, percutientes sibi pectus, dicunt:

mea culpa, mea culpa, mea máxima culpa.

Deinde prosequuntur:

Ideo precor beátam Maríam semper Vírginem,
omnes Angelos et Sanctos,
et vos, fratres, oráre pro me
ad Dóminum Deum nostrum.

Sequitur absolutio sacerdotis:

Misereátur nostri omnípotens Deus
et, dimissís peccátis nostris,
perdúcat nos ad vitam aetérnam.

Populus respondet:

Amen.

Vel:

5. Sacerdos fideles invitat ad actum paenitentialem:

Fratres, agnoscámus peccáta nostra,
ut apti simus ad sacra mystéria celebránda.

Fit brevis pausa silentii.

[*] Die dominica, praesertim tempore paschali, loco consueti actus paenitentialis, quandoque fieri potest benedictio et aspersio aquae in memoriam baptismi, ut in Appendice II.

Penitential Act*

4. Then follows the Penitential Act, to which the Priest invites the faithful, saying:

Brethren (brothers and sisters), let us acknowledge our sins,
and so prepare ourselves to celebrate the sacred mysteries.

A brief pause for silence follows. Then all recite together the formula of general confession:

I confess to almighty God
and to you, my brothers and sisters,
that I have greatly sinned,
in my thoughts and in my words,
in what I have done and in what I have failed to do,

And, striking their breast, they say:

through my fault, through my fault,
through my most grievous fault;

Then they continue:

therefore I ask blessed Mary ever-Virgin,
all the Angels and Saints,
and you, my brothers and sisters,
to pray for me to the Lord our God.

The absolution by the Priest follows:

May almighty God have mercy on us,
forgive us our sins,
and bring us to everlasting life.

The people reply:

Amen.

Or:

5. The Priest invites the faithful to make the Penitential Act:

Brethren (brothers and sisters), let us acknowledge our sins,
and so prepare ourselves to celebrate the sacred mysteries.

A brief pause for silence follows.

* From time to time on Sundays, especially in Easter Time, instead of the customary Penitential Act, the Blessing and sprinkling of water may take place (as in Appendix II) as a reminder of Baptism.

Postea sacerdos dicit:

Miserére nostri, Dómine.

Populus respondet:

Quia peccávimus tibi.

Sacerdos:

Osténde nobis, Dómine, misericórdiam tuam.

Populus:

Et salutáre tuum da nobis.

Sequitur absolutio sacerdotis:

Misereátur nostri omnípotens Deus
et, dimíssis peccátis nostris,
perdúcat nos ad vitam aetérnam.

Populus respondet:

Amen.

Vel:

6. Sacerdos fideles invitat ad actum paenitentialem:

Fratres, agnoscámus peccáta nostra,
ut apti simus ad sacra mystéria celebránda.

Fit brevis pausa silentii.

Postea sacerdos, vel diaconus vel alius minister, sequentes, vel alias, invocationes cum Kyrie, eléison profert:

Qui missus es sanáre contrítos corde: Kyrie, eléison.

Populus respondet:

Kyrie, eléison.

Sacerdos:

Qui peccatóres vocáre venísti: Christe, eléison.

Populus:

Christe, eléison.

Sacerdos:

Qui ad déxteram Patris sedes, ad interpellándum pro nobis: Kyrie, eléison.

The Priest then says:

Have mercy on us, O Lord.

The people reply:

For we have sinned against you.

The Priest:

Show us, O Lord, your mercy.

The people:

And grant us your salvation.

The absolution by the Priest follows:

May almighty God have mercy on us,
forgive us our sins,
and bring us to everlasting life.

The people reply:

Amen.

Or:

6. The Priest invites the faithful to make the Penitential Act:

Brethren (brothers and sisters), let us acknowledge our sins,
and so prepare ourselves to celebrate the sacred mysteries.

A brief pause for silence follows.

The Priest, or a Deacon or another minister, then says the following or other invocations with Kyrie, eleison (Lord, have mercy):

You were sent to heal the contrite of heart:

Lord, have mercy. Or: Kyrie, eleison.

The people reply:

Lord, have mercy. Or: Kyrie, eleison.

The Priest:

You came to call sinners:

Christ, have mercy. Or: Christe, eleison.

The people:

Christ, have mercy. Or: Christe, eleison.

The Priest:

You are seated at the right hand of the Father to intercede for us:

Lord, have mercy. Or: Kyrie, eleison.

Populus:

Kyrie, eléison.

Sequitur absolutio sacerdotis:

Misereátur nostri omnípotens Deus
et, dimíssis peccátis nostris,
perdúcat nos ad vitam aetérnam.

Populus respondet:

Amen.

---

7. Sequuntur invocationes Kyrie, eléison, nisi iam praecesserint in aliqua formula actus paenitentialis.

℣. Kyrie, eléison. ℟. Kyrie, eléison.
℣. Christe, eléison. ℟. Christe, eléison.
℣. Kyrie, eléison. ℟. Kyrie, eléison.

Aliae melodiae in Graduali romano inveniuntur.

8. Deinde, quando praescribitur, cantatur vel dicitur hymnus:

Toni integri in Graduali romano inveniuntur.

Glória in excélsis Deo
et in terra pax homínibus bonae voluntátis.
Laudámus te,
benedícimus te,
adorámus te,
glorificámus te,
grátias ágimus tibi propter magnam glóriam tuam,
Dómine Deus, Rex caeléstis,
Deus Pater omnípotens.
Dómine Fili Unigénite, Iesu Christe,
Dómine Deus, Agnus Dei, Fílius Patris,
qui tollis peccáta mundi, miserére nobis;
qui tollis peccáta mundi, súscipe deprecatiónem nostram.
Qui sedes ad déxteram Patris, miserére nobis.

The people:

Lord, have mercy. Or: Kyrie, eleison.

The absolution by the Priest follows:

May almighty God have mercy on us,
forgive us our sins,
and bring us to everlasting life.

The people reply:

Amen.

---

7. The **Kyrie eleison** (**Lord, have mercy**) invocations follow, unless they have just occurred in a formula of the Penitential Act.

℣. Lord, have mercy. ℟. Lord, have mercy.
℣. Christ, have mercy. ℟. Christ, have mercy.
℣. Lord, have mercy. ℟. Lord, have mercy.

Or:

℣. Kyrie, eleison. ℟. Kyrie, eleison.
℣. Christe, eleison. ℟. Christe, eleison.
℣. Kyrie, eleison. ℟. Kyrie, eleison.

8. Then, when it is prescribed, this hymn is either sung or said:

Glory to God in the highest,
and on earth peace to people of good will.

We praise you,
we bless you,
we adore you,
we glorify you,
we give you thanks for your great glory,
Lord God, heavenly King,
O God, almighty Father.

Lord Jesus Christ, Only Begotten Son,
Lord God, Lamb of God, Son of the Father,
you take away the sins of the world,
  have mercy on us;
you take away the sins of the world,
  receive our prayer;
you are seated at the right hand of the Father,
  have mercy on us.

Quóniam tu solus Sanctus, tu solus Dóminus, tu solus Altíssimus,
Iesu Christe, cum Sancto Spíritu: in glória Dei Patris.
Amen.

9. Quo hymno expleto, sacerdos, manibus iunctis, dicit: Orémus.

Et omnes una cum sacerdote per aliquod temporis spatium in silentio orant.

Tunc sacerdos, manibus extensis, dicit orationem collectam, qua expleta, populus acclamat:

Amen.

For you alone are the Holy One,
you alone are the Lord,
you alone are the Most High,
Jesus Christ,
with the Holy Spirit,
in the glory of God the Father.
Amen.

9. When this hymn is concluded, the Priest, with hands joined, says:

Let us pray.

And all pray in silence with the Priest for a while.

Then the Priest, with hands extended, says the Collect prayer, at the end of which the people acclaim:

Amen.

History of the Latin Text and Rite

John Baldovin

Introduction

The distinguished liturgical historian Robert Taft has noted that the introductory rites of the eucharistic celebration are among those parts of the liturgy that are subject to change. Along with the rites at the preparation of the gifts and the rites surrounding communion, he calls the introductory rites "action" or "soft" points in the development of the liturgy. These he contrasts with the original core of the liturgy, which consisted of readings from Scripture and the EP.[1] Taft discerns that core in the second-century description of the liturgy found in the *First Apology* (nos. 65 and 67) of Justin Martyr (d. *ca.* 165). Justin does not mention any liturgical element prior to the readings from the OT and NT. This piece of evidence alone would not suffice to prove that there were no preliminary rites in the Ante-Nicene liturgy, but as late as the early fifth century we know that St. Augustine (d. 430) wrote in his *City of God* of beginning the liturgy with the greeting and straightaway the readings:

> Then the crowd ran to me where I was sitting, getting ready to enter the church. . . . We went into the people, the church being full and resounding with the voices of those rejoicing: "Thank God, Praise God!" Without exception the people were shouting out on all sides. I greeted them, and again they shouted out all the more. Finally there was silence, and the Holy Scriptures were solemnly read.[2]

The same is true for John Chrysostom in Antioch and Constantinople.[3] Therefore, prior to the fifth century, except for a liturgical greeting like

[1] Robert Taft, "The Structural Analysis of Liturgical Units: An Essay in Methodology," and "How Liturgies Grow," in *Beyond East and West: Essays in Liturgical Understanding*, 2nd ed. (Rome: Pontificium Institutum Orientale, 1997), 199–202, 203–5.

[2] St. Augustine, *The City of God*, 22.8 = Johnson, 3:34.

[3] See Frans van de Paverd, *Zur Geschichte der Messliturgie in Antiocheia und Konstantinopel gegen Ende des vierten Jahrhunderts: Analyse der Quellen bei Johannes Chrysostomos*, Orientalia Christiana Analecta 187 (Rome: Pontificium Institutum Orientalium Studiorum, 1970), 86–87.

"Peace to all," there is no solid evidence of what we know as the entrance rites today.

There is, however, a notice in the *Liber Pontificalis* under Celestine I (d. 432) that he determined "that before the sacrifice the 150 Psalms of David should be performed antiphonally by everyone; this used not to be done, but only St. Paul's epistle and the holy gospel were recited."[4] Medieval liturgical commentators like Rabanus Maurus (d. 856) and Amalarius of Metz (d. *ca.* 850) interpreted the passage to refer to the introit or entrance psalm. This became the commonly accepted theory—i.e., that an antiphonal psalm, later abbreviated, was added to the Roman liturgy in the third decade of the fifth century. This interpretation has recently been challenged by Peter Jeffery who argues that the *Liber Pontificalis* notice could equally refer to the psalm chant between the readings. Jeffery's argument rests on his conviction that Celestine introduced not antiphonal but responsorial psalmody to Rome in imitation of what he experienced in St. Ambrose's Milan toward the end of the fourth century. Since the *Liber Pontificalis* is reliable only from the sixth century, when it was composed, the editors may have mistakenly added "antiphonally" since they knew antiphonal psalmody in the form of the introit chant.[5] On the other hand, we know that in the Christian East a psalm with antiphon preceded the readings at the eucharistic liturgy at least in the early fifth century.[6] So we can say that from the sixth century at the latest the Roman liturgy knew an entrance chant. Before that, except for a greeting, we cannot be sure that there were any entrance rites prior to the reading of the Scriptures.

Entrance Chant (*OM2008*, no. 1)

The first full description of the Roman Mass that we possess is in a document of rubrical directions known as *OR I*. According to its most recent commentator, John F. Romano, this document probably originated in Rome during the pontificate of Sergius I (687–701). *OR I* describes a procession

See also, Robert Cabié, *The Eucharist*, ed. Aimé Georges Martimort, trans. Matthew O'Connell, The Church at Prayer 2 (Collegeville, MN: Liturgical Press, 1986), 50.

[4] Raymond Davis, *The Book of Pontiffs (Liber Pontificalis): The Ancient Biographies of the First Ninety Roman Bishops to AD 715* (Liverpool: Liverpool University Press, 1989), 34.

[5] Peter Jeffery, "The Introduction of Psalmody into the Roman Mass by Pope Celestine I (422-432): Reinterpreting a Passage in the *Liber Pontificalis*," *Archiv für Liturgiewissenschaft* 26 (184): 147–65.

[6] From the Old Armenian Lectionary, which translates the fifth-century liturgy of Jerusalem, see John Wilkinson, *Egeria's Travels*, 3rd ed. (Oxford: Aris & Phillips, 1999), 175–94.

from the Lateran palace to St. Mary Major Church on the Esquiline Hill for the papal (stational) liturgy of Easter Sunday morning. An elaborate entrance procession follows the vesting of the pope in the vesting room near the basilica's entrance. This is how *OR I* describes it:

37. Then the regionary subdeacon, having the pope's liturgical napkin [= maniple] in his left hand wrapped over the chasuble, going out to the portico of the *secretarium*, says: *Choir*. He responds: *I am here.* And he: *Who is singing the Psalm?* He responds: *He and he.*

38. And returning to the pope the subdeacon extends the liturgical napkin to him, bowing to his knees, saying: *The servants of my lord so-and-so a regionary subdeacon is reading the epistle and so-and-so from the choir is singing. . . .*

40. When this is announced, immediately the fourth one of the choir follows the subdeacon, standing in front of the pope's face, until the pope signals to him that they may sing the Psalm; when he signals to him, immediately he goes out in front of the entrance of the *secretarium* and says: *Light [it] on fire.*

41. When they light [it] on fire, immediately the second subdeacon, having the golden censer, places the incense on the outside, so that he travels in front of the pope.

42. And the fourth of the choir comes into the presbytery to the prior of the choir, or the second or the third, after having bowed his head, says: *Lord, command.*

43. Then they, getting up in order, go in front of the altar; the two lines stand in order so far as [it is] according to order, indeed the *parafonistae* on either side on the outside, the children on both sides below in order.

44. And soon the prior of the choir starts the introit, when the deacons hear their voice, immediately they enter to the pope in the *secretarium*.

45. And then the pope, rising, gives his right hand to the archdeacon and the left [hand] to the second [deacon], or who is in order; and they, after having kissed his hands, walk with him in *sustentatio*.

46. Then the second subdeacon with the censer walks in front of him, sending out incense, and the seven acolytes of whose region the day is, carrying seven lit candelabra walk in front of the pope until [they are] in front of the altar.

47. But, before they come in front of the altar, the deacons in the presbytery remove their chasubles and the regionary subdeacon receives them and extends them to the acolytes of the region of which they are deacons.

48. And then two acolytes, holding open receptacles with the Eucharist, and the second subdeacon with them having his hand in the mouth of the receptacle shows the Eucharist to the pope or the deacon who walks in procession. Then, after having bowed his head, the pope or the deacon kisses the Eucharist and looks so that if it is too much, let him command that it is put in the repository.

49. Then passing on, before he comes to the choir, the candelabra are divided, four to the right and three to the left and the pope crosses into the front part of the choir and bows his head to the altar, getting up and praying and making the sign of the cross on his forehead, and gives peace to one bishop of the hebdomadary [bishops] and to the archpriest and to all the deacons.

50. And looking at the prior of the choir he signals to him that he may sing the *Glory*; and the prior of the choir bows to the pope and intones. But the fourth of the choir walks in front of the pope, so that he places the prayer rug in front of the altar; and approaching, the pope prays on it until the repetition of the verse.

51. Now the deacons get up when he says: *As it was*, so that they kiss the sides of the altar, first two by two in turn returning to the pope. And getting up, the pope kisses the evangelary and the altar and approaches his seat and stands turned toward the East.[7]

At this point it is clear that the introit or processional psalm consisted of an antiphon, the verses of the psalm, the singing of the "Glory to the Father and to the Son . . . ," and a repetition of the antiphon. This is typical of antiphonal (as opposed to responsorial) chant. Only as many verses of the psalm are needed until the pope reaches the altar area. This practice seems to be the case, at least in some places, up to the beginning of the twelfth century.[8] At the same time, antiphonaries (chant collections) from the ninth century on suggest that the introit chant could consist only of an

[7] Translation by John F. Romano, online at http://www.medievalliturgy.com/files/J._F._Romano_Translation_of_the_First_Roman_Ordo.pdf (accessed 27 January 2011).

[8] See Vincenzo Raffa, *Liturgia Eucaristica: Mistagogia della Messa: dalla storia e dalla teologia alla pastorale pratica*, Bibliotheca 'Ephemerides liturgicae' Subsidia 100 (Rome: CLV, 2003), 248.

antiphon, psalm verse, *Gloria Patri*, and repetition of the antiphon. This would certainly make sense given the smaller scale of most churches and the elaboration of the melodies of the chants themselves.[9] Josef Jungmann laments the reduction of the introit to the antiphon and first verse of the psalm, since it was often enough another verse of the psalm that made sense of choosing it for a particular occasion.[10] Moreover, in the period after Pentecost the Sunday psalms are chosen for the most part from the Psalter in numerical order (from Ps 12 on the First Sunday up to Ps 118 on the Seventeenth Sunday, followed by selections from the Wisdom and Prophetic Literature).

By the thirteenth century, according to the *Ordo of the Roman Curia* (Lateran), the chant was also read at the altar by the priest.[11]

Sign of the Cross, Greeting, Penitential Act, and *Kyrie* (*OM2008*, nos. 1–7)

As noted above, as elaborate as the procession of the eighth-century papal Mass was, the presider did not actually say anything until he intoned the "Glory to God in the highest" or (in Advent and Lent) the opening prayer. The pope signed his forehead with the sign of the cross, but in silence. The priest tracing the sign of the cross on his body accompanied by the trinitarian formula does not seem to appear until the late Middle Ages in the Sarum (Salisbury) Use in southern England and in the *Ordo* of Burchard of Worms (1502).[12] The practice of people and priest performing the gesture and speaking the trinitarian formula together with the people responding, "Amen," was an innovation introduced into the Missal of Paul VI (1970).[13]

The greeting, "The Lord be with you," is found in *OR I* only before the three presidential prayers (opening prayer, prayer over the gifts, and prayer after communion) and the preface of the EP. We have noted earlier, however, that a greeting ("The Lord be with you" or "Peace to all") marked the beginning of the service at the end of the fourth century in East and West.

[9] See Cyrille Vogel, *Medieval Liturgy: An Introduction to the Sources*, trans. and rev. William G. Storey and Niels Krogh Rasmussen (Washington, DC: Pastoral Press, 1986), 357–60; Richard Crocker, "Chants of the Roman Mass," in *New Oxford History of Music II: The Early Middle Ages to 1300*, ed. Richard Crocker and David Hiley (Oxford: Oxford University Press, 1990), 139–43, 174–80.

[10] Jungmann MRR, 1:327.

[11] Raffa, *Liturgia Eucaristica*, 249.

[12] See ibid., 261. The private penitential prayers of the priest will be dealt with below.

[13] Ibid., 262.

OM1969 added two scriptural greetings as options. Both are derived from Pauline material (2 Cor 13:14 and Phil 1:2).

The current Order of Mass has eliminated the priest's private penitential material that developed in different ways from the Carolingian period (ninth century) on. Instead we have several different forms of introductory material.

First is the *Asperges*. Vincenzo Raffa has suggested that the rite of sprinkling originated in the ancient domestic and monastic circles and was only incorporated into the Roman Rite Mass with the *MR1570*. More accurately, it was added to the introduction of the liturgy. It consisted of an antiphonal unit: antiphon (Ps 51:7), verse (Ps 51:1), *Gloria Patri*, and repetition of the antiphon. During the Easter season, the *Asperges* antiphon was replaced by a verse from Ezekiel 47 (the so-called *Vidi aquam*) followed by a verse from Ps 117. The sprinkling rite was made an option to the penitential act on Sundays in *OM1969*. It has been placed in an appendix in *MR2002*.

The other forms are all options under what is now called "the penitential act." In terms of the Roman Rite, the most ancient penitential element is the repetition of *Kyrie eleison* and *Christe eleison* ("Lord, have mercy" and "Christ, have mercy"). Since the Gallican Synod of Vaison (529) mentions that the Roman use of the *Kyrie* ought to be adapted in the eucharistic liturgy north of the Alps, we can be fairly certain that the Roman liturgy contained some form of the *Kyrie* in the fifth century.[14] In addition, Pope Gregory I defends his adaptation of the Greek usage (to include "Christ . . ." as well as "Lord, have mercy") at the end of the sixth century.[15] The late seventh-century *OR I* tells us the following:

> But the choir, after having finished the antiphon, intones the Lord, have mercy. But the prior of the choir watches the pope, so that he signals to him when he wants to change the number of the litany and bows to the pope.[16]

The *Kyrie* acclamation clearly has some relationship to the litanies in the liturgies of the Christian East. Theories differ as to how the repetition of the *Kyrie* with the invocations of the litany was adopted by the Roman Rite. The most reasonable theory to date has been proposed by Paul De Clerck.[17]

[14] Mansi, *Sacrorum Conciliorum Nova et Amplissima Collectio* (Florence, 1795), 8:727.

[15] Gregory the Great, *Epistola* 9.26 in L. Hartmann, ed., *Monumenta germaniae Historica Epistolae* 2 (Berlin: Wiedmann, 1897).

[16] Romano translation, no. 52.

[17] Paul De Clerck, *La "prière universelle" dans les liturgies latines anciennes: Témoignages patristiques et textes liturgiques*, Liturgiewissenschaftliche Quellen und Forschungen 62

De Clerck argued that the *Kyrie* was originally used as an independent chant similar to the litany of divine peace that is found in Milanese sources. My own theory corroborates De Clerck by suggesting that the source of the independent chant was the Byzantine insistent litany (*ektene*) that was used in stational processions in Constantinople and that, just as the Office of Three Antiphons and *Trisagion* chant were the "remains" of popular processions in that city, so we might understand the similar development of the Roman Rite with regard to the *Kyrie*. Moreover, this origin would mean that the *Kyrie* chant need not necessarily be considered penitential.

We have already noted that it was possible to trope the *Kyrie*. This was certainly reported by Amalarius of Metz in the ninth century.[18] This usage has been recovered in the third form of the penitential act with invocations directed to Christ.

The final element of the penitential act that can be traced to historical sources is the *Confiteor* (I confess). Vincenzo Raffa traces this prayer to penitential rites in the ninth century. Certainly it was common in the early Middle Ages for priests to pray *apologiae* (penitential prayers) on their way to the altar. The *Confiteor* can be found in the *Micrologus* of Bernhold of Constance around 1100.[19] Its use became universal in the Roman Rite in *MR1570* in dialogical form between the priest and ministers. The same prayer formed the basis of the first form of the penitential act in *MR1970*.

Hymn: Glory to God in the Highest (*OM2008*, no. 8)

The hymn, Glory to God in the Highest, has never been an element in each and every celebration of the Eucharist. The text of this hymn does not, in fact, originate from the eucharistic liturgy but rather from morning prayer in the Christian East. Jungmann likens it to the nonscriptural hymns (*psalmi iditiotici*) of the primitive church. Other examples of the genre are the *Te Deum* ("We Praise you") and the evening hymn *Phos Hilaron* ("Joyful Light").[20] Like the *Phos Hilaron*, its antiquity is suggested by the fact that a good part of it is addressed directly to Christ.

(Münster: Aschendorff, 1977), 282–84; also, John Baldovin, "Kyrie Eleison and the Entrance Rite of the Roman Eucharist," in *Worship: City, Church and Renewal* (Washington, DC: Pastoral Press, 1992), 135–50. For a different view, see Raffa, *Liturgia Eucaristica*, 280–87. Raffa believes that the original usage contained tropes or expansions on the *Kyrie* similar to those that we find later in the Middle Ages.

[18] Amalarius of Metz, *De ecclesiasticis officiis* 3.6.2, cited in Raffa, *Liturgia Eucaristica*, 285.

[19] *Micrologus* (*PL* 101:979A), cited in Raffa, *Liturgia Eucaristica*, 273.

[20] Jungmann MRR, 1:346–47. As a morning hymn, see Apostolic Constitutions 7:47.

An ancient form in Latin is found in the late seventh-century *Antiphonary of Bangor*.[21] The Latin of Bangor, which for the most part is the later Latin text in the Roman Mass, is somewhat misleading in that it translates *en anthropois eudokia* as *hominibus bonae voluntatis*, whereas Jungmann insists that the goodwill in question is God's favor toward human beings.[22]

The sixth-century *Liber Pontificalis* notes that the *Gloria* was introduced into the Roman liturgy by Pope Telesphorus (d. 136). Although this is almost certainly not the case since the *Liber* is only reliable from the sixth century on, it does at least indicate that this hymn was in use by the sixth century. Up until the time of the Gregorian Sacramentary (eighth century) the *Gloria* may be sung only at liturgies at which bishops preside and then only on Sundays and feast days. Presbyters were allowed to use it only at Easter.[23] By the end of the eleventh century priests were allowed to use the *Gloria* at any celebration that a bishop could. Jungmann notes that the rubric that up to the ninth century called for the bishop to face the assembly while intoning the *Gloria* is an indication that this hymn was originally meant to be sung by the entire congregation.[24]

The Collect (Opening Prayer) (*OM2008*, no. 9)

The entrance rites conclude with a variable opening prayer. As with the introit chant, we do not know precisely when this prayer was added to the liturgy. We know that it must have been sometime between the evidence of Augustine opening the liturgy simply with a greeting and the middle of the sixth century when a number of the prayers in the *Veronense* seem to have been composed.[25] The later collections of prayers for the Mass (in the so-called Gelasian and Gregorian sacramentaries) contain many more opening prayers for the various Sundays, feasts, and special occasions (e.g., prayers in time of drought). The current name for the prayer is found first north of the Alps in the ninth-century description of Amalarius of Metz.[26] It appears for the first time in the liturgical books of the Roman Rite in the

[21] Jungmann MRR, 1:348–49, citing F. E. Warren, *The Antiphonary of Bangor*, Henry Bradshaw Society 10 (London: HBS, 1892–95), 31.

[22] The Latin text remains the basis for the current translation.

[23] J. Deshusses, ed., *Le sacramentaire grégorien*, Spicilegium Friburgense 16 (Fribourg: Editions Universitaires, 1971), 85 from the *Hadrianum*.

[24] Jungmann MRR, 1:358.

[25] On the *Veronense*, formerly called "The Leonine Sacramentary," see Vogel, *Medieval Liturgy*, 38–45.

[26] *Expositio* I.IV.1 cited in Raffa, *Liturgia Eucaristica*, 296.

ritus servandus of *MR1570*. It was called the "opening prayer" in ICEL1973 despite the fact that the Latin remained *collecta*.

The vast majority of prayers have the following pattern:

- Address to the Father: "Almighty and Eternal God"
- Expansion or description through a relative clause: "who . . ."
- Request: "grant that . . ."
- Conclusion: "Through Jesus Christ, our Lord."

These prayers were composed according to a Roman rhetorical method called the *cursus*.[27]

Vincenzo Raffa lists four different theories as to the original function of the opening prayer:

1. autonomous introduction to the Mass
2. conclusion of a preceding litany
3. introduction to the readings
4. conclusion to the introit psalm.[28]

Jungmann is of the opinion that the collect is the conclusion to the action of the entrance, which is covered by the introit chant.[29] In this way it would be analogous to two other "action points," the presentation of the gifts and the communion procession, which also involved psalmody and action.

[27] For an excellent explanation, see Jungmann MRR, 1:276–79; also G.G. Willis, *Essays on Early Roman Liturgy*, Alcuin Club Collection 46 (London: SPCK, 1964), 111–18.

[28] Raffa, *Liturgia Eucaristica*, 298. For the view that these prayers were attached to the readings, see G. G. Willis, "The Collect" in *Further Essays in Early Roman Liturgy*, Alcuin Club Collection 50 (London: SPCK, 1968), 108–12.

[29] Jungmann MRR, 1:266.

Theology of the Latin Text and Rite

Dominic E. Serra

The theological significance of the introductory rites is found not only in the words spoken but in the entire structure of the liturgical action, both word and gesture. As John Baldovin has previously noted, Augustine provides our earliest evidence of the essential structure: the bishop entered the assembly while the people cried out in praise of God; he took his place before them, greeted them in Christ, and received their greeting in turn. Not long after Augustine we learn from Roman sources that the spontaneous shouts of praise became a prescribed entrance chant (introit) and the greeting introduced a prayer, sometimes called a collect. We also know that the bishop of Rome venerated the altar by prostrating before it in silent prayer and then kissed it. The acolytes too honored the altar by arranging their torches around it. These represent natural developments of the more ancient rite. They grow from it "organically" because they expand the purpose and sense of their source. Reintroduced in *OM1969*, they are again the core of the introductory rites of *OM2008*.[1]

This theological analysis will highlight the essential core of the introductory rites: the procession, veneration of the altar, greeting at the chair, and opening prayer. Elements that further adorn that simple structure also will be considered: the penitential rite, blessing and sprinkling of blessed water, *Kyrie*, and Glory to God. While important elements, these are secondary to the previously noted core elements of the introductory rites.

The Procession (*OM2008*, no. 1)

Orthodox theologian Alexander Schmemann suggested that the entrance procession concludes with the movement of the ministers to the altar but begins when, in response to God's call, we leave behind the separateness of our private homes and apartments and start our trek each Sunday to the place where we will be known by the collective titles of church or People

[1] See Baldovin, 115–23.

of God.[2] The trickle of individuals increases and our "procession" intensifies until our group can be identified as a congregation. Then the entrance of the ordained president of the assembly completes the procession of the People of God hierarchically ordered (GIRM2003, no. 16). Thus we become a sacramental manifestation of the church throughout the world and in every generation. What we do here and now is done by the church, the Body of Christ, the People of God. We sing with full voice during this solemn conclusion to our procession from individuality into community and that very action solidifies our unity by revealing the truth about our sacramental identity (cf. GIRM2003, no. 57).

The first rubric of *OM2008* provides this instruction: *Populo congregato, sacerdos cum ministris ad altare accedit, dum cantus ad introitum peragitur* (no. 1). The opening phrase is an ablative absolute, singular in number and passive in voice: literally, "the people (having been) gathered." The many individuals who show up in the church become a single "people." The passive construction tells us that they do not make themselves a people but that they are congregated by God to be his very own people (1 Pet 2:9-10). This basic ecclesiological premise permeates *LG*: the church does not create itself but is called into existence by God, through the ministry of Christ, in the power of the Holy Spirit (nos. 1–8). Ultimately, we are saved not as individuals but as a communion of believers whose gathering anticipates the eschatological banquet. Our coming together in response to God's call is already the first movement of the creative power of the Eucharist by which the church is created.

Veneration of the Altar (*OM2008*, no. 1)

The priest makes his way through our assembly as if gathering and bringing us to the altar, to Christ. There he bows profoundly, kisses the altar, and may honor it with incense while servers place their candles around it in veneration. The altar receives these signs of honor because it is Christ in our midst; "He is our priest, altar, and sacrificial Lamb."[3] On the day the altar was dedicated, its entire surface was anointed by the bishop with chrism, the very oil used to consecrate new Christians at

[2] Alexander Schmemann, *For the Life of the World: Sacraments and Orthodoxy* (Crestwood, NY: St. Vladimir's Seminary Press, 1973), 26–28.

[3] " . . . *idem sacerdos, altare et agnus exhibuit*," Praefatio Paschalis V, *MR2002* (my translation).

baptism and confirmation and priests and bishops at their ordination.[4] GIRM2003 requires that the altar should "be so placed as to be truly the center toward which the attention of the whole congregation of the faithful naturally turns" (no. 299). This follows from the conviction that the altar is one of the chief manifestations of the presence of Christ in the midst of his church.

Liturgical regulations are quite restrictive about what may be placed upon the altar lest it appear to be nothing more than a convenient resting place for items used in the service. The gifts of bread and wine will be placed here so that they will come to be identified with the self-offering of Christ. The gospel book may be placed on the altar so it will be clear that its proclamation in the assembly derives its power from Christ in our midst. Aside from the offerings and the gospel only those things required for the celebration, such as the Missal, may be placed here. The candles carried in the procession may be placed either on or around the altar. Many parishes have chosen to place these around the altar, not merely because this is the more ancient tradition, but because it expresses more clearly that they are signs of reverence for the altar itself, much the way we may light candles before images of Christ and the saints (GIRM2003, nos. 306–7).

The veneration of the altar consists of three main gestures and one ancillary action. The main gestures are the profound bow, the kiss, and the incensation. When executed in close succession, these rites—powerfully drawing attention to the altar—will not appear to be disjointed, separate actions but rather three expressions by which Christ is greeted. The priest bows as soon as he arrives before the altar; he may step up to it and kiss it (before walking around to the other side), and then he may begin incensing immediately while walking all around it. This will be one act of veneration in three modes of expression. This may also heighten the sense that the altar is approachable from all sides, not just from the side usually occupied by the priest. God's holy people gathered around the altar should sense that the altar belongs to the whole church, a community hierarchically ordered and gathered around Christ, our altar, priest, and sacrifice. This attention to the altar and its centrality in the midst of the assembly will help establish it as a symbol of Christ's presence in our midst.

[4] "The anointing with chrism makes the altar a symbol of Christ . . .; for the Father anointed him with the Holy Spirit and constituted him the High Priest so that on the altar of his body he might offer the sacrifice of his life for the salvation of all" (Dedication of an Altar, no. 22a, in *The Rites of the Catholic Church*, 2 vols. [Collegeville, MN: Liturgical Press, 1991], 2:411).

If the gospel book is carried in procession, it should be placed on the altar just before the tripartite veneration. There are two reasons for this. First, the placement illustrates the inseparable unity that exists between the proclamation of the Word of God and the eucharistic action (GIRM2003, no. 28). Second, when the gospel book will later be taken from the altar and carried to the place of proclamation, it will be the more obvious that the proclamation derives from Christ. The book need not be propped up to be made visible as if it were being placed on a pedestal for veneration. This practice can lead to some confusion about the liturgical symbols. The Word of God is present and active in our assembly primarily in the act of proclamation and it is that action at the ambo that should be the focus of our attention. The gospel book will be visible in the entrance procession; it will be obvious when placed upon the altar where these two symbols of Christ are united as one, and it will again be visible when it is taken from the altar and carried to the place of proclamation. If it is placed on the altar as if enshrined, it could make the altar appear to be a shelf or stand for the book. When the gospel book is taken from the altar at the time of proclamation, it will be clear that the altar is the table at which the faithful are nourished by Word and sacrament.

Greeting at the Chair (*OM2008*, no. 2)

Having greeted the altar, the president goes to the place from which he will preside over the action of the church at prayer. After making the sign of the cross, he takes in the entire congregation with his glance and, extending his arms toward them, greets them saying, "The Lord be with you." These are the very first words addressed to the assembly; the sign of the cross is not really addressed to the gathered church, but these words surely are. They give attention to the assembly's identity as Christ's faithful people, the Lord's dwelling place, and the congregation immediately returns the greeting to Christ's servant who presides. In this simple mutual act of greeting we give expression to the teaching of *SC*, no. 7, which instructs that the presence of Christ in the liturgy is manifold and may be found in the assembly, in the priest, in the proclamation of the Word, and in the eucharistic species of bread and wine. Having venerated Christ our altar of sacrifice and eschatological banquet table, the priest now venerates Christ in the assembly and they in turn honor the same Christ in the priest-presider. In addition to this classical greeting of the Roman liturgy, other greetings taken from the NT may be used. These will introduce a trinitarian element to the greeting that otherwise is primarily christological. As Anscar Chupungco points out, the response, *et cum spiritu tuo*, is meant to address the priest-presider in the fullness of his being.[5] In catechesis, it will be important to point out that the greeting to the priest's "spirit" does not establish a kind of dualism that may suggest that the spirit rather than the body is honored in the greeting. Spirit here has the very opposite sense as the fullness of humanity.

The Penitential Rite (*OM2008*, nos. 4–6)

The historical facts related elsewhere in this commentary indicate that the penitential rite had its start in the Roman liturgy as a private preparatory prayer of the priest and ministers.[6] *OM1969* did away with the private form and provided a new, communal rite in its place. It has an important but secondary place among the introductory rites. It is normally omitted when some other ritual takes place just before or at the beginning of Mass, and on Sundays it may be replaced by the rite of sprinkling blessed water (GIRM2003, no. 51).

OM2008 provides three forms for the penitential rite. Space will not allow a detailed study of each of these but attention to some of the elements common to all three will be instructive. The rite begins with the priest's invitation, *Fratres, agnoscamus peccata nostra, ut apti simus ad sacra mysteria celebranda*. These words were chosen with great care to avoid being misconstrued to be an invitation to an examination of conscience. We are invited instead to acknowledge our sins so that we may be properly prepared to enter into the celebration of the sacred mysteries. Notice that the acknowledgment of our sins, not the forgiveness of our sins, will make us well suited for the celebration of the mysteries.[7] We are well disposed to the celebration when we are aware that we are sinners in need of the healing and forgiving power of the Eucharist. It is not a matter of getting rid of our sins in order to be pure enough to celebrate the mysteries; rather, it is that the general confession makes us capable of being forgiven by the sacrifice we offer and by the banquet of reconciliation. While grave sin must ordinarily first be brought to the sacrament of reconciliation, our minor sins can be healed by the medicine of the Eucharist itself.

This rite may take any one of three forms. The first is a version of the *Confiteor*. It has the advantage of being communal as it makes reference to

[5] See Chupungco, 137–38 below.

[6] See Baldovin, 121 above.

[7] See Chupungco's suggested translation, 138 below.

our brothers and sisters present with us and all the saints. The second form consists of two dialogical invocations. The third expands the *Kyrie* by the addition of invocations addressed to Christ. These are statements of the various ways in which Christ deals with sinners and brings about forgiveness. This is in keeping with the fact that "Lord, have mercy" is primarily an acclamation by which the glorified Christ is acclaimed as both present among us and active in bringing us a share in his glory. While this acclamation includes the sense that sharing in his glory is related to his merciful forgiveness, the emphasis is upon the exalted Lord rather than upon our sinfulness. In keeping with the meaning of the ancient invocation—*Kyrie eleison*—and with the sense of the invitation to the act of penitence, these are invocations, not petitions for forgiveness. The concluding absolution likewise is neither a petition for nor a declaration of forgiveness since it addresses neither God nor the assembly directly. It simply expresses the wish that God will bring us forgiveness and eternal life—gifts that come to those who celebrate the sacred mysteries with an attitude of humility.

On Sundays, the sprinkling of blessed water may replace the penitential act in order to highlight the paschal and baptismal nature of the Lord's Day. It is suggested that this option is especially suitable to the Easter Season.

Lord Have Mercy (*OM2008*, no. 7)

This invocation of the risen Lord was briefly discussed above in connection with its use in the third form of the penitential act. When it is used in that way, it is not repeated at this point in the liturgy. Notice that, when used alone, it follows the absolution and thus is not part of the penitential act. Its independence from that rite makes it clear that the "Lord, have mercy" is an acclamation of the risen Lord whose presence causes us to rejoice in his abundant mercy.

Glory to God (*OM2008*, no. 8)

This ancient text seems to have originated as a morning hymn, which is the role it plays in the fourth-century Apostolic Constitutions, a document reflecting Syrian practice.[8] As a hymn it is best executed as a sung text. Since it is used only on Sundays, feasts, and solemnities there should be no reason to recite it. These are normally occasions of heightened festivity and so should include more communal singing.

[8] Book 7.47.1, ed. Metzger, *Sources chrétiennes* 336:112 = Johnson, 2:244–45.

The text itself is quite unusual in that it addresses both the Father and Christ in successive strophes and then refers to the Holy Spirit in a very brief concluding doxology. In fact, the original text in the Apostolic Constitutions does not even have this small reference to the Spirit. This prayer, like the Roman Canon, comes to us from a time when attention to the role of the Holy Spirit in our redemption was beginning to be spoken of as complementary to that of Christ. In its current form, the whole mystery of salvation in Christ is to be understood as taking place in the Holy Spirit.

The Collect (*OM2008*, no. 9)

The ninth section of the *OM* concerns itself with the first presidential prayer of the Mass, which consists of four elements: (1) the invitation to prayer (*oremus*), (2) the silent prayer, (3) the spoken prayer, and (4) the assembly's "Amen." The reason *OM2008* refers to this as a "presidential prayer" is that it is voiced by the one who presides as an expression of the prayer of the whole congregation (GIRM2003, no. 30). When understood in this way, the opening prayer or collect is the silent prayer of the people, which is then made audible when the text is chanted or recited by the presiding priest. It is concluded by the people's "Amen."

When the silence between the invitation to prayer and the collect is omitted, the text will seem to be the priest's prayer rather than the congregation's, and the delicate balance between the ministry of the whole people and that of the priest will be missed. This pattern is repeated several times in the course of the liturgy and always in association with its most important prayers precisely because they are the prayers of the whole Body of Christ made audible by the one who is ordained to preside in the church's liturgy. This is an exercise of priestly ministry because it is simultaneously an action done in the name of Christ and in the name of the church, which is Christ's Body. These presidential prayers are classically formed in the first person plural, not in the first person singular. They are normally accompanied by the *orans* gesture: hands raised and outstretched, as if simultaneously gathering all present and reaching toward God.

This liturgical prayer is normally addressed to the Father, through the Son, in the Holy Spirit. This is far more than a mere regulation. It has everything to do with our baptismal identity. In baptism we became adopted children of God by means of water and the Holy Spirit so that we might be able to address the Father as does the Son in their eternal, silent conversation of love. This is the other side of the mystery of the incarnation by which the Son assumed our mortal nature so that passing through our death he might bring us with himself to the Father's right hand and introduce us into the trinitarian "conversation of love" in the Spirit. That is what we are doing in the liturgy, and by doing it consciously and actively we are conformed more and more to the image of Christ, our destiny. We are not listening to the priest pray during the liturgy; the priest is attending to the prayer of the whole assembly and raising it up to God as an action of Christ addressing his Father in the Spirit. Since it is the prayer of the congregation, it ends with the people's "Amen."

The collect brings the introductory rites to their conclusion. It is fitting that these rites be concluded by an action that expresses the theological relationships between the priest-presider and the people, and between the whole church and Christ through whom we address the Father in the Holy Spirit. It would be unfortunate if the execution of the prayer would appear anticlimactic and lackluster in comparison with the other introductory rites. There is little question but that the opening song will be sung and, in the proper seasons, the Gloria will be sung as well. The fact that the opening prayer carries so much theological importance suggests that it too be chanted, thus bringing these rites to a rousing conclusion capped by a lively "Amen" as we move on to attend to God's Word proclaimed.

Excursus on Translating *OM2008*

Anscar J. Chupungco

"If I translate word by word, it sounds absurd; if I am forced to change something in the word order or style, I seem to have stopped being a translator."[1] St. Jerome (d. 420) does not conceal his predicament as a translator. Word-for-word translation for the sake of fidelity to the original text often does not make sense, but a change in the meaning of the word can betray the intended meaning of the message. The translation of liturgical texts is perhaps the most delicate and challenging issue arising from Vatican II's decision to allow the use of vernacular languages in the liturgy.

Translation consists basically of transferring into the receptor language the message of the source language. In the liturgy, the vernacular is the receptor language while liturgical Latin is the source language. The message is the doctrine and spiritual riches of the Latin text that the liturgy intends to communicate to a particular assembly. The assembly is the addressee for whose benefit the Latin text was prepared. To help today's liturgical assembly to grasp the meaning of what was originally communicated, the message should be reexpressed using the linguistic patterns proper to the receptor language.

This type of translation follows the theories of "dynamic equivalence"[2] that gained the support of the Consilium in its 1969 instruction, *CLP*. After the publication of *LitAuth* in 2001, *CLP* was considered "dated." Nonetheless, its value as a guideline for liturgical translation stands on solid scientific grounds. According to *CLP*, "a faithful translation cannot be judged on the basis of individual words: the total context of this specific act of communication must be kept in mind, as well as the literary form proper to the respective language" (no. 6). The context, according to *CLP*, includes the message itself, the audience for which the text is intended, and the manner of expression.

[1] St. Jerome, *Eusebii Interpretata Praefatio*, *Eusebius Werke* 7.1, Die griechischen christlichen Schriftsteller der ersten drei Jahrhunderte 47, ed. Rudolf Helm (Leipzig: J. C. Hinrichs, 1954), 2.

[2] See Pecklers and Ostdiek, 59–60 above.

Dynamic equivalence contrasts with the method known as "formal correspondence," which does not normally take into account the culture represented by both the source and the receptor languages. This method merely translates the original text word by word or phrase by phrase with no regard for the cultural underpinnings in them. Although it aims to be faithful to the original text, its fidelity centers almost exclusively on the surface level of the source language and on literal transference into the receptor language.[3] Sometimes formal correspondence tries to recast the grammar of the receptor language in order to conform to the source language. This can do untold violence to the receptor language. Apropos Salvatore Marsili remarks: "We would not regard as scientific a translation based on the belief that the sense of a Latin text could be captured by a simple recourse to a dictionary and the study of the grammatical and logical form in question." He further points out that the text possesses a "genius" of its own, "which is in turn the genius of the people, the age, and the culture giving rise to the text."[4]

This volume contains numerous articles on ICEL2010. I myself offer them on the introductory rites, Liturgy of the Word, preparation of the gifts, EP RI, EP RII, and EP MVN. My analysis is premised on the new ICEL's preference for formal correspondence or literal translation, as directed by *LitAuth*, over the other method known as dynamic equivalence or sense translation. In fairness to those who prefer formal equivalence as a method of translation, it should be admitted that there are a number of instances when it may become necessary to resort to formal correspondence in order to preserve the doctrine of faith. Nevertheless, due respect should always be given to the grammar, lexicon, and syntax of both the source and receptor languages.

For a fuller appreciation of ICEL's attempt to offer a more accurate English translation of the Latin texts, it is useful to refer to ICEL2008, subsequently revised in 2010.

As a rule of thumb, to verify the exactness of an English literal translation, it is a good idea to translate it back to Latin. For example, if a Latin verbal clause, like an ablative absolute, is translated as a prepositional clause, and this is subsequently translated to Latin, the meaning of the Latin sentence will no longer be intelligible. The aim of this exercise is to highlight some problematic instances where the method of literal translation could

[3] Charles H. and Marguerite G. Kraft, *Christianity in Culture: A Study in Dynamic Biblical Theologizing in Cross-cultural Perspective*, rev. ed. (Maryknoll, NY: Orbis, 2005), 205–10, *et passim*.

[4] Salvatore Marsili, "Liturgical Texts for Modern Man," in *The Crisis of Liturgical Reform*, *Concilium* 42 (New York: Paulist Press, 1969), 26.

have rendered the English text closer to the original Latin, had the Latin texts been examined syntactically and contextually. Literal translation considers not only the individual words but also the syntax and punctuation marks like the colon. Sometimes the punctuation mark can identify the declension case of a noun. For example, is the phrase *mea culpa* in the *Confiteor* in the nominative or the ablative case? If it is in the nominative case, it should not be translated as an ablative of means.

In the course of my analysis, as well as that of some of the other scholars in this volume, comparisons with ICEL1973 translation will be made. It appears that occasionally the new translation carried over some of the inaccuracies of the former. It is useful to note that dynamic equivalence, which often marks ICEL1973, is not the same as free translation. Like formal correspondence, it respects the elements of Latin grammar. It is true that dynamic equivalence translates the sense more than the single words that make up a sentence, however, the sense or meaning of a sentence cannot be validly established apart from the correct understanding of grammar. Dynamic equivalence is a serious, scientific form of translation.

It is useful to remember that the majority of Latin texts in the *OM* were written in medieval, not classical, Latin. Medieval Latin, which characterizes much of the Roman Rite, owns a particular lexicon that classical Latin dictionaries do not include. Several other texts are in the form and style of "modern" (sometimes described as classroom) Latin. Those who studied theology in Latin will easily recognize this in the rubrical notes and in new prayer compositions, including the new EPs.

ICEL2010 has been approved for use in English-speaking congregations throughout the world. The ensuing commentaries on this translation will seek to point out the strengths and weaknesses of some of the translations that ostensibly followed the method of formal correspondence. This method is not necessarily flawed, but it requires closer attention to the Latin grammar and lexical usage.

Much work remains to be done on the level of implementation in order to make the new translation intelligible and prayerful. Through catechesis and mystagogy, pastors, liturgists, catechists, and religious educators need to explain the intended meaning of the new English texts in the light of the original Latin. When grappling with the real meaning of the English text, they cannot make the excuse that "this is what the Latin text says." It is possible that the Latin has not been properly translated.

The ICEL2010 Translation

Anscar J. Chupungco

The Sign of the Cross and Greeting (ICEL2010, nos. 1–3)

"When the people are gathered . . ." (no. 1, line 1)

ICEL2010 renders well the sense of the Latin ablative absolute *Populo congregato* with the clause "When the people are gathered." The Latin *congregare* can be translated either as "assemble" or "gather." It is useful to note, however, that unlike the verb "assemble," "gather" does not carry the idea of bringing together a group of people in a particular place for a particular purpose. The liturgy is not merely a gathering of people. It is an assembly convoked for a specific intention, namely, to worship as a body. "Liturgical assembly" has entered the active lexicon of English liturgy and has a deep theological connotation that is not clearly rendered by "liturgical gathering."

"Then the Priest, extending his hands, greets the people . . ." (no. 2, line 1)

ICEL1973 elaborated the rubrics by adding the phrase "facing the people." Perhaps it was useful at that time, but today it is superfluous to direct the priest to face the people when he greets them. Regarding the introduction to the penitential rite, ICEL1973 had alternative formulas for introducing that rite and offers the priest a wide margin of improvisation with "He may use these or similar words." ICEL2010 keeps strictly to the Latin rubrics.

Of grammatical interest is ICEL2010's introduction of a new English orthography presumably for a more sacral effect. It frequently uses capital letters, even when the Latin uses the lowercase: Priest, Sign of the Cross, Entrance Chant, Penitential Act, and so on. The overall effect is distracting for those who are not familiar with the orthography of the German language.

"And with your spirit" (no. 2, line 12)

The greeting "The Lord be [is] with you" is found in Luke 1:28 and some passages in the OT. The answer in both the Greek and Latin liturgies is "And with your spirit" (*pneuma* or *spiritus*). In 2 Timothy 4:22, among others, this formula is addressed to the community as a farewell greeting. The ancient homily that is read on Holy Saturday narrates that when Adam saw Christ, he cried out to everyone in the realm of the dead: "My Lord be with you all." Christ answered him: "And with your spirit."

Hellenistic anthropology recognizes three ascending levels in humans: the body (*soma*), the soul (*psyché*), and the spirit (*pneuma*). The spirit represents the highest and noblest level in a human being. It is not unlikely that Hellenism influenced the formula "And with your spirit." In such a case, it is a courteous way of returning the greeting "The Lord be with you." Perhaps in consonance with the modern holistic view of the human person, ICEL1973 did not translate *spiritu tuo*. Nevertheless, its simplified version, "And also with you," fails to convey the full sense of the original formula.

ICEL2010's literal translation requires a comprehensive catechesis grounded on a theological anthropology that finds resonance in the *Magnificat* ("My spirit rejoices in God my Savior"; Luke 2:48-55). The interpretation that wishes to associate the Holy Spirit or the spirit of the priesthood with this liturgical formula has no solid theological or liturgical basis.

The Penitential Act (ICEL2010, nos. 4–6)

"let us acknowledge our sins, and so prepare ourselves to celebrate the sacred mysteries" (no. 4, lines 3–4)

The Latin verb *aptare*, which is the root word of *apti*, does not mean to prepare or to be in the process or phase of preparation. It means to be in the state of being well-suited for an action. We acknowledge our sins not that we may prepare ourselves for the celebration but that we may in point of fact be worthy to celebrate. "Prepare ourselves" is not the literal translation of *apti simus*. The ICEL2010 retains ICEL1973's "to prepare ourselves," but it corrects its predecessor's weak translation of *agnoscamus* ("let us call to mind our sins").

"through my fault, through my fault, through my most grievous fault" (no. 4, lines 13–14)

Based on Latin syntax, *mea culpa* is in the nominative case, unlike the preceding *cogitatione, verbo, opere et omissione*, which are in the ablative case expressing means or instrumentality. The triple *mea culpa* is separated from the preceding sentence by a colon. The phrase after a colon expands or explains the preceding sentence. Syntactically, therefore, *mea culpa* is in the nominative case with unexpressed or implicit verb. It is not in the ablative case. Other examples of nominatives without verbs are *Dominus vobiscum*, *Verbum Domini*, and *Mysterium fidei*. The nominative case, even without an explicit verb, is not to be translated as ablative of means ("through my fault").

ICEL2010 translates *mea culpa* as if it were a prepositional clause ("through my fault"), making it dependent on the main verb *peccavi* ("I have sinned"). Subsequently ICEL2010 reads: "I have greatly sinned through my fault." The sentence is theologically redundant, if not open to discussion: are there are instances when one commits sin without being at fault or through the fault of another? What the triple *mea culpa* says is, "I am at fault; I am guilty; I have grievously sinned."

The ICEL2010 translators should have considered the grammatical value of punctuation marks. The colon after *omissione* ("in what I have failed to do") calls for a new complete sentence that has a verb expressed or implied. Retaining the colon, the text could have simply kept the nominative case with no verb like the Latin original: "my fault, my fault, my most grievous fault." The Latin *mea culpa* is accepted in English as a formal acknowledgment of personal fault. However it is sometimes said humorously. The inaccuracy of ICEL2010 is a carryover of ICEL1973's "I have sinned through my own fault."

"May almighty God have mercy on us, forgive us our sins, and bring us to everlasting life" (no. 4, lines 21–23)

The Latin ablative absolute *Et, dimissis peccatis nostris* is a verbal clause whose subject is *Deus*. ICEL2008 translated it using the prepositional clause "with our sins forgiven." "With" is a preposition that normally expresses accompaniment. The English language has prepositional clauses that contain verbs ("She knelt with hands raised in prayer"), but the verbs in such cases have a descriptive, modifying function of a verbal adjective. English prepositional clauses with or without verbs are not the equivalent of the Latin ablative absolute.

ICEL2008 placed the phrase "with our sins forgiven" after the personal pronoun "us" ("May almighty God have mercy on us, and lead us, with our sins forgiven, to eternal life"). Syntactically the phrase describes our forgiven condition, not the forgiving action of God. The Latin text places *et, dimissis peccatis nostris* after *Deus*, which is the grammatical subject of the ablative absolute, in order to affirm that God is the subject of the forgiveness of our sins. Literally, the sentence should read: "May almighty God have mercy on us, and having forgiven our sins, lead us to eternal life."

If ICEL2008 is translated back to Latin, the Latin text would read: *cum peccatis nostris dimissis* or "in the company of our forgiven sins." *Cum* is a preposition used with the ablative case to express accompaniment. If *cum* is used as adverb, it requires a complete sentence with a subjunctive verb.

ICEL1973 avoided the problem of translating the tricky ablative absolute by resorting to a verbal clause, which, however, does not render the tense sequence of the ablative absolute. It appears that the awkward ICEL2008 translation ("with our sins forgiven") was an attempt to capture that sequence. ICEL2010 abandoned the 2008 draft text and simply returned to the 1973 version with no further attempt to translate the ablative absolute.

Glory to God (ICEL2010, no. 8)

"and on earth peace to people of good will" (line 3)

The phrase *bonae voluntatis* is in the genitive case, like the original Greek (Luke 2:14). In Latin the genitive case is either possessive (people possess the virtue of good will) or objective (people are the object of God's benevolence or good will). A majority of interpreters prefer the second: peace is God's gift to those whom he favors; it is not God's reward to people who possess good will. The literal translation offered in ICEL2010 does not take the grammatical properties or nuances of the Latin genitive case. In effect it ignores the findings of biblical exegesis by opting for the possessive genitive.

ICEL1973, on the other hand, did not translate *bonae voluntatis* ("and peace to his people on earth"). The possessive pronoun "his" referring to God is not in any way a substitute for the good will or *bona voluntas* of God.

"Lord God, heavenly King, O God, almighty Father" (lines 9–10)

ICEL2010 positions the vocative "Lord God, heavenly King" at the end of a series of five acclamations. This is an unusual English sentence construction. Nonetheless, it complies with the word order of the Latin original that places the vocative *Deus Pater omnipotens* at the end of the acclamations. In fairness to the Latin text, it should be said that the present location of the vocative is probably where it is best. Any other position of the vocative disrupts the flow of the sentence.

There are no grammatical grounds, however, why in a literal translation the place of the vocative noun should not conveniently respect normal English for the sake of clarity and intelligibility. The Latin language has no strict rules about word order because it enjoys the use of declension. In

English, however, it is cumbersome to recite a series of acclamations whose addressee appears only at the end.

The Collect Prayer (ICEL2010, no. 9)

"Then the Priest . . . says the Collect prayer" (lines 4)

Although the Latin *collecta*, which is a prayer that concludes the introductory rites, is found in some medieval sacramentaries, *MR1962* simply calls it *oratio*. This evades the unresolved debate among scholars on the nature, purpose, and position of the *collecta*. The other prayers are called *oratio super oblata* (*OM2008*, no. 30), *oratio post communionem* (*OM2008*, no. 139), and *oratio super populum* (*OM2008*, no. 142). ICEL1973 called it "opening prayer," a misnomer since the prayer actually concludes the introductory rites. It is useful to note that the Liturgy of the Word has no opening prayer; it begins with the first reading. ICEL2010's translation of *oratio* as "Collect prayer" renders the debate among liturgists moot.

In its translation, ICEL1973 inserted the word "sings" ("Then the priest . . . sings or says the opening prayer"). While it is true that the priest is encouraged to sing the greetings, presidential prayers, eucharistic preface, and doxology, the Latin simply says *dicit*. It is hoped that the new translation, which omits the word "sings," will not diminish the established practice of singing the *oratio*, at least on Sundays.

The Mystagogical Implications

Catherine Vincie

Gathering as the Body of Christ

For Christians it is no ordinary thing to come together to celebrate. At our best, expectations are high and we come hungry: to be fed on life-giving Word and saving bread and cup, to be graced by the living God. We come for nothing less than transformation: to become ever more deeply the very Body of Christ whom we celebrate in Word and rite. But how do we gather and give ourselves over to the rites so that they can transform us? Are our gathering rites up to the noble task of shaping us into a praying assembly?

Introductory Rites (ICEL2010, nos. 1–3)

"When the people are gathered" are the opening words of the Mass. While ICEL2010 translates well the Latin *congregato* ("are gathered"), as Chupungco points out, the alternate translation "are assembled" would have put more stress on the purposeful nature of the gathering and connected better to the biblical concept of the *qahal YHWH* or the assembly of God.[1] As will become clear below, the liturgical assembly has a rich biblical and theological meaning.

Notice your community. When you assemble together, are there young and old, poor and of means, of every ethnicity and race, to celebrate the Eucharist, the heart of our faith? Is your assembly a multilingual congregation, made up of a variety of newly arrived immigrants, or is it a more homogenous group with a common language? Does the community begin with a sense of solidarity, already pulled together by a common crisis or celebration, or do the entrance rites have to bear that burden? We are already one in our humanity, one in the image of God, one in our baptism, but gathering to become one people for prayer takes additional work and grace. Gathering starts well before the church door. We come out of the liturgy of the world to this moment of liturgical prayer with our cares, burdens, joys,

[1] See 137 above.

and hopes. If a common concern has not brought us together, we sometimes come with individual mindsets, perhaps not as conscious as we should be of our bondedness in the human family or even within the church community. Something needs to happen to us if we are to become a community of faith and prayer. This is the task of the introductory rites: to gather us as one, uniting our whole selves with Christ as he stands before the Father in praise and intercession, and to help us open ourselves to the transforming love of God made known to us in Christ Jesus.

In coming together we are invited to receive the first grace of the gathered assembly—Christ's real presence in the assembly. This motley crew, at times bedraggled and out of sorts, is no obstacle to Christ who desires to be among us and to hold us in the love of God. Does our gathering space and music ministry lead us to this reality? "I rejoiced when they said to me, 'Let us go to the house of the LORD!' . . . to give thanks to the name of the LORD," proclaims Psalm 122. Does the entrance chant bring the assembly to this sentiment?

Be attentive to the variety of moods and feelings that mark our assemblies over the course of the year. On festive days we may assemble in elaborate procession, the church alive with vibrant colors and joyous song. In Lent we gather more subdued, aware of the conversion from sin to which we have been called. During Advent we gather in quiet expectation of the One who comes to redeem us and show us the way to Divine Mystery. Drawn together from every corner of the earth, we "who were no people" are called to be the new people of God. There is no room in this gathering for distinctions among us, no privileged seats, no special places for any except the poor at the Lord's table. How different this is from our normal gatherings! What a challenge it is for us to let this world become our world.

The shape of the environment and our place in it are also worthy of reflection. Whether round, fan shaped, or rectangular, it hints of the ecclesiology at play within this community. Newly built or renovated spaces that move the community past the baptismal font connect baptismal identity with eucharistic celebration. It does so even more when the font is aligned with altar, ambo, and chair. Entrance into the assembly space—like baptism—is door and pathway to the Eucharist that brings baptism to fullness.

The position of the assembly vis-à-vis altar, ambo, chair, and one another also is layered rich with meaning. Variations in choir style seating (i.e., face-to-face) suggest that when we gaze at one another, we are gazing at the Body of Christ. When ambo and altar project into the midst of the assembly, we declare that the Word of God that gathers us is alive in our midst. While some would argue that priest and people should face the same way to indicate their joint praise of God, the priest facing the people enables him to preside not only over a rite but also over an assembly and its ministers who together celebrate that rite.

When the people are gathered, the ministers process through the assembly and up to the altar, a symbol of Christ, venerating it with a profound bow. Our bodies speak volumes about devotion and desires. While the assembly stands, the ministers symbolically gather the sentiments of the assembly and express reverence for the risen Christ in its name. The priest goes further, venerating the altar with an extravagant symbol reserved for those we love: a kiss. On festive days, we further reverence altar and cross with aromatic clouds of incense, allowing our senses of smell and sight to inform us of the gravity of the occasion. A theological anthropology that says we are embodied spirits and enspirited bodies undergirds our worship. All of our senses and spirit are employed in this corporate praise of the living God. After reverencing the altar the priest then goes to the presider's chair. Not a throne, this simple but dignified chair—along with his vesture—symbolizes his leadership and ministerial ordering within the people of God.

Meanwhile, the choir and assembly (or sometimes choir alone) have been singing an entrance chant or song. Its purpose is to open the celebration and to form the gathering into a community, establishing communion (GIRM2003, no. 47). Music has the potential to move us; as some have said, it is the language of lovers. Through its tones, rhythms, and melodies, music can draw us into the mystery of redemption. Whether through the dancing rhythms of a Mariachi group, the driving beats of a "Life Teen" gathering, or the more subtle strains of Gregorian chant, its purpose remains the same: to gather us into a communion of praise and thanks.

Music's words in our mouths and melodies on our lips make demands on us, calling us beyond our individual feelings to express communally the tone and sentiments of the feast or season. When well done, music can draw us into those sentiments if we allow it. Like trying on clothes, we metaphorically put on garments of sung praise, thanksgiving, and petition so that they become our praise, thanksgiving, and words of desire. We "who were no people" become a united people of praise and thanks, ready to hear the Word of God and more worthily celebrate the Eucharist (GIRM2003, no. 46).

When the entrance chant or song has come to a conclusion, the priest leads the people in the sign of our faith—the sign of the cross.[2] This dramatic

[2] Also see Roll, 636 below.

gesture reminds us of that moment in initiation when we were first claimed by Christ. Over and over throughout our lifetime we make that gesture—this paradox of life in death, of redemption in suffering—with hands pressing onto head, heart, and shoulders. With this gesture we confess our confidence that death will not have the last word; through the cross of Christ we will be led to resurrection and life eternal. The sign of the cross is also the mark of our discipleship; we carry within us the pattern of his dying and rising. Through this bodily sign we also make our allegiance to the triune God made known to us in Christ Jesus and in the power of the Spirit. For many, the experience of the cross is very much their daily reality. Through personal loss or illness, through community trauma from natural or human-made disasters, they know the experience of death in its many manifestations.

Eucharist urges us to make the connection between the cross of Christ and human suffering. Both the death and resurrection of Christ and human suffering are in the mode of "mystery," only grasped with the eyes of faith. Simplistic "explanations" will not do; nor will ideas of an impassible God respond adequately to the crisis of faith that radical suffering brings. The eucharistic liturgy invites reflection on divine "pathos," God's impassioned "suffering with"—not because of some deficiency, but through overflowing love born in solidarity with us and all of creation.

Signed in faith, the priest, with arms extended as if holding us as one body, greets us with one of three greetings. Whichever greeting is chosen, we proclaim the mystery of the gathered assembly! "By this Greeting and the people's response, the mystery of the Church gathered together is made manifest" (GIRM2003, no. 50). We call to mind Christ's presence in and among us, God's love poured out on us, and our communion in the Holy Spirit and acknowledge the mystery of Christ present in the assembly gathered and in the priest leading (*SC*, no. 7). Perhaps we often expect the coming of God in spectacular ways—in thunder and lightning, in earthquake or storm, and in their equivalents in our personal lives. But here, as was true for Elijah (1 Kgs 19:11-12), we wait and discover God in quite ordinary ways. In a typical community gathered for praise, assembly and priest all too human, we find ourselves revealing both the mystery of God present among us and the mystery of the church. How could it be so? Whether gathered in a barrio in South America, in a struggling parish in a US inner city, or in a wealthy suburb of London, the mystery is the same: we are gathered into one by Christ Jesus and we manifest the true nature of the church—a communion of the love of God in Christ Jesus and in the Spirit's power. Gathering rites enacted week after week can lose their luster, yet they have the potential to lift us out of our malaise and become moments of revelation. If we truly heard the words we speak, how could we not be moved?

Penitential Act (ICEL2010, nos. 4–6)

But all is not yet ready. The church, through the priest, calls us to pause and "acknowledge our sins, and so prepare ourselves to celebrate the sacred mysteries." What the rubrics do not stress, yet what is very important, is the ever-abiding mercy of God. It takes a few moments of silence to come to awareness of these two realities. The first we are often loathe to admit, and the second only too glad to embrace. The liturgy invites us to give sufficient attention to both. The time for silence is time for grace to work its ways on us, as we are often oblivious to the ways in which we do not act as Christ's. Once we acknowledge, through God's grace, how far we have missed the mark, more time is needed to accept God's forgiveness. This moment is not for its own sake but renders us more open and ready to celebrate the Word and Eucharist that follow.

In contemporary Catholic theology, grace as God's gift of self (uncreated grace) takes precedence over "created grace" or any habit or quality of the human soul influenced by God.

The universality of this Divine self-communication exists within God's overall desire for the redemption of all. Grace thus conceived is a liberating force not only individually but also socially. Of course, we can only speak about this grace-filled salvation in light of the human experience of sin, finitude, and death. It is against both the propensity to sin and sin itself that God's self-communication comes to us as mercy. With Scripture, we need to emphasize that where sin abounds, grace abounds even more fully (Rom 5:20).

The church puts words into our mouths to enable our transformation from the despair of sin to hope and gratitude for God's mercy. Called by the priest, we may recite as one the *Confiteor*, a formula that acknowledges our sins and calls upon Mary and the communion of saints to intercede for us. In this prayer, we are invited once again to use the ancient bodily gesture of beating our breast at the acknowledgment of our sins. With the changed translation of ICEL2010, one wonders if the reintroduction of this gesture and the added text ("through my fault, through my fault, through my most grievous fault") places too much emphasis on our sinfulness, taking away the rightful emphasis on God's mercy. Of course, we may use options other than the *Confiteor*. The absolution by the priest follows. The priest unites himself with the assembly in these penitential acts. The language is always the plural "we." All of us together stand before God in need of mercy and forgiveness as we go up to the altar of God.

In a comment on the Penitential Act, GIRM2003 makes a curious observation: "The rite concludes with the priest's absolution, which, however, lacks the efficacy of the Sacrament of Penance" (no. 51). One wonders about the efficacy of intercessory prayer and God's response of forgiveness through the ordained minister in this context, but no further hints are given to us. Historically speaking, there have been three traditions using the absolution formula: the ninth-century and later monastic practice of confessing to one another at Prime and Compline that included an absolution formula,[3] after the *Confiteor* in the Mass,[4] and the sacrament of penance. To use sacramental language for all three of these occasions would be anachronistic, but further reflection on the contemporary use of absolution formulas outside of the sacrament of penance is warranted.

Placed again in the appendix of *MR2002*, a rite of sprinkling may replace the penitential rite on any Sunday, especially the Sundays of Easter. Drawn from the rite of baptism, this sprinkling rite reminds us of the washing away of sin and our plunging into the waters of redemption where we died with Christ just as we were raised in him. It also reminds us of patterning ourselves on the baptism of Christ, when the Spirit descended and spoke of Jesus as God's beloved (Matt 3:17). We too have been made the beloved. Baptism is also the great sacrament of reconciliation along with Eucharist, something well remembered each time we come to the Lord's table.

Glory to God (ICEL2010, no. 8)

Penitence makes way for praise. In ICEL2010 the words more rythmically tumble out one upon another; it is as if we cannot say enough to acknowledge the greatness of God: "We praise you, we bless you, we adore you, we glorify you, we give you thanks." Yet we return to penitence, asking Jesus Christ again for mercy and salvation. At this point the more theologically complex "Only Begotten Son" replaces "only Son of the Father" in ICEL2010. It will take careful catechesis to break open the christologically weighty "Only Begotten" in terms that the faithful can understand. The Christian usage of this term (Latin, *unigenitus*) dates from some of the earli-

[3] See Claude Morgand, "La Discipline pénitentielle et l'Officium Capituli d'après le Memoriale Qualiter," *Revue Bénédictine* 72 (1962): 22–60.

[4] See Baldovin, 121 above.

est creeds of our tradition, reflecting baptismal practice since the mid-third century and codified in the "Symbol or Creed of Eusebius" (325). This doctrinal position stands in contrast to those who argued that the Son was created by the Father and thus was a lesser creature. The Nicene Creed at the end of the Liturgy of the Word provides greater theological elaboration than the *Gloria* on this issue, but the doctrinal claim of the Son's identity in being with the Father is clearly set forth here. It is because of this identity we sing that Christ alone is "Holy," "Lord," and "the Most High . . . with the Holy Spirit, in the glory of God the Father. Amen." This hymn of praise may be sung or said, but clearly singing it according to the melody in the *Graduale Romano* or some other melody expresses the sentiments of praise far better than recitation, which too often devolves into a rote exercise. Again, the church puts words into our mouths until they become our words of praise for all that has been given us.

Collect (ICEL2010, no. 9)

One of the three collects in the Mass, the opening collect, gathers the prayer of the people and sets out the character of the celebration. The priest, standing at the chair entreats the people with a call to prayer: "Let us pray." Having become one body for praise, we are asked as a community to gather all of who we are and what we desire and direct it toward our preparation for the eucharistic mystery. This includes silent prayer, and the silence should be profound—a time to go deep within as we pray with one heart in preparation for the mystery we are about to celebrate. The priest needs an ear attuned to the depths of this silence and the prayer being made by the gathered assembly that he will collect. Then, with extended arms in the *orans* position, he gathers in the assembly's prayer and articulates the character of the particular feast. The Alternative Opening Prayer of Christmas Mass at Dawn of the present Sacramentary illustrates this point particularly well:

> Almighty God and Father of Light,
> a child is born for us and a son is given to us.
> Your eternal Word leaped down from heaven
> in the silent watches of the night,
> and now your Church is filled with wonder
> at the nearness of her God.

Yet that is not enough, as praise moves to petition in our praying that the reality of the feast makes a home in us:

Open our hearts to receive his life
and increase our vision with the rising of dawn,
that our lives may be filled with his glory and his peace,
who lives and reigns for ever and ever.

"The people, uniting themselves to this entreaty, make the prayer their own with the acclamation, Amen" (GIRM2003, no. 54). Earlier in the penitential rite, people responded Amen to the prayer of absolution, but now they make an "acclamation," suggesting a more resounding response and signaling that the entrance rites have come to a high point in this collect. We have gathered; we have acknowledged our sin and proclaimed God's mercy; we have praised God on high. Now we collect all of those sentiments into a final prayer of praise and petition, readying ourselves for the Liturgy of the Word.

The Liturgy of the Word

The Latin Text

Liturgia verbi

10. Deinde lector ad ambonem pergit, et legit primam lectionem, quam omnes sedentes auscultant.

Ad finem lectionis significandam, lector acclamat:

Verbum Dómini.

Omnes respondent:

Deo grátias.

11. Psalmista, seu cantor, psalmum cantat vel dicit, populo responsum proferente.

12. Postea, si habenda sit secunda lectio, lector eam ex ambone legit, ut supra.

Ad finem lectionis significandam, lector acclamat:

Verbum Dómini.

Omnes respondent:

Deo grátias.

13. Sequitur Allelúia, vel alter cantus a rubricis statutus, prouti tempus liturgicum postulat.

14. Interim sacerdos incensum, si adhibetur, imponit. Postea diaconus, Evangelium prolaturus, ante sacerdotem profunde inclinatus, benedictionem petit, submissa voce dicens:

Iube, domne, benedícere.

Sacerdos submissa voce dicit:

Dóminus sit in corde tuo et in lábiis tuis:
ut digne et competénter annúnties Evangélium suum:
in nómine Patris, et Fílii, ✠ et Spíritus Sancti.

Diaconus signat se signo crucis et respondet:

Amen.

Si vero non adest diaconus, sacerdos ante altare inclinatus secreto dicit:

Munda cor meum ac lábia mea, omnípotens Deus,
ut sanctum Evangélium tuum digne váleam nuntiáre.

15. Postea diaconus, vel sacerdos, ad ambonem pergit, ministris pro opportunitate cum incenso et cereis eum comitantibus, et dicit:

Dóminus vobíscum.

The English Text

The Liturgy of the Word

10. Then the reader goes to the ambo and reads the First Reading, while all sit and listen.

To indicate the end of the reading, the reader acclaims:

The word of the Lord.

All reply:

Thanks be to God.

11. The psalmist or cantor sings or says the Psalm, with the people making the response.

12. After this, if there is to be a Second Reading, a reader reads it from the ambo, as above.

To indicate the end of the reading, the reader acclaims:

The word of the Lord.

All reply:

Thanks be to God.

13. There follows the Alleluia or another chant laid down by the rubrics, as the liturgical time requires.

14. Meanwhile, if incense is used, the Priest puts some into the thurible. After this, the Deacon who is to proclaim the Gospel, bowing profoundly before the Priest, asks for the blessing, saying in a low voice:

Your blessing, Father.

The Priest says in a low voice:

May the Lord be in your heart and on your lips,
that you may proclaim his Gospel worthily and well,
in the name of the Father and of the Son ✠ and of the Holy Spirit.

The Deacon signs himself with the Sign of the Cross and replies:

Amen.

If, however, a Deacon is not present, the Priest, bowing before the altar, says quietly:

Cleanse my heart and my lips, almighty God,
that I may worthily proclaim your holy Gospel.

15. The Deacon, or the Priest, then proceeds to the ambo, accompanied, if appropriate, by ministers with incense and candles. There he says:

The Lord be with you.

Populus respondet:

Et cum spíritu tuo.

Diaconus, vel sacerdos:

Léctio sancti Evangélii secúndum N.,

et interim signat librum et seipsum in fronte, ore et pectore.

Populus acclamat:

Glória tibi, Dómine.

Deinde diaconus, vel sacerdos, librum, si incensum adhibetur, thurificat, et Evangelium proclamat.

16. Expleto Evangelio, diaconus, vel sacerdos acclamat:

Verbum Dómini.

Omnes respondent:

Laus tibi, Christe.

Deinde librum osculatur dicens secreto:

Per evangélica dicta deleántur nostra delícta.

17. Deinde fit homilia, quae a sacerdote vel diacono habenda est omnibus diebus dominicis et festis de praecepto; aliis diebus commendatur.

18. Homilia expleta, cantatur vel dicitur, quando praescribitur, symbolum seu professio fidei:

Toni integri in Graduali romano inveniuntur.

Credo in unum Deum,
Patrem omnipoténtem,
factórem caeli et terrae,
visibílium ómnium et invisibílium.
Et in unum Dóminum Iesum Christum,
Fílium Dei Unigénitum,
et ex Patre natum ante ómnia saécula.
Deum de Deo, lumen de lúmine, Deum verum de Deo vero,
génitum, non factum, consubstantiálem Patri:
per quem ómnia facta sunt.

The people reply:

And with your spirit.

The Deacon, or the Priest:

A reading from the holy Gospel according to N.

and, at the same time, he makes the Sign of the Cross on the book and on his forehead, lips, and breast.

The people acclaim:

Glory to you, O Lord.

Then the Deacon, or the Priest, incenses the book, if incense is used, and proclaims the Gospel.

16. At the end of the Gospel, the Deacon, or the Priest, acclaims:

The Gospel of the Lord.

All reply:

Praise to you, Lord Jesus Christ.

Then he kisses the book, saying quietly:

Through the words of the Gospel
may our sins be wiped away.

17. Then follows the Homily, which is to be preached by a Priest or Deacon on all Sundays and Holydays of Obligation; on other days, it is recommended.

18. At the end of the Homily, the Symbol or Profession of Faith or Creed, when prescribed, is either sung or said:

An alternate musical setting of the Creed may be found in Appendix I.

I believe in one God,
the Father almighty,
maker of heaven and earth,
of all things visible and invisible.

I believe in one Lord Jesus Christ,
the Only Begotten Son of God,
born of the Father before all ages.
God from God, Light from Light,
true God from true God,
begotten, not made, consubstantial with the Father;
through him all things were made.

Qui propter nos hómines et propter nostram salútem
descéndit de caelis.

Ad verba quae sequuntur, usque ad **factus est**, omnes se inclinant.

Et incarnátus est de Spíritu Sancto
ex María Vírgine, et homo factus est.
Crucifíxus étiam pro nobis sub Póntio Piláto;
passus et sepúltus est,
et resurréxit tértia die, secúndum Scriptúras,
et ascéndit in caelum, sedet ad déxteram Patris.
Et íterum ventúrus est cum glória,
  iudicáre vivos et mórtuos,
cuius regni non erit finis.
Et in Spíritum Sanctum, Dóminum et vivificántem:
qui ex Patre Filióque procédit.
Qui cum Patre et Fílio simul adorátur et conglorificátur:
qui locútus est per prophétas.
Et unam, sanctam, cathólicam et apostólicam Ecclésiam.
Confíteor unum baptísma in remissiónem peccatórum.
Et exspécto resurrectiónem mortuórum,
et vitam ventúri saeculi. Amen.

19. Loco symboli nicaeno-constantinopolitani, praesertim tempore Quadragesimae et tempore paschali, adhiberi potest symbolum baptismale Ecclesiae Romanae sic dictum Apostolorum.

Credo in unum Deum
Patrem omnipoténtem, Creatórem caeli et terrae,
et in Iesum Christum, Fílium eius únicum,
Dóminum nostrum,

Ad verba quae sequuntur, usque ad **María Vírgine**, omnes se inclinant.

qui concéptus est de Spíritu Sancto,
natus ex María Vírgine,
passus sub Póntio Piláto,
crucifíxus, mórtuus, et sepúltus,
descéndit ad ínferos,
tértia die resurréxit a mórtuis,

For us men and for our salvation
he came down from heaven,

At the words that follow up to and including and became man, all bow.

and by the Holy Spirit was incarnate of the Virgin Mary,
and became man.

For our sake he was crucified under Pontius Pilate,
he suffered death and was buried,
and rose again on the third day
in accordance with the Scriptures.
He ascended into heaven
and is seated at the right hand of the Father.
He will come again in glory
to judge the living and the dead
and his kingdom will have no end.

I believe in the Holy Spirit, the Lord, the giver of life,
who proceeds from the Father and the Son,
who with the Father and the Son is adored and glorified,
who has spoken through the prophets.

I believe in one, holy, catholic and apostolic Church.
I confess one Baptism for the forgiveness of sins
and I look forward to the resurrection of the dead
and the life of the world to come. Amen.

19. Instead of the Niceno-Constantinopolitan Creed, especially during Lent and Easter Time, the baptismal Symbol of the Roman Church, known as the Apostles' Creed, may be used.

I believe in God,
the Father almighty,
Creator of heaven and earth,
and in Jesus Christ, his only Son, our Lord,

At the words that follow, up to and including the Virgin Mary, all bow.

who was conceived by the Holy Spirit,
born of the Virgin Mary,
suffered under Pontius Pilate,
was crucified, died and was buried;
he descended into hell;
on the third day he rose again from the dead;

ascéndit ad caelos,
sedet ad déxteram Dei Patris omnipoténtis,
inde ventúrus est iudicáre vivos et mórtuos.
Credo in Spíritum Sanctum,
sanctam Ecclésiam cathólicam,
sanctórum communiónem,
remissiónem peccatórum,
carnis resurrectiónem,
vitam aetérnam. Amen.

20. Deinde fit oratio universalis, seu oratio fidelium.

he ascended into heaven,
and is seated at the right hand of God the Father almighty;
from there he will come to judge the living and the dead.

I believe in the Holy Spirit,
the holy catholic Church,
the communion of saints,
the forgiveness of sins,
the resurrection of the body,
and life everlasting. Amen.

20. Then follows the Universal Prayer, that is, the Prayer of the Faithful or Bidding Prayers.

History of the Latin Text and Rite[1]

Michael Witczak

Liturgy of the Word

The origins of the Liturgy of the Word are rooted in the biblical tradition. Jesus participated in the "liturgy of the word" in the synagogue (Luke 4:16-21), as did Paul (Acts 13:13-43). The proclamation of the Word was part of OT worship, e.g., the ceremony for the establishment of the covenant (Exod 24:3-11) and ceremonies for the renewal of the covenant (Josh 24:1-28; Neh 8:1-8 and 9:3-38). The first Christians were familiar with the synagogue liturgy, but the influence of the synagogue celebration of the word on the development of the Christian Liturgy of the Word is difficult to determine.[2]

One of the earliest full descriptions of the celebration of the Word at the Eucharist is found in the *First Apology* (no. 67) of Justin Martyr (d. *ca.* 165). He gives this brief description of the Sunday worship:

[1] For overviews, Jungmann MRR, 1:391–494; Adrien Nocent, "Storia della celebrazione dell'eucaristia," in *La liturgia eucaristia: Teologia e storia della celebrazione*, ed. Salvatore Marsili, Anamnesis 3:2 (Casale Monferrato: Marietti, 1983), 208–23; Robert Cabié, *The Eucharist*, ed. Aimé Georges Martimort, trans. Matthew O'Connell, The Church at Prayer 2 (Collegeville, MN: Liturgical Press, 1986), 59–75, 131–32, 152–57,197–203; Hans Bernhard Meyer, *Eucharistie: Geschichte, Theologie, Pastoral*, ed. Hans Bernhard Meyer et al., Gottesdienst der Kirche: Handbuch der Liturgiewissenschaft 4 (Regensburg: F. Pustet, 1989), esp. 115–25, 176–77, 182–392; especially helpful is Vincenzo Raffa, *Liturgia Eucaristica: Mistagogia della Messa: dalla storia e dalla teologia alla pastorale pratica*, Bibliotheca 'Ephemerides liturgicae' Subsidia 100 (Rome: CLV, 2003), 259–321.

[2] See Charles Perrot, "La lecture de la bible dans les synagogues au premier siècle de notre ère," *La Maison-Dieu* 126 (1976): 24–41; Carmine di Sante, "The Liturgy of the Synagogue," in *Jewish Prayer: The Origins of Christian Liturgy*, trans. Matthew J. O'Connell (New York: Paulist Press, 1991), 169–82. For cautions about claiming too much about first-century connections between Jewish and Christian worship, see Roger Beckwith, *Daily and Weekly Worship: Jewish to Christian*, Alcuin-GROW Liturgical Study 1 (Bramcote, Nottingham: Grove, 1987); Paul F. Bradshaw and Lawrence A. Hoffman, eds., *The Making of Jewish and Christian Worship*, Two Christian Traditions 1 (Notre Dame, IN: University of Notre Dame Press, 1991); Alistair Stewart-Sykes and Judith H. Newman, *Early Jewish Liturgy: A Sourcebook for Use by Students of Early Christian Liturgy*, Alcuin/GROW Liturgical Study 51 (Cambridge: Grove, 2001); Paul F. Bradshaw, *The Search for the Origins of Christian Worship: Sources and Methods for the Study of Early Liturgy*, 2nd ed. (New York: Oxford University Press, 2002), esp. 21–72.

3. And on the day called Sunday an assembly is held in one place of all who live in town or country, and the records of the apostles or the writings of the prophets are read for as long as time allows.

4. Then, when the reader has finished, the president in a discourse admonishes and exhorts (us) to imitate these good things.

5. Then we all stand up together and send up prayers.[3]

This rudimentary description of ministers (reader and president) and readings (records of the apostles and writings of the prophets) with preaching and prayer remains the only developed description of the celebration of the Word until the emergence of the *Ordines Romani*, *ca*. 700. There are hints of ritual practice and of the slow developing of a lectionary in occasional references in homilies, particularly those of Augustine[4] and Gregory the Great.[5]

The phrase *liturgia verbi* appears for the first time in the official liturgical books of the Roman rite in the post–Vatican II liturgy.

First Reading (*OM2008*, no. 10)

The reading before the gospel used to be the purview of the subdeacon. *OR I* describes the pope and ministers sitting and the subdeacon going up the steps of the ambo to read (no. 56). The reading specified is the *apostolus* or the *epistula* (no. 20). *OR I* has no hint of any readings from the OT. A later version of the *Ordo* from *ca*. 900 specifies that the subdeacon does not ascend all the way into the ambo but should stand on a lower step (*OR V*, no. 29).

The books for the readings have a history of their own: *apostolus*, epistolary, lectionary, evangelary, and so on, developed systems of readings that came to be combined as the centuries unfolded.[6]

[3] Justin Martyr, *First Apology* 67, in *Prex Eucharistica*, 1:70–71 = Jasper & Cuming, 29–30.

[4] Augustine's sermons can be found in *PL* 35 and in the modern edition of Radbodus Willems, *CCL* 36 (1954). See Johnson, 3:1–82 for commentary, bibliography, and many of these texts in English translation.

[5] Gregory's sermons are found in *PL* 76 and in modern editions by Pierre-Patrick Verbraken (Song of Songs and Ezekiel), *CCL* 144 (1963); Marci Adriaen (Ezekiel), *CCL* 412 (1971); Adriaen (Job), *CCL* 143, 143A, and 143B (1979–85); and Raymond Étaix (Gospels), *CCL* 141 (1999). See Johnson, 4:59–81 for commentary, bibliography, and many of these texts in English translation.

[6] See Cyrille Vogel, *Medieval Liturgy: An Introduction to the Sources*, trans. and rev. William G. Storey and Niels Krogh Rasmussen (Washington, DC: Pastoral Press, 1986), 291–355; Aimé Georges Martimort, *Les Lectures liturgiques et leurs livres*, Typologie des sources du moyen âge occidental 64 (Turnhout: Brepols, 1992); Eric Palazzo, *A History of Liturgical Books from the Beginning to the Thirteenth Century*, trans. Madeleine Beaumont (Collegeville, MN: Liturgical

The pattern of the *OR* remains for solemn celebrations throughout the Middle Ages, although in situations where there was no subdeacon, the priest himself would read the epistle. That practice became codified in *MR1570*, promulgated by Pius V after the Council of Trent. The *OM* simply indicates that the epistle, gradual, Alleluia or tract, and sequence follow as the time of the year stipulates (Sodi-Triacca, no. 1407). The details are laid out in the *ritus servandus* printed at the beginning of *MR1570*. There we learn that the priest reads the epistle at the altar, not at the ambo. At the end of the reading, done in an understandable voice, the minister said *Deo gratias* (Sodi-Triacca, no. 25). The *MR1962* expands this slightly to differentiate more carefully the Alleluia and its verse, the rare use of the sequence, and that the use of the sequence is limited to the days for which it is specified (Sodi-Toniolo, no. 1399).

Several changes were introduced in *MR1970*. The role of the lector[7] was reintroduced into ordinary celebrations of the liturgy. The normal place for the reading was returned to the ambo. The rubrics take account of the presence of the faithful, who are directed to sit. At the end of the reading, the phrase *Verbum Domini* is introduced to draw forth the people's response: *Deo gratias*. This shift of the final phrase from priest alone to a dialogue between reader and people is of a piece with Vatican II's overarching desire that "the full and active participation by all the people is the paramount concern" (*SC*, no. 14). The rubric also mentions that the people should sit and listen to the readings. *OR I* had mentioned the ministers sitting to listen. This specific reference to the people's role flows from the clear conciliar directive that the role of the people be included in the rubrics (*SC*, nos. 30–31).

A new book was introduced for the use of the lector (*OLM1969* and *OLM1981*), with its own structure of organizing the readings.

The Psalm (*OM2008*, no. 11)

There is little evidence about a use of the psalms as a response to the reading in the period before the peace of the Church (313 CE).[8] Augustine

Press, 1993), 83–105; Cassian Folsom, "Liturgical Books of the Roman Rite," in *Introduction to the Liturgy*, ed. Anscar Chupungco, Handbook for Liturgical Studies 1 (Collegeville, MN: Liturgical Press, 1998), 245–314, esp. 254–57.

[7] Wilton Gregory, "The Lector—Minister of the Word: An Historical and Liturgical Study of the Office of the Lector in the Western Church," (PhD diss., Athenaeum of Saint Anselm, 1980).

[8] On the introduction of responsorial psalmody into the Eucharist, see Peter Jeffery, "The Introduction of Psalmody into the Roman Mass by Pope Celestine I (422–432): Reinterpreting a

and others provided complete or almost complete commentaries on the psalms that were originally homilies preached at the liturgy. It is clear that psalms loomed large in the imagination of the patristic church.[9]

The order of celebration found in *OR I* describes that one minister ascended the ambo with the *cantatorium* (book for the responsorial music) and said the response and yet another minister said the Alleluia. Other versions of *OR I* amplify the text to mention the cantor by title, specify that the response is *gradale* (i.e., done on the step), and that at the proper season the Alleluia is substituted by the tract. At minimum, the response is done alone. *OR V* describes the cantor singing in alternation with the schola.[10]

The books used by the cantor have their own history. They are variously called *cantatorium, gradale, graduale, antiphonale*, and many other names. The order of chants is related to the order of readings found in the lectionary, epistolary, or *apostolus* but has its own development.[11]

As the Middle Ages progressed, eucharistic celebrations with the priest as the sole minister became more common. In that case, the priest would read the response. The situation was codified in *MR1570* as noted above: the priest reads the epistle, gradual (the name that became traditional for the response), the Alleluia or tract, and the sequence (Sodi-Triacca, no. 1407). In a solemn Mass, the priest would read the gradual and the Alleluia or tract, but these would also be sung by the schola. The pattern of the text of the gradual was eventually fixed as a response, a verse of a psalm, and the response repeated.

The current rubric returns the responsorial psalm to its original configuration: several verses of a psalm rather than a single verse, sung by a psalmist or cantor (the distinction is not clear), with the refrain sung by the people. It can be recited as well. *IGMR2002* also allows for metrical settings of psalms (no. 61). *SC*'s emphasis on participation (no. 14) is an important underpinning to this decision to lengthen the psalm and give the repetition of the antiphon to the people.

Passage in the Liber Pontificalis," *Archiv für Liturgiewissenschaft* 26 (1984): 147–165; cf. Baldovin, 116 above.

[9] Augustine, *Ennarrationes in psalmos*, ed. Eligius Dekkers and J. Fraipont, CCL 38–40 (Turnhout: Brepols, 1956); English translation: Maria Boulding, *Saint Augustine: Expositions of the Psalms*, ed. John E. Rotelle and Boniface Ramsey, The Works of St. Augustine: A Translation for the Twenty-First Century 3:15–20 (Hyde Park, NY: New City Press, 2000–2004).

[10] *OR I*, no. 57 and *OR V*, n. 30 = Andrieu, 2:86 and 2:215.

[11] A basic source is René-Jean Hesbert, ed., *Antiphonale missarum sextuplex* (Brussels: Vromant, 1935); also, see Vogel, *Medieval Liturgy*, 357–62; Palazzo, *A History of Liturgical Books*, 63–82; Folsom, "Liturgical Books of the Roman Rite," in Chupungco, *Introduction to the Liturgy*, 258–61.

The Second Reading (*OM2008*, no. 12)

The use of more than one reading before the gospel is noted in the Apostolic Constitutions (*ca.* 380), where it seems that two OT readings were followed by a responsorial psalm. Then two NT readings ensued (from Acts and the letters?), followed by the gospel.[12] Some interpret Ambrose (d. 397) as proposing two readings before the gospel, but it is not clear if he is describing the celebration or proposing a method of exegesis: from prophet to apostle to gospel.[13] Some early lectionaries hint of more than one reading before the gospel, and the four annual Saturday celebrations of the Ember Days included the possibility of five OT readings, an epistle, and a gospel, shortened to one OT, one NT, and a gospel when ordinations were not celebrated.[14] Other than Ember Days and the Easter Vigil, the Roman Missal had no other days with more than two readings.

Alleluia or Other Chant (*OM2008*, no. 13)

The history of the Alleluia is connected with that of the responsorial psalm. While it was found in all the Eastern liturgies, it seems to have entered the Western liturgy in the second half of the seventh century at a time when the Roman See was occupied by a number of Eastern popes.[15]

OR I speaks of it following the *responsum*. It was replaced during Lent by a longer set of psalm verses called the *tractus*, perhaps a remnant of singing psalms without a responsorial verse.[16] *MR1570* and *MR1962* continued the medieval tradition of this chant being sung by the schola at a solemn Mass, while always recited by the priest.

Another song inserted in the celebration is the sequence. This type of song seems to have evolved out of extensive cantillation on the vowels of the word "Alleluia." To help the singers remember the melody, texts were developed which eventually came to be sung. Ninth-century sources attest to its existence.[17] There was a stunning growth of this form in the ninth

[12] Apostolic Constitutions 2:57, 5–9, ed. Marcel Metzger, *Sources chrétiennes* 320, 329, 336 (Paris: Editions du Cerf, 1985–87); see W. Jardine Grisbrooke, *The Liturgical Portions of the Apostolic Constitutions: A Text for Students*, Alcuin-GROW Liturgical Study 13–14 (Bramcote, Nottingham: Grove, 1990), 15.

[13] *Expositio in Psalmum* 118.17.10; see Raffa, *Liturgia Eucaristica*, 263, n. 11.

[14] See the readings listed, for example, in Sodi-Toniolo, nos. 69–116.

[15] See Cabié, *The Eucharist*, 64–65; Raffa, *Liturgia Eucaristica*, 280–82.

[16] *OR I*, nos. 57–58 = Andrieu, 2:86–87.

[17] See the Antiphonal of St. Blandin (*ca.* 800) in René-Jean Hesbert, ed., *Antiphonale missarum sextuplex* (Brussels: Vromant, 1935), 199; Amalarius of Metz, *Off.* III.16.3 in Jean Michel Hanssens, *Amalarii episcopi Opera liturgica omnia*, Studi e testi, 138–40 (Città del Vaticano:

century and beyond, so that in some traditions virtually every Sunday had an appointed sequence. It was never popular in Rome. In *MR1570* the number of sequences was reduced to only five: Easter, Pentecost, *Corpus Christi*, All Souls (and funerals), and Our Lady of Sorrows. *MR2002* appoints sequences for Easter and Pentecost and gives them as an option for *Corpus Christi* and Our Lady of Sorrows. The *Dies irae* sequence is no longer contained in the Missal but can be used in the Divine Office during the thirty-fourth week of the year.

The Gospel (*OM2008*, nos. 14–16)

The reading of the gospel is the ritual high point of the Liturgy of the Word. The possible use of incense, the blessing, and the optional use of candles and a procession all indicate a key moment. This ceremony takes place during the singing of the chant before the gospel. The church teaches that Christ himself is proclaiming his gospel (*SC*, no. 7).

OR I indicates that the deacon reverences the pontiff, who then blesses the deacon in words virtually identical to those used today. The deacon (or the priest substituting for the deacon) goes to the altar, kisses the gospel book, raises it, and—preceded by subdeacons with incense and acolytes with candles—proceeds to the ambo where the acolytes step aside to allow the deacon to ascend to the top of the ambo.[18] The prayer said by a priest when there is no deacon present is an addition to the ritual that is found beginning in the eighth and ninth centuries. A desire to attach a prayer to every action in order to help the priest remain focused on the meaning of the ritual action arose throughout the Carolingian world. These prayers tended to be composed in the first-person singular and to focus on the unworthiness of the priest and his need for purification to perform worthily the ritual act at that moment.[19]

Biblioteca Apostolica Vaticana, 1948–50), 2:304; and *OR V*, no. 31 = Andrieu, 2:215; also Raffa, *Liturgia Eucaristica*, 288–89.

[18] no. 58 = Andrieu, 2:87–89.

[19] For an overview of this phenomenon, see Bonifaas Luykx, *De oorsprong van het gewone der Mis*, De Eredienst der kerk 3 (Utrecht and Antwerp: Spectrum, 1955), and its German translation as "Der Ursprung der gleichbleibenden Teile der heiligen Messe (Ordinarium Missae)," *Liturgie und Mönchtum* 29 (1961): 72–119; also Joanne M. Pierce, "The Evolution of the *Ordo Missae* in the Early Middle Ages," in *Medieval Liturgy: A Book of Essays*, ed. Lizette Larson-Miller (New York and London: Garland Publishing, 1997), 3–24; helpful for understanding the genre of apology is Adrien Nocent, "Les apologies dans la célébration eucharistique," in *Liturgie et rémission des péchés*, Bibliotheca 'Ephemerides liturgicae' Subsidia 3 (Rome: CLV Edizioni Liturgiche, 1975), 179–96.

As noted above, in the form of eucharistic celebration that developed in the late Middle Ages, a single priest did everything, even repeating chants sung by the schola. That form of celebration is codified in *MR1570*, which also makes provision for a more solemn celebration. The first description in *MR1570* is the solemn one: the deacon places the book of the gospels on the altar and—after the incense is blessed—genuflects and prays the *Munda cor meum* silently. Then he goes with the book to the priest and asks for a blessing, which the priest gives using the text from *OR I*. He kisses the priest's hand and then proceeds with ministers bearing incense and candles to the place where the gospel is read: no longer the ambo but the north (gospel side) of the altar platform. When the celebration is not solemn but celebrated by the priest alone, the Missal is moved from the epistle side (south) to the gospel side (north). The priest stands in the center and says *Munda cor meum, Iube domne,* and *Dominus sit in corde meo* (Sodi-Triacca, nos. 1408–10).

This sequence of actions remains mostly intact in *MR2002*. The ambo, restored to use in *OM1969*, remains the focal point for all the readings. The blessing of the deacon is separate from the quiet prayer of a priest-celebrant before the gospel: not combined as in *MR1570* and *MR1962*. Also new in *OM1969* is the expansion of the conclusion of the gospel into a dialogue between the deacon or priest and the people. The final verse *Laus tibi, Christe,* now recited by the assembly, is in the *ritus servandus of MR1570* (Sodi-Triacca, no. 25). As with the conclusion to the first two readings, the shift of the concluding phrase from something said by a minister to a dialogue between the reader, deacon, or priest and the people expresses the conciliar desire to provide numerous and consistent opportunities for the active participation of the faithful.

Homily (*OM2008*, no. 17)

The homily became a part of the rubrics of *OM1969*. Preaching was an important part of the eucharistic celebration during the patristic period. There are extensive remains of the preaching of Ambrose, Jerome (d. 420), Augustine, Leo the Great (d. 441), Caesarius of Arles (d. 542), and Gregory the Great in the West, as well as of John Chrysostom (d. 407) and others in the East. Preaching was an important part of the bishop's role and was assigned to priests who had pastoral responsibilities.[20]

[20] See Craig Satterlee, *Ambrose of Milan's Method of Mystagogical Preaching* (Collegeville, MN: Liturgical Press, 2002), esp. 87–110; William Harmless, *Augustine and the Catechumenate*

OR I's description of the Eucharist does not include a place for a homily after the gospel. While preaching remained an important part of the life of the church throughout the Middle Ages and into the modern period, it had no official place in the Order of Mass until it was restored by Vatican II (*SC*, no. 52). The rubric of *OM2008* repeats the conciliar stipulation that the homily be given on all Sundays and holy days of obligation and that it is commended on other days. It also specifies that the homily be given by the priest or deacon.[21]

Creed (*OM2008*, nos. 18–19)

The recitation of a creed was originally part of the baptismal liturgy. In the sixth century, the Nicene-Constantinopolitan Creed was added to the celebration of the Eucharist by decree of the Patriarch Timothy (Monophysite?) to combat Arian tendencies.[22] The use of this Creed seems then to have been taken up in Visigothic Spain. During the anti-Adoptionist controversy, when the *Filioque* was added to the Creed (Third Council of Toledo in 589), it began to be used in various places in the Frankish world. Charlemagne (d. 814) decreed the use of the Creed in his imperial chapel but shrugged off the suggestion of Pope Leo III (d. 816) to drop the phrase *Filioque* so as not to anger the Greeks. *OR I* does not include the Creed, but *OR V* (dependent on Amalarius) does. It entered the Roman Order of Mass in 1014 at the request of Emperor Henry II (d. 1024), who was amazed that it was not a part of the Mass. Pope Benedict VIII (d. 1024) acceded to the request.[23]

(Collegeville, MN: Liturgical Press, 1995), esp. 156–93; William Klingshirn, *Caesarius of Arles: The Making of a Christian Community in Late Antique Gaul* (Cambridge: Cambridge University Press, 1994), esp. 146–70; also the helpful articles by Réginald Grégoire in the *Encyclopedia of the Early Church*, ed. Angelo di Berardino, trans. Adrian Walford (New York: Oxford University Press, 1991), s.v. "Homily," "Homilary," "Sermon."

[21] This specification follows a lengthy discussion that culminated in the instruction, "Some Questions Regarding Collaboration of Nonordained Faithful in Priests' Sacred Ministry," issued by the Congregation for the Clergy and signed by seven other dicasteries on 15 August 1997 (*AAS* 89 [1997], 852–77). See the commentary by James Coriden in *New Commentary on the Code of Canon Law*, ed. John Beal, James Coriden, and Thomas Green (New York: Paulist Press, 2000), 924–32; and John Huels, *The Pastoral Companion: A Canon Law Handbook for Catholic Ministry*, 4th ed. (Montreal: Wilson and Lafleur, 2009), 90–93.

[22] Theodore the Lector, *Historia ecclesiastica* 2, fragment 32 and 48 (*PG* 86:201A and 209A); see Raffa, *Liturgia Eucaristica*, 295–96.

[23] See Bernard Capelle, "L'introduction du symbole à la messe," in *Mélanges J. de Ghellinck* 2 (Gembloux: J. Duculot, 1951), 1003–27; repr. in Capelle, *Travaux liturgiques*, 3 vols. (Louvain: Mont César, 1955–67): 3:60–81. See the accounts in Cabié, *The Eucharist*, 131–32 and 145; and Raffa, *Liturgia Eucaristica*, 295–97. Berno of Reichenau (d. 1048) recounts the interchange between

The Creed was sung by the schola and in many places recited by the people. In *MR1570* the priest—who always recited the Creed, even when sung by the schola—genuflected at the words *Et incarnatus est* until *Crucifixus* and made the sign of the cross at the words *Et vitam venturi saeculi* (Sodi-Triacca, nos. 1411–12).

New regulations for the Creed were introduced after Vatican II. *IGMR1969* states that it is recited by priest and people on Sundays and solemnities; when sung, it should be done all together or in alternation (nos. 43–44). *MR2002* changes two elements: it adds melodies with which the priest can intone the beginning of the Creed (the impression from *OM1969* is that the whole text is simply sung or recited together). The second addition is the use of the Apostles' Creed as an option. This ancient Creed developed over several centuries and became firmly ensconced in the Western tradition by the eighth century.[24] Originally a baptismal creed, this is its first introduction into the *OM*, although its use in Masses for children had been permitted since 1973.[25] Several countries had requested permission to have this option also in Masses for adults (e.g., Germany). *MR2002* includes the Apostles' Creed as an option for any Mass, though recommending it for Lent and Easter. It includes a bow at the words referring to the incarnation of Jesus Christ as at the same place in the Nicene-Constantinopolitan Creed.

Prayer of the Faithful (*OM2008*, no. 20)

The history of general intercessions at the celebration of the Eucharist is complex. Justin Martyr speaks of a general prayer that included the newly baptized at their first celebration of the Eucharist and also on every Sunday.[26] ApTrad gives a similar indication at the celebration of the Eucharist after baptism.[27] Apostolic Constitutions also give evidence of this form of prayer.[28] There are passages in the writings of several popes that indicate the exis-

the emperor Henry and Pope Benedict in *De quibusdam rebus ad missae officium spectantibus* 2 (*PL* 142:1060–61).

[24] *The Oxford Dictionary of the Christian Church*, ed. Frank L. Cross and E. A. Livingstone, 3rd ed. (New York: Oxford University Press, 2005), s.v., "Apostles' Creed" and "Old Roman Creed."

[25] Directory for Masses with Children, esp. no. 49 = DOL 2182.

[26] *First Apology* 65 = Johnson, 1:67; and *First Apology* 67 = Johnson, 1:68.

[27] Paul Bradshaw, Maxwell Johnson, and L. Edward Phillips, *The Apostolic Tradition: A Commentary*, ed. Harold W. Attridge, *Hermeneia* series (Minneapolis: Fortress Press, 2002), 120–21.

[28] Book 8.10, ed. Metzger, *Sources chrétiennes* 336:166–72 = Johnson, 2:251–53.

tence of a general prayer between the reading of the gospel and the beginning of the offering of the gifts.[29] A text from Prosper of Aquitaine (d. after 455) serves as a classic reference to the general intercessions.[30] These solemn intercessions pray for seven categories of persons.

By the time of *OR I*, there is no longer a trace of general intercessions between the gospel and the offering of gifts. Where might they have gone? Several theories have been proposed that focus attention on the *Kyrie* at the beginning of Mass and at the intercessions contained in the Roman Canon.[31] During the Middle Ages and early modern period, various responses developed to the need for including the people's intentions within the celebration of the liturgy. Notable in this regard was the *prône*: a kind of vernacular office inserted into the Mass before the offertory that often included a series of intercessions, announcements (e.g., marriage bans), instruction, and even preaching.[32]

Vatican II called for a restoration of the general intercessions especially on Sundays and days of obligation (*SC*, no. 53). *IGMR2002* describes how the prayer should unfold (nos. 69–71). *MR2002* contains sample forms of the general intercessions in an appendix.[33]

[29] See Innocent I, *Epistola* 25 to Decentius of Gubbio (*PL* 20:554A = Johnson, 3:100); Boniface I, *Epistola* 7 to Honorius (*PL* 20:767A); and Celestine I, *Epistola* 23 to Theodosius II (*PL* 50:544BC).

[30] *Indiculus* 8 (*PL* 51:209C).

[31] See Bernard Capelle, "Le Kyrie de la messe et le pape Gélase," *Revue Bénédictine* 46 (1934): 125–33 = Capelle, *Travaux liturgiques* 2:116–34; "Le pape Gélase et la messe romaine," *Revue d'Histoire Ecclésiastique* (1939): 22–34 = *Travaux liturgiques* 2:135–45; "L'oeuvre liturgique de saint Gélase," *Journal of Theological Studies* 52 (1951): 125–44 = *Travaux liturgiques* 2:146–60. See Antoine Chavasse "L'Oraison 'super sindonem' dans la liturgie romaine," in *Revue Bénédictine* 70 (1960): 313–23; Chavasse, "À Rome, au tournant du Ve siècle, additions et remaniements dans l'ordinaire de la messe," *Ecclesia orans* 5 (1988): 25–44; Paul De Clerck, *La "prière universelle" dans les liturgies latines anciennes: Témoignages patristiques et textes liturgiques*, Liturgiewissenschaftliche Quellen und Forschungen 62 (Münster: Aschendorff, 1977); John Baldovin, *The Urban Character of Christian Worship: The Origins, Development, and Meaning of Stational Liturgy*, Orientalia Christiana Analecta 228 (Rome: Pontifical Oriental Institute, 1987), 158–66, 241–51; Baldovin, "Kyrie Eleison and the Entrance Rite of the Roman Eucharist," *Worship* 60 (1986): 334–47; and Raffa, *Liturgia Eucaristica*, 297–321.

[32] See Katherine Lualdi Jackson, "Change and Continuity in the Liturgy of the *Prône* from the Fifteenth to the Seventeenth Century," in *Prédication et liturgie au Moyen Âge* (Turnhout: Brepols, 2008), 373–89; also, Cabié, *The Eucharist*, 155–57.

[33] Appendix 5, 1165–75.

Theology of the Latin Text and Rite

Nathan D. Mitchell and Demetrio S. Yocum

There is an essential connection between the Liturgy of the Word and the Liturgy of the Eucharist. *SC* called this relationship to our attention when it stated: "The two parts which in a sense go to make up the Mass, viz. the liturgy of the word and the eucharistic liturgy, are so closely connected with each other that they form but one single act of worship" (no. 56). Both parts together provide an answer to the fundamental question, "How can we continue to access Jesus?" As Marianne Sawicki cogently argues in her intriguing book *Seeing the Lord*, this was the great crisis facing the disciples after Calvary.[1] Death *ends* access—and yet, in an outrageous reversal of "business as usual," the earliest Christian communities connected *eating Jesus' flesh* with *life*, not with decay.[2] Indeed, the gospels are less biographies than stories about access to One who has died, "someone risen, someone who keeps talking and touching after death—not in spite of *sarka fagein* but because of it."[3] So the challenge was to find strategies of access, or what can be called "cultural technologies" of access. Two primary technologies emerged: the one, *textual* (embodied in stories, Scriptures, catechetical teaching); the other, *bodily* (embedded in sacramental rituals and in their verification through solidarity with the poor and needy).

Among Christians, *bodily* access to Jesus centered on what Sawicki calls "the three tables": The first is *a table of the Word*, where God's new reign or "kingdom" is announced—a "kingdom" that rudely disrupts and overturns all earlier economic, social, and gender arrangements (a table where there is neither Jew nor Greek, slave nor free, male nor female). The second is *a table where thanksgiving or Eucharist is made*—a site of recognition ("they recognized Jesus in the breaking of bread"); a place where people meet in fear and hope; a table that becomes the breast of God, where even the little

[1] Marianne Sawicki, *Seeing the Lord: Resurrection and Early Christian Practices* (Minneapolis: Fortress Press, 1994), 301.

[2] Ibid., 302. Cf. the *sarka phagein* language of John 6:53: "I say to you, unless you eat the flesh [Greek: *ean mē phagēte tēn sarka*] of the Son of Man . . ."

[3] Ibid., 301.

children may rest their heads; a table that becomes "the feet of Jesus" where "instruction flows sweet as kisses and clean as tears."[4] The third Christian table is *"what people have in common who think they have nothing in common."*[5] This table is a tornado, a source of massive disruption, disablement, and dislocation but also an unparalleled source of unity and hope. As Sawicki writes,

> It is the leveling of all flesh by the body's innate fragility and the ravages of time. It is a tabulation of race, class, and gender that reduces privilege to naught. It is the lowest common human denominator—hunger, disability, need—depicted in a riveted tableau of the universal deathbound human condition. The Christian table is the home of the homeless, the larder of the poor. And theirs only.[6]

The strong interconnection of these three Christian tables starts therefore at the table of the Word. It is here that we are given access to the sacramental mystery of the Eucharist and verify our Christian identity in sharing at the table with our neighbors. The importance of the Word, the *logos* of God incarnated in Christ Jesus as our "bread" of salvation, conversion, and sanctification is perhaps nowhere better revealed than in the Liturgy of the Word's dialogic nature: "God himself *speaks* to his people"[7] through the readings, the chants, and the homily, and the people *reply* "actively, fully aware, and devoutly"[8] through their singing, their profession of faith, and their common prayers. Far from being a unilateral discourse imposed upon us from above, it is a mutual dialogue of love, devotion, and renewal of the covenant with the One who has called us friends.

The Scriptural Readings (*OM2002*, nos. 10 and 12)

The three tables delineated by Sawicki, however, should not be taken only figuratively. The strong relationship between the Word of God and the Eucharist, begins precisely at the ambo, from where the assembly listens to the Word of God, which then leads to the altar.[9] We gather at one table and then we move toward the other, "The church has always venerated the

[4] Ibid., 296.

[5] Ibid.

[6] Ibid., 296–97.

[7] *IGMR2002*, no. 29 (emphasis added).

[8] *SC*, nos. 33 and 48.

[9] See *IGMR2002*, no. 58: "In the celebration of the Mass with the congregation, the readings are always proclaimed from the ambo." See also *OLM1981-Pr*, no. 16.

divine scriptures as it has venerated the Body of the Lord, in that it never ceases, above all in the sacred liturgy, to partake of the *bread of life* and to offer it to the faithful from the one *table* of the word of God and the Body of Christ."[10] Hence, the church nourishes its people at a "twofold" table: "from the one it grows in wisdom and from the other in holiness. In the word of God the divine covenant is announced; in the Eucharist the new and everlasting covenant is renewed."[11]

Hence, the ambo is the table where the church, as Body of Christ, receives its sustenance and growth in its encounter with the living Lord, in the Word of God. The church, therefore, makes every effort to ensure that the faithful are more "lavishly" nourished at this table.[12] For this purpose Vatican II established a cycle of scriptural readings repeating every three years for Sundays and every two years for weekdays.[13] This broader and deeper exposure of the assembly to the treasures of the Bible well reflects the intentions of Vatican II, which in composing the order of readings of the Roman Missal had a clear pastoral purpose: "Throughout the liturgical year, but above all during the seasons of Easter, Lent, and Advent, the choice and sequence of readings are aimed at giving Christ's faithful an ever-deepening perception of the faith they profess and of the history of salvation."[14]

Doubtless, one of the most significant improvements initiated by the many post–Vatican II writings in matters concerning God's Word is the introduction of a far richer and consistent fare of OT readings, in particular for Sundays and festive days but for weekdays as well.[15] The two underlying selection principles governing the choice of the orders of readings, namely, the principles of harmony and semicontinuous reading, ensure that the NT and OT texts are chosen for their relation to the gospel reading of the day. As the introduction to the Lectionary states,

[10] *Dei Verbum*, no. 21 (emphasis added).

[11] *OLM1981-Pr*, no. 10.

[12] *SC*, no. 51 and *Dei Verbum*, no. 39.

[13] The readings in *MR1570* recurred after only a single year, covering thus a meager 34.6 percent of the total verses in the Bible. An explanation of the math behind this figure can be found at: http://catholic-resources.org/Lectionary/Roman_Missal.htm (accessed 15 March 2011). A comparison with post–Vatican II can be found at: http://catholic-resources.org/Lectionary/Statistics.htm (accessed 15 March 2011).

[14] *OLM1981-Pr*, no. 60.

[15] OT readings in *MR1570* are used exclusively for the gradual (the Psalms), the Vigil of Easter, the Vigil of Pentecost, the feast of Epiphany and its octave, during Holy Week, and on some weekdays. In 1951 the OT readings for the Vigil of Pentecost were eliminated, and the OT readings for the Easter Vigil were limited to four instead of twelve.

> when in celebrating the Liturgy the Church proclaims both the Old and New Testament, it is proclaiming one and the same mystery of Christ. The New Testament lies hidden in the Old; the Old Testament comes fully to light in the New. Christ himself is the center and fullness of the whole of Scripture, just as he is of all liturgical celebration.[16]

This is in line with the overall view that the gospel is the "high point" of the Liturgy of the Word, where Christ himself, "present in his own word, proclaims the Gospel."[17]

The Responsorial Psalm (*OM2008*, no. 11)

The responsorial psalm, once known as the gradual, has undoubtedly gained momentum deriving from *IGMR2002*'s recognition of its "great liturgical and pastoral significance."[18] Chosen from the Lectionary on the basis of its correspondence with the other readings, the responsorial psalm finds its legitimacy as an "integral part of the liturgy of the word,"[19] when it invites the assembly to "perceive the word of God speaking in the psalms and to turn these psalms into the prayer of the Church."[20] This task is mainly accomplished through the singing of the faithful, which is "a great help toward understanding and meditating on the psalm's spiritual meaning."[21] Singing is thus established as the privileged approach to savoring the theological truth inherent within the lyrical-poetical nature of the psalms.

There are two recognized ways of singing the responsorial psalm: the first and preferential way is the responsorial singing, when the cantor sings the psalm verse and, "as a rule," the assembly sings the response; the other is the direct way, when the cantor sings the psalm "straight through" while the community listens only or they all sing it together.[22] More important, the strong emphasis on the act of singing the responsorial psalm helps the assembly focus on the psalm *as* the Word of God and not just propaedeutic to it.[23] This is what *IGRM2002* unhappily alludes to when it states that the

[16] *OLM1981-Pr*, no. 5; cf. also no. 13: "For this the other readings, in their established sequence from the Old to the New Testament, prepare the assembly."

[17] *IGMR2002*, nos. 60 and 29.

[18] Ibid., no. 61.

[19] Ibid.

[20] *OLM1981-Pr*, no.19.

[21] Ibid., no. 21.

[22] *IGMR2002*, no. 61.

[23] Cf. Edward Foley, "The Structure of the Mass, Its Elements and Its Parts," in *A Commentary on the General Instruction of the Roman Missal*, ed. Edward Foley, Nathan Mitchell, Joanne Pierce (Collegeville, MN: Liturgical Press, 2007), 153.

responsorial psalm "fosters meditation *on* the word of God," reiterating the same concept again later, when it insists that if the psalm "cannot be sung, then it should be recited in such a way that it is particularly suited to fostering meditation *on* the word of God."[24]

The Acclamation and the Gospel Reading (*OM2008*, nos. 13–16)

As the high point of the Liturgy of the Word, the reading of the gospel does not overshadow the other liturgical readings. Rather, its prominence is achieved by revealing in each of the other texts their true and ultimate meaning. We gather around the table where God speaks to hear what referred to Christ, "in all the Scriptures" (Luke 24:27). However, the conspicuous importance of the gospel not only is reflected in harmonizing all other readings to the doctrines and events presented in the evangelic message but is made *visible* in the physical space and other elements that make up the celebration of the Liturgy of the Word as well as through the gestures, language, actions, and "marks of honor" performed by both ministers and faithful.[25] For instance, as the central focus of the proclamation of the Word of God, the ambo's design should reflect, "the dignity and nobility of that saving word," and "draw the attention" of the gathered assembly.[26] In addition, to emphasize the intimate relationship between Word and Eucharist it is recommended that the design of both ambo and altar reflect their "harmonious and close relationship."[27] The area around the ambo should also be spacious enough for the gospel procession with the accompaniment of ministers bearing candles and incense. In keeping with the tradition that confers "the utmost care" and "greater respect" to the Book of the Gospels over the other books of readings, *OLM1981-Pr* recommends the use of "a beautifully designed" Book of the Gospels.[28]

The reverence due to the gospel reading is also evident during the acclamation (e.g., the Alleluia), the procession, and the raising of the Book of

[24] *IGMR2002*, no. 61 (emphasis added).

[25] See *IGMR2002*, no. 60, and *OLM1981-Pr*, nos. 13–18.

[26] In Built of Living Stones: Art, Architecture, and Worship, issued by the USCCB (16 November 2000), chap. 1, nos. 61–62.

[27] *OLM1981-Pr*, no. 32.

[28] "Along with the ministers, the actions, the allocated places, and other elements, the books containing the readings of the word of God remind the hearers of the presence of God speaking to his people. Since in liturgical celebrations the books too serve as signs and symbols of the higher realities, care must be taken to ensure that they truly are worthy, dignified and beautiful" (no. 35).

Gospels. Indeed, there is a strong relationship between the two in that raising the book helps the assembly understand that their acclamation is a profession of faith in Christ "present and speaking to them" and that the procession from altar to ambo is not just a musical interlude.[29] Without the procession, without singing and raising the Book of Gospels, such proclamation of faith is considerably weakened.[30] Moreover, it is recommended for the minister to sing the greeting "The Lord be with you," and "A reading from the holy Gospel according to . . .," and at the end, "The Gospel of the Lord." In so doing the assembly itself is encouraged to sing its acclamations, thus "bringing out the importance of the Gospel reading and of stirring up the faith of those who hear it."[31] It is at this point that the book is incensed and reverenced by the priest who makes the sign of the cross on his forehead, mouth, and breast.[32] In line with a tradition that traces back to the eleventh century, the assembly reproduces the priest's signs of reverence. The absence of any written instruction for the faithful to do so confirms that, as for the singing of the acclamations, the assembly envisions its status of "priestly people" imitating the actions of the priest-celebrant.

The Homily (*OM2008*, no. 17)

According to Paul VI's apostolic constitution promulgating the revised *MR1969*, the homily is one of the elements of Mass that "have suffered injury through accidents of history" and ought to be "restored to the vigor which they had in the days of the holy Fathers."[33] Thus, Vatican II ensured that the homily "regain its proper importance" by stating that it "is strongly recommended since it forms part of the liturgy itself" (*SC*, no. 52). This renewed relevance of the homily is also made clear when *SC* establishes that for Masses celebrated with the participation of the faithful, and specifically on Sundays and feasts of obligation, the homily "should not be omitted except for a serious reason" (no. 52). *MR2002* and *IGMR2002* go even further in stating that the homily is "on other days recommended."[34]

[29] *IGMR2002*, no. 60.

[30] Cf. Foley, "The Structure of the Mass," in Foley et al., *A Commentary on the General Instruction of the Roman Missal*, 154.

[31] *OLM1981-Pr*, no.17.

[32] *IGMR2002*, no. 7; *OLM1981-Pr*, no. 17.

[33] Paul VI, Apostolic Constitution, *Missale Romanum*, at http://www.vatican.va/holy_father/paul_vi/apost_constitutions/documents/hf_p-vi_apc_19690403_missale-romanum_en.html (accessed 27 June 2011).

[34] *MR2002*, no. 17; *IGMR2002*, no. 66.

Moreover, *IGMR2002* is the first to offer a structured hierarchy regulating those entitled to give the homily. Homiletic priority is granted to the priest-celebrant, then to any other concelebrant, and, "occasionally" and "according to circumstances," to deacons. Worth noting here is the fact that this ranking order does not take into account the deacon's traditional role of "heralds of Christ's Gospel."[35] From a canonical perspective, laypeople's preaching is not considered a homily. However, in view of the ongoing crisis in pastoral leadership in parishes worldwide as well as sacerdotal vocations, the preaching of laypeople and religious people, now more than ever before, may have its importance in revealing "the mysteries of faith and the standards of the Christian life" in the sacred texts.[36] Furthermore, as a series of preeminent canonists has clarified, laypeople are allowed by law to engage in the act of liturgical preaching.[37] The gap between liturgical preaching and eucharistic preaching (i.e., homily) is yet to be fully explored theologically. As the preaching act has become increasingly inclusive from a canonical, theological, and pastoral perspective, one wonders how this will inspire and shape the homiletic act.

Perhaps the liturgical significance of the homiletic moment should be seen more in its being "nourishment" by and "encounter" with the living Word of God than as instruction, clarification, or *expositio* of the Word itself. As Louis-Marie Chauvet has stated, "any theology that integrates fully, and *in principle*, the sacramentality of the faith requires a consent to corporality, a consent so complete that it tries to *think about God according to corporality*."[38] Hence, through the person of Christ, who is always "active and present in the preaching of his Church,"[39] we are invited to meet and deepen our relation with the mystery of the God incarnate whose Spirit *is* in the "body" of the Scriptures as well as the other liturgical texts used for the celebration of Mass.

[35] On the diaconal ministry and preaching see Foley, "The Structure of the Mass," in Foley et al., *A Commentary on the General Instruction of the Roman Missal*, 157–58.

[36] *OLM1981-Pr*, no. 24.

[37] See the summary of the work of James Coriden, John Huels, and James Provost in Patricia Parachini, *Lay Preaching: State of the Question*, American Essays in Liturgy (Collegeville, MN: Liturgical Press, 1999), esp. 42–43.

[38] Louis-Marie Chauvet, *Symbol and Sacrament: A Sacramental Reinterpretation of Christian Existence*, trans. Patrick Madigan and Madeleine Beaumont (Collegeville, MN: Liturgical Press, 1995), 155.

[39] *OLM1981-Pr*, no. 24.

The Two Creeds (*OM2008*, nos. 18–19)

After a moment of silent recollection following the readings and the homily, which represent God's Word to the faithful, comes the moment—on Sundays and other solemnities—for the creed, the assembly's joint response of faith to the Word of God, which can be either sung or said.[40] Both the priest-celebrant and the assembly stand as a sign of reverence and promptness to profess the mysteries and doctrines of faith. Standing all together, the assembly becomes one body and church, in an ecumenical action shared with many other churches worldwide. In this gesture we should envision a sign of hope and healing where differences are overcome and the mystical Body of Christ regains its unity.

As Karl Rahner and Herbert Vorgrimler have observed, the creed in its theological connotation is less an act of confessing the faith and more a *formulation* of the content of faith. They recognize that the central "act of confessing" the faith in the Eucharist is the eucharistic prayer.[41] This means that the creed need not be elaborate, but as *symbolum*—a profession of faith and a statement of our most fundamental beliefs—it ought to be simple, meaningful, and intelligible for every faithful gathered. This is also in line with the dimension of collective prayer that is inherent to the creed as a liturgical moment.

MR2002 establishes two standard formulas of faith. By stating that the Apostles' Creed may be used especially during Lent and Easter, *MR2002* implicitly establishes the Nicene-Constantinopolitan Creed as the official and "default" option for the profession of faith. Initially formulated amid the christological and trinitarian controversies of the Council of Nicaea (325 CE), the language of the Nicene Creed is still highly prone to awkward and infelicitous renderings in the vernaculars due in part to the difficulty to translate from the Greek. The more ancient, poetic, and scriptural Apostolic Creed, the "baptismal Symbol of the Roman Church," should therefore *not* be restricted only to Lent and Easter but, as *symbolum*, used more regularly.

The Prayer of the Faithful (*OM2008*, no. 20)

As for the homily and the penitential rite, *SC* and Paul VI's promulgation of *MR1969* clearly identified the general intercessions or prayer of the

[40] *MR2002*, no. 68.

[41] Karl Rahner and Herbert Vorgrimler, *Dictionary of Theology*, trans. Richard Strachan et al. (New York: Crossroad, 1981), 106.

faithful as another element to be restored, in particular on Sundays and feasts of obligation. *MR2002* specifies neither who should preside at the prayer nor who should announce the prayers. The unfolding of this liturgical moment is best described in *IGMR2002*. *SC*, however, does specify, for example, that "the people are to take part" in it (no. 53). As the priestly people's prayer and response to the Word of God, it is thus more than appropriate for these intentions to be announced from the ambo and read by one of the lay faithful (and not only by the deacon or cantor, given precedence by *IGMR2002*, no. 71) while the rest of the assembly stands and responds with a sung invocation or silent prayer.

The prayer of the faithful is a normative element of this part of Mass for two reasons: (1) its "inclusion" within the Eucharist celebration and (2) its "universal" nature. This is in line with the blunt but effective statement of the CCC: "The Eucharist commits us to the poor" (no. 1397). *Cult* and *care* imply one another. Official Christian worship is meaningless unless verified in what Chauvet (borrowing from Emmanuel Levinas) calls the "liturgy of the neighbor,"[42] that is, our daily care for the least and the littlest, the most vulnerable, the widow, the orphan, the stranger—including our "enemies."

As stated in *SC* and *IGMR2002*, the intercessions ought to be made "for the church, for the civil authorities, for those oppressed by various needs, for all humankind, and for the salvation of the entire world." Therefore, the intentions should aspire to go and reach "beyond" the local assembly's needs, intentions (and patriotic sentiments), in order to embrace the aspirations and suffering of all humankind and creation. It is in this "universal" aspiration that the prayer of the faithful is deeply connected with the baptismal call of the priestly people to evangelize and be missionaries, thus fostering participation and responsibility in the "salvation of the entire world."[43] In crafting and announcing these intentions, the whole assembly and the priest-celebrants alike are therefore invited to develop a broader compassion that reaches beyond one's local surroundings and extends to unknown people and places.

[42] Chauvet, *Symbol and Sacrament*, 238; also 75, where Chauvet cites Levinas to define "an invisible God" accessible through justice and approachable "in the humble call of the neighbor." For a summary of Levinas' thought on this, see Jeffrey Bloechl, *Liturgy of the Neighbor* (Pittsburgh: Duquesne University Press, 2000).

[43] *SC*, no. 53; *IGMR2002*, no. 69.

The ICEL2010 Translation

Anscar J. Chupungco

The First Reading (ICEL2010, no. 10)

"Then the reader goes to the ambo . . ." (line 1)

It is odd to begin a new section with the conjunction "then." It translates the Latin *deinde*, which denotes sequence of actions and is a rubrical device to ensure the smooth flow of the rite. *Deinde* appears several times in the rubrics of the Order of Mass. ICEL1973 seldom translated it. In this particular instance there is no need to translate *deinde*, because the heading "The Liturgy of the Word" already separates the new section from the introductory rites.

The technical word for the place where the Scriptures are read is "ambo." In structure and decor it is different from the lectern. Indeed, it shares in some way with the altar's other name, "table" (the table of God's Word and of Christ's Body and Blood). ICEL2010 is a timely correction of the ICEL1973 that translated ambo as lectern.

"To indicate the end of the reading, the reader acclaims" (line 3)

The Latin liturgy uses the substantive *acclamatio* and the verb *acclamo*. The root words are *ad* + *clamo*: "to call to" or "to call attention to." The English verb "acclaim," meaning to applaud or praise, is not the literal equivalent of *acclamo*, even if they sound alike. The Latin rubric *lector acclamat* does not tell the reader to acclaim or applaud the liturgical formula *Verbum Domini*. Rather, it directs the reader to notify the assembly that the reading has ended. The lector does this by reciting *Verbum Domini*.

"The word of the Lord" is an acclamation, a statement of faith that elicits the assembly's response, "Thanks be to God." The odd ICEL2010 rubric, which directs the reader to acclaim the formula of acclamation, stems from an inexact translation of the Latin *acclamat*.

The Blessing before the Gospel (ICEL2010, no. 14)

"that you may proclaim his Gospel worthily and well" (line 7)

The English adverb "well" does not sufficiently translate the Latin *competenter*, which means proficiently, knowledgeably, and adeptly. The deacon is expected to read not only well but with competence. If the English text is translated back to Latin, the result would be: *ut digne et bene annunties Evangelium suum*. The adverb *bene* ("well") is obviously not what the Latin text intends to convey to the deacon. ICEL1973 ("that you may worthily proclaim his gospel") did not translate *competenter*.

"that I may worthily proclaim your holy Gospel" (line 14)

Both ICEL2010 and ICEL1973 overlooked the Latin verb *valeam*: "that I may have the vitality (or strength) to proclaim your gospel worthily." This Latin verb does not appear in the blessing of the deacon, but here the literal translators should not have neglected it. The prayer is an example of medieval apology. *Valeam* expresses the priest's sentiment of humility and inadequacy in respect to his ministry of proclaiming the gospel.

The Gospel (ICEL2010, no. 16)

It is interesting to note that the Latin uses the acclamation *Verbum Domini* ("The Word of the Lord") not only for the first and second readings (*OM2008*, nos. 10 and 12) but also for the gospel. It is equally interesting to note that ICEL2010 (no. 16, line 2) adopts ICEL1973, which translated the third *Verbum Domini* as "The Gospel of the Lord." It is a rare example of dynamic equivalence in the ICEL2010 corpus. Obviously a literal translation could provoke debate, since in liturgical tradition the gospel reading is clearly distinguished from the other readings by special rites, ministry, and book. By using the dynamic equivalence instead of formal correspondence ICEL2010 shows pastoral sensitivity to the assembly that distinguishes the gospel from the other biblical readings.

The Nicene-Constantinopolitan Creed (ICEL2010, no. 18)

"I believe in one God. . . . I believe in one Lord Jesus Christ. . . . I believe in the Holy Spirit . . ." (lines 5, 9, and 30)

The Latin text of this profession of faith is prefaced by the verb *Credo*, which is not repeated in the entire formula. In Latin a single verb for a lengthy sentence does not raise the problem of intelligibility if the preposition after the verb requires the same declension case. In the Latin Creed the verb *credo* is followed by the preposition *in* with nouns in the accusative case: *Credo in Deum . . . in Iesum Christum . . . in Spiritum Sanctum*. This peculiar and uncommon Latin construction that allows a period at the end of several sections of a single sentence does not have an English equivalent.

In the ICEL2008 text of the Creed, the first section referring to God the Father carries the subject and verb "I believe." The section ends with a period. The sections on Jesus Christ and the Holy Spirit, in literal accord with the Latin, have neither subject nor verb and simply start with the conjunction "and." "And in one Lord Jesus Christ" is four lines away from its intended subject and verb but is separated from them by a period. Likewise, the following lines "God from God . . ." has no subject and verb. "And in the Holy Spirit" is twenty-six lines away from its subject and verb and appears after six sentences about Jesus Christ. This formula of profession of faith, which by nature and purpose should be crystal clear, is cumbersome to recite, grammatically incorrect, and lends itself to theological misinterpretation because of the absence of the required subjects and verbs. Happily ICEL2010 reinserted "I believe" before the sections on Jesus Christ and the Holy Spirit.

"I believe in one, holy, catholic and apostolic Church."(line 34)

Theology carefully distinguishes the different structures of the verb *credo*: *credo in* with accusative, *credo* with dative, and *credo* followed by accusative without preposition. *Credo in* with nouns in the accusative case is reserved to the profession of faith in the Holy Trinity: *credo in unum Deum; credo in unum Iesum Christum; credo in Spiritum Sanctum*. But when the object of *credo* is the church, theology uses the accusative without preposition: *credo Ecclesiam*, that is, I acknowledge the nature and authority of the church and accept its teaching.

Rightly ICEL2008, contrary to ICEL1973, does not prefix this section with the preposition *in*: "And [I believe] one, holy, Catholic and apostolic Church." However, the parsimonious use of "I believe" in ICEL2008 makes this section on the church as grammatically anomalous as the preceding trinitarian sections.

ICEL2010 reintroduced the phrase "I believe" also in the case of the church. However, it reinserts the preposition "in," thus overlooking the creedal distinction between *credo in Deum* and *credo Ecclesiam*.

To summarize, the basic grammatical structure of the Creed should consist of the following complete sentences: I believe in one God . . .; I believe in one Lord Jesus Christ . . .; I believe in the Holy Spirit . . .; I believe the one, holy, catholic and apostolic Church; I confess one baptism . . .; and I look forward to the resurrection . . .

"consubstantial with the Father" (line 14)

Since the Creed is *Symbolum fidei* or the dogmatic statement of Christian belief, it can be argued that the closer the translation is to the Latin original, the fewer occasions there will be for error. It is hoped that with catechesis and frequent recitation the word "consubstantial" will cease to be an unfamiliar entry in the liturgical lexicon and a tongue twister for the assembly.

The Apostles' Creed (ICEL2010, no. 19)

"I believe in God, the Father almighty . . . and in Jesus Christ. . . . I believe in the Holy Spirit, the holy catholic Church" (lines 4–5, 7, and 18–19)

Although the Apostles' Creed is a shorter profession of faith, it repeats the verb *credo* before the Holy Spirit after the long discourse on Jesus Christ. Unlike ICEL2010, which follows the original Latin, ICEL1973 repeated "I believe" before the second segment on Jesus Christ and again before the section on the Holy Spirit. It is useful to call attention to the Latin construction that employs the preposition *in* with the accusative for the Holy Trinity but not for the church and the other articles of faith. Both ICEL1973 and ICEL2010 do not give due importance to this.

"he descended into hell" (line 13)

The Latin *inferi* was identified in the past as the limbo of the ancestors, the abode or realm of the dead where the ancestors awaited the coming of the Savior. ICEL2010 revives a former English translation of *inferos* as hell, which does not correspond to the current understanding of hell. Obviously, the new translation will require much catechesis. ICEL1973 was cryptic ("He descended to the dead") and does not fully render the meaning of this article of faith and patristic tradition. It is not, however, as perplexing as "hell."

The Prayer of the Faithful (ICEL2010, no 20)

"Then follows the Universal Prayer, that is, the Prayer of the Faithful or Bidding Prayers." (lines 1–2)

ICEL2010 attaches "Bidding Prayer" to the "Prayer of the Faithful" making it appear as another name of the latter. In point of fact, the two are not synonymous. The prayer of the faithful brings to mind its character as the common prayer of the baptized (the faithful) or the priestly people, while bidding prayer refers to the manner in which the prayer is performed. The prayer of the faithful foresees occasions when the people pray in silence after each intention.

The Latin text speaks of *oratio universalis,* literally, universal prayer. ICEL2010 departs from the commonly accepted translation of ICEL1973 ("Then follow the general intercessions"). The term "general intercessions" is a dynamic interpretation of the *oratio universalis,* which in liturgical practice consists of intercessions of a general character and intention. "Universal Prayer" does not explicitly say this.

The Mystagogical Implications

Catherine Vincie

The Word and Liturgical Anamnesis

Gathered in faith and prepared to listen with open hearts and minds, the community sits to hear God's Word proclaimed. The readings from Scripture are not just a recounting of the history of God's people. In a great act of anamnesis, the church recalls the salvific events of the past not as mere history but as present encounter. In the readings, "God speaks to his people, opening up to them the mystery of redemption and salvation and offering them spiritual nourishment; and Christ himself is present in the midst of the faithful through his word" (GIRM2003, no. 55). Even now, God speaks a revelatory word. The salvific acts of God in Israel's history are now proclaimed for the sake of our salvation. The Gospel proclamation, God's saving work in Christ, is "Good News" for us in this time and place. Its saving, healing, and reconciling word is for us today.

Biblical Theology of the Word

The Word of God has a rich history in biblical theology. Rather than mere information about God, the Scriptures reveal a dynamic communication of God's own self to humanity. The Word of God is both event and content, "living and effective, sharper than any two-edged sword" (Heb 4:12). This understanding is rooted in the Hebrew term *dabar* (word), which means not just ordinary speech but a happening or event. God's Word has meaning and power; it is creative, revelatory, and redemptive. The NT introduces the Greek term *logos*, meaning Jesus' message, which also communicates dynamism as his word saves and initiates God's reign. *Logos* also refers to Jesus himself as the content of the word: the revelation of who God is for us. All God wants to say to us is revealed in Jesus, the Word of God. For Christians, this understanding is normative for comprehending all other references to the Word of God.

In the liturgy, the Word of God is both proclamation and revelation. The church is formed by God's Word but also becomes a sacrament of God. It proclaims to others what it has seen and heard and, by the power of the Holy Spirit, mediates God's revelation of self and salvation. The proclamation of God's Word occurs through God's initiative and is addressed to human freedom. This divine self-offer awaits human response in freedom and love. God's gratuitous gift is a grace (often considered "uncreated" grace); the ability to accept the gift is also a grace. This theological truth is given liturgical expression in structures large and small throughout the Liturgy of the Word.

Lectionary

Wanting the people of God to feast more lavishly from the "table of the Word," the council fathers directed that a more representative selection of the Bible be employed over the course of several years (*SC*, no. 51). On Sundays and other solemnities there are three biblical readings prescribed over a three-year cycle. The first usually comes from the Hebrew Scriptures, except during the Easter season when it is taken from the Acts of the Apostles. The second reading comes from the letters of the apostles or the book of Revelation. The gospels of Matthew, Mark, and Luke are read in years A, B, and C, respectively, with John being read during the Easter Season and to fill in the Sundays as needed for the shorter Gospel of Mark.

It is not enough to say that we have been given fuller fare in the revised Roman Catholic Lectionary, as important as that is. The readings have a christological focus and hermeneutic. In Roman Catholic practice, the order of the readings places the most important last. The gospels have pride of place because they proclaim the great mystery of our salvation—Christ Jesus, fully human and divine, who died and rose for our sake. The Liturgy of the Word proclaims this mystery and places it before the People of God for its reception in faith and action. Conversion and transformation is the hope that can be realized through the grace of God's Spirit and human freedom. Grounding this hope is the belief that God's Word is efficacious, though its realization in this world is gradual and partial; full realization awaits completion only in the eschaton.

The readings from the Hebrew Scriptures and other parts of the NT point to and contextualize the gospel proclamation. The first reading has been chosen to correspond to the gospel, providing directionality to interpreting the Christ mystery. In actuality, the three readings mutually interpret one another: not only do the Hebrew Scriptures point to the gospel, but the gospel helps to interpret the first and second readings. The readings from the Law and the Prophets help the community to understand Christ in a wider context, and the Christ mystery opens up the meaning of these Scriptures as well. The church provides a particular reading of salvation history, which might diverge significantly from a Jewish reading of these same texts but is still a legitimate reading of the Scriptures.

Some have argued that this use of the Hebrew Scriptures does not allow them to speak for themselves, nor does it allow for longer narratives. The *Revised Common Lectionary* (used by many Protestant and Anglican churches) takes this into account and provides for more extended readings from the Hebrew Scriptures. Numerous criticisms have also been leveled at the Roman Lectionary for its treatment of women in the Scriptures, e.g., the omission of women either entirely or by option when a shorter version of a reading is allowed; the question of whether women are included on Sundays and feasts or only on weekdays when few of the People of God attend; the issue of "difficult texts" such as the subordination of women in Ephesians 5:21-33; finally, the critique of the cultural context within which the Lectionary is proclaimed. While a more careful and intentional composition of the Lectionary could have avoided some of these issues, at this point these criticisms need to be dealt with in the homily and/or outside in adult faith formation forums.

As noted above, the whole Liturgy of the Word can be understood within the dynamic of divine offer and human response that characterizes so much of Roman Catholic liturgical theology. This dynamic is apparent within large and small structures of the Liturgy of the Word. The first reading is a proclamation of salvation history before the Christ event, and the people are called to respond with the responsorial psalm. Each reading is followed by an acclamation by the people, a prayer of thanksgiving in the case of the first (and second) reading, and an acclamation of praise after the gospel.

Either instituted male lectors or commissioned women and men proclaim the first and second readings. In either case, such readers need biblical, spiritual, and liturgical formation so that through their ministry an experience of encounter with Christ is facilitated (*OLM1981-Pr*, nos. 52 and 55). Through proper preparation and delivery, the prophets' words should ring clear, and the apostolic letters should take on new life and meaning.

Silence should be part of the Liturgy of the Word, either at the beginning or between readings. If members of the assembly are to take in this salvific word, they need the time and space for the word to resound in their hearts and a response to be made (GIRM2003, nos. 56 and 128). The psalmist invites us to "taste and see that the LORD is good" (Ps 34:9), so we pause to ruminate on this word, that it might take root in our being and that we might respond appropriately to the living God. Silence is the medium for this holy encounter.

SC significantly contributed to our understanding of the word in our liturgies. In addition to traditional understandings of Christ's presence in the minister and eucharistic elements, *SC* also taught that Christ is present in the word "since it is he himself who speaks when the holy scriptures are read in church" (no. 7). This presence in absence underscores the eschatological dimension of sacramentality, for the salvation achieved for us is of the quality of "already" but "not yet." Christ is truly present, but we await the fullness of revelation when we will see Christ face-to-face. In the meantime we have sacraments of his presence, such as his word. The sacramental moments are real encounters following the dynamics of divine offer awaiting human response.

From his or her place either in the sanctuary or the assembly, the lector comes forward to the ambo to proclaim the first reading (ICEL2010, no.10). After allowing the assembly to move into receptive silence, the lector announces the source of the reading and then proclaims the reading in a clear voice. With some rare exceptions, prior to Vatican II we had not heard the Hebrew Scriptures proclaimed in church since the fifth century. As a sign of our continuity with the Chosen people and the covenants made with them, we now taste richer fare from these Scriptures and claim that heritage as our own. "This arrangement best illustrates the basic unity of both Testaments and of the history of salvation" (*OLM1981-Pr*, no. 3a). Because of the priority given to the gospel, readings from the Hebrew Scriptures "have been chosen primarily because of their relationship to the New Testament selections, especially the gospel reading" (*OLM1981-Pr*, no. 3c).

After the first reading, the lector acclaims, "The word of the Lord," to which the assembly responds, "Thanks be to God." Chupungco suggests that the term *acclamatio* would be better reserved for the assembly's response, as the reader does not make an acclamation as much as calls the assembly to do so.[1] ICEL2010 notes that this acclamation signals the end of the reading, but it does so much more (no. 10). Proclaiming that what we have heard is the "word of the Lord" speaks volumes about our understanding of Christ's presence in our midst as we feed at the table of the word. Like the disciples at Emmaus (Luke 24:32), our hearts burn within us as Christ proclaims a saving word. We rejoice because we have seen this day. Our acclamation is most properly, "Thanks be to God."

[1] See 181 above.

Again we are invited into reverential silence where, through the "Holy Spirit, the word of God may be grasped by the heart and a response through prayer may be prepared" (GIRM2003, no. 56). The emphasis now is on preparing for the psalm response that the psalmist or cantor leads from the same ambo. One would hope that on Sundays and solemnities, at least, the people's response in the responsorial psalm would be sung and that the musical settings would bring out the meaning of the psalm and allow the people's prayer to emerge (GIRM2003, no. 61). While the psalm and its response may be taken from various sources, it is preferred that it is taken from the Lectionary because it corresponds to the first reading. If the psalm is to be read, it "should be recited in such a way that it is particularly suited to fostering meditation on the word of God" (ibid). ICEL2010 merely suggests that the psalmist sings or says the psalm with the people's response (no. 11).

Following the psalm and its response, on Sundays we turn to the NT reading from either the letters of the apostles or the book of Revelation, depending on the time of the year. Once again we are invited to "listen with the ear of the heart," as St. Benedict (d. 547) suggests at the beginning of his Rule. After proclaiming the reading, the lector again ends with the acclamation, "The word of the Lord," and the people again respond, "Thanks be to God." Then follows a reverential silence to allow the word to penetrate our hearts.

The gospel, as the highpoint of the Liturgy of the Word, calls for a suitable acclamation, i.e., an Alleluia with verse or another acclamation during Lent (ICEL2010, no. 13). The Alleluia and its verse should be sung; if not, they should be eliminated (GIRM2003, no. 63c). The assembly stands for this acclamation as it prepares to hear the gospel proclaimed. If the gospel book is to be incensed, the thurible is prepared by the deacon or acolyte. A deacon ordinarily reads the gospel, since reading is a ministerial, not a presidential, function. Approaching the priest, the deacon bows his head and asks quietly for a blessing (ICEL2010, no. 14), receiving this blessing by making the sign of the cross. He (or the priest if there is no deacon) then goes to the altar and makes a profound bow and prays for a "clean heart." Lifting up the Book of the Gospels from its place on the altar, he processes to the ambo, often accompanied by two candle bearers and, on festive days, a thurifer.

After the greeting and its response, he announces the source of this day's gospel, followed by the gesture of a small cross on the gospel book, forehead, mouth, and breast. Traditionally copied by the assembly, GIRM2003 for the first time instructs the assembly to do this (no. 134), although ICEL2010 makes no mention of this assembly gesture of pressing into our flesh the symbol of our faith, reminding ourselves again of the cost of discipleship. Then the Book of the Gospels may be incensed, indicating our high esteem for the gospels. After the gospel is proclaimed, there follows the acclamation, "The Gospel of the Lord," with the people's response, "Praise to you, Lord Jesus Christ," and another gesture of reverence: the deacon or priest kissing the Book of the Gospels and saying in a low voice, "Through the words of the Gospel may our sins be wiped away."

Homily

The homily breaks open the word for the particular people who make up this worshiping assembly (ICEL2010, no. 17). We expect a word of consolation when we are weary and a word of challenge when we are complacent, hoping that the homilist can weave the story of our lives together with the story of salvation. Truly listening to the Word never leaves us the same: the Word speaks to our hearts and elicits a response both at the Eucharist and in the days and nights that follow. It offers a vision of how life might be when lived under the power of the Word. When the homily is completed, a brief silence may be observed to let this vision become our vision.

Fulfilled in Your Hearing makes some important points regarding the homily and the homiletic task. It suggests that the homily is preached "in order that a community of believers who have gathered to celebrate the liturgy may do so more deeply and fully—more faithfully—and thus be formed for Christian witness in the world" (no. 40). The homily too has a dynamic of call and response. The homilist must speak from the Scriptures and the liturgy[2] "in such a way that those assembled will be able to worship God in spirit and truth, and then go forth to love and serve the Lord" (no. 49). The human response to the mediation of the Word through preaching remains the same as that of the gospel itself; it must become enfleshed in real lives at the liturgy and beyond the liturgy.

The homily also pulls together the Liturgy of the Word and points the congregation to the Liturgy of the Eucharist that will soon follow. In a sense, the Liturgy of the Word acts as divine offer and the Liturgy of the Eucharist as the human response of thanksgiving, reflecting a Roman Catholic understanding of the liturgy as simultaneously God's work and the church's work. The head and the body of Christ engage in a mutual exchange of

[2] Edward Foley, "The Structure of the Mass, Its Elments and Its Parts," in *A Commentary on the General Instruction of the Roman Missal*, ed. Edward Foley, Nathan Mitchell, Joanne Pierce (Collegeville, MN: Liturgical Press, 2007), 156–57.

gifts, encountering one another through the mediation of Word and sacrament.

If there are catechumens present in the assembly, they are to be kindly dismissed. While there is no mention of this in ICEL2010, the RCIA states this explicitly (nos. 67 and 83.2). There are no instructions for the posture of the assembly, but manners suggest that the assembly stand while catechumens are dismissed.

Creed

Having feasted at the table of the Word, the assembly and priest stand and sing (say) the profession of faith. The creed is sung every Sunday and on more solemn occasions (GIRM2003, no. 68) and takes any of three forms. The Apostles' Creed (recommended for Advent and Lent) is simpler in its summary of the faith, while the Nicene-Constantinopolitan Creed (recommended for all other Sundays and solemnities) is the result of faith reflections in light of the church's struggles to clarify orthodox beliefs. The creed may also take the interrogative form of renewing one's baptismal commitment. In whatever form, it is a response to the proclamation of the word.

The change in ICEL2010 from "We believe" to "I believe" is in some ways troubling. The first-person singular had been reserved to individual baptismal professions of faith, while the plural "we" had been traditionally used to speak of the common faith of the gathered assembly. It is unfortunate that the effort to build an assembly in the introductory rites is not supported by a communal expression of faith in this section of the Liturgy of the Word. On the other hand, having assembly members claiming their faith through the "I" could increase their sense of ownership.

During the creed, the community is invited to reverentially bow at the announcement of the birth of our Lord (GIRM2003, nos. 18–19). Bending low, we acknowledge the great *commercium*, the divine gift of the Son to humanity. A bow seems so small a gesture to respond to this divine offer of the incarnation. We can only hope that this small gesture trains our hearts and minds in gratitude and that we learn to offer ourselves.

Prayer of the Faithful

Praying for the needs of the church and the world is our priestly duty rooted in our baptism. GIRM2003 speaks eloquently of the offer-response dynamic we have been emphasizing and of the priestly office of the People of God. "In the general intercessions or prayer of the faithful, the people respond in some way to the word of God which they have welcomed in faith and exercising an office of their baptismal priesthood, offer prayers to God for the salvation for all" (no. 69). Joining with Christ our High Priest, we make intercession for all those in need in our immediate community and around the world. When well crafted by ministers who know the assembly and the needs of the world, the petitions can be a call to action—in prayer now and in direct service to those in need later on. They can open our eyes to the suffering, the lost, the imprisoned, the sick and dying, and all those crying out for liberation and healing. As we repeat the refrain in litanic form ("Lord, hear our prayer"), we trust with St. Paul that God, who did not spare the only Son, will not refuse us anything we need (Rom 8:32).

The Liturgy of the Word leads us in multiple ways through a dynamic of proclamation and response, of divine offer and human reply. The Word of God seeks a receptive heart, and *OM2008* calls for moments of silence to interiorize this word. We then respond with psalmody and Alleluia or Lenten verse. After the homily we make our faith response in the creed and stay standing for the prayer of the faithful, the prayer of a priestly people, itself a response to the word. Shaped and fed by the Word of God, we turn to the eucharistic table to be fed richly in new and sacramental ways.

The Preparation of the Gifts

The Latin Text

Liturgia eucharistica

21. His absolutis, incipit cantus ad offertorium. Interim ministri corporale, purificatorium, calicem, pallam et missale super altare collocant.

22. Expedit ut fideles participationem suam oblatione manifestent, afferendo sive panem et vinum ad Eucharistiae celebrationem, sive alia dona, quibus necessitatibus Ecclesiae et pauperum subveniatur.

23. Sacerdos, stans ad altare, accipit patenam cum pane, eamque ambabus manibus aliquantulum elevatam super altare tenet, submissa voce dicens:

Benedíctus es, Dómine, Deus univérsi,
quia de tua largitáte accépimus panem,
quem tibi offérimus,
fructum terrae et óperis mánuum hóminum:
ex quo nobis fiet panis vitae.

Deinde deponit patenam cum pane super corporale.

Si vero cantus ad offertorium non peragitur, sacerdoti licet haec verba elata voce proferre; in fine populus acclamare potest:

Benedíctus Deus in saécula.

24. Diaconus, vel sacerdos, infundit vinum et parum aquae in calicem, dicens secreto:

Per huius aquae et vini mystérium
eius efficiámur divinitátis consórtes,
qui humanitátis nostrae fíeri dignátus est párticeps.

25. Postea sacerdos accipit calicem, eumque ambabus manibus aliquantulum elevatum super altare tenet, submissa voce dicens:

Benedíctus es, Dómine, Deus univérsi,
quia de tua largitáte accépimus vinum,
quod tibi offérimus,
fructum vitis et óperis mánuum hóminum,
ex quo nobis fiet potus spiritális.

Deinde calicem super corporale deponit.

Si vero cantus ad offertorium non peragitur, sacerdoti licet haec verba elata voce proferre; in fine populus acclamare potest:

Benedíctus Deus in saécula.

The English Text

The Liturgy of the Eucharist

21. When all this has been done, the Offertory Chant begins. Meanwhile, the ministers place the corporal, the purificator, the chalice, the pall, and the Missal on the altar.

22. It is desirable that the faithful express their participation by making an offering, bringing forward bread and wine for the celebration of the Eucharist and perhaps other gifts to relieve the needs of the Church and of the poor.

23. The Priest, standing at the altar, takes the paten with the bread and holds it slightly raised above the altar with both hands, saying in a low voice:

Blessed are you, Lord God of all creation,
for through your goodness we have received
the bread we offer you:
fruit of the earth and work of human hands,
it will become for us the bread of life.

Then he places the paten with the bread on the corporal.

If, however, the Offertory Chant is not sung, the Priest may speak these words aloud; at the end, the people may acclaim:

Blessed be God for ever.

24. The Deacon, or the Priest, pours wine and a little water into the chalice, saying quietly:

By the mystery of this water and wine
may we come to share in the divinity of Christ
who humbled himself to share in our humanity.

25. The Priest then takes the chalice and holds it slightly raised above the altar with both hands, saying in a low voice:

Blessed are you, Lord God of all creation,
for through your goodness we have received
the wine we offer you:
fruit of the vine and work of human hands,
it will become our spiritual drink.

Then he places the chalice on the corporal.

If, however, the Offertory Chant is not sung, the Priest may speak these words aloud; at the end, the people may acclaim:

Blessed be God for ever.

26. Postea sacerdos, profunde inclinatus, dicit secreto:

In spíritu humilitátis et in ánimo contríto
suscipiámur a te, Dómine;
et sic fiat sacrifícium nostrum in conspéctu tuo hódie,
ut pláceat tibi, Dómine Deus.

27. Et, pro opportunitate, incensat oblata, crucem et altare. Postea vero diaconus vel alius minister incensat sacerdotem et populum.

28. Deinde sacerdos, stans ad latus altaris, lavat manus, dicens secreto:

Lava me, Dómine, ab iniquitáte mea,
et a peccáto meo munda me.

29. Stans postea in medio altaris, versus ad populum, extendens et iungens manus, dicit:

Oráte, fratres:
ut meum ac vestrum sacrifícium
acceptábile fiat apud Deum Patrem omnipoténtem.

Populus surgit et respondet:

Suscípiat Dóminus sacrifícium de mánibus tuis
ad laudem et glóriam nóminis sui,
ad utilitátem quoque nostram
totiúsque Ecclésiae suae sanctae.

30. Deinde sacerdos, manibus extensis, dicit orationem super oblata; qua conclusa, populus acclamat:

Amen.

26. After this, the Priest, bowing profoundly, says quietly:

With humble spirit and contrite heart
may we be accepted by you, O Lord,
and may our sacrifice in your sight this day
be pleasing to you, Lord God.

27. If appropriate, he also incenses the offerings, the cross, and the altar. A Deacon or other minister then incenses the Priest and the people.

28. Then the Priest, standing at the side of the altar, washes his hands, saying quietly:

Wash me, O Lord, from my iniquity
and cleanse me from my sin.

29. Standing at the middle of the altar, facing the people, extending and then joining his hands, he says:

Pray, brethren (brothers and sisters),
that my sacrifice and yours
may be acceptable to God,
the almighty Father.

The people rise and reply:

May the Lord accept the sacrifice at your hands
for the praise and glory of his name,
for our good
and the good of all his holy Church.

30. Then the Priest, with hands extended, says the Prayer over the Offerings, at the end of which the people acclaim:

Amen.

History of the Latin Text and Rite

Michael Witczak

Liturgy of the Eucharist

The Liturgy of the Eucharist has three parts, two primarily actions (the preparation of the gifts and communion) and one primarily verbal (the EP). The two action parts have shown themselves over the centuries to be "soft spots," susceptible to constant change and complexity.[1] The history of the Latin rite and texts of the preparation of the gifts bears out this designation.

The use of headings within the *OM* was first introduced in *OM1969* and continued in *MR1970*, *MR1975*, and *MR2002*. There is not a subheading in *OM2008* indicating that this section is the preparation of the gifts, although that title is used in *IGMR2002* (e.g., nos. 72.1 and 73).

The distinction between *Liturgia verbi* and *Liturgia eucharistica* is relatively new. Formerly the distinction (though not found in the liturgical books themselves) was between the Mass of the Catechumens and the Mass of the Faithful, or between the Foremass and Mass. Neither set of distinctions remains helpful. The first implies that the faithful were not present with the catechumens (an anachronism at best) for the first part of the celebration, and the second implies that the readings were not integral to the celebration. Vatican II addressed this when it taught: "The two parts which in a sense go to make up the Mass, viz. the liturgy of the word and the eucharistic liturgy, are so closely connected with each other that they form but one single act of worship" (*SC*, no. 56 = *IGMR2002*, no. 28).[2]

[1] See Baldovin 115 above.

[2] For an overview of the history of the preparation of the gifts see Jungmann MRR, 2:1–100; Robert Cabié, *The Eucharist*, ed. Aimé Georges Martimort, trans. Matthew O'Connell, The Church at Prayer 2 (Collegeville, MN: Liturgical Press, 1986), 76–84, 132–33, 143–44, 157–64; Adrien Nocent, "Storia della celebrazione dell'eucaristia," in *La liturgia eucaristia: Teologia e storia della celebrazione*, ed. Salvatore Marsili, Anamnesis 3:2 (Casale Monferrato: Marietti, 1983), 225–29; Hans Bernhard Meyer, *Eucharistie: Geschichte, Theologie, Pastoral*, ed. Hans Bernhard Meyer et al., Gottesdienst der Kirche: Handbuch der Liturgiewissenschaft 4 (Regensburg: F. Pustet, 1989), 197, 205, 218; and especially Vincenzo Raffa, *Liturgia Eucaristica: Mistagogia della Messa: dalla storia e dalla teologia alla pastorale pratica*, Bibliotheca 'Ephemerides liturgicae' Subsidia 100 (Rome: CLV, 2003), 323–77.

Offertory Chant and Preparation of the Altar (*OM2008*, no. 21)

The liturgy reformed after Vatican II no longer includes specific texts to be sung at the preparation of the gifts. The *antiphonale* that evolved in the early Middle Ages[3] included texts to be sung while the gifts were prepared. The earliest tradition, e.g., Justin Martyr and ApTrad, mentioned that gifts of bread and wine and sometimes other offerings were placed on the altar.[4]

Medieval liturgical books show a developed form of this offering. *OR I* describes the deacon going to the altar after the reading of the gospel while an acolyte approaches with a chalice covered by a corporal. The deacon takes the corporal and gives it to a second deacon who unfolds it on the altar. The mention of the offertory chant is postponed until the end of the preparation of the gifts, when the pontiff signals the schola to stop.[5] *OR V* from *ca.* 900 is clearer in its description. After the invitation *Oremus* (not followed by prayer), it specifies the singing of the offertory chant with its verse. A subdeacon comes with the paten and chalice with the corporal (or *sindon*) covering them and two deacons spread the corporal over the altar. In neither case are the vessels placed on the altar, because they will be used to take up the offerings of the people.[6]

The shift that occurred in the course of the Middle Ages from a solemn celebration to a parallel celebration in which only the priest and one or two acolytes were ministering (eventually called a "private" Mass) led to changes. *MR1570* codified the celebration in this way. After the greeting, response, and invitation to pray, the priest recited the offertory verse. At a solemn Mass, the chalice, paten, and other items had been prepared before the Mass began and were placed on a side table; the deacon then offered

[3] A basic source is René-Jean Hesbert, ed., *Antiphonale missarum sextuplex* (Brussels: Vromant, 1935); also, see Cyrille Vogel, *Medieval Liturgy: An Introduction to the Sources*, trans. and rev. William G. Storey and Niels Krogh Rasmussen (Washington, DC: Pastoral Press, 1986), 357–62; Eric Palazzo, *A History of Liturgical Books from the Beginning to the Thirteenth Century*, trans. Madeleine Beaumont (Collegeville, MN: Liturgical Press, 1993), 63–82; Cassian Folsom, "The Liturgical Books of the Roman Rite," in *Introduction to the Liturgy*, ed. Anscar Chupungco, Handbook for Liturgical Studies 1 (Collegeville, MN: Liturgical Press, 1998), 258–61.

[4] Justin Martyr, *First Apology* 65 and 67.5 = *Prex Eucharistica*, 1:68–71; ApTrad 4 (at the Eucharist following the ordination of the bishop) 5–6 (offering of oil, cheese, and olives), and 21 (at the liturgy of baptism when bread and wine, water, milk, and honey are offered) = Paul Bradshaw, Maxwell Johnson, and L. Edward Phillips, *The Apostolic Tradition: A Commentary*, ed. Harold W. Attridge, *Hermeneia* series (Minneapolis: Fortress Press, 2002), 38–39, 52–53, and 120–23.

[5] *OR I*, nos. 64 and 85 = Andrieu, 2:89 and 95.

[6] *OR V*, no. 43 = Andrieu, 2:218.

the priest the paten. At a private Mass the priest had already brought the various vessels and liturgical objects with himself and placed them on the altar when he arrived. This is not described in the *OM* but in the *ritus servandus* (Sodi-Triacca, no. 21). The *ritus servandus* also describes the priest removing the veil from the chalice, placing the chalice to the epistle side, removing the pall, and then taking the paten (Sodi-Triacca, no. 26).

IGMR2002 stipulates that the vessels and other objects be placed on a side table before the Mass begins, whether it is a more solemn or less solemn celebration (nos. 117–18). The distinction between a solemn Mass and a private Mass is not continued.

Offering of the Faithful (*OM2008*, no. 22)

The earliest tradition includes an offering made by those present at the celebration. Justin Martyr describes an offering of bread and wine with water. No ministers are named. At the end of the Sunday celebration, the head of the community distributes to the widows and the orphans, the ill and imprisoned what the wealthy members of the community have placed before him.[7] ApTrad describes the deacons presenting the gifts to be offered.[8]

Medieval books reveal a much-developed ceremonial for the offering of the gifts. *OR I* presents the pontiff accompanied by members of the pontifical court going to the *senatorium* and receiving the gifts of the principal men. The archdeacon takes the vessels of wine and pours them into the chalice. A subdeacon follows with a *scyphus* (a larger vessel) into which the full chalice is poured from time to time. A subdeacon receives offerings of bread from the pontiff and in turn places them on the *sindon* (large cotton cloth) being carried by two acolytes. A bishop receives the offerings of those outside the *senatorium*. The pontiff receives the offerings of some of the principal members of his court and then proceeds to receive the gifts of the women on the other side of the *senatorium*. The pontiff returns to his seat and washes his hands. The pontiff's own offering is placed on the altar by the archdeacon.[9]

OR V simplifies the ceremony. A priest receives the offerings of the men, then the women, then the ministers, placing the bread on the *sindon* and the wine in the chalice. These are then brought to the pontiff. He receives

[7] *First Apology*, nos. 65.3 and 67.5–6 = *Prex Eucharistica* 1:68 and 70.

[8] Nos. 4 and 21 = Bradshaw et al., *The Apostolic Tradition*, 38–39 and 120–23.

[9] *OR I*, nos. 61–68 = Andrieu, 2:88–93.

them, and then they are carried to the altar. Oblations are also accepted from the schola. The pontiff meanwhile washes his hands.[10]

The offering of the gifts of bread and wine by the members of the congregation, both the faithful and the ministers, slowly faded from the ritual. During the later Middle Ages, as the celebration by a single priest became common, the gifts were placed on the altar at the start of Mass, as described above. The people no longer had any direct involvement with the placing of the gifts on the altar.

Blessing over the Bread (*OM2008*, no. 23)

The earliest tradition gives no prayer for the priest to say while placing the bread on the altar. The custom emerges in the eighth and ninth century in the form of *apologiae* or private devotional prayers of the priest. Each action of the Mass developed a rubrical description and an attached prayer. The prayer was usually written in the first-person singular and highlighted the personal unworthiness of the priest who was celebrating the Mass.[11] This proved an extremely popular form of prayer, and some books of prayer contained numerous examples that priests could pray at each moment of the preparation of the gifts.[12]

As the Middle Ages proceeded, the number of prayers became reduced and a certain format entered into the usage of various groups, for example, the Roman Curia, local churches, and individual religious congregations such as the Franciscans and Dominicans. The dual impetus of combining all the various books for the celebration of the liturgy into a single missal was paralleled by the inclusion of all ministerial roles into the role of the presiding priest.[13]

MR1570 includes this version of a Carolingian prayer for the taking of the bread: *Suscipe, sancte Pater omnipotens, aeterne Deus, hanc immaculatam*

[10] *OR V*, nos. 43–51 = Andrieu, 2:218–20.

[11] See Adrien Nocent, "Les apologies dans la célébration eucharistique," in *Liturgie et rémission des péchés*, Bibliotheca 'Ephemerides liturgicae' Subsidia 3 (Rome: CLV Edizioni Liturgiche, 1975), 179–96; Cabié, *The Eucharist*, 130–31; Meyer, *Eucharistie*, 204–6.

[12] For example, see Joanne Pierce, "Sacerdotal Spirituality at Mass: Text and Study of the Prayerbook of Sigebert of Minden (1022–1036)," (PhD diss., University of Notre Dame, 1988), 205–31.

[13] For an account of the rise of the Missal see Vogel, *Medieval Liturgy*, 105–6; Palazzo, *A History of Liturgical Books*, 107–10. For an interesting overview of four different celebrations of the preparation of the gifts, see Cabié, *The Eucharist*, 157–64; also Paul Tirot, *Histoire des prières d'offertoire dans la liturgie romaine du VIIe au XVIe siècle*, Bibliotheca 'Ephemerides liturgicae' Subsidia 34 (Rome: CLV-Edizioni Liturgiche, 1985).

hostiam: quam ego indignus famulus tuus offero tibi.[14] The prayer contains the usual apologetic claims of unworthiness and uses the language of offering and mediation. After the prayer, the host would be placed on the corporal and the paten set aside.

The recovery of the early tradition led the *coetus* after Vatican II to propose that the language of offering be limited to the EP and that the preparation of the gifts focus on placing the bread and wine on the altar. The experimental form proposed employing a section of the prayer from *Didache*, no. 9, "As this bread was scattered . . ." The experience of this experimental form was that it was too sparse and perhaps too great a departure from what was in use at the time (i.e., *MR1962*). After some interventions, *OM2008*, no. 23 was adopted in 1968. It is based on Jewish meal prayers and the prayers of the *Didache* and includes a possible response by the people. This last point was one very important to Paul VI.[15] The bread remains on the paten after the prayer.

Commingling (*OM2008*, no. 24)

The use of wine with water is noted as early as the writings of Justin (*First Apology*, nos. 65 and 67). *OR I* describes the *archiparafonista* of the schola as presenting the water, which the archdeacon pours into the wine in the form of the sign of the cross (no. 80). No words were spoken at this moment.

The Carolingian desire to add rubrics and prayers led to the recitation of a text at this moment. Over the centuries, a number of texts were associated with this action. The text finally codified in *MR1570* is adapted from a Christmas prayer attributed to Leo the Great: *Deus, qui humanae substantiae dignitatem mirabiliter condidisti, et mirabilius reformasti: da nobis per huius aquae et vini mysterium, eius divinitatis esse consortes, qui humanitatis notrae fieri dignatus est particeps, Jesus Christus.*[16] The priest blessed the water with the sign of the cross as he said this prayer.

The proposed text in the experimental period after Vatican II was simplified and the sign of the cross omitted: "At the Lord's command, wine was

[14] Sodi-Triacca, no. 1414. "Accept, O Holy Father, Almighty and Eternal God, this spotless host, which I your unworthy servant offer to you."

[15] See Frederick McManus, "The Roman Order of Mass from 1964 to 1969: The Preparation of the Gifts," in *Shaping English Liturgy: Studies in Honor of Archbishop Denis Hurley*, ed. Peter C. Finn and James M. Schellman (Washington, DC: Pastoral Press, 1990), 107–38; also see Bugnini, 337–92, esp. 343, 350, 354, 358, 364–65, 369, 375–76, 379.

[16] Sodi-Triacca, no. 1416; "God, who wonderfully formed the dignity of the human substance and more wonderfully re-formed it: grant that through the mystery of this water and wine we be sharers of his divinity who deigned to become a sharer in our humanity."

made from water: may water mixed with wine become the wedding banquet."[17] The texts were completely redone after some criticism, and the form found in *MR2002* was adopted: it keeps some reference to the Leonine prayer but shortens it and is more to the point.

Blessing over the Chalice (*OM2008*, no. 25)

This section shares a common history with the rubrics and words over the bread (*OM2008*, no. 23). The first evidence of rubrics concerning the wine comes from *OR I* (nos. 70 and 79). The wine collected from the gathered people was placed in the main chalice and in the large *scyphus*. There was no prayer text given. During the eighth and ninth centuries prayers were added to the action. Among the many prayers that served the purpose during the centuries, *MR1570* included the prayer: *Offerimus tibi domine calicem salutaris, tuam deprecantes clementiam: ut in conspectu divinae maiestatis tuae pro nostra et totius mundi salute cum odore suavitatis ascendat*.[18] The rubric that follows (Sodi-Triacca, no. 1418) specifies that the chalice be covered with the pall.

The post–Vatican II *coetus* originally proposed that the wine be placed on the altar with words adopted from Proverbs 9:1-2: "Wisdom has built a house for herself, she has mixed her wine, she has set her table. Glory to you, God, for ever."[19] The reaction to the experimental uses of the rite led to the eventual substitution of the prayer now in the rite, including language of offering and a response by the people.

In spiritu humilitatis (*OM2008*, no. 26)

This apology is one of many private prayers that appeared as part of the offertory rites during the Middle Ages.[20] It is in *MR1570* and has remained as part of the reformed liturgy. It is a typical apology, though converted into the third-person plural; it is said privately by the priest. It names the action as "sacrifice."

[17] McManus, "The Roman Order of Mass," 121.

[18] Sodi-Triacca, no. 1418; "We offer you, Lord, the cup of salvation, begging your mercy: that it rise in the sight of your divine majesty with a sweet odor for the salvation of us and the whole world."

[19] McManus, "The Roman Order of Mass," 123.

[20] It appears as early as the Sacramentary of Amiens of the eighth century. See Victor Leroquais, "L'*ordo missae* du sacramentaire d'Amiens, B.N. lat. 9432," *Ephemerides liturgicae* 41 (1927): 435-445.

Incense (*OM2008*, no. 27)

The role of incense in worship goes back to the OT (e.g., Lev 2:1, 15; 24:7; see Luke 1:9-11). It also was a symbol of prayer and eschatological worship (Ps 141:2; Isa 60:6; Rev 5:8). The use of incense at this moment in the celebration seems not to have been of Roman origin: *OR I* does not include it. The *ordines* influenced by Frankish custom[21] include an incensing of the altar at this point. Slowly over the following centuries the ritual became more complex, including the incensing of the gifts, the cross, the altar, the priest, and the rest of the ministry. This slowly developing custom was codified in *MR1570*. The ritual there specified that solemn celebrations included a blessing of the incense (chosen from among several prayers used for that purpose over the centuries): *Per intercessionem sancti Michaelis archangeli stantis a dextris altaris incensi, et omnium electorum suorum, incensum istud dignetur dominus benedicere, et in odorem suavitatis accipere.*[22] The priest then received the thurible from the deacon and incensed the gifts while saying: *Incensum istud a te benedictum, ascendat ad te domine: et descendat super nos misericordia tua.*[23] Then he incensed the altar saying: *Dirigatur domine oratio mea sicut incensum in conspectu tuo.*[24] Then he would return the thurible to the deacon saying: *Accendat in nobis dominus ignem sui amoris, et flammam aeternae caritatis.*[25] The deacon incensed the priest and then the others in order. The elaborate pattern of incensing of the gifts and altar keyed to the specific words being spoken was schematized by a chart in later editions of the Missal, e.g., *MR1962* (Sodi-Triacca, nos. 174–75).

Vatican II called for a simplification of rituals and the elimination of doublings (*SC*, no. 34). The experimental forms that were developed immediately after the council allowed for the use of incense. A first version called for the incensing of only the offerings (the altar and people had been incensed at the beginning of Mass). Eventually, the ritual expanded with the priest making a single swing of the censer over the gifts, then circling

[21] e.g., *OR V*, no. 55 = Andrieu, 2:220.

[22] Sodi-Triacca, no. 1423; "Through the intercession of St. Michael the Archangel standing to the right of the altar of incense, and [the intercession of] all your elect, may the Lord deign to bless this incense, and accept its sweet odor."

[23] Sodi-Triacca, no. 1424; "May this incense blessed by you rise to you, Lord: and may your mercy descend over us."

[24] Sodi-Triacca, no. 1425; "May my prayer rise before you, O Lord, like incense."

[25] Sodi-Triacca, no. 1426: "May the Lord ignite in us the fire of his love and the flame of eternal charity."

the altar with incense, and finally incensing the people. No texts were provided.[26]

OM2008 allows for the use of incense at any Mass, with the possible incensing of offerings, cross, and altar, then of the priest and the people. More complete rubrics, including a silent sign of the cross over the smoking incense and the proper number of swings of the censer and order of incensing, is contained in *IGMR2002* (nos. 276–77). Adapted from the 1984 *CaerEp*, this section was not in any *IGMR* until 2002. This is one moment when the Carolingian custom of always accompanying an action with a prayer has been abandoned.

Washing of the Hands (*OM2008*, no. 28)

The custom of the priest washing his hands at this part of the celebration is found as early as *OR I*, where it takes place after the pontiff has received the offerings of those in the *senatorium*.[27] Some *ordines* included the hand washing at the beginning of the action (e.g., *OR IV*). Eventually, papal and episcopal Masses had two hand washings: one at the beginning and one, with the disappearance of actual offerings by the people, after the incensing. Several different texts came to accompany the washing. The Roman Rite accepted Psalm 25:6-12 into *MR1570*.[28]

The period of experimentation after Vatican II found the hand washing in different places. The provisional text (1964) placed the washing after the incensing with a new text: "May we not go to prayer with a bad conscience. May the Lord pour clear water over us, and we shall be washed." The normative text of the next year moved the hand washing to the beginning of the preparation of the gifts at the chair and provided no accompanying text. The 1967 version returned the hand washing to after the incensing and added a psalm verse (eventually Ps 51:4, the current text). This form entered *MR1970* and has remained.[29]

Invitation to Prayer (*OM2008*, no. 29)

A dialogical introduction to the prayer over the gifts between the priest and the minister dates to the Carolingian period, which attached prayers

[26] McManus, "The Roman Order of Mass," 121.
[27] *OR I*, no. 76 = Andrieu, 2:92.
[28] Raffa, *Liturgia Eucaristica*, 360–61.
[29] McManus, "The Roman Order of Mass," 120–27.

to each rubric.[30] It entered the Mass of the Roman Curia in the thirteenth century[31] and was incorporated into *MR1570*.

The experiments after Vatican II originally omitted the dialogical introduction, leaving only the invitation to prayer, *Oremus*. Some, including Paul VI, reacted against this omission, noting that it eliminated a possible moment of verbal participation by the people (who are now seen as substituting for the ministers). The form from the previous usage was ultimately retained.[32] *MR2002* specifies that the people stand after the invitation but before their response.

Prayer over the Gifts (*OM2008*, no 30)

A prayer over the gifts is already found in some of the earliest liturgical books, e.g., the *Veronense*, *Gelasianum*, and *Hadrianum*. Its name varies, already bearing the title *Secreta* ("Secret") in the *Gelasianum* (no. 3 *et passim*). *OR I* does not mention the prayer but supposes it because it mentions saying the conclusion (*quando dixit "per omnia saecula . . ."*) aloud.[33] In a solemn Mass, the prayer was said privately, "so that only God and the celebrant can hear it."[34] The custom developed that the dialogue before the preface began with the conclusion to the Secret: the musical typography in *MR1570* makes these elements look like part of one musical act (Sodi-Triacca, no. 1433).

The postconciliar reform immediately transformed the "Secret" into a "Prayer over the Gifts" (ICEL2010 = "Prayer over the Offerings") to be said aloud.[35] The conclusion of the prayer in *OM2008* is now the conclusion of the preparation of the gifts and not the beginning of the dialogue before the preface.

[30] Leroquais, "L'*ordo missae*," 442.

[31] S. J. P. Van Dijk, *The Ordinal of the Papal Court from Innocent III to Boniface VIII and Related Documents*, Spicilegium Friburgense 22, completed by Joan Hazeldon Walker (Fribourg: University Press, 1975), 505.

[32] *OR XV*, no. 35 = Andrieu, 3:102; also, McManus, "The Roman Order of Mass," 120–29; Raffa, *Liturgia Eucaristica*, 363–64.

[33] *OR I*, no. 87 = Andrieu, 2:95.

[34] See Raffa, *Liturgia Eucaristica*, 364.

[35] *InterOec*, no. 48 = DOL 340.

Theology of the Latin Text and Rite

Patrick Regan

Of all the parts of the eucharistic liturgy reformed after Vatican II, this one diverges most from its predecessor in *MR1570*. Many have not yet fully comprehended its originality and do not carry it out as intended. To do so we must grasp the implications of changed nomenclature and carefully notice all details in the rubrics.

Since *OM1969* this part of the Mass has a new name. It is no longer called *Offertorium* ("Offertory") but *Preparatio donorum* ("Preparation of the Gifts").[1] Surprisingly, however, this designation does not appear in *OM2008* or elsewhere in any of the three editions of *MR1970*. We learn of it in *IGMR2002*, explained in nos. 72–77 and mentioned in nos. 33, 43, and 214. Although no longer the name of a part of the Mass, *Offertorium* remains the name of the chant found in the Roman Gradual that is meant to be sung at that point. [2] It appears in *OM2002* as *cantus ad offertorium* (nos. 21, 23, 25) and is translated "Offertory Chant" even as *cantus ad introitum* (no. 1) is rendered "Entrance Chant."[3]

This can be confusing. Equally confusing is that the CCC retrieves the abandoned term, declaring in no. 1333 that "in the Offertory we give thanks to the Creator for bread and wine," and in no. 1350 it employs "The presentation of the offerings (the Offertory)" as a subtitle. Benedict XVI writes in *SacCar* that participants in the 2005 synod of bishops on the Eucharist "drew attention to the presentation of the gifts" (no. 47). Although *Preparatio donorum* is the official designation for this part of the eucharistic celebration, it is not consistently employed even in magisterial documents.

[1] The reasons for this change in terminology are well set forth in Foley, "The Structure of the Mass, Its Elements and Its Parts," in *A Commentary on the General Instruction of the Roman Missal*, ed. Edward Foley, Nathan Mitchell, Joanne Pierce (Collegeville, MN: Liturgical Press, 2007), 124.

[2] Unfortunately, *IGMR2002*, no. 42, combines the two, instructing the faithful to sit *dum fit praeparatio donorum ad offertorium* ("while the Preparation of the Gifts at the Offertory is taking place"). *IGMR2002* uses the expression *ritus ad offertorium* (no. 74), translated "the rite at the offertory," but is here talking about norms for singing.

[3] Here is another instance where ICEL2010 capitalizes a phrase that is not capitalized in *MR2002*; neither *cantus ad offertorium* nor *cantus ad introitum* are capitalized in *MR2002*.

The title *Liturgia eucharistica* above *OM2008*, no. 21, indicates that the *Liturgia verbi* came to an end with the universal prayer or prayer of the faithful (no. 20) and that we have reached the second part of the Mass, the eucharistic liturgy, as outlined in *IGMR2002*, no. 28. The next title in *OM2008* is *Prex eucharistica* after no. 30. The *Preparatio donorum*—the first of the four sections of the eucharistic liturgy—begins after the prayer of the faithful and ends with the prayer over the offerings (in *OM2008*, nos. 21–30). Benedict XVI cautions that "this is not to be viewed as a kind of 'interval' between the liturgy of the word and the liturgy of the Eucharist. To do so would tend to weaken, at the least, the sense of a single rite made up of two interrelated parts" (*SacCar*, no. 47). The words *Liturgia eucharistica* in bold type after the prayer of the faithful, then, is an unmistakable reminder that what follows is the beginning of the eucharistic liturgy, not a prelude to it.

Preparing the Altar (*OM2008*, no. 21)

As soon as the prayer of the faithful is over, *incipit cantus ad offertorium*.[4] Meanwhile, ministers place the corporal, purificator, chalice, pall, and Missal upon the altar.[5] From this we see that preparation of the gifts opens with preparation of the place upon which the gifts are to be placed, the altar. On a grand occasion like the Paschal Vigil, when so much begins anew, it would be well to start the service with the altar completely bare and make spreading the cloth—preferably one that reaches the floor on all four sides—the first act of preparation described in no. 21. This rubric supposes that until now none of the articles enumerated in it have been on the altar. This is seldom the case. Almost always the corporal, purificators, and sometimes even the Missal are set out before Mass; other times cruets, lavabo dish, and finger towel are placed there. Even worse is when matches or a lighter, a missalette, the parish bulletin, or homily notes litter the surface of the table of the Lord. Flowers should be alongside the altar, not on it (*IGMR2002*, no. 305).

[4] Rarely is this chant from the *Graduale Romanum* sung. Much more common is a hymn or other sacred song or, more frequent still, instrumental music. This is also an ideal time for the choir to sing and for the congregation to listen and pray silently. Additionally, this is the moment in most places when the collection, not mentioned in *OM2008* (noted in *IGMR2002*, no. 105c, but without reference to the preparation of the gifts) is taken up.

[5] The pall was not included in *OM1969* or subsequent *OMs* but was added in *MR2002*.

MR2002 contains the texts of the antiphons of the entrance and communion chants because, if they are not sung, they must be read (*IGMR2002*, nos. 48 and 87). The offertory chant is not an antiphon meant to be sung with a psalm, and there is no obligation that it be read when not sung. Thus the words of this chant are not printed in *MR2002*.

Procession with the Gifts (*OM2008*, no. 22)

Once the altar is prepared the faithful bring forth the bread and wine as well as *alia dona* ("other gifts") to serve the needs of the church and the poor. Ordinarily they do so in a procession, not mentioned here but made explicit in *IGMR2002*, no. 74. What is mentioned—and this is in the forefront of the rubric—is the meaning of the action. It expresses their participation in the preparation of the gifts (*participationem suam oblatione*, "their participation by making an offering") at the most fundamental level of furnishing the very matter of the eucharistic banquet and represents on their part an oblation, an act of offering. It also grounds the eucharistic celebration in creation. The CCC teaches that "it commits the Creator's gifts into the hands of Christ who, in his sacrifice, brings to perfection all human attempts to offer sacrifice" (no. 1350). Benedict XVI continues this line of thought: "In the bread and wine that we bring to the altar, all creation is taken up by Christ the Redeemer to be transformed and presented to the Father. In this way we also bring to the altar all the pain and suffering of the world, in the certainty that everything has value in God's eyes" (*SacCar*, no. 47).

Since *IGMR2002* states that it is *Valde optandum est* ("most desirable," no. 85) that priest and people receive communion from hosts consecrated at the same Mass, the amount of bread brought forth should be calculated in view of the number of people expected to receive Holy Communion. The integrity of the eucharistic meal is at stake. Hosts received in communion should be those brought up in the procession with the gifts and over which the consecratory thanksgiving has been pronounced. Communion from the tabernacle should be the exception, not the rule.

Rubrics accompanying the Prayer of Blessing over the Bread (*OM2008*, no. 23)

The previous rubric described an action of the faithful. This one deals with the priest. It says that, standing at the altar, he does three things: he takes (*accipit*) the paten with the bread from the faithful who brought it up; with both hands he holds it (*tenet aliquantulum*) slightly raised above the altar while reciting the formula of blessing in a low voice; then he puts it down (*deponit*), on the corporal.[6]

There are several points to note here. First, the rubric does not say that the priest is offering anything. Second, his act of taking the bread is significant because, as explained in *IGMR2002*, no. 72, it corresponds to Jesus' act of taking the bread (and wine) at the Last Supper. Third, the priest is to recite the blessing while still holding the paten slightly above the altar. Only then is he to put it down on the corporal.

Rubrics accompanying the Preparation of the Chalice and Prayer of Blessing over the Wine (*OM2008*, nos. 24–25)

No. 25 prescribes for the chalice of wine what no. 23 prescribed for the bread, and in almost identical words. The priest *accipit* ("takes") the chalice, with both hands *tenet* ("he holds") it slightly raised above the altar while reciting the blessing in a low voice, and then he *deponit* ("puts [it] down") on the corporal. The actions are the same for both the bread and the chalice. Both terminate with the object being put down *super corporale*. The difference between the two is that the chalice, before being taken by the priest, must be prepared. This is dealt with in no. 24, which states that the deacon or priest pours wine and a little water into it, saying *secreto* ("silently") the prayer, *Per huius aquae et vini mysterium*, an abbreviation of the formula in *MR1570*.[7]

To respect the sense of these actions the chalice should not be prepared while resting on the corporal, raised during the recitation of the blessing, and set back down again on the corporal. Ideally it should be prepared by the deacon at the credence table as *IGMR2002* permits (no. 73), then brought to the priest, who takes it (*accipit*), holds it (*tenet*) above the altar while saying the blessing, then puts it down (*deponit*) on the corporal.

When there is no deacon and the chalice has to be prepared by the priest, when brought to the altar with the corporal, purificator, pall, and Missal (as no. 21 requires), it should be placed not on the corporal but on the right

[6] *MR2002* introduced two changes into this rubric. The first is that the priest is to hold the paten with both hands, missing in *OM1969* and succeeding *OMs*. The second is that he is to recite the blessing *submissa voce* ("in a low voice") instead of *secreto* ("silently") as in *OM1969* (no. 19) and its successors.

[7] *Deus, qui humanae substantiae dignitatem mirabiliter condidist, et mirabilius reformasti: da nobis,* per huius aquae et vini mysterium, eius divinitatis esse consortes, qui humanitatis nostrae fieri dignatus est particeps, *Iesus Christus, Filius tuus, Dominus noster: qui tecum vivit et regnat in unitate Spiritus Sancti Deus: per omnia saecula saeculorum. Amen* (Sodi-Triacca, no. 1170; emphasis added).

side of the altar and prepared there. Then the priest, standing in the middle of the altar, should take it, hold it slightly raised above the altar, say the blessing, and finally set it upon the corporal. The action of presenting and taking the gifts culminates in their being placed upon the corporal. This should be done authoritatively and decisively. Once set down they should not be lifted up again until the institution narrative. Doing so gives the impression of offering them. In fact, they are not being offered here but being placed down upon the altar, symbol of Christ, and henceforth reserved entirely for purposes determined by him.

Consequently, once set upon the altar the bread and wine should not be moved around or even touched until they are again taken by the priest during the institution narrative.[8] This holds especially when there are several patens and chalices and several ministers involved in arranging them. On such occasions, instead of squeezing all the vessels onto one standard-size corporal, it would be better to spread them out graciously either on two or three corporals or on a single large one. Above all, priests must control their tendency to fiddle nervously with the paten and chalice when their arms are not extended. Here, economy of movement is of the utmost importance.

Prayers of Blessing over the Bread and Chalice (*OM2008*, nos. 23 and 25)

Having elucidated the action, we now turn to the two blessings that the priest recites after taking the bread and chalice. Both have the same structure and much of the same wording. Modeled on Jewish meal prayers,[9] they are sometimes called *berakoth* (sing., *berakah*), the Hebrew word for "blessings." They begin, *Benedictus es, Domine, Deus universi. Dominus* is the Latin translation of the unpronounceable personal name of God revealed to Moses in the burning bush (Exod 3:6). The Greek translation is *Kyrios*, in English, "Lord." This opening exclamation, then, is a benediction of the divine name. To it is added, *Deus universi*, "God of all creation," an expression intended to connect the eucharistic celebration not only with salvation but also with creation, inviting us to see creation as ordered to redemption and redemption as the crowning of creation. In as much as the Eucharist actualizes the

[8] The language in the rubric for taking the elements at the institution narrative is very similar to that for the preparation of the gifts: *accipit panem eumque parum elevatum super altare tenens* (*OM2008*, no. 89; cf. no. 90).

[9] Cf. *Prex Eucharistica*, 1:6–7.

mystery of redemption, it also brings to perfection all that God intends for creation.

The prayers then acknowledge that the bread and wine just taken derive from the bountiful munificence of the Creator and are being offered to him, not in their natural state—grain and grapes—but made into cultural products, bread and wine, by the work of human hands.[10] Introduced into the eucharistic action just begun, they are destined for an even more marvelous transformation: becoming for us "bread of life" (John 6:35) and "spiritual drink" (1 Cor 10:4). *Nobis* ("for us") points toward communion and emphasizes that bread and wine are now being presented, taken, and placed on the altar in view of their being shared as Body and Blood of Christ. At the end of each of these blessings, when said aloud, the faithful acclaim, *Benedictus Deus in saecula* ("Blessed be God forever").

We recall that no. 17 above expects the offertory chant to begin after the prayer of the faithful and the two *berakoth* to be said in a low voice. The last sentence in nos. 23 and 25 declares that these blessings may be said aloud (*licet haec verba elata voce proferre*) if the offertory chant is not sung. The word *licet* is important, for it means that when there is no singing or instrumental music the priest may, but is not required to, say the two blessings aloud. He may place the bread and wine on the corporal in silence.

Private Prayer of the Priest (*OM2008*, no. 26)

After setting down the chalice and paten the priest, bowing profoundly, recites *secreto* ("silently") the prayer *In spiritu humilitatis*, taken unchanged from *MR1570*. It asks *suscipiamur* ("that we be accepted") by the Lord and that *sacificium nostrum* ("our sacrifice") be pleasing—expressions that will return in the *Orate, fratres* and *Suscipiat* (no. 29, below). This gesture and prayer is not mentioned in any edition of *IGMR*.

Incensation (*OM2008*, no. 27)

This rubric dealing with the possibility of an incensation designates the bread and wine as *oblata* ("offerings"). Until now they have been called *dona* ("gifts," no. 22). Placing them upon the altar changed their character. The EP will change them even more.

[10] Benedict XVI writes that this "enables us to appreciate how God invites man to participate in bringing to fulfillment his handiwork, and in so doing, gives human labor its authentic meaning, since, through the celebration of the Eucharist, it is united to the redemptive sacrifice of Christ" (*SacCar*, no. 47).

Washing of Hands (*OM2008*, no. 28)

The priest, when washing his hands, now says silently words from Psalm 51:4, considerably shorter than Psalm 25:6-12 required by *MR1570*. This and the *In spiritu humilitatis* (*OM2008*, no. 26) seem incongruous in the context of liturgical action that is essentially corporate and public.

Invitation to Prayer and Prayer over the Offerings (*OM2008*, nos. 29–30)

The congregation has been seated throughout the preparation of the gifts. The priest now calls them to prayer: *Orate, fratres*, a command from him to them, not the usual exhortation to pray together, *Oremus*. They rise and respond by reciting the *Suscipiat*. These two formulas have provoked much discussion in recent years. The previous translation of *meum ac vestrum sacrificium* as "our sacrifice" was criticized for seeming to blur the distinction between the ministerial priesthood and that of the baptized. The current translation of "my sacrifice and yours" is criticized for giving the impression that there are two sacrifices.[11]

The preparation of the gifts concludes with the priest extending his hands and reciting the second of the three presidential prayers, the *Oratio super oblata*: no longer translated as "Prayer over the Gifts" (ICEL1973) but "Prayer over the Offerings" (ICEL2010), which is consistent with the shift from *dona* to *oblata* noted above in no. 27.

[11] Cf. Chupungco, 220 below.

The ICEL2010 Translation

Anscar J. Chupungco

Liturgy of the Eucharist (ICEL2010, no. 21)

ICEL2010 begins this new section, which is separated from the preceding by a new heading, "The Liturgy of the Eucharist," with the temporal clause "When all this has been done" (line 1). To which previous action does "all this" refer? The Latin ablative absolute (*His absolutis*) means all that precedes this part of the celebration. ICEL2010's temporal clause is uncharacteristic of English usage. For clarity ICEL1973 named the Liturgy of the Word ("After the liturgy of the word, the offertory song is begun").

Procession with the Gifts (ICEL2010, no. 22)

The Latin conjunction *sive* (or) in the phrase *afferendo sive panem et vinum . . . sive alia dona* ("bringing forward bread and wine . . . and perhaps other gifts") has a disjunctive function if it is repeated: the people may bring up either bread and wine or other gifts. This disjunctive meaning of *sive* suggests that the people may choose the type of gifts they wish to bring to the celebration. ICEL2010's "and perhaps" does not render the Latin conjunctions *sive . . . sive* accurately. At best, the adverb "perhaps" is a wishful interpretation of the pair *sive . . . sive*, but it is not a literal translation.

Prayers of Blessing over the Bread and Chalice (ICEL2010, nos. 23 and 25)

The Latin text uses the genitive case for both *terrae/vitis* and *operis manuum hominum*: "fruit of the earth/vine and of human labor." Both ICEL2010 as well as ICEL1973 ("which earth has given and human hands have made. . . . fruit of the vine and work of human hands") seem to juxtapose "fruit" and "work," when the Latin text actually calls bread (and wine) the fruit of the earth (of the vine) and of the work of human hands. This is a small point, but when translating literally one needs to pay special attention to the Latin grammar.

Commingling (ICEL2010, no. 24)

The Latin text does not mention the name of Christ, although it is obvious that he is referenced in this prayer. This is another case of ICEL2010's interpretive—not literal—translation, although it is correct.

The translation of *dignatus est* ("who humbled himself") does not carry the full weight of the Latin verb. In this text, borrowed from Leo the Great, the *dignitas* of humankind is extolled. In context, the text means: Christ considered human nature worth the incarnation; it is worth dying for. Sin did not efface human nature's God-given dignity. The stress of the Latin text is not on Christ's humility ("he humbled himself") but on his appreciation of human dignity.

Invitation to Prayer (ICEL2010, no. 29)

ICEL2010's phrase "my sacrifice and yours" is an ambiguous construction: it can mean "my sacrifice and your sacrifice," which is prone to misinterpretation. The Latin conjunction *atque* (*ac* before a consonant) is different from *et*, although both are translated in English with the conjunction "and." In Latin lexical usage *et* enumerates, while *atque* or *ac* joins together nouns, pronouns, and verbs. The Latin text does not say *meum et vestrum sacrificium* ("my sacrifice and your sacrifice"). Rather, it carefully chooses *ac*: "my sacrifice, which is also your sacrifice," or, in short, "our sacrifice" (thus, ICEL1973's "that our sacrifice"). There is only one sacrifice, although there are different ministers and functions within the sacrificial act. The thinking that seeks to distinguish one sacrifice from another based on the difference between an ordained priesthood and the priestly assembly is not supported by the Latin text.

The Mystagogical Implications

Catherine Vincie

Offertory Chant (ICEL2010, no. 21)

When the creed has been said or sung and the prayer of the faithful spoken, the offertory chant may be sung. In spite of the fact that the true "offering" takes place in the EP (GIRM2003, no. 79f.), both the GIRM2003 and the *OM* call this the "Offertory Chant," recalling *MR1570* when true offering prayers were said at this point. Those prayers came to be called the "little canon" because of their close imitation of the offering that took place in the Roman Canon. Returning to this language risks introducing confusion regarding what constitutes the true offering of the Mass.[1]

For dioceses of the United States, the chant is taken from one of the same four resources named for the entrance chant: the Roman Gradual, the Simple Gradual, some other collection of psalms and antiphons, or some other song approved by the bishops (GIRM2003, no. 48). On some occasions, instrumental music may be used, except during Lent; the exception is on the Fourth Sunday (*Laetare Sunday*), solemnities, and feasts (GIRM2003, no. 313). This is music that accompanies ritual action; the offertory chant should continue at least until the gifts are brought to the altar.

Preparation of the Altar (ICEL2010, no. 21)

Meanwhile, the altar is prepared by a minister who places the missal, the chalice, the corporal, the purificator, and the pall on the altar in readiness for the priest-celebrant. In addition, if a single chalice is not enough to hold the Precious Blood for the whole assembly, the minister brings additional cups and places these on the altar as well.[2] These are minor actions; they are supportive of the principal action of bringing up the gifts by the faithful and the preparation of the gifts by the priest that will follow.

[1] See Regan, 211 above.

[2] Norms for the Distribution and Reception of Holy Communion under Both Kinds for the Dioceses of the United States of America (2002), no. 36.

People's Offering of Bread, Wine, and Gifts for the Church and the Poor (ICEL2010, no. 22)

In accord with ancient tradition, the people make an offering of the bread and wine for the eucharistic celebration and additional gifts for the care of the church and of the poor. We cannot receive the self-offering of Christ in the Eucharist if we do not give of ourselves so that others may live. This is only just and right, giving our eucharistic celebration an integrity that it would not otherwise have. The prophetic tradition was adamant that divine worship without justice to the neighbor was no worship at all. Neither one nor the other is sufficient; only both together will do. St. Cyprian criticized those "who come without alms and [in communion] receive part of the sacrifice that a poor person has brought."[3] Thus, a collection from the assembly takes place. The monetary gifts or food for the poor will be part of the procession with the gifts that follows.

Regardless of whether they have made the bread or the wine themselves, it is preferable that the faithful always bring forth the gifts of the Eucharist to show their participation and contribution to the holy meal (GIRM2003, no. 73). Bread and wine are the fruit of nature and the blessings of a good God. In the early church, when threatened with Gnosticism and a rejection of creation as good, St. Irenaeus of Lyons (d. *ca.* 202) wrote, "For we are to present an offering to God, and in all things we are to be grateful to the Creator, doing so with a pure mind, in faith, without hypocrisy, with firm hope, in fervent love, being the first fruits of his own creation. The church alone offers this pure oblation to the Creator, offering it with a thanksgiving that comes from his creation."[4]

We do not bring God's gifts of grain and grapes in their natural state. We transform them into bread and wine, adding our own efforts of labor and culture to the sacrifice. This proclaims not only that nature is good but that human effort and all manner of culture are also good and worthy to be used for praise. The fruit of our work also will be taken up by God and transformed into gifts of eternal life. The world, culture, and history are not opposed to worship; rather, they come together in the simple gesture of offering bread and wine.

This "fruit of the earth and work of human hands" signify the offering of ourselves who, no less than the bread and wine, will be transformed through our eucharistic praying and communion. Ritual action is always

[3] Cyprian, *De opere et eleemosyna*, no. 15 = *PL* 4:612–13.

[4] Irenaeus, *Adversus haereses*, IV.18.4, in *Contre les Hérésies*, ed. Adeline Rousseau et al., *Sources chrétiennes* 100, 2 vols. (Paris: Cerf, 1965), 2:606–7 = Johnson, 1:80.

self-engaging and full of risk. Through our offering gestures we open ourselves to the possibility that we will be changed forever. We cannot pray to the living God to receive us and our gifts without the real possibility that God will accept these offerings and make us and them the Body of Christ. Such is our faith; such is our hope. It is a risk we take in the belief that whatever we have left behind will be repaid a hundredfold in this life and the next. Since we do not live our lives all at once, we come back again and again to Eucharist to offer ourselves and our gifts in order that bit by bit we may be transformed into the very One we receive in communion.

Bringing forth gifts for the eucharistic celebration and for the poor also symbolizes the assembly's true participation with the priest in the offering of Christ. *SC*—which stresses the full, conscious, and active participation of the assembly throughout the Mass—speaks particularly of the offering of Christ and of us:

> The church, therefore, spares no effort in trying to ensure that, when present at this mystery of faith, Christian believers should not be there as strangers or silent spectators. On the contrary, having a good grasp of it through the rites and prayers, they should take part in the sacred action, actively, fully aware, and devoutly. . . . Offering the immaculate victim, not only through the hands of the priest but also together with him, they should learn to offer themselves. (no. 48)

By way of anticipation, the assembly, through its representatives, brings forth what is necessary for the sacrifice of the Mass. Then, through the EP, at the invitation of the priest, "the entire congregation of the faithful should join itself with Christ . . . in the offering of Sacrifice" (GIRM2003, no. 78). Thus they learn to offer themselves, entering into the paschal mystery through, with, and in Christ.

Presenting the Gifts (ICEL2010, no. 22)

The priest receives the gifts of bread and wine, as well as the collection for the church and the poor, from a representative group of the faithful. Those who bring up the gifts represent the many who have contributed either the eucharistic gifts or the collection. The procession streams through the gathered assembly—sometimes led by servers with candles, sometimes not, but always with the dignity that befits an offering for Eucharist. The quality of the eucharistic gifts should be obvious: "The meaning of the sign demands that the material for the Eucharistic celebration truly have the appearance of food" (GIRM2003, no. 321). The bread should be made of wheat flour, unleavened, and recently baked. It ought to be of such shape as to give the appearance that we are all partaking of the one loaf, the one Body given up for us, and it should be sufficient for the communion of all. While many parishes continue to use the wheaten hosts from companies or religious communities who make such, an increasing number are calling upon members of the assembly to supply the bread from their own ovens. This further strengthens the bread symbol as a true gift from the people themselves. The wine should be pure and not mixed with any extraneous substances. It is unlikely, however, that the wine is the actual work of the members of the assembly, but in some cases, this could be the case. It too should be of sufficient quantity to provide for the whole assembly.

Blessing Prayers over the Bread and Wine (ICEL2010, nos. 23–25)

Taking the paten with the bread, the priest elevates it slightly and says quietly the prayer of blessing. There is a slight change in language here ("we have received the bread we offer you"). The addition of "you" makes the object of offering clearer. The change from "which earth has given and human hands have made" to "fruit of the earth and work of human hands"—a more faithful rendering of the Latin text—should hold no pastoral difficulties other than the need to become accustomed to a new text. If the offertory chant is finished or was not sung, the prayer may be said aloud and the people respond, "Blessed be God for ever" (ICEL2010, no. 23). He then places the paten with the bread on the altar.

Next the wine is prepared. Either the priest or the deacon pours a little water into the wine saying: "By the mystery of this water and wine may we come to share in the divinity of Christ who humbled himself to share in our humanity" (ICEL2010, no. 24). Some have argued that "may we come to share" is a weak translation of *efficiamur*, not conveying that it is by the power of God that we come to share divinity. Nonetheless, this prayer effectively proclaims the divine *commercium*, the great exchange of gifts: the mystery of Christ made flesh for us and for our sake. We pray through the priest that the Son of God who took on human flesh will share divinity with us. The prayer is said quietly by the priest, suggesting that it is a minor moment, but the sentiment of the prayer is quite profound and is a foreshadowing of what is to come. It will take on greater importance when it is couched in the epicletic prayer to the Spirit during the EP (e.g., ICEL2010, no. 113, below), that we will be transformed and saved by our communion with the Lord.

The priest raises the chalice of wine a little above the altar and prays a prayer similar to that said over the bread. He then places the chalice on the corporal and makes a profound bow, praying "that he may exercise his ministry with greater attention and devotion" (GIRM2003, no. 143). Note that the prayer (ICEL2010, no. 26) is said in the plural; it is a prayer that we be acceptable to God and that our sacrifice be pleasing. There is only one sacrifice, although there are differences in the ministers and their liturgical functions.

Incensation (ICEL2010, no. 27)

The thurifer, deacon, server, or some other minister brings the incense boat and the thurible to the priest who spoons incense onto the burning coals and blesses the smoke, making the sign of the cross with his hand. The priest then incenses the gifts by making three swings of the thurible toward them or by making the sign of the cross over them. He then goes around the altar and the cross and incenses them. Following this, the priest gives the thurible to the minister who makes a profound bow toward the priest and incenses him with three swings of the thurible and bows again. He likewise comes before the assembly, bows, and incenses them with three swings, bowing again at the end. Incense is a traditional sign of reverence and had been used to bless the gifts and the priest alike; happily, the incensing of the assembly was added to the *OM* after Vatican II (cf. *IGMR1969*, no. 51). It is due to the priest's sacred ministry and the dignity of the People of God by virtue of their baptism that they are incensed (GIRM2003, no. 75). The incensing signifies that the church's prayer and offering rise to God as the incense itself rises upward. We can only pray that we and our gifts will be become acceptable to the living God.

Washing of the Hands (ICEL2010, no. 28)

The priest prays in the name of the church, but there are times during the Eucharist that he prays in his own name, e.g., before the gospel, here at the preparation of the gifts, and also before and after his own communion (ICEL2010, nos. 14, 28, and 131). At this point in the preparation of the gifts the priest moves to the side of the altar and, assisted by a server, washes his hands and dries them with a towel. Though a minor gesture, the authenticity of liturgical signs demands that a reasonable amount of water and a towel of suitable size be used. As the priest washes his hands, he quietly recites a text asking God to cleanse him of sin.

Invitation to Prayer (ICEL2010, no. 29)

The priest and assembly then engage in a dialogue: an invitation to pray and a response by the people. The English text has changed from "our sacrifice" to "my sacrifice and yours." Anscar Chupungco cautions not to interpret "my sacrifice and yours" as two separate sacrifices, as a more literal translation of the Latin texts would read "my sacrifice, which is also your sacrifice."[5] In the people's response the only textual change is the addition of "holy" as a description of the church, a more literal translation of the Latin text.

Here, ritual redundancy is the rule. Having brought our gifts to the altar, the priest and assembly bless God for them. We then incense the gifts in a gesture of reverence, anticipating the offering.

Finally, we pray that our gifts be acceptable to God—but that is not all; we also pray that the gifts we offer redound to us "for our good and the good of all his holy Church." The Eucharist weaves a rhythm of offering and receiving again and again; each time we offer the gifts they are transformed and given back to us in greater measure. In this holy exchange of gifts, we always receive more than we can ever give. The climax of this mutual exchange of gifts is the communion rite during which we receive the Body and Blood of the Lord. From this climactic moment we are sent out to be what we have received, the very Body of Christ. Every Eucharist exhibits this rhythm of a holy exchange of gifts and a sending forth to make the reception of Our Lord fruitful. In a sense, we should not close the Eucharist with the sign of the cross and give the impression that our worship is sufficient in and of itself, for it is not complete until our worship moves toward ethical action.

Prayer over the Offerings (ICEL2010, no. 30)

The priest extends his hands in the *orans* gesture, indicating that this prayer is made to God, as he says the "Prayer over the Offerings"— a more faithful translation of *super oblata* than ICEL1973's "Prayer over the Gifts." This prayer from the Missal is one of the three proper prayers for the day. It basically asks that God may sanctify these gifts, make them holy, and so transform us in our sharing of them. The prayer for the Thursday after January 2 speaks of the holy exchange of gifts mentioned above: "Receive our oblation, O Lord, by which is brought about a glorious exchange that,

[5] See Chupungco, 220 above.

by offering what you have given, we may merit to receive your very self." The people make this prayer their own with the acclamation "Amen." Now that we and our gifts have been prepared, it is time to begin the great EP.

Eucharistic Prayer I

The Latin Text

Prex Eucharistica I
seu Canon Romanus

83. ℣. Dóminus vobíscum.
℟. Et cum spíritu tuo.

℣. Sursum corda.
℟. Habémus ad Dóminum.

℣. Grátias agámus Dómino Deo nostro.
℟. Dignum et iustum est.

Sequitur Praefatio iuxta rubricas proferenda, quae concluditur:

Sanctus, Sanctus, Sanctus Dóminus Deus Sabaóth.
Pleni sunt caeli et terra glória tua.
Hosánna in excélsis.
Benedíctus qui venit in nómine Dómini.
Hosánna in excélsis.

84. Sacerdos, manibus extensis, dicit:

Te ígitur, clementíssime Pater,
per Iesum Christum, Fílium tuum,
Dóminum nostrum,
súpplices rogámus ac pétimus,

iungit manus et dicit:

uti accépta hábeas

signat semel super panem et calicem simul, dicens:

et benedícas ✠ haec dona, haec múnera,
haec sancta sacrifícia illibáta,

extensis manibus prosequitur:

in primis, quae tibi offérimus
pro Ecclésia tua sancta cathólica:
quam pacificáre, custodíre, adunáre
et régere dignéris toto orbe terrárum:

The English Text

Eucharistic Prayer I
(The Roman Canon)

83. ℣. The Lord be with you.
℟. And with your spirit.

℣. Lift up your hearts.
℟. We lift them up to the Lord.

℣. Let us give thanks to the Lord our God.
℟. It is right and just.

Then follows the Preface to be used in accord with the rubrics, which concludes:

Holy, Holy, Holy Lord God of hosts.
Heaven and earth are full of your glory.
Hosanna in the highest.
Blessed is he who comes in the name of the Lord.
Hosanna in the highest.

84. The Priest, with hands extended, says:

To you, therefore, most merciful Father,
we make humble prayer and petition
through Jesus Christ, your Son, our Lord:

He joins his hands and says:

that you accept

He makes the Sign of the Cross once over the bread and chalice together, saying:

and bless ✠ these gifts, these offerings,
these holy and unblemished sacrifices,

With hands extended, he continues:

which we offer you firstly
for your holy catholic Church.
Be pleased to grant her peace,
to guard, unite and govern her
throughout the whole world,

una cum fámulo tuo Papa nostro N.
et Antístite nostro N.*
et ómnibus orthodóxis atque cathólicae
et apostólicae fídei cultóribus.

85. Commemoratio pro vivis.

Meménto, Dómine,
famulórum famularúmque tuárum N. et N.

Iungit manus et orat aliquantulum pro quibus orare intendit.

Deinde, manibus extensis, prosequitur:

et ómnium circumstántium,
quorum tibi fides cógnita est et nota devótio,
pro quibus tibi offérimus:
vel qui tibi ófferunt hoc sacrifícium laudis,
pro se suísque ómnibus:
pro redemptióne animárum suárum,
pro spe salútis et incolumitátis suae:
tibíque reddunt vota sua
aetérno Deo, vivo et vero.

86. Infra Actionem.

Communicántes,
et memóriam venerántes,
in primis gloriósae semper Vírginis Maríae,
Genetrícis Dei et Dómini nostri Iesu Christi:
† sed et beáti Ioseph, eiúsdem Vírginis Sponsi,
et beatórum Apostolórum ac Mártyrum tuórum,
Petri et Pauli, Andréae,
(Iacóbi, Ioánnis,
Thomae, Iacóbi, Philíppi,
Bartholomaéi, Matthaéi,
Simónis et Thaddaéi:
Lini, Cleti, Cleméntis, Xysti,
Cornélii, Cypriáni,
Lauréntii, Chrysógoni,
Ioánnis et Pauli,

* Hic fieri potest mentio de Episcopis Coadiutore vel Auxiliaribus, vel de alio Episcopo, ut in *Institutione generali Missalis Romani*, n. 149, notatur.

together with your servant N. our Pope
and N. our Bishop,*
and all those who, holding to the truth,
hand on the catholic and apostolic faith.

85. Commemoration of the Living.

Remember, Lord, your servants N. and N.

The Priest joins his hands and prays briefly for those for whom he intends to pray.

Then, with hands extended, he continues:

and all gathered here,
whose faith and devotion are known to you.
For them, we offer you this sacrifice of praise
or they offer it for themselves
and all who are dear to them:
for the redemption of their souls,
in hope of health and well-being,
and paying their homage to you,
the eternal God, living and true.

86. Within the Action.

In communion with those whose memory
we venerate,
especially the glorious ever-Virgin Mary,
Mother of our God and Lord, Jesus Christ,
† and blessed Joseph, her Spouse,
your blessed Apostles and Martyrs,
Peter and Paul, Andrew,
(James, John,
Thomas, James, Philip,
Bartholomew, Matthew,
Simon and Jude;
Linus, Cletus, Clement, Sixtus,
Cornelius, Cyprian,
Lawrence, Chrysogonus,
John and Paul,

* Mention may be made here of the Coadjutor Bishop, or Auxiliary Bishops, as noted in the *General Instruction of the Roman Missal*, no. 149.

Cosmae et Damiáni)
et ómnium Sanctórum tuórum;
quorum méritis precibúsque concédas,
ut in ómnibus protectiónis tuae muniámur auxílio.
(Per Christum Dóminum nostrum. Amen.)

COMMUNICANTES PROPRIA

In Nativitate Domini et per octavam

Communicántes,
et (noctem sacratíssimam) diem sacratíssimum celebrántes,
(qua) quo beátae Maríae intemeráta virgínitas
huic mundo édidit Salvatórem:
sed et memóriam venerántes,
in primis eiúsdem gloriósae semper Vírginis Maríae,
Genetrícis eiúsdem Dei et Dómini nostri Iesu Christi: †

In Epiphania Domini

Communicántes,
et diem sacratíssimum celebrántes,
quo Unigénitus tuus, in tua tecum glória coaetérnus,
in veritáte carnis nostrae visibíliter corporális appáruit:
sed et memóriam venerántes,
in primis gloriósae semper Vírginis Maríae,
Genetrícis eiúsdem Dei et Dómini nostri Iesu Christi: †

A Missa Vigiliae paschalis usque ad dominicam II Paschae

Communicántes,
et (noctem sacratíssimam) diem sacratíssimum celebrántes
Resurrectiónis Dómini nostri Iesu Christi secúndum carnem:
sed et memóriam venerántes,
in primis gloriósae semper Vírginis Maríae,
Genetrícis eiúsdem Dei et Dómini nostri Iesu Christi: †

In Ascensione Domini

Communicántes,
et diem sacratíssimum celebrántes,
quo Dóminus noster, unigénitus Fílius tuus,

Cosmas and Damian)
and all your Saints;
we ask that through their merits and prayers,
in all things we may be defended
by your protecting help.
(Through Christ our Lord. Amen.)

PROPER FORMS OF THE *COMMUNICANTES*

On the Nativity of the Lord and throughout the Octave

Celebrating the most sacred night (day)
on which blessed Mary the immaculate Virgin
brought forth the Savior for this world,
and in communion with those whose memory we venerate,
especially the glorious ever-Virgin Mary,
Mother of our God and Lord, Jesus Christ, †

On the Epiphany of the Lord

Celebrating the most sacred day
on which your Only Begotten Son,
eternal with you in your glory,
appeared in a human body, truly sharing our flesh,
and in communion with those whose memory we venerate,
especially the glorious ever-Virgin Mary,
Mother of our God and Lord, Jesus Christ, †

From the Mass of the Easter Vigil until the Second Sunday of Easter

Celebrating the most sacred night (day)
of the Resurrection of our Lord Jesus Christ in the flesh,
and in communion with those whose memory we venerate,
especially the glorious ever-Virgin Mary,
Mother of our God and Lord, Jesus Christ, †

On the Ascension of the Lord

Celebrating the most sacred day
on which your Only Begotten Son, our Lord,
placed at the right hand of your glory
our weak human nature,

unítam sibi fragilitátis nostrae substántiam
in glóriae tuae déxtera collocávit:
sed et memóriam venerántes,
in primis gloriósae semper Vírginis Maríae,
Genetrícis eiúsdem Dei et Dómini nostri Iesu Christi: †

In dominica Pentecostes

Communicántes,
et diem sacratíssimum Pentecóstes celebrántes,
quo Spíritus Sanctus
Apóstolis in ígneis linguis appáruit:
sed et memóriam venerántes,
in primis gloriósae semper Vírginis Maríae,
Genetrícis Dei et Dómini nostri Iesu Christi: †

---

87. Manibus extensis, prosequitur:

Hanc ígitur oblatiónem servitútis nostrae,
sed et cunctae famíliae tuae,
quaésumus, Dómine, ut placátus accípias:
diésque nostros in tua pace dispónas,
atque ab aetérna damnatióne nos éripi
et in electórum tuórum iúbeas grege numerári.

Iungit manus.

(Per Christum Dóminum nostrum. Amen.)

A Missa Vigiliae paschalis usque ad dominicam II Paschae

Hanc ígitur oblatiónem servitútis nostrae,
sed et cunctae famíliae tuae,
quam tibi offérimus
pro his quoque, quos regeneráre dignátus es ex aqua et Spíritu Sancto,
tríbuens eis remissiónem ómnium peccatórum,
quaesumus, Dómine, ut placátus accípias:
diésque nostros in tua pace dispónas,
atque ab aetérna damnatióne nos éripi
et in electórum tuórum iúbeas grege numerári.

Iungit manus.

(Per Christum Dóminum nostrum. Amen.)

which he had united to himself,
and in communion with those whose memory we venerate,
especially the glorious ever-Virgin Mary,
Mother of our God and Lord, Jesus Christ, †

On Pentecost Sunday

Celebrating the most sacred day of Pentecost,
on which the Holy Spirit
appeared to the Apostles in tongues of fire,
and in communion with those whose memory we venerate,
especially the glorious ever-Virgin Mary,
Mother of our God and Lord, Jesus Christ, †

---

87. With hands extended, the Priest continues:

Therefore, Lord, we pray:
graciously accept this oblation of our service,
that of your whole family;
order our days in your peace,
and command that we be delivered from eternal damnation
and counted among the flock of those you have chosen.

He joins his hands.

(Through Christ our Lord. Amen.)

From the Mass of the Easter Vigil until the Second Sunday of Easter

Therefore, Lord, we pray:
graciously accept this oblation of our service,
that of your whole family,
which we make to you
also for those to whom you have been pleased to give
the new birth of water and the Holy Spirit,
granting them forgiveness of all their sins;
order our days in your peace,
and command that we be delivered from eternal damnation
and counted among the flock of those you have chosen.

He joins his hands.

(Through Christ our Lord. Amen.)

---

88. Tenens manus expansas super oblata, dicit:

Quam oblatiónem tu, Deus, in ómnibus, quaésumus,
benedíctam, adscríptam, ratam,
rationábilem, acceptabilémque fácere dignéris:
ut nobis Corpus et Sanguis fiat dilectíssimi Fílii tui,
Dómini nostri Iesu Christi.

Iungit manus.

89. In formulis quae sequuntur, verba Domini proferantur distincte et aperte, prouti natura eorundem verborum requirit.

Qui, prídie quam paterétur,

accipit panem,
eumque parum elevatum super altare tenens,
prosequitur:

accépit panem in sanctas ac venerábiles manus suas,

elevat oculos,

et elevátis óculis in caelum
ad te Deum Patrem suum omnipoténtem,
tibi grátias agens benedíxit,
fregit,
dedítque discípulis suis, dicens:

parum se inclinat

ACCÍPITE ET MANDUCÁTE EX HOC OMNES:
HOC EST ENIM CORPUS MEUM,
QUOD PRO VOBIS TRADÉTUR.

Hostiam consecratam ostendit populo, reponit super patenam, et genuflexus adorat.

90. Postea prosequitur:

Símili modo, postquam cenátum est,

accipit calicem,
eumque parum elevatum super altare tenens, prosequitur:

accípiens et hunc praeclárum cálicem
in sanctas ac venerábiles manus suas,
item tibi grátias agens benedíxit,
dedítque discípulis suis, dicens:

88. Holding his hands extended over the offerings, he says:

Be pleased, O God, we pray,
to bless, acknowledge,
and approve this offering in every respect;
make it spiritual and acceptable,
so that it may become for us
the Body and Blood of your most beloved Son,
our Lord Jesus Christ.

He joins his hands.

89. In the formulas that follow, the words of the Lord should be pronounced clearly and distinctly, as the nature of these words requires.

On the day before he was to suffer,

He takes the bread
and, holding it slightly raised above the altar, continues:

he took bread in his holy and venerable hands,

He raises his eyes.

and with eyes raised to heaven
to you, O God, his almighty Father,
giving you thanks, he said the blessing,
broke the bread
and gave it to his disciples, saying:

He bows slightly.

TAKE THIS, ALL OF YOU, AND EAT OF IT,
FOR THIS IS MY BODY,
WHICH WILL BE GIVEN UP FOR YOU.

He shows the consecrated host to the people, places it again on the paten, and genuflects in adoration.

90. After this, the Priest continues:

In a similar way, when supper was ended,

He takes the chalice
and, holding it slightly raised above the altar, continues:

he took this precious chalice
in his holy and venerable hands,
and once more giving you thanks, he said the blessing
and gave the chalice to his disciples, saying:

parum se inclinat

ACCÍPITE ET BÍBITE EX EO OMNES:
HIC EST ENIM CALIX SÁNGUINIS MEI
NOVI ET AETÉRNI TESTAMÉNTI,
QUI PRO VOBIS ET PRO MULTIS EFFUNDÉTUR
IN REMISSIÓNEM PECCATÓRUM.
HOC FÁCITE IN MEAM COMMEMORATIÓNEM.

Calicem ostendit populo, deponit super corporale, et genuflexus adorat.

91. Deinde dicit:

Mystérium fídei.

Et populus prosequitur, acclamans:

Mortem tuam annuntiámus, Dómine,
et tuam resurrectiónem confitémur, donec vénias.

Vel:

Quotiescúmque manducámus panem hunc
et cálicem bíbimus,
mortem tuam annuntiámus, Dómine, donec vénias.

Vel:

Salvátor mundi, salva nos,
qui per crucem et resurrectiónem tuam liberásti nos.

92. Deinde sacerdos, extensis manibus, dicit:

Unde et mémores, Dómine,
nos servi tui,
sed et plebs tua sancta,
eiúsdem Christi, Fílii tui, Dómini nostri,
tam beátae passiónis,
necnon et ab ínferis resurrectiónis,
sed et in caelos gloriósae ascensiónis:
offérimus praeclárae maiestáti tuae
de tuis donis ac datis
hóstiam puram,
hóstiam sanctam,
hóstiam immaculátam,
Panem sanctum vitae aetérnae
et Cálicem salútis perpétuae.

He bows slightly.

TAKE THIS, ALL OF YOU, AND DRINK FROM IT,
FOR THIS IS THE CHALICE OF MY BLOOD,
THE BLOOD OF THE NEW AND ETERNAL COVENANT,
WHICH WILL BE POURED OUT FOR YOU AND FOR MANY
FOR THE FORGIVENESS OF SINS.
DO THIS IN MEMORY OF ME.

He shows the chalice to the people, places it on the corporal, and genuflects in adoration.

91. Then he says:

The mystery of faith.

And the people continue, acclaiming:

We proclaim your Death, O Lord,
and profess your Resurrection
until you come again.

Or:

When we eat this Bread and drink this Cup,
we proclaim your Death, O Lord,
until you come again.

Or:

Save us, Savior of the world,
for by your Cross and Resurrection
you have set us free.

92. Then the Priest, with hands extended, says:

Therefore, O Lord,
as we celebrate the memorial of the blessed Passion,
the Resurrection from the dead,
and the glorious Ascension into heaven
of Christ, your Son, our Lord,
we, your servants and your holy people,
offer to your glorious majesty
from the gifts that you have given us,
this pure victim,
this holy victim,
this spotless victim,
the holy Bread of eternal life
and the Chalice of everlasting salvation.

93. Supra quae propítio ac seréno vultu
respícere dignéris:
et accépta habére,
sícuti accépta habére dignátus es
múnera púeri tui iusti Abel,
et sacrifícium Patriárchae nostri Abrahae,
et quod tibi óbtulit summus sacérdos tuus Melchísedech,
sanctum sacrifícium, immaculátam hóstiam.

94. Inclinatus, iunctis manibus, prosequitur:

Súpplices te rogámus, omnípotens Deus:
iube haec perférri per manus sancti Angeli tui
in sublíme altáre tuum,
in conspéctu divínae maiestátis tuae;
ut, quotquot ex hac altáris participatióne
sacrosánctum Fílii tui Corpus et Sánguinem sumpsérimus,

erigit se atque seipsum signat, dicens:

omni benedictióne caelésti et grátia repleámur.

Iungit manus.

(Per Christum Dóminum nostrum. Amen.)

95. Commemoratio pro defunctis

Manibus extensis, dicit:

Meménto étiam, Dómine,
famulórum famularúmque tuárum N. et N.,
qui nos praecessérunt cum signo fídei,
et dórmiunt in somno pacis.

Iungit manus et orat aliquantulum pro iis defunctis, pro quibus orare intendit.

Deinde, extensis manibus, prosequitur:

Ipsis, Dómine, et ómnibus in Christo quiescéntibus,
locum refrigérii, lucis et pacis,
ut indúlgeas, deprecámur.

Iungit manus.

(Per Christum Dóminum nostrum. Amen.)

93. Be pleased to look upon these offerings
with a serene and kindly countenance,
and to accept them,
as once you were pleased to accept
the gifts of your servant Abel the just,
the sacrifice of Abraham, our father in faith,
and the offering of your high priest Melchizedek,
a holy sacrifice, a spotless victim.

94. Bowing, with hands joined, he continues:

In humble prayer we ask you, almighty God:
command that these gifts be borne
by the hands of your holy Angel
to your altar on high
in the sight of your divine majesty,
so that all of us, who through this participation at the altar
receive the most holy Body and Blood of your Son,

He stands upright again and signs himself with the Sign of the Cross, saying:

may be filled with every grace and heavenly blessing.

He joins his hands.

(Through Christ our Lord. Amen.)

95. Commemoration of the Dead

With hands extended, the Priest says:

Remember also, Lord, your servants N. and N.,
who have gone before us with the sign of faith
and rest in the sleep of peace.

He joins his hands and prays briefly for those who have died and for whom he intends to pray.

Then, with hands extended, he continues:

Grant them, O Lord, we pray,
and all who sleep in Christ,
a place of refreshment, light and peace.

He joins his hands.

(Through Christ our Lord. Amen.)

96. Manu dextera percutit sibi pectus, dicens:

Nobis quoque peccatóribus fámulis tuis,

et extensis manibus prosequitur:

de multitúdine miseratiónum tuárum sperántibus,
partem áliquam et societátem donáre dignéris
cum tuis sanctis Apóstolis et Martyribus:
cum Ioánne, Stéphano,
Matthía, Bárnaba,
(Ignátio, Alexándro,
Marcellíno, Petro,
Felicitáte, Perpétua,
Agatha, Lúcia,
Agnéte, Caecília, Anastásia)
et ómnibus Sanctis tuis:
intra quorum nos consórtium,
non aestimátor mériti,
sed véniae, quaesumus, largítor admítte.

Iungit manus.

Per Christum Dóminum nostrum.

97. Et prosequitur:

Per quem haec ómnia, Dómine,
semper bona creas, sanctíficas, vivíficas, benedícis,
et praestas nobis.

98. Accipit patenam cum hostia et calicem, et utrumque elevans, dicit:

Per ipsum, et cum ipso, et in ipso,
est tibi Deo Patri omnipoténti,
in unitáte Spíritus Sancti,
omnis honor et glória
per ómnia saécula saeculórum.

Populus acclamat:

Amen.

Deinde sequitur ritus communionis.

96. He strikes his breast with his right hand, saying:

To us, also, your servants, who, though sinners,

And, with hands extended, he continues:

hope in your abundant mercies,
graciously grant some share
and fellowship with your holy Apostles and Martyrs:
with John the Baptist, Stephen,
Matthias, Barnabas,
(Ignatius, Alexander,
Marcellinus, Peter,
Felicity, Perpetua,
Agatha, Lucy,
Agnes, Cecilia, Anastasia)
and all your Saints;
admit us, we beseech you,
into their company,
not weighing our merits,
but granting us your pardon,

He joins his hands.

through Christ our Lord.

97. And he continues:

Through whom
you continue to make all these good things, O Lord;
you sanctify them, fill them with life,
bless them, and bestow them upon us.

98. He takes the chalice and the paten with the host and, raising both, he says:

Through him, and with him, and in him,
O God, almighty Father,
in the unity of the Holy Spirit,
all glory and honor is yours,
for ever and ever.

The people acclaim:

Amen.

Then follows the Communion Rite.

History of the Latin Text and Rite

John Baldovin

Origins

The Roman Canon—or EP I in the current Roman Missal—is one of the most venerable prayers in the Christian tradition. Its remote origins are obscure. It is certainly possible that some of its elements existed in Greek, and we shall explore the relationship between parts of the prayer and the Alexandrian tradition. Important elements of the text as we know it, however, come from the fourth century when the Roman Church first formally adopted Latin as its liturgical language.[1]

The earliest evidence that we have for the Roman Canon comes from the mystagogical lectures of Ambrose of Milan. In his *De sacramentis* 5:21, Ambrose writes:[2]

Vis scire, quam verbis caelestibus consecretur? Accipe, quae sunt verba. Dicit sacerdos:	Do you want to know by what heavenly words it is consecrated? Accept what the words are. The priest says:
Fac nobis, inquit, hanc oblationem scriptam, rationabilem, acceptabilem, quod est figura corporis et sanguinis Domini nostri Jesu Christi.	Make this offering approved, reasonable, and acceptable for us, *because it is the figure of the body and blood of our Lord Jesus Christ.*
Qui pride quam pateretur, in sanctis manibus suis accepit panem, respexit ad caelum, ad te, sancte Pater omnipotens aeterne Deus, gratias agens, benedixit, fregit, fractumque apostolis et discipulis suis tradidit dicens: Accepite et edite ex hoc omnes; hoc est enim corpus meum, quod pro multis confringetur. – Adverte!	Who on the night before he suffered took bread into his holy hands, looked up to heaven, to you holy Father, almighty eternal God, giving thanks, blessed, broke, and handed the broken (bread) to his apostles and disciples saying: Take and eat of this all of you: For this is my body which will be broken for many. (Be attentive!)

[1] See Bryan Spinks, "The Roman Canon Missae," in *Prex Eucharistica*, 3:131–37; also, Ostdiek and Pecklers, 37 above.

[2] Latin text from *Prex Eucharistica*, 1:421–22; literal English translation by the author.

Similiter etiam calicem, postquam cenatum est, pridie quam pateretur, accepit, respexit ad caelum, ad te sancte Pater omnipotens aeterne Deus, gratias agens, benedixit, apostolis et discipulis suis tradidit dicens: Accipite et bibite ex hoc omnes; hic est enim sanguis meus.	Similarly, after supper, on the night before he suffered, he took the cup, looked up to heaven, to you holy Father almighty eternal God, giving thanks, blessed and handed it to his apostles and disciples saying: Take and drink from this all of you, for this is my blood. . . .
Deinde quantum sit sacramentum, cognosce. Vide quid dicat: Quotiescumque hoc feceritis, totiens commemorationem mei facietis, donec iterum adveniam.	Now, learn what a great sacrament this is. See what he says: As often as you do this, so often you make my commemoration until I come again.
Et sacerdos dicit: Ergo memores gloriosissime eius passionis et ab inferis resurrectionis et in caelum ascensionis offerimus tibi hanc immaculatam hostiam, rationabilem hostiam, incruentam hostiam, hunc panem sanctum et calicem vitae aeternae.	And the priest says: Therefore remembering his most glorious passion, his resurrection from the dead and ascension into heaven, we offer to you this spotless victim, reasonable victim, bloodless victim, this holy bread and cup of eternal life.
Et petimus et precamur, uti hanc oblationem suscipias in sublime altare tuum per manus angelorum tuorum, sicut suscipere dignatus es munera pueri tui iusti Abel et sacrificium patriarchae nostri Abrahae et quod obtulit summus sacerdos Melchisedech.	And we beg and pray that you might take this oblation by the hands of your angels to your altar on high, just as you accepted the offerings of your righteous child, Abel, the sacrifice of our patriarch, Abraham, and that which the high priest, Melchizedek, offered.

Ambrose recounts the central portion of the EP as his Milanese neophytes would have heard it prayed on the night of their baptism. The earliest Roman liturgical texts (from the late seventh and the eighth centuries) witness (with some minor variations) to this same basic text—but with one major theological difference as demonstrated by the following chart.[3]

[3] Latin text from *Prex Eucharistica*, 1:433; English translations from Jasper & Cuming, 145 and 164–65, respectively.

Ambrose	**Roman Canon**
Fac nobis, inquit, hanc oblationem scriptam, rationabilem, acceptabilem, quod est figura corporis et sanguinis Domini nostri Jesu Christi.	Roman Canon: Quam oblationem tu, Deus, in omnibus, quaesumus, benedictam, ascriptam, ratam, rationabilem acceptabilemque digneris, ut nobis corpus et sanguis fiat dilectissimi Filii tui Domini Dei nostri Iesu Christi.
The priest says: Make for us this offering approved, reasonable, and acceptable, *because it is the figure of the body and blood of our Lord Jesus Christ.*	Vouchsafe, we beseech you, O God, to make this offering wholly blessed, approved, ratified, reasonable, and acceptable; *that it may become to us the body and blood of your dearly beloved Son Jesus Christ our Lord.*

The theological shift between Ambrose in the late fourth century and the Roman prayer in the early Middle Ages is dramatic. In Ambrose the consecration seems to take place because the bread and wine act as figures of the Body and Blood of the Lord. The later version of the Canon is much more explicit in asking God to consecrate the gifts.[4]

Apart from the witness of Ambrose, the writer known as Ambrosiaster refers to the phrase "your high priest Melchizedek" in the late fourth century.[5] In the late sixth century Gregory the Great affirmed that the prayer was written during the pontificate of Damasus (366–84). On the other hand, Josef Jungmann claims that a number of the prayers of the Canon (*Communicantes, Hanc igitur, Memento etiam,* and *Nobis quoque*) cannot be found at the beginning of the fifth century.[6]

Contemporary research on the EPs suggests that the institution narrative was not a part of any tradition prior to the fourth century and that the *Sanctus* may well be a fifth-century addition to the Roman Canon.[7] Walter Ray has argued that the Roman Canon shares a common ancestry with the

[4] On this question, see Enrico Mazza, *The Celebration of the Eucharist: The Origin of the Rite and the Development of Its Interpretation*, trans. Matthew J. O'Connell (Collegeville, MN: Liturgical Press, 1999), 141–43.

[5] Ambrosiaster, *Quaestiones Veteris et Novi Testamenti 109, De Melchisedec* (*PL* 35:2329); see Enrico Mazza, *The Eucharistic Prayers of the Roman Rite*, trans. Matthew J. O'Connell (New York: Pueblo, 1986), 57–58.

[6] Jungmann MRR, 1:55.

[7] See Matthieu Smyth, "The Anaphora of the So-Called 'Apostolic Tradition' and the Roman Eucharistic Prayer," in *Issues in Eucharistic Praying in East and West*, ed. Maxwell Johnson (Collegeville, MN: Liturgical Press, 2010), 94–97; also Robert Taft, "Mass without the Consecration?" *Worship* 77 (2003): 482–509.

Alexandrian Anaphora of St. Mark by comparing the structure of both with the third-century Strasbourg Papyrus Gk. 254.[8] In terms of content, one of the most interesting parallels between the Anaphora of St. Mark and the Roman Canon involves the preface of Mark and the *Supplices te*:

Anaphora of St. Mark – Greek[9]	**Roman Canon**
Receive, O God, the thank offerings of those who offer the sacrifices, at your holy and heavenly and spiritual altar in the vastnesses of heaven by the ministry of your archangels . . . as you accepted the gifts of your righteous Abel, the sacrifice of our father Abraham, the incense of Zachariah . . .	We humbly beseech you, almighty God, bid these things be borne by the hands of your angel to your altar on high, in the sight of your divine majesty, that all of us who have received the most holy body and blood of your Son, by partaking at this altar may be filled with all heavenly blessing and grace; through Christ our Lord.

It seems clear, therefore, that the Roman Canon was composed of a number of distinct prayers over the course of several centuries. This accounts for the rather confusing structure that it presents to modern-day readers.

It has been noted that the lack of an explicit epiclesis (i.e., invocation of the Holy Spirit) may well be a sign of the Roman Canon's great antiquity. It could be that explicit mention of the Holy Spirit only became part of eucharistic praying in the mid-fourth century when theological debates about the Trinity were in full swing.[10]

A final witness to the antiquity of at least the earliest versions of the Canon is Ambrose's reference to the image (*figura*) of Christ's body and blood. Enrico Mazza has argued that the "image theology" of the sacraments as witnessed in Ambrose and an equally ancient *post pridie* (post–institution narrative) prayer of the Old Spanish tradition is older than the explicit notion of consecration that the prayer later developed.[11]

[8] Walter Ray, "Rome and Alexandria: Two Cities, One Anaphoral Tradition," in Johnson, *Issues*, 99–127.

[9] English translation of the Anaphora of St. Mark from Jasper & Cuming, 62; of the Roman Canon, from Jasper & Cuming, 165. Smyth comments that the Archangel of the St. Mark Anaphora as well as in the homily from St. Ambrose is a figure of Christ ("Anaphora," 78).

[10] See Robert Taft, "From Logos to Spirit: The Early History of the Epiclesis," in *Gratias Agamus. Studien zum eucharistischen Hochgebet. Festschrift Balthasar Fischer*, ed. Andreas Heinz and Heinrich Rennings (Freiburg: Herder, 1992), 489–502; also Smyth, "Anaphora," 84.

[11] See Mazza, *The Eucharistic Prayers*, 68–70. The Old Spanish *post pridie* is: *Quorum oblationem benedictam, ratam, rationabilemque facere digneris que est imago et similitudo corporis et sanguinis*

Content of the Prayer

There seems to be a growing consensus that the classic EPs of the great traditions (Byzantine, Alexandrian, Roman, et al.) were not composed originally as units but rather the result of the fusion of a number of different elements.[12] This would go a long way toward explaining why the Roman Canon lacks clear logical progression. The Canon itself is usually what is referred to as the portion of the prayer that follows the preface and *Sanctus*. Jungmann has shown that the preface was originally considered part of the EP as a whole, as is quite clear in the Eastern traditions, which do not have variable prefaces like the Roman tradition does.[13] The classic Roman Canon contained thirteen elements (to which a memorial acclamation has been added in the Missal of Paul VI):

1. *Te igitur*: a prayer for the acceptance of the offering together with an intercession for the pope, local bishop, and the church as a whole
2. *Memento, Domine*: intercession for the living
3. *Communicantes*: association of the prayer with Mary, the apostles, and a number of local Roman martyrs[14]
4. *Hanc igitur*: another prayer for acceptance, which could contain an embolism for specific individuals, like the newly baptized. The sixth-century collection of prayers known as the *Veronense* contains a distinct formula for each Mass
5. *Quam oblationem*: a plea for consecration, the equivalent of what today would be considered a consecratory epiclesis
6. *Qui, pridie*: the narrative of institution
7. *Unde et memores*: a formula of anamnesis and offering
8. *Supra quae*: a third plea for acceptance
9. *Supplices te*: a second formula of consecration. Here, God is asked to have his angel ("angels" in Ambrose) bring the offering to the heavenly altar.[15] This doubling of the consecration could well be a sign that several prayers were joined to form the Canon

Jhesu Christi Filii tui ac Redemptoris nostri (from Marius Férotin, ed., *Le 'Liber mozarabicus sacramentorum' et les manuscrits mozarabes* 2 [Rome: CLV Edizioni Liturgiche, 1995 (1912)], 1440).

[12] See, for example, Paul Bradshaw, *Eucharistic Origins* (London: SPCK, 2004), 121–23.

[13] Jungmann MRR, 2:101–9.

[14] John XXIII (d. 1963) added St. Joseph in 1962.

[15] See Edward Kilmartin, *The Eucharist in the West*, ed. Robert Daly (Collegeville, MN: Liturgical Press, 1998), 106 and 130.

10. *Memento etiam*: intercession for the dead
11. *Nobis quoque*: another association of the prayer with the saints, including a number of women martyrs of the church in Rome, Sicily, and North Africa
12. *Per quem*: a prayer of blessing, most probably for other gifts brought to the altar[16]
13. *Per ipsum*: the concluding doxology and Amen

The Roman Canon remained stable from the sixth century up until *OM1969* with two exceptions. First, the commemoration of the dead (*Memento etiam*, no. 10 above) was not a feature of every liturgy. It is not found, for example, in the early eighth-century manuscript of the Gregorian Sacramentary, called the *Hadrianum*. On the other hand, the commemoration of the dead does begin to appear in some contemporary eighth-century documents such as the (Irish) Bobbio Missal.[17]

The other change has an even greater theological significance. The commemoration of the living (*Memento, Domine*, no. 2 above) at first read:

Pre-ninth-century Latin	**English translation**
Memento, Domine, famulorum famularumque tuarum et omnium circum adstantium quorum tibi fides cognita est et nota. Qui tibi offerunt hoc sacrificium laudis pro se suisque omnibus. . . .	Remember, Lord, your servants and all who stand around whose faith and devotion are known to you, who offer to you this sacrifice of praise for themselves and for all their own. . . .

However, in the editions of the Gregorian Sacramentary after the ninth century—beginning with the *Hucusque* or Supplement of Benedict of Aniane (d. 821)—the text was transformed to read:

Post-ninth-century Latin	**English translation**
Memento, Domine, famulorum famularumque tuarum et omnium circum adstantium quorum tibi fides cognita est et nota pro quibus offerimus, vel qui tibi offerunt hoc sacrificium laudis. . . .	Remember, Lord, your servants and all who stand around whose faith and devotion are known to you, for whom we offer or who themselves offer to you this sacrifice of praise. . . .

[16] Jungmann MRR, 2:260–61.
[17] Ibid., 2:238–39.

The addition of four words: *pro quibus offerimus, vel* represents a significant shift in the perception of who was doing the offering. Now it seems that the priest can substitute for the assembled faithful in offering the eucharistic sacrifice.

Present State of the Prayer

It is well known that there were a number of suggestions for the revision of the Roman Canon around the time of Vatican II. The proposal of Hans Küng would have abbreviated the prayer by eliminating much of the intercessory material. Karl Amon's proposal would have eliminated the first part of the Canon up until the institution narrative, substituting a short formula like that found at the beginning of EP II. Then the anamnesis and oblation would have taken place, followed by a prayer for acceptance of the sacrifice and the *Supplices te rogamus* and doxology.[18] These proposals would have abbreviated the text of the Canon. According to Annibale Bugnini, the chief architect of the liturgical reform, the Consilium did consider revision of the Roman Canon but ultimately came to the conclusion that one should not tamper with such a venerable text and that in view of the use of multiple anaphoras in the Eastern churches, the Roman Church might adopt several new additional EPs. Paul VI accepted that suggestion, saying, "The present anaphora is to be left unchanged; two or three anaphoras for use at particular specific times are to be composed or looked for."[19]

Thus, the Roman Canon appeared in *MR1970* virtually unchanged. There were two relatively minor changes made to the institution narrative.[20] First, the words *quod pro vobis tradetur* ("which will be given up for you") were added to the words over the bread in order to make the institution formula identical in all of the EPs. Second, the words *mysterium fidei* ("the mystery of faith") were eliminated from the words over the cup and were

[18] Mazza, *The Eucharistic Prayers*, 56.

[19] Bugnini, 449–50.

[20] "Minor" is of course a matter of judgment. The elimination of the words "mystery of faith" caused great consternation among traditionalists who saw this as a betrayal of fifteen hundred years of Catholic tradition. One of the harshest critics of the reformed Mass, for example, says the following: "This change shifts the centre of gravity in the Mass, and clearly shows the fundamental difference between the traditional missal and the new missal: in the former, the Mass is a sacrificial offering of the transubstantiated presence of Christ, while in the latter the Mass is understood as a memorial of Christ's Passover" (The Society of Saint Pius X, *The Problem of the Liturgical Reform: A Theological and Liturgical Study* [Kansas City, MO: Angelus Press, 2001], 12).

instead inserted after the narrative so as to introduce the memorial acclamation.[21] The introduction of a memorial acclamation (e.g., "We proclaim your Death, O Lord, and profess your Resurrection until you come again," ICEL2010, no. 91) is probably the most radical change made to the pre–Vatican II Canon of the Mass. The motive in adding the memorial acclamation (a feature found originally in the Christian East) was to increase the people's active participation in eucharistic praying.[22] The ending *Per Christum Dominum nostrum. Amen* ("Through Christ our Lord. Amen.") was made optional in four cases: at the end of the *Communicantes* (*OM2008*, no. 86), *Hanc igitur* (*OM2008*, no. 87), *Supplices te rogamus* (*OM2008*, no. 94), and *Memento etiam* (*OM2008*, no. 95). It has been retained at the end of the *Nobis quoque peccatoribus* (*OM2008*, no. 96). Finally, in terms of rubrics, some twenty-two signs of the cross were eliminated from the Canon and only one retained in the *Te igitur* prayer (*OM2008*, no. 84).

Conclusion

The Roman Canon remains a major monument of the Western liturgical tradition. The very fact that it has weathered the test of time for some sixteen hundred years is a testimony to its enduring value.

[21] See Witczak, 358.
[22] Bugnini, 454–55.

Excursus on Interpreting Eucharistic Prayers

David Power

In interpreting the EPs of *OM2008* one looks first for the meaning a prayer gives to the act of eucharistic worship as the action of the assembly and second for the way in which it expresses the mystery of salvation being celebrated. Prayers also have a particular background and history. While individual essays on the various EPs now in the Roman Missal will follow, their origins in a given culture and context, as well as their subsequent liturgical history, cannot be ignored.

Liturgical Latin[1] and the Prayer

LitAuth gives high credit to the liturgical meaning conveyed by the style and precision of vocabulary in the Latin of the Roman tradition. While it has the entire range of liturgical pieces in mind, these items are of particular importance in the Roman Canon, given its antiquity, it venerability, and its central place in worship. The Canon of the Mass is a specifically Christian construct that marks the endeavor to bring faith in the mystery of Christ into the context of Rome. In interpreting it we need to be mindful of its style, its vocabulary, the connection between prayer and ritual action, and the theological impact of the prayer as a whole in offering a way of celebrating the Christian mystery of salvation.[2]

[1] For the early development of liturgical Latin, see Christine Mohrmann, *Liturgical Latin: Its Origins and Character* (Washington, DC: The Catholic University of America Press, 1957). Numerous word studies are pertinent to interpretation but notable are two dictionaries still in print: Albert Blaise, *Le vocabulaire latin des principaux thèmes liturgiques* (Turnhout: Brepols, 1966); and Wilfrid Diamond, *Dictionary of Liturgical Latin* (Eugene, OR: Wipf and Stock Publishers, 2008 [1971]).

[2] The impact of the visual and of movement dictated by place and space, though always pertinent to meaning, is not considered here.

Liturgical Style

In writing of the style of Roman prayers, Christine Mohrmann notes the hieratic quality of·speech found in Roman euchology. The Latin of the Roman Mass is not the accustomed Latin of conversation or even business, nor is it tributary to any great extent to the language of the city's religious cults. It has a tone and even vocabulary that may have sounded unaccustomed and difficult to follow for many congregants. However, the distance between common-day speech and liturgical speech should not be exaggerated. The congregation might have been aware—from the style of prayer, from chant, and from the ambience—that they were brought into a world of mystery and of the holy. Yet, they knew this belonged to them because they recognized it as Latin: its style drew upon the potential of this tongue to speak the divine. The people were not held apart, as they would have been by Greek or Syriac, but neither were they rudely deposited into the vulgarities and commonplace of the street. Liturgical Latin exhibits a style that signals that people are invited—and need to be truly and sincerely invited—to pray along with the presider and sing along with the choir, so as to be one congregation with those who give them a collective and representative voice in what is sung or proclaimed.

Liturgical Vocabulary

Mohrmann notes in the emergence of Christian Latin the triple influence of the adoption of Greek terms, the popularization of expressions to make them commonly intelligible, and most fundamentally the biblical translations from Hebrew and Greek.[3] She also notes how liturgical Latin adopted a form all its own, often more juridical and more highly stylized than the Latin of biblical translation, but one that fit into a Roman context where order itself gave rise to awe. Of the Canon in particular, she notes the inclination "to accumulate words with roughly the same meaning, and, in general, to give the early texts [taken perhaps from Milan or even from early Greek texts] a more cumbrous, solemn wording."[4] This occurred even as the Canon borrowed from early Latin translations of the Greek Bible or took on contemporary legal terms consonant with Roman rhetorical or juridical style.

[3] She summarizes this in *Études sur le Latin des Chrétiens* (Rome: Edizioni di Storia e Letteratura, 1958), 98.

[4] Mohrmann, *Liturgical Latin*, 66; also, Mohrmann, *Études*, 83–102.

Mohrmann and Jungmann note the tendency to use an abundance of terms that are not clearly distinct in meaning. The older the Latin and the more authentically Roman, the more likely it is to string words together without wanting to give a precise meaning to each, but rather seeking a collective effect.[5] As for precision, in the composition of early liturgical texts we find that they do not always use the same word to correspond to a given Greek word: for example, to correspond to the Greek word *doxa* we find in different places the three Latin words *gloria*, *claritas*, and *maiestas*.[6] Rather than three words, each with a distinct meaning, they are evidence of the search for an appropriate Latin translation of one and the same Greek term.[7] The meaning of words could also change over time, as Jungmann notes for the term *rationabilis/em*. While in its early Christian usage it corresponded to the Greek *logikon*, by the time of Gregory the Great it meant simply "what was suited to reason or the nature of things."[8]

This raises a problem in interpreting Latin texts, such as the Roman Canon. One is hard put to say that a particular word has the same meaning every time. In word studies for early Roman and medieval sacramentaries, commentators are wont to go to the concordances of Deshusses, or even to the dictionary of Albert Blaise to find a shorter path, to unearth what meaning, or shades of meaning, are generally attached to words. This still has value for looking at contemporary texts, which means also looking at concordances for *MR2002*, such as those of Schnitker-Slaby[9] and Sodi-Toniolo[10] to see how even ancient words are used in it.

In the process of interpreting the Roman Canon, it is also necessary to recognize that it is internally important to that prayer that there be some variation and variability, both in texts and in style. That different texts were used for different occasions is evident in the choice of prefaces and of the forms for the *Communicantes*, *Memento*, and the *Hanc igitur*. Of the earliest

[5] For example, from the Roman Canon: *dignum et justum, aequum et salutare: benedictam, adscriptam, ratam, rationabilem, acceptabilem*. Mohrmann refers to the accumulation of terms in various parts of the Canon as "une recherche d'abondance, dans une accumulation de termes de valeur à peu près égale" (*Études*, 77).

[6] Diamond offers four meanings for *gloria* in his *Dictionary*: glory, honor, majesty, the reward of the saints; in *Le Vocabulaire Latin*, Blaise offers *gloire, majesté, puissance, gloire des élus*. Only context will tell more exactly which is intended.

[7] See Bernard Botte, "Maiestas," in Bernard Botte and Christine Mohrmann, *L'Ordinaire de la Messe. Texte critique, traduction et études* (Paris: Cerf, 1955), 111–13.

[8] Jungmann MRR, 2:189.

[9] Thaddäus A. Schnitker and Wolfgang A. Slaby, *Concordantia Verbalia Missalis Romani. Partes Euchologicae* (Münster: Aschendorff, 1983).

[10] Cf. list of abbreviations under Sodi, above xxi; this is not to be confused with their 2007 edition of *MR1570* referenced in this volume as Sodi-Tonolio.

prefaces found in the *Veronense*, Mohrmann in the works already cited remarks that their style is different from that part of the prayer beginning with *Te igitur*. While there was a more or less set pattern to follow, this part of the thanksgiving was meant to be improvised. What we have in the collection are texts that were likely composed *ad hoc* but thought worthy of repetition as the year went through its recurrent cycle. Even today, variability has to be taken into account in interpreting EP I in *OM2008*, since it retains the prayer's variable parts. Even if there is not the freedom of improvisation, there is the freedom of choice with the resultant effect on what is conveyed.

Prayer and Ritual

The relation between prayer and ritual action is inherent to the interpretation of the text, since the prayer is one to be prayed over the gifts presented in community and it is a prayer of access to the communion table. At the origins of the Roman Rite the presentation of these gifts had been ceremoniously made[11] so that it became clear over what Eucharist is made. It appears that the community was gathered around, led in prayer by the celebrant, since they are called the *circumstantes*. It would also be remarkable if the response to the invitation in the opening dialogue were not accompanied by some kind of bodily movement, significant of the lifting up of heart to be one in prayer with him who proclaims the prayer. Apart from noting that the faithful present the bread and wine, and other gifts (*OM2008*, no. 18), and the implicit invitation to look upon bread and chalice at the words of Jesus in the institution narrative and at the final doxology (*OM2008*, nos. 62, 63, 71), *OM2008* says nothing about the bodily actions or positions of the people.[12] For the priest, however, there are a number of ritual prescriptions that will be noted below.

[11] See Witczak, 203–4 above.

[12] Episcopal conferences have inserted their own directives, which now have a role in interpreting the prayer and its purpose for given congregations; also, the actions and postures of the people are addressed in *IGMR2002*, nos. 42–44, *et passim*.

Theology of the Latin Text and Rite

David Power

Theological Genius of the Roman Canon[1]

Commentators are often influenced by Edmund Bishop's "Genius of the Roman Rite"[2] in the admiration shown for its linguistic contours. Given the undeniable local character of the Roman Rite, one has to ask if there is not something more fundamental to the inspiration for worship found in this rite. In a postconciliar assessment of Bishop's insights, Burkhard Neunheuser suggested that its true genius was more theological than linguistic.[3] He highlighted mainly its christological focus, finding the whole meaning of the liturgy summarized in the phrase, *ad Patrem per Christum, suum Filium*, which expresses a sense of mediation that Neunheuser found maintained through the entire liturgy. This is certainly true of the Roman Canon. Whatever their variability and the possibility of improvisation, early prefaces—even those for the commemoration of martyrs—were centered on the

[1] Indispensable works for a theological commentary on the Roman Canon (in chronological order) are: Jungmann MRR; Louis Bouyer, *Eucharist: Theology and Spirituality of the Eucharistic Prayer* (Notre Dame, IN: University of Notre Dame Press, 1968), 227–43; Enrico Mazza, *The Eucharistic Prayers of the Roman Rite*, trans. Matthew J. O'Connell (New York: Pueblo, 1986), 36–87.

Studies on the history of the text include, Giovanni Di Napoli, "Il lento processo di formazione del canone romano," *Ecclesia orans* 17 (2000): 229–68; Enrico Mazza, *The Origins of the Eucharistic Prayer* (Collegeville, MN: Liturgical Press, 1995), 240–86; Adrien Nocent, "La liturgia dell'eucaristia" in *La liturgia eucaristia: Teologia e storia della celebrazione*, ed. Salvatore Marsili, Anamnesis 3:2 (Casale Monferrato: Casa Editrice Marietti, 1983), 225–70; Nocent, "La celebrazione dell'Eucaristia secondo il canone romano," in *La liturgia eucaristia*, 225–46; Bryan Spinks, "The Roman Canon Missae," in *Prex Eucharistica*, 3:131–37. For a theological-historical commentary also see Dominic Serra, "The Roman Canon: The Theological Significance of its Structure and Syntax," *Ecclesia orans* 20 (2003): 99–128; Josef Schmitz, "*Canon Romanus*," in *Prex Eucharistica*, 3:281–10. On the Roman Canon in the *Stowe Missal*, see Hugh Kennedy, "The Eucharistic Prayer in Early Irish Liturgical Practice," *Prex Eucharistica*, 3:227–32.

[2] In his *Liturgica Historica: Papers on the Liturgy and Religious Life of the Western Church* (Oxford: Clarendon Press, 1918), 1–19.

[3] Burkhard Neunheuser, "Roman Genius Revisited," in *Liturgy for the New Millennium: A Commentary on the Revised Sacramentary*, ed. Mark Francis and Keith Pecklers (Collegeville, MN: Liturgical Press, 2000), 35–48. Bouyer's study of the Roman Canon bears out the primacy of this theological structure in what is specific to Roman liturgy.

priestly mediation of Christ's sacrifice, his taking flesh and the shedding of his blood. This is still apparent in the revised prefaces of *MR2002*.

The *Sanctus* also plays an important part in expressing the sacramental presence of the divine worship established once and for all in Christ. It clearly places the people within this earthly sanctuary of God's abode among his people through his Son and of people's access to God with their gifts through this same Son. The offering of Christ is present sacramentally in the offerings of the church with its thanksgiving, praise, intercession, and earthly gifts. The rhythm of offering (for which the *supra oblata* are important), thanksgiving, praise, intercession, and doxology give the people a participation in the mediation of the Son whom the Father sent. This is still EP I's *lex orandi*. This genius or law of prayer is not tied to its particularly local cultural expression but lies in the deep structures of worship that it embodies.[4]

This does not mean that attention to language is unimportant, but it does mean that for hermeneutics and an appropriation into other cultural and linguistic contexts, interpreters of the Roman liturgy have to be attentive to the deep structures of the commemorative worship expressed. The composition of the Roman liturgy was an endeavor rooted in a reading of the Bible translated into a known language. This translation was a transposition of the received revelation into a context both ancient and new. In the interpretation of this prayer, therefore, it is important to distinguish between linguistic niceties and a basic prayer structure. The latter is more important and enduring than the former.

It is also the genius of the Roman Rite to allow for a change in style according to which particular form of prayer is being prayed.[5] In early EPs it may be that the entire prayer was simply cantillated. With the emergence of the Roman Rite, chant was introduced for the preface, while the text after the *Sanctus* (sung by schola or congregation) was spoken; by at least 750 it was inaudible to all but those closest to the priest. This fit well with the direction taken by the prayer. The first part was clearly a song of praise, a

[4] The strong accent on intercession, and then the placement of the institution narrative within a prayer of intercession rather than of thanksgiving, has been compared to types of memorial Jewish prayer other than the table *berakoth* by Bouyer, *Eucharist*, and Cesare Giraudo, *La struttura letteraria della preghiera eucaristica: Saggio sulla genesis letteraria di una forma*, Analectica Biblica 92 (Rome: Pontificium Institutum Biblicum, 1981). One does not have to settle the historical question of their influence on Christian Eucharist to see the value of the comparison.

[5] Gerard Rouwhorst, "The Design of Sung Eucharistic Prayer in the Tradition," in *Liturgy and Muse: The Eucharistic Prayer*, ed. Anton Vernooij (Leuven-Paris-Dudley, MA: Peeters, 2002), 13–36.

hostia laudis. After the *Sanctus*, however, the priest was occupied with intercessions and offerings, in keeping with what the Lord was remembered to have done at the Last Supper. This he did not so much *in persona Christi* as *in persona ecclesiae*, acting on the people's behalf in setting forth their offerings and in presenting their intercessions.

The modifications made to the Roman Canon in *OM2008* are uncertain in regard to prayer tone. For the most part there is an assumption that the whole prayer may be said in the same tone of voice and with the same position of the hands, though the preface may be sung; *OM2008* further notes that it is permitted to sing the parts of the EP provided with notation, especially the principal parts (no. 32). There is little in style to mark the inner movement within the prayer from thanksgiving and praise to intercession and offering.

Opening Dialogue (*OM2008*, no. 83)[6]

The opening dialogue brings the whole congregation together in the EP, a "prayer of thanksgiving and sanctification" (GIRM2003, no. 78). In the people's response, the Pauline form is adopted, *cum spiritu tuo*, patterned on 2 Corinthians 13:13 and Philippians 4:13—both formulas, interestingly, not of greeting but of farewell.[7] The formula evokes the possession of the Spirit, the particular Christian gift that is necessary to Christian action and here, in particular, to the liturgical action. The invitation *Sursum corda* takes up on this communion in the Spirit, after which the thanksgiving nature of the prayer is at once mentioned in the invitation *Gratias agamus*. Although it is thus designated as thanksgiving, in the body of the texts, elements of praise, offering, and intercession are included, as well as the intention of sanctifying the gifts and the people (*sanctificatio*).

In the invitation *Sursum corda*, the adverb suggests an upward movement. In the response *Habemus ad Dominum*, the verb means to hold, i.e., to hold up and keep held up while the thanksgiving memorial and praise proceed. To have one's heart held up to the Lord is to have one's life focused on God and on spiritual things, in the sense in which Paul contrasts spirit and flesh. Those who have their minds, hearts, and bodies raised heavenward are ready to offer the true spiritual worship of memorial thanksgiving

[6] For further historical information on the dialogue, see Witczak, 355–56 below.

[7] Robert Taft explains that in the Byzantine liturgy the opening verse was originally a trinitarian greeting, based on these greetings in Paul. Robert F. Taft, "The Dialogue before the Anaphora in the Byzantine Eucharistic Liturgy," *Orientialia Christiana Periodica* 52 (1986): 299–324.

and so respond that it is right and just to do so. The priest is to extend his hands in the traditional *orans* position.

While the rubrics describe actions and gestures for the priest here and throughout the EP, nothing is prescribed for the congregation. This leaves a ritual indeterminacy that is open to a variety of corporeal ways of participating, which could express different meanings. When episcopal conferences make prescriptions for their own territories (e.g., GIRM2003, no. 43) this belongs to the performative interpretation of the prayer and the people's part in it.

The dialogue and opening words of the preface (*Vere dignum*) give the prayer its Roman tenor. *Dignum* goes sometimes with *iustum, salutare, aequum*, expressing attitudes of homage, of rendering what is due. The phrase is biblical in origins; such terms are found in both the OT and the NT.

Dignum translates *axion* in 2 Thessalonians 1:3, signifying that in the order of the grace given in Jesus Christ it is meet-proper-fitting to give thanks, for through him faith and charity abound.[8] *Iustum*, as the quality of acts done according to the Law, is more common in the OT, e.g., Deuteronomy 1:16; in the Latin translation of Romans 8:4, however, it is said that the just fulfillment of the Law is done not according to the flesh but in the spirit. *Aequum* is a quality that belongs with judgment (e.g., Lev 24:22) and to the treatment of others: thus *aequum et iustum* translates Paul's admonition about the conduct that a master should exercise in regard to servants, knowing that one has over oneself a Lord in heaven (Col 4:1). In giving thanks there is a rightness comparable to a juridical ordering of life and relationships, which is founded in the nature of things.

To place this ordering within the economy of redemption the word *salutare* is added. Although of itself the word means health-giving, *salus/salutare* regularly renders the Greek terms for the salvation given in and through Jesus Christ (e.g., Luke 1:47; 2:11; 3:6; 2 Pet 2:20). *Salutare* in Roman sacramentaries is attached to the celebration of the mysteries and to what the people do or obtain. For example, in the *Hadrianum* (nos. 101, 112, 177) it is said to be a quality of the mysteries celebrated. *Salus* is used of what is obtained for people or for the world by God's bounty and the work of Christ and sacraments, e.g., *salus populi, mundi* (*Hadrianum*, nos. 95, 103, 159, 160). *MR2002* holds to this usage, as seen from the previously mentioned concordances.[9]

[8] It can also describe other actions of the believer, such as doing penance: one should produce the worthy fruit of penance (Matt 3:8).

[9] Cf. 257 above.

Prefaces[10]

One cannot fully study EP I without reference to the prefaces that introduce the prayer.[11] Unlike the rest of the prayer, these have been variable from the beginning but are nonetheless integral to the understanding of the whole. Schmitz comments that the vast number of prefaces prayed on different occasions, found in the *Veronense* and other sources, include not just thanksgiving but also petition, catechesis, doctrine, and panegyric.[12]

As previously noted, Mohrmann[13] remarks that the style of the earliest prefaces found in the *Veronense* is different from that part of the prayer beginning with *Te igitur*. While there was a more or less set pattern to follow, this part of the prayer was meant to be improvised—to engage the faithful more directly, capture their imagination, and assume into prayer the devotion particular to feast or season. Even days of fast had their proper prefaces to connect that sacrifice of daily living with the sacrifice of the sacramental oblation. For the celebration of the apostles and the local saints or martyrs, the preface allowed the honors given to them by praying at their tombs or holding vigils in their honor to be brought into the great thanksgiving of the eucharistic sacrifice.

From a scholarly point of view the genre fared badly over the centuries, for not all compositions of early or later periods were well in touch with the *mysterium* celebrated in the Mass.[14] The vast number of compositions that emerged over the centuries was cut down in *MR1474* and *MR1570* to retain only those that could be said to be thanksgiving for the mystery of salvation over the cycle of the year or that belonged to special feasts that fitted readily with this mystery, such as those of Mary and the apostles.[15]

Prefaces are again multiplied in *MR1970*. They show a greater seasonal diversification and include texts for saints of different categories, not only of apostles and martyrs as in the *Veronense*. There are two kinds of prefaces. The major type, running through the liturgical calendar, is a memorial thanksgiving for the work of redemption accomplished in the mysteries of

[10] These texts are not included in this volume; cf. *MR2002*, nos. 33–82.

[11] These are also regularly used with EP III and sometimes with EP II, EP RI, and EP RII, although the latter have their own proper prefaces.

[12] *Wenn man die Geschichte der römischen Präfationen überblickt, zeigt sich, dass zahlreiche Formulare der Vergangenheit dem Ideal einer Präfatio nicht gerecht warden* (Josef Schmitz, "Canon Romanus," *Prex Eucharistica*, 3:286).

[13] Cf. her works cited above, 255, n. 1, and 256, n. 3.

[14] However, the christological focus of the prefaces for the commemoration of martyrs in the *Veronense* cannot be overlooked, since it is their testimony to Christ that is lauded.

[15] See *MR1474*, nos. 167–76.

Christ, as they are interpreted within the commemorations of the major cycles. The commemoration of the mystery includes the prefaces for Sundays in Ordinary Time as these singly highlight different aspects of this mystery: within the limits of classification they may be listed as the paschal mystery (I, II, and VII); the restoration of humanity through the humanity of Christ (III and IV); the mystery of creation as a mystery of divine grace lauded by restored humanity (V); the gift of the Spirit as a pledge of heavenly inheritance (VI); and the mystery of salvation as the mystery of the work of the Father, Son, and Spirit (VIII). The other kind of preface is particular to the commemoration of saints. It is a celebration of the communion of saints, as this is brought to life in memory of the deeds of those remembered and in anticipation of the glory to come in which all will be united.

Particular theological problems involving the understanding of the eucharistic action have to be noted in the new prefaces. While in the traditional Canon and in prayers over the gifts there is no hesitation to speak about offering bread and wine or about offering sacrifices of praise and of propitiation, the new prefaces[16] seem to avoid deliberately speaking this way so as to make this clearly a memorial offering. They also avoid the verbs and nouns of sin-offering, e.g., *placare/placatio*, as they avoid the expression *hostia laudis*. When drawing on liturgical sources of varied traditions they modify the terms so as to exclude references to *hostia laudis* and *hostia placationis*. For example, in prefaces 49 and 50, mention is made of the memorial of that act whereby Christ offered himself, but the sources indicated by Anthony Ward and Cuthbert Johnson speak of the prayer itself as the immolation of a sacrifice of praise. Traditionally, the phrase *hostiam laudis iugiter immolantes* includes both the prayer of the church and the death itself in which Christ fulfilled the types of Paschal Lamb, Abel, Abraham, and Melchizedek (*Veronense*, no. 1250; *Gelasianum*, no. 20). Another example of the tendency in the new prefaces to change the source material is found in preface 55 for the dedication of an altar: here the mention of *sacrificium laudis* in the sources becomes a reference to the memorial of the sacrifice of Christ and a *sacrificium in mysterio*. Since it is customary, even yet in Roman prayers, to speak of the Eucharist as a *hostia laudis et placationis*, these new prefaces in their own distinctive terminology are in tension with the rest of EP I and EP III.[17]

[16] Anthony Ward and Cuthbert Johnson, *The Prefaces of the Roman Missal: A Source Compendium with Concordance and Indices* (Vatican City: Tipografia Polyglotta Vatican, 1989).

[17] These issues will be addressed again later in this chapter.

Sanctus[18] (*OM2008*, no. 83)

Putting aside the history of the *Sanctus*, the meaning of this song of the entire congregation can be identified as a way to join them with the heavenly liturgy where choirs of angels sing the divine praises. Whatever the original Hebrew and now Latin biblical meaning of *Deus Sabaoth*, here it means the armies of angels. Under this title they are called in the most ancient tradition a *militia*, which means armies, not choirs, evoking God's power over the universe and against evil.[19] To the praise of God there is added a blessing of the One who comes (i.e., Christ) in *nomine Domini*, in the name of the *Kyrios*, and who is one with the Father in this lordship.

Biblical references in this hymn are to the cherubic liturgy evoked in Isaiah 6 and to Matthew 21:9 and possibly to Malachi 1:11 on the sacrifice among the Gentiles that is worthy of God. While noting the relation of the *Benedictus* to the acclamation offered Jesus on his entry into Jerusalem (Matt 21:9), Louis Bouyer reminds us that this itself can be traced back to Psalm 118 (119), the hymn for the king's royal entry into Jerusalem, which marks out the eschatological sense of the acclamation offered Christ. "[O]n the lips of the celebrants of the Eucharist . . . it is a confession of the divine *Shekinah* entering into the eschatological sanctuary of the Church."[20]

Te Igitur (*OM2008*, no. 84)

The movement from praise and thanksgiving to intercession at this point is understandable in the light of the vision of an ecclesial heavenly sanctuary evoked in the *Sanctus-Benedictus*; Bouyer's comparison with the Jewish synagogue *Tefillah* is also helpful.[21] Invited into this heavenly worship the members of the assembly, led by their priestly celebrant, are conscious of being there with the gifts they have brought. They stand before the divine majesty with these offerings and only God may make them holy or give them and those who offer them a part in his glory and the right to stand in his court. Entry is obtained through the one acclaimed as the blessed of the

[18] For studies on the origins and meaning of the *Sanctus*, see Robert Taft, "The Interpolation of the Sanctus into the Anaphora When and Where? A Review of the Dossier," *Orientalia Christiana Periodica* 57 (1991): 281–308 and 58 (1992): 531–52; Gabriele Winkler, *Das Sanctus über den Ursprung und die Anfange des Sanctus und sein Fortwirken* (Rome Pontifical Oriental Institute, 2002).

[19] Albert Blaise, *Le vocabulaire latin des principaux thèmes liturgiques* (Turnhout: Brepols, 1966), no. 114.

[20] Bouyer, *Eucharist*, 231.

[21] Ibid., 197f.

Lord and so the approach to the Father and the prayer of intercession are made "through Jesus Christ, your Son, our Lord."[22]

In this eschatological and christological setting, the *Te igitur* is clearly a plea for the acceptance of gifts offered to God and is related to the ritual action whereby the gifts are offered by the faithful. While now reference to the gifts can be seen only as reference to the bread and wine, it seems that in early Roman liturgy it was a prayer over three types of gift: those intended for the episcopal household (to meet its needs and that of its charitable works), those that the people wanted blessed for their own use afterward (to which is attached the *per quem* toward the end of the prayer), and those that were to be consecrated as sacrament of Christ's Body and Blood.[23]

As for the phase *offerre pro*, on a first reading it might mean that the gifts or the Mass are being offered for certain persons by way of making intercession for them. However, the term seems to have originally meant representing these persons through the bringing of gifts offered in their place, whether they were present or not. Thus, in any congregation gifts are offered for the bishop of Rome, for the local bishop, for all the bishops in a communion of faith, and for all Catholic faithful,[24] some of these specified in the *Hanc igitur* (*OM2008*, no. 87) and the *Memento* for the living and for the dead. Without the ritual performance of offering gifts named and designated for persons, however, these meanings do not clearly come through. In the prayer as it now stands, therefore, *offerre quo* and *Hanc igitur* sound simply like petitions for some specified individuals or groups of persons, lacking the sense of making an offering on their behalf.

Memento (*OM2008*, no. 85)

During Vatican II and the first phase of postconciliar liturgical renewal, one criticism of the Roman Canon was that the inner sequence of its internal parts was not always clear and that petitions and commemorations inter-

[22] This is also what gives sense to the inclusion of the institution narrative within the intercessory part of the prayer.

[23] Jungmann recalls how Erik Peterson wanted to attach the words *dona, munera, sacrificia illabata* singly to each of these types of gift but the general liturgical use of the terms hardly bears this out. Jungmann MRR, 2:151, n. 16.

[24] There is a connection between *offerre pro* and *Hanc oblationem*, which names those for whom gifts are offered (e.g., newly baptized, newly married, and newly ordained) so that, if physically absent, they too are present in the assembly, or if physically present, they are represented in the offering in a special way appropriate to the occasion being celebrated.

rupted the easy flow of the prayer as a eucharistic offering.[25] Contrarily, placing a special remembrance of the living at this point of the prayer is quite coherent, and this would have been clearer when gifts were offered in the name of the persons or groups remembered. Even now, since in offering the sacrifice for the whole catholic or universal communion of the faithful the *Te igitur* ends with a petition for the Bishop of Rome and for all bishops in communion with him in the apostolic tradition, it is quite logical to pause and pray for others, especially some in the assembly for whom the prayer is being offered for a particular reason this day.

Memento is a form of address that could be directed to people, admonishing them to recall something about themselves (e.g., Ash Wednesday's *memento homo quia pulvis es*), but it is here addressed to God, much as is *recordare* in EP III. Whatever our human fragility, God is asked to remember the good deeds he has done for this people and so to have mercy on those for whom prayer is now made. While relying principally on God's fidelity, both the remembrance of the living and the remembrance of the dead in the Canon include an appeal to the deeds and the faith of those recalled and of those present (*circumstantes*), who are represented in the offerings made through the *sacrificium laudis*, the sacrifice of praise. *Devotio* and *vota* are very comprehensive terms[26] and include prayers of praise and of petition and religious activity such as fasting or deeds of mercy. All of this is assumed into the sacrifice of praise in which all join. What is asked in return is a comprehensive well-being in the service of God. While *salus* has a primarily spiritual connotation, *incolumitas* is inclusive of both spiritual and material welfare.[27]

Communicantes (*OM2008*, no. 86) and *Nobis quoque* (*OM2008*, no. 96)

The communion of the living church, already given expression, is now evoked in the sense of an even larger communion. These two prayers express communion with those who have preceded the faithful in witness to Christ, especially the apostles and the martyrs of the local church. The

[25] Cipriano Vagaggini, *The Canon of the Mass and Liturgical Reform*, trans. Peter Coughlan (Staten Island, NY: Alba House, 1967), 111–14; for a further outline of these criticisms, see Witczak, 354 below.

[26] Cf. Blaise, *Vocabulaire*, s.v. *devotio* and *vota*.

[27] Blaise, *Vocabulaire*, no. 74. As the *Libera* embolism to the Lord's Prayer suggests when it asks that people be freed from intrusions (*perturbatio*) of any sort, both are needed for a life lived in the service of God.

Communicantes harkens back to the preface by alluding to the feast or mystery being celebrated at any precise moment of the liturgical calendar, so that the communion of those venerated and of the living is a communion in the mystery of Christ as marked on the liturgical calendar. The terms *communicantes*, *pars*, *societas*, and *consortium* are different ways of expressing communion in Christ and in the glory of God, now and hereafter. The word *communicatio/communicare*[28] is very expressive because of the different occasions on which it is used, e.g., referring to the rites of breaking the bread, partaking of the eucharistic table, and participation in the passion of Christ. *Consortium*[29] more often speaks of the communion enjoyed by the heavenly blessed, which all hope for and await as they share now in the mystery of Christ. *Societas*,[30] which in English is more properly translated "company" than "society," denotes an earthly communion lived in the anticipation of heavenly sharing in the glory of God.[31]

Quam oblationem[32] (*OM2008*, no. 88)

After much intercession for the acceptance of the gifts, the prayer requests their change into the Body and Blood of Christ: they will be transformed because they are acceptable and made acceptable through the transformation. The verb is *fiant* (*corpus et sanguis*).[33] They become the Body and Blood in virtue of the divine action.

In Greek anaphoras the purpose of the Spirit's action is its agency in simultaneously and correspondingly sanctifying the gifts as sacraments of Christ's offering and gift of his Body and Blood and those who partake of them. In the Roman prayer these are spoken of separately,[34] but were the Ambrosian *figura corporis et sanguinis* to have been retained, it would have been clear that sacramentality is intended. Enrico Mazza is probably right

[28] On the traditional Roman usage of these words, consult Blaise, *Vocabulaire*, s.v. For examples of *communico/communicantes*, apart from the Canon, in *MR2002*, see Sodi, nos. 469, 1361, 1363, 1751, 3156.

[29] For examples in *MR2002*, see Sodi, nos. 507, 510, 1077, 1749, 2439, 2526, 3140, 3152.

[30] For examples in *MR2002*, see Sodi, nos. 570, 760, 1757, 2232, 3215.

[31] The present text of both these prayers allows the omission of the memory of the saints peculiar to the Church of Rome but makes no provision for an inclusion of others. It would be in the logic of the prayer, however, to do so, as done in the Stowe Missal. As previously mentioned, *Hanc igitur* is also variable; regarding its Latin vocabulary, cf. below, 276.

[32] On the *quam oblationem* and the institution narrative, see Serra, "The Roman Canon."

[33] While in the other three prayers this petition becomes an epiclesis for the Spirit, the verb remains, *ut fiant*.

[34] The introduction of the Spirit epiclesis into EP II, III, and IV is done in line with the meaning of the prayer *quam oblationem* in the Roman Canon.

in saying that though *figura* is not used, the same sense is kept because of the focus on the sacramentality of the elements and of their offering. It is in being sacrament—and this includes being offered—that bread and wine are given sacramental being, and it is only by God's beneficence that this is so. This is expressed by the words *benedictam, adscriptam, ratam, rationabilem, acceptabilem*: a rhetorical concatenation of words to indicate the request for God's sacramental action and its effect on the bread and wine.

Institution Narrative (*OM2008*, nos. 89–90)

As distinct from most other liturgical traditions, the institution narrative in the Roman Canon is placed within the intercessory part of the prayer, beginning with the conjunctive pronoun *Qui*, showing that recalling the Supper is linked to the petition for acceptance and transformation of the gifts. Structurally this does not signal a moment for the priest to act out what Jesus did or to speak in his name (i.e., *in persona Christi*). It is rather the introduction of a narrative explanation of what the church is doing; i.e., she is performing a rite that dates back to the Supper and that commemorates the death of the beloved Son of God, the Lord Jesus Christ (*dilectissimus Filius, Dominus noster Jesus Christus*).

Given the emphasis of the prayer (previously in the *Sanctus* and later in the *Supra quae*) on the heavenly sanctuary and on intercession, the narrative relates the Supper and the Eucharist not only to his passion but also to the intercessory exercise of Christ's high priesthood in the heavenly sanctuary, which he entered by shedding his blood. There, in virtue of his voluntary death and obedience—his once-for-all sacrifice—he continually makes the intercession (Heb 7:25; Rom 8:34; 1 John 2:1-2)[35] that allows the faithful access to the Father, trusting in propitiation for their sins and ready to render an acceptable sacrifice of praise.

In each of the four EPs of *OM2008*, the institution narrative is introduced by an allusion to Christ's passion, placing the story of the meal quite clearly into the passion narrative, as is the case in the gospels. The introduction in the Roman Canon is the simplest, locating the narrative in time, the day before he suffered: *pridie quam pateretur*. The form of the words of Jesus (not what surrounds them) is uniform in all the prayers. It is the text of the early

[35] *Semper vivens ad interpellandum pro nobis*: the verb translates *entunchanein* (e.g., Heb 7:25), which means to make appeal to somebody on another's behalf, against some enemy or some ill. Christ makes appeal to the Father, for the people for whom he gave his life, that they may be freed from sin and death and so have confidence in approaching the Father through him. This aptly expresses the *canon actionis* of this Roman prayer.

Roman Canon that is foundational, though this has been completed in *OM2008* by an addition to the words over the bread, *quod pro vobis tradetur*, to make them parallel the words over the cup.[36] While used here in the passive voice, *trado* is found in the NT to express the Father's handing over of the Son and the Son's handing over of himself. Rather than simply referring to the act of his enemies before which Jesus was submissive, *tradetur* thus enhances the perception that the church is remembering the voluntary death of Jesus as sacrifice. It also signals the unity of Supper and passion. This goes readily with the description of the blood, *qui pro vobis et pro multis effundetur*. These two phrases attached to the Body and to the Blood given to the disciples suggest a voluntary sacrifice on Christ's part.

Placing this within the order of divine salvific acts, the chalice of the blood is called the chalice of the new and eternal *testamentum*. This Latin word (rather than *foedus*) is undoubtedly kept because it was the usual biblical term for referencing the covenant and is used in the Latin translations of the Letter to the Hebrews, where the contrast is made between the two covenants and the two priesthoods of these covenants. The reference to the *remissio peccatorum* is essential to the interpretation of Christ's covenantal sacrifice. In speaking of the shedding of his blood *pro multis*, the Pauline contrast between the one and the many (e.g., Rom 5:19) is in mind: the sin and disobedience of many is redeemed through the One, who is God's appointed servant and mediator of the New Covenant.

In expressing the nature of the act of worship performed by Christ, the text says *gratias agens benedixit*. This means that he blessed God in thanking him, which is the traditional Jewish sense of blessing. Over time, with the introduction of signs of the cross it was understood to mean that he blessed the bread and wine by way of doing something to them. In *OM2008* this sign is made before the narrative, not to accompany it as in *MR1570*.

The connection between the Supper and the worship of the assembled church is made by the introduction of the memorial command at the end of the narrative: *hoc facite in meam commemorationem*. It is the action of Christ himself at the Supper and his memorial command that is the foundation and meaning of the church's sacrifice of praise, thanksgiving, and atonement. The Latin *commemoratio* is taken from the Latin translation of anamnesis in the Pauline account of the Supper (1 Cor 11:25).

Although the sign of the cross over the oblations occurs now outside the narrative, it is nonetheless clear that ritual prescriptions attach conse-

[36] The words *mysterium fidei* are also omitted from the narrative itself but are now placed at the end of the narrative as an address to the people about the meaning of the Eucharist.

cratory power to the words of Jesus repeated by the priest. This is first signaled by the rubric inserted before the narrative, instructing the priest that these words should be brought out (*proferantur*) distinctly and openly (*distincte et aperte*). *Aperte* must mean in a clear voice so that the words when heard stand out from their context. On pronouncement of the words of Jesus over the bread that he holds in his hands, and over the cup that he holds in his hands, inclining at the moment of their repetition, the priest is instructed to adore (*genuflexus adorat*).[37] This implies the reason for showing the host and chalice to the people, although of itself the lifting up of the elements could be a sign of offering, as in the final doxology.

Since this interpretation of the words does not follow from the original text found in the Roman tradition, it has to be seen as an exercise of the power of the church in determining sacramental ritual to locate the consecration in the repetition by the priest of the words of Jesus for the practitioners of the Roman Rite. For the interpretation of the prayer as a whole it is rather problematic since it introduces an efficacious symbolic action into a prayer that as a prayer of commemoration is couched in the form of thanksgiving, praise, and intercession. When the words and action of the priest are singled out as the moment in which consecration takes place, it is difficult to consider the prayer as a whole over the gifts offered as the commemorative enactment of the mystery of Christ, since the representation of the mystery is confined to these words pronounced by the ordained minister.

Anamnesis and Acclamation[38] (*OM2008*, no. 91)

The anamnetic acclamation of the people in *OM2008* is new to the Roman Rite. It is addressed to Christ. While the words of the priest (*Mysterium fidei*) are interjected before the acclamation, the people now respond to the command to keep remembrance. In the first two acclamations the commemoration is given a clear eschatological horizon, while the third is a petition addressed to the Savior. Stylistically they are an interruption of a prayer addressed through Christ to the Father. On the other hand, as a first response

[37] To allow place for both epiclesis and the words of Jesus in the act of consecration, *IGMR2002*, no. 79c indicates that to the words of Jesus we have to join the invocation of the Spirit, which precedes the institution narrative.

[38] See Marc Schneiders, "Acclamations in the Eucharistic Prayers," in *Omnes Circumadstantes: Contributions towards a History of the Role of the People in the Liturgy*, ed. Charles Caspers and Marc Schneiders (Kampen: J. H. Kok, 1990), 78–100.

to the command of Christ they allot to the whole assembly the memorial proclamation that fulfills the command.

Inserting an acclamation draws upon the practice of Eastern liturgies to allow for the assembly's intervention in the course of the anaphora.[39] Sometimes these are no more than an occasional *Amen* and usually they are addressed to the Father to whom the prayer is offered. In the Liturgy of St. James, however, this acclamation is addressed to Christ, as is now the case with the three possibilities offered in *OM2008*.

Mortem annuntiare is interpreted in light of the injunction *mortem Domini annunciabitis donec veniat* (1 Cor 11:26), which makes the Eucharist an eschatological act of remembrance. *Annuntiare* designates a public act, one which says that what is proclaimed is done. The word is used of proclaiming the resurrection (Acts 4:2), which means confessing the mystery so as to live by it, give witness to it, and participate in it. The same Greek-Latin term is used to designate the preaching of the Gospel (1 Cor 9:14) or the apostolic testimony to Jesus Christ (1 Cor 2:1). Here, the testimony is to the efficacy of the liturgical action.

In *Resurrectionem confitemur, confiteri* is associated with the wonderful works of God. It means internal belief and external confession with praise. In the Latin of Romans it is associated with making known the resurrection or lordship of Jesus (Rom 10:9; 14:11; 15:9). This is also the case in Philippians 2:11. Such confession might be paraphrased: we confess with our heart and profess with our lips your wondrous resurrection.

Donec venias refers to the expectation of Christ's return in glory and expresses an eschatological hope for the coming of Christ as Lord, when all things are reconciled in him.[40] The phrase resonates with 1 Corinthians 11:26, although Paul refers only to the proclamation of Christ's death.

The people's response to the command to keep remembrance sets the tone for the *Memores* of the priest. It is the proclamatory action of the assembly that is the first response to the Lord's command and so the first public and liturgical making present of the Lord's death. The people are given a sacramental voice whereby they profess not just their faith in the mystery celebrated but also the mystery itself. With this proclamation, made to Christ himself, they are ready to turn to the Father to offer the memorial sacrifice in commemoration of this mystery along with the priest.[41]

[39] Bouyer, *Eucharist*, 450.

[40] Blaise, *Vocabulaire*, par. 178.

[41] In his encyclical *Ecclesia de Eucharistia* (no. 5), Pope John Paul II points to this meaning, i.e., to the acclamation of the reality of the paschal mystery in which Christ is present to his

Unde et memores (*OM2008*, no. 92)

In this prayer the priest explicitly unites the people with himself in making the offering: those who offer are the ministers (*nos servi tui*) and the whole people (*plebs tua sancta*). It is in offering that the church keeps memorial, placing before God what is taken from God's own gifts. In keeping with the *pridie quam pateretur* introducing the institution narrative, it is the passion that is remembered and not simply the death, while the expression *ab inferis resurrectionis* marks the conquest of death that Christ has embraced by his descent into the abode of the dead and from where he has risen. To what was probably the original reference in the Eucharist to the passion and resurrection, the Canon adds the mystery of the ascension, which was marked on the calendar in Rome within the fifty days after Easter.[42]

In referring to the gifts, the prayer echoes the Roman tendency to join several adjectives together, i.e., *pura, sancta, immaculata*. Together they convey the idea that since this is done in remembrance of Christ, the offering or sacrifice is without blemish. It is therefore a holy bread of life everlasting and a chalice of that salvation that never ends. The word *hostia* is not capitalized, contrasting with EP III and IV. It does not refer simply to the offering of Christ's Body and Blood but has the common meaning of the church's praise or *hostia laudis* by which the passion and death are sacramentally represented. It is precisely this which is offered in remembrance: the offering of Christ, which takes on its sacramental form in the offering of the church, inclusive of its gifts and its commemorative praise and thanksgiving.

Supra quae (*OM2008*, no. 93)

Since the sacrifice of the church as a prayer of praise includes a sequel of petition—as in the sequence *Sanctus–Te igitur*—it follows naturally that the offering now leads into prayer for the acceptance of the gifts offered by the church. This highlights the need for propitiation, the nature of the Eucharist as a *hostia placationis*, but it does so in a calm way, referring to God's kind visage, asking him to look with *propitio et sereno vultu*. *Propitio/propitiatio* reflects the need for a righting of an order disturbed by sin, much in

---

people, who respond with amazement at the perennial making present of this mystery. Without reference to the EP, similar ideas are expressed by Benedict XVI, *SacCar*, no. 11.

[42] E.g., we know from Leo the Great that this was an important feast in the Roman Church and was associated with NT texts of the Lord ascending into heaven, or returning to the Father (Synoptics and Eph 4:7-13), where he exercises lordship over earthly and heavenly powers, over evil, and over the Church to which he gives authority and gifts of service.

the sense of *placare/placatio*,[43] but this is offset by the adjective *sereno*, which is elsewhere attached to the divine *pietas* or fatherly mercy and suggests the peaceful and serene countenance of one well pleased by the offering of the church. The prayer beautifully places the sacrifice of the church, offered in memorial of Christ's redemptive mystery and in obedience to his memorial command, into a long dispensation of sacrifice that has its climax in Christ, the Paschal Lamb.[44] The meaning of this sacrifice draws on remembrance of the justice of Abel, the faith of Abraham who is ever the patriarch of those justified by faith, and the offerings of the goods of the earth in thanksgiving by Melchizedek, so often employed to illustrate the priesthood of Jesus Christ.

Supplices (*OM2008*, no. 94)

This is a prayer that has generated much discussion, regarding both its origin and its meaning. The discussion is rehearsed by Mazza, who concludes, "In summary, our celebration is seen as a sharing in the angelic liturgy that goes on in heaven around the heavenly altar. . . . This theology works with an idea of sacrifice and of Eucharistic communion described with the aid of 1 Cor 10:18 . . . and not of 1 Cor 10:16-17."[45] Mazza's reference to 1 Corinthians 10:18 is to what is said of participation at the altar of Christ rather than that of the victims of pagan offerings. The prayer's invocation of the angels places this altar in heaven and suggests a mediatorial role, for in biblical imagery the angels in offering prayer and incense bridge a spatially imagined gap between the inner sanctum and outer court. By Christ's mediation this gap is closed and all are holy in a way that allows them to eat and drink of the gifts placed on the altar, in communion with the heavenly liturgy of the Lamb. One might paraphrase this difficult oration by saying: the people made holy by Christ's blood and mediation are able to share now at this earthly table as a symbol of the heavenly table that awaits them and where they are already in communion with the angels and the saints.

Per quem (*OM2008*, no. 97)

This was the conclusion, coming before the final doxology, to the blessing of such gifts as oil, vegetables, and fruits that served other family and ecclesial purposes. As such, it integrates blessing of all creation and human-

[43] See 276 below.

[44] See *Veronense*, no. 1250.

[45] Mazza, *The Eucharistic Prayers*, 83.

ity's relation to it into the eucharistic memorial. Now, however, it sounds like redundancy or a floating phrase without context, since it is not clear to what "all these good things" refers. If creation is to be included, the sense would be that those blessed through the sacraments of the Lord's Body and Blood hope that God might bless all the good things of creation in which the people share in Christ's name and over which his death, resurrection, and ascension has given him lordship. That sense of blessing, however, does not come through clearly in the text as given.

The Doxological Logic of the Roman Canon

It is fitting to conclude with reflections on how the prayer presents the church's act of commemorative worship. The doxological logic of the Canon as an act of worship, which in praise of the deeds of God in Christ moves through thanksgiving and praise to intercession and offering, has already been mentioned. It is often spoken of in the prayers over the offerings as *hostia laudis et placationis*. This is a thankful praise from which flow offering of gifts and petition, expressive of gratitude but also of the desire to appease and atone for sin. The gifts are offered as *rationabile obsequium servitutis*, meaning the service and devotion of the church gathered for prayer. Offering such service is symbolized in the offering of the gifts—which is possible since it is done through Christ—as a *figura* of his body and blood offered, and so in expectation of its transformation to become nourishing and cleansing food.

While to the chagrin of its critics the prayer was seen to accentuate the church's sacrifice and by its defenders to be properly expressive of Christ's sacrifice when done in the church, the prefaces both past and present make it clear that sacrifice is not the only image or term whereby in the Eucharist Christ's death is remembered. In fact, the term sacrifice applies first and foremost to the church's own commemorative action, to its offering of its gifts and of its praise, in which thanksgiving and petition, even placation, are incorporated. The mystery commemorated is not remembered simply as sacrifice or even as Pasch, and its interpretation should not rely solely on either of these images or categories. The death of Christ in the prefaces that inform the rest of the Canon is diversely interpreted and poetically expressed as the following: victory over death, the culmination of the *commercium* begun in the incarnation and continued in the church's own prayerful devotion and service, a ransom, an end-putting to sin and death, a Pasch of suffering, a Pasch of transition, a placatory sacrifice, a sacrifice of communion, and an obedience to the Father. When sacrifice is used, either as *hostia* or as *sacrificium*, the offering of Christ and the offering of the church are simultaneously placed in line with the deeds of Abel, Abraham, and Melchizedek, thus given a meaning that comes from their insertion into a story line of long duration.

In current interpretations of the Eucharist, ideas of memorial, praise, and thanksgiving have been given due prominence. However, problems arise with regard to what is termed appeasement. That the offering is made as a *placatio* suggests that it is something inherent to prayer for sinful humanity standing before the divine majesty. It is effective because it is done through Christ, in virtue of his redemptive work, but it remains something required of the church in its public devotion and service.

The understanding of the Eucharist as a sacrifice of appeasement or atonement appears to have given pause to those who assembled *MR2002*, as noted above regarding the composition of new prefaces.[46] On the other hand, the traditional text from the *Te igitur* onward is left untouched so that at the heart of the Canon the church in offering its *sacrificium laudis* asks that God may be "pleased because placated" (*ut placatus accipias*) to accept the offering of the gifts proffered and offered.

While the prayer *Hanc igitur* may not always have been included, it was used for special persons, and in all of these cases requesting forgiveness of sins, peaceful days on earth, and eternal life seemed appropriate.[47] Designing the Eucharist as a sacrifice of appeasement or atonement is plentiful in the prayers over the offerings.[48]

Placatus is used in the *Vetus Latina* and in the Vulgate to translate Hebrew words that refer to the appeasement of God's anger toward the people, or of the appeasement of the anger of the king (e.g., Exod 16:53; 28:30; 1 Sam 19:6; 2 Chr 30:20; Jer 42:10; Ezek 16:53). It is found often in the Latin fathers (including Augustine) and is used very frequently in liturgical Latin. The word seems to be imported from the Latin of court and jurisprudence where it was expected that a willing surrender of some penalty was needed to

[46] See 263–64 above.

[47] Now the prayer is always part of the Canon, but not even the most recent translation, supposedly done according to the norms of *LitAuth*, dares to restore the language of sin-offering and finds its way around *placatus* by asking that God "graciously accept" the offering of the Church's service, though the word would be more correctly translated as "appeased," or with the phrase "accept this offering of our service by which you are appeased." To confuse *placare* and *placere* is a rather elementary mistake in interpretation.

[48] Examples are in the Masses of the Day at Christmas, for the Feast of the Holy Family, for the Third Sunday of Lent, for Passion Sunday, for the anniversary Mass for the Dead, for the Mass for a Deceased Pope, and for the Fourth, Twelfth, Nineteenth, and Thirty-Second Sundays in Ordinary Time.

restore right order, especially when dealing with a sovereign or lord. The prayer then takes account of the need for redemptive atonement—whether by reason of Christ's death or by reason of the works undertaken by the church—and the offerings made to turn God's face from human sin and cause him instead to look with pleasure on his Son and those whom he had made his children.

Appeasement is only one of the ways in which the action is described. In prayers over the offering it is also a cleansing sacrifice, sacred exchange, renewal of Christ's redemptive sacrifice, offering of service and devotion, gift and expiation, work of our redemption, honor rendered to God's majesty, purification, revelation of God's mystery, and mystical and sacramental sign. In other prayers it is asked that the gifts may be sanctified and become nourishment, cleansing, a spiritual offering, and an expiation. There can be no synthesis or conceptual reduction: all these ways of indicating the action taken in the Mass are retained but not synthesized. The closest to a single comprehensive description might indeed be best found in the expression *hostia laudis et placationis*, where commemorative praise and appeasement come together to say what is taking place. The imagery of atonement and appeasement is, therefore, integral to EP and cannot be left out of its interpretation, for it is also integral to our Roman heritage. The Latin tendency in medieval and pre-Reformation times was to reduce the offering of the Mass to this aspect of satisfaction or appeasement, but dissatisfaction with this should not lead to an annulment of this idea when it is kept alongside others.

Conclusion

An examination of EP I shows that its interpretation requires attention to the Latinity of a past age, which is now cut loose of its local ecclesial moorings. It has also lost something of its ritual framework, which was the performative offering of gifts by those who belonged in the assembly. Despite these difficulties, this study reveals how inclusive the memorial offering is intended to be in its sacramentality. The offering or sacrifice is a memorial, done in obedience to Christ's command to keep remembrance of him. While always enacted in communion with his voluntary and sacrificial obedience to the Father, it quite deliberately includes an offering of praise, of devotion in its various expressions, and of earthly goods. These together are the sacramental stuff, transformed into the sacrament of Christ's Pasch and of his Body and Blood. If they are not verbally and intentionally included in the sacrifice, as the sacrifice of Christ, head and members, the memorial fails in its sacramentality.

To isolate the offering of Christ as victim, made sacramentally present, from the sacrifice of the people offered in its own sacramental form, would exclude the sacramental expression of how a people is made holy in its being, its deeds, and its prayer through its redemptive communion with and in Christ. This is untrue to the tradition of the Roman liturgy. The holy and spotless *hostia* is the sacramental offering of the church as Christ's people, and the bread of life and chalice of salvation are representative of its communion in the redemption and life of Christ, in the offering of the body and the shedding of the blood at Supper and on the cross.

We further noted problems found in the composition of *MR2002*, especially in the prefaces, regarding images of appeasement or atonement. If, however, the traditional meaning of EP I is to be kept, this has to be retained.

Finally, while the interpretation of the text has to deal with the cultural particularities of ecclesiastical Latin, it was shown that the fundamental prayer structure does not depend on the vocabulary as such but reflects its deep structure, with its particular conjunction of praise, thanksgiving, offering, and petition. It is this which is most important in the genius of the Roman Rite, not the use of a rather idiosyncratic vocabulary. For translations and fresh compositions in the Roman tradition this is important to remember.

The ICEL2010 Translation

Gilbert Ostdiek

Introduction

Translating the Roman Canon presents unique challenges. As noted above,[1] it took shape over many centuries, from its initial formulation in fourth-century classical Roman Latin style through redactions and insertions that continued well into the early Middle Ages. Translation thus needs to address not only evolving Latin style and vocabulary but also, more importantly, changing cultural and theological contexts.

SC called for rites marked by "noble simplicity," free from "useless repetitions," and "within people's powers of comprehension" (no. 34). In keeping with those directives and the guidelines laid down in *CLP*, ICEL1973 adopted a restrained pastoral approach in translating this venerable prayer. When revision of this prayer was undertaken in the 1980s, ICEL retained that approach. Because ICEL1973 had become so familiar, revisions were kept to a minimum and only were considered when required theologically or by fuller rendering of the Latin. Before this revision was approved, Rome had announced a new *editio typica* of the *MR* with new translation guidelines (*LitAuth*), adopting a literal, word-for-word approach.[2] ICEL2010 is the product of this new approach.

Opening Dialogue (ICEL2010, no. 83)[3]

The opening greeting and response are the same as in the introductory rites.[4] The response is a more literal translation of the Latin than ICEL1973. In light of the orthography of *spiritu* (lower case "s"), it would be unwarranted to interpret this text as attributing a special gift of the Holy Spirit to the priest-celebrant.

[1] See Baldovin, 247–54, esp. 250 above.

[2] For a historical overview of these developments, see 63–69 above.

[3] Also, see Chupungco, 475–76 below.

[4] See Chupungco, 137–38 above.

ICEL2010's translation of *Sursum corda* and its response remains the same as ICEL1973 and will be familiar to congregants. A 2003 draft had read, "Let our hearts be lifted high. We hold them before the Lord." The intent behind the translation of the response was to stress the present continuing action of *habemus*. The unfamiliarity of that version of the ritual exchange, however, would have been pastorally disruptive (*LitAuth*, no. 64).

The third invitation to "give thanks" is the same as ICEL1973. Although the prayer to follow offers more than thanks, this translates the Latin accurately. The people's response requires congregants to learn a new response. "It is right and just" is a more exact translation of *dignum et iustum est* than "It is right to give him thanks and praise" (ICEL1973). Bernard Botte and Christine Mohrmann suggest that *dignum* and *iustum* can be seen as synonymous.[5] The variable prefaces that follow normally begin by reaffirming these words of the assembly's response, then adding a second pair *aequum et salutare* ("our duty and our salvation").

Sanctus (ICEL2010, no. 83)

The ICEL1973 translation of the *Sanctus* remains unchanged except that "Lord God of power and might" is replaced by "Lord God of hosts." *Sabaoth*, a Hebrew loan word in the plural, has many shades of meaning: hosts, armies, a multitude, or, by extension, God's angelic army.[6] In view of its etymological roots in the Hebrew verb "to wage war," the translators wisely chose to leave the word "hosts" unspecified. This word may at first seem puzzling to some and will need catechesis. Nonetheless, the translation reads well.

Te igitur (ICEL2010, no. 84)

"To you, therefore, most merciful Father, we make humble prayer and petition" (lines 2–3)

ICEL2010 follows the Latin more closely than the ICEL1973 free translation: "We come to you, Father, with praise and thanksgiving." The connective adverb *igitur* was left untranslated in ICEL1973 and ICEL1998.[7] In

[5] Bernard Botte and Christine Mohrmann, *L'Ordinaire de la Messe. Texte critique, traduction et études* (Paris: Cerf, 1955), 74, n. 1.

[6] See Power, 265 above.

[7] Botte and Mohrmann, *L'Ordinaire de la Messe*, 75, n. 9, was cited in support of this decision. They held that *igitur* had become very weak in the Latin of the fourth century. Postconciliar French, Italian, and Spanish translations adopted that same position.

keeping with *LitAuth* (no. 57), it is translated here to preserve the full meaning of the connection between thanksgiving and the offering that follows.[8] A contrast is well drawn between God (*clementissime*, an imperial title borrowed by Christians) and the humble petitioners (*supplices*). A delicate grammatical rearrangement renders *supplices rogamus ac petimus* into "we make humble prayer and petition."

"that you accept and bless these gifts, these offerings, these holy and unblemished sacrifices" (lines 6–10)

ICEL1973 pared this phrase down considerably: "to accept and bless these gifts we offer you in sacrifice." ICEL2010 has restored the triple Latin designation of the gifts, a Latin rhetorical device to add stress. The threefold naming of the gifts has been interpreted in varying ways. Jungmann sees a gradation in the way the three terms designate the material offerings: the gifts themselves (*dona*) presented as a public service (*munera*) to be offered in tribute to God (*sacrificia*).[9] Mazza sees them rather as offerings for the dead (*dona*), for the living (*munera*), and offerings to be used in the sacrifice (*sacrificia*).[10] How to translate *illibata* has also been widely discussed: literally, "un-poured," but by extension "complete, integral, without blemish." Choice of the last meaning in ICEL2010 may evoke a resonance with the Passover lamb (Exod 12:5). In Mohrmann's view "unblemished" need not be understood as alluding to a sacrificial animal.[11]

"which we offer you firstly" (line 12)

The translation of *in primis* as "firstly" is not felicitous. An earlier version read "which we offer first of all," like the postconciliar Italian (*anzitutto*), French (*avant tout*), and Spanish (*ante todo*) translations. Otherwise, this line reads well. Priests will also be pleased that this paragraph has been broken into two sentences midway through: "Be pleased. . . ."

[8] Jungmann notes the difficulty some have in seeing the internal link between the preface and this petition for acceptance of the offering. He suggests that ancient Christian thought saw an inner link between the concepts of thanksgiving and offering, in Jungmann MRR, 2:148–49. Enrico Mazza likewise sees historical grounds for a link between thanksgiving (preface) and the offertorial theme of the *Te igitur* (*The Origins of the Eucharistic Prayer* [Collegeville, MN: Liturgical Press, 1995], 260).

[9] Jungmann MRR, 2:150–51.

[10] Enrico Mazza, *The Eucharistic Prayers of the Roman Rite*, trans. Matthew J. O'Connell (New York: Pueblo, 1986), 59; cf. Power, 266, n. 23, above.

[11] She holds that it does not have a cultic or ritual sense but rather the general meaning of "*non effleuré, entier*" (Botte and Mohrmann, *L'Ordinaire de la Messe*, 115).

"and all those who, holding to the truth, hand on the catholic and apostolic faith." (lines 19–20)

This translation reads somewhat awkwardly. *Cultor(ibus)*, a noun form of the verb *colere*—"to plant, to guard, to have care of," and by extension "to worship"—is rendered in English by a present participle instead of a noun. Botte and Mohrmann suggest that the phrase *catholicae et apostolicae fidei cultoribus* reinforces and specifies *orthodoxis*, to which it is attached in apposition by *atque*.[12] Historically, this phrase refers to the college of bishops, who share with the pope the role of *cultores fidei*. An alternate wording might have been "and all faithful guardians of the catholic and apostolic faith"[13] or "and for all who hold and teach the catholic faith that comes to us from the apostles" (ICEL1973). Those alternatives have the advantage of not limiting *orthodoxis* to "holding to the truth" whose root (*doxa*) means both belief and practice.

***Memento* (ICEL2010, no. 85)**

"For them, we offer you this sacrifice of praise or they offer it for themselves and all who are dear to them." (lines 8–10)

ICEL2010 here follows the Latin closely. Not knowing the historical context in which the Latin was written, congregants will find it hard to make sense of these lines. As Mazza notes, they appeared in the first half of the ninth century, a time when the celebration was increasingly left in the hands of the priest. Not knowing Latin, people "attended" with little active participation in the rite itself. By offering a stipend for the Mass, people could still "take part" in the offering, whether or not they were present at the celebration. Mazza concludes, "the word 'or' (*vel*) is rubrical, that is, it points to an alternative: either the offerers themselves are present, or they are absent, in which case the celebrant offers the sacrifice of praise in their stead."[14] Given that obscurity, ICEL1973 opted for a simpler and clearer wording: "We offer you this sacrifice of praise for ourselves and those who are dear to us."

"and paying their homage to you" (line 13)

This translation loses the parallel between the verb forms *offerunt* and *reddunt*, but in view of the distance between them in the text, the participial

[12] Ibid., 77, n. 2.

[13] Mazza, *The Eucharistic Prayers*, 49.

[14] Ibid., 65; also, Power, 266 above.

form "paying" may make the connection clearer to hearers. An earlier draft had read "and fulfilling their vows to you." That wording was prone to being heard by the lay faithful as referring to vowed religious. "Paying homage" is less subject to misunderstanding, but "homage" paraphrases the Latin *vota*.[15] *Vota* means "desires, prayers, petitions," so there might have been other, more accurate alternatives, such as "and offer you their desires" or "longings" or "prayers."[16]

Communicantes (ICEL2010, no. 86)

"In communion with those whose memory we venerate"[17] *(lines 2–3)*

The parallel between *communicantes* and *venerantes* is lost in this translation. Mazza notes that a literal translation can bring this out: "sharing in one holy fellowship and venerating the memory."[18] ICEL2010 clearly identifies the *communicantes* with Mary and the communion of saints they are venerating. ICEL1973—like the French and Italian translations—placed them with "the whole Church."

"Mother of our God and Lord, Jesus Christ, and blessed Joseph, her Spouse" (lines 5–6)

The word order of the first phrase, following that of the Latin, does not flow as naturally as did ICEL1973 translation: "Mother of Jesus Christ, our God and Lord."[19] Although not as close to the Latin, ICEL2010's "blessed

[15] By the fourth century *vota* had become synonymous with *preces* or *oratio* (Botte and Mohrmann, *L'Ordinaire de la Messe*, 77, n. 6).

[16] Jungmann called attention to the complex redaction history of this paragraph (MRR 2:159–69). He suggests that the phrase *tibique reddunt vota sua* is meant to be a restatement, using other words, of the phrase *qui tibi offerunt hoc sacrificium laudis* four lines earlier, although these two phrases became separated by later insertion of the intervening lines. The same two ideas are immediately conjoined in Ps 50:14—*immola Deo sacrificium laudis et redde Altissimo vota sua*—where the second phrase doubles the first. The second phrase in EP I may, in fact, have served to tie the *memento* of the living to the *communicantes* of the saints that follows, thus joining the earthly assembly with the communion of saints in offering God the sacrifice of praise. If we accept Jungmann's identification of this doubling, a translation of *tibique reddunt vota sua* might have repeated the idea of offering and underlined the element of promise-obligation intimated in *vota*, e.g., "and they offer the sacrifice of praise that is due to you, the eternal God, living and true." This is an example of how the redaction history of EP I can complicate the goal of straightforward literal translation.

[17] The parentheses allowing the optional omission of some of the listed saints was a decision taken by the Consilium in 1968 to simplify the text.

[18] Mazza, *The Eucharistic Prayers*, 66.

[19] ICEL2003 faultily translated *Genetricis Dei et Domini nostri Iesu Christi* as "Mother of God and our Lord, Jesus Christ." This could imply a dual maternity, separating Jesus' divinity and

Joseph, her Spouse" reads much more felicitously than ICEL2008's discarded "blessed Joseph, Spouse of the same Virgin."

"we ask that through their merits and prayers, in all things we may be defended" (lines 19–20)

The Latin is grammatically incomplete. The subject of *communicantes* and *venerantes* is not specified; they cannot modify the implied subject of *concedas*, i.e., God.[20] On the premise that the subject of these participles is governed indirectly by an unexpressed *quaesumus* or by *muniamur*—the last line of the *Communicantes*—ICEL2010 has inserted "we ask that," which makes the subject of the participles explicit but leaves *concedas* untranslated.[21] This approach transfers the agency of "through their merits and prayers" from God (*concedas*) to us (*quaesumus*). The prepositional phrase "in all things" is also awkwardly placed. It would help to reword these lines to read "grant that through their merits and prayers we may be defended in all things."

Proper forms of the *Communicantes* (ICEL2010, no. 86, lines 23–54)

There are proper forms of the *Communicantes* for five major celebrations: Christmas, Epiphany, Easter Vigil through Easter week, Ascension, and Pentecost. On these occasions, the Latin text introduces the festal commemoration with *celebrantes* and inserts it between *communicantes* and *venerantes* with the list of saints. Because of how it chose to translate *communicantes et memoriam venerantes*, ICEL2010 had to depart from the Latin sequence. It places "celebrating . . ." first and then continues with "in communion with those whose memory we venerate." Because of the number and grammatical form of the phrases inserted in the texts for Epiphany and Ascension, effective proclamation requires careful preparation.

humanity, the exact opposite of what the Council of Chalcedon (451 CE) intended by the term *theotokos*.

[20] In view of the complicated history of the connection between the *Communicantes* and the *Memento* (see Jungmann MRR, 2:170–79), an earlier draft of this translation had chosen to strike out the third-person subject and to leave it open-ended. The final version restored the third-person plural in the conclusion (*concedas ut*; "we ask that"). The postconciliar French and Italian missals chose to translate *venerantes* with a verb form in the first-person plural, as did ICEL1973.

[21] By changing *venerantes* from a participle form into a declarative verb in the first-person plural, the postconciliar romance language texts named the implied subject of the participles and were able to translate *concedas ut* literally.

Hanc igitur (ICEL2010, no. 87, lines 2–9)

ICEL2010 inverts the sequence of the Latin, producing a more pleasing English phrasing. The contrast of *servitutis nostrae, sed et cunctae familiae tuae* is not fully captured in "of our service, that of your whole family," which places the two members in apposition. In its original context, the Latin distinguished the service of the clergy and that of the assembly.[22] That distinction is less apropos in current eucharistic theology and practice, which sees the whole assembly, congregants and priest, as the subject (*leitourgos*) of the liturgical action (CCC, no. 1188) along with the risen Lord (Heb 8:2). *Oblatio* is translated here as "oblation." In the following prayer, it is translated as "offering," a more readily understood word that also allows for greater nuance of meaning.[23]

Proper *Hanc igitur* (ICEL2010, no. 87, lines 10–21)

The Johannine text on which this translation draws (John 3:5) uses the preposition *ex* with a passive verb form: *nisi quis natus fuerit ex aqua et Spiritu*.[24] In the NABRE translation of this passage ("without being born of water and Spirit") the preposition "of" works because of the passive verb form. Translating *regenerare ex* as "give birth of" can be heard as shifting the meaning of the preposition "of" from origin-agency into a possessive genitive, as though this is the birth of the water and the Holy Spirit. Prepositions such as "from," "out of," "through," or "by" would be clearer.

Quam oblationem (ICEL2010, no. 88)

This prayer well exemplifies the difficulties facing a translator. The history of its redaction and vocabulary is complex. The sequence of five adjectives—*benedictam, adscriptam, ratam, rationabilem, acceptabilemque*—illustrates the difficulty of doing a simple literal translation of terms evolving over time. Unlike the first, fourth, and fifth adjectives, which have biblical resonances, *adscriptam* and *ratam* are drawn from Roman civil usage. *Adscribere* refers to officially enrolling or listing someone, such as a soldier or a citizen, in a registry (and thus their being accepted as such), and *reor* has to do with

[22] Botte and Mohrmann, *L'Ordinaire de la Messe*, 79, n. 2.

[23] *Oblatio* can mean both that which is offered and the act of offering. In the latter sense, the prayer asks God to accept our act of offering, *oblatio servitutis nostrae*.

[24] *Nova Vulgata*.

fixing, establishing, confirming, or ratifying something. Taken together from this Roman usage, these two words might well be translated as "accept [ratify] and approve this offering." The meaning of *rationabilis* has also been contested by scholars.[25] In Romans 12:1 and 1 Peter 2:2 it is used to translate the Greek *logikos*, with the meaning of "spiritual." Mohrmann argues that by the time of its use in the Roman Canon this biblical meaning had given way to the classical philosophical or juridical meaning of "reasonable" or "rational." Botte holds otherwise. Mazza sums up Botte's position thus: "In his analysis, Dom Botte points out that in the present *Quam oblationem*, the word *rationabilem* is accompanied by *acceptabilemque* and that in the Canon the particle *-que* combines the two and only two terms. *Acceptabilis* is a typical sacrificial word and, since it is so closely associated with *rationabilis*, we are compelled to assign a sacrificial meaning to it as well."[26] ICEL2010 has chosen to use the older biblical meaning of "spiritual."

Qui, pridie (ICEL2010, no. 89)

ICEL2008's rendering of the rubric *parum se inclinat* as "He bows slightly," was revised in ICEL2010 to the strange-sounding "He bends slightly," in which the reflexive object has been lost. This change, which appeared in the text that received the *recognitio* in March of 2010, was then reversed and the text received by US publishers in late 2010 again says, "He bows slightly." Standard wording in traditional liturgical usage would have been "He makes a slight body bow" (*se inclinans*) in contrast to "a head bow" (*caput inclinans*).

ICEL2010 has restored "and venerable" (*ac venerabiles*) to the institution narrative, and also added "O" to the phrase "to you, O God" for euphony. ICEL2010 has also restored *ex* ("eat *of* it") and *enim* in the text over the bread ("*for* this is my Body") and wine ("*for* this is the chalice of my Blood," *OM2008*, no. 90). Priests will need to be attentive until this new wording of the institution account has become familiar.

[25] See Botte and Mohrmann, *L'Ordinaire de la Messe*, 117–22.

[26] Mazza, *The Eucharistic Prayers*, 72. Botte had argued that in the Latin usage of the time, *que* joins only these two terms, separating them from the other three and coloring the meaning of *rationabilis*. Mazza also notes that the theology underlying this prayer has evolved over time and influences how we interpret its meaning within the Canon (ibid., 68–72).

Simili modo (ICEL2010, no. 90)

Using "chalice" instead of the familiar translation "cup" in this prayer will sound strange, even archaic, to the faithful,[27] evoking images of medieval jeweled chalices. The Greek and Latin of all the institution accounts (Matt 26:27; Mark 14:23; Luke 22:20; 1 Cor 11:25) have *potērion* and *calix*, respectively. In classical Latin, *calix* meant "cup, goblet, drinking vessel."[28] Recent scholarship on the historical background of these terms sheds light on the proper translation of *hunc praeclarum calicem*.[29] After discussing the range of primary and transferred meanings of *calix* in classical and ecclesiastical use, the author notes, "In the missal's euchology, *cup* more accurately and consistently reflects the meanings of *calix*, and neither its bluntness nor its common usage outside the liturgy in any way diminishes its appropriateness or value in our liturgy."[30] The study also questions the translation of *praeclarum* as "precious" and concludes that "[f]ailing the acceptance of other solutions, *taking the cup of wine* . . . is clear, and is faithful to the core of the tradition."[31]

ICEL2003 translated *qui pro vobis and pro multis effundetur* as "which will be poured out for you and for all."[32] ICEL2010 text reads "for many." Although literal to the Latin, this wording is sure to be a focus of further discussion.[33]

Mysterium fidei (ICEL2010, no. 91)

Following the lead of Consilium's revision,[34] *MR1970* had excised these words from the institution account and transposed them into an invitation

[27] The word "cup" is used in the approved Scripture translations familiar to most people, especially in the institution accounts proclaimed on Palm Sunday and Holy Thursday.

[28] See Charlton T. Lewis and Charles Short, *A Latin Dictionary* (Oxford: Clarendon Press, 1998), who give the same range of meanings for *poculum*.

[29] Barry M. Craig, "Potency, Not Preciousness: Cyprian's Cup and a Modern Controversy," *Worship* 81, no. 4 (2007): 290–313.

[30] Ibid., 293.

[31] Ibid., 313. Studies such as this suggest that the translation of the *OM* might well have benefitted from exposure to wider discussion and attained greater maturation in the process. As Craig notes, strict word-for-word translation of terse Latin formulations may fail to capture the fuller theological implications and richness found in their original and historical contexts (ibid., 292).

[32] ICEL2003 (n. 14), cited *Notitiae* 6 (1970): 39–40, 138–40, and the example of postconciliar Italian, German, Portuguese, and Spanish translations as rationale for retaining "for all." ICEL2008 already had "for many."

[33] See Elich, 330–31 below, and especially Chupungco, 480–81.

[34] Bugnini, 379 and 382.

for the memorial acclamation by the assembly, which ICEL1973 rendered as "Let us proclaim the mystery of faith." ICEL2010 has pared the invitation down to an exact translation of the Latin words. The popular first acclamation ("Christ has died, Christ is risen, Christ will come again") was an original ICEL text and has been dropped in keeping with the current restrictions on original compositions (*LitAuth*, nos. 98 and 106). The translation of the three remaining Latin acclamations has been changed, requiring adjustments on the part of the assembly and in musical settings. In the first and second acclamations, the ICEL1973 translation of *donec venias* as "until you come in glory" has been changed to the somewhat more literal "until you come again," although "again" is an expansion. The use of "cup" for *calix* in the second acclamation is inconsistent with the words of institution.

***Unde et memores* (ICEL2010, no. 92)**

Unde, which connects this prayer with the dominical command *hoc facite* (*OM2008*, no. 90), literally means "wherefore"; substituting "therefore" (*igitur*) makes the text more pleasing for proclamation. The Latin *memores* has been turned into a subordinate clause "as we celebrate." ICEL2010 has also significantly rearranged the Latin, delaying the translation of *nos servi tui, sed et plebs tua sancta* until the sixth line in English (line 7). This was rendered more felicitously by ICEL1998: "we celebrate the memory of Christ, your Son. We, your holy people and your ministers, call to mind." ICEL1998 and ICEL2010 both honor the ancient distinction between ministers and congregants noted earlier,[35] while preserving the sense of the unity of the assembly in making the offering. The Latin adversative *sed et* is downplayed by placing "your servants and your holy people" in apposition to "we."

"offer to your glorious majesty . . . this spotless victim" (lines 8–12)

Mazza has suggested "splendor of your glory" as an alternate translation to ICEL2010's "glorious majesty."[36] The word *hostia* is famously difficult to translate. Niermeyer specifies its meaning in medieval Christian usage as "Eucharistic sacrifice."[37] Commenting on this prayer, Mazza writes:

[35] See 285 above.

[36] Mazza, *The Eucharistic Prayers*, 78; also the discussion in Botte and Mohrmann, *L'Ordinaire de la Messe*, 111–13.

[37] J. F. Niermeyer, *Mediae Latinitatis Lexicon Minus* (Leiden: Brill, 2002).

> In like manner, the text of the Canon will become clearer if we take the three attributes [*puram, sanctam, immaculatam*] as referring to the *hostia* or "victim" in the two senses of the term: "victim" as meaning "sacrifice" and "victim" as meaning the bread and wine when seen in light of the special theological concern manifested in the above cited passage from Irenaeus. In other words, the three attributes apply not only to the sacrificial act but to the material of sacrifice as well.
>
> But is "victim" a suitable translation? It seems not. This "victim," after all, is immediately described as "the sacred bread of everlasting life and the chalice of eternal salvation." In everyday speech, even for a person with some education, it is difficult to understand how bread and chalice are a "victim" or of what they are a victim. It would be preferable, therefore, to translate *hostia* as "sacrifice" or even "worship and sacrifice," or something similar.[38]

Cipriano Vagaggini (d. 1999) also uses "sacrifice" in his literal translation of this part of EP I.[39]

Supra quae (ICEL2010, no. 93)

Grammatically the pronoun *quae* ("these offerings") refers to *Panem sanctum vitae aeternae et Calicem salutis perpetuae* in the previous paragraph (no. 92), which is the direct object of *offerimus*. This allows the shorthand reference here to "these offerings" that makes proclamation less cumbersome. The word "kindly" is perhaps too weak an equivalent for *propitio*, which means "merciful, forgiving, favorably inclined."

The addition of "once" in line 4 (not in the Latin) enhances the euphony. "Abel the just" in the following line may sound like an appellation not in the Latin and is better rendered "your just servant, Abel."

This text again raises the question of how to translate *hostia*. Mazza's literal translation is, "and that which your great priest Melchizedek offered to you, a holy sacrifice, a spotless offering."[40] What Melchizedek offered was bread and wine, not a sacrificial animal (Gen 14:18). It might be noted that Mazza's rendering also avoids the grammatical problem of apposition in ICEL2010.

[38] Mazza, *The Eucharistic Prayers*, 79.

[39] Cipriano Vagaggini, *The Canon of the Mass and Liturgical Reform*, trans. Peter Coughlan (Staten Island, NY: Alba House, 1967), 37.

[40] Mazza, *The Eucharistic Prayers*, 52.

Supplices (ICEL2010, no. 94)

The introduction of sense lines in ICEL1973 as a form of "visual punctuation" to indicate sense units has been of great service to effective proclamation. In the text that bears the 2010 *recognitio*, "receive" was at the end of line 7 after the word "altar"; in the version sent to publishers in late 2010, however, "receive" has been rightly moved to the beginning of line 8, keeping verb and object together. *Sumpserimus* is future perfect tense, not present. A more accurate translation would be that "those of us who shall have received . . . may be filled." Here, the simple future "shall receive" would be adequate.

Memento (ICEL2010, no. 95)

Mazza notes that "[t]he 'sign of faith' with which the dead have gone before us is baptism."[41] Jungmann also states that *signum fidei* "is not just a 'sign of faith' in an indefinite and general sense; it is the seal which in Baptism is impressed upon the profession of faith; thus it is Baptism itself."[42] Vagaggini renders *signum fidei* as "sealed with the sign of faith," a much clearer reference to baptism.[43] To convey the full baptismal theological meaning of the prayer, an implied verb, such as "sealed" or "marked," needs to be supplied. ICEL1973 and ICEL1998 read, "and have gone before us marked with the sign of faith."

"a place of refreshment, light and peace" (line 11)

In some parts of the English-speaking world "place of refreshment" is a euphemism for a pub. That is unfortunate, since this phrase has become liturgically memorable in many other parts of the English-speaking world. The root meaning of *refrigerare*—"to cool off" or, in a transferred sense, "to grow cool or become languid"—does not offer much help. *Refrigerium* has taken on the primary meaning of "solace, comfort, consolation, refuge."[44] Mazza's literal translation uses "place of comfort,"[45] but that could also be heard to suggest the contemporary euphemism of a "comfort station." To capture the note of solace and safe refuge in a poetic turn of phrase,

[41] Ibid., 84.

[42] Jungmann MRR, 2:242.

[43] Vagaggini, *Canon of the Roman Mass*, 38.

[44] See Niermeyer, *Mediae Latinitatis Lexicon Minus*; also Lewis and Short, *A Latin Dictionary*.

[45] Mazza, *The Eucharistic Prayers*, 52.

ICEL1998 used "a haven of light and peace." In the end "solace" might have been the translator's best choice.

Nobis quoque peccatoribus (ICEL2010, no. 96)

This opening line is fractured and does not flow well. ICEL2008, "To us, also, your sinful servants," flowed much better. Jungmann comments that there is ample evidence that *peccator* was once a standard self-designation, especially a self-designation of the clergy, and that this line refers to the ministers, not the whole assembly.[46] For that reason, it would be better to translate *quoque* not as "also," but rather "especially."[47]

Given the length of EP I, priests often use the option of omitting the names of the saints in brackets here, as in the *Communicantes*. Unfortunately, that leaves only the names of men in these two commemorations.

Per quem haec omnia (ICEL2010, no. 97)

Jungmann notes that this prayer is a remnant from a time when natural products were brought forward and blessed before the end of the Canon. In that context, *haec omnia* would have referred to these natural products as well, not only to the eucharistic species as it does now.[48] Translating *creas* as "make" may seem pedestrian to some. ICEL2003 was expressed more felicitously: "Through whom you ever create all these good things, O Lord, you make them holy and fill them with life, you bless them and give them to us."

Per ipsum (ICEL2010, no. 98)

The rubric at the head of the doxology was changed from ICEL2008's "elevating both" (chalice and paten with the host) to ICEL2010's "raising both." This provides resonance with the ritual action here and with the rubrics and ritual actions during the institution account.

The doxology, so straightforward in Latin, is not easy to translate into English. Difficulties arise both from following the Latin syntax and from the hendiadys (a figure of speech in which two words express a single idea,

[46] The postconciliar Italian translation expresses this clearly: *Anche a noi, tuoi ministri, peccatori.* The rubric calling for the priest alone to strike his breast reinforces this self-designation.

[47] Jungmann MRR, 2:249–50; Mazza accepts his position (*The Eucharistic Prayers*, 85).

[48] See Jungmann MRR, 2:259–64.

hence governing a verb in the singular). For example, ICEL2010's translation "O God, almighty Father" turns *tibi Deo Patri*, an indirect object in the dative case, into a vocative of address. ICEL2008 was particularly fractured and hard to proclaim effectively: "Through him, and with him, and in him, to you, O God, almighty Father, in the unity of the Holy Spirit, is all honor and all glory, forever and ever."[49] ICEL2003 read: "Through him, and with him, and in him, in the unity of the Holy Spirit, all glory and honor is yours, almighty God and Father, for ever and ever." Although it did not follow the Latin word order exactly, this version would have been much easier to proclaim.

Conclusion

The translators of ICEL2010 have at times, and wisely so, departed from the principle of strict formal equivalence, as *LitAuth* (no. 20) allows. Even so, the language of EP I often does not flow naturally for an English speaker. It is one of the longer and more grammatically complex prayers in the entire *MR2002* and requires priests to prepare and practice it aloud for effective proclamation.

[49] For example, "is all honor and all glory" is much harder to enunciate than "all glory and honor is yours."

The Mystagogical Implications

Mark E. Wedig

Mystagogy is a specific kind of interpretation of liturgy. By trying to explain the various meanings of an ecclesial ritual in a uniquely holistic way, mystagogy carries the weight of the cultural reception of the rite, the assortment of theological meanings conveyed, and the ways the prayer elicits conversion together in one presentation or reflection. Therefore, in order to create a proper mystagogy for EP I it is necessary to address a number of factors and their interrelatedness: the prayer's liturgical purpose and context, the meaning of the language in relationship to the assembly, the dominant theological themes that the prayer conveys when prayed by the assembly, and the kind of Christian spirituality elicited when its usage is regular and in the life of the local church.

Purpose and Context of a Mystagogy for EP I

The purpose of developing a mystagogy for EP I is to assist in engendering the assembly's full, conscious, and active participation in it. Therefore, where, when, and how the prayer is prayed is determinative of its vitality in the life of the church. All prayer arises out of an ecclesial context, both as a text and as prayer alive in its contemporary usage. EP I's contextual meanings span the life of the prayer from its ancient praxis to its reception in the life of contemporary local churches. The prayer exhibits the specific religious and theological concerns of the Roman Church of late antiquity. Praying this ancient Roman prayer also creates a unique dynamic as contemporary public prayer. Moreover, the contemporary dynamism of the prayer is more important for developing a mystagogy than its history.

The *Communicantes* (ICEL2010, no. 86) set up a normative liturgical context for praying EP I. There are proper *Communicantes* for Christmas and its Octave, Epiphany, from the Easter Vigil to the Second Sunday of Easter inclusive, Ascension, and Pentecost. EP I is meant to be prayed during these ancient and most venerated solemnities. There is also a proper *Hanc igitur* (ICEL2010, no. 87) for use from the Easter Vigil to the Second Sunday of Easter inclusive. These special forms set a normative context for praying this most ancient Roman Catholic EP during the more solemn liturgies of the liturgical year. The liturgical maxim that more ancient prayer texts take precedence over newer ones applies to the suggested usage of EP I for the most solemn liturgies of the church.

EP I has a particular purpose and context in the ordination rites of the Roman Catholic Church. The rubric for the ordination rites directs the use of EP I for these occasions. There are proper *Communicantes* from the ordination rites themselves specifying that God accept the offering from God's whole family and from the one God has chosen for the order of deacon, priest, and bishop.[1] The rites again give precedence to this most ancient Western anaphora for these solemn occasions.

In the actual life and practice of the church, however, more often than not EP I is not regularly prayed during these solemn liturgies—perhaps with the exception of the ordination rituals. Moreover, it is likely that EP I is seldom prayed in local parishes, and in most places it is not prayed at all.[2] Enrico Mazza notes, "Though theoretically in use, it has become marginal in practice; its use today is so minimal as to be statistically irrelevant. The Canon, whose text was most characteristic of the Roman liturgy from the fourth century on, is now practically unused."[3] The prayer in effect has dropped out of the assembly's consciousness. As a result, it has been rendered an artifact and object of historical reference more than an actual prayer in the life of the church.

A mystagogy for EP I, therefore, needs to recognize and take into consideration the basic evaporation of this prayer in the life of the post–Vatican II church. Because of its absence from the consciousness and practice of most contemporary Catholic Christians, negation and vacuum need to characterize reflection on the prayer. This mystagogy has to address this absence, admitting that the prayer is pastorally unknown to contemporary

[1] *The Rites of the Catholic Church*, 2 vols. (Collegeville, MN: Liturgical Press, 1991), 2:36, 47, and 76.

[2] For the purposes of gathering information for the essays in this volume, the author conducted three different focus groups to gauge people's experience of the EPs of the Roman Rite. The three groups of ten persons each, were composed of separate "populations" of churchgoers. Group 1 was made up of presbyters, ordained between five and thirty years. Group 2 was composed of graduate students in theology and ministry at a local Catholic university. Group 3 was made up of a range of persons who make up the regular membership of the eleven o'clock Sunday morning Eucharist at a local parish. My greatest astonishment came from the experience of Group 1. Of the ten presbyters, only one claimed to pray EP I on any regular basis; nine out of ten said they never prayed EP I in their parishes; two claimed they never prayed the prayer at all, even as a concelebrant of their own ordination.

[3] Enrico Mazza, *The Eucharistic Prayers of the Roman Rite*, trans. Matthew J. O'Connell (New York: Pueblo, 1986), xxxi.

generations. Furthermore, since the prayer, if prayed at all, can be thought to be used only for the most rare and arcane reasons, one need admit that this is mystagogy for a prayer that is not a part of the regular consciousness of the faithful.

In developing such a mystagogy, one could be tempted to create an apologetics for its contemporary relevance, as if the prayer's fading in the life of the faithful had to do with a social and cultural failure to appreciate the character of the prayer's language and the nuances of its structures. There are multiple contemporary commentaries and blogs that do so, lamenting the prayer's absence from the life of the church and attributing its demise to a certain disdain for the prayer that originated in members of the Consilium and that continues in the contemporary ecclesial context, especially among priests who have received little or no instruction concerning the prayer.[4] Yet such an apologetics is not helpful for seeing why EP I has often faded into the ecclesial background and been avoided pastorally. Instead, a mystagogy for EP I needs to examine critically both the strengths and weaknesses of the prayer's euchological language and theological meaning in order to clarify why the prayer has evaporated from use and how its revival might hinge on teaching about its pastoral and theological strengths.

Language of EP I

The language of EP I is central to both its affective strength as a prayer and the problem of its usage. Its language is evocative and unusual, making it emotionally appealing at one level but not resonant with everyday speech and problematic for participative listening at another level. The *Te igitur* (ICEL2010, no. 84), for example, evokes awe with a mystifying and formal tone, separated from everyday language. At one level there is a certain appeal to the majesty of such language. One also can construe that otherness is a fundamental characteristic of the holy, particularly if sacredness is understood strictly as an otherworldly and daunting presence.

Yet most people are not accustomed to such esoteric and obscure discourse and find it difficult to pray words that speak in such anachronistic hues and tones. For instance, in its *Supra quae*, EP I prays, "Be pleased to look upon these offerings with a serene and kindly countenance" (ICEL2010, no. 93). The phrase "serene and kindly countenance" does not resonate with the speech of twenty-first-century people. Most would pass over such

[4] www.adoremus.org/9-11-96 (accessed 27 December 2010).

language and dismiss its ability to mean anything to them. Such language makes it easier to steer away from praying EP I for pastoral reasons in that the prayer creates dissonance between liturgy and life.

Nonetheless, mystagogy is important for EP I since its structure and theological themes reverberate throughout EP II, EP III, and EP IV. The Roman Canon is significant in that it provides the foundational structure for the other EPs of the Roman Rite. The three other EPs that appeared in *MR1970* respond to the metaphors of sacrifice that punctuate EP I. Thus EP III—the prayer prayed most often on Sundays—was specifically written as a kind of corrective to the theological and linguistic flaws of the Roman Canon. Therefore, a proper mystagogy can examine EP I and EP III in relationship to one another.

Theological Discourse of EP I

A discourse of sacrifice predominates throughout EP I; it is therefore impossible to develop the mystagogical implications of this prayer without addressing the theological meaning of sacrifice for the prayer text itself and for contemporary Christians. To *approve* and to *accept* the sacrifice offered is of the essence of the prayer. What does it mean for human beings to come before God and present themselves as vulnerable and open to the compassionate will of the One who created them? There is nothing magical or directly consequential about our prayer that will persuade or coerce God. The prayer for acceptance leads to extended intercession and petition for the church, to protect it, to unify it, and to grant peace to it. It prays to remember the dead and those present at the liturgy who offer their sacrifice of praise. And in communion with all who have gone before this assembly, may they be defended by God's protecting help.

The mystagogical implications of EP I demand an extended reflection on the value of sacrifice as a fundamental way to pray eucharistically. Such an excursus first needs to militate against understandings of sacrifice that propitiates and barters with God in order to please the divine. For Christianity there was only one sacrifice of love in Christ Jesus and therefore all other sacrifices join themselves to that one sacrifice. EP I accentuates this. The prayer beckons God to accept and approve the nonbloody sacrifice of the Christian community as its vulnerable and most authentic posture of humility before the Creator.

Finally, a mystagogy of EP I must contend with the fragmented and discontinuous makeup of the prayer. It is difficult to view EP I as a theological aggregate or whole. It originates from multiple euchological texts that were collected into one prayer. It does not follow like a text that was written and composed by a single author.[5] Because of this it is more historically interesting than it is pastorally effective. Mystagogically, it is difficult to present the prayer as an ideal way to involve the faithful in praying in a participative manner. Instead, the prayer represents a highly redacted prayer that contains sometimes disparate shards of theological meaning. It is a text that collected and absorbed the valuable traditions of the early church that then was canonized as the central euchological prayer for the Roman Church for centuries after its acceptance.

Spirituality of EP I

A liturgical spirituality develops when the official public prayer of the church enters into the consciousness and imagination of an assembly. One can derive a spirituality of the liturgy from the language and theological meaning of liturgical prayer when it resonates with and is correlated to the struggles and hopes of the Christian people. When the fundamental rhythms and lyrics of the paschal mystery are enacted in prayer, and that prayer becomes a medium for knowing Christian life, one can view the liturgy as a locus of conversion. How and when can the assembly's praying of EP I function in the capacity to catalyze growth in the paschal mystery?

The Canon as a Foundational Euchological Spirituality of the West

Western eucharistic spirituality rests largely on the historical precedence of the Roman Canon for both good and bad. Without a living memory of this euchology, liturgy in the West—both Catholic and Protestant—cannot situate itself historically or understand its developments and reforms. For instance, Martin Luther's original EP was a radical redaction of the Roman Canon, leaving the preface, institution narrative, and final doxology as the principal structure of his prayer. Even though all references to sacrifice were extricated from his *Formula Missae*, Luther's reforms are still a reaction to the Roman Canon, and a Lutheran liturgical spirituality has deep roots in this prayer. Moreover, modern Roman Catholic reform of its euchology can be understood as both a response to and reaction against the Roman Canon. The other EPs of *MR1970* provided euchology that would give the faithful a more comprehensive and complete participation in eucharistic praying than the Canon could provide.

[5] Mazza, *The Eucharistic Prayers*, 55; also Baldovin, 251 above.

For a long period of the church's history, the Roman Canon, especially in its performance, underscored the hieratic and priestly role of the presider. The priest's actions, especially during the Canon, helped to determine a particularly sacerdotal understanding of ordained ministry. This was accentuated by the way the priest-celebrant was understood to mediate the presence of the divine in a unique way. For centuries, the Roman Canon was the prayer of the priest and not that of the assembly. How does praying EP I today preserve what was valuable and good about that understanding of the priestly ministry and how does praying it today inappropriately emphasize the role of the priest more as the unique mediator of the divine?

Along with this understanding of the EP as an essentially sacerdotal prayer, the Roman Canon also strongly emphasized the church's participation in a heavenly liturgy. EP I, by its words and gestures, casts a vivid image of the humbleness of humanity in a supplicant relationship to a sublime mystery that permeates both heaven and earth. Given that contemporary reforms have attempted to move away from the hierarchical understanding of the Eucharist as an act of priestly mediation and emphasize more the work of the assembly in union with priest, how does the contemporary church still preserve some of the strong hieratic tones, gestures, and images that join our worship with that of heaven? What parts of contemporary worship have underplayed the eschatological power of the Mass as set by EP I and what should be done to retrieve that?

If EP I is not to remain simply an ecclesial artifact but continue to represent part of the living euchological spirit of the church, how and when does praying it make sense in the life of the church? How does the church preserve what has been so valuable in its tradition while downplaying what has been problematic? The prayer itself is not likely to take a central role in the imagination of the Sunday assembly, but can it be considered a useful part of the tradition that is prayed and given precedence during the most solemn occasions of the church year? Moreover, EP I may also be preserved in the imaginations of the faithful when a liturgical catechesis of the other EPs demonstrates how the Roman Canon is an undeniable foundation upon which all other Roman EPs have been constructed.

This Holy and Living Sacrifice

The language of sacrifice that permeates EP I gives impetus to contemporary Roman Catholics for shaping an authentic mystagogy about the sacramental and eucharistic significance of sacrifice. This is not a matter of avoiding the terminology or concept, or even—á la Luther—extricating all references to it in our praying. Rather, this means learning to teach what is valuable about the discourses of sacrifice in Judaism and Christianity, especially concerning the Eucharist. There is an abundance of theological literature that emphasizes the great value of sacrifice in Christian history and for contemporary Christian spirituality.[6]

A retrieval of the NT understandings of sacrifice reveals that the original Christian usage of the term refers more to a moral disposition than to a ritual action. Similar to theological interpretations in Judaism contemporaneous with Jesus, early Christianity used the language of sacrifice to connote a disposition of the Christian who imitates Christ's self-giving love. Against that setting, one can understand how Christianity developed a "sacramental" notion of sacrifice. It was not until centuries into Christian history that the cultic activity of offering and expiation became interpreted through a sacrificial lens. Nevertheless, in Christian history the idea of sacrifice has suffered under that later connotation, clearly atypical from a NT perspective.

A proper mystagogy for EP I in sacrificial mode should focus on the idea of sacrifice as only the gift of Christ and that Christ through his abiding Spirit is the principal agent in the eucharistic sacrifice. This being said, EP I is pneumatologically defective in its overall construction placing an overemphasis on the eucharistic action as being christologically mediated to the detriment of the Spirit. Likewise, a proper mystagogy should strongly militate against the erroneous yet popular Christian misconception that the priest is the primary mediator offering the sacrifice in the person of Christ. EP I does not emphasize the latter even though it uses sacrificial terminology. A mystagogy of the prayer needs to demonstrate how a proper understanding of sacrifice punctuates the prayer.

Conclusion

This chapter has suggested that, in order to address the mystagogical implications of EP I, it is necessary to address a number of factors: the prayer's liturgical purpose and contexts, the meaning of the language in relationship to the assembly, the dominant theological themes that the prayer itself conveys when prayed, and the kind of spirituality the anaphora

[6] E.g., Robert J. Daly, *Sacrifice Unveiled: The True Meaning of Christian Sacrifice* (New York: Continuum, 2009); David N. Power, *The Eucharistic Mystery: Revitalizing the Tradition* (New York: Crossroad, 1994); Power, *The Sacrifice We Offer: The Tridentine Dogma and Its Reinterpretation* (London: T&T Clark, 1989); James Alison, *Raising Abel: The Recovery of the Eschatological Imagination* (New York: Crossroad, 1996).

can elicit. The degree that these factors can be distilled into a synthetic understanding of EP I will, to a large measure, determine the effectiveness of a proper and holistic interpretation of the prayer.

One faces a number of comprehensive challenges in rendering EP I alive and relevant to the imagination of today's assemblies: How does one integrate the prayer's ancient historical significance with the contemporary evaporation of its usage? How does one amalgamate the highly affective language of the prayer with the unfamiliarity of its discourse to contemporary people? How does one assimilate the significance of this archetypal text for all other Roman Catholic EPs while at the same time acknowledge that it is rendered pastorally irrelevant by so many pastors and people? How can one make the prayer's sacrificial discourse resonate with a proper spiritualization of that discourse? At the same time, believers still want and need to appropriate the richness of the prayer, especially through a contemporary liturgical spirituality that will enliven a greater appreciation for it. May the Roman Canon continue to find a place in the religious imaginations of prayerful and faithful assemblies.

Eucharistic Prayer II

The Latin Text

Prex Eucharistica II

99. Quamvis praefatione propria instructa sit, Prex eucharistica haec adhiberi potest etiam cum aliis praefationibus, cum iis praesertim quae mysterium salutis compendiose repraesentant, v. gr. cum praefationibus communibus.

℣. Dóminus vobíscum.
℟. Et cum spíritu tuo.

℣. Sursum corda.
℟. Habémus ad Dóminum.

℣. Grátias agámus Dómino Deo nostro.
℟. Dignum et iustum est.

Vere dignum et iustum est, aequum et salutáre,
nos tibi, sancte Pater,
semper et ubíque grátias ágere
per Fílium dilectiónis tuae Iesum Christum,
Verbum tuum per quod cuncta fecísti:
quem misísti nobis Salvatórem et Redemptórem,
incarnátum de Spíritu Sancto et ex Vírgine natum.

Qui voluntátem tuam adímplens
et pópulum tibi sanctum acquírens
exténdit manus cum paterétur,
ut mortem sólveret et resurrectiónem manifestáret.

Et ídeo cum Angelis et ómnibus Sanctis
glóriam tuam praedicámus, una voce dicéntes:

Sanctus, Sanctus, Sanctus Dóminus Deus Sábaoth.
Pleni sunt caeli et terra glória tua.
Hosánna in excélsis.
Benedíctus qui venit in nómine Dómini.
Hosánna in excélsis.

100. Sacerdos, manibus extensis, dicit:

Vere Sanctus es, Dómine, fons omnis sanctitátis.

101. Iungit manus, easque expansas super oblata tenens, dicit:

Haec ergo dona, quaesumus,
Spíritus tui rore sanctífica,

The English Text

Eucharistic Prayer II

99. Although it is provided with its own Preface, this Eucharistic Prayer may also be used with other Prefaces, especially those that present an overall view of the mystery of salvation, such as the Common Prefaces.

℣. The Lord be with you.
℟. And with your spirit.

℣. Lift up your hearts.
℟. We lift them up to the Lord.

℣. Let us give thanks to the Lord our God.
℟. It is right and just.

It is truly right and just, our duty and our salvation,
always and everywhere to give you thanks, Father most holy,
through your beloved Son, Jesus Christ,
your Word through whom you made all things,
whom you sent as our Savior and Redeemer,
incarnate by the Holy Spirit and born of the Virgin.

Fulfilling your will and gaining for you a holy people,
he stretched out his hands as he endured his Passion,
so as to break the bonds of death and manifest the resurrection.

And so, with the Angels and all the Saints
we declare your glory,
as with one voice we acclaim:

Holy, Holy, Holy Lord God of hosts.
Heaven and earth are full of your glory.
Hosanna in the highest.
Blessed is he who comes in the name of the Lord.
Hosanna in the highest.

100. The Priest, with hands extended, says:

You are indeed Holy, O Lord,
the fount of all holiness.

101. He joins his hands and, holding them extended over the offerings, says:

Make holy, therefore, these gifts, we pray,
by sending down your Spirit upon them like the dewfall,

iungit manus

et signat semel super panem et calicem simul, dicens:

ut nobis Corpus et ✠ Sanguis fiant
Dómini nostri Iesu Christi.

Iungit manus.

102. In formulis quae sequuntur, verba Domini proferantur distincte et aperte, prouti natura eorundem verborum requirit.

Qui cum Passióni voluntárie traderétur,

accipit panem,

eumque parum elevatum super altare tenens, prosequitur:

accépit panem et grátias agens fregit,
dedítque discípulis suis, dicens:

parum se inclinat

ACCÍPITE ET MANDUCÁTE EX HOC OMNES:
HOC EST ENIM CORPUS MEUM,
QUOD PRO VOBIS TRADÉTUR.

Hostiam consecratam ostendit populo, reponit super patenam, et genuflexus adorat.

103. Postea prosequitur:

Símili modo, postquam cenátum est,

accipit calicem,

eumque parum elevatum super altare tenens, prosequitur:

accípiens et cálicem
íterum tibi grátias agens dedit discípulis suis, dicens:

parum se inclinat

ACCÍPITE ET BÍBITE EX EO OMNES:
HIC EST ENIM CALIX SÁNGUINIS MEI
NOVI ET AETÉRNI TESTAMÉNTI,
QUI PRO VOBIS ET PRO MULTIS EFFUNDÉTUR
IN REMISSIÓNEM PECCATÓRUM.

HOC FÁCITE IN MEAM COMMEMORATIÓNEM.

Calicem ostendit populo, deponit super corporale, et genuflexus adorat.

He joins his hands
and makes the Sign of the Cross once over the bread and the chalice together, saying:

so that they may become for us
the Body and ✠ Blood of our Lord Jesus Christ.

He joins his hands.

102. In the formulas that follow, the words of the Lord should be pronounced clearly and distinctly, as the nature of these words requires.

At the time he was betrayed
and entered willingly into his Passion,

He takes the bread
and, holding it slightly raised above the altar, continues:

he took bread and, giving thanks, broke it,
and gave it to his disciples, saying:

He bows slightly.

TAKE THIS, ALL OF YOU, AND EAT OF IT,
FOR THIS IS MY BODY,
WHICH WILL BE GIVEN UP FOR YOU.

He shows the consecrated host to the people, places it again on the paten, and genuflects in adoration.

103. After this, he continues:

In a similar way, when supper was ended,

He takes the chalice
and, holding it slightly raised above the altar, continues:

he took the chalice
and, once more giving thanks,
he gave it to his disciples, saying:

He bows slightly.

TAKE THIS, ALL OF YOU, AND DRINK FROM IT,
FOR THIS IS THE CHALICE OF MY BLOOD,
THE BLOOD OF THE NEW AND ETERNAL COVENANT,
WHICH WILL BE POURED OUT FOR YOU AND FOR MANY
FOR THE FORGIVENESS OF SINS.

DO THIS IN MEMORY OF ME.

He shows the chalice to the people, places it on the corporal, and genuflects in adoration.

104. Deinde dicit:

Mystérium fídei.

Et populus prosequitur, acclamans:

Mortem tuam annuntiámus, Dómine,
et tuam resurrectiónem confitémur, donec vénias.

Vel:

Quotiescúmque manducámus panem hunc
et cálicem bíbimus,
mortem tuam annuntiámus, Dómine, donec vénias.

Vel:

Salvátor mundi, salva nos,
qui per crucem et resurrectiónem tuam liberásti nos.

105. Deinde sacerdos, extensis manibus, dicit:

Mémores ígitur mortis et resurrectiónis eius,
tibi, Dómine, panem vitae
et cálicem salútis offérimus,
grátias agéntes quia nos dignos habuísti
astáre coram te et tibi ministráre.

Et súpplices deprecámur
ut Córporis et Sánguinis Christi partícipes
a Spíritu Sancto congregémur in unum.

Recordáre, Dómine, Ecclésiae tuae toto orbe diffúsae,
ut eam in caritáte perfícias
una cum Papa nostro N. et Epíscopo nostro N.*
et univérso clero.

---

* Hic fieri potest mentio de Episcopis Coadiutore vel Auxiliaribus, vel de alio Episcopo, ut in *Institutione generali Missalis Romani*, n. 149, notatur.

104. Then he says:

The mystery of faith.

And the people continue, acclaiming:

We proclaim your Death, O Lord,
and profess your Resurrection
until you come again.

Or:

When we eat this Bread and drink this Cup,
we proclaim your Death, O Lord,
until you come again.

Or:

Save us, Savior of the world,
for by your Cross and Resurrection
you have set us free.

105. Then the Priest, with hands extended, says:

Therefore, as we celebrate
the memorial of his Death and Resurrection,
we offer you, Lord,
the Bread of life and the Chalice of salvation,
giving thanks that you have held us worthy
to be in your presence and minister to you.

Humbly we pray
that, partaking of the Body and Blood of Christ,
we may be gathered into one by the Holy Spirit.

Remember, Lord, your Church,
spread throughout the world,
and bring her to the fullness of charity,
together with N. our Pope and N. our Bishop*
and all the clergy.

---

* Mention may be made here of the Coadjutor Bishop, or Auxiliary Bishops, as noted in the *General Instruction of the Roman Missal*, no. 149.

In Missis pro defunctis addi potest:

Meménto fámuli tui (fámulae tuae) N.,
quem (quam) (hódie) ad te ex hoc mundo vocásti.
Concéde, ut, qui (quae) complantátus (complantáta) fuit
similitúdini mortis Fílii tui,
simul fiat et resurrectiónis ipsíus.

Meménto étiam fratrum nostrórum,
qui in spe resurrectiónis dormiérunt,
omniúmque in tua miseratióne defunctórum,
et eos in lumen vultus tui admítte.
Omnium nostrum, quaésumus, miserére,
ut cum beáta Dei Genetríce Vírgine María,
beátis Apóstolis et ómnibus Sanctis,
qui tibi a saéculo placuérunt,
aetérnae vitae mereámur esse consórtes,
et te laudémus et glorificémus

iungit manus

per Fílium tuum Iesum Christum.

106. Accipit patenam cum hostia et calicem, et utrumque elevans, dicit:

Per ipsum, et cum ipso, et in ipso,
est tibi Deo Patri omnipoténti,
in unitáte Spíritus Sancti,
omnis honor et glória
per ómnia saécula saeculórum.

Populus acclamat:

Amen.

Deinde sequitur ritus communionis.

In Masses for the Dead, the following may be added:

Remember your servant N.,
whom you have called (today)
from this world to yourself.
Grant that he (she) who was united with your Son in a death like his,
may also be one with him in his Resurrection.

Remember also our brothers and sisters
who have fallen asleep in the hope of the resurrection,
and all who have died in your mercy:
welcome them into the light of your face.
Have mercy on us all, we pray,
that with the Blessed Virgin Mary, Mother of God,
with the blessed Apostles,
and all the Saints who have pleased you throughout the ages,
we may merit to be coheirs to eternal life,
and may praise and glorify you

He joins his hands.

through your Son, Jesus Christ.

106. He takes the chalice and the paten with the host and, raising both, he says:

Through him, and with him, and in him,
O God, almighty Father,
in the unity of the Holy Spirit,
all glory and honor is yours,
for ever and ever.

The people acclaim:

Amen.

Then follows the Communion Rite.

History of the Latin Text and Rite

John Baldovin

As Annibale Bugnini wrote in his chronicle of the post–Vatican II liturgical reform, "Once euchological pluralism and rubrical flexibility had been rediscovered after centuries of fixism, it was unthinkable that a monolithic approach to the EP should long endure."[1] Of the three new anaphoras added to the *OM1969* of Paul VI, EP II contains a great deal of ancient material. This prayer was intended to be a modern adaptation of the example of a EP found in ApTrad.

The Apostolic Tradition

The anaphora of ApTrad is imbedded within the rite for the ordination of a bishop. ApTrad itself, an early "church order," is a very complex document with a fascinating history. First published in the early twentieth century, until recently it was considered the work of Hippolytus, a third-century Roman presbyter and theologian. That attribution has been seriously challenged. It now seems that this is a document of "living literature" compiled in stages. The most complete manuscript is a Latin translation that dates from the end of the fifth century.[2] Therefore, it is erroneous to make sweeping generalizations about the anaphora such as: this is *the Roman* anaphora of the *early third century*. It is fairly clear that the author was not the early third-century Roman presbyter, Hippolytus.[3] It is not altogether clear that the document is Roman at all, nor that every feature of it comes from the third century. In fact, there is a growing consensus that the institution narrative in this prayer was a fourth-century addition.[4]

[1] Annibale Bugnini, *The Reform of the Liturgy: 1948–1975*, trans. Matthew J. O'Connell (Collegeville, MN: Liturgical Press, 1990), 448.

[2] Paul Bradshaw, Maxwell Johnson, and L. Edward Phillips, *The Apostolic Tradition: A Commentary*, ed. Harold W. Attridge, *Hermeneia* series (Minneapolis: Fortress Press, 2002), 7–15.

[3] Regarding the question of "which Hippolytus," see John Baldovin, "Hippolytus and the *Apostolic Tradition*: Recent Research and Commentary," *Theological Studies* 64 (2003): 520–42.

[4] See Matthieu Smyth, "The Anaphora of the So-Called 'Apostolic Tradition' and the Roman Eucharistic Prayer," in *Issues in Eucharistic Praying in East and West*, ed. Maxwell Johnson (Collegeville, MN: Liturgical Press, 2010), 71–97.

This last point is extremely important and a sensitive issue as well. The anaphora of ApTrad is often used as evidence that "our first full text" of a EP contains the institution narrative. But contemporary research into the origin of eucharistic praying leans toward the conviction that the institution narrative was actually an embolism or expansion that was used as a scriptural warrant for the prayer itself, along the lines that Deuteronomy 8:10 serves as a scriptural warrant for the prayer found in the *Didache*, and Malachi 1:11 for the prayer of the Strasbourg Papyrus Gk. 258.[5] In this way one can understand the 2002 Vatican decision to accept the validity of another ancient prayer, the Anaphora of Addai and Mari (East Syrian tradition)—a prayer that does not contain an explicit institution narrative.[6]

In addition, ApTrad itself makes it quite clear (at least in the Coptic, Arabic, and Ethiopic versions) that the anaphora is an exemplar, not a prayer that must be repeated word for word. Until at least the fourth century EPs were improvised.[7] Here is the text of the anaphora in the Verona Latin and English translations.[8]

Verona Latin	English Translation
Dominus vobiscum	The Lord be with you.
Et omnes dicant; Et cum spiritu tuo.	*And all shall say:* And with your spirit.
Sursum corda.	Up with your hearts.
Habemus ad Dominum.	We have (them) with the Lord.
Gratias agamus Domino.	Let us give thanks to the Lord.
Dignum et iustum est.	It is fitting and right.
Et sic iam prosequatur:	*And then he shall continue thus:*
Gratias tibi referimus, Deus, per dilectum puerum tuum, Jesum Christum,	We render thanks to you, O God, through your beloved child Jesus

[5] For a fine summary of the state of research on the institution narrative and the early Eucharist, see Paul Bradshaw, "Did Jesus Institute the Eucharist at the Last Supper?" in Johnson, *Issues in Eucharistic Praying*, 1–19.

[6] See the comprehensive summary of the issues by Nicholas Russo, "The Validity of Addai and Mari: A Critique of the Critiques," in Johnson, *Issues in Eucharistic Praying*, 21–62.

[7] Cf. Allan Bouley, *From Freedom to Formula: The Evolution of the Eucharistic Prayer from Oral Improvisation to Written Texts* (Washington, DC: Catholic University of America Press, 1981); also, Vincenzo Raffa, *Liturgia Eucaristica: Mistagogia della Messa: dalla storia e dalla teologia alla pastorale pratica*, Bibliotheca 'Ephemerides liturgicae' Subsidia 100 (Rome: CLV, 2003), 497–531, esp. see his note on free composition, 512–13.

[8] Latin as reproduced in *Prex Eucharistica*, 1:80–81; English translation from Jasper & Cuming, 34–35.

quem in ultimis temporibus misisti nobis salvatorem et redemptorem et angelum voluntatis tuae, qui est Verbum tuum inseparabile, per quem omnia fecisti, et <cum> beneplacitum tibi fuit, misisti de caelo in matricem virginis; quique, in utero habitus, incarnatus est et Filius tibi ostensus est, ex Spiritu sancto et virgine natus.	Christ, whom in the last times you sent to us as a savior and redeemer and angel of your will; who is your inseparable Word, through whom you made all things, and in whom you were well pleased. You sent him from heaven into a Virgin's womb; and conceived in the womb, he was made flesh and was manifested as your Son, being born of the Holy Spirit and the Virgin.
Qui voluntatem tuam complens et populum sanctum tibi adquirens, extendit manus, cum pateretur, ut a passione libareret eos qui in te crediderunt.	Fulfilling your will and gaining for you a holy people, he stretched out his hands when he should suffer, that he might release from suffering those who have believed in you.
Qui cumque traderetur voluntariae passioni, ut mortem solvat et vincula diaboli dirumpat, et inferum calcet et iustos illuminet, et terminum figat et resurrectionem manifestet, accipiens panem, gratias tibi agens dixit: Accipite, manducate, hoc est corpus meum quod pro vobis confringetur.	And when he was betrayed to voluntary suffering that he might destroy death, and break the bonds of the devil, and tread down hell, and shine upon the righteous, and fix a term, and manifest the resurrection, he took bread and gave thanks to you, saying: "Take, eat, this is my body, which shall be broken for you."
Similiter et calicem dicens: Hic est sanguis meus, qui pro vobis effunditur. Quando hoc facitis, meam commemorationem facitis.	Likewise also the cup, saying: "This is my blood, which is shed for you; when you do this, you make my remembrance."
Memores igitur mortis et resurrectionis eius, offerimus tibi panem et calicem, gratias tibi agens, quia nos dignos habuisti adstare coram te et tibi ministrare.	Remembering therefore his death and resurrection, we offer to you the bread and the cup, giving you thanks because you have held us worthy to stand before you and minister to you.
Et petimus, ut mittas Spiritum tuum sanctum in oblationem sanctae	And we ask that you would send your Holy Spirit upon the offering of your

Ecclesiae; in unum congregans, des omnibus qui percipient <de> sanctis in repletionem Spiritus sancti, ad confirmationem fidei in veritate, ut te laudemus et glorificemus per puerum tuum Iesum Christum: per quem tibi gloria et honor Patri et Filio cum sancto Spiritu in sancta Ecclesia tua et nunc et in saecula saeculorum. Amen.	holy Church;[9] that, gathering her into one, you would grant to all who receive the holy things (to receive) for the fullness of the Holy Spirit for the strengthening of faith in truth; that we may praise and glorify you through your child Jesus Christ; through whom be glory and honor to you, to the Father, and the Son, with the Holy Spirit, in your holy Church, both now and to the ages of ages. Amen.

In comparison with our contemporary EP II several aspects of this prayer stand out. In the first place there is no *Sanctus*. It is impossible to know with certainty when the threefold Holy was introduced into eucharistic praying. Since developed EPs may well be a combination of different original units put together, the *Sanctus* unit may have been joined to a prayer like that of ApTrad.[10]

A second feature of note is the nature of the epiclesis that follows the oblation and simply asks for the gift of the Holy Spirit upon the church and the recipients of communion.

Finally, it is not altogether clear whether the phrase *adstare coram te et tibi ministrare* ("to stand before you and minister to you") refers to the newly ordained bishop or to the faithful as a whole. The nominative plural ("we") of traditional liturgical praying normally refers to the entire assembly. On the other hand, this prayer is offered as a specific example of how one *might* pray at the ordination of a bishop.

Although the intention was to adapt the prayer from ApTrad, the result was evidently a very different prayer altogether that retained some of ApTrad's imagery from its praise section. Enrico Mazza has argued extensively and persuasively that much of the theology and vocabulary of ApTrad's anaphora is derived from the paschal homilies of the second century, such as the *Peri Pascha* of Melito of Sardis (d. *ca.* 190), the homily on the resurrection of Pseudo-Epiphanius, and the *Peri Pascha* of Pseudo-Hippolytus (after the fourth century CE). Some of the phrases that Mazza finds in both the second-century homilies and in the anaphora of ApTrad

[9] Jasper & Cuming note here (n. 35) that the Latin is virtually untranslatable.

[10] See Gabriele Winkler, "On Angels, Humans, the Holy, and its Perversions: Greetings from Faust," *Studia liturgica* 34 (2004): 63; see also Paul Bradshaw, *Eucharistic Origins* (London: SPCK, 2004), 128.

are: "the angel of your will" (Pseudo-Hippolytus), "whom you sent from heaven to a Virgin's womb" (Melito; fragment), "your inseparable word" (both Pseudo-Hippolytus and Melito), and "to break the bonds of death" (Pseudo-Hippolytus, Melito, and Pseudo-Epiphanius). He does not so much argue a direct dependence of the anaphora on these homilies as note a common stock of imagery in use during the second century. That would make the origin of a good part of this prayer very early.[11] At the same time, we need to be cautious about the idea that there were any "canonized" prayers in the first three centuries.

The decision by the Consilium to adopt a common structure for all EPs in the Roman Rite made it impossible to retain the prayer found in ApTrad.[12]

The Prayer Today

The prayer we know as EP II is quite different from the anaphora of ApTrad which served as its inspiration. The architect of the post–Vatican II liturgical reform, Annibale Bugnini, gives the following account of the common structure of the new EPs in *MR1970*:

1. Preface (changeable in EPs II and III, unchanging in IV)
2. Transition from the *Sanctus* to the consecratory epiclesis (very short in II, short in III, lengthy in IV)
3. Consecratory epiclesis
4. Account of institution
5. *Anamnesis* and offering of the divine Victim
6. Prayer for acceptance of the offering and for a fruitful communion

7 and 8. Commemoration of the saints and intercessions (or intercessions and commemoration of the saints)

9. Doxology[13]

A comparison of the text of ApTrad with EP II shows that very little of the former has been retained. In its preface EP II has several phrases from the

[11] Enrico Mazza, *The Origins of the Eucharistic Prayer* (Collegeville, MN: Liturgical Press, 1995), 107–27.

[12] As Bugnini himself acknowledges, 456.

[13] Ibid., 451.

"paschal homily" material of ApTrad: *quem . . . misisti nobis salvatorem et redemptorem . . . ex Spiritu sancto et virgine natus. Qui voluntatem tuam complens et populum sanctum tibi adquirens, extendit manus, cum pateretur . . . resurrectionem manifestaret.*[14] The institution narrative contains a few phrases that can be found in ApTrad. The anamnesis and oblation section that follows the memorial acclamation, however, is taken from ApTrad virtually verbatim: *Memores igitur mortis et resurrectionis eius, offerimus tibi panem et calicem, gratias tibi agentes, quia nos dignos habuisti adstare coram te et tibi ministrare.*[15] There is also a faint resemblance between ApTrad's epiclesis and the second epiclesis of EP II, which asks that the Holy Spirit gather the church.

The "new" material in EP II, therefore, consists of the addition of the *Sanctus* with its introduction; a bridge from the *Sanctus* to the remainder of the prayer, employing the typical West Syrian anaphoral connecting word "Holy"; a consecratory epiclesis before the institution narrative; the reformulation of the institution narrative; the memorial acclamation; and the intercessions. Many of the more difficult phrases that figured in the anaphora of ApTrad were eliminated by the liturgical reform. The phrase *terminum figat* ("set a limit")—which Matthieu Smyth translates as "to fix the rule of this sacrifice"[16]—stands out.

This prayer is relatively brief and was intended for weekday use. Its main virtues are that (at least theoretically) it honors an ancient prayer of the church and it is filled with scriptural resonances.

[14] "whom you sent as our Savior and Redeemer, incarnate by the Holy Spirit and born of the Virgin. Fulfilling your will and gaining for you a holy people, he stretched out his hands as he endured his Passion [so as to break the bonds of death and] manifest the resurrection" (ICEL2010, no. 99; the bracketed words are not in the Verona text of ApTrad).

[15] "Therefore, as we celebrate the memorial of his Death and Resurrection, we offer you, Lord, the Bread of life and the Chalice of salvation, giving thanks that you have held us worthy to be in your presence and minister to you" (ICEL2010, no. 105). It seems that the translators have opted to translate *tibi ministrare* in a way that favors the minister as subject; see Power 323–24 below.

[16] Smyth, "Anaphora," 90.

Theology of the Latin Text and Rite[1]

David Power

Introduction

In interpreting the new prayers of *MR1970* and its successors, one must keep in mind that they are not prayers that evolved within church communities but are commissioned compositions. Hence, they cannot be related to any particular culture or territory that can be examined in order to see what gives rise to them, as can be done with the Roman Canon. Rather, they are scholarly attempts that draw on the fruits of studies of a variety of other liturgical traditions, Eastern and Western, in order to make up for what were seen as defects in the Canon. While taking from what was thought to be the best Latin of the liturgical tradition, they borrowed from an abundance of sources spread out over time, including Greek, Syriac, Gallican, and Old Spanish, as well as Roman.

In their format, they are made to fit the model of the Roman Canon, which is a sequence of short prayers rather than a single literary unit. The institution narrative is placed within the intercessions so that it is preceded by a petition for the sanctification of the gifts, now modified to include a plea for the sending of the Spirit. The intercessions after the anamnesis include reference to communion with the Bishop of Rome. In a theological hermeneutic one needs to take account of the narrative foundation for remembrance before and after the *Sanctus* and the connections between thanksgiving, praise, institution narrative, offering, and intercessions.[2]

Paradigm for EP II

In composing EP II, the authors drew on the EP found in ApTrad.[3] This was ecumenically inspired in that many churches in the revision of their

[1] For studies of this prayer, see Enrico Mazza, *The Eucharistic Prayers of the Roman Rite*, trans. Matthew J. O'Connell (New York: Pueblo, 1986), 88–122, and the literature he quotes.

[2] What has been said in the previous essay on items common to all four prayers is not repeated here, see 261–75 above.

[3] On the enigmatic status of that document in liturgical history, see Baldovin, 311 above.

eucharistic liturgies were ready to take this prayer as a springboard from which they could reach some convergence. In truth, EP II wanders considerably from it, both in structure and in meaning, and has to be examined as an original text with its own distinctive style and content.

To express the nature and meaning of the prayer, several terms, largely borrowed from the early Latin tradition of Rome, are used to express what the church does in its worship: it is to give thanks (*gratias agere*), in order to give glory to God or to proclaim his glory (*gloriam praedicare*); in conjunction with giving thanks, it offers the oblation or sacrifice of the gifts sanctified (*offerimus, gratias agentes*); it anticipates the eternal praise (*te laudemus et glorificemus*) to which the community looks forward. It follows what Burkhard Neunheuser pointed to as the genius of the Roman Rite, inviting the assembly to offer through Christ and ascribing continual mediation to him in heavenly worship.[4] The movement of prayer is from what is predominantly thanksgiving for what has been done to praising and glorifying God and in remembering the saints and praying for the deceased anticipating the companionship in eternal life (*vitae aeternae consortes*) where praise and glory are offered to God through the Son (*te laudemus et glorificemus*).[5] Thanksgiving dominates earthly worship, when God's deeds are remembered, but what is anticipated is eternal praise and glorification when God's glory is seen. It is in this prayerful anticipation that the gathered community approaches the table, where it is one in the communion of Christ's Pasch that is remembered.

Preface (*OM2008*, no. 99)

The opening dialogue and first words of the prayer are the same as EP I, examined above. In the movement of thanksgiving in the pre-*Sanctus* the prayer remembers the work of Christ in both creation and redemption and in this way names the one whose memorial is kept. He is God's beloved Son and his Word. The words *Filium dilectionis tuae* evoke the baptism of Jesus (e.g., Mark 1:11) and the transfiguration (e.g., Mark 9:7), where the voice from above proclaims him God's beloved Son, as these accounts are found in Latin translations of the NT. *Dilectio* translates the divine *agape*, the love pronounced by the Father for the Son, the love that is given to

[4] Burkhard Neunheuser, "Roman Genius Revisited," in *Liturgy for the New Millennium: A Commentary on the Revised Sacramentary*, ed. Mark R. Francis and Keith F. Pecklers (Collegeville, MN: Liturgical Press / Pueblo, 2000), 35–48.

[5] This is also found in EPs III and IV.

those who are beloved in Christ, through whom the church gives thanks. The words *Verbum tuum per quod cuncta fecisti* recall the Johannine prologue, which through mention of the beloved is collated with Colossians 1:15ff.: Christ, Lord of all creation and head of the church, is the Word and Beloved Son of the Father.[6]

The prayer has a trinitarian orientation and expresses how the liturgical action participates in the life of the triune God. The incarnation of God's beloved is the work of the Spirit and this reference to the Spirit carries over into the prayers for sanctification that occur in the intercessory part of the prayer. In describing the work of Christ, *Salvator et Redemptor* is a deliberate pairing to express the mystery of what Christ has wrought. The two words, either as nouns or in their form as verbs, are found in the Latin Vulgate[7] to translate what is said of the saving act that gives grace, the redemption or ransom or price paid to free humanity from sin and death.[8]

As for the meaning given to the mystery being celebrated, what stands out in the text of ApTrad is the voluntary suffering of Christ by which he freed the world from suffering and set a term to the power of death. In evoking this, EP II accentuates the Son's submission to the will of the Father (*voluntatem tuam adimplens*). Christ was sent to dissolve death (*ut mortem solveret*), or put an end to its empire, and to manifest the resurrection (*et resurrectionem manifestaret*), and in so doing he purchased a holy people at the price of his suffering (*populum acquirens*).

Both *solvere*[9] and *acquirere* render the images used in NT Greek to express salvation through the death of Christ "at a cost." *Acquirere*[10] also has the sense of making a purchase, or metaphorically obtaining something by

[6] In *MR2002* God is called *conditor et redemptor* (e.g., Sodi, nos. 107, 1861, 3159, 3174), and Christ the *Redemptor* whom God has sent (e.g., Sodi, nos. 147, 856, 618), but he is not called *conditor* except in the hymn *Crux fidelis* (Sodi, no. 601). This respects the understanding that God the Father is the origin and Christ the one *through* whom he acts. This holds for what is said of Christ's role in creation in the EPs II, III, and IV.

[7] While other Latin translations predate the Vulgate, for ready reference it may serve to see how Latin terms translate Greek. For *salvator* see Luke 2:11; John 4:42; Eph 5:23. A classical instance of *redimere* is 1 Pet 1:18-19; see also Gal 3:3.

[8] For *salvator* in *MR2002* biblical antiphons, see Sodi, nos. 6, 152, 160; in prayers for Advent, Sodi, nos. 1240, 1570, 1660, 1863.

[9] Several instances of linking *solvere* with release are found in *MR2002*, as seen in the Sodi concordance under this word: *vincula solvat, damni ligni ut solveret, solvere debitum populi tui, adae debitum solvit*. While it connotes a debt rendered, *solvere mortem* means to release from death's hold.

[10] The two words are put together in Eph 1:14, *in redemptionem acquisitionis*. In Roman sacramentaries the verb *acquirere* and the substantive *acquisitio* is used of what the people obtain through the observance of prayer and solemnities; e.g., *Hadrianum*, nos. 32, 219, 313, 718, 994, which does not quite render the sense given the word here as something done by Christ.

striving, seeking, and searching without restraint, so that the people may be Christ's and God's own.[11] The sense of strife, of the pain suffered by Christ in surrendering to willing suffering, is much stronger in ApTrad but is not lost in EP II because of the phrase *extendit manus cum pateretur*.[12]

The locution *Manifestare resurrectionem* puts the resurrection in the order of public display: it reveals Christ's power over death as he enters into new life. In its use in *MR2002*, this meaning of *manifestare* shows up first in biblical antiphons[13] and is found most often in Advent prayers.[14] It is also used of the transfiguration, pointing to it as a manifestation of the *claritas* (glory shown in light) that God has given to the Son.[15] *Manifestare* is used in NT Latin to express the revelation of Christ to the Gentiles, the glory of God shown in Christ, God's revelation through the nativity, the epiphany, the transfiguration, and the Supper, and the glory that the Spirit gives to the Son. It is sometimes used with *clarificare*, one of the set of verbs used to express what in NT Greek is called *doxa*. It is only by the resurrection manifested, proclaimed, made clear for its victory over death that the power of Christ's overcoming of death by his death is known and that his glory as God's Son is made clear.[16]

Post-*Sanctus* (*OM2008*, no. 100)

The *Sanctus* having been sung, the holiness of the people acquired then becomes a theme, for it is in virtue of their holiness that they participate in the very holiness of God. Phrases that return like a refrain through the prayer are *Populus sanctus, sanctus Deus, vere sanctus, fons sanctitatis, Spiritus tui rore sanctifica, dona sancta*. This could be compared to a verbal treatise on the marvel of holiness, which is communicated as a share in divine holiness and is then made sacrament in the sanctification of the bread and wine

[11] In *MR2002* there is one case of *sanguine acquisivit* attributed to the action of Christ's eternal high priesthood: Sodi, no. 2969. Often, there is reference to the *populus acquisitionis*, following 1 Pet 2:9, cf. Sodi, nos. 555, 587, 1206, 1268, 1369, etc. To "win" is rather feeble a translation; to "gain" also fails to evoke the full sense.

[12] For *Extendens manus suas*, compare EP RI's *brachia eius inter caelum et terram extenta* (appendix, no. 3, lines 16–17).

[13] E.g., Sodi, nos. 6, 152, 160.

[14] E.g., Sodi, nos. 1240, 1570, 1660, 1863.

[15] Sodi, no. 1652.

[16] For the full meaning of bringing about the dissolution of death and manifesting the resurrection, one could look at 2 Tim 1:9-11: here *inluminatio* is associated with manifestation. This translates the Greek word used for "appearance"/"epiphany" and indeed interprets it by choosing to call it "enlightenment": this casting of light on the world is given in the advent of the Savior and is shown forth in the life bestowed, a life that will not know corruption.

for the holy people, made into the Body and Blood of Christ, a *panis vitae*, a *calix salutis*.

Epiclesis (*OM2008*, no. 101)

The introduction of the Spirit epiclesis into EP II, III, and IV is done in line with the meaning of the prayer *quam oblationem* in the Roman Canon. Thus the same theological issues return but are complicated by the use of an epiclesis for the Spirit both before and after the institution narrative. Ritual prescriptions, as previously noted,[17] appear to attach consecratory power to the words of Jesus repeated by the priest, though *IGMR2002* (no. 79c) indicates that to the words of Jesus we have to join an invocation of the Spirit.[18] As in EP I, the supplication before the institution narrative does not of itself point to an act of consecration but could read as motive for asking for the acceptance of the oblation. The twofold epiclesis becomes theologically problematic not in itself but because of the performative prescriptions that accompany the institution narrative, changing its meaning from what is textually suggested. It is more in keeping with tradition to say that the Spirit acts by making holy "the people and their gifts," respecting the action of bringing the gifts rather than isolating the gifts as things in themselves.

In the *Vere Sanctus* the prayer moves from the holiness of God who is source of all holiness to the sanctification of the gifts through the Spirit. The bread and wine are rather dispassionately referred to simply as *dona* without further qualification. This is similar to EP IV (*munera*) but less expressive than either EP I or EP III, both of which speak of what the community has first done to the gifts before the action of God or Spirit is asked.

In petitioning for the action of the Spirit, the phrase *Spiritus tui rore* is unusual. Liturgical Latin usually uses the words *virtute* or *gratia* when referring to the workings of the Spirit. The best known case for the use of dew as metaphor of divine action in Latin texts is that of Isaiah 45:8, *rorate caeli desuper, et nubes pluant justum*. Otherwise, Hosea speaks of God as "dew to Israel" (Hos 14:5), and Deuteronomy 32:2 compares the effect of Moses' teaching in God's name to dew on the grass.[19] Nowhere in biblical Latin, however, is this associated with the action of the Spirit. As used in EP II, it

[17] See Power, 271 above.

[18] Paul De Clerck, "Les epiclèses des nouvelles prières eucharistiques du rite romain. Leur importance théologique," *Ecclesia orans* 16:2 (1999): 189–208.

[19] Mazza, *The Eucharistic Prayers*, 109.

conjures up an image of the Spirit resting on the gifts as dew rests on the grass, as it is said that the Spirit comes upon or rests or remains on the Son.[20]

In the description of the action of the Spirit on the gifts we find the word *fiant*. In the Greek anaphoras of Basil and John Chrysostom, *anadeixai* is used to express what is implied in the sacramental representation of the bread and wine, since it means holding something up to God so that it may be changed.[21] This helps us to see the meaning of what the *fiant* of the Latin text expresses: God has to act on the bread and wine held up, offered by the people, through the action of the Spirit who sanctifies. The visibility of the action is important, the work of the Spirit giving sacramental form to the Body and Blood, resting upon the bread and wine as dew upon the earth. The bread and wine are offered as holy gifts, but with thanksgiving, and they are offered as a sacrament through the grace of the Spirit that transforms them truly and sacramentally into the Body and Blood given over and shed for the holy people.[22]

A paraphrase of the *Vere Sanctus* in EP II would be:

> God truly holy and source of all holiness, the people whom your Son acquired by his suffering have placed before you their offerings of bread and wine. As the dew rests upon the earth and makes it fertile, so may the Spirit of holiness descend upon the gifts and make them fecund with an abiding holiness, so that they are made for us the body and blood of our Lord (creator and redeemer whom you sent) Jesus Christ.

Institution Narrative (*OM2008*, no. 102)

In introducing the institution narrative, the text recalls Christ's voluntary suffering: it was when he was about to hand himself over to the voluntary suffering of his passion that he gave thanks and handed the bread and wine to his disciples. The institution narrative itself is introduced, as in EP III, by reference to the night in which Jesus Christ was betrayed (*in qua nocte tradebatur*). The reference to *tradere* (handing over, betrayal) comes from the biblical accounts of the Supper where the word refers to the act of the disciple, Judas, and this reference remains in the prayer. By connotation, how-

[20] Mark 1:10; Luke 3:22; Matt 3:16 in the Vulgate. The neo-Vulgate omits *manentem*, which may be in keeping with the Greek but makes the metaphor less forceful.

[21] Louis Bouyer, *Eucharist: Theology and Spirituality of the Eucharistic Prayer* (Notre Dame, IN: University of Notre Dame Press, 1968), 299.

[22] All this is given more lively expression in EPs I and III, where the action of the Church in offering the gifts is expressed in a way comparable to the Byzantine anaphoras.

ever, with the clear sense of Jesus' own willingness to give himself over, *tradere* recalls the will of the Father in handing over his Son more explicitly than in EP I.[23] The text uses no adjectives of the *panem* and the *calicem* but to have called them holy would have pursued the image of holiness in its diverse manifestations introduced in the *Vere Sanctus*. As it is, this holiness of the gifts is expressed in the anamnesis where the bread is called *panis vitae* and the chalice *calix salutis*.

Anamnesis-Offering (*OM2008*, no. 105, lines 2–6)

After the people's acclamation,[24] the *memores* (anamnesis-oblation) is restricted to memory of the *mors et resurrectio*. There is no mention of the ascension as in EP I. Some think this is a sign of the antiquity of ApTrad. Whatever the reason, in EP II the mention of death and resurrection alone harmonizes with the earlier part of the prayer that focused on the voluntary death and on what is made manifest in the resurrection. The lordship of Christ expressed in other prayers through remembrance of the ascension is sufficiently referenced in remembering what the resurrection makes manifest.

The *memores* expands on ApTrad, borrowing from EP I for what is offered in the phrase *panem vitae et calicem salutis*. If a consecratory value is attached to the repetition of the words of Jesus this affects the meaning, but the sacramental sense of the offering of the bread of life and chalice of salvation remains: it is the memorial offering of the church, the pure worship of Malachi 1:11, the offering with thanksgiving of the bread and wine so that it is the sacrament of Christ's offering (Supper and cross) and of the church's self-offering in and with him—in Augustine's words, the sacrifice of the whole body, head and members.

One may ask who makes the offering according to this text. *Qui dignos habuisti astare coram te et ministrare. Ministrare/ministerium* are typically expressive of service. While in ecclesiastical Latin the word stands for any service offered for the worship of the church, the text of ApTrad suggested the priestly service of the ordained; EP II also seems to attend to the work of the ordained minister.[25] In *MR2002 ministerium* usually refers to this service, although for the March 19 feast of Saint Joseph—a rather late addition

[23] With the Latin use of *tradere* in NT translations, the Father is said to hand over the Son (Rom 8:32) and the Son to hand himself over in obedience to the Father (Gal 2:20; Eph 5:2).

[24] See Power, 271–72 above.

[25] See Baldovin 314 above for a different reading of ApTrad.

to liturgical repertory—it means the service of all the people (Sodi, no. 1454). A proper grasp of the minister's service does not exclude the congregation in whose name the priest prays through the Son.

Epiclesis and Intercessions (*OM2008*, no. 105, lines 7–31)

The second epiclesis asks that all may be gathered or congregated as one in the sharing of the one bread and the one cup, thus highlighting a desire for communion and unity.

The petition beginning with *recordare* that follows the epiclesis tells us that the congregation asks for God's remembrance of the people. In the Vulgate the word is used to denote prayers whereby to ask God to remember those who have served him, even in the face of the weakness and suffering of the people or of their sins.[26] While in Roman sacramentaries and *MR2002* the verb is commonly used of the remembrance of the church or congregation rather than of God's remembering, EP II employs the sense given the word in biblical Latin.

The ecclesial communion of those who worship is suggested in several ways: *congregare in unum*, to be brought together as one through the Spirit in sharing in the sacramental Body and Blood of Christ; to be one in charity, *in caritate una cum Papa et Episcopo*. Sacramental communion and communion in charity go together. In praying for the pope along with the local bishop, the prayer expresses the sense of Catholic communion that encompasses churches spread across the world, all united in charity through the action of the Spirit.

Communion is perfected, or brought to perfection, in charity. *Perficere* is another word from biblical Latin often used in Roman liturgies. It means that God brings something to completion that has been begun in those who serve him: it is he who completes the work rather than the agents themselves.[27] It can also mean bringing to perfection what is done in worship, either to complete the act of worship or to carry over what is expressed in worship into people's lives.[28]

In the *memento* for the dead that leads to the final doxology, this sense of communion prevails. What is asked is that the dead who are remembered

[26] See Exod 13:29; 32:13; Deut 9:27; Job 4:7; Jer 14:21; 15:15; Lam 3:19.

[27] In the Vulgate we find this sense, e.g., in Rom 7:18; Phil 2:13; 2 Cor 8:6; Ps 16:5; 79:16; Eccl 3:19. As to its use in sacramentaries, we find it in *Veronense*, nos. 124, 142, 201, 213, 216, 222, 352, etc.; also in *Hadrianum*, nos. 127, 209, 233, 283, 432, 536.

[28] As in *Hadrianum*, nos. 536, 539, 719, 967. In *MR2002* there are many instances of this usage noted in the Sodi-Toniolo concordance.

may be the *consortes* or companions of those who have attained glory in a common praise and glorification of God. *Consortes* means being partakers in the one destiny, in the one fellowship in which God is praised and glorified.[29] Its euchological use is based on 1 Peter 1:4, where the baptized are called *divinae naturae consortes* on account of their redemption by Jesus Christ, signifying also that although living in this world the faithful aspire to what is beyond it. This is the destiny to which the EP aspires, in and through Jesus Christ and in the unity of the Spirit, as expressed in the doxology.

Conclusion

In this most succinct of the prayers, in keeping memory the accent is on what is done through the death and resurrection of the Son, who is Creator and Word Incarnate and sent by the Father. As for what this means to the church, this is expressed through the imagery of holiness—a holiness that originates in God and through the Spirit enfolds the people and their sacramental gifts, perfecting them sacramentally in a communion of charity and so anticipating the holiness of the eternal participation in the glory given to God. To correspond to this, the act of worship proceeds from thanksgiving, through intercession, to glorifying God together with the blessed. The Latinity of the prayer is borrowed to a great extent from the tradition of liturgical Latin, but this falls into a kind of liturgical vacuum, and there is no recourse to the abundant style of EP I. It does not supply for this with any fullness of imaginative and rhetorical expression. Apart from the invitation to a communion of prayer in the opening dialogue and the power of the *Sanctus* to bring the whole congregation together, the prayer offers little by way of an inner rhetorical cogency, though some of the imagery is vivid enough in its fidelity to biblical Latin.

[29] For *consortes* in *MR2002*, see Sodi, nos. 37, 113, 340, 367, 507, etc.

The ICEL2010 Translation

Tom Elich

Preface and *Sanctus* (ICEL2010, no. 99)

The preface dialogue and *Sanctus* are common to all the EPs. The key changes ("It is right and just" and "Lord God of hosts") translate the actual words without making the translation into an explanation.[1] The word "just" does not correspond to common English usage, but this terse response is amplified by the beginning of the preface when "right" and "just" are juxtaposed with "duty" and "salvation."

In the opening protocol of the preface, several christological affirmations are now placed in apposition with the naming of Christ. It makes for a long sentence, but it is grammatically straightforward. With admirable concision, Christ's role in creation, redemption, and incarnation are summarized in several lines. ICEL2010's "you made all things" (line 13) is probably not an improvement on ICEL1973's "you made the universe," since *cuncta* really has a collective sense of the whole. ICEL1998 had already emphasized the link between the flesh and the Spirit ("He took flesh by the Holy Spirit and was born of the Virgin Mary"). This was not clear in ICEL1973 where taking flesh seemed to be linked more to Christ's birth of the Virgin Mary. In this new text, "incarnate" (a technical but accessible term) is clearly linked with the work of the Holy Spirit.

The thought pattern in the second section of ICEL1973's rendering of the preface needed better expression. ICEL2010 suffices, although ICEL1998[2] is clearer, not least in the image, "he stretched out his arms on the cross." The present text, "he stretched out his hands as he endured his Passion" does not paint the picture quite so vividly for the hearer. "Break the bonds

[1] *LitAuth*, no. 20: ". . . in the most exact manner . . . without paraphrases or glosses"; also, *"Ratio Translationis" for the English Language* (Congregation for Divine Worship and the Discipline of the Sacraments: Vatican City, 2007), 51.

[2] "To accomplish your will and gain for you a holy people, he stretched out his arms on the cross, that he might break the chains of death and make known the resurrection."

of death" is a strong phrase. Having done away with death, Christ manifests the resurrection to those who have died and forms a "holy people."[3]

The phrase "Lord God of hosts" will become familiar if not quite transparent.[4] It is a prophetic title regularly used in a number of common Scripture translations. The danger is that people will supply a meaning from their experience, in this case relating it either to hospitality or to particles of bread. One serious consequence of these changes is that they abandon the common ecumenical texts we have shared with other churches.[5]

Post-*Sanctus* (ICEL2010, no. 100)

The first four words of the very brief post-*Sanctus* are the same in EP III. It is an emphatic beginning, but the translators have been unable to retain a linguistic parallel with the beginning of the preface: the *Vere* of the preface is rendered "truly" whereas the post-*Sanctus* has "indeed." Fortunately, the eccentric ICEL2006 attempt to make this a substantive ("Holy One")—on the grounds that *Sanctus* was capitalized—was changed in ICEL2010 to the adjective "Holy." This retains the link with what has gone before: "Holy, Holy, Holy Lord God of hosts," a triple adjective, capitalized both in Latin and English.[6]

The second phrase adds a concrete image. Since ICEL1973's "fountain" might be mistaken for an item of decorative landscaping, the shift to "fount" is welcome with its evocation of a spring or source, although ICEL2006's "wellspring" was also most attractive—a genuinely English word with an impeccable pedigree.

Epiclesis (ICEL2010, no. 101)

The unchanged English translation "Make holy" strengthens the verbal link between the *Sanctus*, post-*Sanctus*, and epiclesis. One could argue that this renders the "therefore" in the first line unnecessary in English. Certainly

[3] See Power's discussion of the "holiness of the people," 320–21 above.

[4] On "host" (*Sabaoth*) as a multitude or army, which possibly identifies God as the Lord of Creation, see John McKenzie, "Aspects of Old Testament Thought," NJBC, 77:14; also Power, 265 above.

[5] Cf. English Language Liturgical Consultation and International Consultation on English Texts, *Praying Together: A Revision of* Prayers We Have in Common *(ICET 1975); Agreed Liturgical Texts*, rev. ed. (Norwich: Canterbury Press, 1990). The preparation of common liturgical texts is urged by the Pontifical Council for Promoting Christian Unity, *Directory for the Application of Principles and Norms on Ecumenism* (1993), no. 187.

[6] On capitalizations in ICEL2010, see 137 and 211, n. 3, above, 331–32 below.

"Make holy, therefore, these gifts, we pray," with its four discrete phrases will encourage a staccato proclamation.

ICEL2010 was determined to express the sanctifying work of the Holy Spirit in terms of the beautiful poetic image of the settling dew (*Spiritus tui rore*). Expressed in a matter-of-fact way in ICEL1973 ("come upon") and ICEL1998 ("send down"), ICEL2006 prayed that the gifts be made holy "by the dew of your Spirit." Some found this problematic, suggesting that it would be misheard as "due" or as some other variant; the USCCB rejected the line.[7] ICEL2010 turns the crisp metaphor into a wordy and prosaic sentence: "by sending down your Spirit upon them like the dewfall."

Institution Narrative (ICEL2010, nos. 102 and 103)

In Latin, the institution narrative begins with the relative pronoun "who" (*Qui*). This little word directly connects the words of institution with the epiclesis and stitches the narrative into the grand sweep of eucharistic praise and thanksgiving. This in turn shapes our understanding of the way in which the consecration of the bread and wine take place in the EP and its relation to the words of Christ on the one hand and the invocation of the Holy Spirit on the other.[8] A brave attempt was made to retain this feature in ICEL2006, but an English sentence that begins with a relative pronoun is ungrammatical and, therefore, unacceptable in formal liturgical speech. It was eliminated in ICEL2010, but two subordinate clauses ("At the time . . . and entered willingly . . .") are once again allowed to intervene between the epiclesis and the subject of the institution narrative over the bread, "he."

To establish the context for the Lord's Supper, the verb *tradere* is used in both EP II and III.[9] ICEL2006 opted for "handed over," but they were changed in ICEL2010 to the more particular and concrete "betrayed," the common biblical translation of *tradere* in the passion narratives.[10] Only ICEL1973's translation of EP II recognized that *tradere* is also used in the words over the bread: "Before he was *given up* to death . . . this is my body which will be *given up* for you." This significant verbal parallel between table and cross would have been worth preserving in translation. The

[7] For a defense of the image and its background in Scripture, see the address to the US bishops' conference by ICEL chairman, Bishop Arthur Roche (15 June 2006), available at www.liturgyoffice.org.uk/Resources/Missal/US+AR.shtml (accessed 1 April 2010).

[8] Cf. Power, 269 and 271 above.

[9] Cf. Power, 322–23 above.

[10] E.g., Matt 26:24; Mark 14:21; Luke 22:23; John 18:2.

passive sense of "betrayed" is balanced by the active phrase, "entered willingly into his Passion." The capitalized "Passion" here should be understood to include both Jesus' suffering and death, although this will be difficult for some for whom the word's primary meaning of ardent emotion might be a distraction.

The institution narrative is common to all EPs. The two small changes in wording over the bread ("eat of it, for this") and a change in punctuation are not very significant.[11] The same cannot be said for the changes in the words of institution over the cup.

First is the usage of the word "chalice" instead of ICEL1973's "cup." In ICEL2006, "chalice" was used for the first occurrence in this text and "cup" for the second ("he took the chalice. . . . this is the cup of my Blood"); both became "chalice" in ICEL2010. When rubrics or *IGMR2002* refer to a liturgical vessel in the form of a goblet, *calix* is rightly translated "chalice" (e.g., GIRM2003, no. 73). In relation to the biblical narrative, every modern English version of Scripture uses "cup" where the Vulgate has *calix*: in the Synoptic accounts of the Last Supper, at the agony in the garden, and in 1 Corinthians 11. This is not a question of sacred in preference to secular vocabulary. "Cup" is the ordinary English translation for the term as it appears throughout Scripture (*potérion, calix, kos*).[12] Ironically, "cup" is retained in ICEL2010's translation of the second acclamation following the institution narrative (no. 104) when "chalice" might have been used, while "chalice" recurs in ICEL2010's translation of the offering (no. 105).[13]

A second change that is misleading in English is ICEL2010's translation of *pro multis* as "for many." In English, this wording seems to contradict the Roman Catholic belief that Christ died for all.[14] Originally, the translation "for all" was defended by the Holy See.[15] A 2006 circular letter from CDWDS, however, points out that the Scriptures say "many" and the Latin liturgy has always used *pro multis* and not *pro omnibus*. " 'For many' is a faithful translation of *pro multis* whereas 'for all' is rather an explanation of the sort that belongs properly to catechesis."[16] The strangeness of other possible translations such as "for the many" or "for the multitude"

[11] "Eat of it" expresses the sharing of the bread among "all of you" and parallels the words over the cup, "drink from it"; cf. Ostdiek, 286 above.

[12] Greater problems are presented by EP I where the phrase *hunc praeclarum calicem* is found. See Craig, "Potency, not Preciousness"; also Ostdiek, 287 above.

[13] The phrase, *the cup of salvation*, is well known in the liturgy from Ps 116:13, and it is difficult to see why it would not be retained.

[14] 2 Cor 5:14-15; also CCC, no. 605, and Chupungco 480–81 below.

[15] *Notitiae* 50 (1970): 39.

[16] Prot. N. 467/05/L, in *Notitiae* 481–82 (2006): 444–46.

would at least have given some space for a more adequate theological understanding.

Other changes are well explained by the notes provided with ICEL2006. In view of the classic distinction between eternity and perpetuity, "everlasting" has been replaced by "eternal." In Latin the *qui* that is the subject of *effundetur* can refer either to the cup or the blood. "Poured out" may also refer to both and so retains in English the ambiguity of the Latin. The final phrase "for the forgiveness of sins" is a simple balanced expression of Christ's work of reconciliation.

The Mystery of Faith (ICEL2010, no. 104)

The people's acclamations are introduced by a straightforward announcement, "The mystery of faith." This parallels the direct statements used at the end of the readings and in giving Holy Communion. The acclamations, addressed to Christ, are given in a crisp memorable translation. "Let us proclaim," which was part of ICEL1973's invitation, is reintroduced to the first acclamation. "Proclaim your Death . . . profess your Resurrection" will become a memorable phrase, as will "Save us, Savior of the world."

Anamnesis (ICEL2010, no. 105, lines 2–3)

A single line completes the anamnesis of Jesus' death and resurrection. ICEL1973's translation of this line referred back to "Do this in memory of me"—even though the Latin word is not the same. ICEL2010's translation of the adjective *memores* creates a whole phrase, "as we celebrate the memorial."[17] The simplest and most direct version seems to be ICEL1998, "Remembering, therefore, his death and resurrection . . ." but in ICEL2010 this may have been deemed incompatible with the present participle "giving thanks" that follows.

The capitalization of words such as "Bread," "Cup," "Chalice," "Cross," "Death," "Resurrection" in ICEL2010 has no basis in the Latin of *MR2002*, is not consistent, and raises questions about how these words ought to be proclaimed. No doubt it is meant to affirm the sacred reality of the Real

[17] On the significance of this shift, Mazza writes, "The 'memorial' is part of the action being celebrated; 'mindful' is an attribute of the persons who are performing the action of offering" (*The Eucharistic Prayers of the Roman Rite*, trans. Matthew J. O'Connell [New York: Pueblo, 1986], 111).

Presence for those who are uncomfortable with references to bread and cup after the words of institution, but this consistent usage in Roman EPs is an important part of Roman Catholic sacramental theology. The sacramental sign is integral to the Real Presence of Christ—when the first ceases to exist, so does the second.

Offering and Epiclesis (ICEL2010, no. 105, lines 4–7)

As we make the memorial, we offer. The single sentence continues, combining "we offer" (line 4) with "giving thanks" (line 6). This is a rich expression of the church's offertory, placing it in the broader context of thanksgiving and making it clear that we are able to make this extraordinary offering by divine grace, for it is God who has deemed us worthy to serve in God's presence. The gift of grace is amplified in what is sometimes called a second epiclesis: by partaking of the Body and Blood of Christ, we plead that the Holy Spirit will make us one, i.e., the one Body of Christ whose offering on the cross we remember. It is as the Body of Christ that we stand in God's presence to offer "the Bread of life and the Chalice of salvation" (line 5). The section needs to be read as a whole[18] because the theological logic is reversed in the text: the bold statement of what "we offer" to God is only made possible by what is proclaimed in the five lines that follow.

ICEL2006 offered a strong translation, preserving a memorable line from ICEL1973: "giving thanks that you have deemed us worthy to stand in your presence and serve you." Three unhelpful changes were made in ICEL2010. First, "deemed" is changed to "held" (line 6). While this is a correct translation of *habuisti*, "held" risks carrying a coercive connotation, whereas "deemed" expresses more clearly the blessing of divine election. Second, "stand" is changed to "be" (line 7), presumably to avoid any literal reference to the posture of the assembly before the consecrated elements. Not only is "stand" a more literal translation of *astare* but, more important, in "stand" we ought hear an echo of our boldness in approaching the throne of grace because we have a great high priest, Jesus Christ, who has passed through the heavens (Heb 4:14–5:10). Third, "serve" is changed to "minister to" (line 7). This expression might seem closer to the Latin, but "minister to" actually means "to attend to someone's needs" or "to take care of."

[18] There are two sentences in English and Latin. The Latin is able to link them together by beginning the second sentence with *et* ("and"), but it would be inappropriate to begin a sentence with "And" in English.

Supplices deprecamur is given its full force in ICEL2010's "Humbly we pray" (line 8). The section concludes with a line found in ICEL1998 ("we may be gathered," line 10), emphasizing Eucharist as the corporate action of the gathered church.

Intercessions (ICEL2010, no. 105, lines 11–33)

The intercessions commend to God the church spread throughout the world, with specific mention of the pope, the local bishop, and all the clergy. The use of the personal pronoun "her" (line 13) for something like the church is rare in contemporary English but in this context is meant to evoke images of the church as our mother and the bride of Christ.[19] ICEL1998's translation of the verb *perficias* as "perfect" may have been rejected because it could be confused with the adjective with the stress placed on the wrong syllable; "bring to fullness" is a good translation. However, to translate *caritas* with the English look-alike "charity" (line 13) is a mistake. Pope Benedict XVI's encyclical *Deus Caritas* ("On Christian Love")[20] makes it clear that charitable works are only one part of Christian love. Using "love" as a verb but not as its corresponding noun will cause confusion in English, for "charity" is too narrow in its meaning and can even be perceived as pejorative.[21] Virtually all modern versions of Scripture translate the Vulgate's *caritas* with "love."[22]

The *memento* of the dead includes both those who have died in the explicit hope of the resurrection and all those who have died in God's mercy. We ask that God will welcome them into the light. The anthropomorphic metaphor in the Latin (*in lumen vultus*) provides a strong image in English: "the light of your countenance" (ICEL2006), subsequently changed to "the light of your face" (ICEL2010, line 25).[23] The interpolation for Masses for the Dead has a misleading phrase: the deceased is said to be united with Christ "in a death like his" (line 20), although they would not have died by crucifixion.[24]

[19] *LG*, nos. 6–7; also Eph 5:23-32. This was a specific request of *LitAuth*, no. 31.d, reiterated in *"Ratio Translationis" for the English Language*, no. 124.

[20] See www.vatican.va/holy_father/benedict_xvi/encyclicals/documents/hf_ben-xvi_enc_20051225_deus-caritas-est_en.html (accessed 1 April 2010).

[21] For example, in the expression, "As cold as charity."

[22] E.g., Paul's famous discourse on love in 1 Cor 13:1-13; or 1 John 4:6-21.

[23] ICEL2010 is inconsistent. For the same Latin word *vultus*, ICEL2006's "countenance" was here changed to *face*, while in EP I (no. 93) ICEL2006's "gaze" was changed to "countenance."

[24] The extended metaphor of Rom 6 is lost in this simple statement, which recurs in the interpolation in Masses for the Dead in EP III, no. 115.

The final sentence (lines 26–33) is long and complex, with three lines—referencing the Virgin Mary, the apostles, and the saints—coming between the conjunction "that" and the subject "we." The phrase referencing the saints ("who have pleased you") is less felicitous than ICEL1998's version ("who had found favor with you"), which emphasizes God's kindness more than the actions of the saints. The greatest difficulty in a difficult sentence, however, is changing ICEL1973's "worthy to share eternal life"—a good translation of *aeternae vitae mereamur esse consortes*—to "merit to be coheirs to eternal life" (line 30). This will push the limits of intelligibility. The priest needs to be absolutely sure of its meaning if it is to be conveyed to the people: any "merit" we may have is the result of God's mercy (four lines earlier, in line 26); we ask to become coheirs "with" the Virgin Mary, the apostles, and the saints as made clear from the three preceding lines (27–29).

Final Doxology (ICEL2010, no. 106)

The strong, formal language of the doxology is restructured to end with "all glory and honor is yours, for ever and ever." It will soon become well-loved and known by heart.

Conclusions

EP II is concise; this means that the expression of the rich but difficult theology of anamnesis, sacrifice, and offering tends to be quite dense. ICEL2010 in general handles the theology well without becoming obscure. One of the most delightful surprises it offers are the strong and concrete images that it uncovers from the Latin text (e.g., "break the bonds," "fount," "dewfall, "face"). Studying successive versions of ICEL's translations certainly helps understand the text and demonstrates the range of possibility in the translation process. In the final analysis, of course, one can only use a single form of words. It should quickly be possible for the Body of Christ to make this text its own and to pray it worthily.

The Mystagogical Implications

Joyce Ann Zimmerman

In word count the shortest of all the EPs, EP II is the one most often chosen to be prayed, even on Sundays. Yet this prayer is by no means the "shortest" in theology or mystagogical implications. Perhaps we need to change our mind-set and begin to choose this prayer not for its brevity but for the unique richness and challenge it puts forth. From its preface to the final Amen, this prayer draws us into the mystery of salvation and challenges us to embrace holy lives in such a way that we may one day "praise and glorify" God forever.

The Preface (ICEL2010, no. 99)

The opening rubric notes that this prayer has its own preface, which suggests that the thematic thrust of its preface is carried forth through the rest of the prayer. This is the case, and this same rubric note alerts us to what exactly that thematic thrust is: "this Eucharistic Prayer may also be used with other Prefaces, especially those that present an overall view of the *mystery of salvation*" (emphasis added). Indeed, the word "salvation" appears in the very first line of the preface and is repeated a number of times throughout the prayer using the word "salvation" (twice) or analogous terms such as "Savior" (twice), "Redeemer," and "Passion" (twice). In its own way EP II goes on to make clear and concrete what it is we must do to gain salvation.

There is a beautiful parallelism in the first line of the preface that reads, "It is truly right and just, our duty and salvation." Pairing the first two terms of the two couplets, we have right-duty and just-salvation. "Right" here means fitting or appropriate, and so our "duty" is to do what is fitting and appropriate. The second pairing suggests for what this duty reaches: just-salvation. Rather than a social justice–limited meaning, "just" is a biblical term (Hebrew, *zdk*) that points to right relationship not only with God but also among God's people. "Salvation" is also a biblical term (Hebrew, *yasa*) and generally means spaciousness or an enlargement, the effect of overcoming whatever binds or encloses. Whenever any kind of trouble is overcome, "salvation" occurs, effecting health and well-being. The preface specifically names the "beloved Son, Jesus Christ" as "our Savior." All of Jesus' healing miracles can be interpreted as acts of salvation. Christ-the-Healer is Christ-the-Savior.

The preface goes on to state quite concretely how we come to healing and wholeness: through Jesus' fulfilling his Father's will, by "stretch[ing] out his hands" on the cross and embracing all humanity, by "endur[ing] his Passion." Jesus bound himself to God's will—he chose suffering and death—and in so doing he broke open "the bonds of death." Jesus' self-giving creates the spaciousness of a new covenantal relationship with God and each other, "a holy people" gained for God's "glory." Salvation is God's gift to us when we graft our lives onto Christ's life, when we break the fetters of whatever binds us, when we are healed of alienation and divisions. Salvation occurs when we do as Jesus did, stretching out our arms to embrace the sick and suffering, the alienated and outcast, the downtrodden and downcast. Already in these words of the preface we are challenged to change how we think about God's good creation—who "made all things" through the Word—and how we must live in our world. Before we ever get to the points in the prayer where we ask the Holy Spirit to transform the gifts and us (the epicleses), we are already nudged toward "the fullness of charity," which is the mark of the presence of Christ in his church and the well-being of salvation made visible.

This preface rehearses for us an attitude toward God that is fitting as we continue our great prayer of thanksgiving. The mystery we celebrate is a mystery of obedience and self-giving. We give God thanks and "declare [God's] glory" because of the gift of salvation Jesus has already gained for us. We call God "most holy" and sing with the angels "Holy, Holy, Holy" because Jesus' saving acts have made of us a "holy people" fitting to be the presence of the risen Christ in our world today. The preface, then, is more than a rehearsing of salvation events; it draws us into those same events and begs us to be obedient and self-giving as Jesus, to enlarge our world to a spaciousness that embraces all with "stretched out" hands and arms.

Fount of All Holiness (ICEL2010, nos. 100–103)

There is no abrupt thematic change when we conclude the "Holy, Holy, Holy" acclamation and begin the great thanksgiving proper. There are only two sentences preceding the institution narrative, and they continue the salvation and holiness thematic prevailing in the preface. These two sentences are powerful and must be prayed in such a way that they do not slip by us without notice. They must be prayed slowly and deliberately, with a slight pause before moving on to the institution narrative.

This prayer is addressed to "O Lord," but the text makes clear that we are addressing the First Person of the Trinity by mentioning both the Holy Spirit and Jesus separately. What is especially rich in these two sentences is the occurrence of "holy" twice and "holiness" once (especially coupling this with the double occurrence of "holy" in the preface and its triple occurrence in the previous acclamation). We not only call God "holy" but acknowledge God as the "fount of all holiness." From God are these gifts made holy; from God are we made holy. God's holiness is pervasive for those who open themselves and surrender their wills to God's holiness, to receive it as God's gift. The prayer asks that the Spirit come upon the gifts (including ourselves) "like the dewfall." This is an active image: not like dew, but dew*fall*. The Spirit's transformative work is ongoing and pervasive. The dewfall covers everything; it is refreshing coolness; it is nourishment; it is life-giving. We can point to an allusion to the manna in the desert by which God nourished the Chosen People in the desert:

> In the morning there was a layer of dew all about the camp, and when the layer of dew evaporated, fine flakes were on the surface of the wilderness, fine flakes like hoarfrost on the ground. On seeing it, the Israelites asked one another, "What is this?" for they did not know what it was. But Moses told them, "It is the bread which the LORD has given you to eat." (Exod 16:13b-15)

Our holiness is an effect of salvation; we share in God's very life when we allow God's presence to be dewfall enveloping us and drawing us to the divine Son. There is a cost, however, to opening ourselves to the dewfall coming upon these gifts. The institution narrative (no. 102) begins in the usual way of placing us in the context of the Last Supper: "At the time he was betrayed." This is followed by another line that is entirely in keeping with the thematic of this whole prayer: "and entered willingly into his Passion" (a reference to the passion is also made in the preface). God's gifts of holiness, nourishment, and life (really, all one gift) come at a cost: we must submit our wills to God's will; we must lose our life to find it; we must be faithful as Jesus was, even to "stretch[ing] out [our] hands" to embrace what we would not choose. This passion context delivers an appropriate balance between God's holiness in which we share by the power of the Spirit and our own constant need to overcome our human weakness and sinfulness.

In light of this salvation and holiness reflection, the most fitting eucharistic acclamation would be the third: "Save us, Savior of the world, for by your Cross and Resurrection you have set us free" (no. 104). This acclamation not only continues the salvation theme introduced already in the preface but also helps make an easy transition to the third part of the prayer.

Giving Thanks (ICEL2010, no. 105)

The anamnesis, which begins the last part of EP II, once again makes clear that our remembering and thanksgiving is for Jesus' "Death and Resurrection" (in the third memorial acclamation the language is "Cross and Resurrection"). This is what we celebrate, but more is said. We offer "the Bread of life and the Chalice of salvation." No longer is the dewfall manna of old; this "Bread of life" is a new manna, the very Body and Blood of our Savior Jesus Christ. Moreover, our offering returns to us in Holy Communion to nourish and strengthen us to carry forward Jesus' saving ministry.

In the preface we prayed that it is our right and duty to give God thanks. Now we repeat our "giving thanks," first because God has "held us worthy" to be in the divine presence. Our worthiness is not due to what we accomplish in deeds but founded on surrendering ourselves to God's will and thus allowing the dewfall of the Spirit to come upon us and make us holy. Our worthiness, our holiness, is God's work for us and within us. We are "held . . . worthy" because God has bestowed divine life on us through Christ and the Spirit.

We also give thanks that we are held worthy to "minister to" God. What does this mean? It sounds odd, indeed, to think that we "minister to" God. Yet we do! To minister means to serve or attend to. But God cannot be seen or touched or otherwise physically encountered. We hear the words of the writer of the first letter of John: "for whoever does not love a brother whom he has seen cannot love God whom he has not seen. This is the commandment we have from him: whoever loves God must also love his brother" (1 John 4:20b-21). We minister to God when we attend to others whom we do physically encounter. We minister to God through others by being who we were re-created in baptism to be: members of the Body of Christ. The way to the Father is through the Son (see John 14:6). By identifying with the Son, all that we do serves God as Jesus served God.

Contrasted with God holding us worthy, we also bow before God in "humbly" beseeching that the Spirit come upon us. It is the Spirit's divine indwelling that makes us one in the Body of Christ, identifies us with Christ, and so enables us to serve God in others. We pray, then, for the "Church, spread throughout the world," that we come to "the fullness of charity" by our Christlike lives. This awesome task of being called to worthiness and service, of being visible signs of the risen Christ's presence among us is the corporate task of the whole church.

At the conclusion of the prayer (before the great doxology) we look to Mary, the apostles, and all the saints for the inspiration to be faithful to our call to thankfulness and holiness. Like those who have already died, we long to be in the "light of [God's] face," that is, to bask in God's countenance, presence, glory. We desire to be "coheirs to eternal life" so that we may "praise and glorify" God now through our thankfulness and service but also forever in the life to come.

Conclusion

We come full circle in EP II. In the preface we "declare [God's] glory" as we acclaim with one voice God's holiness. We conclude the prayer with the desire that we "may praise and glorify" God forever. Pouring forth in every breath praise and glory of God is also what is to mark our Christian living. The EP is for far more than consecrating the elements of bread and wine so that they become for us truly the Body and Blood of our Lord Jesus Christ. In EP II we come face-to-face with the salvation God offers us and also with the challenge that we gain eternal life only when we surrender ourselves to God's gifts of life, holiness, and worthiness.

The very paucity of words serves to underscore the plentifulness of EP II. It is as though the church is inviting us to eliminate all unnecessary words, all bounding distractions, all that might cause us to swerve from the essential truth of God's holiness and our call to share in that gift of grace. This prayer invites us to the spaciousness of all the world and all life and all peoples within. This prayer invites us to bring healing and wholeness to anyone and everyone we meet. This prayer invites us to worthiness and humility, service and giftedness, thankfulness and willingness. May we respond to these invitations with our whole hearts, every day of our lives, and thus offer God "all glory and honor . . . for ever and ever."

Eucharistic Prayer III

The Latin Text

Prex Eucharistica III

107. ℣. Dóminus vobíscum.
℟. Et cum spíritu tuo.
℣. Sursum corda.
℟. Habémus ad Dóminum.
℣. Grátias agámus Dómino Deo nostro.
℟. Dignum et iustum est.

Sequitur Praefatio iuxta rubricas proferenda, quae concluditur:

Sanctus, Sanctus, Sanctus Dóminus Deus Sabaóth.
Pleni sunt caeli et terra glória tua.
Hosánna in excélsis.
Benedíctus qui venit in nómine Dómini.
Hosánna in excélsis.

108. Sacerdos, manibus extensis, dicit:

Vere Sanctus es, Dómine,
et mérito te laudat omnis a te cóndita creatúra,
quia per Fílium tuum,
Dóminum nostrum Iesum Christum,
Spíritus Sancti operánte virtúte,
vivíficas et sanctíficas univérsa,
et pópulum tibi congregáre non désinis,
ut a solis ortu usque ad occásum
oblátio munda offerátur nómini tuo.

109. Iungit manus, easque expansas super oblata tenens, dicit:

Súpplices ergo te, Dómine, deprecámur,
ut haec múnera, quae tibi sacránda detúlimus,
eódem Spíritu sanctificáre dignéris,
iungit manus
et signat semel super panem et calicem simul, dicens:
ut Corpus et ✠ Sanguis fiant
Fílii tui Dómini nostri Iesu Christi,
iungit manus
cuius mandáto haec mystéria celebrámus.

The English Text

Eucharistic Prayer III

107. ℣. The Lord be with you.
℟. And with your spirit.

℣. Lift up your hearts.
℟. We lift them up to the Lord.

℣. Let us give thanks to the Lord our God.
℟. It is right and just.

Then follows the Preface to be used in accord with the rubrics, which concludes:

Holy, Holy, Holy Lord God of hosts.
Heaven and earth are full of your glory.
Hosanna in the highest.
Blessed is he who comes in the name of the Lord.
Hosanna in the highest.

108. The Priest, with hands extended, says:

You are indeed Holy, O Lord,
and all you have created
rightly gives you praise,
for through your Son our Lord Jesus Christ,
by the power and working of the Holy Spirit,
you give life to all things and make them holy,
and you never cease to gather a people to yourself,
so that from the rising of the sun to its setting
a pure sacrifice may be offered to your name.

109. He joins his hands and, holding them extended over the offerings, says:

Therefore, O Lord, we humbly implore you:
by the same Spirit graciously make holy
these gifts we have brought to you for consecration,

He joins his hands
and makes the Sign of the Cross once over the bread and chalice together, saying:

that they may become the Body and ✠ Blood
of your Son our Lord Jesus Christ,

He joins his hands.

at whose command we celebrate these mysteries.

110. In formulis quae sequuntur, verba Domini proferantur distincte et aperte, prouti natura eorundem verborum requirit:

Ipse enim in qua nocte tradebátur

accipit panem
eumque parum elevatum super altare tenens, prosequitur:

accépit panem
et tibi grátias agens benedíxit,
fregit, dedítque discípulis suis, dicens:

parum se inclinat

ACCÍPITE ET MANDUCÁTE EX HOC OMNES:
HOC EST ENIM CORPUS MEUM,
QUOD PRO VOBIS TRADÉTUR.

Hostiam consecratam ostendit populo, reponit super patenam, et genuflexus adorat.

111. Postea prosequitur:

Símili modo, postquam cenátum est,

accipit calicem,
eumque parum elevatum super altare tenens, prosequitur:

accípiens cálicem,
et tibi grátias agens benedíxit,
dedítque discípulis suis, dicens:

parum se inclinat

ACCÍPITE ET BÍBITE EX EO OMNES:
HIC EST ENIM CALIX SÁNGUINIS MEI
NOVI ET AETÉRNI TESTAMÉNTI,
QUI PRO VOBIS ET PRO MULTIS EFFUNDÉTUR
IN REMISSIÓNEM PECCATÓRUM.

HOC FÁCITE IN MEAM COMMEMORATIÓNEM.

Calicem ostendit populo, deponit super corporale, et genuflexus adorat.

112. Deinde dicit:

Mystérium fídei.

Et populus prosequitur, acclamans:

Mortem tuam annuntiámus, Dómine,
et tuam resurrectiónem confitémur, donec vénias.

110. In the formulas that follow, the words of the Lord should be pronounced clearly and distinctly, as the nature of these words requires.

For on the night he was betrayed

He takes the bread
and, holding it slightly raised above the altar, continues:

he himself took bread,
and, giving you thanks, he said the blessing,
broke the bread and gave it to his disciples, saying:

He bows slightly.

TAKE THIS, ALL OF YOU, AND EAT OF IT,
FOR THIS IS MY BODY,
WHICH WILL BE GIVEN UP FOR YOU.

He shows the consecrated host to the people, places it again on the paten, and genuflects in adoration.

111. After this, he continues:

In a similar way, when supper was ended,

He takes the chalice
and, holding it slightly raised above the altar, continues:

he took the chalice,
and, giving you thanks, he said the blessing,
and gave the chalice to his disciples, saying:

He bows slightly.

TAKE THIS, ALL OF YOU, AND DRINK FROM IT,
FOR THIS IS THE CHALICE OF MY BLOOD,
THE BLOOD OF THE NEW AND ETERNAL COVENANT,
WHICH WILL BE POURED OUT FOR YOU AND FOR MANY
FOR THE FORGIVENESS OF SINS.

DO THIS IN MEMORY OF ME.

He shows the chalice to the people, places it on the corporal, and genuflects in adoration.

112. Then he says:

The mystery of faith.

And the people continue, acclaiming:

We proclaim your Death, O Lord,
and profess your Resurrection
until you come again.

Vel:

Quotiescúmque manducámus panem hunc
et cálicem bíbimus,
mortem tuam annuntiámus, Dómine, donec vénias.

Vel:

Salvátor mundi, salva nos,
qui per crucem et resurrectiónem tuam liberásti nos.

113. Deinde sacerdos, extensis manibus, dicit:

Mémores ígitur, Dómine,
eiúsdem Fílii tui salutíferae passiónis
necnon mirábilis resurrectiónis
et ascensiónis in caelum,
sed et praestolántes álterum eius advéntum,
offérimus tibi, grátias referéntes,
hoc sacrifícium vivum et sanctum.

Réspice, quaésumus, in oblatiónem Ecclésiae tuae
et, agnóscens Hóstiam,
cuius voluísti immolatióne placári,
concéde, ut qui Córpore et Sánguine Fílii tui refícimur,
Spíritu eius Sancto repléti,
unum corpus et unus spíritus inveniámur in Christo.

Ipse nos tibi perfíciat munus aetérnum,
ut cum eléctis tuis hereditátem cónsequi valeámus,
in primis cum beatíssima Vírgine, Dei Genetríce, María,
cum beátis Apóstolis tuis et gloriósis Martyribus
(cum Sancto N.: Sancto diei vel patrono)
et ómnibus Sanctis,
quorum intercessióne
perpétuo apud te confídimus adiuvári.

Haec Hóstia nostrae reconciliatiónis profíciat,
quaésumus, Dómine,
ad totíus mundi pacem atque salútem.
Ecclésiam tuam, peregrinántem in terra,
in fide et caritáte firmáre dignéris

Or:

When we eat this Bread and drink this Cup,
we proclaim your Death, O Lord,
until you come again.

Or:

Save us, Savior of the world,
for by your Cross and Resurrection
you have set us free.

113. Then the Priest, with hands extended, says:

Therefore, O Lord, as we celebrate the memorial
of the saving Passion of your Son,
his wondrous Resurrection
and Ascension into heaven,
and as we look forward to his second coming,
we offer you in thanksgiving
this holy and living sacrifice.

Look, we pray, upon the oblation of your Church
and, recognizing the sacrificial Victim by whose death
you willed to reconcile us to yourself,
grant that we, who are nourished
by the Body and Blood of your Son
and filled with his Holy Spirit,
may become one body, one spirit in Christ.

May he make of us
an eternal offering to you,
so that we may obtain an inheritance with your elect,
especially with the most Blessed Virgin Mary, Mother of God,
with your blessed Apostles and glorious Martyrs
(with Saint N.: the Saint of the day or Patron Saint)
and with all the Saints,
on whose constant intercession in your presence
we rely for unfailing help.

May this Sacrifice of our reconciliation,
we pray, O Lord,
advance the peace and salvation of all the world.
Be pleased to confirm in faith and charity
your pilgrim Church on earth,

cum fámulo tuo Papa nostro N. et Epíscopo nostro N.,[*]
cum episcopáli órdine et univérso clero
et omni pópulo acquisitiónis tuae.

Votis huius famíliae, quam tibi astáre voluísti,
adésto propítius.
Omnes fílios tuos ubíque dispérsos
tibi, clemens Pater, miserátus coniúnge.

† Fratres nostros defúnctos
et omnes qui, tibi placéntes, ex hoc saéculo transiérunt,
in regnum tuum benígnus admítte,
ubi fore sperámus,
ut simul glória tua perénniter satiémur,

iungit manus

per Christum Dóminum nostrum,
per quem mundo bona cuncta largíris. †

114. Accipit patenam cum hostia et calicem, et utrumque elevans, dicit:

Per ipsum, et cum ipso, et in ipso,
est tibi Deo Patri omnipoténti,
in unitáte Spíritus Sancti,
omnis honor et glória
per ómnia saecula saeculórum.

Populus acclamat:

Amen.

Deinde sequitur ritus Communionis.

---

115. Quando haec Prex eucharistica in Missis pro defunctis adhibetur, dici potest:

† Meménto fámuli tui (fámulae tuae) N.,
quem (quam) (hódie) ad te ex hoc mundo vocásti.

[*] Hic fieri potest mentio de Episcopis Coadiutore vel Auxiliaribus, vel de alio Episcopo, ut in *Institutione generali Missalis Romani*, n. 149, notatur.

with your servant N. our Pope and N. our Bishop,*
the Order of Bishops, all the clergy,
and the entire people you have gained for your own.

Listen graciously to the prayers of this family,
whom you have summoned before you:
in your compassion, O merciful Father,
gather to yourself all your children
scattered throughout the world.

† To our departed brothers and sisters
and to all who were pleasing to you
at their passing from this life,
give kind admittance to your kingdom.
There we hope to enjoy for ever the fullness of your glory

He joins his hands.

through Christ our Lord,
through whom you bestow on the world all that is good. †

114. He takes the chalice and the paten with the host and, raising both, he says:

Through him, and with him, and in him,
O God, almighty Father,
in the unity of the Holy Spirit,
all glory and honor is yours,
for ever and ever.

The people acclaim:

Amen.

Then follows the Communion Rite.

---

115. When this Eucharistic Prayer is used in Masses for the Dead, the following may be said:

† Remember your servant N.
whom you have called (today)
from this world to yourself.

* Mention may be made here of the Coadjutor Bishop, or Auxiliary Bishops, as noted in the *General Instruction of the Roman Missal*, no. 149.

Concéde, ut, qui (quae) complantátus (complantáta)
fuit similitúdini mortis Fílii tui,
simul fiat et resurrectiónis ipsíus,
quando mórtuos suscitábit in carne de terra
et corpus humilitátis nostrae
configurábit córpori claritátis suae.
Sed et fratres nostros defúnctos,
et omnes qui, tibi placéntes, ex hoc saéculo transiérunt,
in regnum tuum benígnus admítte,
ubi fore sperámus,
ut simul glória tua perénniter satiémur,
quando omnem lácrimam abstérges ab óculis nostris,
quia te, sícuti es, Deum nostrum vidéntes,
tibi símiles érimus cuncta per saécula,
et te sine fine laudábimus,

iungit manus

per Christum Dóminum nostrum,
per quem mundo bona cuncta largíris. †

Grant that he (she) who was united with your Son in a death like his,
may also be one with him in his Resurrection,
when from the earth
he will raise up in the flesh those who have died,
and transform our lowly body
after the pattern of his own glorious body.
To our departed brothers and sisters, too,
and to all who were pleasing to you
at their passing from this life,
give kind admittance to your kingdom.
There we hope to enjoy for ever the fullness of your glory,
when you will wipe away every tear from our eyes.
For seeing you, our God, as you are,
we shall be like you for all the ages
and praise you without end,

He joins his hands.

through Christ our Lord,
through whom you bestow on the world all that is good. †

History of the Latin Text and Rite

Michael Witczak

Introduction

As previously noted, the Roman liturgy knew of only one EP once liturgical books came into existence. Versions of the Roman Canon are found as early as the late seventh century, and the text was stabilized by the end of the ninth century. Its literary antecedents reach back to Ambrose, who cited a prayer very much like the Roman Canon in his postbaptismal catecheses.[1] Also previously noted, at its origin eucharistic praying was extemporized.[2] The Western tradition of EPs continued to have variable elements that seem to emerge from this extemporized tradition. The Gallican and Old Spanish prayers provided for three variable moments within a stable core (the dialogue, the *Sanctus*, the words of institution, and the final doxology). The Roman Rite had variable prefaces and also some other prayers (*Hanc igitur* and *Communicantes*).[3]

The period after the Council of Trent was a time of recovering the church's scriptural, patristic, and liturgical past and reintroducing the richness and variety of the EP tradition to scholarship and pastoral concern.[4] This wider view of the tradition led a number of commentators around the

[1] On the history of the Roman Canon (EP I), see Baldovin, 247–54 above; also Power, 259–78 above.

[2] Ibid.

[3] For an example of Gallican prayers, see *Prex Eucharistica*, 1:461–93; English translation of one prayer and bibliography in Jasper & Cuming, 147–50. For Old Spanish prayers see *Prex Eucharistica*, 1:494–513; English translation of one prayer in Jasper & Cuming, 151–54; also, Power, 263 above.

[4] For an account, see Burkhard Neunheuser, "Il movimento liturgico: panorama storico e lineamenti teologici," in *La Liturgia, momento nella storia della salvezza*, ed. Salvatore Marsili, Anamnesis 1 (Casale Monferrato: Marietti, 1974), 11–30; Keith Pecklers, "History of the Roman Liturgy," in *Introduction to the Liturgy*, ed. Anscar Chupungco, Handbook for Liturgical Studies 1 (Collegeville, MN: Liturgical Press, 1998), 153–78; Keith Pecklers, *The Unread Vision: The Liturgical Movement in the United States of America: 1926–1955* (Collegeville, MN: Liturgical Press, 1998), esp. 1–23; André Haquin, "The Liturgical Movement and Catholic Ritual Revision," OHCW, 696–720, esp. 696–704, and bibliography.

time of Vatican II to suggest changes to the Roman Canon.[5] Cipriano Vagaggini brought together a number of criticisms and suggestions and identified what he called merits and defects of the Roman Canon. Its merits included its antiquity and traditional character, its treasury of prefaces, its theology of offering, and its literary style. The defects included a structure that seemed to lack unity, a lack of logical progression of ideas, the seemingly random location of intercessions in various parts of the prayer, an exaggerated emphasis on offering, the disorder of epicletic-type prayers, the lack of a theology of the Holy Spirit's role, deficiencies in the wording of the institution narrative, the lists of saints, and the lack of an overarching presentation of the history of salvation.[6]

After various proposals, Paul VI made the decision to keep the Roman Canon as it was and to add additional prayers. Three new prayers were promulgated in 1969. (EP II and EP IV are treated extensively in other places in this commentary.) EP III, examined here, seems based on a proposal made by Vagaggini.[7] Some see traces of Gallican influence,[8] others Oriental,[9] and others call it neo-Roman.[10]

The overall structure of the prayer is laid out concisely in *IGMR2002* (no. 79): thanksgiving, acclamation (*Sanctus*), epiclesis of the Holy Spirit, institution narrative and consecration, anamnesis, offering, intercessions, and doxology. All of the new Roman EPs since 1969 have followed this outline.[11] In some ways, the structure is Antiochene, with the intercessions

[5] See the overview and extensive bibliography in Cipriano Vagaggini, *The Canon of the Mass and Liturgical Reform*, trans. Peter Coughlan (Staten Island, NY: Alba House, 1967), 17–24; see the proposed revisions of the Roman Canon by Hans Küng, "Das Eucharistiegebet: Konzil und Erneuerung der römischen Liturgie," *Wort und Wahrheit* 18 (1963): 102–7; and by Karl Amon, "Gratias Agere: Zur Reform des Messcanons," *Liturgiesches Jahrbuch* 15 (1965): 79–98; also, cf. Power, 266–67 above.

[6] Vagaggini, *The Canon of the Mass*, 84–107.

[7] Bugnini, 448–65; Enrico Mazza, *The Eucharistic Prayers of the Roman Rite*, trans. Matthew J. O'Connell (New York: Pueblo, 1986), 123–25; Vincenzo Raffa, *Liturgia Eucaristica: Mistagogia della Messa: dalla storia e dalla teologia alla pastorale pratica*, Bibliotheca 'Ephemerides liturgicae' Subsidia 100 (Rome: CLV, 2003), 601–4.

[8] Bernard Botte, *From Silence to Participation: An Insider's View of the Liturgical Renewal*, trans. John Sullivan (Washington, DC: Pastoral Press, 1988), 149. See the comment in Bugnini, 457; Vagaggini, *The Canon of the Mass*, 140, 155; Raymond Moloney, *Our Eucharistic Prayers in Worship, Preaching and Study*, Theology and Life Series 14 (Wilmington, DE: Michael Glazier, 1985), 123–24.

[9] See Adrien Nocent, "Le nuove preghiere eucaristiche," in *La Liturgia, Eucaristia: teologia e storia della celebrazione*, ed. Salvatore Marsili, Anamnesis 3:2 (Casale Monferrato: Marietti, 1983), 253; Mazza, *The Eucharistic Prayers*, 123.

[10] Mazza, *The Eucharistic Prayers*, 125; Raffa, *Liturgia Eucaristica*, 614.

[11] Some would say too rigorously, e.g., Nocent, "Le nuove preghiere eucaristiche," 253–54.

gathered after the words of institution. In other ways, it is Alexandrian,[12] with an epiclesis both before and after the words of institution. Some expressions may come from Gallican sources. The particular structure and thematic emphases emerge from concerns that were important at the time of the council and its aftermath.[13]

Opening Dialogue and *Sanctus* (*OM2008*, no. 107)

The presented text includes the opening dialogue, reference to the preface, and the text of the *Sanctus*. Previous editions of the postconciliar *OM* had presented the dialogue immediately after the preparation of the gifts with the title *Prex Eucharistica* (*OM1969*, no. 27); then followed the prefaces and finally the texts of the four EPs. The dialogue and *Sanctus* were not repeated with EP III but were presumed from their initial presentation. The advantage of the current arrangement is that the structure of the prayer is presented clearly and avoids the misapprehension that the EP somehow "begins" after the *Sanctus* rather than with the dialogue.

The dialogue is found in some of the most ancient examples of EPs, e.g., ApTrad and Addai and Mari.[14] The earliest Roman liturgical books sometimes began with the second interchange, *Sursum corda*.[15] The tradition emerged during the eighth and ninth centuries of saying the prayer over the gifts silently (eventually called *Secreta*)[16] and singing the conclusion, *Per omnia saecula saeculorum*. The manuscripts presented this as an integral part of the dialogue before the preface. This tradition continued until the reforms after Vatican II.[17]

[12] For a further exploration of Alexandrian elements, see Baldovin, 249 above.

[13] See Nocent, "Le nuove preghiere eucaristiche," 247–48, 253–57; Bugnini, 448–65, especially as he details the desire to have a "Roman" structure for a EP. Vagaggini in discussing the merits and defects of the Roman Canon often makes reference to an "ideal" structure of a canon that every EP must embody.

[14] See ApTrad, no. 4, in Paul Bradshaw, Maxwell Johnson, and L. Edward Phillips, *The Apostolic Tradition: A Commentary*, ed. Harold W. Attridge, *Hermeneia* series (Minneapolis: Fortress Press, 2002), 38–39. The text of Addai and Mari can be found in Anthony Gelston, *The Eucharistic Prayer of Addai and Mari* (Oxford: Clarendon, 1992), text at 48–49, commentary at 76–80.

[15] See the texts and variants of the *Gelasianum* in Leo Eizenhöfer, *Canon Missae Romanae*, 2 vols., Rerum Ecclesiasticarum Documenta, Series Minor, Subsidia Studiorum 1 and 7 (Rome: Herder, 1966 [1954]), 1:22–23.

[16] See my comments, 209 above.

[17] See Eizenhöfer, *Canon Missae Romanae*, 1:22–23; Sodi-Triacca, no. 1433 *et passim*; and Sodi-Toniolo, no. 1428 *et passim*.

The *Sanctus* is a liturgical composition based on Isaiah 6:2 and the gospel accounts of Palm Sunday (Matt 21:9 and Mark 11:9). The language of the angels worshiping God eternally and the acclamation of the crowds as Jesus entered Jerusalem mounted on a donkey combine to punctuate the initial praise of the prayer.[18]

Post-*Sanctus* (*OM2008*, no. 108)

The prayer repeats the *Sanctus* and intensifies it: *Vere sanctus*, an introductory phrase common in Old Spanish, Gallican, and Eastern prayers.[19] On the one hand, this section is a transition from the preface and *Sanctus* to the epiclesis. On the other hand, it is elegant in its trinitarian theology and blending of themes. God's holiness consists in conferring life and holiness on creation (in the Son through the Holy Spirit). Likewise, God constantly (*non desinis*) gathers a people to make their offering. All this is worthy of praise.

The text is close to the proposal made by Vagaggini in 1966. It is reminiscent of Paul (1 Cor 2:1-4) and John (1:1-4).[20] It concludes with a reference to Malachi 1:11: "From the rising of the sun to its setting, / my name is great among the nations; Incense offerings are made to my name everywhere, / and a pure offering; / For my name is great among the nations, / says the LORD of hosts." This is the first appearance of a theme that will return throughout the prayer: the sacrificial character of the Eucharist.[21]

Epiclesis (*OM2008*, no. 109)

The gestures in this prayer highlight its epicletic meaning. The imposition of hands in the Roman Canon occurred during the *Hanc igitur* and may have served as an indicative gesture keyed to the words ("this therefore"). Signs of the cross had multiplied in the Roman Canon. *MR1962* indicated that the priest made the sign of the cross over the bread and wine twenty-five times, often when the text spoke of "blessing." *SC*, no. 34, called for

[18] See the commentary and bibliography in Raffa, *Liturgia Eucaristica*, 559–60 (introductory dialogue) and *Sanctus* (564–70); curiously Mazza has no commentary on the dialogue; on the *Sanctus* see Mazza, *The Eucharistic Prayers*, 47–48; also, see Bryan Spinks, *The Sanctus in the Eucharistic Prayer* (Cambridge, UK: Cambridge University Press, 1991) and Power, 260–61 above.

[19] See examples in *Prex Eucharistica*, 1; see Vagaggini, *The Canon of the Mass*, 154–57.

[20] See Mazza, *The Eucharistic Prayers*, 126–27.

[21] See the comment in Raffa, *Liturgia Eucaristica*, 615–16; Mazza, *The Eucharistic Prayers*, 127–28.

the elimination of duplications. *OM2008* uses the sign of the cross only one time during EP III, i.e., during this first epiclesis. The combination of the imposition of hands over the gifts and the sign of the cross serve to highlight this moment.

The text shares some phrases with the text proposed by Vagaggini, which was consciously modeled on the *Quam oblationem* of the Roman Canon.[22] The major change is the explicit reference to the work of the Holy Spirit (*eodem Spiritu sanctificare digneris*), the same Spirit invoked in the previous trinitarian part of the prayer. The prayer refers to the gifts we have brought (*munera quae detulimus*) and connects the action to Christ's command (*cuius mandato haec mysteria celebremus*). The prayer continues the trinitarian emphasis we saw in the transition above: the Father (*Domine*) is asked that the gifts become Christ's Body and Blood by the power of the Spirit.[23]

Institution Narrative (*OM2010*, nos. 110–11)

The gestures for these two sections of the institution narrative and consecration modify the gestures found in the *MR1570* and *MR1962*. A major change is the stipulation that the words be said distinctly and openly (*distincte et aperte*) while the previous tradition was to say the prayer silently.[24] The gestures of reverence have been simplified: there is only one genuflection after the consecrated host and chalice have been shown to the people. The rubric directing the priest to keep thumb and forefinger joined together until after the ablution after his communion is no longer included. The rubrics shifted terminology here already in *OM1969*: the priest takes the "bread" at the start (*accipit panem*) but shows (*ostendit*) the consecrated "host" to the people (*hostiam consecratam*).

The text is virtually identical to that found in all the postconciliar EPs. The introductory words, however, vary from prayer to prayer. EP III begins with a reminiscence of 1 Corinthians 11:23 (*in qua nocte tradebatur*), where EP I sets the stage with *Qui, pridie quam pateretur* ("on the day before he was to suffer"). According to Vincenzo Raffa, the double use of *tradebatur/tradetur*

[22] See Baldovin, 249 above; also Power, 268–69 above.

[23] See comments in Raffa, *Liturgia Eucaristica*, 616–18; Mazza, *The Eucharistic Prayers*, 129–30.

[24] The silent recitation of the Canon goes back at least to the *OR V*, no. 58 (*et tacito intrat in canonem*) of the ninth century, based on the commentary of Amalarius = Andrieu, 2:221.

at the beginning and end of the words over the bread highlights the voluntary quality of Christ's action.[25]

Mysterium fidei (*OM2008*, no. 112)

The insertion of an acclamation by the people was new for the Roman Rite in *OM1969*. Such acclamations, however, were known in other rites.[26] After Vatican II they were inserted as a means of increasing the participation of the people.[27] The acclamation is introduced by the phrase *Mysterium fidei*, found in the words over the cup in the historical text of the Roman Canon but considered to be difficult to understand by many commentators.[28] The solution was to extract it from the institution narrative and use it here.

The first acclamation is based on the anaphora of St. James and is reminiscent of 1 Corinthians 11:26; the second is based more directly on 1 Corinthians 11:26; the third is a blend of phrases from Revelation 5:9 and 1 Peter 1:18-19.[29] Within a prayer directed to the Father, the acclamations are directed to Christ. They recall the paschal mystery of Christ's dying and rising and situate the life of the community within that mystery, expressed by the use of the first-person plural, "we" and "us" (*annuntiamus, confitemur, manducamus, bibimus, salva nos*).

OM2008 provides chant notation for the invitation *Mysterium fidei*, with two possible melodies; *MR1970*, on the other hand, provided no such musical notation. The alternative forms of the memorial acclamation were not included within *MR1975* but were placed in an appendix after the *OM*.

[25] Raffa, 618; Mazza, *The Eucharistic Prayers*, 130–31; also Power, 270 above.

[26] See, for example, in *Prex Eucharistica*, 1: Alexandrian anaphora of St. Mark, 113; Antiochene anaphora of James the Brother of the Lord (Greek version), 249, etc. See also the comment in Cesare Giraudo, *Eucaristia per la chiesa: Prospettive teologiche sull'eucaristia a partire dalla "lex orandi,"* Aloisiana 22 (Rome: Gregorian University Press, 1989), 427–28; also Power, 272 above.

[27] See Bugnini, 454–55; Raffa, *Liturgia Eucaristica*, 583–85. See also Andreas Heinz, "Anamnetische Gemeindeakklamationen im Hochgebet," in *Gratias Agamus. Studien zum eucharistischen Hochgebet. Festschrift Balthasar Fischer*, ed. Andreas Heinz and Heinrich Rennings (Freiburg: Herder, 1992), 129–47; Hans Bernhard Meyer, *Eucharistie: Geschichte, Theologie, Pastoral*, ed. Hans Bernhard Meyer et al., Gottesdienst der Kirche: Handbuch der Liturgiewissenschaft 4 (Regensburg: F. Pustet, 1989), 352; James Dallen, "The Congregation's Part in the Eucharistic Prayer," in *Living Bread, Saving Cup: Readings in the Eucharist*, ed. R. Kevin Seasoltz, rev. ed. (Collegeville, MN: Liturgical Press, 1987), 113–25, esp. 116–21; Cesare Giraudo, *Preghiere Eucaristiche per la Chiesa di Oggi: Reflessioni in Margine al Commento del Canone Svizzero-Romano*, Aloisiana 23 (Rome: Gregorian University Press, 1993), 116–19: while a commentary on EP MVN, it is pertinent to the acclamations in all EPs.

[28] See Vagaggini, *The Canon of the Mass*, 104, with bibliography.

[29] Also see Power's biblical analysis of these texts above, 272.

Anamnesis and Offering (*OM2008*, no. 113, lines 2–8)

The theme of anamnesis continues after the acclamation of the people. The tradition reveals that a memorial of the dying and rising of Christ is ordinary at this point.[30] The text is reminiscent of the Roman Canon and also of the project of Vagaggini. The phrase "remembering [*memores*] . . . we offer [*offerimus*]" is found as early as ApTrad and is typical of many prayers.[31] The text extends the memorial of the paschal mystery to include also the awaited second coming of Christ (*praestolantes alterum eius adventum*). This addition continues the thought of the people's memorial acclamation: *donec venias*, until you come.

The offering is made not only in the context of remembering but also of giving thanks (*gratias referentes*). The vocabulary of praise is extensive and mutually enriching in its diversity.[32]

Second Epiclesis (*OM2008*, no. 113, lines 9–14)

The sacrificial theme of EP III continues: here within three lines of text we find *oblationem*, *Hostiam*, and *immolatione* (offering, victim, immolation) and the prayer that begs that the Lord be pleased to accept this gift. The theology of acceptance of the sacrifice was considered both a merit and, because of its overuse, a defect by commentators at the time of Vatican II.[33] Vagaggini's project served as a starting point for this part of the prayer but was significantly simplified, removing some phrases he had taken from the Roman Canon (e.g., *Hostiam puram, Hostiam sanctam*, etc.).

The lack of a Spirit epiclesis in the Roman Canon was considered a defect, as noted above. The solution contained in the new prayers was to surround the institution narrative with a double epiclesis, the first asking God to transform the bread and wine into the Body and Blood of Christ

[30] See the examples in *Prex Eucharistica*, 1, e.g., ApTrad, 81; Anaphora of St. Mark the Evangelist, 112–15; Anaphora of John Chrysostom, 276–77; and, the Anaphora of Addai and Mari, 380.

[31] Texts in *Prex Eucharistica*, 1:81 and 380, although Addai and Mari is not so clear.

[32] See Raffa, *Liturgia Eucaristica*, 618–20; also Robert J. Ledogar, *Acknowledgment: Praise-Verbs in the Early Greek Anaphora* (Rome: Herder, 1968); Thomas J. Talley, "From *Berakah* to *Eucharistia*: A Reopening Question," in Seasoltz, *Living Bread, Saving Cup*, 80–101.

[33] Vagaggini, *The Canon of the Mass*, 87–89 and 96–97; also Power's extensive discussion on the sacrificial nature of EP I, 275–77 above.

and the second to beg for a life of communion in Christ, both by the power of the same Spirit.[34]

The final phrase, *unum corpus et unus spiritus inveniamur in Christo*, has some scriptural resonance with Acts 4:31-32 and 1 Corinthians 12:17.[35] The phrase is drawn from the Alexandrian Anaphora of St. Basil, which in turn had taken it from Ephesians 4:3-4.[36]

Commemoration of the Saints (*OM2008*, no. 113, lines 15–22)

The influence of Vagaggini's proposal continues in this section. The lists of saints from the Roman Canon is substituted by this very short list, with the possibility of adding the saint of the day or the patron of the church or diocese or other group celebrating.[37] The mention of the saints is introduced by a reference to the *munus aeternum* ("eternal sacrifice"). This phrase is taken from a prayer over the gifts for Pentecost from the *Veronense* (no. 216) and seems to reflect Colossians 1:24, where Paul speaks of filling up what is lacking in the suffering of Christ on behalf of his Body, the church.[38] The gift spoken of here is the *munus* of the whole Christian life (Rom 12:1).[39] This section of the prayer provides a rich understanding of the Eucharist as a celebration of the whole church: the saints and elect in heaven and those on earth who follow them (*consequi*).

Intercessions for the Living (*OM2008*, no. 113, lines 23–34)

This section of the prayer (beginning *Haec Hostia nostrae reconciliationis proficiat*) is less dependent on Vagaggini's proposal. The sacrifice of reconciliation is for the whole world (*totius mundi*), a strong universalizing sense (see John 6:51). The tradition of the Roman Canon, naming the pope and local bishop, is continued, with the new possibility of mentioning auxiliary or other bishops. The teaching of *LG* on the church as the People of God on pilgrimage (nos. 9, 48–51) is taken up here.[40] Some criticize the order of the

[34] Vagaggini, *The Canon of the Mass*, 100–101 and 104–5; John H. McKenna, *The Eucharistic Epiclesis: A Detailed History from the Patristic to the Modern Era*, 2nd ed. (Chicago: Hillenbrand Books, 2009).

[35] Raffa, *Liturgia Eucaristica*, 620–21.

[36] *Prex Eucharistica*, 1:353; also, see Mazza, *The Eucharistic Prayers*, 142.

[37] Vagaggini's list of saints included Joseph, John the Baptist, and the apostles Peter and Paul (*The Canon of the Mass*, 127).

[38] Raffa, *Liturgia Eucaristica*, 622.

[39] Mazza, *The Eucharistic Prayers*, 143.

[40] Ibid., 146.

last phrases for not following the order found in *LG*: the people of God first, then those in orders who lead and guide it.[41]

The paragraph beginning *Votis huius familiae* diverges from Vagaggini in this section. The attention to those *astare* (literally, "standing present")[42] continues the consideration that the Roman Canon gives to the gathered assembly of believers (*circumstantes*). The attention to "this family" (*huius familiae*) flows from the concerns of Vatican II to vitalize the particular church and the local community.[43] The contrast between "this family" and "all your children" (*omnes filios*) is striking: the image of a family gathered and wherever dispersed (*ubique dispersos*) also hints at the image of the flock and the shepherd who goes out to gather the lost (see Luke 15:4-7; Matt 18:12-14; esp. John 11:52). In the context of this language about family, God is called *Pater* (Father) rather than *Dominus* (Lord) here.

Intercessions for the Dead (*OM2008*, no. 113, lines 35–41, and no. 115)

The typographical marks indicate that this section can have a substitute text in Masses for the dead (see next paragraph). The first part of this prayer for the dead does not reflect Vagaggini's proposal, but the last part does. The universal character introduced in the previous section continues, as we pray for the members of our family (*fratres nostros*) and all the dead who please God (*omnes . . . tibi placentes*). The body of the prayer concludes with a reference to the good things in the created world (*mundo bona cuncta*) as it had begun after the *Sanctus* (*a te condita creatura . . . vivificas et sanctificas universa*).

The insertable text that is allowed (*Quando haec Prex eucharistica in Missis pro defunctis adhibetur*) is an amalgamation of the prayer for the dead discussed in the paragraph above along with a number of scriptural reminiscences to make it appropriate for Masses for the dead. It begins with a specific mention of the person who has died. The Roman Canon provided a place for mentioning the deceased by name (although it was seldom used), and the *memento* of the dead was one of the last parts of the Canon to become a regular part of the prayer.[44] The *coetus* responsible for the EP considered

[41] Nocent, "Le nuove preghiere eucaristiche," 253–54; for a different view see Raffa, *Liturgia Eucaristica*, 623–24; Mazza, *The Eucharistic Prayers*, 147–48.

[42] On the translation of *astare* as "summoned before you," see Elich, 382 below.

[43] See *SC*, no. 42; *LG*, no. 26; *Apostolicam Actuositatem*, no. 10; see the discussion on parishes in John Beal, James Coriden, and Thomas Green, ed., *New Commentary on the Code of Canon Law* (New York: Paulist Press, 2000), 673–78.

[44] See the notes in Eizenhöfer, *Canon Missae Romanae*, 1:38–39; Jungmann MRR, 2:237–48, esp. 237–40.

prayers for the dead to be appropriate for an embolism at this point, since a similar addition occurs in EP II.[45] A phrase from Romans 6:5 follows and Philippians 3:21, Revelation 7:17, and 1 John 3:2. This litany of hope can be sustaining for the bereaved. Some wonder if it might not be too much: Adrien Nocent calls it a bit melodramatic.[46]

Doxology (*OM2008*, no. 114)

The doxology is identical in all postconciliar EPs. A doxological conclusion to prayers is found from the earliest tradition of the EPs.[47] Unlike the Roman Canon, where the only mention of the Holy Spirit was in the doxology, EP III has been trinitarian throughout. The doxology thus caps the prayer with a sense of inclusion as well as exclamation.[48]

The actions during the doxology in the postconciliar EPs have been simplified. *MR1962*, for instance, included removing the pall from the chalice, genuflecting, making three signs of the cross with the consecrated Host above the chalice, then two signs of the cross with the Host between himself and the chalice, then elevating host and chalice slightly during the phrase *omnis honor, et gloria*. The *MR1962* rubrics go on to describe another genuflection and the conclusion of the silent prayer with a vocalized final phrase *per omnia saecula saeculorum* that immediately continues into the introduction to the Lord's Prayer.

Despite the fact that textually the Roman Canon was the fusion of various and sometimes disparate elements,[49] the ritual of *MR1570* and *MR1962* creates a seamless flow from *Secreta* to preface dialogue at the beginning and from doxology to Lord's Prayer at the end. The ritual flow is continuous. The reforms of Vatican II, however, seem to intend a sense of ritual units with clearly noted junctions and transitions.

We have already noted that *SC*, no. 34, called for the elimination of duplications; thus, the doxology no longer includes the multiple signs of the cross. The elevation, described in *MR1962* as *parum* (literally "a little," hence the designation for this ritual moment as the "minor elevation") is now replaced by the straightforward designation *utrumque elevans* ("elevat-

[45] Bugnini, 455.

[46] Nocent, "Le nuove preghiere eucaristiche," 254.

[47] See examples in *Prex Eucharistica*, 1, e.g., ApTrad, 81; Anaphora of St. Mark the Evangelist, 114–15; Anaphora of John Chrysostom, 278–79; and, the Anaphora of Addai and Mari, 409.

[48] *Pace* Raffa, *Liturgia Eucaristica*, 596.

[49] See Baldovin, 250, and Power, 317 above.

ing both [paten with host and chalice]"). The distinction between the "showing" of the species at the consecration (*ostendit populo, OM2008,* nos. 110 and 111) and their "elevation" here requires careful reflection.

The chant notation for the doxology here and in all of the EPs in *MR2002* underscores the lyrical nature of this moment and the importance of singing the doxology.

Conclusion

This prayer is a good example of a prayer resulting from reflection on the EP tradition at the time of Vatican II. It is rooted in a deep reading of the tradition and manifests a clear sense of what makes a prayer "Roman," e.g., the split epiclesis and the prominence of sacrificial language.

Theology of the Latin Text and Rite

David Power

What is particular to EP III comes after the *Sanctus*, since like EP I it has a variable preface. What model was used in its composition is disputed.[1] What is of particular interest for theological interpretation is that it was thought that new prayers needed to be written in Latin to keep within the Roman tradition, drawing on what was considered the best in the traditions of liturgical Latin, whether these be fragments that are known prior to the composition of the Roman Canon, the Roman tradition itself as known from the *Veronense*, or Old Spanish and Gallican liturgies.[2]

Whatever this veneration for the Latin tradition, however, there was a readiness to look to Syriac and Greek sources for inspiration. Citing Bernard Botte, Enrico Mazza[3] looks for such influence in the (split) epiclesis for the Spirit where it may have been intended to imitate the Alexandrian anaphora. Citing Adrien Nocent, Mazza thinks that this borrowing from the Alexandrian anaphora is incorporated into the model of the Antiochene tradition. On the other hand, he also refers to the opinion of Theodor Schnitzler and Herman Wegman that the prayer is modeled on the Roman Canon. With all these opinions afloat, the prayer has to be seen as an eclectic borrowing from different founts, with an effort to blend what is borrowed into a unified literary sequence, following as well as possible the style of an evolving liturgical Latin.

The different sections of the prayer show the same fundamental pattern as found in EP II and will be presented accordingly, without repeating matters discussed in my essay on EP I.

[1] Cipriano Vagaggini, *The Canon of the Mass and Liturgical Reform*, trans. Peter Coughlan (Staten Island, NY: Alba House, 1967). Although the prayer cannot be ascribed as it stands to Vagaggini, it echoes some of the discussions in this book; see Witczak, 354 above.

[2] Vagaggini, *The Canon of the Mass*, 148–50. From Vagaggini's account some in the aftermath of the council thought that there would be a further phase of liturgical renewal marked by the composition of prayers in vernacular languages but that this was not the immediate concern of the postconciliar liturgical enactment.

[3] Enrico Mazza, *The Eucharistic Prayers of the Roman Rite*, trans. Matthew J. O'Connell (New York: Pueblo, 1986), 123–49.

Post-*Sanctus* (*OM2008*, no. 108)

As in EP II, this part of the prayer leads into an epiclesis for the sanctification of the gifts, which is meant to parallel the *Quam oblationem* of the Roman Canon. The commemoration of God's works in the preface is assumed but, unlike in EP II, before the petition there is room for a further recall of God's deeds and an invitation to a prayer of praise. The priest, voicing the mind of the assembly, evokes the praise given to God by the whole of creation (*te laudat omnis a te condita creatura*). The use of *laudare* rather than *gratias agere* may owe something to what scholarship has at times seen as the Jewish distinction between blessing for creation and thanksgiving for redemption. Here, however, it is creation that is said to praise God—not specifically humans in beholding creation—and the praise is addressed to the Lord for the works of both creation and redemption, seeing that all life and holiness comes from him, through Christ and the work of the Spirit.

The trinitarian perspective of the prayer is to be noted in the proclamation of the work of the three persons in the works of salvation. The Father is the source of life and holiness. The gifts of life and holiness and the gathering of God's people are given or done *per Filium, Spiritus Sancti operante virtute.* Son and Spirit are also at work in the gathering of the church as a holy people for the offering of the clean oblation from sunrise to sunset, obviously a reference to Malachi 1:11 taken from a long ecclesiastical tradition. In the tradition of the EP the Eucharist began to be spoken of as a sacrifice by reason of the assimilation of this prophecy into Christian theology and euchology.[4] The Eucharist is indeed a sacrifice but of a new sort, so that sacrifice is primarily the sacrifice of praise offered by those of pure heart, even as they bring their gifts before God in the memorial of Christ and the invocation of the Spirit. The ultimate purpose of creation and sanctification lies in giving glory to God, but this is now done by God's people and will be completed when all are satiated with God's own glory, as it is put toward the end of the prayer in the petition for the dead.

The phrase *vivificas et sanctificas universa* in conjunction with mention of all creation (*omnis a te condita creatura*) has considerable implications for the purpose and reality of creation. The combination of the two words is borrowed from the end of the Roman Canon, where it originally concluded

[4] See Strasbourg Papyrus Gk. 254 in Jasper & Cuming, 53–54; also, Bryan D. Spinks, "A Complete Anaphora? A Note on Strasbourg Gr. 254," *The Heythrop Journal* 25 (1984): 51–55.

the blessing of the different kinds of earth's produce brought by the people before concluding the eucharistic blessing itself.[5] The gathering of the people to give worship is related to the holiness and the life given to all created things, and the clean oblation that is made has to be the voice not only of the holy people but of all creation.[6]

The purpose of this clean oblation of praise made by God's people is indicated in its being offered to the divine name (*nomini tuo*). Following scriptural sources, in biblical and liturgical Latin the name stands for the reality of God as this is made known in all of creation, and not only in the call of the human race to life and holiness.[7] This offers a good perspective on the spiritualization of cult or worship, as rooted in a reading of Malachi. The true offering resides not in the making of material gifts but in the praise given to God, and yet gifts are rendered and material creation is included in the praise because it too enjoys the life and the holiness that is poured out through the Son and the Spirit. Rather disappointingly, as with EP II, the creation motif is dropped when the prayer proceeds to the intercessions, where creatures other than humans are not mentioned and nothing is said of the effect of sin on creation, nor therefore of their redemption through the Son and Spirit.

Epiclesis (*OM2008*, no. 109)

The reference to the simultaneous work of Christ and of the Spirit in creation and redemption is ground for a connection in the sacramental action itself between the work of the Spirit, requested in the epiclesis over the gifts, and the actions and words of Christ recalled in the institution narrative. Neither acts without the other and they work in liaison. Some find a justification for a twofold epiclesis in the Alexandrian anaphora, which is often compared with the Roman Canon. While this may have influenced the prayer's composition, the sense is different from what is found in the Liturgy of Mark, where the first as well as the second epiclesis invokes the Spirit over both the people and their gifts. Both are offered in

[5] Nowhere else are the two words conjoined, either in early sacramentaries or in *MR2002*.

[6] This echoes a particularly Eastern theology that sees humankind as the voice of all God's works; see Elizabeth Theokritoff, *Living in God's Creation: Orthodox Perspectives on Ecology* (Crestwood, NY: St Vladimir's Seminary Press, 2009), 155–80. The author references Alexander Schmemann, *For the Life of the World* (Crestwood, NY: St Vladimir's Seminary Press, 1973).

[7] For the praise rendered to God in *MR2002*, see Sodi, nos. 1264, 1270; for creation's praise because it too is redeemed in humanity's redemption, see Sodi, nos. 1150, 1228, 1275, 1349.

the sacrifice, with no separating the sanctification of gifts and people as could be understood of the split epiclesis of the new Roman prayers.[8]

To describe what is done through the Spirit, the word *sacranda* in EP III is more cultic than juridical but conveys the sense of an order to be observed as is found in the more juridical vocabulary of the Canon. The verb *detulimus* in conveying that the gifts have been "lifted up" heightens the cultic and ritual sense of the action and adds to the understanding of what constitutes the full sacramental representation of Christ's own Pasch and sacrifice.[9] The people have brought their gifts of bread and wine and placed them before God in the hope and trust that they be made holy things through the action of the Spirit, sacraments of the Body and Blood of Christ.

Institution Narrative (*OM2008*, no. 110)

The institution narrative itself is introduced, as in EP II, by reference to the night in which Jesus Christ was betrayed, *in qua nocte tradebatur*.[10]

Anamnesis-Offering (*OM2008*, no. 113, lines 2–8)

The *Memores-offerimus* calls the offering of the assembly *hoc sacrificium vivum et sanctum*. In this way the imagery of a holiness descending from God and embracing creation evoked earlier in the prayer returns. The sacrifice is the sacramental offering of the church in memorial of the work of Christ. The work of Christ here remembered includes his death, resurrection, ascension, and indeed his second coming to which the church looks forward (*praestolantes*). This Latin word means an attitude of living in view of something not yet realized but to be expected, or the attitude of living in expectation.[11] It is only with the return of Christ, his second coming (*alterum adventum*), that the work of redemption is completed, the fullness of the mystery revealed. Since this is expressed at this point one has to remark with some disappointment that the end of the prayer, in the plea for the dead, does not retrieve the imagery of the full plenitude of Christ

[8] Mazza discusses the composition of the Alexandrian anaphora at length in *The Origins of the Eucharistic Prayer* (Collegeville, MN: Liturgical Press, 1995), 177–85.

[9] While a more detailed discussion of translation will follow (375–82 below), something has to be said here about the need to respect the meaning of the original Latin. In ICEL2010, "we have brought to you for consecration" suggests an apparent impasse. Better are English translations of the Byzantine anaphoras: "we have set forth."

[10] See my commentary on this text, 322–23 above.

[11] For other examples in *MR2002*, see Sodi, nos. 140, 143, 1268, 1349, 3261.

manifest at the end of time but talks only of partaking of eternal life in praise and glorification (as in EP II).[12]

Epiclesis (*OM2008*, no. 113, lines 9–14)

The epiclesis in this prayer could be said to be only a quasi-epiclesis since it does not directly ask for the Spirit but rather that the people filled with the Spirit may be made one through the sacrament. This reference to the Spirit occurs within intercessions for the church.

As noted above, what is offered is called a *sacrificium vivum et sanctum.* This could mean the memorial offering of the church in which the once-and-for-all sacrifice of Christ is represented. Its meaning, however, is modified by placing the power of consecration (as in the other prayers) in the words of Christ as spoken by the priest. This focus on the presence and offering of the Body and Blood resulting from the consecration seems to be suggested by the use of the word *Hostia* (with capital *H*) in the epiclesis and the intercessions, which begin with *Respice.* God is asked to look upon the *Hostia* set before him. *Respice* means asking a favorable glance from God.[13]

The *Hostia,* which is Christ himself as sacrificial victim through his own self-offering and whose sacramental Body and Blood are laid upon the altar, is here remembered. Its place in the economy of salvation is expressed through the phrase *cuius voluisti immolatione placari,* which seems to refer to the once-and-for-all offering of Christ himself, who is now sacramentally present as a victim.[14] The reference to Christ himself as victim is reinforced in the intercession that follows the epiclesis when it is asked that the *Hostia nostrae reconciliationis*—i.e., the sacrifice on which God has been asked to look favorably—may be of benefit to the church. This is a clear enough use of the biblical reference to the death of Christ by which he became the victim offered for reconciliation from sin (2 Cor 5:19-21).

According to Mazza there was some discussion about using the word "victim," which would have more clearly referred to Christ in his state as sacrificial offering, but in choosing *Hostia* the prayer makes it possible to include the fuller sense of what is offered. Though it may refer immediately to the offering of the immolated Body and Blood of Christ by the church,

[12] EP IV is more suggestive when it sees the end of Christ's work as the freedom of all creation from the corruption of sin and death in the Father's kingdom.

[13] See Gerard Moore, *Vatican II and the Collects for Ordinary Time: A Study in the Roman Missal (1975)* (San Francisco-London-Bethesda: Catholic Scholars Press, 1998), 206–7.

[14] The idea of God handing over his Son for the purpose of human redemption and being satisfied by his immolation is taken up here.

it still includes its multiple signification as a sacramental offering or sacrifice; i.e., being the offering of the church it recalls and represents the offering of Christ and allows a place for the offering of praise and atonement and the devotion of the people shown in their many works.

The church's prayer is sometimes called an *immolatio*, even an *immolatio laudis*, because it is the sacrament of Christ's immolation, but as the inclusion of praise indicates, it goes beyond that to include the work of his people. While reference is made to Christ who was sacrificed—as in *Pascha nostrum immolatus est Christus*, derived from 1 Corinthians 5:7[15]—there is also abundant use of more inclusive expressions such as *laudis tibi hostias immolamus*[16] or *oblatio quam immolando*, where what is intended is the church's sacramental offering.[17] Given the multivalence of the language of immolation, in praying EP III other meanings are not to be ignored in the living interpretation of the prayer, even if they are seen to be secondary.

In this quasi-epiclesis *immolatio* together with *respice* includes a reference to making atonement, even appeasement. It goes with *propitius* and completes *placare*. In *MR2002 respice* goes often with *propitius*:[18] God is to be propitiated by that which he sees offered. This inclusion of appeasement or atonement in the work of redemption is found in the NT, where it is said that Christ offers himself according to the will of the Father as an atonement or appeasement. While this leaves intact the gracious and merciful initiative of the Father, it still means that because of sin and offence there has to be a setting right of the due order of humanity's relation to God. Images of God's anger and desire for atonement are not simply rejected but taken over into the NT and liturgy to suggest restoring a right order of humankind's compensation for sin through communion with

[15] This meaning is found in sundry places in the Missal (e.g., Sodi, nos. 643, 651, 1200), including references to communion, when it is said that we eat the flesh immolated for us: *carnem pro nobis immolatam sumimus* (Sodi, no. 1214).

[16] Sodi, nos. 1594, 3049.

[17] Sodi, no. 1723. For the meaning that emerges from a varied use of *immolatio*, one notable example is the *super oblata* for Feria IV of the second week of Advent: *Devotionis nostrae tibi, Domine, quaesumus hostia iugiter immoletur, quae et sacri peragat instituta mysterii, et salutare tuum nobis potenter operetur.* The connection here is between the immolation of what is offered as a sign of the Church's devotion and as its praise, and the immolation of Christ the Paschal Lamb, of which it is a sacramental representation and a memorial.

[18] E.g., Sodi, nos. 107, 279, 321. It seems that in the composition of these prayers, the commission thought of *adesto propitius* and similar phrases as meaning nothing other than looking favorably, but the adverb has inevitable links with propitiation.

Christ. The remorse that goes with thankful remembrance is motivated by a sense of justice.[19]

Intercessions (*OM2008*, no. 113, lines 15–42)

In keeping with this understanding, in EP III the Body and Blood of Christ in sacramental form are offered in atonement. The offering renders God propitious to sinners, and by divine power God makes of these gifts the sacramental mystery of Christ's work and atonement in which salvation is celebrated and efficacious. If God looks propitiously or mercifully on this sacramental sacrifice, then by the power of the Spirit they who eat and drink to salvation of his Body and Blood are made one in Christ, as his Body united in the Spirit. Perfected in charity by the Holy Spirit (see EP II) the communicants in the Body and Blood (*Ipse nos*) become an eternal *munus* to God, i.e., an offering or gift, so that they may enter into their inheritance with the *electi*. *Munus* is usually the offering made by the church, but it is also the sacramental gift that God gives. There are three senses of gift at work: that which the church makes; that which the people receive when it is sanctified; and that which they become, here and hereafter, when perfected by the Spirit.[20]

The plea for communion motivates an appeal to the intercession of Mary and the saints with whom communion is already enjoyed but is to be made complete. For the dead, the church asks that they, as a perfect gift, may receive their inheritance *cum electis*. The elect are usually the already blessed,[21] but the term harkens back to baptism, the candidates for which are called the elect, and the church itself is a *genus electum*, borrowing from 1 Peter 2:9.[22]

Reference to the victim of reconciliation, the *Hostia nostrae reconciliationis*, introduces the prayer for the church on earth and for the world. What is sought through this victim offered for our reconciliation is peace and the communion of the Pilgrim Church, united visibly in faith and charity in episcopal communion. This is a communion of the whole people, the *populus*

[19] This combination of the offering of *hostiae* and appeasement is well expressed in the *supra oblata* for December 21: *Ecclesiae tuae, Domine, munera placatus assume, quae et misericors offerendi tribuisti, et in nostrae salutis efficis potenter transire mysterium.*

[20] See Sodi, nos. 719, 751, 874, 1030. The Spirit itself is called a *munus* ("gift") in *MR2002* (Sodi, no. 924), but this is not very prominent in the euchology of *MR2002*.

[21] Sodi, nos. 1268, 1508, 1541, 1871, 1970.

[22] Sodi, nos. 629, 1206, 3245.

acquisitionis, or the people won by the immolation of Christ here remembered and sacramentally present.

In praying for the church, the assembly prays for the whole world, seeking peace and salvation. *Pax et salus* means peace that comes from above and echoes the greeting at the beginning of the prayer.[23] The source and nature of this peace is spelled out in the Latin text of Ephesians 2:14-15.[24]

In the Roman euchological tradition peace often means freedom from external interferences that would disrupt the life and worship of the Christian people.[25] Hence, it is associated (as in the embolism to the Lord's Prayer) with freedom from *perturbatio*, meaning external incursions that would hinder the freedom of religion or religious practice.[26] More deeply, *pax* is an inner disposition, *spiritus virtutis et pacis*.[27] It goes with devotion in this life and culminates in the *somnum pacis* of the deceased. As Moore states, "the divine *pax* is a gift of God's love, associated with his merciful propitiation for sin. The term is used to denote the inner peace that is related to freedom from sin, civil peace, and eternal life."[28]

In the interests of such peace among the peoples of the world, the Pilgrim Church needs to remain in a communion of faith and charity, promoted by communion with the pope and the episcopal order. The petition that God hear the prayers (*vota*) of the people is replete with propitiatory language: God is to be *clemens, miseratus*. This seems to presume many hindrances to peace and to communion of the people whom God has acquired and to the gathering of the dispersed into one. The combination of love with mercy and the remedy of propitiation, as Moore notes, goes back to the Latin version of Ephesians 2:4-6: God *dives in misericordia* out of his great love gave us death to sin and life in Christ.[29] As the exercise of God's love, *miserando* and *parcendo* go together in response to the *propitiatio* offered in Christ's death and in the sacrament of this death. God is simultaneously *iustus*,

[23] See Sodi, nos. 152, 1168.

[24] *Ipse enim est pax nostra, qui fecit utraque unum . . . duos condat in semetipso in unum novum hominem, faciens pacem*: "For he [Christ] is our peace, he who made both one . . . that he might create in himself one new person in the place of the two, thus establishing peace."

[25] See *Veronense*, nos. 553, 590, 872, 961, 963, 1033.

[26] Also *Veronense*, nos. 327, 444, 497, 590, 626, 874; *Hadrianum*, nos. 850, 930. In *MR2002* this combination is found in Sodi, nos. 1306, 2377, 3284.

[27] As in *Veronense*, nos. 1056 and 1311.

[28] Moore, *Vatican II and the Collects*, 477.

[29] Ibid., 377–78.

misericors, miserator toward his people: just and merciful, i.e., merciful but exacting what is necessary to right order.[30]

Finally, in EP III there is the prayer for *gloria* for the deceased, as in other prayers. It is quite comprehensive in its scope since it is given not only to those who on earth were of the church (*fratres*) but to all who pleased God in this life. Several expressions are used to describe this glory. Clearly referencing Revelation 20:3-4, it is a state in which there is no sorrow or mourning. This is because the blessed will see God and will be like him and so can praise him (*laudabimus*) forever. The place of Christ in this praise concludes the petition, for it is offered through him, our Lord, through whom God bountifully gives all good things (*largiris*).[31] This harkens back to the *Vere Sanctus* wherein Christ is proclaimed as the one through whom, by the power of the Spirit, God creates and sanctifies everything. The congregation of the faithful to give voice on earth to the praise of all creatures is perfected through Christ in blessedness, and Christ himself perfects his work in the heavenly and eternal praise.

Conclusion

While this prayer borrows lavishly from other sources, in its structure and liturgical vocabulary it remains within the orbit of the Roman tradition. What is offered to God in memorial of Christ's sacrifice includes praise, thanksgiving, and appeasement. The prayer is more comprehensive than EP II in its expression of holiness and in its inclusion of all created things in the work of Christ as the one through whom God acts. It also joins very readily the work of Christ and the Spirit in creation and reconciliation. While creation in its entirety is attributed to Christ and Spirit, when the prayer speaks of reconciliation its compass is narrower and appears to be confined to humankind, without including creation as a whole in this work. Another of the prayer's virtues is that it shows how the holiness given through Christ and Spirit to the elect is begun in baptism, perfected in faith and charity in the living communion of the church, and reaches its apex in

[30] *Veronense*, nos. 232, 366, 1019. The coupling *misericors-miserator*, is typical of the redundancy of words found in Roman liturgical Latin. On mercy and justice, see *Veronense*, nos. 232, 366, 1019. *Miseratio* for sinners is a response to the offering of the sacrifice and is also at work in the effect of communion (Sodi, nos. 662, 3150) and finally in the beatitude given to the dead (Sodi, nos. 3172, 3233).

[31] As Albert Blaise notes in his translation, the term denotes abundance, generosity, profusion, liberality (*Le Vocabulaire Latin des principaux thèmes liturgiques* [Turnhout: Brepols, 1966], s.v. *largiris*).

eternal glory. EP III follows this trajectory, moving from the clean oblation of the Eucharist to the eternal praise of God in a share in divine glory. Even as it includes a distinctive accent on appeasement, as a whole the prayer could be read as a kind of mini-treatise on holiness, a *lex orandi* that could generate a sacramental perception of the whole of creation as embodiment of the holiness of God, lived now in eschatological anticipation and given voice in the liturgy of the church. Finally, the prayer is quite insistent in its various expressions on the offering of the Body and Blood of Christ, reinforcing the consecratory power attributed to the words of Christ repeated in the institution narrative.

The ICEL2010 Translation

Tom Elich

EP III is used with a variable preface and its rather elaborated expression makes it especially suitable for use on Sundays and feast days. A EP always encapsulates complex and rich theological ideas: anamnesis and sacrifice with notions of time, past, present, and future; epiclesis and the mysterious action of the Holy Spirit in sacrament and church. ICEL2010's version of EP III makes a serious attempt to express this theology in a full and nuanced way.

The form of the English text also provides a challenge in its complexity and vocabulary. Priests will need to study it carefully and understand its articulation. Then, unlike the collects for the liturgical seasons, the prayer will be repeated frequently. Through the use of the text over months and years, the assembly will have the opportunity to become familiar with it and meditate on it, so that, with the support of suitable catechesis, they may come to immerse themselves in the richness of eucharistic praying. The prayer is unlikely to be transparent in its meaning at the first hearing but is not impenetrable.

Post-*Sanctus* (ICEL2010, no. 108)

The three sentences of ICEL1973 are combined into a single sentence in ICEL2010 without becoming turgid. The relationship of ideas expressed in this way is theologically powerful: God is the beginning and end of all that is good and holy; in particular, God convenes our liturgical assembly, placing our perpetual sacrifice into the context of the cosmic praise of all creation and making this offering pure through the sacrifice of Jesus Christ and life-giving by the working of the Holy Spirit.

The first line reinforces the affirmation of the *Sanctus* that the Lord God is holy.[1] ICEL1973 addressed the prayer to the Father to emphasize the trinitarian structure of liturgical praying and to employ a more personal,

[1] The adjective "Holy" is important in making this link (ICEL2006 tried to use the substantive "Holy One"). The address "O Lord" prevents people from hearing "Holy Lord."

biblical title.[2] The title "Father" is implied a few lines later in ICEL2010 when Jesus Christ is called "your Son" (line 5). ICEL2010 helpfully retains some familiar phrases (e.g., "rightly gives you praise . . . working of the Holy Spirit . . . gather a people to yourself"), but what was rather static has become more dynamic: instead of "all creation" we have "all you have created," and "all life, all holiness" becomes "you give life to all things and make them holy." ICEL2010 retains "working of the Holy Spirit"[3] and strengthens it by the addition of the word "power."

At the beginning of line 5, the conjunction "for" links together God's work of creating, redeeming, and empowering, and at the beginning of line 8, the conjunction "and" draws the liturgy into the context of the work of the Trinity. Many will be sad to lose the balanced time-place imagery of ICEL1973—"From age to age . . . from east to west"—but in its place is the beautiful and vivid image from the Latin, "from the rising of the sun to its setting." The last line is unusual: "a pure sacrifice may be offered to your name" (line 10); ICEL1973 had an offering "made to the glory of your name." Glorifying God's name is familiar (e.g., "Hallowed be thy name"). Since the ineffable name actually signifies the transcendent God, an offering to God's name is actually an offering to God. The offering, of course, does not actually take place here but is about to happen. The sacrifice is "pure" because it is God who gives life, makes holy, and gathers a people.

This opening passage emphasizes the power of the liturgical assembly, the church gathered by the Father in the unity of the Trinity, to give voice to the praise of all created things.

Epiclesis (ICEL2010, no. 109)

Just as the single sentence of the thanksgiving draws the eucharistic offering into the whole work of creation, so too the adjective "same" ("by the same Spirit") links the epiclesis to the creative working of the Holy Spirit celebrated in the post-*Sanctus* by which God gives "life to all things and make[s] them holy." Here, by the Holy Spirit, God is asked to make holy the gifts of bread and wine and to give them life in a particular sense, namely, that they become the Body and Blood of the living Christ. People will need focused attention to appreciate this connection because the idea spans half a dozen lines of text (lines 3–12).

[2] ICEL2010's substitution of "Lord" for ICEL1973's "Father" also occurs in the epiclesis and anamnesis; in all three cases the Latin is *Domine*.

[3] ICEL2006 used "work."

Due deference in making a request of God is expressed strongly with "humbly implore" (line 3), reinforced by "graciously" in the next line. Perhaps the more restrained ICEL1998 "humbly pray" would have sufficed since excess quickly appears insincere in English, though ICEL1973's "we ask you" is certainly too bald. The phrase "for consecration" (line 5) is a surprise in this translation because it has not been explicitly represented in the English text until now.[4] The verb makes it clear that the gifts are brought and set aside at this point but not yet offered. The meaning of the words is amplified by the gestures outlined in the rubrics: the laying on of hands is the ritual sign of invoking the Holy Spirit, and the sign of the cross at the words "Body and Blood of your Son" links the Eucharist with Jesus' death and resurrection.

The epiclesis concludes with a reference to the Last Supper and the command of Christ to "Do this in memory of me" (Luke 22:19). The change from ICEL1973's "this eucharist" to "these mysteries" at first glance seems to be the simple choice of a look-alike word: *mysteria* for "mysteries." *Mysterium* can mean mystery in concepts such as the "mystery of salvation" or the "paschal mystery," but it also has a very close relationship with *sacramentum*, and the two are often interchangeable.[5] Given the liturgical setting and the reference to the command of Christ, one might reasonably assume that the particular sacrament of the Eucharist is the intended meaning. ICEL's notes for the bishops' conferences in 2006, however, explained that ICEL1973's "this Eucharist" only refers to the celebration actually taking place whereas ICEL2010 wished to say that whenever and wherever we celebrate the Mass, we do so at Christ's command.[6]

Institution Narrative (ICEL2010, nos. 110 and 111)

The reference to the command of Christ leads into the institution narrative and is verbally connected to it by the conjunction "for" and the emphatic "himself." Again in this prayer the actions of the Holy Spirit and of Christ are joined in the consecration of the bread and wine. The present text retains the strong word "betrayed," after both ICEL1998 and ICEL2006

[4] The concept is expressed explicitly in the French and Portuguese, but was considered to be already included in the "make holy" (Latin, *sanctificare*) in English and its parallels in the Italian, Spanish, and German translations.

[5] See Collins and Foley, 89 above.

[6] This usage is consistent with the epiclesis in EP IV and the invitation to the eucharistic acclamation.

translated *tradetur*[7] as "handed over"; this makes the word order a little more comfortable by comparison with ICEL2006.

The phrase in EP III, "giving you thanks, he said the blessing," corresponds to the one found in EP I; it introduces the words over the bread and is repeated before the words over the cup. Giving thanks and blessing are two aspects of the one act of praise. The actual words of institution are the same in each of the EPs.[8]

Anamnesis, Offering, and Epiclesis (ICEL2010, no. 113, lines 2–15)

The anamnesis begins in the same way in each of the principal EPs with the people's acclamation of Jesus' death and resurrection. It is significant that the whole assembly takes such an important part in the EP. As the priest resumes his proclamation on behalf of all, the opening word "Therefore" relates the just completed acclamation (no. 112) by the assembly with the communal offering ("we offer") being made in union with Christ. The priest reaffirms that while we "offer" (*offerimus*), we do this action remembering the passion, resurrection, and ascension and waiting for the second coming. Perhaps ICEL2010's introduction of the verbs "celebrate" and "look forward" is meant to recall the Lord's memorial command; in fact, however, what we actually do as we remember is offer.[9] This is a surprising lapse in the way the English is structured on the Latin model.

What we offer in thanksgiving is the "holy and living sacrifice" (line 8). This entire phrase has remained unchanged since ICEL1973. It expresses well that our eucharistic offering is actually the sacrifice that Christ accomplished on the cross and of which we have been urged to be mindful as we join our lives to his.

The amplification of this idea in the following lines (9–11) presents dense theological ideas to the assembly; its difficult vocabulary will challenge people's comprehension even further. We ask God, in looking upon the offering on the altar, to see what it represents, namely, the sacrifice of Christ on the cross by which God has chosen to reconcile the world to himself (2 Cor 5:18-19). In ICEL2008 *oblationem* was translated as "oblation" rather than "offering" for the first time. Apart from resembling the Latin word

[7] On the theological significance of *tradetur*, see Power, 270 above.

[8] See Ostdiek's and my comments, 287 and 329–30 above, and Chupungco 479–81 below.

[9] See Enrico Mazza, *The Eucharistic Prayers of the Roman Rite*, trans. Matthew J. O'Connell (New York: Pueblo, 1986), 132.

more closely, it is unclear what advantage this obscure word brings. Perhaps we should be grateful that the following line did not use "immolation" for the same reason. However, the translation of this line shows great uncertainty, as indeed it did when it was originally composed in Latin.[10]

ICEL1973	ICEL1998	ICEL2006	ICEL2008	ICEL2010
and see the Victim whose death has reconciled us to yourself	and see the Victim by whose sacrifice you were pleased to reconcile us to yourself.	and, recognizing the Victim by whose sacrificial death you willed to be reconciled,	and, recognizing the sacrificial Victim by whose death you willed to reconcile us to yourself,	and, recognizing the Victim by whose death you willed to reconcile us to yourself,

Using the metaphor of sacrifice, these lines give explicit expression to the divine will by which reconciliation is achieved in the death of Christ, and, rightly, it is we who are reconciled with God, although the Latin text just has the passive infinitive (*placari*) more properly rendered as "to be reconciled." The reorganization of the sense lines in ICEL2010 brings the text into line with the arrangement of the Latin, which emphasizes the person of Christ. The two difficult words here are *Hostiam* and *immolatione. Immolatio* means "a sacrificing," and the simple rendering as "death" seems insufficient. *Hostia* refers to a "victim" offered in a sacrifice. Both words then arise from an unambiguous context of sacrifice, which has paled in ICEL2010 with the omission of any explicit mention of sacrifice. The word "victim" by itself is also misleading because "nowadays a 'victim' is one who has suffered injustice or whose lot is a wretched one; it has lost all its original cultic flavour."[11] The word is capitalized, a useful visual cue, but this is not heard in the proclamation. It may be that the translation is no more ambiguous than the Latin original, but only catechesis will enable the assembly to understand and pray these lines.

These difficult lines serve as introductory clauses to the second (communion) epiclesis (lines 12–15), which prays for the unity of the church. A few attempted changes in ICEL2006 were unsuccessful and the memorable lines from ICEL1973 basically remain. Placing the word "may" (line 15) after the mention of the Holy Spirit, however, means that the phrase no

[10] See ibid., 136–37.

[11] Ibid.

longer exactly constitutes an invocation of the Holy Spirit.[12] Nonetheless, it makes a fine connection with the first epiclesis, linking the Spirit with the Body and Blood of the Christ: as we are restored by receiving the sacrament, we are, in fact, filled with the Holy Spirit. The body-spirit link is continued as we pray for oneness in body and spirit.

Intercessions (ICEL2010, no. 113, lines 16–45)

The intercessions in EP III are quite extensive. ICEL2010 is at pains to bring out the strong eschatological elements in the text, and the theme of reconciliation recurs.

The opening phrase has been translated and arranged in various ways, none of them very satisfying:

ICEL1973	ICEL1998	ICEL2006	ICEL2008	ICEL2010
May he make us an everlasting gift to you;	Let him make us an everlasting gift to you;	May he bring us to perfection as an eternal gift to you;	May he make of us an eternal offering to you;	May he make of us an eternal offering to you.

It clearly references the communion epiclesis and reaches back to the idea of the "oblation of your Church." It is more easily understood if one goes to the draft texts considered at the time of its composition in 1967.[13] Originally following the offering of "this holy and living sacrifice," the text read, "and with it, ourselves and all we have, for we are yours and all things are yours." The sentence is based on *SC*, which urges people to take part with conscious and full involvement by "Offering the immaculate victim, not only through the hands of the priest but also together with him, they should learn to offer themselves" (no. 48). These lines are crucial to an appreciation of a self-offering integrated with the eucharistic offering of the church, although the text makes it clear that such an offering is not something achieved independently of the action of Christ.

The purpose of recognizing ourselves in the eternal offering is that we obtain an inheritance with the Virgin Mary and the saints (the "elect").[14]

[12] Power calls it a "quasi-epiclesis," 369 above.

[13] For a discussion, see Mazza, *The Eucharistic Prayers*, 135–36; for the draft texts, see 149–53.

[14] This idea is now expressed in a similar way at the end of EP II: (with the Virgin Mary, the apostles and all the saints) "we may merit to be coheirs to eternal life."

We participate in the offering of the cross so that we may share in the glory of Christ with the saints. Provision is made for the inclusion by name of the saint of the day or patron saint. This section evokes the eschatological dimension of the eucharistic celebration for, by the hope of our inheritance with the elect, we benefit from their intercession before God to receive God's unfailing help. The addition in the final two lines of "in your presence" (line 23) and "unfailing" (line 24) to ICEL1973 enriches the content and endows the phrase with a solemn cadence.

There follow intercessions for the world and the church. The ICEL1973 parallel between "our peace" and that of the world is no longer found in ICEL2010. In return, we have a continuation of the theme of reconciliation. ICEL2006 translated *Hostia* here as "Victim," as it is two paragraphs earlier; this was reversed in ICEL2010 by a return to "Sacrifice."[15] The petition therefore draws "the peace and salvation of all the world" within the scope of "this Sacrifice of our reconciliation," a useful counterbalance to any possible misunderstanding of the changed words of institution over the cup, "for many for the forgiveness of sins."[16]

The final translation of the intercession for the church is less felicitous. The memorable phrase from ICEL1973, kept in ICEL2006, "strengthen in faith and love your pilgrim Church on earth" is spoiled by the choice of the look-alike word "confirm" (line 28) in rendering *firmare* and the problematic translation of *caritate* as "charity";[17] happily the second part of ICEL1973's translation remains. The whole is introduced by the somewhat stiff "Be pleased," a translation of *digneris* that does not mean quite the same thing as "may you see fit" or "deign." The term "Order of Bishops" (line 31) will be foreign to many people. ICEL2006's version of the final line ("the entire people you make your own") was more straightforward than ICEL2010's (line 32).

The idea of a "pilgrim Church" and the "entire people" is continued as we ask the merciful and compassionate Father to listen to these prayers and gather together his children scattered throughout the world (lines 36–37).[18] The idea has an eschatological reference to the great throng of people from every nation, race, tribe, and language who stand before the

[15] Although the English terminology of "reconciliation" is used both here and in the earlier paragraph in conjunction with *Hostia*, in this case the Latin word is *reconciliationis*, whereas previously the verb was *placari*.

[16] See 378, n. 8 above.

[17] See my comments, 333 above.

[18] ICEL2006 had "earth" instead of "world." Both words occur in the previous paragraph. In fact the Latin simply says *ubique dispersos* ("scattered wheresoever").

throne of God (Rev 7:9). This context is essential for the commemoration of the departed that immediately follows. The Latin *quam tibi astare voluisti,* meaning "whom you have called to stand before you" was rendered by the somewhat stern "summoned before you" (line 34). This loses a powerful biblical allusion (e.g., Rev 7:9) for fear of making a superficial reference to the posture of the liturgical assembly.

The intercession for the departed is structured so that it builds toward the mention of God's kingdom and the fullness of glory we too hope to share. Nevertheless, the phrase "give kind admittance to your kingdom" (line 41) is disappointing to those accustomed to ICEL1973's strong beginning, "Welcome into your kingdom," or who saw ICEL2006's "Lovingly receive into your kingdom." The phrase "their passing from this life" (line 40) is an accurate translation of *ex hoc saeculo transierunt* but carries the burden of the euphemism "passing."[19] The final sentence provides a strong conclusion ("bestow on the world all that is good," line 45) and the rhetorical force of a repeated "through" leads naturally into the doxology.

Final Doxology (ICEL2010, no. 114)

The formal doxology is common to all the EPs. It provides a solemn ending with a clear rhetorical structure that builds to a forceful climax. It evokes well the people's "Amen."

[19] The interpolation for Masses for the Dead draws on strong Pauline imagery, cf. Rom 6 and Phil 3.

The Mystagogical Implications

Joyce Ann Zimmerman

A tendency for many members of the Catholic liturgical assembly is to narrow down the meaning and intent of the EPs to only the act of consecration, which most people locate at Jesus' words of institution: "this is my Body . . . this is the chalice of my Blood." Without detracting from this great mystery—that the bread and wine are changed into the Body and Blood of the risen Christ—we also want to widen our appreciation for the dynamic movement unfolding in the EP. The challenge is to experience the prayer as revealing to us God's wondrous saving deeds on our behalf, God's invitation into living this mystery of our faith, and God's promise of bringing us to "the fullness of [divine] glory."

Another tendency by all too many is that the EP is a long recitation by the priest during which we get lost in the many words that carry little or no meaning beyond consecration. The prayer's various structural parts are largely unknown to all too many Catholics, and so when the priest prays this central prayer the people sometimes turn to private prayer, their minds wander, or they limit their focus on one or more phrases or words that have particular meaning for them. The challenge is to experience the prayer as a seamless whole drawing us into the mystery of God confirming the "faith and charity" marking our efforts to be faithful followers of Jesus.

Yet another tendency is that the EP is so focused on the action of the Holy Spirit changing the bread and wine into the Body and Blood of our Lord Jesus Christ that we easily miss how we ourselves are also transformed by this same Holy Spirit. The challenge is to experience the prayer as our own joining with the unending offering of Jesus in "this holy and living sacrifice." The challenge is to experience the prayer as drawing us into the "one body, one spirit in Christ" whereby we are able to *live* as Jesus himself did.

The essential catechesis needed is to see the entire prayer as consecratory, i.e., as making sacred all of life, all of creation, the bread and wine, the people God has chosen to gather into one with the divine Self. Authentic mystagogical preaching and reflection always lead us back to the originating events "of the saving Passion of [the] Son, his wondrous Resurrection and Ascension into heaven, . . . as we look forward to his second coming." A mystagogical reflection on EP III brings us directly into Jesus' mission of salvation. This prayer especially brings to mind the motifs of creation, holiness, sacrifice, all brought about by the "power and working of the Holy Spirit." Let us see how these three motifs capture the dynamic of the prayer and urge us to live the transformation that God brings about in each of us.

Creation

At a time when global warming cries out for responsible stewardship of the resources of our world, when human catastrophes such as oil spills pollute the environment, when many of us live in concrete jungles, this prayer's language about "creation," "all things," "the world," and "the earth" is a reminder that everything in our world is a good given us by God and "that all creation is groaning in labor pains even until now; and not only that, but we ourselves, who have the firstfruits of the Spirit, also groan within ourselves as we wait for adoption, the redemption of our bodies" (Rom 8:22-23). This prayer helps us utter our groan as part of all God has created that brings God praise and thanksgiving; it helps us see that all life comes from God and the divine intent is that it be holy.

This prayer's frequent mention of creation and the world reminds us that Jesus' saving deeds redeem all of life and creation. At the beginning of the prayer, as we call to mind God's wondrous deeds on our behalf, we acknowledge that all creation "rightly gives [God] praise" and that it is God who gives life. This motif of the goodness of creation is revisited toward the end of EP III where we make intercession to God. Here we ask God to "advance the peace and salvation" that only God can give and to gather all God's children who are "scattered throughout the world." This ardent intercession is really about unity; when we are one in the human family, then the breakdown in relationships that sows discord and violence and wars gives way to the peace that marks our being one with each other because we are one in God.

Our full, conscious, and active participation in praying EP III requires of us that we grow in our appreciation for the life and goodness of creation as God's gifts to us and for which we are to be responsible stewards. As Jesus lived a simple life, so must we. As Jesus reached out to heal alienation and pain, so must we. As Jesus drew all things to himself, so must we. These ways of living the Gospel are reinforced in this EP. It behooves us to hear with open hearts our prayer that God "advance the peace and salvation of all the world." Praying this means that we pledge ourselves to receive God's promise and cooperate in making all creation to be the good God created.

Holiness

In EP III we extol God as holy, we confirm that God has made all things holy, and we ask God through the Holy Spirit to make the gifts of bread and wine holy. We are quite comfortable saying that God is holy and that the bread and wine become the Body and Blood of our Lord Jesus Christ are holy. Some are quite uncomfortable admitting that they themselves are holy. True, we do not make ourselves holy—God makes us holy by the divine gift of grace—but holy we are!

The prayer has a double epiclesis, which includes words and gesture calling down the Holy Spirit. Before the institution narrative (those words of Jesus we recall from the Last Supper) the priest extends his hands over the bread and wine and prays that "the same Spirit graciously make holy these gifts." These words and gesture make clear to us that changing the bread and wine into the Body and Blood of our Lord Jesus Christ is not the action of this community, nor even the action of the priest. It is the action and power of the Holy Spirit. Because of the gesture of extended hands, most of us are familiar with this element of the EP, although we might not understand its full meaning.

Fewer people, however, key into a second epiclesis that takes place after the institution narrative, possibly because the priest does not repeat the gesture of extending his hands. This second epiclesis is not over the gifts of bread and wine but over the assembled community. The priest prays that the members of the assembly be "filled with [the] Holy Spirit, [and] become one body, one spirit in Christ." Just as the Holy Spirit transforms the gifts of bread and wine, so does that same Holy Spirit transform us. The prayer for unity is one that begs us to be united to each other by being united to Christ, and we are so united only by the gracious outpouring of Christ's Spirit upon us. The epiclesis over the people is a kind of perpetual Pentecost.

Our holiness, then, is a grace-gift from God that makes us one with Christ and, thus, in right relationship with God. As we hear the words of the epiclesis over us, we ought to be moved to live up to our relationship in Christ and with each other. We are transformed not for our own sakes but so that we can be Christ's presence wherever we live and work and play. So united with Christ, we are a living Gospel proclaiming God's grace-gift of holiness. The mystery of the Eucharist extends beyond the wondrous gift of the risen Christ's Body and Blood given to us for our nourishment. The mystery of the Eucharist includes our own receiving of these gifts and our own transformation into being more perfect members of the Body of Christ.

St. Augustine long ago captured the wonder of our receiving Christ at the eucharistic celebration. He boldly proclaims (in Sermon 272) that we receive the mystery, the Body of Christ, our very selves. Then he challenges us: when we say Amen, make sure that we are faithful members of Christ's Body and that our Amen is true. We say Amen at any number of times during Mass. Each one is a rehearsal for when we say the great Amen that is our pledge of faithful Gospel living. When we hear the Holy Spirit called upon us at the epiclesis, our hearts ought to be filled with Amen. When we hear in the preface dialogue the invitation *Sursum corda* (literally, "upward hearts"), to lift up our hearts, our response must be more than a halfhearted "We lift them up to the Lord." Our response is an Amen, a *Habemus ad Dominum*—we *have* our hearts toward the Lord, not simply at this moment at Mass, but at every moment of our lives.

This is holiness: having our hearts turned toward the Lord at every breathing moment of our lives. This is holiness: receiving the Holy Spirit who transforms us to be more deeply related to God and each other in the Body of Christ. This is holiness: the grace-gift of the very life of God. Amen! Let it be true by the way we live the Eucharist every day, in all circumstances, in all the world!

Sacrifice

It is no surprise that EP III is rich in sacrifice-oblation-offering language because the word "sacrifice" comes from the Latin meaning "to make holy." Specifically, its use in this prayer refers both to Christ's sacrifice on the cross and "the oblation of your Church."

The first use of sacrifice occurs in the post-*Sanctus* part of EP III: "from the rising of the sun to its setting a pure sacrifice may be offered." The phrase comes from the prophet Malachi and is a good example of how liturgy draws on Sacred Scripture: "For from the rising of the sun to its setting, / my name is great among the nations; / Incense offerings are made to my name everywhere, / and a pure offering; / For my name is great among the nations, / says the LORD of hosts" (Mal 1:11).

This image abounds with meaning. The sun's rising and setting are natural signs framing our days; sacrifice is offered all day. This suggests that, first, our sacrifice—our self-giving in union with Christ—not simply is embraced during Mass but informs all our daily living. It also suggests that Christ's sacrifice is liturgically remembered perpetually—at some place and at each moment of the day Christ's faithful followers are lifting their voices in thanksgiving and praise during Mass—just as Malachi suggests. Yet the prophet says more: our perpetual sacrifice is offered to God because God's name (presence) is great. God's presence draws forth from us praise.

Another element of a EP is called the anamnesis, a Greek word meaning "to remember." After the institution narrative of EP III we "celebrate the memorial of" (make memory of) Jesus' saving deeds, and our remembering brings us to "offer [God] in thanksgiving this holy and living sacrifice." Perhaps the most important word here is "living." Jesus' suffering and death on the cross were once-and-for-all historical events, but the event is not over. It continues in the faith and liturgical actions of the church. We recognize Jesus as the sacrificial victim who reconciles us to God, but more, we pray that God look "upon the oblation of [the] Church." We ourselves join with Christ in offering ourselves to God. Sacrifice is a "making holy" because we join ourselves to Christ in his perfect self-offering to the Father.

Sometimes we have an attitude that "sacrifice" is negative—we give up something cherished in order to gain something we want more. Liturgically, this is not quite right. Rather than "give up" we "give over." We give ourselves over to God through Christ in the Spirit because this is how we are made "an eternal offering" to God, how we "obtain an inheritance" with all the saints in heaven, how we "hope to enjoy for ever the fullness" of God's glory. Thus the motif of sacrifice has an eschatological thrust: the eternal life and holiness we hope one day to gain is already being realized through our union with Christ and his eternal self-giving.

After the institution narrative the priest invites us to proclaim the mystery of faith. We know there are several choices for this acclamation, and usually it is those who prepare the liturgy who make the choice. In light of our comments about sacrifice, here is a choice that marvelously anticipates what we pray after this acclamation: "Save us, Savior of the world, for by your Cross and Resurrection you have set us free." All we need do is join ourselves to our Savior's eternal selfgiving. This is our perpetual sacrifice. This is our pledge of glory.

Conclusion

The EPs are rich, indeed. We have taken just three striking motifs from EP III for our reflection. It would be daunting to think that we can keep in mind all this and so much more at hand in the prayer each time we join our hearts to the priest's voice in praying it. So let's consider some suggestions for how we can pray EP III more fervently.

First, it would be good to sit with the prayer text outside of Mass and pray it ourselves slowly. We can stop at words or phrases that strike us. We can identify its various elements such as the epiclesis over the gifts and the one over the people, the institution narrative, the remembering and offering, the intercessions. We can relate the meaning of the text to what the element is suggesting and come to a deeper understanding of what we are praying.

Second, we might memorize the opening few words of each EP so that when we hear them we click into the unique features of the particular prayer. When we hear "You are indeed Holy, O Lord, and all you have created rightly gives you praise," we would instantly be reminded of the motifs of creation, holiness, and our sacrifice of praise.

Third, we must be gentle with ourselves. Rather than try and internalize all the sentiments of the EP, we might choose one word or phrase and keep it in mind during Mass throughout the prayer as a kind of interpretive stance of our hearts. What is crucial is bringing ourselves to a resounding Amen! at the conclusion of the great doxology. May that Amen be true!

Eucharistic Prayer IV

The Latin Text

Prex Eucharistica IV

116. Praefatio huius Precis eucharisticae mutare non licet ratione structurae ipsius Precis, quae summarium historiae salutis praebet.

℣. Dóminus vobíscum.
℟. Et cum spíritu tuo.

℣. Sursum corda.
℟. Habémus ad Dóminum.

℣. Grátias agámus Dómino Deo nostro.
℟. Dignum et iustum est.

Vere dignum est tibi grátias ágere,
vere iustum est te glorificáre, Pater sancte,
quia unus es Deus vivus et verus,
qui es ante saécula et pérmanes in aetérnum,
inaccessíbilem lucem inhábitans;
sed et qui unus bonus atque fons vitae cuncta fecísti,
ut creatúras tuas benedictiónibus adimpléres
multásque laetificáres tui lúminis claritáte.

Et ídeo coram te innúmerae astant turbae angelórum,
qui die ac nocte sérviunt tibi
et, vultus tui glóriam contemplántes,
te incessánter gloríficant.

Cum quibus et nos et, per nostram vocem,
omnis quae sub caelo est creatúra
nomen tuum in exsultatióne confitémur, canéntes:

Aliae melodiae in Graduali romano inveniuntur.

Sanctus, Sanctus, Sanctus Dóminus Deus Sábaoth.
Pleni sunt caeli et terra glória tua.
Hosánna in excélsis.
Benedíctus qui venit in nómine Dómini.
Hosánna in excélsis.

117. Sacerdos, manibus extensis, dicit:

Confitémur tibi, Pater sancte,
quia magnus es et ómnia ópera tua

The English Text

Eucharistic Prayer IV

116. It is not permitted to change the Preface of this Eucharistic Prayer because of the structure of the Prayer itself, which presents a summary of the history of salvation.

℣. The Lord be with you.
℟. And with your spirit.

℣. Lift up your hearts.
℟. We lift them up to the Lord.

℣. Let us give thanks to the Lord our God.
℟. It is right and just.

It is truly right to give you thanks,
truly just to give you glory, Father most holy,
for you are the one God living and true,
existing before all ages and abiding for all eternity,
dwelling in unapproachable light;
yet you, who alone are good, the source of life,
have made all that is,
so that you might fill your creatures with blessings
and bring joy to many of them by the glory of your light.

And so, in your presence are countless hosts of Angels,
who serve you day and night
and, gazing upon the glory of your face,
glorify you without ceasing.

With them we, too, confess your name in exultation,
giving voice to every creature under heaven,
as we acclaim:

Holy, Holy, Holy Lord God of hosts.
Heaven and earth are full of your glory.
Hosanna in the highest.
Blessed is he who comes in the name of the Lord.
Hosanna in the highest.

117. The Priest, with hands extended, says:

We give you praise, Father most holy,
for you are great

in sapiéntia et caritáte fecísti.
Hóminem ad tuam imáginem condidísti,
eíque commisísti mundi curam univérsi,
ut, tibi soli Creatóri sérviens,
creatúris ómnibus imperáret.
Et cum amicítiam tuam, non oboédiens, amisísset,
non eum dereliquísti in mortis império.
Omnibus enim misericórditer subvenísti,
ut te quaeréntes invenírent.
Sed et foédera plúries homínibus obtulísti
eósque per prophétas erudísti in exspectatióne salútis.

Et sic, Pater sancte, mundum dilexísti,
ut, compléta plenitúdine témporum,
Unigénitum tuum nobis mítteres Salvatórem.
Qui, incarnátus de Spíritu Sancto
et natus ex María Vírgine,
in nostra condiciónis forma est conversátus
per ómnia absque peccáto;
salútem evangelizávit paupéribus,
redemptiónem captívis,
maestis corde laetítiam.
Ut tuam vero dispensatiónem impléret,
in mortem trádidit semetípsum
ac, resúrgens a mórtuis,
mortem destrúxit vitámque renovávit.

Et, ut non ámplius nobismetípsis viverémus,
sed sibi qui pro nobis mórtuus est atque surréxit,
a te, Pater, misit Spíritum Sanctum
primítias credéntibus,
qui, opus suum in mundo perfíciens,
omnem sanctificatiónem compléret.

118. Iungit manus, easque expansas super oblata tenens, dicit:

Quaésumus ígitur, Dómine,
ut idem Spíritus Sanctus
haec múnera sanctificáre dignétur,

and you have fashioned all your works
in wisdom and in love.
You formed man in your own image
and entrusted the whole world to his care,
so that in serving you alone, the Creator,
he might have dominion over all creatures.
And when through disobedience he had lost your friendship,
you did not abandon him to the domain of death.
For you came in mercy to the aid of all,
so that those who seek might find you.
Time and again you offered them covenants
and through the prophets
taught them to look forward to salvation.

And you so loved the world, Father most holy,
that in the fullness of time
you sent your Only Begotten Son to be our Savior.
Made incarnate by the Holy Spirit
and born of the Virgin Mary,
he shared our human nature
in all things but sin.
To the poor he proclaimed the good news of salvation,
to prisoners, freedom,
and to the sorrowful of heart, joy.
To accomplish your plan,
he gave himself up to death,
and, rising from the dead,
he destroyed death and restored life.

And that we might live no longer for ourselves
but for him who died and rose again for us,
he sent the Holy Spirit from you, Father,
as the first fruits for those who believe,
so that, bringing to perfection his work in the world,
he might sanctify creation to the full.

118. He joins his hands and, holding them extended over the offerings, says:

Therefore, O Lord, we pray:
may this same Holy Spirit
graciously sanctify these offerings,

iungit manus
et signat semel super panem et calicem simul, dicens:

ut Corpus et ✠ Sanguis fiant
Dómini nostri Iesu Christi

iungit manus

ad hoc magnum mystérium celebrándum,
quod ipse nobis relíquit in foedus aetérnum.

119. In formulis quae sequuntur, verba Domini proferantur distincte et aperte, prouti natura eorundem verborum requirit.

Ipse enim, cum hora venísset
ut glorificarétur a te, Pater sancte,
ac dilexísset suos qui erant in mundo,
in finem diléxit eos:
et cenántibus illis

accipit panem,
eumque parum elevatum super altare tenens, prosequitur:

accépit panem, benedíxit ac fregit,
dedítque discípulis suis, dicens:

parum se inclinat

ACCÍPITE ET MANDUCÁTE EX HOC OMNES:

HOC EST ENIM CORPUS MEUM,

QUOD PRO VOBIS TRADÉTUR.

Hostiam consecratam ostendit populo, reponit super patenam, et genuflexus adorat.

120. Postea prosequitur:

Símili modo

accipit calicem,
eumque parum elevatum super altare tenens, prosequitur:

accípiens cálicem, ex genímine vitis replétum,
grátias egit, dedítque discípulis suis, dicens:

parum se inclinat

ACCÍPITE ET BÍBITE EX EO OMNES:
HIC EST ENIM CALIX SÁNGUINIS MEI
NOVI ET AETÉRNI TESTAMÉNTI,

He joins his hands
and makes the Sign of the Cross once over the bread and chalice together, saying:

that they may become
the Body and ✠ Blood of our Lord Jesus Christ

He joins his hands.

for the celebration of this great mystery,
which he himself left us
as an eternal covenant.

119. In the formulas that follow, the words of the Lord should be pronounced clearly and distinctly, as the nature of these words requires.

For when the hour had come
for him to be glorified by you, Father most holy,
having loved his own who were in the world,
he loved them to the end:
and while they were at supper,

He takes the bread
and, holding it slightly raised above the altar, continues:

he took bread, blessed and broke it,
and gave it to his disciples, saying:

He bows slightly.

TAKE THIS, ALL OF YOU, AND EAT OF IT,
FOR THIS IS MY BODY,
WHICH WILL BE GIVEN UP FOR YOU.

He shows the consecrated host to the people, places it again on the paten, and genuflects in adoration.

120. After this, he continues:

In a similar way,

He takes the chalice
and, holding it slightly raised above the altar, continues:

taking the chalice filled with the fruit of the vine,
he gave thanks,
and gave the chalice to his disciples, saying:

He bows slightly.

TAKE THIS, ALL OF YOU, AND DRINK FROM IT,
FOR THIS IS THE CHALICE OF MY BLOOD,
THE BLOOD OF THE NEW AND ETERNAL COVENANT,

QUI PRO VOBIS ET PRO MULTIS EFFUNDÉTUR
IN REMISSIÓNEM PECCATÓRUM.

HOC FÁCITE IN MEAM COMMEMORATIÓNEM.

Calicem ostendit populo, deponit super corporale, et genuflexus adorat.

121. Deinde dicit:

Mystérium fídei.

Et populus prosequitur, acclamans:

Mortem tuam annuntiámus Dómine,
et tuam resurrectiónem confitémur, donec vénias.

Vel:

Quotiescúmque manducámus panem hunc
et cálicem bíbimus,
mortem tuam annuntiámus, Dómine, donec vénias.

Vel:

Salvátor mundi, salva nos,
qui per crucem et resurrectiónem tuam liberásti nos.

122. Deinde sacerdos, extensis manibus, dicit:

Unde et nos, Dómine, redemptiónis nostrae
memoriále nunc celebrántes,
mortem Christi
eiúsque descénsum ad ínferos recólimus,
eius resurrectiónem
et ascensiónem ad tuam déxteram profitémur,
et, exspectántes ipsíus advéntum in glória,
offérimus tibi eius Corpus et Sánguinem,
sacrifícium tibi acceptábile et toti mundo salutáre.

Réspice, Dómine, in Hóstiam,
quam Ecclésiae tuae ipse parásti,
et concéde benígnus ómnibus
qui ex hoc uno pane participábunt et cálice,
ut, in unum corpus a Sancto Spíritu congregáti,
in Christo hóstia viva perficiántur,
ad laudem glóriae tuae.

WHICH WILL BE POURED OUT FOR YOU AND FOR MANY
FOR THE FORGIVENESS OF SINS.

DO THIS IN MEMORY OF ME.

He shows the chalice to the people, places it on the corporal, and genuflects in adoration.

121. Then he says:

The mystery of faith.

And the people continue, acclaiming:

We proclaim your Death, O Lord,
and profess your Resurrection
until you come again.

Or:

When we eat this Bread and drink this Cup,
we proclaim your Death, O Lord,
until you come again.

Or:

Save us, Savior of the world,
for by your Cross and Resurrection
you have set us free.

122. Then, with hands extended, the Priest says:

Therefore, O Lord,
as we now celebrate the memorial of our redemption,
we remember Christ's Death
and his descent to the realm of the dead,
we proclaim his Resurrection
and his Ascension to your right hand,
and, as we await his coming in glory,
we offer you his Body and Blood,
the sacrifice acceptable to you
which brings salvation to the whole world.

Look, O Lord, upon the Sacrifice
which you yourself have provided for your Church,
and grant in your loving kindness
to all who partake of this one Bread and one Chalice
that, gathered into one body by the Holy Spirit,
they may truly become a living sacrifice in Christ
to the praise of your glory.

Nunc ergo, Dómine, ómnium recordáre,
pro quibus tibi hanc oblatiónem offérimus:
in primis fámuli tui, Papae nostri N.,
Epíscopi nostri N.,* et Episcopórum órdinis univérsi,
sed et totíus cleri, et offeréntium,
et circumstántium,
et cuncti pópuli tui,
et ómnium, qui te quaerunt corde sincéro.

Meménto étiam illórum,
qui obiérunt in pace Christi tui,
et ómnium defunctórum,
quorum fidem tu solus cognovísti.

Nobis ómnibus, fíliis tuis, clemens Pater, concéde,
ut caeléstem hereditátem cónsequi valeámus
cum beáta Vírgine, Dei Genetríce, María,
cum Apóstolis et Sanctis tuis
in regno tuo, ubi cum univérsa creatúra,
a corruptióne peccáti et mortis liberáta,
te glorificémus per Christum Dóminum nostrum,

iungit manus,

per quem mundo bona cuncta largíris.

123. Accipit patenam cum hostia et calicem, et utrumque elevans, dicit:

Per ipsum, et cum ipso, et in ipso,
est tibi Deo Patri omnipoténti,
in unitáte Spíritus Sancti,
omnis honor et glória
per ómnia saécula saeculórum.

Populus acclamat:

Amen.

Deinde sequitur ritus Communionis.

---

* Hic fieri potest mentio de Episcopis Coadiutore vel Auxiliaribus, vel de alio Episcopo, ut in *Institutione generali Missalis Romani*, n. 149, notatur.

Therefore, Lord, remember now
all for whom we offer this sacrifice:
especially your servant N. our Pope,
N. our Bishop,* and the whole Order of Bishops,
all the clergy,
those who take part in this offering,
those gathered here before you,
your entire people,
and all who seek you with a sincere heart.

Remember also
those who have died in the peace of your Christ
and all the dead,
whose faith you alone have known.

To all of us, your children,
grant, O merciful Father,
that we may enter into a heavenly inheritance
with the Blessed Virgin Mary, Mother of God,
and with your Apostles and Saints in your kingdom.
There, with the whole of creation,
freed from the corruption of sin and death,
may we glorify you through Christ our Lord,

He joins his hands.

through whom you bestow on the world all that is good.

123. He takes the chalice and the paten with the host and, raising both, he says:

Through him, and with him, and in him,
O God, almighty Father,
in the unity of the Holy Spirit,
all glory and honor is yours,
for ever and ever.

The people acclaim:

Amen.

Then follows the Communion Rite.

---

* Mention may be made here of the Coadjutor Bishop, or Auxiliary Bishops, as noted in the *General Instruction of the Roman Missal*, no. 149.

History of the Latin Text and Rite

John Baldovin

Introduction

The third of the new EPs in *MR1970* was the result of a desire for a prayer that would express the fullness of salvation history and at the same time represent an opening to the rich euchological tradition of the Christian East.[1] One of the most significant prayers of the Christian East was chosen as the basis of this new EP: the Alexandrian Anaphora of St. Basil.

Alexandrian (Egyptian) Anaphora of St. Basil

This anaphora has been recognized (along with the East Syrian Anaphora of Addai and Mari) as possibly one of the earliest EP texts that we know.[2] Even though first known to us from Coptic manuscripts, this prayer does not reflect the Egyptian anaphoral tradition so much as what has come to be known as the West Syrian or Antiochene tradition. Other prayers in that tradition include the Greek Byzantine version of St. Basil, the Anaphora of St. John Chrysostom, and the Anaphora of St. James, which may well have used a good deal of material from Alexandrian Basil.[3]

The use of the St. Basil anaphora makes EP IV the only current Roman EP that is traceable to a historical figure. St. Basil was the bishop of Casearea in Cappadocia from 370–379. He was a theological giant in his own time, especially with regard to the debate over the divinity of the Holy Spirit, as well as a major influence in the formation of rules for monastic life. John Fenwick has pointed to a few sources that suggest Basil may have been the author of liturgical prayers. Certainly the anaphora bearing his name has

[1] Bugnini, 458–59.

[2] Jasper & Cuming, 67. Jasper & Cuming also consider the Anaphora of ApTrad in the same category, but more recent research casts doubt on that opinion.

[3] See John R. K. Fenwick, *The Anaphoras of St. Basil and St. James: An Investigation into their Common Origin*, Orientalia Christiana Analecta 240 (Rome: Pontificium Institutum Orientale, 1992); also, Fenwick, *Fourth Century Anaphoral Construction Techniques*, Grove Liturgical Study 45 (Bramcote, Nottingham: Grove Books, 1986).

been attributed to him since the sixth century.[4] The Byzantine Greek version of the Basil Anaphora (used in the Orthodox churches) is greatly expanded from the Alexandrian version (used in the Coptic Church). Most of the expansion is theological and reflects the theological concerns of the three Cappadocian Fathers: Basil, his brother St. Gregory of Nyssa (d. *ca.* 395), and their friend St. Gregory of Nazianzus (d. *ca.* 390).

It is possible that Basil himself was the author of the shorter (Alexandrian) text that he himself later expanded. Thus the axiom, held by liturgical scholars for a long time, that longer texts were original and then abbreviated because people found them tedious has been disproven—especially by the careful work of Hieronymus Engberding.[5] The various versions of the Anaphora of Basil have been the subject of a good deal of scholarship in recent years.[6]

The West Syrian anaphoral tradition in general is characterized by its logical and coherent development of themes. Here is the typical structure:

West Syrian Anaphoral Structure
Dialogue
Pre-*Sanctus* Praise of God
Sanctus
Post-*Sanctus* Salvation History, with "Holy" as bridge word
Institution Narrative
Anamnesis-Oblation
Epiclesis
Intercessions
Doxology-Amen

[4] See Fenwick, *Anaphoras*, 19–24.

[5] Hieronymus Engberding, *Das eucharistische Hochgebet der Basileiosliturgie. Textgeschichtliche Untersuchungen und kritische Ausgabe* (Münster: Aschendorff, 1931).

[6] See Achim Budde, *Die ägyptische Basileios-Anaphora: Text-Kommentar-Geschichte* (Münster: Ascendorff, 2004); Gabriele Winkler, *Die Basilius-Anaphora: Edition der beiden armenischen Redaktionen und der relevanten Fragmente, Übersetzung und Zusammenschau aller Versionen im Licht der orientalischen Überlieferungen*, Anaphorae Orientales 2 (Rome: Pontificium Institutum Orientale, 2005); D. Richard Stuckwisch, "The Basilian Anaphoras," in *Essays on Early Eastern Eucharistic Prayers*, ed. Paul F. Bradshaw (Collegeville, MN: Liturgical Press, 1997), 109–30; Anne Vorhes McGowan, "The Basilian Anaphoras: Rethinking the Question," in *Issues in Eucharistic Praying in East and West*, ed. Maxwell Johnson (Collegeville, MN: Liturgical Press, 2010), 219–61.

These prayers move smoothly from thanksgiving and the praise of God to the anamnesis of God's work in Christ to invocation of the Holy Spirit. This structure fits very well with the fourth-century development of trinitarian theology and accounts in particular for the replacement of earlier forms of petition for God to "come" upon the offerings with a specific invocation of the Holy Spirit, whose divinity was dogmatically settled at the Council of Constantinople (381).[7] Further, it is possible to see in the prayers of this tradition a theology that takes account of past, present, and future: the past represented by thanksgiving and anamnesis for creation and salvation, the present by the return-gift of the oblation, and the future by the invocation of the Holy Spirit and intercessions.[8] What follows is a translation of the Coptic text (both in Bohairic and Sahidic) of the Anaphora of St. Basil.[9] Elements of this text that have been adapted for EP IV are printed in bold.

Alexandrian Anaphora of St. Basil

Bishop: The Lord be with you all.

People: And with your spirit.

Bishop: Let us lift up our hearts.

People: We have them with the Lord.

Bishop: Let us give thanks to the Lord.

People: It is fitting and right.

Bishop: **It is fitting and right**, fitting and right, truly it is fitting and right, I AM, truly Lord God, existing before the ages; you dwell on high and regard what is low; you made heaven and earth and the sea and all that is in them. Father of our Lord and God and Savior Jesus Christ, through whom you made all things visible and invisible, you sit on the throne of your glory; you are adored by every holy power. Around you stand angels and archangels, principalities and powers, thrones, dominions and virtues; around you stand the cherubim with many eyes and the seraphim with six wings, forever singing the hymn of glory and saying:

[7] See Robert Taft, "From Logos to Spirit: On the Early History of the Epiclesis," in *Gratias Agamus. Studien zum eucharistischen Hochgebet. Festschrift Balthasar Fischer*, ed. Andreas Heinz and Heinrich Rennings (Freiburg: Herder, 1992), 489–502. I presuppose here the basic contemporary approach to the development of eucharistic praying outlined in my article on EP II (315–16 above). EPs in various traditions were patched together over time, coalescing into the basic traditions that appear in the late fourth century.

[8] A similar contemporary analysis can be found in Louis-Marie Chauvet, *Symbol and Sacrament*, trans. Patrick Madigan and Madeleine Beaumont (Collegeville, MN: Liturgical Press, 1995).

[9] Jasper & Cuming, 70–73. The editors note that the Coptic is a translation from a Greek original.

People: Holy, holy, holy Lord . . .

Bishop: Holy, holy, holy you are indeed, Lord our God. **You formed us and placed us in the paradise of pleasure; and when we had transgressed your commandment through the deceit of the serpent, and had fallen from eternal life, and had been banished from the paradise of pleasure, you did not cast us off forever, but continually made promises to us through your holy prophets; and in these last days you manifested to us who sat in darkness and the shadow of death your only-begotten Son, our Lord and God and Savior, Jesus Christ. He was made flesh of the Holy Spirit and of the holy Virgin Mary, and became man**; he showed us the ways of salvation, granted us to be reborn from above by water and the Spirit, and made us a people for our own possession, sanctifying us by his Holy Spirit. **He loved his own who were in the world,** and gave himself for our salvation to death who reigned over us and held us down because of our sins.

. . . [Sahidic text] by his blood. From the cross he descended into hell and rose from the dead, and on the third day, he ascended into heaven and sat at the right hand of the Father; he appointed a day on which to judge the world with justice and render to each according to his works.

And he left us this great mystery of godliness: for when he was about to hand himself over to death for the life of the world, he took bread, blessed, sanctified, broke, and gave it to his holy disciples and apostles saying: "**Take and eat from this all of you; this is my body, which is given for you** and for many for forgiveness of your sins. Do this for my remembrance."

Likewise, also the cup after supper: he mixed wine and water, blessed, sanctified, gave thanks, and again gave it to them, saying: "**Take and drink from it, all of you; this is my blood which shall be shed for you and for many for forgiveness of your sins. Do this for my remembrance.** For as often as you eat this bread and drink this cup, you proclaim my death until I come."

We, therefore, remembering his holy sufferings, and his resurrection from the dead, and his ascension into heaven, and his session at the right hand of the Father, and his fearful and glorious coming to us (again), have set forth before you your own from your own gifts, this bread and this cup. And we, sinners and unworthy and wretched, pray you, our God, in adoration that in the good pleasure of your goodness your Holy Spirit may descend upon us and upon these gifts that have been set before you, and may sanctify them and make [Greek, *anadeixai* = "reveal"][10] them holy of holies.

Make us all worthy to partake of your holy things for sanctification of soul and body, that we may become one body and one spirit, and may have a portion with all the saints who have been pleasing to you from eternity.

[10] My translation.

> Remember, Lord, also your one holy, catholic, and apostolic Church: give it peace, for you purchased it with the precious blood of Christ; and remember all orthodox bishops in it. . . .[11]

As one can easily see, not a great deal of the content of Alexandrian Basil was taken word for word into EP IV. The biblical–salvation history spirit of the Basil Anaphora is, however, quite evident.

EP IV Structure and Content

As with EP II, the decision by the Consilium to add a consecratory epiclesis to the prayer results in a significant structural shift. The structure of Alexandrian Basil is clearly (and I would add deliberately) trinitarian, with the invocation of the Holy Spirit coming only after the institution narrative and anamnesis-oblation—a structure, as we have seen, that is common in the West Syrian–Antiochene tradition of eucharistic praying. In EP IV we have an example of a "split epiclesis" with the petition for the gathering of the church separated from the request for consecration by the institution narrative. This approach reflects the different historical emphases in East and West vis-à-vis the primacy of the epiclesis or the words of institution.

In addition, Alexandrian Basil has several elements that suggest a greater antiquity, many of which have been lost in EP IV. First, as in the Egyptian tradition in general, the verbs of offering-sacrifice are in the aorist tense (e.g., "gifts that *have been set* before you") suggesting that the entirety of the action-prayer—and not just one moment—are considered the eucharistic sacrifice. Second, the Greek verb used in the epiclesis of Alexandrian Basil is *anadeixai*, which means "to show forth." Combined with the notion of a unified prayer-action, the idea of manifesting the reality of the transformed gifts is somewhat different from a moment of consecration in which the Holy Spirit is asked to "make" the gifts the Body and Blood of Christ. The latter idea is quite clearly evident in the Byzantine version of the Basil Anaphora and, of course, in EP IV.[12]

[11] I have omitted most of the intercessory material.

[12] On the subject of the development of a sacramental theology of consecration in the course of the fourth century, see Enrico Mazza, *The Celebration of the Eucharist: The Origin of the Rite and the Development of Its Interpretation*, trans. Matthew J. O'Connell (Collegeville, MN: Liturgical Press, 1999), 139–60.

Another striking difference between Alexandrian Basil and EP IV is the wording of the oblation:

Alexandrian Basil	**EP IV**
We, therefore, remembering . . . have set forth before you your own from your own gifts, this bread and this cup.	Therefore, O Lord, as we now celebrate the memorial of our redemption . . . we offer you his Body and Blood, the sacrifice acceptable to you which brings salvation to the whole world.

As far as I can tell, the explicit offering of Christ's Body and Blood as opposed to phrases like "the Bread of life and the Chalice of salvation" (EP II) or "this holy and living sacrifice" (EP III) is unique in the history of eucharistic praying.[13] While it is not incorrect to say "we offer his Body and Blood," it would have been more respectful of the traditions of the Christian East to use "your own from your own," which reflects the *de tuis donis ac datis* ("from the gifts you have given us") of EP I.

An adaptation of the text that respects the West Syrian pattern with a single epiclesis following the institution narrative and a wording of the oblation much closer to Alexandrian Basil was made by an ecumenical group of liturgical scholars. It is included in the Episcopal (Prayer D), United Methodist (A Common EP), Evangelical Lutheran, and other contemporary liturgical books.

Conclusion

EP IV represents a remarkable first step toward the enrichment of the Roman Rite with texts from the Christian East. In Late Antiquity the Roman Church was quite accustomed to borrowing liturgical material from the (more inventive) Christian East, e.g., the *Kyrie* litany and a number of feasts like the Assumption of Mary and Epiphany. The prayer also represents an admirable attempt to have a scripturally rich prayer for use especially on Sundays.[14]

[13] For Mazza's explanation of this choice of words, see his *The Eucharistic Prayers of the Roman Rite*, trans. Matthew J. O'Connell (New York: Pueblo, 1986), 179–80.

[14] Although *IGMR2002* (no. 365) makes it quite clear that EP IV (unlike EP II) is to be used integrally and, therefore, may not be used with a proper preface.

Theology of the Latin Text and Rite[1]

David Power

Introduction

In its structure and content, this prayer draws considerably from Eastern anaphoras,[2] but it is divided much as the other two new prayers into the pre-*Sanctus*, the post-*Sanctus*, the institution narrative, the anamnesis-offering, the epiclesis, and the intercessions, continuing the pattern of the Roman Rite. While the prayer is one of praise and thanksgiving, as Enrico Mazza points out, it has elements of a confession or profession of faith. This is displayed through use of the word *confitemur*, a feature borrowed no doubt from the Syro-Antiochene sources put to use in its composition.

Preface (*OM2008*, no. 116, lines 9–23)

This part of the prayer is devoted to the praise of the eternal and ineffable mystery of God, while the post-*Sanctus* is the thankful remembrance of God's works. In this first part of the prayer certain images and ideas are introduced that affect the entire prayer. They may be noted by singling out key terms: the address *Pater sancte*, and the words *gloria, lumen, claritas, glorificare, confiteri.*

The address to God as *Pater sancte* is used throughout the prayer, connecting its various parts to each other. This is the name given to the ineffable one to whom praise is given when the assembly gazes upon the inaccessible light of the one true God, the source of all life and creator of all that is in heaven and on earth. It is also the name that is confessed in the post-*Sanctus* when divine deeds of restoration and redemption are recalled, the name of God who sent his Son into the world in the fullness of time out of love for the world. It is the name of the one who, having sent his Son, sends the Spirit to believers as firstfruits of redemption and to perfect the work of the

[1] Enrico Mazza, *The Eucharistic Prayers of the Roman Rite*, trans. Matthew J. O'Connell (New York: Pueblo, 1986), 154–90; Joseph Gelineau, "La quarta preghiera eucaristica," *Le nuove preghiere eucaristiche*, Parola per l'assemblea festiva 1 (Brescia: Queriniana, 1969), 51–68.

[2] See Baldovin, 401–05 above.

Son, giving them a share in God's own *claritas* or luminous glory. It is the name recalled in the institution narrative as the one who glorifies his Son in the hour of his death. It is the name that will be hymned for eternity by those who receive their heavenly inheritance, together with the whole of creation. It is substituted once by the appellation *Clemens Pater*, when at the commemoration of the dead heavenly and eternal heritage is requested for all.[3]

For the mutual glorification of Father and Son, or for the glory given God in the mysteries, *MR2002* prefers *glorificare*: the Latin *clarificare* is kept in antiphons taken from these Johannine texts and occurs once in a preface, that for the dedication of a church. Both are used in biblical Latin to translate *doxazein*. They are not, however, synonyms but represent the attempt to find a suitable Latin term to translate the Greek. Bernard Botte considers *gloria/glorificare* more banal than the coupling *claritas/clarificare* because of the suggestion of divine brightness and beauty in the latter terms.[4]

The full significance of this usage comes from John's gospel. The inaccessible *lux* (light) in which God dwells goes with the *luminis claritas*, or splendor of light, by which he fills creation. Two significant texts are found in John 12:28 and John 17:1-12, where *doxazó* is rendered in biblical Latin as *clarificare*. There is a mutual glorification: the Son glorifies the Father; the Father, the Son. In this mutual glorification, Jesus addresses God as *Pater sancte* (John 17:11) and prays for those whom the Father has given him.[5]

In the initial address to God the adjectives used are *unus, vivus, verus*, but they are not common to Latin euchology. They have NT roots, as noted by Mazza. *Deus unus* comes from 1 Corinthians 8:4 and *Deus vivus* from Romans 9:26, while *Deus verus* occurs in John 17:3. The adjectives are always associated with the work of redemption, indeed with God's work through the Son whom he has sent or given. The unity, truth, life of God is known

[3] As well as in this prayer, *Pater sancte* is common in prefaces of *MR2002* and also occurs in other texts, e.g., in the nuptial blessing (Sodi, no. 2528) or in postcommunion prayers (e.g., Sodi, nos. 2694, 2741, 2743). In the prefaces it goes often with *omnipotens, sempiterne* (e.g., Sodi, nos. 287, 332, 339, 376, 555), expressing at one and the same time the eternal mystery of the ineffable Godhead and the work by which he is at work in the universe as the power that governs all things.

[4] Bernard Botte and Christine Mohrmann, *L'Ordinaire de la Messe. Texte critique, traduction et études* (Paris: Cerf, 1955), 111–13, s.v. "*Maiestas*."

[5] Of these texts Hans Bietenhard says that this refers to the revelation given to the world in the Son and that the name and the glory and the address to the Father are so interconnected that they have to be expounded together. See *Theological Dictionary of the New Testament*, ed. Gerhard Kittel, Gerhard Friedrich, Geoffrey William Bromiley, 10 vols. (Grand Rapids: Eerdmans, 1964), 5:272; also, ibid., s.v. *doxa*, 2:247–53.

through the Son, and in EP IV this refers to the work of creation as well when God is named in this way in the prayer's initial address.

Apart from the initial address to the Father, *gloria/glorificare* recurs throughout the prayer, as in *te glorificare*. Of the angels it is said that they behold the face of God's glory and in so doing glorify him without ceasing (*vultus tui gloriam contemplantes, te incessanter glorificant*). The institution narrative (no. 119) is introduced by saying of Jesus, *cum hora venisset ut glorificaretur a te*. In the intercessory prayer *respice* (no. 122, line 11), it is asked that the church be made one in Christ and Spirit, *ad laudem gloriae tuae*, and the eternal inheritance of the blessed is expressed in the wish for all that they may glorify God through Christ (*te glorificemus per Christum*).[6]

In this introductory part of the prayer leading to the *Sanctus*, the verb used to express the church's worship is *confiteri*,[7] as it is also used in the post-*Sanctus*.[8] *Confiteri* has roots in Latin versions of Philippians 2:11: the name of Jesus as Lord to the glory of God is confessed by all tongues, indicating a combination of faith, acknowledgment, and hymnic praise. In *MR2002* the word is often combined with *laudare* in the last words of the prefaces, just before *Sanctus*. Elsewhere it expresses confession of faith in words, deeds, and praise.[9] This is to be linked with the meaning of glorification and the praise of the divine name. The church confesses God's name and glory, i.e., it proclaims in hymnic praise the name of God.

Post-*Sanctus* (*OM2008*, no. 117)

This part of the prayer does not begin with the words *Vere Sanctus* as in EP II and III but with *confitemur*, thus indicating the link between profession of faith and the thanks rendered. It first professes faith in the work of creation as a work of divine wisdom and love and goes on to profess God's saving work after humankind had sinned. The use of the word *dispensatio* toward the end of this narrative remembrance suggests that the story from creation to Christ's Pasch is remembered as God's economy of salvation. The word is rare in biblical Latin, the most well-known case being that of Ephesians 3:9 where the whole economy of salvation through Christ is

[6] Apart from John's gospel, in Christian Latin as found in the NT, *doxa* is often translated as *gloria:* Rom 1:23; 9:23; Phil 4:19; Col 1:27; Eph 1:18. In Col 1:11, however, it is rendered as *claritas*. The Latin *gloria* is also used for that which is to be revealed in the last times and in which the blessed shall share with Christ: Matt 16:27; Mark 8:38; 10:37; Luke 19:38.

[7] *nomen tuum in exsultatione confitemur, canentes* (line 23).

[8] *Confitemur tibi, Pater sancte* (*OM2008*, no. 117, line 2).

[9] See Sodi, nos. 1375, 1991, 2767.

referred to as the *dispensatio sacramenti* hidden in God from the foundation of the world.[10] While the remembrance includes creation, the covenants of the Old Law, the work of the prophets, and the ministry of Christ himself, it is his death and the resurrection from the dead by which he destroyed death itself that is said to complete or fulfill this entire economy (*ut tuam dispensationem impleret, in mortem tradidit semetipsum*).

In remembering creation the prayer is attentive to the place of humanity in the total work of bringing the world to being and in providing for its continuing care. This attention to the place of human beings within the totality of creation may derive from the Apostolic Constitutions (book 8), but it remains much less developed in this prayer,[11] which, however, intimates that the whole dynamic of humanity's relation to creatures depends on their being made unto the image of God, for it is as such that they are to care for creatures. As with EP III, the theme of creation is not pursued when it comes to the recall of sin and the work of redemption.[12]

The two words used in EP IV to express humankind's relation as made in God's image to creation are *cura* (*commisit mundi curam universi*) and *imperare* (*creaturis omnibus imperaret*). *Cura* and *imperium* in *MR2002*—as found in Sodi—most often refer to God's fatherly love for the universe or to the role given to the Son in his resurrection from the dead.[13] In biblical Latin, these terms are used in the book of Wisdom to describe humanity's responsible action in creation according to the dispositions of divine wisdom (Wis 6:19; 9:1; 12:13). *Imperium* is less clear in its meaning, since it may be used of earthly rule. A certain benignity in humanity's relation to creation is suggested by the fact that *cura* and *imperium* are exercised in service of the Creator, who is the holy and loving Father. What happens to creation when the human who is to exercise *imperium* is himself subjected to the rule of death (*mortis imperio*) is not said, and how restoration of right rule occurs is not said either. This is all the more curious since sin is described as loss of God's friendship (*amicitia*), a very potent description of humanity's initial relation to God, and redemption is effected through God's love and through Christ's love.

Enrico Mazza also sees a connection between this section of EP IV on creation and humanity's part in it as image of God and the anaphoras of

[10] The Greek word in this case is *oikonomia*.

[11] Mazza, *The Eucharistic Prayers*, 165–66, elaborates at length on this theme but he draws on an array of Eastern texts and theologies, not on what EP IV says.

[12] See 367 above.

[13] Otherwise, *cura* denotes the relation of a bishop to the people of his church, certainly not meant to be one of domination.

James and Basil, so that we can see humankind giving voice to the praise of all creation. There is, however, a considerable difference between this Greek tradition and its Latin rendering in EP IV. The Greek anaphoral tradition allows humans the delight of paradise, the enjoyment of created things, but the Latin of EP IV emphasizes humanity's power over other things, however benign if it is done in the service of the one Creator. Mazza is probably influenced by the connection he sees in the traditions through the use of words expressing confession and praise.[14]

After praising creation, the post-*Sanctus* of EP IV proceeds to the narrative of God's works, from creation to the sending of the Spirit, and then asks for the sanctification (coincides with *Pater sancte, Spiritus Sanctus*) of the gifts brought, so that the mystery may be celebrated in obedience to Christ's memorial command in the sacrament of his Body and Blood.

In the narrative of salvation leading to the petition for the sanctification of the gifts by the Spirit, the defining terms are *foedus* and *per prophetas. Foedus* not only regards covenant with Israel but expresses God's relation with all people (*omnibus*). Possibly the prayer refers to the covenants from Noah, through Abraham, to Moses, and prophecy denotes the universal role of Israel to which prophets recall the people or the address of the prophets to the nations or even the incursion of prophets like Jonas into Gentile territories. The role of the prophets is to instruct (*erudire*)[15] in the expectation of salvation, which is to highlight hope instilled and kept alive. *Erudire* is not limited to instruction in doctrines but means teaching the way of salvation or how to live by God's economy, with the expectation of the salvation (given in Christ) to the fore.

The exercise of the Father's love and of Christ's love is expressed in this narrative remembrance by using several words. First, it is said that God created all things in wisdom and love (*caritas*). Then the relation between God and humanity in creation is dubbed *amicitia*. The sending of the Son is done through the Father's love for the world (*mundum dilexisti*). Finally, the act of Jesus in leaving the eucharistic sacrament to the church is portrayed as his final act of earthly love (*in finem dilexit eos*) for those whom he had chosen from the world at the hour of his glorification. Within this economy of love, the role of the Spirit whom Christ sent as firstfruits of

[14] The relation between humanity and creation is more developed in *MR2002*'s Preface V for Sundays in Ordinary Time of the present Missal. There it is said that all the wonders of creation are subjected to humanity, which acts as God's vicar in exercising dominion (*dominaretur omnibus quae creasti*), but then its duty is to give praise for the marvels (*magnalia*) of God's works.

[15] This is the way in which the work of the prophets is evoked in the Liturgy of James.

redemption is to bring his work in the world to perfection and to complete the work of making all holy (*sanctificatio*).

Diligere/dilexit is often used in biblical Latin and in the liturgy for the love shown for God by the redeemed. Used of God's love or of Christ's love in *MR2002*, it occurs most often in biblical antiphons[16] and in EPs.[17] This means not only the love the Father and Son have for each other but the Father's or Son's love for the world.[18] This use of *dilectio* renders the uses of *agape* in the Greek NT and reminds us in a special way of the gospels of baptism and transfiguration, where Jesus, sent by the Father, is declared his beloved Son. God's faithful love for the world first embraces his Son who in turn loves his own in the world.[19]

When the prayer extols the Father in remembrance of the sending of the Son it includes the mystery of the incarnation by the Spirit and his preaching and witness of the jubilee, as couched in the reading from the scroll of Isaiah in Luke 4:18-19, before coming to remembrance of his death and resurrection and the sending of the Spirit. In this the prayer shows the influence of the prayer in book 8 of the Apostolic Constitutions and possibly of the anaphora of Basil, which are quite elaborate in recalling the ministry of the Savior. Such prayer responds well to the desire, nourished by the liturgical reading of the NT, to connect the death and resurrection to the incarnation and to the entire work of Jesus Christ in the days of his ministry.

Institution Narrative[20] (*OM2008*, nos. 119 and 120)

When the institution narrative is introduced, it is by reference to the celebration of the mystery as a covenant. *Foedus*, already used in the thanksgiving narrative, is used in preference to *testamentum* (*quod ipse nobis reliquit in foedus aeternum*) since this makes the relation to the foregoing clearer. This is the loving act of God's beloved Son, a love shown at the hour when he is to be glorified in his death by the Father and perpetuated in the Eucharist.[21]

[16] E.g., Sodi, nos. 1842, 2235.

[17] Ibid., nos. 1212, 3300, 3303, 3305.

[18] Ibid., nos. 172, 244, 1104, 1273, 1397.

[19] In the anaphora of John Chrysostom the mystery of Christ is summarized in this sole phrase, "God so loved the world that he sent his only-begotten Son."

[20] For discussion of the epiclesis and of elements in the institution narrative, see 268–71 and 321–23 above.

[21] Outside the EP, *foedus* refers to the new covenant announced by the prophets (Sodi, nos. 637, 3237), and the marital bond is proclaimed a symbol of the divine *foedus* (Sodi, nos. 2516, 2528).

Anamnesis-Offering (*OM2008*, no. 122, lines 2–10)

The memorial in this prayer is more ample than in the others, after the manner of Byzantine prayers. It includes the death of Christ, his descent among the dead (*ad inferos*), his resurrection, his ascension to God's right hand, and the expectation of his advent in glory. That which is offered in this memorial is starkly declared the Body and Blood of Christ and dubbed the acceptable sacrifice, a salutary offering for the whole world. This is followed up in the epiclesis by asking God to look on the *Hostia* (capitalized) that Christ has prepared for the church, meaning the acceptable sacrifice of his Body and Blood, which the church in turn can offer, becoming herself a *hostia* (small letter) *viva*, a living sacrifice in Christ. She is this because through the Spirit she is one Body, participating in the one bread and the one chalice.

Regarding these references to *Hostia* here and in EP III,[22] some further theological comment can be made. The sacramental eucharistic offering and its relation to Christ's own presence can be understood in three ways in light of the Latin theological tradition: (1) Christ truly present in the sacramental offering, i.e., in the sacrament that represents his once-and-for-all paschal sacrifice; (2) Christ present through the sacramental representation of the eternal offering of Christ, ever-present before the Father in the presence at his side of the high priest and victim; (3) Christ sacramentally and truly present through the consecration by a word that proclaims the mystery of his death and symbolically represents his immolation, so that he is then offered by the church in the offering of the transformed bread and wine. The euchology of the prayers does not force a choice between these meanings, but with a performative focus that locates consecration in the words of Jesus, and with the language referring to the *corpus et sanguis* and to the *Hostia* that follows, EP IV, like EP III, favors the third understanding. Ecumenically, this raises some problems about the relation to Christ's once-and-for-all sacrifice on the cross, since it suggests an ecclesial offering of Christ done by the church distinct from that of the cross, however dependent on the cross the former is said to be. It is not a common manner of speaking in liturgical traditions, but neither is it totally absent.[23] When used it must always be carefully related to the memorial and sacramental character of whatever is done in the Eucharist.

[22] See 369 above.

[23] See Ethiopian and Armenian anaphoras in *Prex Eucharistica*, 1:157, 322, 329, 335.

Second Epiclesis (*OM2008*, no. 122, lines 11–17)

This mention of the Spirit and what it does in the church, as in EP III,[24] is not properly speaking an epiclesis since there is no petition to the Father for its sending. Nevertheless, it relates to the earlier petition for the Spirit to sanctify the gifts, when the prayer asked for the sending of the Spirit by the risen Christ to perfect his work. The mention of the Spirit at this point is addressed specifically to the unity of the church and to the transformation of the communicants into a living sacrifice (*hostia viva*). The play on words is Pauline, relating communion from the one bread and the one chalice to gathering those who partake into one body and one sacrifice in Christ. This is done to the praise of God's glory, which is a retrieval of the terms *laus* and *gloria* from the early part of the prayer. What is done from the beginning to the praise of God's glory is completed in the communion of the church.

Intercessions (*OM2008*, no. 122, lines 18–38)

The intercessions follow the trajectory of EP II and III. The one distinctive point to be noted here is the extension of the church's concern beyond its own boundaries to include all the living who seek God with sincere hearts and all the dead who, in ways known to God alone, may have lived some form of faith. The final petition is for all present and for all the Father's children, asking for them an eternal inheritance with the saints. This petition concludes in the same vein as that in which the prayer began, asking that these children may glorify God with all creatures in God's kingdom, through Christ through whom he dispenses every good. The prayer thus concludes with acknowledgment of the universal mediating role of Christ—in the work of creation, in the work of redemption, and in the work of giving the Father eternal praise.

In the other prayers there was some movement from thanksgiving, through intercession, to praise. In this prayer the movement is more complex, starting with the praise of the angels who contemplate God in divine ineffable light, moving to the church's thanksgiving for God's deeds, and then progressing through intercession to communion with the eternal praise of divine glory by the blessed. This is perfectly in keeping with what Burkhard Neunheuser saw as the specific genius of the Roman Rite,[25]

[24] See 369 above.
[25] See 318 above.

namely, its stress on Christ's mediation, in divine action and in prayer, leading from creation to the works of salvation, to the life and prayer of the church, and to eternal participation in God's glory. EP IV joins this focus on Christ's mediation with the work of the Holy Spirit at all stages of this divine drama.

Conclusion

The outstanding theological perspective of this prayer, arising from attention to the Latin text, is its theology of glory and glorification as a way of referring both to the work of the liturgy and to the eternal dispensation of God in creating, redeeming, and bringing both humanity and creation as a whole into a sharing in the eternal divine glory. Second, the Father and Son are united in the Spirit in that eternal mutual glorification, which was given visibility in the incarnation and the redeeming work of Jesus Christ. A third notable feature is the understanding given to holiness as divine holiness disseminated at large by reason of God's all-embracing and ever-operative love. Fourth is the mediation attributed to Christ, in creation, in redemption, in the sanctification and prayer of the church, and in the eternal work of God's glorification. A final noteworthy theological point is the way of positing the relation between humanity and creatures, in the act of creation, in redemption, and in eternity, though this is not fully developed.[26] Along with these theological perspectives there is also the focus on the offering of the Body and Blood of Christ, raising the issues noted in this essay. As far as style and language are concerned, the prayer suggests a more profound sense of awe before the divine glory and its manifestation than do the other prayers.

[26] It need also be noted that the difficulty with a theology that locates consecration in the words of Jesus stands out even more clearly in this prayer than in the others.

The ICEL2010 Translation

Gilbert Ostdiek

The Preface (ICEL2010, no. 116, lines 10–25)[1]

The preface for EP IV is invariable (*IGMR2002*, no. 365d). It can be effectively proclaimed as priests become accustomed to its lengthy first sentence and familiar with its unexpected phrasings. The address *Pater sancte*, drawn from John 17:11, is used throughout EP IV. "Father most holy" follows the Latin phrasing, avoiding the confusion the normal English word order, "Holy Father," would cause. The addition of "most" (the Latin has *sancte*, not the superlative *sanctissime*) heightens the solemnity and aids proclamation.

"and bring joy to many of them by the glory of your light" (line18)

ICEL1973's "and lead all men to the joyful vision of your light" was a felicitous turn of phrase but also a paraphrase. This version is closer to the Latin. Adding "of them" expresses the delimiting of *creaturis* (all creatures blessed by God) implied in *multas* (those to whom God gives joy). The choice of "glory" to translate *claritate* echoes the use of *glorificare-gloriam-glorificant* at the beginning and end of the preface. However, this reverses the directive in *LitAuth* (nos. 50d–51) calling for consistency in translating important words yet allowing for some variety. In this case, uniformity has replaced the verbal variety found in *OM2008*. An alternate translation of *claritate* might have drawn on the biblical image of the light that overcomes and shines forth out of the darkness (John 1:5; 2 Cor 4:6), the light of God in which there is no darkness (1 John 1:5), the marvelous light into which we are called out of the darkness (1 Pet 2:9).

[1] On the preface dialogue, see 279–80 above; on the characteristic vocabulary introduced in the preface, see Power, 407–9 above; also, Enrico Mazza, *The Eucharistic Prayers of the Roman Rite*, trans. Matthew J. O'Connell (New York: Pueblo, 1986), 59.

"And so, in your presence are countless hosts of Angels." (line 19)

This translation is somewhat awkward. Inversion of subject and verb would work better in English, and *astant*, here translated as "are," might more literally have been translated with *coram te* as "stand before you" or "stand in your presence."

Post-*Sanctus* (ICEL2010, no. 117)

"We give you praise, Father most holy" (lines 2–5)

"We give you praise" is certainly an acceptable translation of *confitemur tibi*. The translation of *confitemur* at the end of the preface as "acclaim" might have been repeated here to echo the doubling of *dignum et iustum* at the beginning of the preface. Thus Enrico Mazza's literal translation: "We acclaim you, Father, because you are great and have performed all your works in wisdom and love."[2] Translating *caritate* as "love" is appropriate here, although elsewhere in ICEL2010 it is normally translated as "charity."

"he might have dominion over all creatures" (line 9)

This translation captures well the pleasing resonance between *imperaret* and *imperio*: "have dominion" and "domain." Nevertheless, this is one of two aspects of this paragraph that will require careful catechesis (*LitAuth*, no. 29). In the context of current Roman Catholic teaching about social justice and care of the earth, it is important to respect the balance between the two accounts of creation alluded to in this paragraph. In the first, God gives the *adam* "dominion over . . . all the creatures" (Gen 1:26, 28)—here *creaturis omnibus imperaret*. In the second account, God places the *adam* in the garden "to cultivate and care for it" (Gen 2:15)—here *eique commisisti mundi curam universi*. Care and dominion go together. Dominion is not domination, nor is it without accountability; it is to be exercised as the servant-agent for God who cares for all—here *ut, tibi soli Creatori serviens*.

Another aspect needing attention here is how the faithful will hear the abrupt shift in this paragraph from "man" to "all/those/them." Even though words once considered collective are to be retained in translations (*LitAuth*, no. 30), such language shifts certainly raise concerns on the pastoral level.

"Made incarnate by the Holy Spirit" (lines 20–23)

"Made incarnate" may sound strange at first. The wording in the Creed works better because it did not have to supply an auxiliary verb: *Et incar-*

[2] Mazza, *The Eucharistic Prayers*, 154.

natus est de Spiritu Sancto, "and by the Holy Spirit was incarnate." In translating *conversatus* more of the richness of *conversatio morum* found in the Catholic tradition of spirituality might have been drawn in. Similarly, *nostra condicionis forma* embraces not only our "human nature"—a more abstract concept appropriately expressed in Latin as *natura humana*—but also the concrete circumstances of human life. Mazza's literal translation captures these nuances much more effectively: "he shared our condition in every respect save sin."[3]

"And that we might live no longer for ourselves" (lines 31–36)

This translation, like ICEL1998, has restored the second line (line 32) inadvertently omitted in ICEL1973. This paragraph, however, presents two problems. The first is the lack of clarity about the referents for the personal pronouns in the last two lines. Fleeting proclamation of the text does not allow hearers time to clarify that ambiguity. The problem stems in part from the decision to translate *qui* as a conjunction of purpose, "so that," rather than a relative pronoun. According to the rules of English grammar, the immediate antecedent of "his work" would be the "Holy Spirit" rather than Christ ("he sent"). This makes it ambiguous whether the referents of "his work in the world" and "he might sanctify" are the same or different. By translating *qui* as a relative pronoun, Mazza's literal translation of these lines makes it clear that the Holy Spirit is the subject of *perficiens* and *compleret*, leaving *opus suum* to refer to Christ: "he sent from you, Father, as the first fruits for believers, the Holy Spirit who would finish his work in the world and bring all holiness to completion."[4] Catechesis may have to bring that kind of clarity to this text (*LitAuth*, no. 29).

Furthermore, the Latin does not attribute *omnem sanctificationem* to "creation." That word is not in the Latin and has been inserted. Sanctification is proper to rational creatures. Like the Latin, Mazza's literal translation leaves it open: "and bring all holiness to completion."[5] One might reason further that *omnem sanctificationem* refers specifically to Jesus' followers. Given the Johannine flavor of EP IV, one can see here an allusion to John 17:17-19:

[3] Ibid., 155.

[4] Ibid. The postconciliar French and Italian translations enjoy that same clarity: *il a envoyé d'après de toi, comme premier don fait aux croyants, l'Esprit qui poursuit son oeuvre dans le monde et achève toute sanctification*, and *ha mandato, o Padre, lo Spirito Santo, primo dono ai credenti, a perfezionare la sua opera nel mondo e compiere ogni santificazione*. ICEL2003 was even clearer: "he sent the Holy Spirit from you, Father, as first fruits for those who believe, so that in completing the work of Christ in the world he might bring to fulfillment all sanctification."

[5] Likewise, the French and Italian texts previously noted.

Sanctifica *eos in veritate; sermo tuus veritas est. Sicut me misisti in mundum, et ego misi eos in mundum; et pro eis ego* sanctifico *meipsum, ut sint et ipsi* sanctificati *in veritate* (*Nova Vulgata*, emphasis added).[6]

This passage comes from the final section of the Jesus' Last Supper discourse, which NABRE entitles "The Prayer of Jesus" (John 17:1-26). This prayer focuses on the disciples and their relation to Jesus. His mission is to be theirs; as the Father sent him, so he has sent them (John 17:18). His "holiness" is fulfilled by his total gift of self in love and in service of the coming of God's reign. That is to be their model for mission, their way to "holiness." The world (*in mundo*), into which both Jesus and his disciples are sent, is the arena in which the holiness of total self-giving in service of God's plan is fulfilled, both for Jesus and for them. His work in carrying out that plan, his sanctification, was completed when he gave himself up in death and "handed over the spirit" (John 19:30). The Spirit who guided Christ will abide with his disciples (John 14:16-17; 14:26; 16:13) to guide them, bringing Christ's work to completion in the world (*opus suum in mundo perficiens*) through them, thus bringing them to complete holiness.[7]

In this light, the petition in these lines is for Jesus' disciples now—for ourselves—so that, through the working of the Holy Spirit "sent . . . as the first fruits for those who believe," we might give ourselves totally in love and thus carry on the mission of Jesus. This reading is supported by lines 31–32, drawn from 2 Corinthians 5:15: "And that we might live no longer for ourselves but for him." In keeping with that topic sentence for this paragraph, the sense of lines 33–36 would be: "he sent from you, Father, as the first fruits for those who believe, the Holy Spirit who, completing his work in the world, would bring them [believers] to full holiness" in carrying on his work.

Epiclesis (ICEL2010, no. 118)

The note of purpose expressed in the gerundive construction *ad celebrandum* is ambiguous when translated "for the celebration." ICEL1998 ex-

[6] "Consecrate them in the truth; your word is truth. As you sent me into the world, so I sent them into the world. And I consecrate myself for them, so that they also may be consecrated in truth." NABRE uses "consecrate" rather than "sanctify" (found, for example, in NRSV) to translate the Greek *hagiazo*, Latin *sanctificare*.

[7] For another perspective on the theology underlying this image of holiness, see Mazza, *The Eucharistic Prayers*, 160–61; also, Raymond E. Brown, *The Gospel according to John (xiii–xxi)*, The Anchor Bible 29A (Garden City, NY: Doubleday, 1970), 765–67; Francis J. Moloney, *The Gospel of John*, Sacra Pagina Series 4 (Collegeville, MN: Liturgical Press, 1998), 471–72; Rudolf Schnackenburg, *The Gospel according to St. John*, trans. David Smith and G. A. Kon (New York: Crossroad, 1987), 3:187–88; *The New Interpreter's Bible* (Nashville: Abingdon Press, 1995), 9:793–94.

pressed this more clearly: "that we may celebrate the great mystery which he left us as an everlasting covenant."[8]

Institution Narrative over the Bread (ICEL2010, no. 119)

"For when the hour had come" (lines 3–5)

The parallel between *venisset ac dilexisset* has been lost, but this adaptation expresses the temporal sequence of the two verbs well and is better suited for proclamation. ICEL1998 had made the same adaptation.

"he took bread, blessed and broke it, and gave it to his disciples, saying" (lines 10–11)

This is the only instance in the words over the bread and cup in EP I, III, and IV where *benedixit* is translated as "blessed."[9] In EP I and III *benedixit* is preceded by *et tibi gratias agens* translated as "giving you thanks he said the blessing." This and other changes in the words over the bread and cup may trip up priests who proclaim them from memory. Translating *benedixit* as "said the blessing" instead of "blessed and broke it" would be more consistent (*LitAuth*, no. 50d), and it would avoid two potential problems: (1) that "it" (the bread) might be heard as the object of both "blessed" and "broke," an understanding not in keeping with the NT texts (Matt 26:26; Mark 14:22; Luke 22:19; 1 Cor 11:24), and (2) that the presider might be tempted to make the sign of the cross over the bread, as rubrics had once required.

Institution Narrative over the Cup (ICEL2010, no. 120, lines 2–14)

For comments on the translation of *calix* as "chalice," see my observations above.[10]

"which will be poured out for you and for many" (line 12)

For *pro multis*, ICEL2003 had read "which will be poured out for you and for all."[11] Soon thereafter, CDWDS sent a circular letter to episcopal

[8] Mazza, *The Eucharistic Prayers*, 155, offers a similar translation. He states that these words bring out the theological motivation for the account of the institution, which is then bracketed by a parallel expression in the anamnesis prayer that follows (ibid., 173).

[9] In EP II *benedixit* is missing, see *OM2008*, no. 102 above.

[10] See 287 above.

[11] The draft of 2003–2004, footnote 14, had cited *Notitiae* 6 (1970): 39–40, 138–40, and the example of postconciliar Italian, German, Portuguese, and Spanish translations as the rationale for retaining "for all"; also see 330–31 above and 480–81 below.

conferences requiring the precise translation of *pro multis* as "for many."[12] ICEL2010 follows that directive. In the context of the eucharistic celebration of Christ's sacrifice, *effundetur* might better have been translated "will be shed."

Anamnesis-Offering (ICEL2010 no. 122, lines 2–11)

"we offer you his Body and Blood" (line 9)

This translation is literally faithful to the Latin. Catechesis will be required (*LitAuth*, no. 29) to ensure that "offer you his Body and Blood" is not understood as a new act of offering separate from that of Christ himself and that its memorial and sacramental character is honored.[13]

Epiclesis (ICEL2010, no. 122, lines 12–18)

Following the Latin, these seven lines form one continuous sentence that tests the skills of the priest. *Hostia* and *hostia viva* are well translated as "Sacrifice" (of Christ) and "living sacrifice" (of Christians). *Parasti* ("you yourself have provided") might better be translated "you have prepared." *Qui participabunt* (translated as "who partake") is future tense rather than the present, literally, "who will partake."

Intercessions for the Living and the Dead (ICEL2010, no. 122, lines 19–41)

"all for whom we offer this sacrifice"(line 20)

The ICEL2008 draft had read "all for whom we make this offering." The 2010 text changed "offering" (*oblationem*) to "sacrifice," perhaps to avoid the redundancy of "offer this offering." The wording of ICEL2008, noted above, had avoided that redoubling.

"all the clergy, those who take part in this offering, those gathered here before you" (lines 23–25)

Circumstantium is well translated as "those gathered here before you." But to whom does *offerentium* refer? Are they the same as the *circumstantium*? In that case, "those who take part" and "those gathered here" would be

[12] *Notitiae* 42 (2006): 444–46.

[13] This literal expression of what the Church now offers is unusual in Western liturgical tradition and has raised ecumenical concerns; see Baldovin, 406 above.

redundant. Mazza reasons that *offerentium* refers rather to "the priestly celebrants"[14] since they are listed after "all the clergy" and before "those gathered here." ICEL2008's rendering of "those who make this offering," would have been much clearer than the present text.

"To all of us, your children" (lines 32–41)

Dividing these eight lines of text into two sentences makes them easier to proclaim, but at a cost. *Glorificemus*, in the subjunctive mood, is governed by *ut* at the beginning of this paragraph and is parallel to *valeamus* ("that we may enter"). This translation loses that parallel and uses the weak construction "may we" instead of "that we may."

Conclusion

EP IV, like EP II and III, follows a more straightforward sequence from narrative remembrance to intercessory petition than does EP I. This is a decided advantage for effective proclamation, though it is offset to an extent by the translation's fidelity to the principles of literal equivalence. Long unbroken sentences and a word order taken over from *OM2008* can inhibit the smooth flow of the prayer for priests who have not carefully prepared the proclamation in advance. As noted above, effective catechesis is needed as well if God's people are to hear EP IV with full spiritual benefit. Nonetheless, it can be cherished as one of the most beautiful and powerful of the EPs.

[14] Mazza, *The Eucharistic Prayers*, 339, note 238.

The Mystagogical Implications

Mark E. Wedig

Effective mystagogy enables the Christian community to draw deeply on the spiritual wellspring of the liturgy. The successful mystagogue enlivens the collective imagination of the Christian people to recognize the value of the metaphors and symbols in the liturgy in ways that make something that is ancient religious experience ever new. More specifically, a mystagogy of the EP can enable the assembly and priest to appreciate their collective participation in ecclesial worship. In other words, the church can be uniquely embodied through its prayerful participation and self-realization in this prayer. Hence, this essay will emphasize how a mystagogy of EP IV contributes uniquely to ecclesial awareness through the active participation of priest and assembly.

In creating a mystagogy for EP IV a number of factors will help to draw out the riches from its reservoir of meaning. First, one examines the ecclesial character that is created and shaped by praying the EP. When is it most appropriate to pray the prayer and for what occasions was it intended and fashioned? Second, this prayer is splendid in biblical imagery and especially weaves an intricate tapestry of themes from salvation history. What theological meaning can be drawn from this complex scriptural fabric and how can the prayer enhance our Sunday and other festive worship? Third, one can decipher spirituality from the distinctive Jewish and Christian anthropology of EP IV. Can the communities of faith that receive a formative mystagogy of this prayer become more attuned to the particular vision of humanity created by God that is so fundamental to this prayer?

Ecclesial Context of EP IV

Prayer mediates church. It is not so much that the church simply offers and has prayer but that the church at prayer brings about distinct ecclesial self-realization. As basic and obvious as this might seem, one cannot come to appreciate the highly formative influence of prayer on our ecclesial awareness unless we are educated in the meaning of it. As the priest and assembly pray the eucharistic anaphora and in turn learn about its meaning, together they become more fully the Body of Christ incarnate and realized. What kind of church does EP IV fashion through its symbols, metaphors, theological motifs, and spiritual riches? How can one grow ecclesially through what the prayer has to offer?

Because of its rich treasury of theological themes narrated in the context of salvation history, EP IV has a singularly instructive and edifying effect on those praying it. This prayer can serve the church uniquely when there is the explicit opportunity and occasion to teach and form others in the faith. The liturgical times when catechumens and candidates are being instructed in the mysteries of the faith are excellent occasions for regularly praying EP IV. Consequently, the prayer calls for coordination between the liturgy committee of the parish, the priest, and the catechumenate in order to organize this effect. An authentic mystagogy depends on preparation and foresight. Much of the onus here rests on the cooperation and appreciation of liturgy planning and coordination, which militates against the priest's personal piety determining the choice of the eucharistic anaphora at the Sunday liturgy.

Another occasion when the local church could benefit greatly from praying EP IV is when it celebrates baptism in the context of the Sunday liturgy. The rite of baptism with its profession of faith would be accentuated by the priest and assembly's praying of EP IV. In fact, the profession of faith in the rite of baptism would be extended more explicitly to the prayer at the altar through EP IV's narration of the great themes of salvation history, which in turn enables the faithful to make a more direct association between baptism and Eucharist, or between font and altar.

Though more frequently employed in our worship life than EP I,[1] EP IV also is not prayed nearly as frequently as EP II or EP III, especially on Sundays and solemnities. Some of this can be attributed to its length and complex theological discourse; maybe priests have abstained from praying this prayer more out of habit than intentional avoidance.[2] Maybe EP II and EP III are prayed much more frequently because of an "automatic pilot" response of the priest. That being said, one must remember that mystagogy is not just for the assembly but also for the clergy who need to be renewed

[1] See my discussion of how EP I has evaporated from the life of the Church, 294 above.

[2] For the purposes of gathering information for the essays in this volume, the author conducted three different focus groups to gauge people's experience of the EPs of the Roman Rite. The three groups of ten persons each, were composed of separate "populations" of churchgoers. Group 1 was made up of presbyters who were ordained between five and thirty years; group 2 was composed of graduate students in theology and ministry at a local Catholic university; group 3 was made up of a range of persons in age that make up the regular membership of the eleven o'clock Sunday morning eucharistic liturgy at a local parish. Group 1 revealed that they tended to not pray EP IV simply "out of habit of praying EP III."

in their appreciation of the liturgy's riches. Moreover, an effective mystagogy needs to examine some of the liturgical habits, routines, and patterns that communities can develop that can prevent a broader participation in what the church has offered us. One of the purposes of mystagogy is to help us revisit perfunctory performances and predictable responses to the many options provided in our official worship.

Theological Meaning of EP IV

EP IV is a theological masterpiece of sorts. It is a complete and unified prayer from beginning to end. It also serves as a profession of faith at the altar that is narrated through and stylized by an assemblage of scriptural references. Its symphony of metaphors from the OT and NT are ordered by the theological motifs that are woven throughout the text. The theological weightiness of its design rests in the preface that glorifies God the creator and the post-*Sanctus* anamnesis of salvation that professes the faith of the church. The extended proclamation of God's name, which expounds on the glory, illumination, and grandeur of God's magnificence, draws priest and assembly into the *Sanctus* uniting the eucharistic assembly with the heavenly banquet. The post-*Sanctus* profession of faith, which is also a soteriological anamnesis, is ordered by an extended reflection on all God has done for humanity in utter faithfulness, constantly desiring to restore humanity to God's original created intention. Consequently, the culmination of God's restorative favor for humanity is the salvific love of the incarnation.

Part of appreciating EP IV involves understanding the prayer's uniquely patristic approach to the Bible. Biblical references are often organized according to a "typological" interpretation.[3] In other words, biblical passages are used to interpret other passages. The texts of the Hebrew Scriptures in particular are seen to foreshadow Christian revelation. Events in the OT are deemed as prefiguring Christ in the NT, and the real purpose of the OT texts are viewed in light of that prefiguration. In EP IV, OT and NT biblical references are intertwined to create a symphony of relations. They are seen as compatible and interchangeable so as to narrate a cohesive soteriological textual whole.

A mystagogy of EP IV needs to point out that the early church or a patristic typological interpretation of OT passages can be problematic for contemporary interfaith sensibilities. Appreciation of the prayer does need

[3] John J. O'Keefe and R. R. Reno, *Sanctified Vision: An Introduction to Early Christian Interpretation of the Bible* (Baltimore: Johns Hopkins University Press, 2005) 69–88.

to carry with it a certain note of caution concerning its appropriation of Jewish salvation history. In other words, contemporary exegesis of OT texts lets the Hebrew Scriptures stand on their own terms. That being said, the biblical approach of EP IV can be valued and appreciated on its own terms as long as one is aware of the contemporary critique. It is important to note that the NT texts themselves often approach the Hebrew Scriptures typologically.

EP IV is particularly instructive about Jewish and Christian anthropologies. One might say that the strongest theological motif of the prayer is God's desire to return humanity to its intended state and the ultimate accomplishment of this in Christ Jesus. Moreover, that love is extended in the continuous offer of that same grace in the Eucharist. In EP IV there is a protracted prayerful contemplation of God's creation of humanity in the image and likeness of the Creator. In contrast, sin is humanity's contradiction and rejection of God's anthropological intention. EP IV emphasizes humanity's rejection of its authentic and true condition by refusing to accept the true design and intent of God's creation.

There is a direct connection between the theological anthropology of EP IV and the activity of breaking bread and sharing the chalice. The narrative of salvation in which God continuously calls humanity back to its intended state eventually leads to the meal before Jesus' death, which in turn directly relates to the love poured out in the eucharistic action. In remembering all that God has done for humanity and desired for humanity, the ultimate restorative action is the cross and the consequential love poured out in the eucharistic action. The love manifest on the cross and the love manifest in the eucharistic action each mirror the way God has restored the human condition through Jesus Christ.

Spirituality of EP IV

The spiritual treasures of EP IV emanate from its theological mastery, especially its Jewish and Christian anthropologies. The prayer has the potential of leading presider, preacher, and assembly into contemplative reflection on the fundamental beauty and sacredness of the human person. Spirituality and theological anthropology are uniquely related in that most spiritualities project a specific perspective of the human condition. Of course not all spiritualities view the human condition the same. They cover the continuum of depraved to highly exalted. That being said, the exalted perspective of the human condition in EP IV can serve as a way to emphasize a sacramental spirituality that is grounded in the *imago Dei*.

It is not an exaggeration to say that much of the contemporary world does not proceed with a positive theological anthropology. It would be more accurate to say that postmodern cultures continually operate out of a fundamentally negative and pessimistic view of human nature. Human beings are not looked upon as fundamentally good and, much less, created in God's image and likeness. Humanity is often viewed from a utilitarian perspective at best and too often seen as a commodity, allowing people to be treated as dispensable goods. This contemptible and even shameful view of the human condition arises out of ways the hyperindustrialized and overly commercialized world renders humanity a product to be sold, traded, or bartered.

Authentic Christian spirituality in a postmodern world demands contemplation and renewed focus on modest but intelligible realisms about the human condition as well as resistance to those forces that supplant such intelligibility.[4] This means that the teachers and custodians of the Christian tradition have the responsibility to challenge false illusions about humanity and the exigence to fashion rhetoric and environments that help others take the time and space to realize the given sacredness of their condition. That is not an easy charge in a world that considers the human person through economic generalizations and industrial abstractions. It is not a simple task to hold on to moderate realisms about humanity, which constitute affirming the God-giveness and intrinsic value of a human life. Accordingly, the Catholic Christian tradition has long-standing and extensively articulated understandings and practices representative of such viewpoints.

Might prioritizing the praying of EP IV in the regular life of the church and instructing the faithful of its intrinsic value engender and nurture eucharistic spiritualities that link the altar with an exalted view of the human condition? Could not a greater communal appreciation of praying EP IV be seen as a way to renew Christian solidarity with the contemplative realisms that militate against the harsh and cruel anthropologies of our world? Communities of faith that feed off of the rich biblical narrative and metaphor of the anaphora, instead of flat allegories of the postmodern information highway, model a resistance to the forces that dehumanize our societies and cultures. The mystagogical implications of EP IV directly relate to the reassertion of how the Holy Spirit has been given to us to sanctify and restore all of creation to God's original intention, as EP IV asserts in its preamble to the first epiclesis:

[4] Albert Borgmann, *Crossing the Postmodern Divide* (Chicago: University of Chicago Press, 1992), 110–26.

And that we might live no longer for ourselves
but for him who died and rose again for us,
he sent the Holy Spirit from you, Father,
as the first fruits for those who believe,
so that, bringing to perfection his work in the world,
he might sanctify creation to the full. (ICEL2010, no. 117, lines 31–36)

Conclusion

In this essay we have delineated the mystagogical implications of EP IV by considering how the prayer forms an ecclesial context, mediates a unique theological perspective, and emphasizes a particular spirituality. The essay suggests that the prayer can mediate a unique ecclesial character when its rich treasury of theological themes, narrated in the context of salvation history, are highlighted and accentuated. EP IV can have a singularly instructive effect on the assembly, thereby making it an ideal prayer for liturgical settings when catechumens are present, when the Sunday assembly celebrates a baptism, or other occasions when the faithful are being particularly instructed in the faith.

This essay also emphasized that EP IV is a theologically splendid prayer that narrates Christian belief through its biblical tapestry. The prayer mediates its theology through scriptural metaphors from both the NT and OT. Therefore, it provides a wonderful opportunity for the faithful to encounter key theological concepts through a biblical-patristic typology. One of the strong theological motifs of the prayer is how God has continually summoned humanity back to its intended and original condition despite humanity's disobedience of that mystery and tendency to undermine its own giftedness.

Finally, the spiritual richness of EP IV arises out of the theological anthropology that particularly thematizes the prayer. EP IV emphasizes that God fundamentally views the human condition as good and has created humanity in the image and likeness of the divine. This exalted perspective of the human condition embodied in the narrative of EP IV can serve as the fulcrum of a Christian spirituality that understands religious conversion to be the ongoing reintegration of human persons with God's original and fundamental intention for humanity. In other words, humanity is not an obstacle to God but the very vehicle to a graced existence in God. Thus, EP IV militates against any spiritualities that view the human condition as fundamentally flawed and depraved. Instead, EP IV engenders a spirituality born out of an intrinsically optimistic view of human capability when aligned with God's original intentions.

Eucharistic Prayers for Reconciliation

The Latin Text

PRECES EUCHARISTICAE « DE RECONCILIATIONE »

Preces eucharisticae « de Reconciliatione » adhiberi possunt in Missis, quibus mysterium reconciliationis peculiari modo fidelibus insinuatur, v. gr. in Missis pro concordia fovenda, pro reconciliatione, pro pace et iustitia servanda, tempore belli vel eversionis, pro remissione peccatorum, ad postulandam caritatem, de mysterio Sanctae Crucis, de SS.ma Eucharistia, de pretiosissimo Sanguine D.N.I.C. necnon in Missis tempore Quadragesimae. Quamvis praefatione propria instructae sint, adhiberi possunt etiam cum aliis praefationibus, quae ad paenitentiam et conversionem referuntur, uti v. gr. cum praefationibus Quadragesimae.

I

1. ℣. Dóminus vobíscum.
℟. Et cum spíritu tuo.

℣. Sursum corda.
℟. Habémus ad Dóminum.

℣. Grátias agámus Dómino Deo nostro.
℟. Dignum et iustum est.

Vere dignum et iustum est
nos tibi semper grátias ágere.
Dómine, sancte Pater,
omnípotens aetérne Deus:

Qui ad abundantiórem vitam habéndam
nos incitáre non désinis,
et, cum sis dives in misericórdia,
véniam offérre persevéras
ac peccatóres invítas
ad tuae solum indulgéntiae fidéndum.

A nobis autem,
qui foedus tuum tóties violávimus,
numquam avérsus,
humánam famíliam

The English Text

EUCHARISTIC PRAYERS FOR RECONCILIATION

The Eucharistic Prayers for Reconciliation may be used in Masses in which the mystery of reconciliation is conveyed to the faithful in a special way, as, for example, in the Masses for Promoting Harmony, For Reconciliation, For the Preservation of Peace and Justice, In Time of War or Civil Disturbance, For the Forgiveness of Sins, For Charity, of the Mystery of the Holy Cross, of the Most Holy Eucharist, of the Most Precious Blood of our Lord Jesus Christ, as well as in Masses during Lent. Although these Eucharistic Prayers have been provided with a proper Preface, they may also be used with other Prefaces that refer to penance and conversion, as, for example, the Prefaces of Lent.

I

1. ℣. The Lord be with you.
℟. And with your spirit.

℣. Lift up your hearts.
℟. We lift them up to the Lord.

℣. Let us give thanks to the Lord our God.
℟. It is right and just.

It is truly right and just
that we should always give you thanks,
Lord, holy Father, almighty and eternal God.

For you do not cease to spur us on
to possess a more abundant life
and, being rich in mercy,
you constantly offer pardon
and call on sinners
to trust in your forgiveness alone.

Never did you turn away from us,
and, though time and again we have broken your covenant,
you have bound the human family to yourself

per Iesum Fílium tuum, Redemptórem nostrum,
novo caritátis vínculo tam arcte tibi iunxísti,
ut nullo modo possit dissólvi.

Nunc quidem tempus grátiae et reconciliatiónis
pópulo tuo praebes,
eíque ad te ánimum converténti
in Christo Iesu speráre concédis
cunctísque homínibus tríbuis deservíre,
dum plénius Spirítui Sancto se cóncredit.
Et ídeo, admiratióne perfúsi,
tui amóris virtútem extóllimus
nostrúmque de salúte gáudium profiténtes,
cum innúmeris caeléstium turbis hymnum concínimus,
sine fine dicéntes:

Sanctus, Sanctus, Sanctus, Dóminus Deus Sábaoth.
Pleni sunt caeli et terra glória tua.
Hosánna in excélsis.
Benedíctus qui venit in nómine Dómini.
Hosánna in excélsis.

2. Sacerdos, manibus extensis, dicit:

Vere Sanctus es, Dómine,
qui ab orígine mundi semper operáris
ut, sicut Sanctus es ipse,
sanctus fiat homo.

3. Iungit manus, easque expansas super oblata tenens, dicit:

Réspice, quaésumus, múnera pópuli tui
et super ea Spíritus tui virtútem effúnde

iungit manus

et signat semel super panem et calicem simul, dicens:

ut Corpus et ✠ Sanguis fiant

iungit manus

dilécti Fílii tui, Iesu Christi,
in quo et nos fílii tui sumus.

through Jesus your Son, our Redeemer,
with a new bond of love so tight
that it can never be undone.

Even now you set before your people
a time of grace and reconciliation,
and, as they turn back to you in spirit,
you grant them hope in Christ Jesus
and a desire to be of service to all,
while they entrust themselves
more fully to the Holy Spirit.

And so, filled with wonder,
we extol the power of your love,
and, proclaiming our joy
at the salvation that comes from you,
we join in the heavenly hymn of countless hosts,
as without end we acclaim:

Holy, Holy, Holy Lord God of hosts.
Heaven and earth are full of your glory.
Hosanna in the highest.
Blessed is he who comes in the name of the Lord.
Hosanna in the highest.

2. The Priest, with hands extended, says:

You are indeed Holy, O Lord,
and from the world's beginning
are ceaselessly at work,
so that the human race may become holy,
just as you yourself are holy.

3. He joins his hands and, holding them extended over the offerings, says:

Look, we pray, upon your people's offerings
and pour out on them the power of your Spirit,

He joins his hands and makes the Sign of the Cross once over the bread and chalice together, saying:

that they may become the Body and ✠ Blood

He joins his hands.

of your beloved Son, Jesus Christ,
in whom we, too, are your sons and daughters.

Quamvis vero olim pérditi
tibi appropinquáre nequirémus,
summo nos amóre dilexísti:
Fílius enim tuus, qui solus est Iustus,
morti trádidit seípsum,
ligno crucis pro nobis non dedignátus affígi.

Sed ántequam bráchia eius
inter caelum et terram exténta
efficeréntur tui foéderis indelébile signum,
ipse cum discípulis suis Pascha vóluit celebráre.

4. In formulis, quae sequuntur, verba Domini proferantur distincte et aperte, prouti natura eorundem verborum requirit.

Convéscens autem,

accipit panem

eumque parum elevatum super altare tenens prosequitur:

accépit panem
et tibi grátias agens benedíxit,
fregit et dedit illis, dicens:

parum se inclinat:

ACCÍPITE ET MANDUCÁTE EX HOC OMNES:
HOC EST ENIM CORPUS MEUM,
QUOD PRO VOBIS TRADÉTUR.

Hostiam consecratam ostendit populo, reponit super patenam, et genuflexus adorat.

5. Postea prosequitur:

Simíliter, postquam cenátum est,
sciens se ómnia in seípso reconciliatúrum
per sánguinem suum in cruce fundéndum,

accipit calicem,
eumque parum elevatum super altare tenens, prosequitur:

accépit cálicem, genímine vitis replétum,
et íterum tibi grátias agens
discípulis suis trádidit, dicens:

parum se inclinat

ACCÍPITE ET BÍBITE EX EO OMNES:
HIC EST ENIM CALIX SÁNGUINIS MEI
NOVI ET AETÉRNI TESTAMÉNTI,

Indeed, though we once were lost
and could not approach you,
you loved us with the greatest love:
for your Son, who alone is just,
handed himself over to death,
and did not disdain to be nailed for our sake
to the wood of the Cross.

But before his arms were outstretched between heaven and earth,
to become the lasting sign of your covenant,
he desired to celebrate the Passover with his disciples.

4. In the formulas that follow, the words of the Lord should be pronounced clearly and distinctly, as the nature of these words requires.

As he ate with them,

He takes the bread
and, holding it slightly raised above the altar, continues:

he took bread
and, giving you thanks, he said the blessing,
broke the bread and gave it to them, saying:

He bows slightly.

TAKE THIS, ALL OF YOU, AND EAT OF IT,
FOR THIS IS MY BODY,
WHICH WILL BE GIVEN UP FOR YOU.

He shows the consecrated host to the people, places it again on the paten, and genuflects in adoration.

5. After this, he continues:

In a similar way, when supper was ended,
knowing that he was about to reconcile all things in himself
through his Blood to be shed on the Cross,

He takes the chalice
and, holding it slightly raised above the altar, continues:

he took the chalice, filled with the fruit of the vine,
and once more giving you thanks,
handed the chalice to his disciples, saying:

He bows slightly.

TAKE THIS, ALL OF YOU, AND DRINK FROM IT,
FOR THIS IS THE CHALICE OF MY BLOOD,
THE BLOOD OF THE NEW AND ETERNAL COVENANT,

QUI PRO VOBIS ET PRO MULTIS EFFUNDÉTUR
IN REMISSIONEM PECCATÓRUM.

HOC FÁCITE IN MEAM COMMEMORATIÓNEM.

Calicem ostendit populo, deponit super corporale, et genuflexus adorat.

6. Deinde dicit:

Mystérium fídei:

Et populus prosequitur, acclamans:

Mortem tuam annuntiámus, Dómine,
et tuam resurrectiónem confitémur, donec vénias.

Vel:

Quotiescúmque manducámus panem hunc
et cálicem bíbimus,
mortem tuam annuntiámus, Dómine, donec vénias.

Vel:

Salvátor mundi, salva nos,
qui per crucem et resurrectiónem tuam liberásti nos.

7. Postea, extensis manibus, sacerdos dicit:

Mémores ígitur Fílii tui Iesu Christi,
qui Pascha nostrum est et pax nostra certíssima,
mortem eius et resurrectiónem ab ínferis celebrámus
atque, beátum eius advéntum praestolántes,
offérimus tibi, qui fidélis et misericors es Deus,
hóstiam, quae hómines tecum reconcíliat.

Réspice, benígnus, clementíssime Pater,
quos tibi coniúngis Fílii tui sacrifício,
ac praesta ut, Spíritus Sancti virtúte,
ex hoc uno pane et cálice partícipes,
in unum corpus congregéntur in Christo,
a quo omnis auferátur divísio.

WHICH WILL BE POURED OUT FOR YOU AND FOR MANY
FOR THE FORGIVENESS OF SINS.

DO THIS IN MEMORY OF ME.

He shows the chalice to the people, places it on the corporal, and genuflects in adoration.

6. Then he says:

The mystery of faith.

And the people continue, acclaiming:

We proclaim your Death, O Lord,
and profess your Resurrection
until you come again.

Or:

When we eat this Bread and drink this Cup,
we proclaim your Death, O Lord,
until you come again.

Or:

Save us, Savior of the world,
for by your Cross and Resurrection
you have set us free.

7. Then the Priest, with hands extended, says:

Therefore, as we celebrate
the memorial of your Son Jesus Christ,
who is our Passover and our surest peace,
we celebrate his Death and Resurrection from the dead,
and looking forward to his blessed Coming,
we offer you, who are our faithful and merciful God,
this sacrificial Victim
who reconciles to you the human race.

Look kindly, most compassionate Father,
on those you unite to yourself
by the Sacrifice of your Son,
and grant that, by the power of the Holy Spirit,
as they partake of this one Bread and one Chalice,
they may be gathered into one Body in Christ,
who heals every division.

In communióne mentis et cordis
nos semper serváre dignéris
una cum Papa nostro N. et Epíscopo nostro N.*
Adiuva nos, ut simul advéntum regni tui praestolémus
usque ad horam qua tibi adstábimus,
sancti inter sanctos in sede caelésti,
cum beáta Vírgine Dei Genetríce María,
beátis Apóstolis et ómnibus Sanctis
atque frátribus nostris defúnctis,
quos tuae misericórdiae supplíciter commendámus.

Tum vero, a corruptiónis vúlnere tandem liberáti
et nova plene constitúti creatúra,
gaudéntes tibi canémus gratiárum actiónem

Iungit manus:

Christi tui, in aetérnum vivéntis.

8. Accipit patenam cum hostia et calicem, et utrumque elevans, dicit:

Per ipsum, et cum ipso, et in ipso,
est tibi Deo Patri omnipoténti,
in unitáte Spíritus Sancti,
omnis honor et glória
per omnia saécula saeculórum.

Populus acclamat:

Amen.

Deinde sequitur ritus Communionis.

* Hic fieri potest mentio de Episcopis Coadiutore vel Auxiliaribus, vel de alio Episcopo, ut in *Institutione generali Missalis Romani*, n. 149, notatur.

Be pleased to keep us always
in communion of mind and heart,
together with N. our Pope and N. our Bishop.*
Help us to work together
for the coming of your Kingdom,
until the hour when we stand before you,
Saints among the Saints in the halls of heaven,
with the Blessed Virgin Mary, Mother of God,
the blessed Apostles and all the Saints,
and with our deceased brothers and sisters,
whom we humbly commend to your mercy.

Then, freed at last from the wound of corruption
and made fully into a new creation,
we shall sing to you with gladness

He joins his hands.

the thanksgiving of Christ,
who lives for all eternity.

8. He takes the chalice and the paten with the host and, raising both, he says:

Through him, and with him, and in him,
O God, almighty Father,
in the unity of the Holy Spirit,
all glory and honor is yours,
for ever and ever.

The people acclaim:

Amen.

Then follows the Communion Rite.

* Mention may be made here of the Coadjutor Bishop, or Auxiliary Bishops, as noted in the *General Instruction of the Roman Missal*, no. 149.

PREX EUCHARISTICA « DE RECONCILIATIONE »

II

1. ℣. Dóminus vobíscum.
℟. Et cum spíritu tuo.

℣. Sursum corda.
℟. Habémus ad Dóminum.

℣. Grátias agámus Dómino Deo nostro.
℟. Dignum et iustum est.

Vere dignum et iustum est
nos tibi grátias ágere atque laudes persólvere,
Deus Pater omnípotens,
pro ómnibus, quae in hoc mundo operáris,
per Dóminum nostrum Iesum Christum.

Cum enim genus humánum
dissensióne sit atque discórdia divísum,
experiéndo tamen cognóvimus te ánimos fléctere,
ut sint ad reconciliatiónem paráti.

Per Spíritum namque tuum pérmoves hóminum corda,
ut inimíci íterum in collóquia véniant,
adversárii manus coniúngant,
pópuli sibi óbviam quaerant veníre.

Tua operánte virtúte fit étiam, Dómine,
ut ódium vincátur amóre, últio cedat indulgéntiae,
discórdia in mútuam dilectiónem convertátur.

Quaprópter cum choris caeléstibus
grátias tibi indesinénter agéntes
maiestáti tuae in terris sine fine clamámus:

EUCHARISTIC PRAYER FOR RECONCILIATION

II

1. ℣. The Lord be with you.
℟. And with your spirit.

℣. Lift up your hearts.
℟. We lift them up to the Lord.

℣. Let us give thanks to the Lord our God.
℟. It is right and just.

It is truly right and just
that we should give you thanks and praise,
O God, almighty Father,
for all you do in this world,
through our Lord Jesus Christ.

For though the human race
is divided by dissension and discord,
yet we know that by testing us
you change our hearts
to prepare them for reconciliation.

Even more, by your Spirit you move human hearts
that enemies may speak to each other again,
adversaries join hands,
and peoples seek to meet together.

By the working of your power
it comes about, O Lord,
that hatred is overcome by love,
revenge gives way to forgiveness,
and discord is changed to mutual respect.

Therefore, as we give you ceaseless thanks
with the choirs of heaven,
we cry out to your majesty on earth,
and without end we acclaim:

Holy, Holy, Holy Lord God of hosts.

Sanctus, Sanctus, Sanctus, Dóminus Deus Sábaoth.
Pleni sunt caeli et terra glória tua.
Hosánna in excélsis.
Benedíctus qui venit in nómine Dómini.
Hosánna in excélsis.

2. Sacerdos, manibus extensis, dicit:

Te ígitur, Pater omnípotens,
benedícimus per Iesum Christum Fílium tuum,
qui in tuo nómine venit.
Ipse est pro homínibus Verbum salútis,
manus, quam peccatóribus pórrigis,
via, qua pax tua nobis praebétur.
Cum nosmetípsos a te, Dómine,
propter peccáta nostra avertissémus,
ad reconciliatiónem nos reduxísti,
ut ad te tandem convérsi nos ínvicem diligerémus
per Fílium tuum, quem in mortem pro nobis tradidísti.

3. Iungit manus, easque expansas super oblatas tenens, dicit:

Et nunc reconciliatiónem
a Christo nobis allátam celebrántes,
te deprecámur:
Spíritus tui effusióne haec dona sanctífica,

iungit manus
et signat semel super panem et calicem simul, dicens:

ut fiant Corpus et ✠ Sanguis Fílii tui,
cuius mandátum implémus
haec celebrántes mystéria.

Iungit manus.

4. In formulis, quae sequuntur, verba Domini proferantur distincte et aperte, prouti natura eorundem verborum requirit.

Ipse enim, vitam cum esset datúrus,
ut nos liberáret,
discúmbens

accipit panem,
eumque parum elevatum super altare tenens, prosequitur:

Heaven and earth are full of your glory.
Hosanna in the highest.
Blessed is he who comes in the name of the Lord.
Hosanna in the highest.

2. The Priest, with hands extended, says:

You, therefore, almighty Father,
we bless through Jesus Christ your Son,
who comes in your name.
He himself is the Word that brings salvation,
the hand you extend to sinners,
the way by which your peace is offered to us.
When we ourselves had turned away from you
on account of our sins,
you brought us back to be reconciled, O Lord,
so that, converted at last to you,
we might love one another
through your Son,
whom for our sake you handed over to death.

3. He joins his hands and, holding them extended over the offerings, says:

And now, celebrating the reconciliation
Christ has brought us,
we entreat you:
sanctify these gifts by the outpouring of your Spirit,

He joins his hands and makes the Sign of the Cross once over the bread and chalice together, saying:

that they may become the Body and ✠ Blood of your Son,
whose command we fulfill
when we celebrate these mysteries.

He joins his hands.

4. In the formulas that follow, the words of the Lord should be pronounced clearly and distinctly, as the nature of these words requires.

For when about to give his life to set us free,
as he reclined at supper,

He takes the bread
and, holding it slightly raised above the altar, continues:

accépit panem in manus suas
et tibi grátias agens benedíxit,
fregit dedítque discípulis suis, dicens:

parum se inclinat

ACCÍPITE ET MANDUCÁTE EX HOC OMNES:
HOC EST ENIM CORPUS MEUM,
QUOD PRO VOBIS TRADÉTUR.

Hostiam consecratam ostendit populo, reponit super patenam, et genuflexus adorat.

5. Postea prosequitur:

Símili modo véspere illo

accipit calicem,
eumque parum elevatum super altare tenens, prosequitur:

accépit cálicem benedictiónis in manus suas,
tuam cónfitens misericórdiam
dedítque discípulis suis, dicens:

parum se inclinat

ACCÍPITE ET BÍBITE EX EO OMNES:
HIC EST ENIM CALIX SÁNGUINIS MEI
NOVI ET AETÉRNI TESTAMÉNTI,
QUI PRO VOBIS ET PRO MULTIS EFFUNDÉTUR
IN REMISSIÓNEM PECCATÓRUM.

HOC FÁCITE IN MEAM COMMEMORATIÓNEM.

Calicem ostendit populo, deponit super corporale, et genuflexus adorat.

6. Deinde dicit:

Mystérium fídei:

Et populus prosequitur, acclamans:

Mortem tuam annuntiámus, Dómine,
et tuam resurrectiónem confitémur, donec vénias.

Vel:

Quotiescúmque manducámus panem hunc
et cálicem bíbimus,
mortem tuam annuntiámus, Dómine, donec vénias.

he himself took bread into his hands,
and, giving you thanks, he said the blessing,
broke the bread and gave it to his disciples, saying:

He bows slightly.

TAKE THIS, ALL OF YOU, AND EAT OF IT,
FOR THIS IS MY BODY,
WHICH WILL BE GIVEN UP FOR YOU.

He shows the consecrated host to the people, places it again on the paten, and genuflects in adoration.

5. After this, he continues:

In a similar way, on that same evening,

He takes the chalice
and, holding it slightly raised above the altar, continues:

he took the chalice of blessing in his hands,
confessing your mercy,
and gave the chalice to his disciples, saying:

He bows slightly.

TAKE THIS, ALL OF YOU, AND DRINK FROM IT,
FOR THIS IS THE CHALICE OF MY BLOOD,
THE BLOOD OF THE NEW AND ETERNAL COVENANT,
WHICH WILL BE POURED OUT FOR YOU AND FOR MANY
FOR THE FORGIVENESS OF SINS.

DO THIS IN MEMORY OF ME.

He shows the chalice to the people, places it on the corporal, and genuflects in adoration.

6. Then he says:

The mystery of faith.

And the people continue, acclaiming:

We proclaim your Death, O Lord,
and profess your Resurrection
until you come again.

Or:

When we eat this Bread and drink this Cup,
we proclaim your Death, O Lord,
until you come again.

Vel:

Salvátor mundi, salva nos,
qui per crucem et resurrectiónem tuam liberásti nos.

7. Deinde sacerdos, extensis manibus, dicit:

Memóriam ígitur agéntes
Fílii tui mortis et resurrectiónis,
qui hoc pignus dilectiónis suae nobis relíquit,
tibi quod nobis tribuísti offérimus
perféctae reconciliatiónis sacrifícium.

Pater sancte, súpplices deprecámur,
ut nos quoque accéptos hábeas cum Fílio tuo
et in hoc salutári convívio
eiúsdem Spíritum nobis praestáre dignéris,
qui ómnia áuferat quae nos ínvicem aliénant.

Ipse Ecclésiam tuam inter hómines
signum effíciat unitátis pacísque tuae instruméntum,
et nos in communióne consérvet
cum Papa nostro N. et Antístite nostro N.*
et cunctis Epíscopis et univérso pópulo tuo.

Quemádmodum nunc ad mensam Fílii tui nos congregásti,
ita nos cóllige cum gloriósa Dei Genetríce Vírgine María,
beátis Apóstolis tuis et ómnibus Sanctis,
cum frátribus nostris,
atque homínibus cuiúsvis stirpis et sermónis
in tua amicítia defúnctis,
ad perpétuae unitátis convívium,
in caelis novis et terra nova,
ubi plenitúdo pacis tuae refúlget,

Iungit manus:

in Christo Iesu Dómino nostro.

* Hic fieri potest mentio de Episcopis Coadiutore vel Auxiliaribus, vel de alio Episcopo, ut in *Institutione generali Missalis Romani*, n. 149, notatur.

Or:

Save us, Savior of the world,
for by your Cross and Resurrection
you have set us free.

7. Then the Priest, with hands extended, says:

Celebrating, therefore, the memorial
of the Death and Resurrection of your Son,
who left us this pledge of his love,
we offer you what you have bestowed on us,
the Sacrifice of perfect reconciliation.

Holy Father, we humbly beseech you
to accept us also, together with your Son,
and in this saving banquet
graciously to endow us with his very Spirit,
who takes away everything
that estranges us from one another.

May he make your Church a sign of unity
and an instrument of your peace among all people
and may he keep us in communion
with N. our Pope and N. our Bishop*
and all the Bishops
and your entire people.

Just as you have gathered us now at the table of your Son,
so also bring us together,
with the glorious Virgin Mary, Mother of God,
with your blessed Apostles and all the Saints,
with our brothers and sisters
and those of every race and tongue
who have died in your friendship.
Bring us to share with them the unending banquet of unity
in a new heaven and a new earth,
where the fullness of your peace will shine forth

He joins his hands.

in Christ Jesus our Lord.

* Mention may be made here of the Coadjutor Bishop, or Auxiliary Bishops, as noted in the *General Instruction of the Roman Missal*, no. 149.

8. Accipit patenam cum hostia et calicem, et utrumque elevans, dicit:

Per ipsum, et cum ipso, et in ipso,
est tibi Deo Patri omnipoténti,
in unitáte Spíritus Sancti,
omnis honor et glória
per omnia saécula saeculórum.

Populus prosequitur:

Amen.

Deinde sequitur ritus Communionis.

8. He takes the chalice and the paten with the host and, raising both, he says:

Through him, and with him, and in him,
O God, almighty Father,
in the unity of the Holy Spirit,
all glory and honor is yours,
for ever and ever.

The people acclaim:

Amen.

Then follows the Communion Rite.

EP RI and II

History of the Latin Text and Rite

Richard E. McCarron

EP RI and EP RII, originally promulgated in 1974 and granted limited use *ad experimentum*, now appear in *MR2002* as part of the appendix to *OM2008*, not in the *OM* itself.

This essay—treating them together, as their histories are largely inseparable—traces the foreground of their composition, their development for the Holy Year 1974–75, their promulgation and reception as EPs *de reconciliatione*, and their revision and insertion into *MR2002*.

Creation of New EPs after 1970

The preparation and promulgation of two new EPs for the occasion of the Holy Year 1974–1975 is best understood within the creativity and debate about the composition of new vernacular EPs in the late 1960s and early 1970s. The period was marked by a proliferation of freely composed EPs and the publication of collections of unofficial EPs for various themes, events, and seasons.[1] The defects of many overshadowed the merits of some, which raised the concern of the CDW. Local spontaneity and creativity also begged questions of regulation and oversight: What role do the local conferences of bishops have? What is the responsibility of the Holy See?

Several factors contributed to the creative ferment. First, historical research on the EP had led to a recovery of the variety of forms of EPs in the early church and the collection of historical witnesses.[2] Second was the

[1] Bugnini, 465–67; see also Frederick McManus, foreword to Enrico Mazza, *The Eucharistic Prayers of the Roman Rite*, trans. Matthew J. O'Connell (New York: Pueblo, 1986), xi. For example, in the United States, see John Mossi, ed., *Bread Blessed and Broken: Eucharistic Prayers and Fraction Rites* (New York: Paulist, 1974).

[2] Albert Gerhards calls attention to the importance of the collection *Prex Eucharistica* in 1968, not only as fruit of the liturgical renewal of the Roman church, but for Reformed churches as well. See his "Entstehung und Entwicklung des Eucharistichen Hochgebets im Spiegel der

experience of praying the whole EP in the vernacular, conceded by *Tres Abhinc Annos* in 1967.[3] The perceived difficulties in style and vocabulary of the Roman Canon itself had already led to the preparation and promulgation of EPs II, III, and IV. Third, the guidelines issued for the promulgation of the four major EPs of the Roman Rite issued in 1968 extolled the value of the addition of new texts of the EP besides the Roman Canon for pastoral, spiritual, and liturgical reasons.[4] Fourth, the 1969 instruction on translation *CLP* recognized the limits of texts translated from other languages "for the celebration of a fully renewed liturgy" and stated, "The creation of new texts will be necessary" (no. 43). This led not only to official endeavors of composition with local conferences of bishops approving prayers but to grassroots creativity as well, mostly without any episcopal oversight.

Response of the Holy See

As Annibale Bugnini explains in his account of the implementation of the conciliar liturgical renewal, the Holy See felt obliged to address the proliferation of unapproved, locally composed EPs and the question of oversight and approval of new prayers.[5] There was tension among the dicasteries between granting the authority to the local conferences of bishops to give the approval and reserving that authority to the Holy See. While the practice at the time was for the local bishops' conferences to grant approval (see *SC*, no. 22.2), a number of conferences of bishops (e.g., Germany, Zambia, Switzerland) did turn to the CDW for approval (citing *SC*, no. 40). The CDW had given approval to a number of different prayers or adaptations for diverse groups and needs around the world.[6] However, the number of and reasons for the requests, the poor quality of many of the texts in circulation, and the continued use and publication of unapproved prayers led the congregation to further action.

The CDW appealed to Paul VI in an audience on 27 May 1971, asking him to permit the CDW to study the matter carefully in order to offer an

neueren Forschung: Der Beitrag der Liturgiewissenschaft zur liturgischen Erneuerung," in *Gratias Agamus. Studien zum eucharistischen Hochgebet. Festschrift Balthasar Fischer*, ed. Andreas Heinz and Heinrich Rennings (Freiburg: Herder, 1992), 76–77. A third amended edition of *Prex Eucharistica* was published in 1998.

[3] *Tres Abhinc Annos* (4 May 1967), no. 28 in *AAS* 59 (1967), 442–48.

[4] *Au cours des derniers mois*, no. 4; French text in *Notitiae* 4 (1968): 148–55, English in DOL 1945–63.

[5] Bugnini, 465.

[6] See ibid., 465–67.

informed response.[7] The pope replied affirmatively on 22 June 1971. A study group was assembled in September 1971 and met four times until March 1972. In December 1971 the group circulated a working document it had produced of some one hundred pages. In addition to studies of the nature of the EP, the document examined the problems with the proliferation of EPs of private origin and presented in its final section criteria for the composition and evaluation of EPs.[8] The study group joined the consultors of the CDW at their meeting on 26–28 January 1972. Bugnini indicates that the discussion was lively and that several of the consultors were opposed to the idea of new EPs. A vote was taken at the end of the meeting, which revealed a consensus that there should be more EPs in the Roman Rite. What was less clear was the role the CDW should play in their approval.

A turning point in the deliberations came with the response of the CDF and the decision of Paul VI that the Holy See would reserve to itself the right to approve any further EPs: "'No' to further experiments. The Holy See *reserves to itself* the creation of new Eucharistic Prayers in particular cases."[9]

EuchPar

The final outcome of the deliberations and debate was the circular letter on EPs (*EuchPar*) sent to the presidents of the conferences of bishops by the CDW in April 1973. The document aims to strike a compromise between local initiative and the authority of the Holy See. In the circular letter, the congregation notes the proliferation of new prayers for various reasons: to meet the needs of various groups and peoples, to allow for a more contemporary expression (rather than translation of older texts), and to provide theoretical models for future composition. The letter further notes the continued practice, despite prohibition, of privately composed texts (no. 4) and explains that conferences of bishops may not have "a general permission to compose or approve new EPs" (no. 5). The primacy of the four EPs in *MR1970* is affirmed and use of any unapproved prayer is deemed unlawful (no. 6).

EuchPar does, however, envision the possibility of new EPs. It explains that while the "Apostolic See reserves to itself the right to regulate" EPs,

[7] The section relies on ibid., 467–75.
[8] Ibid., 467–68; detailed contents are described at 468, n. 28.
[9] Ibid., 475, n. 33 (emphasis in original).

the Apostolic See "will not refuse to consider lawful requests" (*legitimas postulationes considerare non renuent*) for new prayers (no. 6). The Apostolic See assures that "it will accord every consideration to the petitions submitted by the conferences of bishops for the possible composition in special circumstances of a new eucharistic prayer and its introduction into the liturgy" (no. 6).[10]

As part of its response to the expressed need for more EPs evidenced by the numbers of requests, the CDW continued to receive and to head off further local compositions and proposed to take initiative to prepare EPs for the approaching Holy Year and for Masses with Children as mentioned by the 1973 Directory for Masses with Children (no. 52).[11]

Holy Year 1975

Paul VI announced on 9 May 1973 that 1975 would be a Holy Year for the church, with 1974 being a time of preparation to culminate in Rome in 1975. The Holy Year was to be devoted to "the renewal of humanity and their reconciliation with God."[12] The pope envisioned a conversion of mind and heart, which leads in turn to a social reconciliation in all aspects of life and relationships—individual, familial, and national—as a leaven of peace and unity.[13] The themes of spiritual renewal of all humanity, ongoing conversion, the promptings of the Spirit to enable humanity to experience the fruits of redemption, and the social dimensions of reconciliation highlighted by the pope are the foreground for the themes that appear in the EPs prepared for the Holy Year.

The papal approval for work on EPs for the Holy Year came in 1973, with the formal letter issued by the secretary of state dated 23 October 1973. On 29 October the secretary of state officially communicated to the CDW the formal approval of the pope for a EP for the Holy Year.[14]

[10] One certainly thinks here of the challenges of inculturation and liturgy. The *Prière Eucharistique pour les Diocèses du Zaïre* approved in 1988 is a case in point. What was submitted and what was approved show some of the tensions between the local church and the Apostolic See that can arise. Some conferences were rejected or still await approval of a EP composed in the local style and idiom, e.g., the requests of the church of the Philippines.

[11] Bugnini, 478. The *Directory for Masses with Children* noted that the Holy See would make other provision for EPs for Masses with children (no. 52).

[12] See the letter of indiction, *AAS* 65 (1973), 312–13.

[13] Paul VI, "Letter of Paul VI to Cardinal Massimiliano de Furstenberg, President of the Central Committee for the Holy Year" (31 May 1973). Available in Italian at http://www.vatican.va/holy_father/paul_vi/letters/1973/documents/hf_p-vi_let_19730531_card-de-furstenberg_it.html (accessed 30 July 2010).

[14] Cited with the protocol numbers in Bugnini, 478.

Composition and Criteria

A study group was quickly established whose first meeting was held in November 1973.[15] Two prayers for the Holy Year were deliberated. The first text was composed originally in French and proposed to the group by Didier Rimaud.[16] It was a very poetic text, reflecting a biblical theology of reconciliation in the euchological style of EP IV.[17] The second text presented came from the work of a study group of the German Liturgical Commission and had already been approved by the German conference of bishops.[18] This text started with a theological reflection on the signs of the times in view of the mystery of reconciliation, attending to the "joys and hopes, griefs and anxieties" (*GS*, no. 1) of the world in a mode of thanksgiving and hope.[19]

The criteria that the study group employed in the work on the texts include: (1) creation of a text that could be easily assimilated by the assembly so to aid their participation; (2) use of biblical language that was free from jargon and would situate reconciliation in the economy of salvation; (3) sobriety of language around eucharistic doctrine so that all could easily understand; (4) reduction of the language of intercession, given the role of the prayer of the faithful; (5) use of the preface and intercessions to carry the theme.[20] What is clear in the texts eventually adopted is that the "theme" or "intention" of reconciliation is drawn into the dynamic of memorial thanksgiving and intercession that marks the other EPs of *MR1970*. These are not prayers "about reconciliation." Rather the prayers take up reconciliation and conversion as particular lenses to narrate and remember the whole economy of salvation, which culminates in the paschal mystery of Christ.

Bugnini explains that these base texts were then translated into English, Italian, and Spanish and sent to forty-nine experts around the world for

[15] The members of the study group are listed by Bugnini: Balthasar Fischer, Luigi Agustoni, Philippe Béguerie, Peter Coughlan, André Haquin, Gottardo Pasqualetti, Reiner Kaczynski, Vicente Pedrosa, Heinreich Rennings, Didier Rimaud, Joseph Gelineau, Antoine Dumas. The chair for the Holy Year was Didier Rimaud with A. Dumas serving as secretary (Bugnini, 478, n. 41). However, Heinreich Rennings explains that it should be *Gilberto* Agustoni, not his brother *Luigi* (Heinrich Rennings, "Votivhochgebet Versöhnung II," in *Gratias Agamus*, ed. Heinz and Rennings, 421, n. 8).

[16] Vincenzo Raffa, *Liturgia Eucaristica: Mistagogia della Messa: dalla storia e dalla teologia alla pastorale pratica*, Bibliotheca 'Ephemerides liturgicae' Subsidia 100 (Rome: CLV, 2003), 764.

[17] Irmgard Pahl, "Das erste Versöhnungshochgebet," in *Gratias Agamus*, ed. Heinz and Rennings, 355–56; also, Rennings, "Votivhochgebet Versöhnung II," 408; and Raffa, *Liturgia Eucaristica*, 764.

[18] Rennings, "Votivhochgebet Versöhnung II," 408.

[19] See Raffa, *Liturgia Eucaristica*, 765.

[20] From ibid., and Rennings, "Votivhochgebet Versöhnung II," 410–11.

evaluation.[21] A second meeting of the study group was held 16–18 January 1974, with two "observers" from the CDF present. At the request of the Secretariat of State, a Latin version of the texts was prepared by Abbot Karl Egger, who worked for the Secretariat. After a third consultation with the leaders of the study group, the CDW, and the translator from the Secretariat of State, the prayers were sent to the CDF on 7 March 1974. The CDF's reply came on 10 May and insisted that only one prayer for reconciliation be proposed (and one for children as well). Likewise, its use was to be restricted to the Holy Year and was not foreseen to become part of the Missal itself. As Piero Marini explains, Bugnini "did his utmost to obtain approval for the five texts [three for children, two for the Holy Year], putting pressure both on the Secretariat of State and on the Congregation for the Doctrine of the Faith."[22]

Promulgation of the Prayers

The final decision of Paul VI came on 26 October 1974, promulgated in the decree *Postquam de Precibus*.[23] With regard to the EPs for the Holy Year, both texts were authorized for use *ad experimentum* until 1977 but "may not be inserted into official editions of the Roman Missal."[24] The pope further indicated that when these Masses *de reconciliatione*[25] were sent to the presidents of the conferences of bishops, they should be told that they were to choose only one of the two for use in each conference.[26] On 26 January 1975, after the request of conferences who found the choice of only one to be difficult, the secretary of state explained that "the Holy See, however, will give every consideration, in individual cases, to reasonable requests for the use of more than one of these prayers."[27] The texts could be translated "with a degree of freedom. . . . It may differ somewhat from the Latin texts" except with regard to the "formularies of consecration."[28] Further the pope explained that that Holy Year prayer chosen by the conference of bishops could also be used for Masses for penitential occasions.

[21] Bugnini, 479. What follows in this paragraph is dependent on ibid.

[22] Piero Marini, *A Challenging Reform: Realizing the Vision of the Liturgical Renewal*, ed. Mark Francis and Keith Pecklers (Collegeville, MN: Liturgical Press, 2007), 147. See Bugnini, 480–81.

[23] DOL 1994–1998.

[24] *Postquam de Precibus*, no. 1 = DOL 1995.

[25] This title had been proposed by the CDW, given that the Holy Year would be nearing its close when they finally made their appearance. See Bugnini, 481.

[26] *Postquam de Precibus*, no. 2 = DOL 1996.

[27] DOL 1996, n. 3.

[28] *Postquam de Precibus*, no. 3 = DOL 1997.

Postquam de Precibus, the *praenotanda*, and the texts of the prayers were first issued as a mimeographed, typewritten manuscript.[29] It was foreseen that the prayers would be used "when there are special celebrations with the theme of reconciliation and penance, especially during Lent and on the occasion of a pilgrimage or a religious meeting."[30] The texts of the two EPs were laid out first with the Latin text followed by a *schema versionis*: for prayer I this included a French text, and for prayer II a German text. These were intended to assist the translators in their task of preparing vernacular editions.[31] In 1975, the decree and *praenotanda* were published in *Notitiae*.[32] In 1977, the use of the EPs for Masses for Reconciliation was extended for another three years. On 15 December 1980, permission was given for indefinite use of the prayers "until otherwise directed."[33]

By 1977 some forty conferences of bishops had received approval for use of one or both of the prayers.[34] Even though the decree had maintained that the bishops' conferences were to choose between the prayers, the approval of both texts for numbers of conferences in practice overruled that directive. Likewise, though the directive that they not be included in the *MR* was maintained still in 1977, vernacular books did come to include them as an appendix of some kind.[35]

Reissuing of the Texts

John Paul II declared a jubilee year "of Redemption" in 1983. The themes of penance and reconciliation were highlighted, and these also served as themes for the synod of bishops held in October 1983. In his apostolic letter *Aperite Portas Redemptori* declaring the year, John Paul II promoted communal celebrations on various themes associated with the year and encouraged the use of "either of the EPs for reconciliation" (no. 11). The CSDW took the occasion to reissue the texts of EP RI and EP RII in Latin.[36] The

[29] Sacra Congregatio Pro Culto Divino, *Preces Eucharisticae pro Missis cum Pueris et De Reconciliatione* (Rome: 1 November 1974), 49-page typewritten manuscript. It carries no protocol number.

[30] Ibid., no. 1 = DOL 1995.

[31] *Praenotanda*, no. 4: "Ad utilitatem eorum, qui versiones in linguas populares parare debent, pro unaquaque Prece versio in aliqua lingua occidentali additur," from page 34 of manuscript noted above in n. 29.

[32] *Notitiae* 11 (1975): 4–6, 12.

[33] *Notitiae* 17 (1981): 23.

[34] See Rennings, "Votivhochgebet Versöhnung II," 409, n. 17.

[35] Ibid., 409.

[36] *Notitiae* 19 (1983): 270–79; also the comments of Mazza, *The Eucharistic Prayers*, 192–93.

rubrics in this reissued version were brought into editorial and linguistic harmony with the EPs of *MR1975*,[37] and there were two minor textual changes from the original prayer texts published in 1974. One editorial change to EP RII—apart from some minor shifting of spacing between paragraphs—was a grammatical change in its preface from *ut voluntate pacis amante rixae sedentur* to *ut voluntate pacis amanter rixae sedentur.* The opening rubrical notes to the prayers recommend Mass formularies with which they may be used and indicate that while the prayers have their own preface, the prayers may also be used with other prefaces that have the theme of penance and conversion, like those of Lent.

U.S. English-Language Texts

The first English version of the prayers was prepared by ICEL and granted *recognitio* on 5 June 1975, which allowed use of both EPs. This permission was extend three years more in 1977 and indefinitely in 1980.[38] When the 1985 Sacramentary was published, the prayers were included in appendix 6, even though they did not appear in *MR1975*. As part of the revision project of the Sacramentary, ICEL offered a new English translation of the texts working from the Latin and the respective French and German versions of the texts. The commission also followed the principle that accompanied the original promulgation of the texts, namely, that the translation can be made more freely to correspond to the style of the target language. These texts were approved by the U.S. bishops and sent to Rome for approval as part of the 1998 Sacramentary revision, ultimately rejected as a whole by the CDWDS in March 2002.[39]

Editio Tertia

EP RI and EP RII were placed in the *Appendix ad Ordinem Missae* of *MR2002*. The official Latin text was heavily revised from the text published in 1974 and slightly amended in 1983. These changes include harmonization

[37] E.g., the deletion of *Omnes acclamant* at the *Sanctus*; insertion of a rubric parallel to *MR1975* regarding the tone of voice at *Sed antequam brachia eius*; indication of the other acclamations other than *Mortem tuam*; the division of rubrics to have the priest join hands before saying *supplici tibi confessione canemus* in EP RI.

[38] From the notice given by John Cummins, then chairman of the Bishops' Committee on the Liturgy, 17 May 1984, in the front matter of the booklet with the prayers published as *Eucharistic Prayers for Masses with Children and for Masses of Reconciliation* (Washington, DC: USCC, 1984).

[39] See the time line, xxv–xxvi above.

of wording with the four major EPs, rewording of sections, changes in grammar for literary style, and the addition of new phrases or specifications of existing words either to draw out more theological or biblical significance or to employ more sacral terminology.

In EP RI, for example, the beginning and ending of the preface have been reworded to harmonize with the dominant literary style of the corpus of prefaces in *MR2002*.[40] In a stronger biblical allusion, God is *dives in misericordia* (Eph 2:4) rather than the previous *Deus bonitatis et misericoridae*. Humankind is joined more specifically by a bond of love through Christ, who is named our redeemer (*per Iesum Filium tuum, Redemptorem nostrum, novo caritatis vinculo . . . iunxisti*). The post-*Sanctus* now begins with the incipit, *Vere Sanctus es, Domine*, harmonizing with EP II and EP III (*OM2008*, nos. 100 and 108). In the first epiclesis, God is asked now to look specifically on the *munera populi* rather than on the *populum hic adunatum* as in the previous versions.[41] The institution narrative has a new introduction: Christ gives the chalice to his disciples rather than his friends as in the previous versions. The second epiclesis has the phrase *ex hoc uno pane et calice particeps* to specify how the assembly is gathered into the Body of Christ. Mary is identified as the Mother of God, and the apostles are now invoked as blessed. The transition to the doxology has been reworded.[42]

In EP RII there is a similar harmonizing of the beginning and ending of the preface. The order of the signs by which we see God's power at work has been changed.[43] The first epiclesis now asks for the *effusione* of the Spirit rather than the *rore* (EP II, *OM2008*, no. 101) and asks specifically for the gifts to become *Corpus et Sanguis Filii tui*. Jesus takes the *calix benedictionis*. There is a harmonizing of the anamnesis-offering with the other major EPs.[44] The banquet is specified as *in hoc salutari convivio*. The intercessory section *Quemadmodum* has been reworked, with the addition of the phrases *in tua amicitia defunctis* and *in caelis novis*, making an explicit commemoration of the dead.[45]

[40] At the opening, *Vere dignum et iustum est nos tibi semper gratias agere* has replaced *Vere dignum et iustum est, Domine sancte Pater, nos tibi gratias agere.* At the ending, the phrase *cum innumeris caelestium turbis hymnum concinimus, sine fine dicentes* is inserted.

[41] Also, the word *munera* is used instead of *dona* as in the 1974 and 1983 versions.

[42] *Tum vero, a corruptionis vulnere tandem liberati et nova plene constituti creatura, gaudentes tibi canemus gratiarum actionem Christi tui, in aeternum viventis* replaces the previous *Tum vero, constituti in nova creatura, a corruptionis vulnere tandem liberata, gratiarum actionem Christi tui, in aeternum viventis, supplici tibi confessione canemus.*

[43] *Odium-ultio-discordia* for the previous version's *rixae-odium-ultio* (note the change from *rixae* to *discordia*).

[44] *Memoriam igitur agentes . . . offerimus* (*OM2008*, no. 105; cf. nos. 113, 122).

[45] The Italian edition of the prayer (*Messale Romano* 1983) inserted an explicit *memento* of the dead just before this section.

Conclusion

EP RI and II (together with the EPs for children) are the first generation of EPs redacted and promulgated following the publication of *MR1970*. Unlike EP MVN, which originated from the bishops of Switzerland and would later also be included in an appendix of *MR2002*,[46] the EPs for reconciliation originated with the initiative of the CDW and were intended for use throughout the world (upon request). The base texts for the work of the study group on the prayers came from French and German sources and were later translated into Latin. After further revision, some of which sought to harmonize them with the four principal EPs and to hone their literary and liturgical style, the Latin texts have become part of an appendix to *OM2008*.

The development, approval, and appropriation of these prayers are an important chapter in the history of the postconciliar liturgy for three main reasons. First, the process shows an attempt on the part of the Holy See to strike a balance between unity and diversity in liturgical practice. In the early 1970s the CDW sought to address creatively two pressing issues: on the one hand, the pastoral, liturgical, and spiritual value of new EPs for the Roman Rite that could respond to contemporary pastoral exigencies and proclaim the mystery of Christ in a variety of ways;[47] on the other, the proliferation of privately and freely composed prayers, unauthorized collections of EPs, and the growing number of requests from bishops' conferences for prayers in contemporary local idiom or for special circumstances.

Second, the process demonstrates the negotiation and reception of the principles of *SC*, no. 23. The inclusion of three EPs alongside the Roman Canon, which had been the sole anaphora of the Roman Rite, itself occasioned hesitation and debate.[48] The desire to expand the anaphoral repertoire beyond those four led to further debate and division. The EPs for reconciliation offered a model of how *sana traditio* could be retained while the *via legitimae progressioni* can evolve for the good of the church. The anaphoral structure of the four EPs of *MR1970* can serve as the frame for contemporary vernacular composition that gives expression in contemporary idiom to ways of remembering the paschal mystery of Christ in light of the signs of contemporary times. The question remains open, however, if there can be a *profundior Liturgiae aptatio* (*SC*, no. 40) with

[46] See 549 below.

[47] See *Au Cours des Derniers Mois,* no. 4 = DOL 1954.

[48] See Bugnini, 448–65; also Witczak, 353–54 above.

regard to the literary structure of the EP, particularly suited to the genius of local cultures.

Third, the insertion of the EPs for Masses for reconciliation in *MR2002* is a contemporary example of the historical dynamic of the Roman Rite to adopt and adapt diverse local liturgical traditions to itself and to receive into its euchology prayers fashioned in one place and time for use in diverse places and new times.[49] EPs originally prepared for the Holy Year were received beyond that event in the life of the church as EPs for reconciliation. The world still remains "divided by dissension and discord" and the plea that the church be "a sign of unity and an instrument of your peace among all people" (EP RII, no. 7, lines 13–14) remains ever timely.

[49] A classic example is the life of the euchology fashioned in response to Lupercalia at the time of Pope Gelasius: see Gilbert Pomarès, ed., *Lettre contre les Lupercales et Dix-huit Messes du Sacramentaire léonien: Introduction, texte critique, traduction, et notes, Sources chrétiennes* 65 (Paris: Cerf, 1959).

EP RI

Theology of the Latin Text and Rite

Susan K. Roll

Introduction

As noted in the previous essay, EP RI and EP RII were new compositions, each composed originally in a modern language and subsequently translated into the Latin. EP RI was composed in an elegant, poetic style of French[1] and this transferred well into Latin. Nevertheless, the lyrical flow of the text caused difficulties for translators and may have been one reason why it was not immediately promulgated in the German-speaking countries, since an accurate rendition in German would have resulted in numerous redundancies.[2] Its content challenges translators as well, since at various points the sense lines do not flow logically; the end of one strophe can leave an incomplete thought and raise questions about the underlying theology.

The main strengths of EP RI are its biblical imagery and its emphasis on reconciliation as a free gift of God. However much humanity may desire peace and reconciliation, we cannot accomplish it definitively on our own. God's endless mercy and willingness to forgive is illustrated in the long history of the covenant made with the Hebrews. Christians find this covenant ratified on a cosmic level in the death and resurrection of Christ. The theme of the New Covenant runs consistently through the main parts of this prayer.

The Preface (*OM2008*, appendix, no. 1, lines 7–34)

The content of the preface in which the interlocked themes of covenant and reconciliation first emerge is well integrated with the whole of the EP;

[1] Its composition is attributed to Didier Rimaud; see above, 457.

[2] Irmgard Pahl, "Das erste Versöhnungshochgebet," in *Gratias Agamus. Studien zum eucharistischen Hochgebet. Festschrift Balthasar Fischer*, ed. Andreas Heinz and Heinrich Rennings (Freiburg: Herder, 1992), 355–56.

while the preface is variable, employing this proper preface with EP RI enhances the persistence of these themes. God is addressed in a multiplicity of titles: *Domine, sancte Pater, omnipotens aeterne Deus*. Later in this prayer the titles of address will become greatly softened.

The second paragraph, beginning *Qui ad abundantiorem vitam* (lines 11–16) incorporates the beautiful NT reference to God as *dives in misericordia* (Eph 2:4) and the source of abundant life. At the same time, that paragraph introduces three separate ideas, the second and third of which do not proceed directly from the first. God's consistency in motivating (*incitare*[3]) the people to have life abundantly may be mirrored in God's consistent offer of pardon and forgiveness. The assembly is left to wait until the next paragraph to hear that abundant life is possible only because of God's persistent invitation to forgiveness no matter how often we turn away.

The covenant is introduced in the third paragraph (lines 17–23) by means of two quite different words. *Foedus* is normally used as the technical term for the covenant,[4] also for a treaty or agreement, while *vinculum* means chains, fetters, or a bond (for example, of marriage). If humans are capable of repeatedly breaking their covenant with God, they must be capable of some degree of mutuality, albeit between two infinitely unequal parties, as well as a high degree of personal responsibility. To use *vinculum* by way of parallel construction as a synonym for the covenant implies that humans have no freedom of choice, although perhaps the intended parallel is precisely with the bond of marriage as a *caritatis vinculum*. *Caritatis* is an addition in *MR2002*.[5] In *OM2008* the word for breaking the covenant is *violare*; in the previous Latin version of EP RI the word was the simpler, less violent *frangere*.[6]

The fourth paragraph (*Nunc quidem*, lines 24–29) presents another somewhat loosely connected series of good and appropriate statements linking the forgiveness granted in the past to that offered in the present. God offers in the present a *tempus gratiae et reconciliationis* in which to turn again to God. Three key ideas, each familiar in itself—people's hope in Jesus Christ, God's gift that enables them to serve all others, while trusting more fully in the Holy Spirit—are linked more by way of association than by consequence with the lead phrase *tempus gratiae et reconciliationis*. In a surprising change (or perhaps a typographical error in the Latin?) *respirare* has been

[3] The previous *editio typica* uses the somewhat richer verb *provocare* instead of *incitare*.

[4] See Power, 411 above.

[5] Consult the index of this volume, s.v., *caritas*.

[6] On the history of this text and its various versions, see McCarron, 457–61 above.

changed to *sperare*; while "to hope in Christ Jesus" is entirely appropriate, "to breathe in Christ Jesus" alluded to the Holy Spirit and introduced brilliantly evocative prayer language.

The final sentence (*Et ideo*, lines 30–34) bursts forth rather unexpectedly in strong images of joy and praise leading into the *Sanctus*. Here, as in several other places in EP RI, the word order is markedly different from the previous version, and multiple words have been replaced (e.g., *extollimus* in line 31, instead of the previous *exaltamus*).

Post-*Sanctus* (*OM2008*, appendix, no. 2)

The post-*Sanctus* opens with a more elaborate address: *Vere Sanctus es, Domine* instead of the simple, even flat, *Deus*, followed by a statement about the human race (*homo*) in the third person. The statement has grammatically rearranged the Latin from the 1983 version, but this does not obscure the profound beauty of the idea that God has, from the beginning of the world, arranged that humanity should become holy, just as God is holy—a poetic reiteration of the *Sanctus* as well as a striking affirmation of human dignity.

Epiclesis (*OM2008*, appendix, no. 3, lines 2–9)

The introduction to the epiclesis over the bread and wine has been rewritten so that the simple gifts presented by the people (*dona* in the 1983 version) have become *munera*, a much weightier designation allied with duty. God is asked to look, not upon the people gathered here (*populum tuum hic adunatum*), but upon the gifts themselves. The prayer is for the power of the Spirit to be poured out upon the gifts, not—as implied in the construction of the original Latin—upon the people, in order that the (people's) gifts may become the Body and Blood of Jesus Christ. This shift is translated somewhat ambiguously as "Look, we pray, upon your people's offerings and pour out on them," leaving open what "them" references. The substitution of *virtus* for *potentia* in *OM2008* sets up a near-parallel between *amoris virtutem* in the Preface (line 31) and *Spiritus tui virtutem* here. The otherwise remarkable thematic consistency of EP RI has been interrupted here in favor of the functional act of calling down the Spirit over the gifts.[7]

[7] Alan F. Detscher, "The Eucharistic Prayers of the Roman Catholic Church," in *New Eucharistic Prayers: An Ecumenical Study of their Development and Structure*, ed. Frank C. Senn (New York and Mahwah, NJ: Paulist Press, 1987), 43.

Introduction to Institution Narrative (*OM2008*, appendix, no. 3, lines 10–19)

The introduction to the institution narrative and consecration introduces the idea that "we," the people, were once lost (as were the Israelites during their wanderings in the desert) and unable to find (here, *appropinquare*, "approach") God. Both the previous and the present EP RI speak of the *summo amore* with which God loves us. While "highest love" would work well metaphorically to express a love transcendent to all others, the English text evades this nuance: "greatest love" in ICEL2010 ("you loved us more than ever," in ICEL's original 1975 translation). The ensuing independent clause (*Filius enim*, lines 13–15) brings together striking images: the Just One who surrenders to death, the wood of the cross, and the element of atonement theology, "for us."

Equally arresting is the visual image that on the cross the arms of Jesus were *inter caelum et terram extenta efficerentur* (lines 17–18). This image comes directly from several versions of ApTrad,[8] although the corresponding passage in EP II refers only to Christ's voluntary suffering (*OM2008*, no. 102, line 3). Christ's agency in his own crucifixion is left in question here because of the passive voice (*efficerentur*); this is the case in the *OM2008* but not in ICEL's previous translation ("Yet before he stretched out his arms between heaven and earth"). This powerful image evokes both the christological and cosmic dimensions of reconciliation, yet at the same time the assembly is required to shift its understanding very quickly from this poignant combination of the historical and metaphorical to the Last Supper narrative, which can be heard as a historical account of a Passover meal. Nonetheless, the image of Christ stretching out his arms between (i.e., in order to reconcile) heaven and earth is richly metaphoric—as we do not live on a flat earth, and "heaven and earth" are not fundamentally spatial concepts.

Two other linked concepts enrich what in other EPs is a more concise introduction to the institution narrative and consecration: covenant (here *foedus*) and the Passover meal (*Pascha*). A biblical link, not brought out in the text of EP RI, could draw a line between the image of Christ's arms outstretched between heaven and earth, and the rainbow given to Noah as

[8] Specifically, the Latin and Ethiopic versions and the *Testamentum Domini* all make reference to the arms of Jesus stretched out to suffering in order to release his people in turn from their suffering. See Paul Bradshaw, Maxwell Johnson, and L. Edward Phillips, *The Apostolic Tradition: A Commentary*, ed. Harold W. Attridge, *Hermeneia* series (Minneapolis: Fortress Press, 2002), 38–40.

a (cosmic) sign of the eternal covenant (Gen 9:12). In this three-part sentence (lines 16–19) the attention moves from a cosmic-visual image of the crucifixion as reconciliation to the covenant to a fairly flat narrative about Jesus' wish to eat a final meal with his disciples. This third part provides the immediate introduction to the institution narrative.

Anamnesis-Offering (*OM2008*, appendix, no. 7, lines 2–7)

The anamnesis makes a second reference to the *Pascha*, this time expanded and identified with the person and redemptive act of Christ, who is called not only "our Passover" but also *pax nostra certissima*—"our certain peace." The idea that the act of sacrifice creates peace requires some comment. The founding account of the Passover in Exodus 12 says nothing about the sacrifice of the lambs causing peace but rather liberation from slavery in Egypt. Paul in 1 Corinthians 5:7 calls Christ "our Pasch" but speaks of the "unleavened bread of sincerity and truth" (*azumois eilikrineias kai alētheias*, 5:8), not peace. In Ephesians 2:14 Christ is called "our peace" (*autos gar estin ē eirēnē ēmōn*), the one who has reconciled Jewish and Gentile followers of Christ through his death on the cross, specifically by abolishing the Law. The question of whether the Eucharist functions as a propitiatory sacrifice to appease the wrath of a just God by recalling the sacrifice of an innocent victim who offers himself to be killed, thus bringing peace, has been greatly nuanced by a number of Catholic theologians with much work yet to be done. Theologians have recast the language and concept of sacrifice attached to the Eucharist in a specifically trinitarian interpretation as the generous self-offering of the Father that calls forth a response from the Son and a correlated response from all Christians,[9] or have pointed to the sacrifice of Christ as a rupture in the cycle of violence and thus antisacrificial,[10] or have spoken instead of a model of exchange, "gift-reception-return gift."[11] Significant evidence from anthropological research identifies the act of sacrifice cross-culturally as a male ritual to ratify patrilineal succession and to supersede the female act of giving birth.[12] Questions

[9] Robert J. Daly, *Sacrifice Unveiled: The True Meaning of Christian Sacrifice* (New York: Continuum, 2009); also, Edward Kilmartin, *The Eucharist in the West*, ed. Robert Daly (Collegeville, MN: Liturgical Press, 1998).

[10] Mary Barbara Agnew, "A Transformation of Sacrifice," *Worship* 61, no. 6 (1987): 493–509.

[11] Louis-Marie Chauvet, *The Sacraments: The Word of God at the Mercy of the Body* (Collegeville, MN: Liturgical Press / Pueblo, 1997), 133–45.

[12] Nancy Jay, *Throughout Your Generations Forever: Sacrifice, Religion and Paternity* (Chicago: University of Chicago Press, 1992).

raised by Roman Catholic theologians about the symbolism of blood or the exclusion of women from contact with the Holy, as well as broader androcentric presuppositions that lie under the surface, are creating new theological trajectories that can potentially transform our understanding of Eucharist.[13]

Epiclesis (*OM2008*, appendix, no. 7, lines 8–13)

The opening address in this epiclesis (*Respice, benignus, clementissime Pater*) marks a softening of tone: God is now addressed in tender terms expressing an abject plea on the part of the community. Here again the sequence of thoughts does not flow quite logically, although each phrase makes sense as a component on its own. A third reference to *virtus*, here the power of the Holy Spirit named as such, expands the references in the preface and the introduction to the epiclesis over the gifts. A significant and understandable change in this text is the addition of *in Christo* (line 12), making clear that Christians may be gathered into one Body, free of division, precisely in Christ. The reference to *divisio*, reinforces the common thematic thread of reconciliation throughout this prayer.

Intercessions (*OM2008*, appendix, no. 7, lines 14–28)

At this point the explicit theme of reconciliation fades in prominence while the functional elements of the intercessions come forward. Yet, consistent with its theme, EP RI echoes motifs found in EP II—praying that the full communion *mentis et cordis* of all the church be made visible so that the Eucharist may truly become a sacrament of unity.[14] Praying that the community may wait expectantly together (but not, as in the earlier translation, "work together"), for the coming of the reign of God echoes faintly the theme of oneness. In a fine expression recalling "be holy, for I am holy" (Lev 11:44), the community prays to become *sancti inter sanctos* (note it is capitalized in ICEL2010 as "Saints among the Saints," in heaven).

[13] Authors include Susan A. Ross, *Extravagant Affections: A Feminist Sacramental Theology* (New York: Continuum, 1998); Elizabeth Johnson, *She Who Is: The Mystery of God in Feminist Theological Discourse* (New York: Crossroad, 1992); Elisabeth Schüssler Fiorenza, *Jesus: Miriam's Child, Sophia's Prophet* (New York: Continuum, 1995); and Kristin De Troyer et al., eds., *Wholly Woman Holy Blood: A Feminist Critique of Purity and Impurity* (Harrisburg, PA: Trinity Press International, 2003).

[14] Here the prayer flows directly from the prayer for unity in the epiclesis and follows the thought of EP II, that the Eucharist should become the sacrament of unity in the church. See Pahl, "Das erste Versöhnungshochgebet," 359–60.

In a circumlocution suggesting that Christ has freed us from bodily death and decay (*a corruptionis vulnere liberati*,[15] line 24), the specter of the always difficult to explain resurrection of the body sets up the closing hymn of praise. This final strophe, though again marked by a tenuously integrated sequence of thought, provides a joyous crescendo leading into the doxology.

Summary

The brokenness and conflict from which humanity seeks healing and reconciliation in this EP is located largely within the Christian community's relationship to God in and through Christ. The prayer expresses hope that all of humanity may be made holy and reconciled to God in Christ without reference to the need for reconciliation among persons, groups, and nations. Its primary focus is on reconciliation between God and humanity, which contrasts with the more global scope of EP RII. The community itself appears considerably more receptive than active. The strongest thematic elements of this EP are the hoped-for unity within the church community and, in return, a restored relationship of the community with God in Christ, accomplished by the power of the Holy Spirit.

[15] This can be found in *Iesu corona virginum*, a hymn text ascribed to Ambrose and used for Vespers in the Common of Virgins. Paul Turner, "Formation for Eucharist: Eucharistic Prayer for Reconciliation," *Celebrate!* 49, no. 5 (Sept.–Oct. 2010): 15.

Excursus on the Eucharistic Prayers for Reconciliation

Anscar J. Chupungco

The two EPs for reconciliation are not the best examples of Latin euchology. They are not literary pieces that even attempt to imitate the style of the more classic Roman prayers. There is a noticeable absence of rhetorical devices like binary succession, symmetry, antithesis, and conciseness that make the Latin orations—especially the prefaces—a delightful read. Like EP IV, also a new composition, these texts recount at length the history of God's relationship with humankind. But the similarity ends there. The Latin EP IV is elegant, stylish, and pleasant to the ears, because of the choice of words, symmetry in the sentence construction, and the balance in the length of each line.

Content-wise, EPs RI and RII are quite disappointing. Sentences are not brimming with profound doctrine, and their literary quality is not arresting enough to make them memorable. There are no references to the gospel stories of forgiveness or to the parables that illustrate God's compassion toward repentant sinners. These EPs would have been perfect occasions to translate into prayer the parables of the prodigal son, the lost sheep, and the lost coin. In this regard, EP IV is a model of biblical quotations and allusions.

The literary poverty and the scarce doctrinal content of these two EPs do not augur well for literary vernacular translations. Nonetheless, in 1975 ICEL was able to produce a satisfactory version that is literary, suited for proclamation, and easy to comprehend. That was because the method of translation employed by ICEL in 1975 was dynamic equivalence, which the 1969 principles of translation (*CLP*) had endorsed. It does not translate word for word or phrase by phrase but according to the sense or message of the source document. A textual analysis of the 1975 translation leads us to conclude that the rearrangement of lines, moderate amount of elaboration, and the use of dynamic equivalence do not intrude upon the intended message of the Latin text. After the publication of *LitAuth*, however, all this has become moot and academic.

LitAuth is of the persuasion that literal translation is the best way to preserve the doctrine that the Latin text tries to communicate to the faithful of today. For this reason, conferences of bishops were encouraged to do a new translation of the entire corpus of *MR2002* independently of the existing translations, which were sometimes branded as new compositions rather than translations because they employ dynamic equivalence.

The following essay and the subsequent essay on EP RII are not meant to cast doubt on the authority of *LitAuth*. Its intention is to point out how some instances of literal translation could have been more faithful to the Latin original if this had been read and analyzed more stringently. The errors are, to be sure, nothing earthshaking. Actually, several of them are minor, even negligible, but, put together, the large number of them can be annoying.

The problem, however, is deeper. When the original text is deficient in content and literary style, literal translation is bound to be equally deficient in content and literary style. Dynamic equivalence may do the trick, but *dura lex, sed lex*.

EP RI

The ICEL2010 Translation

Anscar J. Chupungco

Introduction

EPs RI and RII position themselves significantly between Paul VI's apostolic constitution *Paenitemini* (February 1966) and John Paul II's post-synodal exhortation *Reconciliatio et Paenitentia* (December 1984). Those were twenty years of intensive drive by the hierarchy to reawaken among the faithful the spirit of penance as a way of life and to promote the sacrament. Although these EPs are strongly recommended for use during the season of Lent, they are a timely yearlong reminder that the church is permanently in need of penance.

Except for some traditional elements like the opening dialogue, the *Sanctus*, the institution narrative, and the doxology, these EPs are new Latin compositions. By and large there is a noticeable attempt on the part of the drafters to blend them with the medieval texts that make up the largest section of the *MR2002*. Every now and then, however, one catches instances of Latinized phrases typical of modern Latin. This makes the work of vernacular translation relatively easier. For example, the words *in medio nostri* (post-*Sanctus* of EP MVN I) appear like a literal translation of the Italian *in mezzo a noi*. The Latin *medium*, however, unlike *apud* (in our midst), connotes material space rather than rapport.

As we shall have occasion to note, some texts of these new Latin EPs are a mouthful not only in length but also in the number of thoughts compressed into a single sentence. This makes literal translation that undertakes to render the original text word by word and to reproduce in the vernacular the Latin syntax a daunting exercise.

The Opening Dialogue (ICEL2010, appendix, no. 1, lines 1–6)[1]

The Roman and Oriental liturgies introduce the EP with this ancient dialogue between the priest and the assembly. In the Oriental tradition

[1] Also, see Ostdiek, 279–80 above.

there are slight textual variations, but the overall effect is the same. The priest invites the assembly to raise their hearts (*sursum corda*) in thanksgiving (*gratias agamus*) to God so that they may join the angels in their triumphant hymn before God's throne. ApTrad, traditionally attributed to Hippolytus of Rome,[2] carries the wording whose Latin version became the standard text of the opening dialogue in the Roman Canon and the new EPs.

For a commentary on "And with your spirit," see my work above.[3]

"It is right and just" (line 6)*:*

The Latin text is the equivalent of the Greek *áxion kaì díkaion*: it is a worthy and proper thing to do. *Dignum est* is a classical Latin phrase to signify the worthiness of an action or a thing. ICEL2010 is short and succinct like the original. The word "right," however, includes not only the sense of doing the correct thing in relation to God but also the nuanced meaning of *dignum*: God deserves to be thanked. Likewise, the word "just" takes account of what the words *iustum* and *díkaion* imply: we do what is righteous when we thank God. In a word, our act of thanking God in the Eucharist is worthy of him (*dignum*) and has a sanctifying or justifying (*iustum*) effect on us.

ICEL1973 elaborated the word *dignum*, but in the process it left out *iustum*: "it is right to give him thanks and praise." It is interesting to note that the Byzantine anaphora of St. John Chrysostom expands *áxion kaì díkaion*: "It is right and just to worship the Father, the Son, and the Holy Spirit, the consubstantial and undivided Trinity."

Preface (ICEL2010, appendix, no. 1, lines 7–34)

"almighty and eternal God" (line 9)

This is a minor grammatical observation. There is a tendency when translating the Latin phrase *omnipotens aeterne Deus* to insert "and" between "almighty" and "eternal." The adjective *omnipotens* defines *aeterne Deus*: eternal God who is almighty.

As noted previously,[4] ICEL2010 has introduced a new English orthography presumably for a more sacral effect. It frequently uses the capital letter, even when the Latin uses the lowercase: Priest, Sign of the Cross,

[2] On this attribution, see Baldovin, 311–12 above.

[3] Chupungco, 137–38 above.

[4] See 137 above.

Entrance Chant, Penitential Act, and so on. In this EP every noun referring to Christ is in the upper case: Death, Cross, Resurrection, blessed Coming, Kingdom. The overall effect is distracting.

"Never did you turn away from us" (lines 16–18)

A literal rendering of the Latin text should be: "Never turning away from us who time and again broke your covenant, you bound the human family to yourself." ICEL2010 wrongly joins the clause *qui foedus tuum . . . violavimus* to the main clause *humanam familiam . . . iunxisti*. The translation of the clause "with a new bond of love so tight that it can never be undone" is awkward. To "undo a bond" is an unusual expression in English to mean dissolution of a bond or the breaking of a chain (*vinculum dissolvi*).

"as they turn back to you in spirit" (line 24)

ICEL2010 freely translates *animum* (in the accusative case, the direct object of *convertenti*) with the prepositional phrase "in spirit," which renders weakly the doctrine about the conversion of the whole person rather than merely a conversion "in spirit." The Latin *animus*, which is the seat of human mind and reason, can be rendered correctly as "heart," suggesting the translation "conversion of heart" as appropriate here.

"we join in the heavenly hymn of countless hosts" (line 33)

Caelestium is the genitive plural of *caelestis*. Here is it used as a substantive adjective ("of the heavenly beings" or simply "of heaven"). Its position between *innumeris* and *turbis* indicates that it defines *innumeris turbis* (countless hosts), not *hymnum*. Hence the text should read: "with the countless hosts of heaven we sing the hymn."

Sanctus (ICEL2010, appendix, no. 1, lines 35–39)

There were two versions of the Latin *Sanctus* in *MR2002*. The first was in EPs I–IV; the second was in the EP RI–II and EP MVN. In the former the third *Sanctus* was joined to *Dominus*. In the latter a comma separated the third *Sanctus* from *Dominus Deus Sabaoth*. This punctuation mark intimates that the *Trisagion* or the "Thrice Holy" (in its simplest and primitive form) is an independent component of the acclamation rather than a mere adjective that describes God. While the gray book of 2007 included the comma, it was removed in the 2008 amended version of the *editio tertia* and is not in *OM2008*. It is noteworthy that the Latin puts the three *Sanctus*es in capitals, thereby suggesting that they are not simple modifiers: they stand on their own. In all other instances divine adjectives in Latin are in the lower key.

Reginald Heber's nineteenth-century lyric for the hymn "Holy, holy, holy! Lord God Almighty!" interprets perfectly the syntactic structure of the *Sanctus*. In compliance with the norms of formal correspondence advocated by *LitAuth*, the English *Sanctus* for EP RI in ICEL2010 ("Holy, Holy, Holy, Lord God of hosts") appropriately corrects its 2007 gray book translation of this prayer (Holy, Holy, Holy is the Lord God of hosts).

The *Sanctus* became an integral part of the Roman Canon in the first half of the fifth century. It traces parentage from the Antiochene anaphora whose *Sanctus* consists of two parts. The first ("Holy, holy, holy") is taken from Isaiah 6:13, while the second ("Blessed is he who comes") is from Matthew 21:9. Crucial to exact translation is how to render the Hebrew words *Yahweh Sabaoth*. The Latin Vulgate translates them as *Dominus exercituum* ("Lord of armies"). Surprisingly, the Latin liturgical version retains *Sabaoth*. However, it affixes *Deus* to *Dominus*, as the Clementine Vulgate does, so that the phrase reads *Dominus Deus Sabaoth*.

ICEL1973 avoided the martial or combative nuance of the word "hosts" by the nonmilitary, neutral phrase "God of power and might." Unfortunately, it fails to communicate the prophet Isaiah's vision of *Yahweh Sabaoth*, the Lord of the heavenly armies. ICEL2010's "God of hosts" is closer to the mark. "Hosts," meaning an army, is archaic, though it possesses literary quality. Its meaning may not be obvious to many.[5] "God of heavenly hosts" could be a neat solution, except that it would not pass for a literal translation.

Institution Narrative over the Bread (ICEL2010, appendix, no. 4)

"Take this, all of you, and eat of it" (line 10)

The rubrical note for the words of institution reminds the priest to pronounce clearly and distinctly "the words of the Lord" as the nature of these words requires. Something similar may be said regarding their translation: they should be rendered in the receptor language as closely as possible to the source language. This is one occasion when literal translation might be necessary, provided the grammar, syntax, and meaning of the original text are correctly understood and interpreted and no violence is inflicted upon the grammar of the receptor language.

We deal here with the formula of the eucharistic institution in the EP. It is in Latin. It does not correspond entirely to any of the Latin Vulgate's formulas of institution in Matthew 26:26-28; Mark 14:22-24; Luke 22:19-20; and 1 Corinthians 11:23-25. It appears that the liturgical version of the words

[5] See Ostdiek, 280 above.

that Christ pronounced over the bread and the cup at the Last Supper had a life of its own, as do the four biblical versions.

The Latin formula for the bread is *Accipite et manducate ex hoc omnes*. Its literal translation is "Take and eat of this, all [of you]." The formula is straightforward. It echoes the simplicity of Matthew's account, "Take and eat; this is my body." *Accipite* does not even have an explicit object. The prepositional phrase *ex hoc* (of this) after *manducate* does not appear in any of the institution narratives. The discourse on the bread of life (John 6:48-51), however, uses it: *ex 'autou* and *ek toutou tou 'artou*, which the NRSV renders respectively as "eat of it" (6:50) and "eats of this bread" (6:51), while the NABRE has "eat it" and "eats this bread," respectively.

ICEL1973's version, "Take this, all of you, and eat it," is elegant and well designed for public proclamation as befits the solemn sacred formula. It is not a literal translation, but it effectively communicates in the receptor language the message of the original text. It does honor to the method of dynamic equivalence. Except for the insertion of the preposition "of" ("eat of it") to comply with the norms of *LitAuth*, ICEL2010 adopts its predecessor's version instead of doing a more literal translation: "Take and eat of this, all of you."

"for this is my Body, which will be given up for you" (lines 11–12)

In Latin liturgical usage, *tradere* is often the language of betrayal and sacrifice. We recall the stunning words of the *Exsultet* (*Ut servum redimeres, filium tradidisti*, lit., "In order to ransom a slave, you handed over your Son"). Likewise, EP II (*Qui cum Passioni voluntarie traderetur, OM2008*, no. 102), EP III (*Ipse enim in qua nocte tradebatur, OM2008*, no. 110), and EP IV (*in mortem tradidit semetipsum, OM2008*, no. 117) employ the verb *tradere* to call attention to the appalling mystery of Christ's being betrayed and handed over to a violent death. Both ICEL1973 and ICEL2010 translate *tradetur* with "given up." Whether this English verb sufficiently carries the weight of the Latin is open to discussion. ICEL2010 is correct to translate *enim* (for), which is the conjunction that corroborates the previous statement.

Institution Narrative over the Cup (ICEL2010, appendix, no. 5)

"Take this, all of you, and drink from it, for this is the chalice of my Blood" (lines 11–12)

The preceding commentary (no. 4, lines 11–12) applies, *mutatis mutandis*, to this text. ICEL2010 uses "chalice" in place of "cup" in a bid to uphold the liturgy's sacral language.[6] "Cup" is regarded as being too secular for worship, while "chalice" has been hallowed by liturgical usage and hence belongs to the sacred vocabulary. For some reason ICEL2010 shifts back to "cup" in the second acclamation after the institution narrative: "When we eat this Bread and drink this Cup," although the Latin has *calicem*.

"which will be poured out for you and for many" (line 14)

The Latin verb *effundere* can mean "pour out" or "shed." The English phrase "to pour out" does not always include the condition of hurt or pain and can simply mean to empty out. It familiarly means expressing volubly and at length one's thoughts or feelings of anger or sorrow. Unlike the verb "to shed" (shed tears, shed blood), "to pour out" does not necessarily suggest sacrifice or suffering.

In the context of the Last Supper of Jesus, *effundere* has a decidedly sacrificial undertone, which should not be passed over in translation. ICEL1973 was correct in rendering it with the strong verb "to shed" ("It will be shed for you and for all"). It is unfortunate that ICEL2010 opted for the less specific verb "to pour out," unmindful of its possible negative impact on the theology of eucharistic sacrifice.

On 17 October 2006 the CDWDS sent a letter to the presidents of the conferences of bishops regarding the translation of *pro multis*. It directed them to correct the current translation "for all," because the Latin text says "for many." It affirmed that the phrase "for many" is the exact translation, while "for all" is not a translation but a catechetical explanation of the words Jesus pronounced over the cup.

The biblical sources of *pro multis* are Matthew 26:28 (*perì pollon*) and Mark 14:24 (*hyper pollon*); Luke 22:20 and 1 Corinthians 11:25 do not insert the phrase. The EP in ApTrad omits it. Daniel Harrington explains that the phrase *hyper pollon* in Mark "means for all, not just for a few." He cites as the basis for Mark and Matthew the words of Second Isaiah 53:12: the Servant by his suffering "Bore the sins of many." "Many" is a collective, not restrictive, word: it means "all."[7]

Biblical exegete Albert Vanhoye points out that the corresponding Hebrew word *rabim* indicates a great number without specifying whether it includes many or all. According to him, in the Hebrew *rabim* there is no dialectic opposition between "many" and "all," which is not the case with modern languages like English where these words are not mutually inclu-

6 See Ostdiek, 287 above.

7 Daniel Harrington, "The Gospel according to Mark," NJBC, 41:95.

sive. Vanhoye reminds us that the intention of Jesus at the Last Supper was not directed to a specific group of people, however numerous: his intention as the Savior of the world was universal.[8] Whether or not everyone will welcome Jesus' universal offer of salvation ultimately depends on human freedom. In a word, "all" does not imply that every individual person will automatically be saved.

The ICEL2010 "for many" is a literal translation that takes no account of the biblical *rabim*. It ignores the exegetical context of the words Jesus pronounced at the Last Supper. In effect, it limits the universal offer of salvation.

It is worthy of note, however, that the aforementioned letter of the congregation admits that "indeed, the formula 'for all' would undoubtedly correspond to a correct interpretation of the Lord's intention expressed in the text. It is a dogma of faith that Christ died on the Cross for all men and women." Nevertheless, it is not a "faithful translation of *pro multis*" but "rather an explanation of the sort that belongs properly to catechesis."

We can reverse the observation of the 2006 letter of the CDWDS: the phrase "for all" is the exact translation, while "for many" is not a translation but a catechetical explanation. We can only hope that when the priest pronounces the words "for many," everyone in the assembly will realize that what they hear is not what the priest is saying. In the entire corpus of the ICEL2010 Order of Mass, this is probably the most regrettable example of a slavish application of literal translation.

Anamnesis (ICEL2010, appendix, no. 7, lines 2–6)

ICEL2010 translates the adjective *memores* as a noun ("memorial"). The result is the clumsy repetition of "we celebrate" in the same sentence: "Therefore, as we celebrate the memorial of your Son Jesus Christ . . . we celebrate his Death and Resurrection from the dead."

Epiclesis (ICEL2010, appendix, no. 7, lines 10–16)

ICEL2010 takes liberty with the Latin text *in unum corpus congregentur in Christo, a quo omnis auferatur divisio*, whose literal meaning is: "they may be gathered into one Body in Christ, from which may every division be

[8] Cardinal Albert Vanhoye, "Non c'è contrapposizione dialettica tra *pro multis* e *per tutti*," *30Giorni* (2010): 4 (online at http://www.30giorni.it/it/articolo.asp?id=22501; accessed 17 January 2011).

removed." It is obvious that *a quo* refers to *corpus*, not to *Christo*. There can be no division in Christ in the first place. The Latin text does not say that Christ "heals" every division. The verb "to heal" is not a dynamic equivalent, much less a literal translation of *auferatur*. What is prayed for is that all division be eliminated from the community, the body gathered into one in Christ. It is curious that the word "Body" (of the faithful) is capitalized.

Intercessions (ICEL2010, appendix, no. 7, lines 17–33)

"Help us to work together for the coming of your Kingdom" (lines 20–21)

ICEL2010 takes a proactive stand when it prays that we work for the coming of God's kingdom. "Help us to work together for the coming of your Kingdom." That is not, however, what the Latin says. *Praestolari* means "to wait for," although it is to be desired that we work for the coming of God's kingdom as well.

"freed at last from the wound of corruption" (line 28)

The Latin text *a corruptionis vulnere tandem liberati* is a good example of the use of mixed concepts and images. What is "the wound of corruption"? Are we freed from rather than healed of a wound? The 1975 ICEL version translates *corruptionis vulnus* as "shadow of death." The original Latin is, of course, hardly recognizable in it. *Corruptio* can have the transferred meaning of sin: "wound of sin" might be closer to the original phrase and easier to understand.

Doxology (ICEL2010, appendix, no. 8)

This solemn doxology, which concludes the EP, elaborates the ancient formula "Glory to the Father through the Son in the Holy Spirit" by inserting "Through him, and with him, and in him" in reference to Christ and "in the unity of" in reference to the Holy Spirit. The doxology is addressed to almighty God the Father. The punctuation mark is relevant. The Latin text does not put a comma after *Deo*: it reads *Deo Patri omnipotenti* (almighty God the Father), not *Deo, Patri omnipotenti* (God, almighty Father). We come across the same thing in the Latin version of the Gloria: *Deus Pater omnipotens* (*OM2008*, no. 8, line 11). In both instances *omnipotens* describes *Deus* who is *Pater*. ICEL2010 misses this theological refinement of the doxology, as did the 2007 translation of this text ("Through him, and with him, and in him, to you, O God, almighty Father, in the unity of the Holy Spirit, is all honor and glory, for ever and ever") and ICEL1973 ("Through him, with him, in him, in the unity of the Holy Spirit, all glory and honor is yours, almighty Father, for ever and ever") previously.

The Latin formula positions the Holy Spirit after God the Father. This is a semiotic arrangement that relates the three Persons of the Holy Trinity to one another. The ICEL2008 translation and ICEL2010 are on target. On the other hand, ICEL1973 places the phrase "in the unity of the Holy Spirit" after "through him, with him, in him." In effect, this says that it is in the unity of the Holy Spirit that we raise to God the Father the sacraments of Christ's mediating sacrifice.

EP RI

The Mystagogical Implications

Edward Foley

Introduction

Consistently throughout this volume we have presented mystagogy as a form of theological reflection rooted in the liturgical action and liturgical texts. While mystagogical reflections can be offered for the sake of increased understanding on the part of ministers and assembly, the primary reason for pursuing the mystagogical path is to fulfill that central liturgical mandate of Vatican II, i.e., to aid the full, conscious, and active participation of the people (*SC*, no. 14). Such participation is not simply a liturgical exercise, however, but is for the sake of our participation in the *missio Dei*. Active participation in the church's official liturgy rehearses us for active participation in what Karl Rahner called the "liturgy of the world."[1] Thus, mystagogy is less about "information" and more about "formation" for the sake of "transformation."

While every aspect of the eucharistic liturgy holds great promise for such formation and transformation, EPs are particularly rich and pivotal. If the eucharistic liturgy can be reckoned as the summit and fount of the church's life (*SC*, no. 10), we might envision EPs as the "center of the center." While that lofty assessment is theologically sound, it might not be pastorally accurate. Many times the EP is less the center of the active participation of the faithful and more what one researcher called the "dullest part" of the liturgy.[2] While there are many contributing factors for such a perception, one may be that many of the faithful perceive the EP as primarily that liturgical moment when the bread and wine are consecrated into the Body and Blood of Christ. Since most of the faithful do not believe that they have

[1] Karl Rahner, "Considerations on the Active Role of the Person in the Sacramental Event," in *Theological Investigations XIV: Ecclesiology, Questions in the Church, The Church in the World*, trans. David Bourke (New York: Seabury Press, 1976), 169.

[2] John Baldovin, "Pastoral Reflections on the Study," in *The Awakening Church*, ed. Lawrence Madden (Collegeville, MN: Liturgical Press, 1992), 107.

any role in the consecratory act—it is something only the priest does—they often perceive their role during the EP as one of prayerful observation.

From Consecration to Creed

While there is no doubt that the elements of bread and wine are consecrated through the invocation of the Holy Spirit and the institution narrative, the EP is more than a complicated prayer setting for the consecration. At its heart, it is also fundamentally the community's creed, a eucharistic profession of faith. While we did not recite an explicit creed in the Mass of the Roman Rite for the first millennium—as we do not in most weekday Eucharists—that did not mean these were "creed-less" celebrations. The central and original creed in our eucharistic gatherings has traditionally been the great act of thanksgiving, when the pillars of our faith are announced and affirmed—particularly the death and resurrection of the Lord. Thus, GIRM2003 explicitly notes that the meaning of this prayer is that "the entire congregation of the faithful should join itself with Christ in *confessing the great deeds of God* and in the offering of Sacrifice" (emphasis added, no. 78). Inviting the faithful to consider the EP as a pivotal profession of faith not only promotes a richer degree of active participation in that part of the Mass, but also promotes a more profound mode of eucharistic living in light of these central beliefs.

Every EP in the Roman Rite, no matter when it was composed, how it is translated, or where it is celebrated, professes basic beliefs. First, in full preface mode, we profess that it is a just and proper act to give thanks and praise because of the preemptive love of a Creator who has never turned away from us, even though we have broken God's covenant. In the first eucharistic acclamation we admit not only that God is holy but that God's holiness permeates "heaven and earth"; consequently, we are prompted to care for and respect sister earth and all of creation. In the first prayer for the Holy Spirit (consecratory epiclesis) we not only affirm that it is by the Spirit's power that earthly gifts are transformed into heavenly gifts but more fundamentally announce that the Holy Spirit is present to us, the church, and the world in a dynamic way. In the institution narrative we confess that the bread and wine have become the Body and Blood of Christ, in the hope that the baptized might become the same. At the "mystery of faith," we announce the great summary of the paschal creed, soon made explicit in the anamnesis or solemn remembering. This remembering is always linked to offering: both Christ's eternal offering perfectly revealed in human history in his dying and rising, as well as our own self-offering as affirmed by *SC*, which defines the eucharistic event (like every liturgy) as an action of Christ, head and members (no. 7). The second Spirit prayer (communion epiclesis) admits that the same God-act that transformed gifts of creation and work of human hands into the Body and Blood of Christ is at work transforming the baptized "into one Body in Christ." In the final intercessory prayers for the living and the dead, we profess ourselves an ecclesial communion of heart and mind, living and dead, sinful and purified. The doxological climax brings this eucharistic believing to a final act of eucharistic praising in full trinitarian mode.

Reconciling Beliefs

Besides these central and repeated professions of faith at the center of all EPs, each prayer also articulates particular aspects of believing and the living out of God's mission in our lives. While there are innumerable creedal ways we could interrogate every EP, we will employ three in considering EP RI. First of all, how does this EP define reconciliation? Second, who are the agents of reconciliation? Finally, what does this reconciling lens reveal about the very nature of the eucharistic action this prayer serves?

Defining Reconciliation

EP RI provides a sweeping vision of reconciliation: as sweeping as Jesus' summation of the whole law in the injunction to love God and our neighbor (Mark 12:30-31). Reconciliation is clearly turning back to God (preface: "Even now you set before your people a time of grace and reconciliation . . . as they turn back to you"), having our sins forgiven (institution narrative: "for the forgiveness of sins"), and being "freed . . . from the wound of corruption" (transition to final doxology). Being reconciled with God, however, is only half of the vision of healing and peace proclaimed in this prayer. Equally important (cf. Matt 22:39) is our communion with each other—and the "other" here is strikingly defined. Certainly there is an *ad intra* ecclesial image here that we are to be "in communion of mind and heart, together with N. our Pope and N. our Bishop." Such communion is not merely cognitive assent to official teachings but, in the language of the preface of EP RII, an exercise of "mutual respect." Given all of the public discord within the church, including sometimes polarizing debates about the very translation of the new Roman Missal, this image of communion, mutual respect, and peace at the very heart of our eucharistic action is chastening.

What may be even more shocking here, however, is the very broad *ad extra* mandate for reconciliation embedded in this prayer. While turning back to God is critical, we are also challenged "to be of service to all" (preface). The "all" envisioned in this prayer is not only the baptized but—as explicated in the preface—the whole "human family" that is bound to God through Christ. This broad reconciling vision is echoed in the anamnesis when we recall how Jesus Christ reconciles "the human race" to God. Given the theological debate about the translation of *pro multis* as "for many" in the institution narrative,[3] there is mystagogical delight in discovering that EP RI invites us to profess not only that Christ's reconciling living, dying, and rising is for all humankind but that those who take on Christ in baptism are similarly called to a reconciling embrace with every "other" human being—no matter what "race" or "tongue" (EP RII, no. 7, line 24), gender or religion.

There are ecological overtones in this prayer as well, prompting us to think of reconciliation as an appropriate stance toward nature. The pre-institution narrative metaphor of Jesus stretching out his arms "between heaven and earth" as "the lasting sign" of God's covenant with us can be interpreted as symbolizing that the entire universe is under the reconciling power of the new covenant in Christ.[4] In the "Holy" we sing that the heavens and earth are full of God's glory, reminiscent of their primal beauty and goodness at the dawn of creation. Human greed and neglect have contributed to the scarring of sister earth and the growing toxicity of our own biosphere. As EP RI calls all to be a "new creation" (no. 7, line 29), so does it remind us—consonant with the *berakoth* prayers from the preparation of the gifts and the creational chant from the Holy—that we are commissioned to be reconciled not only with God and one another but also with the cosmos, which reflects the holiness of the divinity.

Agents of Reconciliation

EP RI leaves little doubt that reconciliation is first of all something that God does. The preface is especially lavish with images of this divine initiative. It is God who "does not cease to spur us on to possess a more abundant life." "Rich in mercy," God constantly offers pardon and calls "on sinners to trust in [God's] forgiveness alone." One startling aspect of the eternal nature of this sacred enterprise is that, despite humankind's gift for fracturing the covenant and spurning the divine onslaught, God is a Gibraltar of love even though we have jilted God like some she-camel in heat—in the

[3] See especially Chupungco, 480–81 above.

[4] See Roll, 468 above.

words of the Prophet Jeremiah—sniffing about for some other mate in the desert air (Jer 2:23-24).

The creedal euchology is richly trinitarian in its imaging of God's reconciling work. God's merciful engagement with humankind, so amply documented in the preface, is clearly the divine mission of the First Person of the Trinity. God the "Father," however, is not envisioned in this prayer as being the sole divine agent of reconciliation. The Second Person of the Trinity is central to reestablishing harmony with humankind and all of creation. It is "through Jesus" that the new bond of love is established with such steadfastness "that it can never be undone" (preface). The very institution narrative acknowledges that Jesus faced death "knowing that he was about to reconcile all things in himself through his Blood to be shed on the Cross" (no. 5). This stance is echoed in the anamnesis, which acknowledges the Christ as the one who reconciles the human race to God. Finally, it is through the power of the Holy Spirit that earthly gifts are transformed into the Body and Blood of Christ so that the baptized themselves might "be gathered into one Body in Christ" (no. 7, line 15).

Collectively, these reflections about the divine agency in initiating reconciliation announce that the reconciling mission is not only a trinitarian work but also a revelation of the trinitarian essence. EP RI announces gifts of trust, love, service, unity, and communion because these are our inadequate words for the very nature of the Godhead. The Trinity is the ultimate image of reconciliation, because of its uncompromised unity even in its diversity. The very invitation to reconciliation, therefore, is not only to assume some noncombative stance in the world but to become peaceable—even holy—just as God is holy (no. 2, lines 5–6).

While reconciliation is clearly God's initiation and revelatory of the very nature of the Trinity, this prayer does not dispense the community from the hard work of harmony, concord, mutual respect, and love that punctuates the journey from division to holy embrace. Note the active verbs predicated of those who follow Christ. We are to "turn back" to God and "entrust" ourselves to the Holy Spirit (no. 1, lines 24 and 27). As the baptized, who "offer" the "sacrificial Victim" (no. 7, lines 7–8), we are not simply handing the Crucified and Resurrected Christ back to God but must wed our own sacrifices on behalf of peace and just living to those of Christ. This is made explicit in the intercessions for the living when—admittedly, with God's help—we profess belief in and commitment to working together for the coming of God's kingdom (no. 7, line 21). Effectively, this EP places the ministry of reconciliation at the very heart of Roman Catholic belief. Not the optional endeavor of a few elite volunteers, reconciliation is at the heart of the *Missio Dei* and is thus a defining characteristic of how the baptized must conduct themselves in the world.

Eucharist as Reconciliation

One way to think about the church's liturgy in general or the eucharistic liturgy in particular is that it is a prayerful encounter that "prepares" us to go out and live gospel lives, to go out and be reconcilers and peacemakers. The liturgy of the church not only is a rehearsal for living the "liturgy of the world," however, but is itself to be a reconciling act. Thus, these new[5] EPs for reconciliation point to an ancient belief: the first sacrament of reconciliation has always been the Eucharist. Long before the church was baptizing people for the forgiveness of sins, Jesus was reconciling sinners at table. The one charge leveled at him across the gospel landscape is not that he baptizes sinners, or that he hears their confessions, but rather that he dines with them, he breaks bread with them, he makes Eucharist with them. Consequently, long before the church had evolved to the stage that we were offering penitents one-on-one confession with absolution, the church celebrated the precious reconciling sacrament of Eucharist. Many Roman Catholics have been taught that only baptism or the sacrament of penance are the church's fundamental sacraments of reconciliation. EP RI reminds us, however, that the eucharistic action itself was the aboriginal reconciling ritual for believers who accepted a body broken and a cup poured out for the forgiveness of sins.

This is an especially poignant insight, given all of the controversies and even divisions over the content and style of our eucharistic liturgy, even this new translation of *MR2002*. Mystagogical engagement with these texts—controverted though the translation might be—is an invitation to engage in eucharistic praying and eucharistic living without polemic or prejudice, rancor or rejection. By collectively engaging and praying these texts with peaceable hearts and in mutual respect, the church promises us that such peaceability and mutuality will flourish both within the liturgy of the church and in the liturgy of the world.

[5] See McCarron, 453–63 above.

EP RII
History of the Latin Text and Rite

See Richard E. McCarron, "EP RI and II: History of the Latin Text and Rite," above, pp. 453–63.

EP RII

Theology of the Latin Text and Rite

Susan K. Roll

Originally composed in German[1] and subsequently translated into the Latin *editio typica*, EP RII moves gracefully in tripartite, interlinked rhetorical images. Within the context of the eucharistic liturgy as a whole—in which the *Kyrie eleison*, the introductory dialogue to the EP, and the *Agnus Dei* all shape the verbal rhythm of worship—these tripartite rhythms as they reappear as a rhetorical element in the EP almost create a sense of peace in their very performance. Examples of such tripartite rhythms are twice found in the preface: first with *inimici . . . adversarii . . . populi* (no. 1, lines 17–19) and again with the triple binaries of *odium-amore, ultio-indulgentiae, discordia-mutuam dilectionem* (lines 21–22). A third triplet is found in the post-*Sanctus*, when the Christ is named as *Verbum . . . manus . . . via* (no. 2, lines 5–7). The text embodies what it states: a certain resolution of tension and a coming to rest.

Throughout these literary devices, the predominant motif is that of reconciliation among humankind and, as a consequence, peace as the gift of God through the Spirit. What is remarkable here is the emphasis, right from the first strophe of the preface, on the living and efficacious work of God in our world here and now (no. 1, especially lines 9–11). Songs of praise addressed to God and focused on the present do not appear elsewhere in the Roman liturgical tradition before 1974. This prayer asserts that God is indeed alive and active even in a secular world where God is often experienced as absent.[2] The time and geographical setting for the composition of EP RII was one in which the Iron Curtain still sharply divided Europe with little prospect of reconciliation between the two halves of the continent. While the immediate reason for its composition, the Holy Year 1975, focused

[1] Its composition is attributed to Heinrich Rennings; for a more detailed discussion of this history, see McCarron, 457 above.

[2] Heinrich Rennings, "Votivhochgebet Versöhnung II," in *Gratias Agamus. Studien zum eucharistischen Hochgebet. Festschrift Balthasar Fischer*, ed. Andreas Heinz and Heinrich Rennings (Freiburg: Herder, 1992), 412.

on personal reconciliation in terms of the sacrament of penance—a theme that would come more clearly to the fore in the 1983 Synod on Reconciliation and Penance[3]—the scope envisaged in this prayer is no less than global in nature. This arguably constitutes the real strength of this particular EP. God's gracious mercy is poured out in secular matters as well as religious, on private relationships as well as world crises, and on persons without regard for their individual characteristics or circumstances. God works in the present no less than in the past.

While much of the text for this prayer in *MR2002* remains nearly the same as the original 1974 Latin text, several paragraphs have been edited. In some cases, this amounts merely to a rearrangement of the Latin text that may emphasize one or another component but does not change the underlying meaning. Here and there new Latin text has been added or a word changed. The theological content stands to be affected by these changes, though more implicitly than explicitly.

Preface (*OM2008*, appendix, no. 1, lines 7–25)

One noticeable difference between the 1974 text and that found in *MR2002* appears in the very first line of the preface. *MR2002* begins with a new insertion, *Vere dignum et iustum est*. This echoes the last response of the people (*Dignum et iustum est*) and smoothes the transition into the reason why God is to be praised and thanked: because God alone has the power to make peace by calling forth conversion of mind and heart. The changes in the word order of that first strophe in Latin might point to an intended shift of emphasis:

1974 Text	MR2002
 Tibi, Deus et Pater omnipotens, gratias agimus teque laudamus per Dominum nostrum Iesum Christum, pro operatione tua in mundo.	Vere dignum et iustum est nos tibi gratias agere atque laudes persolvere, Deus Pater omnipotens, pro omnibus, quae in hoc mundo operaris per Dominum nostrum Iesum Christum.

[3] See Chupungco, 475 above.

Pro omnibus, quae in hoc mundo operaris, while a richer expression than *pro operatione tua in mundo*, is almost buried as a sense line as the fourth of five lines of a strophe that ends with the emphasis now on *Dominum nostrum Iesum Christum*. God's involvement in the world proceeds through Jesus, the Christ.

The following paragraph (lines 12–15) employs a rhythmic alliteration that serves to name the evil afflicting all of humankind: *dissensione sit atque discordia divisum*—alliteration well captured in ICEL2010's "divided by dissension and discord." A breath of hope emerges in the next phrase, testifying to human experience and memory as a basis for faith that God, by calling human minds to conversion, will prepare the ground for reconciliation. One might ask, why emphasize the cognitive level (*cognovimus*) when the more usual expression in prayer language would speak of converting hearts: *animos* implies both. In diplomatic relations, economic developments, and military strategies the "head" takes primacy of place, relegating the "heart" to private and personal relations. This formula illustrates that neither is impermeable to God's power.

Each of the following two strophes (lines 16–19 and 20–22) have been constructed with an introductory line referring to God's active work through the Spirit, followed by the previously mentioned triplet parallelisms, each of which names a concrete example of reconciliation drawn from human experience that results from God's initiative and not from human capacities or powers. Line 16 (*Per Spiritum* . . .) makes direct reference to the conversion of human hearts, while the three lines that follow progress from an extreme example (*inimici* . . .) to a more moderate one (*adversarii* . . .) to a mild expression (*populus* . . .) of a movement toward human unity. *Inimici iterum in colloquia veniant* suggests a richer range of occasions for conflict resolution than ICEL2010's "enemies can speak to each other again." Military enemies who cease hostilities and come to the negotiating table is certainly one possible example, but employers and union leaders sitting at the bargaining table is another. ICEL2010's rendering of *adversarii manus coniungant* as "adversaries may join hands" lacks the more explicit image of two persons shaking hands as a greeting, as a pledge of honesty, or as a binding ratification of mutual commitment and promise.[4] The third image (*populi* . . .) is equally vague in Latin and ICEL2010's rendering but does allude to diplomatic relations and makes clear that this prayer emerges from the hard practicalities of this world.

[4] Rennings suggests soccer players from opposing teams shaking hands after a game in his "Votivhochgebet Versöhnung II," 413.

Strophe four (lines 20–22) picks up the same theme but uses three more abstract examples to develop and extend the results of God's active presence. Hatred is overcome by love (*vincatur*, passive voice), revenge gives way to forgiveness (*cedat*, active voice), and discord is transformed (*convertatur*, passive voice) into mutual *dilectio* or "love,"[5] translated here as "respect." While the English word misses the mark as an accurate translation, it strikes a necessary note to support the theological credibility of this strophe. All three of these events hinge on the full mutual respect of the parties involved. Love without respect could lead to condescension. Forgiveness without respect has too often marked the counsel given to abused wives and children: the victim was to forgive the perpetrator and not ask for equal respect.

Sanctus (*OM2008*, appendix, no. 1, lines 26–30)

Because God is not absent but ever present in all aspects of human life and relations today, the people of God join in the eternal hymn of thanksgiving and praise with all of creation, known and unknown, the *Sanctus*.

A significant theological nuance disappears in ICEL2010's rendering of the opening line of the *Sanctus* as "Holy, Holy, Holy Lord God of hosts." While the reference is to the Hebrew *Sabaoth* as the powers of heaven,[6] the original German used in EP RII—and published as a schematic version by the CDW to aid translators[7]—was *Herr aller Mächte und Gewalten*, literally, "Lord of all powers and authorities." This text clearly sets Christ's triumph over every futile earthly claim to dominating power as a precondition to full and true reconciliation. In his resurrection Christ destroys every power and authority, turning them over to God his Father. Only in this way is peacemaking among humans and human institutions and governments possible.[8] In the NT, these earthly powers prevent reconciliation, and we see today too many situations of oppression and exploitation across the globe that thwart any lasting peace. One might recall the words of Paul VI, "If you want peace, work for justice."[9]

[5] See Power, 318–19 above.

[6] Cf. Power's "armies of angels," 265 above.

[7] See McCarron, 459 above.

[8] Rennings, "Votivhochgebet Versöhnung II," 415.

[9] Message for the Celebration of the Day of Peace (1 January 1972), online at http://www.vatican.va/holy_father/paul_vi/messages/peace/documents/hf_p-vi_mes_19711208_v-world-day-for-peace_en.html (accessed 18 January 2011).

Post-*Sanctus* (*OM2008*, appendix, no. 2)

The post-*Sanctus* begins with a transitional sentence that now casts the action of God in terms of the incarnation of the Son of God in Jesus the Christ. A previously noted tripartite enumeration, this time of metaphors for Christ that illustrate God's living presence, follows in a fairly smooth rhythm with striking parallels to the first of the tripartite strophes above:

> *Ipse est pro hominibus Verbum Salutis* (line 5), echoes
> *inimici iterum in colloquia veniant* (no. 1, line 17)
>
> *manus, quam peccatoribus porrigis* (line 6), parallels
> *adversarii manus coniungant* (no. 1, line 18)
>
> *via, qua pax tua nobis praebetur* (line 7), resonates with
> *populi sibi obviam quaerant venire* (no. 1, line 19)

This last parallelism is especially true if *via* is understood more as "path" and not as a "means." Biblically literate hearers of this text might recall Jesus' own triplum "I am the way and the truth and the life" (John 14:6) or the song of Zachariah, "to guide our feet into the path of peace" (Luke 1:79).

"Cum nosmetipsos" (lines 8–12)

This next sentence moves into a reference to salvation history and perhaps especially the prophets of Israel. Newly inserted in *MR2002*'s version is the phrase *propter peccata nostra*: the people, our ancestors and we, turned away from God in a culpable act. God's ceaseless forgiveness contrasts sharply with human sinful resistance and rebellion. The phrase *ut ad te tandem conversi nos invicem diligeremus* sets all forms of human reconciliation in the context of unity with God, while the next sentence (*per Filium tuum, quem in mortem pro nobis tradidisti*) shifts the emphasis to a distinctly Christian and atonement-centered coloration.

Institution Narrative over the Bread (*OM2008*, appendix, no. 4)

A key phrase in the first sentence of the institution narrative—*ut nos liberaret*—appears in both the original Latin text of 1974 and *MR2002*, although ICEL's 1975 translation did not include it; ICEL2010 renders it as "to set us free." While conventional prayer language would suggest freedom from sin and death, the broad context of this particular EP may evoke, for example, associations with freedom from the suffering caused by sinful political repression or economic exploitation.

Anamnesis-Offering (*OM2008*, appendix, no. 7, lines 2–6)

The last line of the anamnesis-offering, *perfectae reconciliationis sacrificium*, adverts in Christian tradition to the death of Christ by the will of his Father. In contemporary society we have learned to be cautious of using "sacrifice" in too facile a manner: soldiers are said to sacrifice their lives for their country and for freedom but all too often do so for political mistakes and diplomatic failures; sacrifices in health, security, and well-being may be asked of poor families but not of the rich. Similarly, there are many theological cautions about the nature of sacrifice and the sometimes inappropriate images of God or discipleship it can convey.[10]

Epiclesis (*OM2008*, appendix, no. 7, lines 7–11)

This prayer for the Spirit *qui omnia auferat quae nos invicem alienant* echoes the line in the preface *Per Spiritum namque tuum permoves hominum corda* (no. 1, line 16) and, in a sense, forms a distant *inclusio*. This is explicitly "his Spirit," that of Christ, and calls for the removal of "everything"—any misunderstandings, grudges, or unforgiven faults—that would prevent the reconciliation of individuals or groups. Again the broad context of this EP further expands the frame of reference for this epiclesis. The opening line of the intercessions, *Ipse Ecclesiam tuam inter homines signum efficiat unitatis pacisque tuae instrumentum*, comes from *LG* (no. 1).

Two frames of reference can be seen at work here: reconciliation, unity, and peace within the church, and in turn the church as a maker of peace in the larger world. This should not be understood in a triumphal manner as if it implies that God can only work through the church. In an eschatological sense this is an expression of hope for what the church might be or might become: a statement of what has been accomplished in the spiritual order by Christ's death and resurrection and what may yet be accomplished on this earth as we move into the future with confidence in God's love.

Commemoration of the Saints (*OM2008*, appendix, no. 7, lines 17–27)

The rich phrasing that closes the commemoration of the saints has been cut short. The familiar English text "gather people of every race, language, and way of life" has been reduced from three dimensions of the diversity

[10] See my commentary, 469–70 above.

of humankind down to two. The original 1974 Latin text *cuiusvis ordinis coetusque, cuiusvis stirpis atque sermonis* has now been changed to *cuiusvis stirpis et sermonis* (line 21, "those of every race and tongue," ICEL2010, line 24). Interestingly, the original German text cites four variables including *Schichten*, social classes or walks of life.[11]

Conclusion

While this EP is situated firmly in the realities of world politics, economics, and social structures, its vision of reconciliation is anything but utopian. Any hope of reconciliation on earth at any national or social level comes from God through the Spirit of Jesus Christ working in human hearts and minds. Humankind does not merely acquiesce passively to this action but is constantly bound up with it, both as those who are called to work for peace and those who praise and thank God from their hearts.

[11] *Wie du uns hier am Tisch deines Sohnes versammelt hast, in Gemeinschaft mit der seligen Jungfrau und Gottesmutter Maria und allen Heiligen, so sammle in der neuen Welt deines immerwährenden Friedens die Menschen aller Schichten und Gruppen, aller Rassen und Sprachen zum Gastmahl der ewigen Versöhnung durch unsern Herrn Jesus Christus.*

EP RII

The ICEL2010 Translation

Anscar J. Chupungco

Introduction

This brief section supplies specific commentaries on particular aspects of the ICEL2010 translation of EP RII. For a general introduction to the EPs for reconciliation, and the challenges of their translation, see my "Excursus on the Prayers for Reconciliation" (473–74 above).

For my specific commentaries on shared elements of these and the other EPs commented on in this volume see my essay, "Eucharistic Prayer for Reconciliation I: The ICEL2010 Translation," which encompasses:

The Opening Dialogue (475–76 above)
Sanctus (477–78 above)
The Institution Narrative (478–81 above)
The Doxology (482–83 above)

The commentary of the elements particular to EP RII now follows.

Preface (ICEL2010, appendix, no. 1, lines 14–15)

ICEL2010's rendering of "yet we know that by testing us you change our hearts" is flawed. The literal sense of the Latin text is: "yet we have known by experience that you change hearts." *Experiendo* is a gerund whose implied subject is that of *cognovimus* (*nos*), not of *flectere*. Had the Latin text intended what the ICEL2010 says, it would have made this construction: *cognovimus tamen te animos experiendo flectere*. In this case, *experior* can have the classical meaning of "to test." As the Latin text stands, however, *experiendo* simply means "by experience": we have known by experience.

Post-*Sanctus* (ICEL2010, appendix, no. 2, lines 2–3)

The Latin opening line here (*Te igitur, Pater omnipotens*) is solemn, like the Roman Canon's classic *Te igitur, clementissime Pater*, which it attempts to reproduce. When this word order, which is peculiar to Latin grammar, is kept in the translation, however, the result is an unusual English sentence construction: "You, therefore, almighty Father, we bless through Jesus Christ."

Commemoration of the Saints and of the Dead (ICEL2010, appendix, no. 7, lines 19–30)

The Latin text is long-winded and can be a real challenge to translate into flowing and comprehensible English. In Latin this is only one sentence; the 1975 ICEL translation divided it into two paragraphs, and ICEL2010 divides it into two sentences but presents it as one paragraph. ICEL2010's first sentence puts the period in the wrong place, however, so that the sentence is left hanging: "Just as you have gathered us now . . . so also bring us together, with the glorious Virgin Mary . . ." [to the unending banquet of unity]. The new English version begins the next sentence repeating the verbal phrase *ita nos collige*: "Bring us to share." On the other hand, the 1975 ICEL original translation of EP RII significantly rearranged the Latin sentence and shortened it by omitting the lengthy commemoration of the saints, except the Blessed Virgin Mary, and the dead. Actually, it is this commemoration that interrupts the flow of the Latin sentence.

Ultimately the problem lies in the Latin text, which is largely devoid of rich theological content and memorable literary quality. ICEL2010 gives us what the Latin says. What EP RII and EP RI say, however, does not echo Paul VI's apostolic constitution *Paenitemini* and John Paul II's post-synod exhortation *Reconciliatio et Paenitentia*.[1]

[1] On the importance of these texts as markers on a twenty-year process of reflection on reconciliation, see my comments 475 above.

EP RII

The Mystagogical Implications

Joyce Ann Zimmerman

A score of countries have established truth and reconciliation commissions that are authorized to deal with grave violations of human rights. The best known and perhaps best model for these commissions was established in 1995 in South Africa by President Nelson Mandela with Archbishop Desmond Tutu after apartheid was abolished in that country. The goal of the commission is the acknowledgment of wrongdoing, reconciliation through forgiveness (some perpetrators were granted amnesty), and a peaceful community.

EP RII might function as a sort of "truth and reconciliation commission" for the liturgical assembly. It too brings us face-to-face with grave violations, not only of human rights, but of divine rights. Acknowledgment of our sinfulness, reconciliation with God and each other, and coming to peace and unity with God and each other are the hallmarks of this prayer.

But why would we have a EP so focused on reconciliation? Is not Eucharist itself the sacrament of reconciliation par excellence?[1] The answers to these questions raise a number of important points for coming to a deeper appropriation of the prayer. Yes, Eucharist is a sacrament of reconciliation because the ritual movement helps us call to mind our sinfulness, to offer ourselves to God in an act of self-giving by uniting ourselves with Christ and his perfect offering of self, and to effect reconciliation because God transforms us through union with Christ's Body and Blood. Although we do not want to dwell unduly on our sinfulness at Mass, acknowledging what estranges us from God is a truth that opens us to God's presence and healing. Further, by making present Jesus Christ's paschal mystery, we ourselves are drawn deeper into this same mystery that we first experienced in the death-dealing and life-giving waters of baptism. Any making memory of Christ's saving deeds invites confession and reconciliation from us. At the same time, Eucharist is a sacrament of peace: it effects what it signifies.

[1] Cf. Foley, 490 above.

Our union with God through Christ in the Holy Spirit is a real experience of the peace that we seek to live in our daily work and leisure.

A EP focused specifically on reconciliation can have a practical import for the community. While every EP at least has a sub-motif of forgiveness and reconciliation, EP RI and EP RII reinforce certain days and seasons that have a particularly penitential aspect to them. So, for example, it would be appropriate to use a reconciliation EP for all the Fridays of the year (except during Easter or if there is a feast or solemnity falling on Friday). Friday is a day of the cross; every Friday we unite ourselves with Christ's ultimate self-giving sacrifice on the cross in preparation for celebrating resurrection every Sunday. Uniting ourselves with Christ's passion and death means that we acknowledge our own actions and attitudes that cry out for redemption. Another example: Lent is the church's season of penitence, and so the EPs for reconciliation are most appropriate for use during this liturgical season. At other times a reconciliation or forgiveness motif in the gospel might suggest the choice of a EP for reconciliation.

There is a clear difference between the penitential act during the introductory rites that have the intent of preparing us to celebrate the sacred mysteries and the acknowledgment of wrongdoing and reconciliation prayed during this EP. Obviously, the EP is no longer preparatory. We are at the heart of the celebration, making a clear proclamation of God's saving deeds on our behalf. The movement toward reconciliation captures our movement toward God. Reconciliation opens us to God's grace-gift being offered, helps us embrace God's presence, and sets right our relationship with God and each other. Let us look at how the movement from acknowledging sinfulness to reconciliation to peace unfolds in the prayer.

Truth: Acknowledgment of Wrongdoing

There is an amazing parallel between the unfolding of reconciliation in the preface for EP RII and the post-*Sanctus* part of the prayer (ICEL2010, appendix, no. 2). This is particularly poignant for its clear acknowledgment of our wrongdoing, which it does by explicating a general condition of the human race rather than specific human acts. The preface begins by naming the "human race" to be "divided by dissension and discord." It invites us to pray about enemies not "speak[ing] to each other" and helps us recognize that sometimes we are adversaries far apart from peace and unity. In perhaps the strongest language, we acknowledge in the preface our "hatred" and propensity for "revenge." After the *Sanctus* we acknowledge that we are sinners and "on account of our sins" have "turned away from" God and each other. Sin is divisive because it alienates. Sin is a disruption in the right relationship we have with God and each other. Sin "estranges us from one another."

This last phrase comes from the second ("communion") epiclesis (no. 7) and is the only mention of sinfulness as we move toward the final doxology. As we make memory of the Son's saving death and resurrection, we offer "the sacrifice of perfect reconciliation." The transformation of ourselves during the prayer is from sinfulness to reconciliation, from estrangement to unity, from discord to peace.

The rupture of our sinfulness is healed by conversion. The preface prays that God "make [our] minds change," a phrase capturing the etymology of the word "conversion." The post-*Sanctus* prayer specifically mentions being "converted to" God. Reconciliation is brought about by God, but we must allow the Holy Spirit to "move human hearts" so that God's grace-gift might wash over us.

Reconciliation: Community

EP RII over and over again mentions love and the Spirit. It is through the Spirit's power at work that "hatred is overcome by love" (no. 1) so that we can once again "love one another" (no. 2). Love is the visible sign of reconciliation. But we are not speaking of mere human love here; we are speaking of the "pledge of [Christ's] love" (no. 7), which is the Holy Spirit. Christ's Spirit is a Spirit of love. It is the work of the Spirit to "take away everything that estranges us from one another" (no. 7) and bring about reconciliation. Restored unity ("peoples seek to meet together," no. 1) and reconciliation ("enemies may speak to each other again," no. 1) are possible because of the power of the Spirit.

The preface (no. 1) comes to a conclusion with a "Therefore." We ceaselessly give [God] thanks on earth because of the reconciliation brought about by God's graciousness, Christ's saving deeds, and the love of the Spirit poured forth into our hearts so that we are moved to "love," "forgiveness," and "mutual respect" (no. 1).

A beautiful image is used twice in this EP to underscore the reconciliation that the prayer seeks. In the preface (no. 1) we pray that the Holy Spirit "move human hearts" so that "adversaries may join hands." The post-*Sanctus* (no. 2) acknowledges that Jesus Christ is "the hand [God] extend[s] to sinners." During Mass we are the Body of Christ extending our hands to each other at the sign of peace. The prayer preceding the invitation to exchange a sign of peace gives us the context for this gesture: it is reminiscent of John 19:21a and 23, a post-resurrection passage where peace and forgiveness are clearly linked. We visibly join hands at the sign of peace, making known by this gesture that the fruit of forgiveness and reconciliation is peace.

Peace: Fruit of Truth and Reconciliation

The word "peace" does not occur in the preface, which at first reading may seem strange. The sentiment is surely not absent, however. At the conclusion of the preface we join our voices to those of the heavenly choir to sing our acclamation to the thrice-holy God. We sing that "Heaven and earth are full of your glory," not unlike the "multitude of the heavenly host" who sang at Jesus' birth "Glory to God in the highest and on earth peace to those on whom his favor rests" (Luke 2:13-14). The first occurrence of the word "peace" comes after the *Sanctus* where God's peace is offered us through Jesus Christ, the hand extended to us.

After the institution narrative the word "peace" occurs twice more. First, we pray for the unity of the church and that the church be "an instrument of [God's] peace among all people" (no. 7). Peace is possible only because of unity, because God "keep[s] us in communion" with God's "entire people" (no. 7). This peace is nothing less than the outpouring of the Holy Spirit to effect reconciliation.

The desire for unity continues as we move toward the great doxology. God has "gathered us now," has brought "us together" in "the unending banquet of unity" (no. 7). Clearly the prayer joins us with all the people "of every race and tongue who have died in [God's] friendship." Friendship is a beautiful image of intimate and abiding relationship, of mutual love and respect, of genuine caring and sharing. The "unending banquet of unity" is the messianic banquet, that eternal feast of God's presence. The prayer uses a line drawn from Revelation 21:1: "a new heaven and a new earth." The context in this last book of the NT is the celebration by all the heavenly hosts of the victory of the Lamb.

Jesus' victory over death is announced by the resurrection. He is the paschal Lamb slain to secure our reconciliation. His promise of our own share in this new, risen life—a life of love and communion—makes clear that the old order has passed away and now we have "a new heaven and a new earth." In this newness of life "the fullness of [God's] peace will shine forth in Christ Jesus our Lord" (no. 7). Here we have a strong eschatological thrust. Perhaps this is the greatest impulse for us to embrace a way of life characterized by reconciliation. What is at stake is even more than unity, peace, and concord in this life. What is at stake is our very salvation, our journey toward a share in the victory of the Lamb, an experience of the glory of new life celebrated for all eternity in the life to come.

All too often our "Amen" response to the great doxology that concludes all EPs is rather unenergetic. As we reflect on the movement through EP RII we ought to be stirred to make our "Amen" response with great zest, with full throat. We are not only affirming God's reconciling, transforming action during this prayer but also expressing our eager anticipation of one day participating eternally in "the unending banquet of unity." One day we will share in the eternal peace of the Lamb. This is the promise of truth and reconciliation.

Conclusion

The full, conscious, and active participation called for by EP RII is truly a *kenosis*, a self-emptying. We pray that "we might love one another through [the] Son, whom for our sake [God] handed over to death" (no. 2). Jesus' *kenosis* led him to the cross but, through his death, to victory over death and being raised to new life. He allowed himself to be "handed over to death" by his "almighty Father." Our own *kenosis* must be a similar self-emptying, a similar faithfulness to God's will. This self-emptying is nothing less than daily self-giving for the sake of others. But a prerequisite for that kind of life-giving self-giving is righteousness—right relationship with God and all others. Embracing a kenotic life means that we first empty ourselves of all "dissension and discord," all hatred and revenge, all that keeps us from loving one another as Jesus loves us. Then can we be filled with the Spirit of Christ, the peace of God dwelling within us.

This kind of reconciling conversion and transformation does not happen once and for all. It is an ongoing openness to the Holy Spirit bringing us to truth and unity. One practical challenge of praying this EP is that it truly calls us to examine our relationships, to ferret out whatever keeps us from loving communion, and humbly to acknowledge our faults and failings. Only with this kind of truth and action can we reach for another's hand in forgiveness, reconciliation, and peace. We only need listen to the nightly news, look at the headlines on an internet site, or read the newspapers to be faced with the overwhelming need for reconciliation in our families, workplaces, cities, nations, and world. This prayer transforms us to make that reconciliation happen.

Reconciliation cannot start with us. Lasting reconciliation begins with deepening our relationship with God. We must remember that reconciliation is always the gift of unity and peace brought about by the action of the Holy Spirit. Jesus' whole life and saving mission was to bring about reconciliation among God's beloved. Our own efforts at reconciliation in a real and concrete way continue Jesus' saving mission. Without constantly seeking reconciliation we are fooling ourselves about being faithful followers of Jesus Christ.

EP RII in its English translation has a poetic ring to it that draws us into the "new heaven and a new earth" that is the promise of reconciliation. Its carefully crafted phrases, parallel images, and short lines are all aids for us to hear and pray with new hearts. It must be prayed with a poetic attitude, freeing us to engage with the images and respond to the gentle invitations that are being opened up to us. If we find ourselves stopping to dwell on a word or phrase that strikes us during Mass, that is fine. The Spirit of love speaks to us profoundly in such pauses. The language of this prayer consists less of imperatives—demands and commands—than language couched in invitation and desire for us to embark on the kind of *kenosis* that promises communion with each other now and a share in the fullness of God's glory and peace to come.

Eucharistic Prayer for Use in Masses for Various Needs

The Latin Text

PREX EUCHARISTICA QUAE IN MISSIS PRO VARIIS NECESSITATIBUS ADHIBERI POTEST

I

Ecclesia in viam unitatis progrediens

1. Sequens forma huius Precis eucharisticae convenienter adhibetur cum formulariis Missarum v. gr. pro Ecclesia, pro Papa, pro Episcopo, pro eligendo Papa vel Episcopo, pro Concilio vel Synodo, pro sacerdotibus, pro seipso sacerdote, pro ministris Ecclesiae, in conventu spirituali vel pastorali.

℣. Dóminus vobíscum.
℟. Et cum spíritu tuo.

℣. Sursum corda.
℟. Habémus ad Dóminum.

℣. Grátias agámus Dómino Deo nostro.
℟. Dignum et iustum est.

Vere dignum et iustum est tibi grátias ágere
tibíque glóriae et laudis hymnum cánere,
Dómine, Pater infinítae bonitátis.

Quia verbo Evangélii Fílii tui,
ex ómnibus pópulis, linguis et natiónibus
unam Ecclésiam collegísti,
per quam, Spíritus tui virtúte vivificátam,
omnes hómines in unum congregáre non désinis.

Ipsa tuae dilectiónis testaméntum maniféstans,
spem beátam regni incessánter largítur
ac véluti signum tuae fidelitátis respléndet
quam in Christo Iesu Dómino nostro,
in aetérnum promisísti.

The English Text

EUCHARISTIC PRAYER FOR USE IN MASSES FOR VARIOUS NEEDS

I

The Church on the Path of Unity

1. The following form of this Eucharistic Prayer is appropriately used with Mass formularies such as, For the Church, For the Pope, For the Bishop, For the Election of a Pope or a Bishop, For a Council or Synod, For Priests, For the Priest Himself, For Ministers of the Church, and For a Spiritual or Pastoral Gathering.

℣. The Lord be with you.
℟. And with your spirit.

℣. Lift up your hearts.
℟. We lift them up to the Lord.

℣. Let us give thanks to the Lord our God.
℟. It is right and just.

It is truly right and just to give you thanks
and raise to you a hymn of glory and praise,
O Lord, Father of infinite goodness.

For by the word of your Son's Gospel
you have brought together one Church
from every people, tongue, and nation,
and, having filled her with life by the power of your Spirit,
you never cease through her
to gather the whole human race into one.

Manifesting the covenant of your love,
she dispenses without ceasing
the blessed hope of your Kingdom
and shines bright as the sign of your faithfulness,
which in Christ Jesus our Lord
you promised would last for eternity.

Et ídeo, cum ómnibus caelórum Virtútibus,
in terris te iúgiter celebrámus,
cum univérsa Ecclésia una voce dicéntes:

Sanctus, Sanctus, Sanctus Dóminus Deus Sábaoth.
Pleni sunt caeli et terra glória tua.
Hosánna in excélsis.
Benedíctus qui venit in nómine Dómini.
Hosánna in excélsis.

2. Sacerdos, manibus extensis, dicit:

Vere Sanctus es et glorificándus,
amátor hóminum Deus,
qui semper illis ades in itínere vitae.
Vere benedíctus Fílius tuus,
qui praesens est in médio nostri
cum ab eius amóre congregámur,
et sicut olim pro discípulis
nobis Scriptúras áperit et panem frangit.

3. Iungit manus, easque expansas super oblata tenens, dicit:

Rogámus ergo te, Pater clementíssime,
ut Spíritum Sanctum tuum emíttas,
qui haec dona panis et vini sanctíficet,

iungit manus
et signat semel super panem et calicem simul, dicens:

ut nobis Corpus et ✠ Sánguis fiant

iungit manus

Dómini nostri Iesu Christi.

4. In formulis, quae sequuntur, verba Domini proferantur distincte et aperte, prouti natura eorundem verborum requirit.

Qui prídie quam paterétur,
in suprémae nocte Cenae,

accipit panem
eumque parum elevatum super altare tenens prosequitur:

accépit panem et benedíxit ac fregit,
dedítque discípulis suis, dicens:

parum se inclinat

And so, with all the Powers of heaven,
we worship you constantly on earth,
while, with all the Church,
as one voice we acclaim:

Holy, Holy, Holy Lord God of hosts.
Heaven and earth are full of your glory.
Hosanna in the highest.
Blessed is he who comes in the name of the Lord.
Hosanna in the highest.

2. The Priest, with hands extended, says:

You are indeed Holy and to be glorified, O God,
who love the human race
and who always walk with us on the journey of life.
Blessed indeed is your Son,
present in our midst
when we are gathered by his love,
and when, as once for the disciples, so now for us,
he opens the Scriptures and breaks the bread.

3. He joins his hands and, holding them extended over the offerings, says:

Therefore, Father most merciful,
we ask that you send forth your Holy Spirit
to sanctify these gifts of bread and wine,

He joins his hands and makes the Sign of the Cross once over the bread and chalice together, saying:

that they may become for us
the Body and ✠ Blood

He joins his hands.

of our Lord Jesus Christ.

4. In the formulas that follow, the words of the Lord should be pronounced clearly and distinctly, as the nature of these words requires.

On the day before he was to suffer,
on the night of the Last Supper,

He takes the bread and, holding it slightly raised above the altar, continues:

he took bread and said the blessing,
broke the bread and gave it to his disciples, saying:

He bows slightly.

ACCÍPITE ET MANDUCÁTE EX HOC OMNES:
HOC EST ENIM CORPUS MEUM,
QUOD PRO VOBIS TRADÉTUR.

Hostiam consecratam ostendit populo, deponit super patenam, et genuflexus adorat.

5. Postea prosequitur:

Símili modo, postquam cenátum est

accipit calicem,
eumque parum elevatum super altare tenens, prosequitur:

accípiens et cálicem,
tibi grátias egit,
dedítque discípulis suis, dicens:

parum se inclinat

ACCÍPITE ET BÍBITE EX EO OMNES:
HIC EST ENIM CALIX SÁNGUINIS MEI
NOVI ET AETÉRNI TESTAMÉNTI,
QUI PRO VOBIS ET PRO MULTIS EFFUNDÉTUR
IN REMISSIÓNEM PECCATÓRUM.

HOC FÁCITE IN MEAM COMMEMORATIÓNEM.

Calicem ostendit populo, deponit super corporale, et genuflexus adorat.

6. Deinde dicit:

Mystérium fídei:

Et populus prosequitur, acclamans:

Mortem tuam annuntiámus Dómine,
et tuam resurrectiónem confitémur, donec vénias.

Vel:

Quotiescúmque manducámus panem hunc
et cálicem bíbimus,
mortem tuam annuntiámus, Dómine, donec vénias.

Vel:

Salvátor mundi, salva nos,
qui per crucem et resurrectiónem tuam liberásti nos.

TAKE THIS, ALL OF YOU, AND EAT OF IT,
FOR THIS IS MY BODY,
WHICH WILL BE GIVEN UP FOR YOU.

He shows the consecrated host to the people, places it again on the paten, and genuflects in adoration.

5. After this, he continues:

In a similar way, when supper was ended,

He takes the chalice and, holding it slightly raised above the altar, continues:

he took the chalice, gave you thanks
and gave the chalice to his disciples, saying:

He bows slightly.

TAKE THIS, ALL OF YOU, AND DRINK FROM IT,
FOR THIS IS THE CHALICE OF MY BLOOD,
THE BLOOD OF THE NEW AND ETERNAL COVENANT,
WHICH WILL BE POURED OUT FOR YOU AND FOR MANY
FOR THE FORGIVENESS OF SINS.

DO THIS IN MEMORY OF ME.

He shows the chalice to the people, places it on the corporal, and genuflects in adoration.

6. Then he says:

The mystery of faith.

And the people continue, acclaiming:

We proclaim your Death, O Lord,
and profess your Resurrection
until you come again.

Or:

When we eat this Bread and drink this Cup,
we proclaim your Death, O Lord,
until you come again.

Or:

Save us, Savior of the world,
for by your Cross and Resurrection
you have set us free.

7. Postea, extensis manibus, sacerdos dicit:

Unde et nos, Pater sancte,
mémores Christi Fílii tui Salvatóris nostri,
quem per passiónem et mortem crucis
ad resurrectiónis glóriam perduxísti
et ad déxteram tuam sedére fecísti,
opus tuae caritátis annuntiámus, donec ipse véniat,
tibíque panem vitae et cálicem benedictiónis offérimus.

In oblatiónem Ecclésiae tuae,
in qua paschále Christi sacrifícium
nobis tráditum exhibémus,
réspice propítius, et concéde,
ut virtúte Spíritus caritátis tuae,
inter Fílii tui membra,
cuius Córpori communicámus et Sánguini,
nunc et in diem aeternitátis numerémur.

Ecclésiam tuam, Dómine, (quae est N.),
lúmine rénova Evangélii.
Vínculum unitátis confírma
inter fidéles et pastóres plebis tuae,
una cum Papa nostro N. et Epíscopo nostro N.*
et univérso órdine episcopáli,
ut pópulus tuus,
hoc in mundo discórdiis laceráto,
unitátis et concórdiae
prophéticum signum elúceat.

---

* Hic fieri potest mentio de Episcopis Coadiutore vel Auxiliaribus, vel de alio Episcopo, ut in *Institutione generali Missalis Romani*, n. 149, notatur.

7. Then the Priest, with hands extended, says:

Therefore, holy Father,
as we celebrate the memorial of Christ your Son, our Savior,
whom you led through his Passion and Death on the Cross
to the glory of the Resurrection,
and whom you have seated at your right hand,
we proclaim the work of your love until he comes again
and we offer you the Bread of life
and the Chalice of blessing.

Look with favor on the oblation of your Church,
in which we show forth
the paschal Sacrifice of Christ that has been handed on to us,
and grant that, by the power of the Spirit of your love,
we may be counted now and until the day of eternity
among the members of your Son,
in whose Body and Blood we have communion.

Lord, renew your Church (which is in N.)
by the light of the Gospel.
Strengthen the bond of unity
between the faithful and the pastors of your people,
together with N. our Pope, N. our Bishop,*
and the whole Order of Bishops,
that in a world torn by strife
your people may shine forth
as a prophetic sign of unity and concord.

* Mention may be made here of the Coadjutor Bishop, or Auxiliary Bishops, as noted in the *General Instruction of the Roman Missal*, no. 149.

Meménto fratrum nostrórum (N. et N.),
qui in pace Christi tui dormiérunt
omniúmque defunctórum,
quorum fidem tu solus cognovísti:
eos ad lumen vultus tui fruéndum admítte
et in resurrectióne dona eis vitae plenitúdinem.

Concéde nos quoque,
terréna exácta peregrinatióne,
ad aetérnam perveníre mansiónem,
ubi tecum semper vivémus
et cum beáta Vírgine Dei Genetríce María,
cum Apóstolis et martyribus,
(cum Sancto N.: Sancto diei vel patrono)
Sanctísque ómnibus communicántes,
te laudábimus et magnificábimus

Iungit manibus

per Iesum Christum, Fílium tuum.

8. Accipit patenam cum hostia et calicem, et utrumque elevans, dicit:

Per ipsum, et cum ipso, et in ipso,
est tibi Deo Patri omnipoténti,
in unitáte Spíritus Sancti,
omnis honor et glória
per ómnia saécula saeculórum.

Populus acclamat:

Amen.

Deinde sequitur ritus Communionis.

Remember our brothers and sisters (N. and N.),
who have fallen asleep in the peace of your Christ,
and all the dead, whose faith you alone have known.
Admit them to rejoice in the light of your face,
and in the resurrection give them the fullness of life.

Grant also to us,
when our earthly pilgrimage is done,
that we may come to an eternal dwelling place
and live with you for ever;
there, in communion with the Blessed Virgin Mary, Mother of God,
with the Apostles and Martyrs,
(with Saint N.: the Saint of the day or Patron)
and with all the Saints,
we shall praise and exalt you

He joins his hands.

through Jesus Christ, your Son.

8. He takes the chalice and the paten with the host and, raising both, he says:

Through him, and with him, and in him,
O God, almighty Father,
in the unity of the Holy Spirit,
all glory and honor is yours,
for ever and ever.

The people acclaim:

Amen.

Then follows the Communion Rite.

II

Deus Ecclesiam suam in viam salutis conducens

1. Sequens forma huius Precis eucharisticae convenienter adhibetur cum formulariis Missarum v. gr. pro Ecclesia, pro vocationibus ad sacros Ordines, pro laicis, pro familia, pro religiosis, pro vocationibus ad vitam religiosam, ad postulandam caritatem, pro familiaribus et amicis, pro gratiis Deo reddendis.

℣. Dóminus vobíscum.
℟. Et cum spíritu tuo.

℣. Sursum corda.
℟. Habémus ad Dóminum.

℣. Grátias agámus Dómino Deo nostro.
℟. Dignum et iustum est.

Vere dignum et iustum est, aequum et salutáre,
nos tibi semper et ubíque grátias ágere:
Dómine, sancte Pater,
mundi creátor et fons omnis vitae:

Qui ópera sapiéntiae tuae numquam derelínquis,
sed in médio nostri adhuc próvidus operáris.
In manu poténti et bráchio exténto
pópulum tuum Israel per desértum duxísti;
nunc autem Ecclésiam tuam in mundo peregrinántem,
Spíritus Sancti virtúte semper comitáris,
eámque per témporis sémitas
in gáudium aetérnum regni tui condúcis,
per Christum Dóminum nostrum.

Unde et nos cum Angelis et Sanctis
hymnum glóriae tuae cánimus,
sine fine dicéntes:

Sanctus, Sanctus, Sanctus Dóminus Deus Sábaoth.
Pleni sunt caeli et terra glória tua.
Hosánna in excélsis.

II

God Guides His Church along the Way of Salvation

1. The following form of this Eucharistic Prayer is appropriately used with Mass formularies such as, For the Church, For Vocations to Holy Orders, For the Laity, For the Family, For Religious, For Vocations to Religious Life, For Charity, For Relatives and Friends, and For Giving Thanks to God.

℣. The Lord be with you.
℟. And with your spirit.

℣. Lift up your hearts.
℟. We lift them up to the Lord.

℣. Let us give thanks to the Lord our God.
℟. It is right and just.

It is truly right and just, our duty and our salvation,
always and everywhere to give you thanks,
Lord, holy Father,
creator of the world and source of all life.

For you never forsake the works of your wisdom,
but by your providence are even now at work in our midst.
With mighty hand and outstretched arm
you led your people Israel through the desert.
Now, as your Church makes her pilgrim journey in the world,
you always accompany her
by the power of the Holy Spirit
and lead her along the paths of time
to the eternal joy of your Kingdom,
through Christ our Lord.

And so, with the Angels and Saints,
we, too, sing the hymn of your glory,
as without end we acclaim:

Holy, Holy, Holy Lord God of hosts.
Heaven and earth are full of your glory.
Hosanna in the highest.

Benedíctus qui venit in nómine Dómini.
Hosánna in excélsis.

2. Sacerdos, manibus extensis, dicit:

Vere Sanctus es et glorificándus,
amátor hóminum Deus,
qui semper illis ades in itínere vitae.
Vere benedíctus Fílius tuus,
qui praesens est in médio nostri
cum ab eius amóre congregámur,
et sicut olim pro discípulis
nobis Scriptúras áperit et panem frangit.

3. Iungit manus, easque expansas super oblata tenens, dicit:

Rogámus ergo te, Pater clementíssime,
ut Spíritum Sanctum tuum emíttas,
qui haec dona panis et vini sanctíficet,

iungit manus
et signat semel super panem et calicem simul, dicens:

ut nobis Corpus et ✠ Sánguis fiant

iungit manus

Dómini nostri Iesu Christi.

4. In formulis, quae sequuntur, verba Domini proferantur distincte et aperte, prouti natura eorundem verborum requirit.

Qui prídie quam paterétur,
in suprémae nocte Cenae,

accipit panem
eumque parum elevatum super altare tenens prosequitur:

accépit panem et benedíxit ac fregit,
dedítque discípulis suis, dicens:

parum se inclinat

ACCÍPITE ET MANDUCÁTE EX HOC OMNES:
HOC EST ENIM CORPUS MEUM,
QUOD PRO VOBIS TRADÉTUR.

Hostiam consecratam ostendit populo, deponit super patenam, et genuflexus adorat.

Blessed is he who comes in the name of the Lord.
Hosanna in the highest.

2. The Priest, with hands extended, says:

You are indeed Holy and to be glorified, O God,
who love the human race
and who always walk with us on the journey of life.
Blessed indeed is your Son,
present in our midst
when we are gathered by his love
and when, as once for the disciples, so now for us,
he opens the Scriptures and breaks the bread.

3. He joins his hands and, holding them extended over the offerings, says:

Therefore, Father most merciful,
we ask that you send forth your Holy Spirit
to sanctify these gifts of bread and wine,

He joins his hands and makes the Sign of the Cross once over the bread and chalice together, saying:

that they may become for us
the Body and ✠ Blood

He joins his hands.

of our Lord Jesus Christ.

4. In the formulas that follow, the words of the Lord should be pronounced clearly and distinctly, as the nature of these words requires.

On the day before he was to suffer,
on the night of the Last Supper,

He takes the bread and, holding it slightly raised above the altar, continues:

he took bread and said the blessing,
broke the bread and gave it to his disciples, saying:

He bows slightly.

TAKE THIS, ALL OF YOU, AND EAT OF IT,
FOR THIS IS MY BODY,
WHICH WILL BE GIVEN UP FOR YOU.

He shows the consecrated host to the people, places it again on the paten, and genuflects in adoration.

5. Postea prosequitur:

Símili modo, postquam cenátum est

accipit calicem,
eumque parum elevatum super altare tenens, prosequitur:

accípiens et cálicem,
tibi grátias egit,
dedítque discípulis suis, dicens:

parum se inclinat

ACCÍPITE ET BÍBITE EX EO OMNES:
HIC EST ENIM CALIX SÁNGUINIS MEI
NOVI ET AETÉRNI TESTAMÉNTI,
QUI PRO VOBIS ET PRO MULTIS EFFUNDÉTUR
IN REMISSIÓNEM PECCATÓRUM.

HOC FÁCITE IN MEAM COMMEMORATIÓNEM.

Calicem ostendit populo, deponit super corporale, et genuflexus adorat.

6. Deinde dicit:

Mystérium fídei:

Et populus prosequitur, acclamans:

Mortem tuam annuntiámus Dómine,
et tuam resurrectiónem confitémur, donec vénias.

Vel:

Quotiescúmque manducámus panem hunc
et cálicem bíbimus,
mortem tuam annuntiámus, Dómine, donec vénias.

Vel:

Salvátor mundi, salva nos,
qui per crucem et resurrectiónem tuam liberásti nos.

7. Postea, extensis manibus, sacerdos dicit:

Unde et nos, Pater sancte,
mémores Christi Fílii tui Salvatóris nostri,
quem per passiónem et mortem crucis
ad resurrectiónis glóriam perduxísti
et ad déxteram tuam sedére fecísti,

5. After this, he continues:

In a similar way, when supper was ended,

He takes the chalice and, holding it slightly raised above the altar, continues:

he took the chalice, gave you thanks
and gave the chalice to his disciples, saying:

He bows slightly.

TAKE THIS, ALL OF YOU, AND DRINK FROM IT,
FOR THIS IS THE CHALICE OF MY BLOOD,
THE BLOOD OF THE NEW AND ETERNAL COVENANT,
WHICH WILL BE POURED OUT FOR YOU AND FOR MANY
FOR THE FORGIVENESS OF SINS.

DO THIS IN MEMORY OF ME.

He shows the chalice to the people, places it on the corporal, and genuflects in adoration.

6. Then he says:

The mystery of faith.

And the people continue, acclaiming:

We proclaim your Death, O Lord,
and profess your Resurrection
until you come again.

Or:

When we eat this Bread and drink this Cup,
we proclaim your Death, O Lord,
until you come again.

Or:

Save us, Savior of the world,
for by your Cross and Resurrection
you have set us free.

7. Then the Priest, with hands extended, says:

Therefore, holy Father,
as we celebrate the memorial of Christ your Son, our Savior,
whom you led through his Passion and Death on the Cross
to the glory of the Resurrection,
and whom you have seated at your right hand,

opus tuae caritátis annuntiámus, donec ipse véniat,
tibíque panem vitae et cálicem benedictiónis offérimus.

In oblatiónem Ecclésiae tuae,
in qua paschále Christi sacrifícium
nobis tráditum exhibémus,
réspice propítius, et concéde,
ut virtúte Spíritus caritátis tuae,
inter Fílii tui membra,
cuius Córpori communicámus et Sánguini,
nunc et in diem aeternitátis numerémur.

Ad mensam ergo tuam convocátos, Dómine,
nos in unitáte confírma:
ut, una cum Papa nostro N. et Epíscopo nostro N.,*
cum ómnibus Epíscopis, presbyteris, diáconis
et univérso pópulo tuo,
in fide ac spe per sémitas tuas ambulántes,
gáudium et fidúciam in mundum effúndere valeámus.

Meménto fratrum nostrórum (N. et N.),
qui in pace Christi tui dormiérunt
omniúmque defunctórum,
quorum fidem tu solus cognovísti:
eos ad lumen vultus tui fruéndum admítte
et in resurrectióne dona eis vitae plenitúdinem.

Concéde nos quoque,
terréna exácta peregrinatióne,
ad aetérnam perveníre mansiónem,
ubi tecum semper vivémus
et cum beáta Vírgine Dei Genetríce María,
cum Apóstolis et martyribus,
(cum Sancto N.: Sancto diei vel patrono)
Sanctísque ómnibus communicántes,
te laudábimus et magnificábimus

Iungit manibus

per Iesum Christum, Fílium tuum.

---

* Hic fieri potest mentio de Episcopis Coadiutore vel Auxiliaribus, vel de alio Episcopo, ut in *Institutione generali Missalis Romani*, n. 149, notatur.

we proclaim the work of your love until he comes again
and we offer you the Bread of life
and the Chalice of blessing.

Look with favor on the oblation of your Church,
in which we show forth
the paschal Sacrifice of Christ that has been handed on to us,
and grant that, by the power of the Spirit of your love,
we may be counted now and until the day of eternity
among the members of your Son,
in whose Body and Blood we have communion.

And so, having called us to your table, Lord,
confirm us in unity,
so that, together with N. our Pope and N. our Bishop,*
with all Bishops, Priests and Deacons,
and your entire people,
as we walk your ways with faith and hope,
we may strive to bring joy and trust into the world.

Remember our brothers and sisters (N. and N.),
who have fallen asleep in the peace of your Christ,
and all the dead, whose faith you alone have known.
Admit them to rejoice in the light of your face,
and in the resurrection give them the fullness of life.

Grant also to us,
when our earthly pilgrimage is done,
that we may come to an eternal dwelling place
and live with you for ever;
there, in communion with the Blessed Virgin Mary, Mother of God,
with the Apostles and Martyrs,
(with Saint N.: the Saint of the day or Patron)
and with all the Saints,
we shall praise and exalt you

He joins his hands.

through Jesus Christ, your Son.

* Mention may be made here of the Coadjutor Bishop, or Auxiliary Bishops, as noted in the *General Instruction of the Roman Missal*, no. 149.

8. Accipit patenam cum hostia et calicem, et utrumque elevans, dicit:

Per ipsum, et cum ipso, et in ipso,
est tibi Deo Patri omnipoténti,
in unitáte Spíritus Sancti,
omnis honor et glória
per ómnia saécula saeculórum.

Populus acclamat:

Amen.

Deinde sequitur ritus Communionis.

III

Iesus via ad Patrem

1. Sequens forma huius Precis eucharisticae convenienter adhibetur cum formulariis Missarum v. gr. pro evangelizatione populorum, pro christianis persecutione vexatis, pro patria vel civitate, pro rempublicam moderantibus, pro coetu moderatorum nationum, initio anni civilis, pro populorum progressione.

℣. Dóminus vobíscum.
℟. Et cum spíritu tuo.

℣. Sursum corda.
℟. Habémus ad Dóminum.

℣. Grátias agámus Dómino Deo nostro.
℟. Dignum et iustum est.

Vere dignum et iustum est, aequum et salutáre,
nos tibi semper et ubíque grátias ágere,
sancte Pater, Dómine caeli et terrae,
per Christum Dóminum nostrum.

Quia per Verbum tuum mundum creásti
et univérsa in aequitáte moderáris.
Ipsum, carnem factum, nobis mediatórem dedísti,
qui verba tua nobis est locútus

8. He takes the chalice and the paten with the host and, raising both, he says:

Through him, and with him, and in him,
O God, almighty Father,
in the unity of the Holy Spirit,
all glory and honor is yours,
for ever and ever.

The people acclaim:

Amen.

Then follows the Communion Rite.

III

Jesus, the Way to the Father

1. The following form of this Eucharistic Prayer is appropriately used with Mass formularies such as, For the Evangelization of Peoples, For Persecuted Christians, For the Nation or State, For Those in Public Office, For a Governing Assembly, At the Beginning of the Civil Year, and For the Progress of Peoples.

℣. The Lord be with you.
℟. And with your spirit.

℣. Lift up your hearts.
℟. We lift them up to the Lord.

℣. Let us give thanks to the Lord our God.
℟. It is right and just.

It is truly right and just, our duty and our salvation,
always and everywhere to give you thanks,
holy Father, Lord of heaven and earth,
through Christ our Lord.

For by your Word you created the world
and you govern all things in harmony.
You gave us the same Word made flesh as Mediator,
and he has spoken your words to us

et ad sui sequélam nos vocávit;
ille via est quae nos ad te ducit,
véritas quae nos líberat,
vita quae gáudio nos replet.

Per Fílium tuum hómines,
quos ad glóriam tui nóminis fecísti,
sánguine crucis eius redémptos
et Spíritus sigíllo signátos
in unam cólligis famíliam.

Quaprópter nunc et usque in saeculum,
ómnibus cum Angelis glóriam tuam praedicámus,
iucúnda celebratióne clamántes:

Sanctus, Sanctus, Sanctus Dóminus Deus Sábaoth.
Pleni sunt caeli et terra glória tua.
Hosánna in excélsis.
Benedíctus qui venit in nómine Dómini.
Hosánna in excélsis.

2. Sacerdos, manibus extensis, dicit:

Vere Sanctus es et glorificándus,
amátor hóminum Deus,
qui semper illis ades in itínere vitae.
Vere benedíctus Fílius tuus,
qui praesens est in médio nostri
cum ab eius amóre congregámur,
et sicut olim pro discípulis
nobis Scriptúras áperit et panem frangit.

3. Iungit manus, easque expansas super oblata tenens, dicit:

Rogámus ergo te, Pater clementíssime,
ut Spíritum Sanctum tuum emíttas,
qui haec dona panis et vini sanctíficet,

iungit manus
et signat semel super panem et calicem simul, dicens:

ut nobis Corpus et ✠ Sánguis fiant

and called us to follow him.
He is the way that leads us to you,
the truth that sets us free,
the life that fills us with gladness.

Through your Son
you gather men and women,
whom you made for the glory of your name,
into one family,
redeemed by the Blood of his Cross
and signed with the seal of the Spirit.

Therefore now and for ages unending,
with all the Angels,
we proclaim your glory,
as in joyful celebration we acclaim:

Holy, Holy, Holy Lord God of hosts.
Heaven and earth are full of your glory.
Hosanna in the highest.
Blessed is he who comes in the name of the Lord.
Hosanna in the highest.

2. The Priest, with hands extended, says:

You are indeed Holy and to be glorified, O God,
who love the human race
and who always walk with us on the journey of life.
Blessed indeed is your Son,
present in our midst
when we are gathered by his love
and when, as once for the disciples, so now for us,
he opens the Scriptures and breaks the bread.

3. He joins his hands and, holding them extended over the offerings, says:

Therefore, Father most merciful,
we ask that you send forth your Holy Spirit
to sanctify these gifts of bread and wine,

He joins his hands and makes the Sign of the Cross once over the bread and chalice together, saying:

that they may become for us
the Body and ✠ Blood

iungit manus

Dómini nostri Iesu Christi.

4. In formulis, quae sequuntur, verba Domini proferantur distincte et aperte, prouti natura eorundem verborum requirit.

Qui prídie quam paterétur,
in suprémae nocte Cenae,

accipit panem
eumque parum elevatum super altare tenens prosequitur:

accépit panem et benedíxit ac fregit,
dedítque discípulis suis, dicens:

parum se inclinat

ACCÍPITE ET MANDUCÁTE EX HOC OMNES:
HOC EST ENIM CORPUS MEUM,
QUOD PRO VOBIS TRADÉTUR.

Hostiam consecratam ostendit populo, deponit super patenam, et genuflexus adorat.

5. Postea prosequitur:

Símili modo, postquam cenátum est

accipit calicem,
eumque parum elevatum super altare tenens, prosequitur:

accípiens et cálicem,
tibi grátias egit,
dedítque discípulis suis, dicens:

parum se inclinat

ACCÍPITE ET BÍBITE EX EO OMNES:
HIC EST ENIM CALIX SÁNGUINIS MEI
NOVI ET AETÉRNI TESTAMÉNTI,
QUI PRO VOBIS ET PRO MULTIS EFFUNDÉTUR
IN REMISSIÓNEM PECCATÓRUM.

HOC FÁCITE IN MEAM COMMEMORATIÓNEM.

Calicem ostendit populo, deponit super corporale, et genuflexus adorat.

6. Deinde dicit:

Mystérium fídei:

Et populus prosequitur, acclamans:

Mortem tuam annuntiámus Dómine,
et tuam resurrectiónem confitémur, donec vénias.

He joins his hands.

of our Lord Jesus Christ.

4. In the formulas that follow, the words of the Lord should be pronounced clearly and distinctly, as the nature of these words requires.

On the day before he was to suffer,
on the night of the Last Supper,

He takes the bread and, holding it slightly raised above the altar, continues:

he took bread and said the blessing,
broke the bread and gave it to his disciples, saying:

He bows slightly.

TAKE THIS, ALL OF YOU, AND EAT OF IT,
FOR THIS IS MY BODY,
WHICH WILL BE GIVEN UP FOR YOU.

He shows the consecrated host to the people, places it again on the paten, and genuflects in adoration.

5. After this, he continues:

In a similar way, when supper was ended,

He takes the chalice and, holding it slightly raised above the altar, continues:

he took the chalice, gave you thanks
and gave the chalice to his disciples, saying:

He bows slightly.

TAKE THIS, ALL OF YOU, AND DRINK FROM IT,
FOR THIS IS THE CHALICE OF MY BLOOD,
THE BLOOD OF THE NEW AND ETERNAL COVENANT,
WHICH WILL BE POURED OUT FOR YOU AND FOR MANY
FOR THE FORGIVENESS OF SINS.

DO THIS IN MEMORY OF ME.

He shows the chalice to the people, places it on the corporal, and genuflects in adoration.

6. Then he says:

The mystery of faith.

And the people continue, acclaiming:

We proclaim your Death, O Lord,
and profess your Resurrection

Vel:

Quotiescúmque manducámus panem hunc
et cálicem bíbimus,
mortem tuam annuntiámus, Dómine, donec vénias.

Vel:

Salvátor mundi, salva nos,
qui per crucem et resurrectiónem tuam liberásti nos.

7. Postea, extensis manibus, sacerdos dicit:

Unde et nos, Pater sancte,
mémores Christi Fílii tui Salvatóris nostri,
quem per passiónem et mortem crucis
ad resurrectiónis glóriam perduxísti
et ad déxteram tuam sedére fecísti,
opus tuae caritátis annuntiámus, donec ipse véniat,
tibíque panem vitae et cálicem benedictiónis offérimus.

In oblatiónem Ecclésiae tuae,
in qua paschále Christi sacrifícium
nobis tráditum exhibémus,
réspice propítius, et concéde,
ut virtúte Spíritus caritátis tuae,
inter Fílii tui membra,
cuius Córpori communicámus et Sánguini,
nunc et in diem aeternitátis numerémur.

Huius participatióne mystérii, omnípotens Pater,
nos Spíritu vivífica
et imágini Fílii tui confórmes fíeri concéde
atque in vínculo communiónis confírma
una cum Papa nostro N., et Epíscopo nostro N.*
cum céteris Epíscopis, cum presbyteris et diáconis
et univérso pópulo tuo.

Fac ut omnes Ecclésiae fidéles,
témporum signa lúmine fídei perscrutántes,

* Hic fieri potest mentio de Episcopis Coadiutore vel Auxiliaribus, vel de alio Episcopo, ut in *Institutione generali Missalis Romani*, n. 149, notatur.

until you come again.

Or:

When we eat this Bread and drink this Cup,
we proclaim your Death, O Lord,
until you come again.

Or:

Save us, Savior of the world,
for by your Cross and Resurrection
you have set us free.

7. Then the Priest, with hands extended, says:

Therefore, holy Father,
as we celebrate the memorial of Christ your Son, our Savior,
whom you led through his Passion and Death on the Cross
to the glory of the Resurrection,
and whom you have seated at your right hand,
we proclaim the work of your love until he comes again
and we offer you the Bread of life
and the Chalice of blessing.

Look with favor on the oblation of your Church,
in which we show forth
the paschal Sacrifice of Christ that has been handed on to us,
and grant that, by the power of the Spirit of your love,
we may be counted now and until the day of eternity
among the members of your Son,
in whose Body and Blood we have communion.

By our partaking of this mystery, almighty Father,
give us life through your Spirit,
grant that we may be conformed to the image of your Son,
and confirm us in the bond of communion,
together with N. our Pope and N. our Bishop,*
with all other Bishops,
with Priests and Deacons,
and with your entire people.

Grant that all the faithful of the Church,

* Mention may be made here of the Coadjutor Bishop, or Auxiliary Bishops, as noted in the *General Instruction of the Roman Missal*, no. 149.

in servítium Evangélii
cohaerénter se impéndere váleant.
Ad cunctórum hóminum necessitátes redde nos inténtos
ut luctus eórum et angóres,
gáudium et spem participántes,
núntium salútis illis fidéliter afferámus
et cum eis in viam regni tui progrediámur.

Meménto fratrum nostrórum (N. et N.),
qui in pace Christi tui dormiérunt
omniúmque defunctórum,
quorum fidem tu solus cognovísti:
eos ad lumen vultus tui fruéndum admítte
et in resurrectióne dona eis vitae plenitúdinem.

Concéde nos quoque,
terréna exácta peregrinatióne,
ad aetérnam perveníre mansiónem,
ubi tecum semper vivémus
et cum beáta Vírgine Dei Genetríce María,
cum Apóstolis et martyribus,
(cum Sancto N.: Sancto diei vel patrono)
Sanctísque ómnibus communicántes,
te laudábimus et magnificábimus

Iungit manibus

per Iesum Christum, Fílium tuum.

8. Accipit patenam cum hostia et calicem, et utrumque elevans, dicit:

Per ipsum, et cum ipso, et in ipso,
est tibi Deo Patri omnipoténti,
in unitáte Spíritus Sancti,
omnis honor et glória
per ómnia saécula saeculórum.

Populus acclamat:

Amen.

Deinde sequitur ritus Communionis.

looking into the signs of the times by the light of faith,
may constantly devote themselves
to the service of the Gospel.

Keep us attentive to the needs of all
that, sharing their grief and pain,
their joy and hope,
we may faithfully bring them the good news of salvation
and go forward with them
along the way of your Kingdom.

Remember our brothers and sisters (N. and N.),
who have fallen asleep in the peace of your Christ,
and all the dead, whose faith you alone have known.
Admit them to rejoice in the light of your face,
and in the resurrection give them the fullness of life.

Grant also to us,
when our earthly pilgrimage is done,
that we may come to an eternal dwelling place
and live with you for ever;
there, in communion with the Blessed Virgin Mary, Mother of God,
with the Apostles and Martyrs,
(with Saint N.: the Saint of the day or Patron)
and with all the Saints,
we shall praise and exalt you

He joins his hands.

through Jesus Christ, your Son.

8. He takes the chalice and the paten with the host and, raising both, he says:

Through him, and with him, and in him,
O God, almighty Father,
in the unity of the Holy Spirit,
all glory and honor is yours,
for ever and ever.

The people acclaim:

Amen.

Then follows the Communion Rite.

IV

Iesus pertransiens benefaciendo

1. Sequens forma huius Precis eucharisticae convenienter adhibetur cum formulariis Missarum v. gr. pro profugis et exsulibus, tempore famis vel pro fame laborantibus, pro affligentibus nos, pro captivitate detentis, pro detentis in carcere, pro infirmis, pro morientibus, ad postulandam gratiam bene moriendi, in quacumque necessitate.

℣. Dóminus vobíscum.
℟. Et cum spíritu tuo.

℣. Sursum corda.
℟. Habémus ad Dóminum.

℣. Grátias agámus Dómino Deo nostro.
℟. Dignum et iustum est.

Vere dignum et iustum est, aequum et salutáre,
nos tibi semper et ubíque grátias ágere,
Pater misericordiárum et Deus fidélis:

Quia Iesum Christum Fílium tuum,
Dóminum ac redemptórem nobis dedísti.

Semper ille misericórdem se osténdit
erga párvulos et páuperes,
infírmos et peccatóres
atque próximum se fecit
oppréssis et afflíctis.

Verbo et ópere mundo nuntiávit
te esse Patrem
omniúmque filiórum tuórum curam habére.

Et ídeo cum Angelis et Sanctis univérsis
te collaudámus et benedícimus
hymnúmque glóriae tuae cánimus,
sine fine dicéntes:

Sanctus, Sanctus, Sanctus Dóminus Deus Sábaoth.
Pleni sunt caeli et terra glória tua.
Hosánna in excélsis.

IV

Jesus, Who Went About Doing Good

1. The following form of this Eucharistic Prayer is appropriately used with Mass formularies such as, For Refugees and Exiles, In Time of Famine or For Those Suffering Hunger, For Our Oppressors, For Those Held in Captivity, For Those in Prison, For the Sick, For the Dying, For the Grace of a Happy Death, and In Any Need.

℣. The Lord be with you.
℟. And with your spirit.

℣. Lift up your hearts.
℟. We lift them up to the Lord.

℣. Let us give thanks to the Lord our God.
℟. It is right and just.

It is truly right and just, our duty and our salvation,
always and everywhere to give you thanks,
Father of mercies and faithful God.

For you have given us Jesus Christ, your Son,
as our Lord and Redeemer.

He always showed compassion
for children and for the poor,
for the sick and for sinners,
and he became a neighbor
to the oppressed and the afflicted.

By word and deed he announced to the world
that you are our Father
and that you care for all your sons and daughters.

And so, with all the Angels and Saints,
we exalt and bless your name
and sing the hymn of your glory,
as without end we acclaim:

Holy, Holy, Holy Lord God of hosts.
Heaven and earth are full of your glory.
Hosanna in the highest.

Benedíctus qui venit in nómine Dómini.
Hosánna in excélsis.

2. Sacerdos, manibus extensis, dicit:

Vere Sanctus es et glorificándus,
amátor hóminum Deus,
qui semper illis ades in itínere vitae.
Vere benedíctus Fílius tuus,
qui praesens est in médio nostri
cum ab eius amóre congregámur,
et sicut olim pro discípulis
nobis Scriptúras áperit et panem frangit.

3. Iungit manus, easque expansas super oblata tenens, dicit:

Rogámus ergo te, Pater clementíssime,
ut Spíritum Sanctum tuum emíttas,
qui haec dona panis et vini sanctíficet,

iungit manus
et signat semel super panem et calicem simul, dicens:

ut nobis Corpus et ✠ Sánguis fiant

iungit manus

Dómini nostri Iesu Christi.

4. In formulis, quae sequuntur, verba Domini proferantur distincte et aperte, prouti natura eorundem verborum requirit.

Qui prídie quam paterétur,
in suprémae nocte Cenae,

accipit panem
eumque parum elevatum super altare tenens prosequitur:

accépit panem et benedíxit ac fregit,
dedítque discípulis suis, dicens:

parum se inclinat

ACCÍPITE ET MANDUCÁTE EX HOC OMNES:
HOC EST ENIM CORPUS MEUM,
QUOD PRO VOBIS TRADÉTUR.

Hostiam consecratam ostendit populo, deponit super patenam, et genuflexus adorat.

Blessed is he who comes in the name of the Lord.
Hosanna in the highest.

2. The Priest, with hands extended, says:

You are indeed Holy and to be glorified, O God,
who love the human race
and who always walk with us on the journey of life.
Blessed indeed is your Son,
present in our midst
when we are gathered by his love
and when, as once for the disciples, so now for us,
he opens the Scriptures and breaks the bread.

3. He joins his hands and, holding them extended over the offerings, says:

Therefore, Father most merciful,
we ask that you send forth your Holy Spirit
to sanctify these gifts of bread and wine,

He joins his hands and makes the Sign of the Cross once over the bread and chalice together, saying:

that they may become for us
the Body and ✠ Blood

He joins his hands.

of our Lord Jesus Christ.

4. In the formulas that follow, the words of the Lord should be pronounced clearly and distinctly, as the nature of these words requires.

On the day before he was to suffer,
on the night of the Last Supper,

He takes the bread and, holding it slightly raised above the altar, continues:

he took bread and said the blessing,
broke the bread and gave it to his disciples, saying:

He bows slightly.

TAKE THIS, ALL OF YOU, AND EAT OF IT,
FOR THIS IS MY BODY,
WHICH WILL BE GIVEN UP FOR YOU.

He shows the consecrated host to the people, places it again on the paten, and genuflects in adoration.

5. Postea prosequitur:

Símili modo, postquam cenátum est

accipit calicem,
eumque parum elevatum super altare tenens, prosequitur:

accípiens et cálicem,
tibi grátias egit,
dedítque discípulis suis, dicens:

parum se inclinat

ACCÍPITE ET BÍBITE EX EO OMNES:
HIC EST ENIM CALIX SÁNGUINIS MEI
NOVI ET AETÉRNI TESTAMÉNTI,
QUI PRO VOBIS ET PRO MULTIS EFFUNDÉTUR
IN REMISSIÓNEM PECCATÓRUM.

HOC FÁCITE IN MEAM COMMEMORATIÓNEM.

Calicem ostendit populo, deponit super corporale, et genuflexus adorat.

6. Deinde dicit:

Mystérium fídei:

Et populus prosequitur, acclamans:

Mortem tuam annuntiámus Dómine,
et tuam resurrectiónem confitémur, donec vénias.

Vel:

Quotiescúmque manducámus panem hunc
et cálicem bíbimus,
mortem tuam annuntiámus, Dómine, donec vénias.

Vel:

Salvátor mundi, salva nos,
qui per crucem et resurrectiónem tuam liberásti nos.

7. Postea, extensis manibus, sacerdos dicit:

Unde et nos, Pater sancte,
mémores Christi Fílii tui Salvatóris nostri,
quem per passiónem et mortem crucis
ad resurrectiónis glóriam perduxísti
et ad déxteram tuam sedére fecísti,

5. After this, he continues:

In a similar way, when supper was ended,

He takes the chalice and, holding it slightly raised above the altar, continues:

he took the chalice, gave you thanks
and gave the chalice to his disciples, saying:

He bows slightly.

TAKE THIS, ALL OF YOU, AND DRINK FROM IT,
FOR THIS IS THE CHALICE OF MY BLOOD,
THE BLOOD OF THE NEW AND ETERNAL COVENANT,
WHICH WILL BE POURED OUT FOR YOU AND FOR MANY
FOR THE FORGIVENESS OF SINS.

DO THIS IN MEMORY OF ME.

He shows the chalice to the people, places it on the corporal, and genuflects in adoration.

6. Then he says:

The mystery of faith.

And the people continue, acclaiming:

We proclaim your Death, O Lord,
and profess your Resurrection
until you come again.

Or:

When we eat this Bread and drink this Cup,
we proclaim your Death, O Lord,
until you come again.

Or:

Save us, Savior of the world,
for by your Cross and Resurrection
you have set us free.

7. Then the Priest, with hands extended, says:

Therefore, holy Father,
as we celebrate the memorial of Christ your Son, our Savior,
whom you led through his Passion and Death on the Cross
to the glory of the Resurrection,
and whom you have seated at your right hand,

opus tuae caritátis annuntiámus, donec ipse véniat,
tibíque panem vitae et cálicem benedictiónis offérimus.

In oblatiónem Ecclésiae tuae,
in qua paschále Christi sacrifícium
nobis tráditum exhibémus,
réspice propítius, et concéde,
ut virtúte Spíritus caritátis tuae,
inter Fílii tui membra,
cuius Córpori communicámus et Sánguini,
nunc et in diem aeternitátis numerémur.

Ecclésiam tuam, Dómine,
in fide et caritáte perfícere dignéris,
una cum Papa nostro N., et Epíscopo nostro N.,*
et cunctis Epíscopis, presbyteris et diáconis,
et omni pópulo acquisitiónis tuae.

Aperi óculos nostros
ut necessitátes fratrum agnoscámus;
verba et ópera nobis inspíra,
ad laborántes et onerátos confortándos;
fac nos sincére ipsis inservíre,
Christi exémplo eiúsque mandáto.
Ecclésia tua vivum testimónium exsístat
veritátis et libertátis,
pacis atque iustítiae,
ut omnes hómines in spem novam erigántur.

Meménto fratrum nostrórum (N. et N.),
qui in pace Christi tui dormiérunt
omniúmque defunctórum,
quorum fidem tu solus cognovísti:
eos ad lumen vultus tui fruéndum admítte
et in resurrectióne dona eis vitae plenitúdinem.

Concéde nos quoque,
terréna exácta peregrinatióne,
ad aetérnam perveníre mansiónem,

* Hic fieri potest mentio de Episcopis Coadiutore vel Auxiliaribus, vel de alio Episcopo, ut in *Institutione generali Missalis Romani*, n. 149, notatur.

we proclaim the work of your love until he comes again
and we offer you the Bread of life
and the Chalice of blessing.

Look with favor on the oblation of your Church,
in which we show forth
the paschal Sacrifice of Christ that has been handed on to us,
and grant that, by the power of the Spirit of your love,
we may be counted now and until the day of eternity
among the members of your Son,
in whose Body and Blood we have communion.

Bring your Church, O Lord,
to perfect faith and charity,
together with N. our Pope and N. our Bishop,[*]
with all Bishops, Priests and Deacons,
and the entire people you have made your own.

Open our eyes
to the needs of our brothers and sisters;
inspire in us words and actions
to comfort those who labor and are burdened.
Make us serve them truly,
after the example of Christ and at his command.
And may your Church stand as a living witness
to truth and freedom,
to peace and justice,
that all people may be raised up to a new hope.

Remember our brothers and sisters (N. and N.),
who have fallen asleep in the peace of your Christ,
and all the dead, whose faith you alone have known.
Admit them to rejoice in the light of your face,
and in the resurrection give them the fullness of life.
Grant also to us,
when our earthly pilgrimage is done,
that we may come to an eternal dwelling place

[*] Mention may be made here of the Coadjutor Bishop, or Auxiliary Bishops, as noted in the *General Instruction of the Roman Missal*, no. 149.

ubi tecum semper vivémus
et cum beáta Vírgine Dei Genetríce María,
cum Apóstolis et martyribus,
(cum Sancto N.: Sancto diei vel patrono)
Sanctísque ómnibus communicántes,
te laudábimus et magnificábimus

Iungit manibus

per Iesum Christum, Fílium tuum.

8. Accipit patenam cum hostia et calicem, et utrumque elevans, dicit:

Per ipsum, et cum ipso, et in ipso,
est tibi Deo Patri omnipoténti,
in unitáte Spíritus Sancti,
omnis honor et glória
per ómnia saécula saeculórum.

Populus acclamat:

Amen.

Deinde sequitur ritus Communionis.

and live with you for ever;
there, in communion with the Blessed Virgin Mary, Mother of God,
with the Apostles and Martyrs,
(with Saint N.: the Saint of the day or Patron)
and with all the Saints,
we shall praise and exalt you

He joins his hands.

through Jesus Christ, your Son.

8. He takes the chalice and the paten with the host and, raising both, he says:

Through him, and with him, and in him,
O God, almighty Father,
in the unity of the Holy Spirit,
all glory and honor is yours,
for ever and ever.

The people acclaim:

Amen.

Then follows the Communion Rite.

History of the Text

Richard E. McCarron

EP MVN appears in the appendix to the Order of Mass in *MR2002*. The Latin *editio typica* of the prayer was approved in 1991. The prayer was first approved for use in Switzerland in 1974 in its German, French, and Italian versions and from then was quickly adopted and given permission for use throughout the world. Given its origins, it has been referred to as the "Swiss Synod Prayer" or the "Swiss Anaphora." As it was approved in different locales, it took different names, e.g., "Plegaria eucarística V" in Spanish-speaking countries, "Prière pour des rassemblements" in France. Since the Latin *editio typica* of 1991, it carries the title *Prex Eucharistica quae in Missis pro Variis Necessitatibus Adhiberi Potest*. This section traces the development of the prayer, its reception beyond Switzerland, the promulgation of the *editio typica*, and its introduction in *MR2002*.

The Development of the Prayer

The circular letter *EuchPar* (1973) allowed for conferences of bishops to submit requests for new EPs for special circumstances (no. 6). Switzerland was the first conference to make a request after the circular letter, and Paul VI granted them permission to prepare a special prayer on 14 February 1974.[1] The occasion was the 1972–75 synod of the bishops of Switzerland, referenced as "Synod '72."[2] This was envisioned as an "ecclesial event of the highest importance," bringing a time of renewal of faith and unity for the whole church of Switzerland; the bishops wanted this renewal to take root and grow in the Swiss church.[3] Their hope was that "the purpose of the synod should find expression in all areas of life, especially in worship."[4] Thus the foreground for the composition of the prayer is a church "that

[1] Bugnini, 477, n. 36.

[2] See Anton Hänggi, "Das Hochgebet «Synode '72» für die Kirche in der Schweiz," *Notitiae* 27 (1991): 436. Hänggi was bishop of Basel from 1968–82.

[3] Ibid., 451 and 437.

[4] Hänggi, citing the summary of the letter of Bishop Nestor Adam to the Congregation for Divine Worship, requesting permission to compose a new EP (ibid., 444).

finds itself of one mind to live a period of ecclesial growth."[5] This growth is nourished and sustained by the Eucharist, and thus the prayer is "a text . . . that reflects in the form of a prayer, the thanksgiving, the invocation, the participation in the sacrifice of Christ of the Christian community that intends to join more sincerely, 'here and now', their journey to the person of Christ."[6]

The text of the prayer was drafted by the Swiss Liturgical Commission (Liturgische Kommission der Schweiz/LKS) in the three working languages of the conference: German, French, and Italian. The *leitmotif* of the prayer—being together on the way, coming together, traveling together—came from the root meaning of the word "synod."[7] The OT themes of the Pilgrim People, the NT themes of a people sent (Mark 16:15) and of a people on journey to the Heavenly Jerusalem, and Vatican II's emphasis on the pilgrim character of the church (e.g., *LG*, nos. 6, 7, 8) provide the foundation, unifying vision, and specific themes of the prayer.[8]

The prayer was composed as a single prayer whose structure is identical with EPs I–IV of *MR1970*. This one prayer has a fixed central section and two variable sections. The fixed elements are the post-*Sanctus*, first epiclesis, institution narrative, anamnesis-offering, the second epiclesis, and the doxology. The variable sections are the preface and the intercessions. Within the two variable sections there are four variations with different accents: originally designated as "God Guides the Church," "Jesus Our Way," "Jesus Passes by No Distress—Jesus, Model of Love,"[9] "The Church on the Way to Unity." The preface and the intercessions of each of these variants are linked with each other by these themes.[10]

This structure—the concept of one prayer with variable parts—can be likened to the tradition of a variable proper preface with a proper *Communicantes* or *Hanc Igitur* from the Roman Canon for certain liturgical feasts.[11] It has, however, led some to identify this as four different prayers, rather than one prayer, perhaps because each of the four variable texts was often individually printed together with the fixed texts for ease of use in celebration (designated as A–D in French and Italian and I–IV in German

[5] Corrado Maggioni, "Coordinate Spazio-Temporali della Preghiera Eucaristica «Synode '72». Dal Sinodo Svizzero al Testo Tipico Latino (1974–1991)," *Notitiae* 27 (1991): 464.

[6] Ibid., 464.

[7] After Hänggi, "Das Hochgebet," 452.

[8] This section summarizes ibid., 452–53.

[9] The first title is from the German and the second from the French and Italian.

[10] The use of "variable" and "variation" follow ibid., 453.

[11] Cf. *OM2008*, nos. 86 and 87 above; the concept of variability and fixity within one prayer also marks the anaphora in the Gallican and Old Spanish Rites.

versions of the published approved texts). This even caused some complaint from the CDF at the time.[12]

Approval and Dissemination of the Prayer

When the text had been approved by the Swiss bishops, it was brought to Rome by a delegation to the CDW in June 1974.[13] It was reviewed and approved with a few corrections by the CDF on 20 July 1974 and by Paul VI on 5 August 1974. The CDW issued its decree on 8 August 1974.[14] With the decree were published the German and French versions of the prayer. The prayer was used for the first time on 8 September 1974.[15] The Italian version received approval on 15 November 1974.[16]

While the decree indicated that the use of EP MVN was limited to the duration of the synod of the Swiss church, the prayer soon "became part of the patrimony of the Church in Switzerland."[17] Likewise, because it was approved in three widely used languages,[18] the prayer soon drew interest from other local churches. By 1987, it had been approved for use in twenty-seven countries and in twelve languages.[19] The text was approved for use in Italy in 1980, with some adjustments to the original Italian approved for Switzerland.[20] An English-language version was approved for use in the Philippines in 1979, originally for their synod; it was extended for use indefinitely in 1985.[21] In 1985 a Spanish translation was approved for the *texto unico* of the *OM* for all Spanish-speaking countries, with a new first epiclesis text.[22] Maggioni

[12] See Bugnini, 477, n. 36.

[13] The details and sections of correspondence are in Hänggi, "Das Hochgebet," 446–47.

[14] Bugnini, 477, n. 36.

[15] Hänggi, "Das Hochgebet," 437.

[16] See Hänggi, "Das Hochgebet," 450.

[17] Maggioni, "Coordinate Spazio-Temporali," 464.

[18] Approved German text: Liturgisches Institut Zürich and Institutum Liturgicum Salzburg, 3rd printing (Zürich: Benziger AG, 1976); French text: Centre Romand de Liturgie (Fribourg: St Paul, 1974); Italian: Centro di Liturgia Lugano (Lugano: Cassarate, 1974).

[19] Maggioni assembles the dates of the decrees and traces the expanded use of the prayer. He notes that 1978 and 1986 saw the most numerous adoptions, connected to French- and Spanish-speaking countries.

[20] The 1983 Italian Missal placed the prayer in an appendix as *Preghiera Eucaristica V*.

[21] *Notitiae* 21 (1985): 583.

[22] The congregation required the wording of the first epiclesis submitted "*que envíes tu Espíritu sobre este pan y este vino,* para que tu Hijo Jesucristo realice en medio de nosotros la presencia de su Cuerpo y de su Sangre" (based on the wording of the French text) be replaced with "*que envíes tu Espíritu sobre este pan y este vino,* de manera que sean para nosotros Cuerpo y Sangre de Jesucristo, Hijo tuyo y Señor nuestro." See the decree in *Notitiae* 22 (1986): 832, no. 4.

offers several observations about its widespread adoption.[23] Early on, its usage seemed related to pastoral needs in view of local synods or congresses. Sometimes it was adopted by a neighboring language-area to Switzerland (e.g., early adoption by Luxembourg and Austria) or by a country that shared a common language with one of the original texts (e.g., French-speaking countries in Africa and French-speaking Canada). Once the Spanish version was approved, many Spanish-speaking countries in the Americas adopted it. A further factor was the desire to enrich local euchology with a contemporary prayer, and the fact that this prayer carried Vatican approval made it a good choice. Maggioni and others note the popularity of its style and its use of language that evokes realities of the contemporary world; it has been deemed easy to understand, which made it very appealing as well.[24]

Editio Typica 1991

This wide reception of the text and the use of the French-, German-, and Italian-language versions as a base for translations are the two key reasons for the preparation and promulgation of an *editio typica* in 1991.[25] Because the three original language texts differed among themselves, there was diversity among the translations into the various languages depending on which text one took as a base. Furthermore, theological questions about some expressions in the text had arisen, in particular around the wording of the first epiclesis,[26] the language of offering and sacrifice, and concern

[23] The rest of this section summarizes his analysis, "Coordinate Spazio-Temporali," 473–74.

[24] Maggioni, "Coordinate Spazio-Temporali," 474; also Mazza, "Its ideas are clear and deal with realities which the faithful recognize in themselves." Mazza goes on to cite Jakob Baumgartner, ". . . [the anaphora's] principal aim is to lead the participants to the highest possible degree of existential involvement" (Enrico Mazza, *The Eucharistic Prayers of the Roman Rite*, trans. Matthew J. O'Connell [New York: Pueblo, 1986], 218). As a counterpoint, Maggioni (474) questions the concept of a unified modernity and wonders if any single contemporary text can really speak across the plurality of cultures. The same qualities also garnered criticism, as noted below.

[25] In *Notitiae* 27 (1991): 388–99; the decision to prepare an *editio typica* was made at the plenary session of the CDW in January 1991, cf. *Notitiae* 27 (1991): 294–95.

[26] See Vincenzo Raffa, *Liturgia Eucaristica: Mistagogia della Messa: dalla storia e dalla teologia alla pastorale pratica*, Bibliotheca 'Ephemerides liturgicae' Subsidia 100 (Rome: CLV, 2003), 783–84; also, Cesare Giraudo, *Preghiere Eucaristiche per la Chiesa di Oggi: Riflessioni in Margine al Commento del Canone Svizzero-Romano*, Aloisiana 23 (Rome: Gregorian University Press, 1993), 21–22; Paul De Clerck, "Epiclèse et formulation du mystère eucharistique: Brèves réflexions sur le langage liturgique à partir de la prière eucharistique du Synode Suisse," in *Gratias Agamus. Studien zum eucharistischen Hochgebet. Festschrift Balthasar Fischer*, ed. Andreas Heinz and Heinrich Rennings (Freiburg: Herder, 1992), 53–56.

that the text was too horizontally focused on the church immediately gathered.[27] Additionally, the distanciation of the prayer from the Swiss synod context or from any local synodal context merited some reconsideration of the thematic material.[28]

The decree and *praenotanda* accompanying the *editio typica* formally situate the prayer within the context of the Masses and prayers *pro variis necessitatibus vel ad diversa*. The decree notes the roles that intercessory formulae play, in particular in ritual Masses where there are often embolisms for the EP. Given that the origins of the prayer itself were to "respond to different circumstances," the decree formally links the prayer to be used "together with the formularies of the Masses for various needs" of *MR1975*. The decree explains that all future translations must "faithfully" follow the *editio typica* and that "all vernacular versions already approved must in the future be made to agree with this Latin typical edition when the new particular editions of the *Missale Romanum* are published in these languages."[29]

The *editio typica* itself is a composite created from the German, French, and Italian texts, together with phrasing from existing Roman euchology. The creation of the *editio typica* was envisaged as a process of "harmonization of the [Eucharistic] Prayer with the others of the Roman rite" and "enrichment of the text by making more explicit several theological elements" of the prayer.[30] These include the notion of offering, the role of the Holy Spirit, and the eschatology of the prayer. While the prefaces and intercessions more closely correspond to the originals, the fixed sections are more in harmony with traditional Roman euchology.[31]

In view of the prayer's relationship with the Masses for Various Needs, the redactors of the *editio typica* provided new thematic headings and rearranged the sequence of the prayers from the original texts. This new order was seen to correspond better with the way that the euchology for the Masses for Various Needs is arranged in the Missal.[32] Thus the order of the variants are now:

[27] See the comments in Mazza, *The Eucharistic Prayers*, 217–24, drawing upon Salvatore Marsili, "Una Nuova Preghiera per la Chiesa Italiana," *Rivista Liturgica* 67 (1980): 465–78.

[28] See further Pere Tena [i Garriga], "Commentarium," *Notitiae* 27 (1991): 421–22.

[29] "Omnes autem versiones linguis vernaculis iam approbatae posthac accommodari debebunt praesenti textui typico latino, quando novae editiones particulares *Missalis Romani* . . . typis imprimentur."

[30] Tena, "Commentarium," 421.

[31] See Tena on the attempt to balance the contemporary language that made the prayer popular and harmony of the text with the existing EPs (ibid., 420–21).

[32] Ibid., 422–23.

I "The Church on the Path of Unity"
II "God Guides His Church along the Way of Salvation"
III "Jesus, the Way to the Father"
IV "Jesus, Who Went about Doing Good"[33]

Use in Diocese of the United States

An interim English translation of the prayer was prepared by ICEL, approved by the NCCB on 16 November 1994 and received the *recognitio* on 9 May 1995.[34] The designation "interim" referred to the anticipation of the confirmation of the new translation of the *MR*, under deliberation at the time (what was referred to as the 1998 Sacramentary). When the edition was finally published as a separate booklet, provision had been made as well for the inclusion of additional acclamations by the assembly in the chant setting of the prayer provided in the back of the booklet.[35] Since the Spanish-language had already been approved in 1985 and incorporated into the *texto unico* of the Ordinary of the Mass for Spanish-speaking countries, the Spanish-language version of the prayer had been in use in the United States since 1989 as *Plegaria Eucarística V* in the *Misal Romano*. A few changes were introduced in the English translation of the prayer for inclusion in the 1998 Sacramentary, approved by the USCCB but rejected by Rome in 2002.[36]

MR2002

The *editio typica* (1991) of the prayers was included in *MR2002*'s *Appendix ad Ordinem Missae*, following EP RII. Rubrics indicate which of the formulas for MVN are appropriately used with the prayer, corresponding to the indications in the *praenotanda* given in 1991.[37] The variable and fixed sections are arranged together to aid celebration and assigned Roman numerals

[33] The current I = original German IV, French-Italian D; current II = original German I, French-Italian A; current III = original German II, French-Italian B; current IV = original German III, French-Italian C. It also assigned them new theme statements.

[34] *Eucharistic Prayers for Masses for Various Needs and Occasions*, prepared by International Commission on English in the Liturgy (Collegeville, MN: Liturgical Press, 1996).

[35] The acclamations were located after the post-*Sanctus* before and after the first epiclesis; after the second epiclesis and the variable intercessory section; and with the *memento* for the dead.

[36] See the time line, xxv–xxvi above.

[37] In *Notitiae* 27 (1991): 389–90.

I–IV. The texts are identical to those published in 1991, with two exceptions. First, in addition to the acclamation, *Mortem tuam*, each prayer adds the two other acclamations given with the other EPs of *MR2002* (*Quotiescumque manducamus* and *Salvator mundi*). Second, in the first variant, *Ecclesia in viam unitatis progrediens*, part of the intercessory material from variant IV was included (*Aperi oculos nostros . . . existat*, 690). The 2008 emended edition of *MR2002* corrected this mistake by deleting that section. Third, in variant III, a grammatical correction was made to the preface (*caro factum . . . dedisti* was changed to *carnem factum . . . dedisti*).

The Gift from Switzerland

What had been received as a gift from Rome to Switzerland in 1974 has now been received back as a gift from Switzerland to the church throughout the world.[38] The incorporation of the Swiss Synod EP into *MR2002* is a noteworthy moment in postconciliar liturgical history and a fascinating case study in the hermeneutics of reception and recontextualization of euchology and a contemporary model of anaphora construction. In terms of reception and recontextualization, a EP that originated for the particular needs and circumstances of the Swiss church in the time of ecclesial renewal occasioned by the Synod '72 was quickly received and eventually spread throughout various sectors of the world far removed from the particular intentions of the Swiss synod. The prayer underwent a transformation from the "Swiss Anaphora" to "EP V" in some local churches to the EP MVN in the *editio typica* in 1991. With insertion of the prayer into *MR2002*, linked as an appendix to the Order of Mass (not as an appendix to the *MR* itself) the prayer has been secured a place in the *lex orandi* of the Roman Rite.

The EP is also noteworthy for the process of its composition. Unlike EP I–IV, the prayer was first composed in vernacular languages, using a contemporary style that wove together biblical, conciliar, and theological language. It is not directly derived from a historical text as is EP IV, for example. Nevertheless, it follows classical anaphoral patterns and the canon of eucharistic praying elaborated in *IGMR*, no. 79. The form of a single prayer with four "variations on a theme" reveals a unique and expansive way the contemporary Roman Rite seeks to balance the interplay between fixity and variability in anaphoral structure. The creation of the *editio typica* from the existing vernacular editions with the integration of more classical liturgical literary patterns and phrasing demonstrates the vision of *SC*, "In order

[38] Hänggi refers to the prayer as "das Geschenk aus Rom" in "Das Hochgebet," 455.

that sound tradition be retained, and yet the way remain open to legitimate progress" (no. 23). It also raises the question of the complications that arise when faced with translating a vernacular to Latin back to a vernacular again. It further occasions thought about the shape that EPs might take in the future.[39]

EP MVN, employing the *leitmotif* of the Christian journey, shows how legitimate progress has been made in continuing liturgical renewal, the dynamism of liturgical tradition, and the challenges of its continuous appropriation in the life of the local churches.

[39] See Giraudo, *Preghiere Eucaristiche*, chap. 14.

Theology of the Latin Text and Rite

Richard E. McCarron

EP MVN has a unique structure compared to the other EPs in *MR2002*. It is a single prayer, with four variations on the theme of the pilgrim journey of the church on the path to salvation through Christ. Within the four variations, there are a variable preface and an intercessory unit that are linked by the common theme of the variation. The fixed elements of EP MVN are: post-*Sanctus*, epiclesis I, institution narrative, anamnesis-offering, epiclesis II, intercession for the dead, and commemoration of the saints.

While it is one prayer with four variations, the *editio typica* prints the variable preface and intercessory units together with the fixed sections as four complete prayers to aid proclamation in liturgical celebration. They are labeled *Forma I–IV* and titled with the theme of the variation.

This commentary first takes up variation I with the fixed parts included. For variations II–IV, only the variable prefaces and intercessions are examined. Since this prayer shares the same anaphoral structure and ritual actions as the major prayers (especially EP II–IV) and the theological and literary issues concerning the dialogue, *Sanctus*, the epiclesis, institution narrative, acclamations, and doxology have been covered in the other contributions in this volume, attention here will be focused on the particularities of the text of this prayer, in relation to the German, French, and Italian originals as needed.[1]

Form I: *Ecclesia in viam unitatis progrediens*

Preface (*OM2008*, appendix, I:1, lines 12–24)

The opening of the preface has been harmonized with the corpus of prefaces in *MR2002* by the conventional Roman transition *Vere dignum et*

[1] Approved German text: *Hochgebet für die Kirche in der Schweiz «Gott fürht die Kirche»*, 3rd printing, Liturgisches Institut Zürich and Institutum Liturgicum Salzburg (Zürich: Benziger AG, 1976). French: Synodes des Catholiques de Suisse, *Prière Eucharistique*, Centre Romand de Liturgie (Fribourg: St. Paul, 1974). Italian: Sinodo dei cattolici in Svizzera, *Preghiera Eucaristica*, Centro di Liturgia Lugano (Lugano: Cassarate, 1974).

iustum est tibi gratias agere.[2] The primary motive for thanksgiving in variation I is the mystery of the church, "brought together" (*collegisti*, perfect tense) by God through the Gospel of Christ. The church is enlivened by the Holy Spirit (*Spiritus tui virtute vivificatam*) and continues today to be the way to unity (*omnes homines in unum congregare non desinis*). On the one hand, the unity of the church is seen as God's gift, through the Spirit; on the other, it seems to imply that the church is the *telos* of the unity of all people.[3] An eschatological note is sounded with the allusion to Revelation 5:9 in line 16 and the OT prophetic sign of the Messianic reign with the ingathering of the nations (see Ezek 20:34).

These eschatological and prophetic dimensions are drawn out in the next section of the preface (lines 20–24), which introduces the theme of covenant. The section is strongly focused on the church's action.[4] The church (referent of *Ipsa)* manifests the *dilectionis testamentum*. The theme of the covenant was explicitly present in the Italian original, there specified as "the covenant promised and realized in Jesus Christ."[5] To the motif of covenant are linked the themes of fidelity (line 22) and promise (line 24).[6] The sacramental nature of the church is recalled (*veluti signum tuae fidelitatis*), echoing the opening of *LG*.[7] The word *resplendet* also resonates with *LG*, which explains that the light of Christ *super faciem Ecclesiae resplendente* (no. 1). The church mirrors that light to the world.

[2] The original texts in German, French, and Italian begin with the transition from the *Gratias agamus* of the dialogue, placing the accent on thanksgiving. This reflects the EP of ApTrad (*Gratias tibi referimus, Deus*), which is noteworthy for not using the *Vere Dignum* as a transition. See the comments of Cesare Giraudo, noting that the Swiss redactors may have drawn inspiration from ApTrad here, in his *Preghiere Eucaristiche per la Chiesa di Oggi: Riflessioni in Margine al Commento del Canone Svizzero-Romano*, Aloisiana 23 (Rome: Gregorian University Press, 1993), 53, n. 2.

[3] Enrico Mazza, *The Eucharistic Prayers of the Roman Rite*, trans. Matthew J. O'Connell (New York: Pueblo, 1986), 222, quotes Salvatore Marsili: "To what extent does the unity of all people have the Church as its common denominator?"

[4] Giraudo sees this as excessive and a departure from the standard convention of the preface to focus on the *mirabilia Dei*; see *Preghiere Eucaristiche*, 56, esp. n. 6. He also sees a structural problem with the attention to ecclesial unity that he locates more appropriately in the second epiclesis. Further, Giraudo critiques this polarization of attention on the Church as perfect and united, which he understands as more of a process and fruit of the eucharistic celebration itself (54–56). It seems to me the link of the preface with the intercessions is not fully taken into consideration.

[5] *Così la Chiesa risplende come segno della tua fedeltà all'alleanza promessa e attuata in Gesù Cristo, nostro Signore.*

[6] Fidelity is a key attribute of God in the OT with regard to the covenant relationship (e.g., Deut 7:9).

[7] *Cum autem Ecclesia sit in Christo veluti sacramentum seu signum et instrumentum intimae cum Deo unionis totiusque generis humani unitatis*, no. 1.

Post-*Sanctus* (*OM2008*, appendix, I:2)

The post-*Sanctus* adopts a literary convention of the Old Spanish and Gallican anaphoral tradition with the pairing of *Vere Sanctus* (line 2) to acclaim the Father and *Vere benedictus* (line 5) to acclaim the Son.[8] The original texts had flowed into continued praise in a style more akin to EP IV. The *editio typica* reworks the ideas of the originals into a new frame. By introducing a more traditional liturgical phasing with the pairing *Vere Sanctus . . . Vere benedictus*, however, the *editio typica* divides what the original languages held in relation through an adverbial construction. The current phrasing first asserts that God the Father is present to us on the journey, but then the *Vere benedictus* stresses Christ's presence.[9]

The attributions in lines 2–3 emphasize the immanence of God as one who accompanies us on the journey and Christ's presence in our midst. God is named as *amator hominum*, the God who loves humanity, a biblical image frequently used in Eastern liturgies (*philanthrópós*). God is named as being *semper illis ades in itinere vitae*. The relational being of God is stressed by the verb *adesse*. That nearness and relationality are echoed in Christ's action of being present in our midst (*qui praesens est in medio nostri*), and the accent is placed on love once more, a love that gathers us together (a reference to the hymn *Ubi Caritas*).[10]

The post-*Sanctus* next introduces an allusion to the Emmaus narrative (Luke 24:13-35). The original German and Italian placed an explicit reference to Emmaus in parentheses, while the French included it in the text. As Enrico Mazza points out, this allusion to the Emmaus narrative carries with it certain theological convictions.[11] Citing François-Xavier Durwell, Mazza emphasizes that the "Eucharist is the permanent manifestation of the risen Jesus."[12] The narrative of Emmaus unfolds a discovery of the presence of Christ through accompaniment, word, and table that leads the

[8] See Pere Tena [i Garriga], "Commentarium," *Notitiae* 27 (1991): 421–22, 423, on how this literary form enabled the linking of the themes of the originals. See the texts in *Prex Eucharistica*, 1:469, 473, 478, 501, 503.

[9] Paul De Clerck, "La Révision de la Prière Eucharistique «Suisse»," *La Maison-Dieu* 191 (1992): 64.

[10] *Ubi caritas et amor, Deus ibi est. Congregavit nos in unum Christi amor*; see Tena, "Commentarium," 423.

[11] Giraudo, however, registers some reservations about the Emmaus allusion. Among his concerns are: the reference may give the impression that Emmaus was a full Eucharist, though the event of Pentecost had not yet transpired; it may stress too closely the identity of the action of minister and Christ. See Giraudo, *Preghiere Eucaristiche*, 84–86.

[12] Mazza, *The Eucharistic Prayers*, 222.

disciples to bear witness to that presence to others.[13] The allusion also stresses the action of Christ in the liturgical event: *Scripturas aperit et panem frangit*.[14] The theological vision of the passage reflects *SC*, no. 7—the multiple modes of Christ's presence in the liturgical celebration. Christ is present in the assembly, the Word, the ministers, and the breaking of the bread and is acting now in the liturgical event.

Taken as a whole, the unit stresses the relationship of the triune God with humankind and a theology of accompaniment, as the prayer moves from naming God the Father to thanksgiving for the Son's action to the invocation of the Holy Spirit for the transformation of the gifts in the next unit.

Consecratory Epiclesis (*OM2008*, appendix, I:3)

The first epiclesis is ordered logically to the post-*Sanctus (ergo,* line 2) to provide a trinitarian progression from the presence and action of the Father and the Son to the mission and action of the Spirit. The epiclesis has been significantly reworked from the originals, the phrasing of which had raised a number of doctrinal concerns.[15] The *editio typica* makes the first epiclesis consistent with those of EPs II, III, and IV as well as RI and RII. It reflects rephrasing introduced in 1986 to the Spanish-language edition.[16] God is invoked as *Pater clementissime*, as in the *Te Igitur* of EP I (*OM2008*, no. 84), while the original texts named God as "almighty." The Father is asked to send out the Holy Spirit (*emittas*) for the sanctification of the gifts. While the verb *sanctificare* (line 4) is consistent with EPs II, III, IV, and RII, the verb *emittere* (line 3) is not used in any other EP in *MR2002*.[17] The *editio typica*

[13] Mazza enlists the exegesis of Jacques Dupont (ibid., 224).

[14] See Tena, "Commentarium," 423.

[15] Paul De Clerck summarizes these concerns, especially with regard to the French version, in terms of a "triple dissatisfaction." First, the action of Christ and the action of the Spirit are juxtaposed rather than imbricated. Second, the phrasing lends itself to understand Christ, his presence, and his Body and Blood as three different realities and to reify the sacramental species. Third, the French verb *réaliser* attenuates the Eucharist as self-gift of Christ himself, also making the Eucharist into object. See De Clerck, "Epiclèse et formulation du mystère eucharistique," in *Gratias Agamus. Studien zum eucharistischen Hochgebet. Festschrift Balthasar Fischer*, ed. Andreas Heinz and Heinrich Rennings (Freiburg: Herder, 1992), 53–54. Concern had also been expressed about the German phrasing, asking that Christ "be present in our midst with his Body and Blood" (*mit Leib und Blut in unserer Mitte gegenwärtig wird*).

[16] *Te rogamos, pues, Padre todopoderoso que envíes tu Espíritu sobre este pan y este vino, de manera que sean para nosotros Cuerpo y + Sangre de Jesucristo, Hijo tuyo y Señor nuestro*. See *Misal Romano* (Conferencia Episcopal Mexicana, 1986); see the decree in *Notitiae* 22 (1986): 832, no. 4.

[17] See De Clerck's comments, "Epiclèse et formulation," 56.

does not introduce the language of "presence" here as the originals did. The text now makes explicit that it is through the action of the Holy Spirit that the gifts of bread and wine are transformed into the Body and Blood of Christ.[18] Also, the *editio typica* does not continue the literary allusion to the Emmaus narrative evoked in the post-*Sanctus*, as perhaps it could have to give a stronger continuity between the sections.[19]

Together the post-*Sanctus* and the first epiclesis have a theological coherence. As Pere Tena explains, they maintain the flow and connection of "the Presence of God on the journey of human life, the presence of Christ in the assembly joined in his name; the real and substantial presence—body and blood—of Christ by the power of the Spirit under the sacramental signs of bread and wine."[20]

Institution Narrative (*OM2008*, appendix, I:4–5)

The transition to the institution narrative in no. 4 (lines 3–4) has been harmonized with the transition found in EP I and its particularly Roman formulation, *qui pridie quam pateretur.* Thus the prayer maintains the literary connection between the first epiclesis and the institution narrative through a relative clause construction. The expression *supremae nocte Cenae* (no. 4, line 4) that has been added echoes the hymn *Pange Lingua*, verse 3.[21] This addition more explicitly links the Last Supper, the passion, and the Eucharist (cf. *SC*, no. 47). The addition of the expression *postquam cenatum est* (no. 5, line 2) also harmonizes the narrative with EPs I, II, III, and RI (reflecting the narratives of Luke and 1 Cor). The *editio typica* makes a distinction between Jesus' saying the blessing over the bread (*benedixit*, without direct object, no. 4, line 7) and giving thanks to God (*tibi gratias egit*, no. 5, line 6) for the cup, reflecting the progression in the institution narratives of Matthew and Mark.

Anamnesis-Offering (*OM2008*, appendix, I:7, lines 2–8)

The anamnesis-offering segment has been extensively reworked from the originals to make more explicit the nature of eucharistic anamnesis and

[18] See CCC, no. 1353.

[19] See De Clerck, "Epiclèse et formulation," in *Gratias Agamus*, ed. Heinz and Rennings, 56; also, his "La Révision de la Prière Eucharistique «Suisse»," 65.

[20] Tena, "Commentarium," 424.

[21] *In supremae nocte cenae recumbens cum fratribus observata lege plene cibis in legalibus, cibum turbae duodenae se dat suis manibus*; see Tena, "Commentarium," 424.

offering. The unit is now explicitly structured *memores-annuntiamus-offerimus*, thus framing the proclamation and offering within the action of memorial. The formulation *Unde et nos* parallels EPs I and IV, making a clear structural link with the memorial command in the institution narrative. Christ is named as both Son and our Savior (*Christi Filii tui et Salvatoris nostri*). The language of reconciliation present in the three originals has been deleted, and the object of the act of remembrance has been specified more explicitly as the passion, death, resurrection, and being seated at God's right hand. The paschal mystery of Christ is named as God's *opus caritatis* and is also the object of the act of proclamation tied to the memorial. An eschatological dimension, absent from the French and German originals but present by allusion in Italian, is now added with the Pauline expression *donec veniat* (1 Cor 11:26). The language of the offering (*panem vitae et calicem benedictionis offerimus*) echoes EP II in its sacramental terminology; while *panem vitae* alludes to John 6, *calicem benedictionis* recalls 1 Corinthians 10:16.

Communion Epiclesis (*OM2008*, appendix, I:7, lines 9–16)

There has been considerable theological advance in the *editio typica* with regard to the second epiclesis compared to the originals. Structurally, the second epiclesis now functions as a distinct unit, rather than serving as an introduction to the variable intercessory sections as it did in the originals. Further, the second epiclesis more fully makes the connection between the transformation of the elements and the transformation of the communicants to which the first transformation is ordered. The *res* of the Eucharist is more fully articulated in terms of the interrelationship of the sacramental Body and the ecclesial Body. The Spirit is invoked *ut virtute Spiritus caritatis tuae*, akin to phrasing found in an ancient collect now used as a *postcommunio*.[22] A distinct eschatological note is sounded with the allusion to 2 Peter 3:18.[23] The praying assembly asks not only to be united now in the Holy Communion to which the EP is ordered but also *in diem aeternitatis*, alluding to the great *communio sanctorum*. As Cesare Giraudo points out, *in diem aeter-*

[22] See *Gelasianum*, no. 1330. It appears in the *MR2002* as a prayer after communion for the Easter Vigil, for the Second Sunday in Ordinary Time, and in the ritual Mass for Confirmation C.

[23] Tena ("Commentarium," 426) points to the prayer after communion of Lent V in *MR2002* and 2 Pet 3:18 as the source for the phrasing. Prayer: *Quaesumus, omnipotens Deus, ut inter eius membra semper numeremur, cuius Corpori communicamus et Sanguini. Qui vivit et regnat in saecula saeculorum* (*Veronense*, no. 1116). The *Nova Vulgata* text of 2 Pet 3:18 reads: *crescite vero in gratia et in cognitione Domini nostri et Salvatoris Iesu Christi. Ipsi gloria et nunc et in diem aeternitatis. Amen.*

nitatis should be understood as *usque ad Diem Domini unde aeternitas incipit*.[24] This reading conveys the sense of gradual growth and transformation of the church through the regular celebration of the Eucharist.[25]

The language of oblation and sacrifice has also been more explicitly developed compared to the originals. Line 10 (*in qua paschale Christi sacrificium*) alludes to the language of *SC*, no. 47, to describe the nature of the sacrifice. Further, the use of the verb *exhibere* echoes the Anaphora of Saint Basil, where it is the central petition of the epiclesis.[26] In Basil, its use suggests an epiphanic theology, whereby the action of the Spirit makes the gifts manifest Christ's presence.[27] While the language of representation is traditional with regard to Roman Catholic doctrine of the relation of the Eucharist to the once-for-all sacrifice of Christ on the cross,[28] this prayer offers a more expansive approach to sacrifice by employing a theology of manifestation. Nevertheless, there is a certain redundancy here in relation to line 9.[29]

This revised section both draws out more clearly the relationship of the Spirit, the Eucharist, and the formation of the church and makes the oblation of the church more explicit.[30]

Intercessions for the Living (*OM2008*, appendix, I:7, lines 17–36)

The intercessions of variation I should be read in light of the preface and with recollection of the themes of the synod.[31] The synod was envisioned as an event of ecclesial renewal, which is precisely the petition here (lines 17–18), following the original Italian more closely.[32] The focus of the original language versions was on the local church and a spiral of relations, which the intercession of the *editio typica* has shifted to accent the communion of the universal church.[33] The *editio typica* has conformed the intercession for the church to the wording of the major anaphoras: the pope is named first, followed by the local ordinary. Of note here is the naming of the *universo ordine episcopali*—a text that recalls the vision of hierarchical communion

[24] He is following Max Zerwick's exegesis; see Giraudo, *Preghiere Eucaristiche*, 122, n. 6.

[25] Tena also notes the progressive growth of the church ("Commentarium," 426).

[26] *anadeixai*; text in *Prex Eucharistica*, 1:236.

[27] See William Crockett, *Eucharist: Symbol of Transformation* (New York: Pueblo, 1989), 59.

[28] Cf. Council of Trent, Session 22 (1562), chap. 1 = Tanner 2:733.

[29] See further in Giraudo, *Preghiere Eucaristiche*, 121.

[30] See Tena, "Commentarium," 425.

[31] See 550 above.

[32] . . . *Si rinnovi nella luce del vangelo*.

[33] See Tena, "Commentarium," 427.

from *LG* (no. 22)—after the local ordinary. In the original context of the local church at synod, the intercessions started with the local bishop. The *editio typica* expresses ecclesial communion from the "universal" to the local.[34] This communion is imaged as a *vinculum unitatis* (line 19), which joins the people and their leaders together.

The purpose for asking for this strengthening in unity is that the church may shine as a *propheticum signum* (line 26) *unitatis et concordiae* (line 25) *in mundo discordiis lacerato* (line 24). In the preface, the church is named *signum tuae fidelitatis* (no. 1, line 22). The praying church (named as *populus tuus*) now seeks to be a prophetic sign. Sharing in Christ's prophetic office, the people of God are called to witness to the wounded world.[35] The *editio typica* follows the wording of the Italian here; the German and French named the church an *instrument*, which highlights the church's action more strongly. While the unity of the church is contrasted to the divided world (rendered in a standard Roman euchological convention of antithesis: *Concordia-discordia*), the fact that strengthening in unity is the object of prayer does not allow one to gloss over the internal divisions in the church. Unity is not a human achievement alone but a gift from God nurtured through sacramental communion.

Intercession for the Dead (*OM2008*, appendix, I:7, lines 27–32)

The memento for the dead has been recast. While the German spoke of the homecoming of the dead, in line with the root metaphor of the anaphora, the *editio typica* follows more closely the original Italian version. The traditional phrasing *in pace Christi tui dormierunt* (line 28) recalls the phrasing of EP I (*OM2008*, no. 95). The requests for *lumen* (line 31) and for the gift of *vitae plenitudinem* (line 32) also reflect traditional themes and imagery in the prayer for the dead.[36] There is an expansive note sounded here in the remembrance of all the dead (line 29).

Commemoration of the Saints (*OM2008*, appendix, I:7, lines 33–43)

The root metaphor of the pilgrim journey inspires the final section of this EP (*terrena exacta peregrinatione*, line 34). The church asks to be admitted

[34] See Tena's comments that the universalizing of the prayer required a different expression of hierarchical communion from the originals (ibid.).

[35] See *LG*, nos. 12 and 35.

[36] E.g., *Gelasianum*, nos. 1672 and 1684.

ad aeternam . . . mansionem, alluding to John 14:2 and John 14:23, and so to share in the great communion of the saints. The plea for ecclesial unity sounded in the intercessions is extended now to an ever greater eschatological communion (lines 37–40, echoing EP I). The *editio typica* has shifted the tense of the originals to the future (*te laudabimus et magnificabimus*, line 51), underscoring the eschatological finale of the anaphora. The section thus draws out the nature of the eucharistic celebration as a pledge of future glory, imaged as reaching the eternal dwelling after the long journey, living in the true communion of which the Eucharist is the foretaste, and praising God eternally.

Form II: *Deus Ecclesiam suam in viam salutis conducens*

Preface (*OM2008*, appendix, II:1, lines 12–27)

The imagery of creation and re-creation frames God's action of guiding the church. God is named in the opening as *mundi creator et fons omnis vitae*, following the Italian version. God, as *fons* (see Jer 2:13; John 4:14; and Rev 21:6), continues to bring forth life and sustain all creation. God's creating action is named *opera sapientiae*, and the preface gives thanks for God's continued providential care (line 17).

The preface adopts a typological motif, recalling God's having led Israel through the desert with *manu potenti et brachio extento* (line 18). The "hand of God" is a traditional metaphor for the Holy Spirit, stressing the action of God in the world through the power of the Spirit. Through the adverb *nunc*, the connection is made with the church *in mundo peregrinantem* whom God now accompanies *Spiritus Sancti virtute* (lines 20–21), on a journey headed *in gaudium aeternum* (line 23), perhaps an allusion to Hebrews 13:14. While there is risk of conflating *populus Israel* with *Ecclesia* here, the thematic frame of the preface stresses more the economy of God as faithful guide from creation to its fulfillment.

Thus, the preface strives to balance the interplay of past, present, and future. The standard convention for most prefaces is to recall the past in the mode of thanksgiving and praise, recognizing the salvation wrought for us by God through Christ in the Spirit. The preface here recalls what God has done and gives thanks for what God continues to do here and now with a view toward its fulfillment in eternity.[37] Here, a theological reflection on the contemporary experience of the church—a reading of the signs

[37] Giraudo thinks that the eschatological theme would be more appropriate to the second epiclesis and intercessions. See his *Preghiere Eucaristiche*, 58–59.

of the times—provides the motive for memorial thanksgiving together with recollection of the Creator God's providential care in the past.

Intercessions for the Living (*OM2008*, appendix, II:7, lines 17–23)

The object of the intercessions—as in each of the four variations in EP MVN—follows the themes of the preface. The *ecclesiam tuam in mundo peregrinantem* of the preface (line 20) is now *ad mensam . . . convocatos* (line 17). The intercessions, linked to the second epiclesis by *ergo*,[38] open up the implications of the second epiclesis (*inter Filii tui membra . . . numeremur*, lines 14 and 16). The relation of the sacramental Body of Christ to the ecclesial Body of Christ is announced through a petition for the gift of unity flowing from our communion in the sacramental Body.

The ecclesial communion is an ordered communion; while variation 1 mentions the pope, the local ordinary, and the whole order of bishops, this variation (along with 3 and 4) includes presbyters and deacons, although the language of *ordo* is not used. Being strengthened in unity, we can in turn witness to the world as we continue the journey.

This journey is specifically the Christian passage through time on the way of God (*in fide ac spe per semitas tuas*, line 22).[39] The image of the Eucharist as food for the journey is implicit, fortifying the *ambulantes*. The fruits of our Holy Communion enable us *gaudium et fiduciam in mundum effundere* (line 23). A parallel is struck between our walking the journey *in fide ac spe* and the fruits of *gaudium et fiduciam*. These are the fundamental qualities of our pilgrim journey as Christians.

Form III: *Iesus via ad Patrem*

Preface (*OM2008*, appendix, III:1, lines 12–31)

The preface of the third variation is strongly christological in character. The memorial thanksgiving here recalls the history of salvation from creation to incarnation to redemption in Christ and the mission of the Holy

[38] Giraudo observes this is unusual for the anaphoral traditions and suggests the construction may have been inspired by EP IV (*Nunc ergo, Domine, omnium recordare*, *OM2008*, no. 122, line 18). It was missing, however, from an earlier draft of the *editio typica*. See his *Preghiere Eucaristiche*, 130, n. 7.

[39] This follows the original French and Italian's language of "faith" more closely; also, see Tena, "Commentarium," 427–28.

Spirit. The controlling metaphor is Christ as mediator, complemented by elements of Johannine Christology.

In the opening strophe God is invoked as *Domine caeli et terrae* (line 14), echoing the prayer of Jesus in Matthew 11:25-27.[40] The next strophe picks up this theme with *mundum creasti* (line 16), now given a christological focus, *per Verbum tuum*.[41] Creation through the Word is connected to incarnation through *Ipsum, carnem factum* with its clear Johannine echo (John 1:14). The gift of Christ is specified through the metaphor of mediator. The preface then makes explicit the way Christ exercises his mediatorship through the triplum *via-veritas-vita* (lines 21–23, cf. John 14:6). The preface plays on Christ as *Verbum* (John 1:1) and *verba tua nobis est locutus* (John 14:10).

The flow of tenses in the preface strikes a balance between remembering the past and naming the present. The past tense (lines 16–20) shifts to present tense forms (lines 21–23 and 28). The economy of salvation is connected to God's continued action through Christ in our day and time.

After naming what Christ is doing in our midst as mediator, the preface shifts to give thanks that God *per Filium tuum homines . . . in unam colligis familiam* (lines 24 and 28). The themes of creation, redemption, and sacramental life are evoked in the intervening relative clause that qualifies *homines* (lines 25–27). The imagery of the blood and the seal of the Spirit reinforce the saving action of God as constituting a people (e.g., Exod 12:23 and Eph 1:13-14). This imagery is drawn from the original Italian version "to complete the description of the work of Christ the mediator."[42] The closing strophe offers an eschatological note with the phrase *et usque in saeculum*.

Intercessions for the Living (*OM2008*, appendix, III:7, lines 17–32)

The intercessions of variation III open with an invocation for the Holy Spirit (*nos Spiritu vivifica*), giving this first section of the intercessions a strongly epicletic casting. This may well be a residual phrasing from the originals, whose intercessory units opened with the second epiclesis. The opening phrase uses the technical term *mysterium*, whose semantic range

[40] *Nova Vulgata: In illo tempore respondens Iesus dixit: "Confiteor tibi, Pater, Domine caeli et terrae, quia abscondisti haec a sapientibus et prudentibus et revelasti ea parvulis."*

[41] Giraudo sees this as an unfortunate duplication of the *per Christum Dominum nostrum* in the opening strophe; see his *Preghiere Eucaristiche*, 61–62.

[42] Tena, "Commentarium," 428.

in the euchological tradition is the whole sacramental action. *Mysterium* signifies participation in the whole liturgical action, not just the sacramental elements to which this refers. In line 19, *imagini Filii tui conformes fieri* alludes to Romans 8:29 and, in this context, to the continual deifying effect of participation in the sacraments. Participation in the sacramental action effects ecclesial unity (*in vinculo communionis confirma*, line 20), stressing the Eucharist as the sacrament of unity.[43] The phrasing of the hierarchical ordering of the church parallels the intercessions of variations II and IV.

The second section of the intercessory unit is a clear transfer of the language of *GS* to liturgical prayer.[44] Line 25 (*temporum signa*) adopts the language of *GS*, no. 4, shifting the lens of interpretation from *sub Evangelii luce* of *GS* to *lumine fidei*.[45] This is ordered to *servitium Evangelii*, connecting discernment to mission. Our mission and witness is not only to the church but *ad cunctorum hominum*, echoing the missionary commitments of *GS* (e.g., no. 11).

Lines 29–30 (*ut luctus eorum et angores, gaudium et spem participantes*) evoke the vocabulary of *GS*, no. 1, and the themes of *GS* as a whole,[46] as do the ensuing lines. To be *imagini Filii tui conformes* and to be strengthened *in vinculo communionis* (lines 19–20) entails a commitment to service, attention to the needs of all, witness to the Gospel (*nuntium salutis*), and accompaniment *in viam regni* on the pilgrim journey. We are not spectators but *participantes* in the lives of all women and men. The communion of all in the church and in Christ leads out to the world. The intercessory unit offers a vision of the Christian life that flows *huius participatione mysterii* (line 17).

Form IV: *Iesus pertransiens benefaciendo*

Preface (*OM2008*, appendix, IV:1, lines 12–28)

The attribution of God the Father at the opening of the preface (*Pater misericordiarum et Deus fidelis*) sets the tone for variation IV. The mercy and faithfulness of God are shown to us in the gift of his Son, who is *Dominum ac redemptorem*. This hendiadys follows the Italian original, while the French and German versions named Jesus as Lord and brother. While adopting a

[43] See Augustine, *In Ioannis Evangelium Tractatus*, 26:13, ed. Radbodus Willems, 2nd ed., *CCL* 36 (1990 [1954]), 266; and Thomas Aquinas, *Summa Theologica* III.73.2 *sc*.

[44] Tena, "Commentarium," 428–29; Giraudo, *Preghiere Eucaristiche*, 134.

[45] . . . *per omne tempus Ecclesiae officium incumbit signa temporum perscrutandi et sub Evangelii luce interpretandi* (*GS*, no. 4; cf. *GS*, no. 11).

[46] See *GS*, nos. 1, 4, 7, 47, 75, 77; Giraudo refers to the themes of *angor-angustia-angere* as the *leitmotiv* of *GS* in his *Preghiere Eucaristiche*, 134–35.

higher christological term, the preface explicates that Christ's redemptive action occurs through his merciful care for the marginalized (lines 17–21). Lines 20–21 (*proximum se fecit oppressis et afflictis*) are an allusion to the parable of the Good Samaritan (Luke 10:30-37). Christ is the Good Samaritan, who does not pass by the ones in need.[47]

This extension of mercy *verbo et opere* (line 22) reveals God as Father (line 23). The Latin here follows the Italian original. The French and German texts stress first God's action of care for all people, modified by the example of a father's care for his children. Given the Lukan allusions in the section immediately prior, this metaphor might best be read through the lens of Luke's parable of the lost son (15:11-32).

The preface emphasizes a Christology of compassion. The revelatory words and deeds of Christ manifest the divine economy as mercy made flesh, marked by care even for sinners (line 19). For a church on the journey, the overarching theme of the EP MVN,[48] the road from Jerusalem to Jericho (Luke 10:30) is evoked, showing the ethical responsibility of our being *proximum . . . oppressis et afflictis* (lines 20–21). Our liturgical anamnesis of Christ who is compassion summons as well our remembrance of those passed by in a world of suffering and distress.

Intercessions for the Living (*OM2008*, appendix, IV:7, lines 17–31)

The intercessions extend the themes of the preface and flow from the second epiclesis. The unit opens, asking that we—whom the second epiclesis prays may be counted among the members of God's Son (line 14)—may be brought *in fide et caritate perficere* (line 18), a grace of the sacramental communion and the working of the Holy Spirit. The phrase *omni populo acquisitionis tuae* (line 21) alludes to 1 Peter 2:9 and the relationship forged in baptism. The theme of perfection in charity draws on the classical theological explanation of the *res* of the Eucharist.[49]

The petition, *Aperi oculos nostros ut necessitates fratrum agnoscamus* (lines 22–23), calls the church to be attentive like the Good Samaritan, alert to those beset by suffering and need. As Christ acted in word and deed (preface, line

[47] See Tena, "Commentarium," 429; Raffa also notes the coherence of the preface with the portrait of Christ in the gospel of Luke (Vincenzo Raffa, *Liturgia Eucaristica: Mistagogia della Messa: dalla storia e dalla teologia alla pastorale pratica*, Bibliotheca 'Ephemerides liturgicae' Subsidia 100 [Rome: CLV, 2003], 798).

[48] Raffa, *Liturgia Eucaristica*, 798.

[49] See Thomas, *Summa Theologica* III.73.3 ad. 3.

22), so the church seeks that God inspire us in words and deeds (line 24). Line 25 recalls the invitation of Jesus to the excluded and oppressed in Matthew 11:28.[50] The church pleads to follow the example of Christ and his command, namely, the great *mandatum* of love (John 13:15, 34).[51]

This intercessory unit concludes with an appeal that the church *vivum testimonium exsistat* (line 28). The church's attention to those in need serves as a visible manifestation of God's reign (*veritatis et libertatis, pacis atque iustitiae,* lines 29–30). To speak of the church and the *populo acquisitionis* (line 21) as a living witness recalls conciliar imagery for the church.[52] Out of ecclesial and eucharistic communion flow our living witness to the world. This witness to God's reign is a new hope (line 31). The Latin follows the German here; the Italian specifies that this is hope in a new world. The intercessions that opened with an appeal to be perfect in faith and charity end with an appeal for hope.

[50] *Nova Vulgata*: *Venite ad me, omnes, qui laboratis et onerati estis, et ego reficiam vos.*
[51] Tena, "Commentarium," 429.
[52] E.g., *LG*, no. 12 and *Ad Gentes*, no. 21.

The ICEL2010 Translation

Anscar J. Chupungco

EP MVN is the only one of its kind in the corpus of EPs. It has four variable prefaces that are thematic and four variable *communicantes* that correspond in a loose way to the themes of the prefaces. The Roman Canon too has several forms of *communicantes*. These are seasonal (Christmas, Epiphany, Holy Thursday, Easter, Ascension, and Pentecost) and in this sense are likewise thematic.

The first two prefaces speak about the Pilgrim Church on its way toward unity under God's guidance "along the paths of time." The last two prefaces present Jesus as the way to the Father and as the compassion of God. The four prefaces narrate the NT history of salvation in inverted order. The christological could have preceded the ecclesiological.

What is remarkable in this prayer is the frequent allusion to Sacred Scripture. The post-*Sanctus* recalls the Emmaus story and throughout the prefaces are familiar biblical phrases: "from every people, tongue, and nation" (Form I, preface); "with mighty hand and outstretched arm" (Form II, preface); "redeemed by the Blood of his Cross" (Form III, preface); "always showed compassion" (Form IV, preface).[1]

The Latin text of this EP is elegant and easy to read even when it employs classical Latin sentence construction and word order. Except for the less appropriate use of *in medio* (instead of *apud*) in the post-*Sanctus* of Form I, and the dense post-consecratory anamnesis prayer repeated in all four forms of this prayer, it is an impeccable piece of modern liturgical Latin.

The rich biblical and doctrinal content as well as the well-crafted Latin of the EP MVN augur well for good English translation. With due respect for *LitAuth*, the ICEL1998 version of this prayer matches the Latin original in content and literary quality. We are dealing here with a mature ICEL compared, for example, to the 1973 translation of the Order of Mass. Unfortunately, it is alleged that ICEL1998 was "unfaithful" to the Latin,

[1] For a more detailed exploration of the biblical allusions in this prayer, see McCarron, 557–70 above.

because it translates the sense rather than individual words and phrases.[2] A new translation had to be made in accord with the principle of formal correspondence.

The aim of this exercise is to comment on a few instances in ICEL2010's version of this EP that call for improvement. These comments are concerned with the fixed elements of the prayer that are the same across all four variations.[3]

Institution Narrative over the Bread (ICEL2010, appendix, I:4)

The Latin has two temporal clauses (*Qui pridie quam pateretur, in supremae nocte Cenae*), one following the other. They present in great detail the time when the Eucharist was instituted: on the day before the passion and at night. Two consecutive temporal clauses is a knotty construction, but it is perfectly all right in Latin because *pridie* does not require the preposition *in* unlike *nocte*. The aural affect is thus not impaired by what would have been a successive repetition of *in*.

ICEL1998 solved this linguistic problem by the use of sense translation: "On the eve of his passion and death, while at table with those he loved." "On the eve" is inclusive of the two temporal clauses; "while at table" refers to *supremae Cenae*. What ICEL1998 leaves out as understood is the Last Supper with the disciples.

ICEL2010, on the other hand, translates both temporal clauses without modification: "On the day before he was to suffer, on the night of the Last Supper." This clumsy English construction could have been avoided by a less literal translation.

Anamnesis-Offering (ICEL2010, appendix, I:7, lines 2–9)

The typical Latin post-consecratory prayer consists of two elements: recalling the paschal mystery and subsequently offering the consecrated bread and wine. While we recall, we offer. This formula is the reason why the post-consecratory prayer is lengthy and conceptually drawn out. ICEL1998 divided the sentence into two for easier communication:

[2] See the discussion of dynamic equivalency, in my "Excursus on Translation of the New *Ordo Missae*," 133–35 above.

[3] For a more detailed overview of the fixed elements in the various forms of this prayer, see McCarron, 559–65 above.

And so, Father most holy,
we celebrate the memory of Christ, your Son,
whom you led through suffering and death on the cross
to the glory of the resurrection
and a place at your right hand.
Until Jesus, our Savior, comes again,
we proclaim the work of your love,
offering you the bread of life and the cup of blessing.

ICEL2010 keeps the Latin structure with several dependent clauses in the first part (recalling) and concludes the long sentence with the other clauses about the offering.

Communion Epiclesis (ICEL2010, appendix, I:7, lines 10–16)

This Latin text echoes the Pauline expression of communion in the Body and Blood of Christ (1 Cor 10:16). ICEL2010 correctly translates it as "in whose Body and Blood we have communion," (line 16) but ICEL1998 used the more familiar expression: "whose body and blood we share."

Conclusion

A celebrated passage from the 1969 instruction *CLP* on the translation of liturgical texts fittingly concludes this short study and brings to a conclusion my previous remarks on translation included in this volume.[4] It will be remembered that this instruction guided the herculean work of liturgical translation across the globe until the appearance in 2001 of *LitAuth*. *CLP* is now considered "dated," but its value as a guideline for liturgical translation stands on solid scientific grounds. According to the 1969 instruction, "a faithful translation cannot be judged on the basis of individual words: the total context of this specific act of communication must be kept in mind, as well as the literary form proper to the respective language" (no. 6). The context includes the message itself, the audience for which the text is intended, and the manner of expression.

[4] See 133–35, 137–41, 181–85, 219–20, 473–74, 475–83, and 501–2 above.

The Mystagogical Implications

Mark E. Wedig

Developing a mystagogy for a EP means entering into that prayer's world of meaning. It denotes teasing out symbolic, linguistic, and theological perspectives that the prayer generates and embodies, especially when a community intentionally incorporates it into its regular and normative liturgical life. One could ask, what was the original intention of the prayer for those who authored it, and how does the prayer connote new meanings for communities who actively pray the prayer today? What particular kind of assembly does the prayer shape by its symbols, language, and theological themes? What are the unique pastoral assets and challenges of praying the prayer? These questions will be addressed in this essay, with particular attention to EP MVN.

Placing EP MVN—also known as the "Swiss Synod Prayer" or "Swiss Anaphora"[1]—in the appendix of *OM2008* along with the EP RI and EP RII begs the question of their usage in relationship to EP I–IV.[2] In light of this placement, it is worth noting that the EPs for children, while still approved for use, are not part of *MR2002* at all. As appendices to the *OM* (and not simply appendices to *MR2002*),[3] the two reconciliation prayers and the one for various needs are designated for specified occasions and particular moments in the life of the local church. What are the various needs that call the local church to pray EP MVN?

The Social, Ecclesial, and Eschatological Meanings of EP MVN

As noted in previous commentaries,[4] EP MVN is conceived as a single EP with four variable thematic parts represented by unique prefaces and intercessions. The prayer as a single and unified prayer expresses a thematic

[1] For the background of these names, see McCarron, 549 above.

[2] On the way various language groups have incorporated EP MVN into the regular body of its eucharistic euchology (e.g., in the 1989 Spanish-language Missal), see McCarron, 554 above.

[3] On this distinction, see McCarron, 555 above.

[4] For example, see McCarron and Chupungco above, 550 and 571, respectively.

unity concerning the Pilgrim Church, to be addressed in greater detail below. Nevertheless, the various titles for each of the four forms of EP MVN give clear indications as to how each of the four variations of this EP may be employed, specifically in their reference to the various Mass formularies found in *MR2002*:

- Form I: "The Church on the Path of Unity" is appropriately used with Mass formularies such as for the church, the pope, the bishop, the election of a pope or bishop, a council or synod, for priests, for ministers of the church, and for a spiritual or pastoral meeting
- Form II: "God Guides His Church along the Way of Salvation" is appropriately used with Mass formularies such as for the church, vocations to holy orders, the laity, family, religious, vocations to religious life, charity, relatives and friends, and giving thanks to the Lord
- Form III: "Jesus, the Way to the Father" is appropriate with Mass formularies such as for evangelization of peoples, persecuted Christians, a nation or state, those in public office, a governing assembly, the beginning of the civil year, and the progress of peoples
- Form IV: "Jesus, Who Went about Doing Good" is appropriately used with Mass formularies such as for refugees and exiles, in time of famine or for those who suffer from famine, for our oppressors, those held in captivity, prisoners, the sick, the dying, the grace of a happy death, and in any need

In giving the example of all of the possible Mass formularies that match the variations in this EP, one might wonder who or what is left out. Might the prayer be intended for all people and all occasions, realizing that the church is always in need?

An appropriate mystagogy of EP MVN requires sifting through the rubric's exhaustive examples of possible ecclesiastical and pastoral uses and discovering the prayer's core ecclesiological purpose. In examining its invariable parts,[5] EP MVN explores metaphors of the road, path, pilgrimage, and journey. The metaphor of Jesus Christ walking "on the journey of life"[6] with the faithful resonates through the invariable parts of EP MVN and is thematized in all four variations of the prayer. Praying from the

[5] For a more detailed discussion of the invariable and variable parts, see McCarron, 557–70 above.

[6] Post-*Sanctus* of Form I = ICEL2010, appendix, 1:2, line 4.

perspective of the earthly pilgrimage is accentuated in each of the texts and it is uniquely eschatological. Here, EP MVN echoes *LG*'s emphasis (no. 48) on the People of God who come to know Jesus Christ through their faithful pilgrimage on earth. There is the need for the church to view itself as a Pilgrim People who journey together with Christ on the road. Such an ecclesiology seems to characterize the entire prayer.

Form I: Unity

To what or where does that pilgrimage go? EP MVN answers definitively that the journey leads to unity, salvation, the Father, and doing good. How might we break open the significance of the church on a trajectory toward harmony and accord, salvation, God, and virtue and apply that to the life of local assemblies? First of all, without simply stating the obvious, mystagogical reflection in this case requires a critical examination of how and when the local church would face unique instances of disunity, strife, and division. EP MVN asks for reflection on the fact that the church, as our world, can experience disruptive and alienating discord that asks the local assemblies to praise God for the healing of division as well as to supplicate for ongoing reconciliation.

LG recognizes such strife:

> [U]ntil the arrival of the new heavens and the new earth in which justice dwells the pilgrim church, in its sacraments and institutions, which belong to this present age, carries the mark of the world which will pass, and it takes its place among the creatures which groan and until now suffer the pains of childbirth and await the revelation of the children of God. (no. 48)

The Pilgrim People, the People of God, uniquely share the sufferings of the world as they journey through the present age.

The unity and healing called for by EP MVN can be understood as a unity and healing that is more systemic and socio-religious than that reflected in EP RI and RII. The injury of discord that is the subject of EP MVN can be viewed less about the disobedience of a penitential people and more about how a people can experience deep and comprehensive disharmonies that militate against the very accord needed to be a church and a society. Such concern, it is suggested, is a uniquely modern and postmodern concern of peoples ravaged by war, racism, sexual abuse and other systemic social scandal, and disenfranchisement.

This EP expresses the awareness of the Christian assembly that knows the power of the paschal mystery to overcome the deepest societal, political, and religious divisions of the human condition. It mirrors the consciousness of a people who know that the alienation caused by forces as powerful as modern war, a Nazi Holocaust, and nuclear destruction cannot obliterate the loving relationship of the triune God.

Form II: Salvation

Second, the path to salvation as expressed by EP MVN is a realized eschatological one. In other words, salvation is experienced as an earthly reality in which the Pilgrim Church, the People of God, is led by Christ "along the paths of time to the eternal joy"[7] of God's kingdom. The world as known by the present human community is the place where salvation is worked out. The soteriological promise is not something remote or hidden but a reality evident in the quotidian experiences of a people who live out justice, peace, joy, and trust.

EP MVN teaches that the salvific process in Christianity militates against the placing of hope for fulfillment in another place and time. The prayer itself conveys the urgency and immediacy of experiencing the kingdom of God breaking forth in the present age. Therefore, the Eucharist not simply foreshadows a heavenly banquet and a communion on the other side of death but instead engenders a feast celebrating God's reign now. This challenges a traditional Roman Catholic perspective on eucharistic worship, which has focused on an earthly communion feasting on heavenly realities. In fact, EP MVN indicates just the opposite where heavenly companions visit an earthly assembly anticipating a heavenly reunion.

A realized eschatology of eucharistic worship is an important focus for contemporary Catholic Christians who see the pressing needs of a global community. One of the great liabilities of being a citizen in a postmodern world is that we are apt to realize the perils of the entire globe at every instance and situation. YouTube allows us to gaze with unrelenting horror at our world's hunger and desperation, creating in us great anxiety and despair. Such worldwide access compels us to link the Eucharist directly to social justice and every movement intent on reversing the trends of global destruction. Communion with each other, thematized in EP MVN, beckons an abiding hope in realized eucharistic justice and truth.

Form III: To the Father

Third, a mystagogy of EP MVN affords the church the opportunity to emphasize that all of Christian prayer is fundamentally trinitarian and

[7] Preface, Form II = ICEL2010, appendix 2:1, lines 22-23.

therefore to the Father, through the Son, and in the Spirit. The community of relations in the Godhead is lived in the extant reality of the church. Moreover, the Trinity is not just an abstract formula or neat schemata about God. EP MVN helps the church make a precise connection between the Trinity and efforts for justice and peace. In other words, trinitarian belief has everything to do with living in the world with specific intentions and objectives concerning the realization of the kingdom of God.

EP MVN accentuates that the Pilgrim Church's path to the Father through Jesus Christ and in the Holy Spirit will always be attentive to the needs of the world around it and be capable of announcing good news to a people and share in their pain. Thus, the intercessions in form III pray:

> Keep us attentive to the needs of all
> that, sharing their grief and pain,
> their joy and hope,
> we may faithfully bring them the news of salvation
> and go forward with them
> along the way of your Kingdom.[8]

Praying as the Pilgrim Church underscores how a contemporary people long for a great reversal in societies across the globe.

Trinitarian faith has practical implications for the pilgrimage on which we find ourselves. Those on the path to the Father tread through landscapes that anticipate the kingdom of God. Without the company of the risen Christ through the Holy Spirit that journey is impossible and that pilgrimage is bound to fail. Again *LG* so aptly explains this life in the Trinity:

> The promised and hoped for restoration, therefore, has already begun in Christ. It is carried forward in the sending of the holy Spirit and through him continues in the church in which, through faith, we learn the meaning of our earthly life while, as we hope for the benefits which are to come, we bring to its conclusion the task allotted to us in the world by the Father, and so work out our salvation. (no. 48)

Form IV: Doing Good

Finally, the spirituality of EP MVN is one of a Pilgrim People, focused on the path to "doing good" that is particularly embodied in giving heed to a fundamental option for the poor. The liberation of people who are captive to societal injustice and oppression is the foundation of a Christian

[8] ICEL2010, appendix, 3:7, lines 29–34.

spirituality as expressed in the EP. The preface to variation IV of EP MVN reminds the assembly of that calling lived out in the life of Jesus Christ:

> He always showed compassion
> for children and for the poor,
> for the sick and for sinners,
> and he became a neighbor
> to the oppressed and the afflicted.[9]

The life of Jesus, which was uniquely focused on the poor, the sick, and the suffering, is the model for all Christians.

Likewise, for the followers of Jesus Christ, the griefs and anxieties of the poor are also to become their griefs and anxieties (*GS*, no. 1). EP MVN engenders a liturgical spirituality that makes the sufferings and hardships of the poor the immediate concerns of the assembly. It petitions that our eyes be opened to recognize the needs of our brothers and sisters so that we may be inspired by words and actions to comfort those who labor and are burdened. The prayer echoes the solidarity and shared aims of so many of our communities who labor for social justice and to alleviate poverty in our cities.

EP MVN in the Life of the English-Speaking Church

The inclusion of EP MVN in *MR2002* provides an opportunity for the church to be evangelized into seeing itself evermore as a Pilgrim People. The ecclesiology articulated in *LG*—especially through the metaphor of the People of God, holy yet imperfect, who journey together and live in the hope of God's kingdom—is strongly emphasized by EP MVN. Moreover, the prayer provides a strong eschatological underpinning for this ecclesiology by stressing the imminence of that reign and the opportunity of the church to do the good works that reverse the plight of a society that faces grave needs and exigencies.

Unknown to Known Prayer in the Life of the Local Church

EP MVN has existed in the dioceses of the United States as an approved "interim" prayer since 1995.[10] It was promulgated for use in booklet form and therefore has remained relatively inaccessible in the life of the English-

[9] ICEL2010, appendix, 4:1, lines 17–21.

[10] The prayer was deemed interim because of the expected approval of the English-language 1998 Sacramentary; on this history, see McCarron, 554 above.

speaking church. In fact, many clergy and laity even now do not know of its existence or that it has been approved for public prayer for the last fifteen years.[11]

Different from the English-language experience, clergy and assemblies in the Spanish-speaking church are quite familiar with EP MVN because of its existence in their Sacramentary since 1989 as *Plegaria Eucarística V*.[12] In particular, Spanish-speaking clergy and liturgy-planning groups have integrated EP MVN into the life of the local assembly as a regular part of their Sunday euchology. In some cases the prayer has become the preferred EP for the Sunday assembly because the "language of the prayer resonates with the people and their experience."[13] Since it is understood by many clergy as one of the primary euchological texts of the Sacramentary, the prayer has been more easily incorporated into the regular Sunday experience of US Catholics in Spanish-speaking contexts.

A Contemporary Church in Need

By incorporating EP MVN into the regular prayer life of the church, the People of God are afforded the opportunity to recognize that in many, if not most, of our gatherings, Catholics experience themselves as a people desperately in need. As stated above, one of the challenging opportunities of a postmodern world is that it calls our attention evermore to the exigencies of a world where people are desperate for justice, harmony, and nonviolence. Christians who gather for Sunday Eucharist, even in the comfort of middle-class environments, find it harder and harder to anesthetize themselves to the suffering of our world. Moreover, the scandals of racism,

[11] For the purposes of gathering information for the essays in this volume, the author conducted three different focus groups to gauge people's experience of the EPs of the Roman Rite. The three groups of ten persons each were composed of separate "populations" of churchgoers. Group 1 was made up of presbyters who were ordained between five and thirty years. Group 2 was composed of graduate students in theology and ministry at a local Catholic university. Group 3 was made up of a range of persons in age that make up the regular membership of the eleven o'clock Sunday morning eucharistic liturgy at a local parish. Only two out of ten from group 1 realized that EP MVN was approved by the USCCB for prayer in English. Those two clergy were familiar with the prayer because they often prayed the prayer in the Spanish-language Sacramentary. Three out of ten from group 2 were aware of the option of praying EP MVN in English. No members of group 3 were aware of the existence of EP MVN.

[12] For this history, see McCarron, 554 above.

[13] For the sake of this essay I gathered a focus group of ten clergy from the Miami area who use the Spanish-language Sacramentary as a regular part of the public prayer of the local church. From this group there was an overwhelming positive experience of *Plegaria Eucarística V* in the *Misal Romano*. In the case of four clergy it was the preferred prayer for the Sunday assembly.

sexism, sexual abuse, and other power abuses have captured our imaginations and shocked our senses of harmony, trust, and justice. Disenchantment with both secular and religious institutions has often placed us on the brink of despair and cynicism.

This context provides all the more reason for incorporating into our shared spiritualities eucharistic metaphors that return our imaginations to the pilgrimage that we share with the risen but wounded Christ. The language of EP MVN affirms and reassures the assembly that their experience of the harsh inequities of the world between rich and poor, educated and illiterate, free and oppressed can be brought to the communion table where the church proclaims and hopes for a radically different social and religious order from their everyday lives. The discourse of EP MVN eloquently represents the sensibilities of contemporary communities of faith that constantly gaze on the seemingly irreconcilable social and political differences that find reconciliation only in the paschal mystery.

Mystagogical reflection on EP MVN might give rise to lament that this anaphora is placed in an appendix in *MR2002*. By understanding the place and significance of its language and themes, might the prayer not warrant regular use in the assembly? Would it not be more appropriate to consider it as a fifth EP—like *Plegaria Eucarística V* in the *Misal Romano*—rather than a prayer for extraordinary purposes? In fact, we are a church in need. The circumstances of our world ask us to pray in a way that never overlooks the inequities of our communion, whether they are local or universal. The metaphor of church as the Pilgrim People pilgrimaging toward a more just and nonviolent social order is eloquently articulated in EP MVN.

The Communion Rite

The Latin Text

Ritus communionis

124. Calice et patena depositis, sacerdos, iunctis manibus, dicit:

Praecéptis salutáribus móniti,
et divína institutióne formáti,
audémus dícere:

Extendit manus et, una cum populo, pergit:

Alii toni in Appendice.

Pater noster, qui es in caelis:
sanctificétur nomen tuum;
advéniat regnum tuum;
fiat volúntas tua, sicut in caelo, et in terra.
Panem nostrum cotidiánum da nobis hódie;
et dimítte nobis débita nostra,
sicut et nos dimíttimus debitóribus nostris;
et ne nos indúcas in tentatiónem;
sed líbera nos a malo.

125. Manibus extensis, sacerdos solus prosequitur, dicens:

Líbera nos, quaésumus, Dómine, ab ómnibus malis,
da propítius pacem in diébus nostris,
ut, ope misericórdiae tuae adiúti,
et a peccáto simus semper líberi
et ab omni perturbatióne secúri:
exspectántes beátam spem
et advéntum Salvatóris nostri Iesu Christi.

Iungit manus.

Populus orationem concludit, acclamans:

Quia tuum est regnum,
et potéstas, et glória
in saécula.

The English Text

The Communion Rite

124. After the chalice and paten have been set down, the Priest, with hands joined, says:

At the Savior's command
and formed by divine teaching,
we dare to say:

He extends his hands and, together with the people, continues:

Our Father, who art in heaven,
hallowed be thy name;
thy kingdom come,
thy will be done
on earth as it is in heaven.
Give us this day our daily bread,
and forgive us our trespasses,
as we forgive those who trespass against us;
and lead us not into temptation,
but deliver us from evil.

Or:

Alternate musical settings of the Lord's Prayer may be found in Appendix I of the *Missal*.

125. With hands extended, the Priest alone continues, saying:

Deliver us, Lord, we pray, from every evil,
graciously grant peace in our days,
that, by the help of your mercy,
we may be always free from sin
and safe from all distress,
as we await the blessed hope
and the coming of our Savior, Jesus Christ.

He joins his hands.

The people conclude the prayer, acclaiming:

For the kingdom,
the power and the glory are yours
now and for ever.

126. Deinde sacerdos, manibus extensis, clara voce dicit:

Dómine Iesu Christe, qui dixísti Apóstolis tuis:
Pacem relínquo vobis, pacem meam do vobis:
ne respícias peccáta nostra,
sed fidem Ecclésiae tuae;
eámque secúndum voluntátem tuam
pacificáre et coadunáre dignéris.

Iungit manus.

Qui vivis et regnas in saécula saeculórum.

Populus respondet:

Amen.

127. Sacerdos, ad populum conversus, extendens et iungens manus, subdit:

Pax Dómini sit semper vobíscum.

Populus respondet:

Et cum spíritu tuo.

128. Deinde, pro opportunitate, diaconus, vel sacerdos, subiungit:

Offérte vobis pacem.

Et omnes, iuxta locorum consuetudines, pacem, communionem et caritatem sibi invicem significant; sacerdos pacem dat diacono vel ministro.

129. Deinde accipit hostiam eamque super patenam frangit, et particulam immittit in calicem, dicens secreto:

Haec commíxtio Córporis et Sánguinis
Dómini nostri Iesu Christi
fiat accipiéntibus nobis in vitam aetérnam.

130. Interim cantatur vel dicitur:

Aliae melodiae in Graduali romano inveniuntur.

Agnus Dei, qui tollis peccáta mundi: miserére nobis.

Agnus Dei, qui tollis peccáta mundi: miserére nobis.

Agnus Dei, qui tollis peccáta mundi: dona nobis pacem.

126. Then the Priest, with hands extended, says aloud:

Lord Jesus Christ,
who said to your Apostles:
Peace I leave you, my peace I give you,
look not on our sins,
but on the faith of your Church,
and graciously grant her peace and unity
in accordance with your will.

He joins his hands.

Who live and reign for ever and ever.

The people reply:

Amen.

127. The Priest, turned towards the people, extending and then joining his hands, adds:

The peace of the Lord be with you always.

The people reply:

And with your spirit.

128. Then, if appropriate, the Deacon, or the Priest, adds:

Let us offer each other the sign of peace.

And all offer one another a sign, in keeping with local customs, that expresses peace, communion, and charity. The Priest gives the sign of peace to a Deacon or minister.

129. Then he takes the host, breaks it over the paten, and places a small piece in the chalice, saying quietly:

May this mingling of the Body and Blood
of our Lord Jesus Christ
bring eternal life to us who receive it.

130. Meanwhile the following is sung or said:

Lamb of God, you take away the sins of the world,
have mercy on us.
Lamb of God, you take away the sins of the world,
have mercy on us.
Lamb of God, you take away the sins of the world,
grant us peace.

Quod etiam pluries repeti potest, si fractio panis protrahitur. Ultima tamen vice dicitur: **dona nobis pacem**.

131. Sacerdos deinde, manibus iunctis, dicit secreto:

Dómine Iesu Christe, Fili Dei vivi,
qui ex voluntáte Patris,
cooperánte Spíritu Sancto,
per mortem tuam mundum vivificásti:
líbera me per hoc sacrosánctum Corpus et Sánguinem tuum
ab ómnibus iniquitátibus meis et univérsis malis:
et fac me tuis semper inhaerére mandátis,
et a te numquam separári permíttas.

Vel:

Percéptio Córporis et Sánguinis tui, Dómine Iesu Christe,
non mihi provéniat in iudícium et condemnatiónem:
sed pro tua pietáte prosit mihi
ad tutaméntum mentis et córporis,
et ad medélam percipiéndam.

132. Sacerdos genuflectit, accipit hostiam, eamque aliquantulum elevatam super patenam vel super calicem tenens, versus ad populum, clara voce dicit:

Ecce Agnus Dei, ecce qui tollit peccáta mundi.
Beáti qui ad cenam Agni vocáti sunt.

Et una cum populo semel subdit:

Dómine, non sum dignus, ut intres sub téctum meum, sed tantum dic verbo, et sanábitur ánima mea.

133. Et sacerdos, versus ad altare, secreto dicit:

Corpus Christi custódiat me in vitam aetérnam.

Et reverenter sumit Corpus Christi.

Deinde accipit calicem et secreto dicit:

Sanguis Christi custódiat me in vitam aetérnam.

Et reverenter sumit Sanguinem Christi.

Or:

The invocation may even be repeated several times if the fraction is prolonged. Only the final time, however, is **grant us peace** said.

131. Then the Priest, with hands joined, says quietly:

Lord Jesus Christ, Son of the living God,
who, by the will of the Father
and the work of the Holy Spirit,
through your Death gave life to the world,
free me by this, your most holy Body and Blood,
from all my sins and from every evil;
keep me always faithful to your commandments,
and never let me be parted from you.

Or:

May the receiving of your Body and Blood,
Lord Jesus Christ,
not bring me to judgment and condemnation,
but through your loving mercy
be for me protection in mind and body
and a healing remedy.

132. The Priest genuflects, takes the host and, holding it slightly raised above the paten or above the chalice, while facing the people, says aloud:

Behold the Lamb of God,
behold him who takes away the sins of the world.
Blessed are those called to the supper of the Lamb.

And together with the people he adds once:

Lord, I am not worthy
that you should enter under my roof,
but only say the word
and my soul shall be healed.

133. The Priest, facing the altar, says quietly:

May the Body of Christ
keep me safe for eternal life.

And he reverently consumes the Body of Christ.

Then he takes the chalice and says quietly:

May the Blood of Christ
keep me safe for eternal life.

And he reverently consumes the Blood of Christ.

134. Postea accipit patenam vel pyxidem, accedit ad communicandos, et hostiam parum elevatam unicuique eorum ostendit, dicens:

Corpus Christi.

Communicandus respondet:

Amen.

Et communicatur.

Eo modo agit et diaconus, si sacram Communionem distribuit.

135. Si adsint sub utraque specie communicandi, servetur ritus suo loco descriptus.

136. Dum sacerdos sumit Corpus Christi, inchoatur cantus ad Communionem.

137. Distributione Communionis expleta, sacerdos vel diaconus vel acolythus purificat patenam super calicem et ipsum calicem.

Dum purificationem peragit, sacerdos dicit secreto:

Quod ore súmpsimus, Dómine, pura mente capiámus, et de múnere temporáli fiat nobis remédium sempitérnum.

138. Tunc sacerdos ad sedem redire potest. Pro opportunitate sacrum silentium, per aliquod temporis spatium, servari, vel psalmus aut aliud canticum laudis aut hymnus proferri potest.

139. Deinde, stans ad altare vel ad sedem, sacerdos, versus ad populum, iunctis manibus, dicit:

Orémus.

Et omnes una cum sacerdote per aliquod temporis spatium in silentio orant, nisi silentium iam praecesserit. Deinde sacerdos, manibus extensis, dicit orationem post Communionem. Populus in fine acclamat:

Amen.

134. After this, he takes the paten or ciborium and approaches the communicants. The Priest raises a host slightly and shows it to each of the communicants, saying:

The Body of Christ.

The communicant replies:

Amen.

And receives Holy Communion.

If a Deacon also distributes Holy Communion, he does so in the same manner.

135. If any are present who are to receive Holy Communion under both kinds, the rite described in the proper place is to be followed.

136. While the Priest is receiving the Body of Christ, the Communion Chant begins.

137. When the distribution of Communion is over, the Priest or a Deacon or an acolyte purifies the paten over the chalice and also the chalice itself.

While he carries out the purification, the Priest says quietly:

What has passed our lips as food, O Lord,
may we possess in purity of heart,
that what has been given to us in time
may be our healing for eternity.

138. Then the Priest may return to the chair. If appropriate, a sacred silence may be observed for a while, or a psalm or other canticle of praise or a hymn may be sung.

139. Then, standing at the altar or at the chair and facing the people, with hands joined, the Priest says:

Let us pray.

All pray in silence with the Priest for a while, unless silence has just been observed. Then the Priest, with hands extended, says the Prayer after Communion, at the end of which the people acclaim:

Amen.

History of the Latin Text and Rite

John Baldovin

Introduction

As with the entrance rites and those surrounding the presentation of the gifts and preparation of the altar, the rites surrounding communion are sometimes referred to as "action-points" or "soft-points" in the liturgy. These rites have had a tendency to expand and change over time in a way that the core (readings, EP) has not.[1] This essay will trace the history of the communion rite from our earliest evidence up to the significant rearrangement that occurred with the *MR1970*.

Aside from St. Paul's admonitions to the Corinthians with regard to refraining from eating and drinking before the communal celebration of the Lord's Supper, our earliest set of data for the communion rite comes from Justin Martyr's *First Apology* (*ca.* 150). The first is a description of the Eucharist that follows a baptism:

> And when the president has given thanks, and all the people have assented, those whom we call deacons give to each of those present a portion of the bread and wine and water over which thanks have been given, and take them to those who are not present.[2]

Justin's second description of the Eucharist deals with the ordinary Sunday assembly:

> The elements over which thanks have been given are distributed, and everyone partakes; and they are sent through the deacons to those who are not present.[3]

The rite is rather elaborate by the beginning of the eighth century and the full exposition of the Roman Rite Eucharist in *OR I*. Here are the elements

[1] Robert Taft, "The Structural Analysis of Liturgical Units: An Essay in Methodology," and "How Liturgies Grow," in his *Beyond East and West: Essays in Liturgical Understanding*, 2nd ed. (Rome: Pontificium Institutum Orientale, 1997), 199–202, 203–5.

[2] Justin Martyr, *First Apology* 65:1 = Jasper & Cuming, 29.

[3] Ibid., 67:1 = Jasper & Cuming, 30.

that this order of service lists following the elevation of the gifts and the doxology of the Roman Canon. The elements in parentheses are implied:

- (Lord's Prayer)
- Embolism
- (Fraction)
- Commingling with formula "May the peace of the Lord be always with you"
- Peace given in order: archdeacon to first (suffragan) bishop and so forth
- Second description of fraction by the pope after which he returns to his chair
- Lamb of God chant is begun
- Pope notifies his household officials of those to be invited to table
- General fraction by bishops and presbyters into sacks held open by acolytes
- Pope receives communion at his chair from the deacon
- The pope breaks off a piece of the consecrated bread he receives for communion and drops it into the chalice with the formula: "Let the mixture and consecration of the body and blood of our Lord Jesus Christ make we who receive it enter into eternal life. Amen" (*Fiat commixtio*)[4]
- Followed by the dialogue: "Peace be with you. And with your spirit"
- The pope receives communion from the chalice
- The archdeacon announces the place of the next stational Eucharist[5]

[4] *OR I*, nos. 94–126, following the translation of John F. Romano: http://www.medievalliturgy.com/files/J._F._Romano_Translation_of_the_First_Roman_Ordo.pdf (accessed 15 December 2010).

[5] Romano takes this to mean the station for communion, but I think a better explanation is the announcement of the next day's stational church. On the stational character of the liturgy, see my *The Urban Character of Christian Worship: The Origins, Development, and Meaning of Stational Liturgy*, Orientalia Christiana Analecta 228 (Rome: Pontifical Oriental Institute, 1987).

- The suffragan bishops receive communion from the pope at the chair, then the presbyters do likewise
- The archdeacon communicates the people from a smaller chalice by using a liturgical straw
- Before this the pope has descended first to the men's side and then to the women's to give communion to the notables. The rest of the people receive communion as well from the deacons
- As soon as the pope comes down from his chair to distribute communion, the schola begins the antiphonal psalm for communion. The pope signals the choir to bring the antiphonal chant to an end with the *Gloria Patri* when communion is finished
- At the end of the singing the pope returns to the altar for the prayer after communion
- The archdeacon then says: "Go, the Mass is ended," and the people respond: "Thanks be to God"
- The liturgy ends with a silent procession back to the sacristy near the door of the church. On the way the pope gives his blessing to individuals.

The eighth-century liturgy contains many of the elements that became part of the medieval and later Tridentine Order of Mass. This description is, of course, greatly complicated by the scale of the papal stational liturgy. The Roman *OM* in the later medieval period (up to *MR1962*) is based on the scaled-down liturgy of the Lateran Curia from the twelfth century onward. We shall briefly survey the contents of the communion and postcommunion rites in *MR1962* before dealing with the history of the individual elements in *MR2002*.

MR1962

The communion rite begins with the priest singing or reciting the *per omnia saecula saeculorum*, which in *OM2008* is understood as the end of the EP. The Lord's Prayer follows, with the choir responding *Sed libera nos a malo* ("But deliver us from evil") at the end of the prayer. The priest then continues with a silent recitation of the embolism to the Lord's Prayer. During this prayer he signs himself with the paten (the Host lies on the corporal) and then breaks the Host over the chalice. He places the right half of the Host on the paten then breaks off a particle of the remaining half. He holds the particle over the chalice while he sings or says aloud the end of the embolism: *Per omnia saecula saeculorum*. He then makes the sign of the cross three times over the chalice while saying or singing: *Pax + Domini sit + semper vobis + cum* ("May the peace of the Lord be always with you"). The priest then drops the particle into the chalice while silently reciting a prayer, which is first found in the Sacramentary of Amiens (ninth century)[6] and is later transformed in *MR1570*: *Haec commixtio, et consecratio Corporis et Sanguinis Domini nostri Jesu Christi fiat accipientibus nobis in vitam aeternam. Amen.* ("May the commingling and consecration of the Body and Blood of our Lord Jesus Christ be eternal life for us who receive it.")[7] The priest then covers the chalice with the pall, genuflects, and strikes his breast three times while saying the *Agnus Dei*, identical to that found in *MR2002*.

Then follows the prayer for peace found in *MR2002*. After this prayer, the priest kisses the altar and then says: *Pax Domini sit semper vobiscum. R. Et cum spiritu tuo* ("May the peace of the Lord be always with you." R. "And also with you"). Two private preparatory prayers follow; these are also found in *MR2002*. The priest then genuflects, rises, says a prayer for receiving the Host, and then says: *Domine non sum dignus* [and silently] *ut intres sub tectum meum: sed tantum dic verbum et sanabitur anima mea* ("Lord, I am not worthy that you should come under my roof: but only say the word and my soul will be healed"). He says a formula for receiving communion and consumes both parts of the Host. He then uncovers the chalice, genuflects, collects any fragments of the Host with the paten, and puts them in the chalice while saying another prayer (*Quid retribuam Domino . . .*; "What shall I return to the Lord . . . "). He takes the chalice in his right hand and making the sign of the cross with it over himself he says the formula for receiving the chalice and consumes the Precious Blood. Then follows a

[6] See Vincenzo Raffa, *Liturgia Eucaristica: Mistagogia della Messa: dalla storia e dalla teologia alla pastorale pratica*, Bibliotheca 'Ephemerides liturgicae' Subsidia 100 (Rome: CLV, 2003), 556.

[7] Jungmann's comment on this prayer is worth quoting in full: "the formula could be construed as though, in consequence of it, the Body and Blood of Christ would be united to each other only after the commingling, and not already at the consecration of the two species, so that the Utraquists had grounds for arguing that Communion under one kind was insufficient. So the change to the present reading was proposed: *Haec commixtio . . . fiat accipientibus nobis in vitam aeternam*; here there is no longer any possible question of a commingling taking place beyond the visible performance; it is now merely the expression of a wish that this external ceremonial commingling may avail us for salvation. It has been established that this is the only change in the Tridentine Missal that was aimed at the Reformers. The word *consecratio*, which stayed in the text in spite of the objections brought against it, and in spite of the fact that it was missing in some medieval texts here and there, must be rendered by 'hallowing' in the sense that through the commingling a sacred token or symbol is effected in the sacramental species and immediately in the Body and Blood of Christ" (Jungmann MRR, 2:315–16).

rubric that, in part, says simply: *Quo sumpto, si qui sunt communicandi, eos communicet, antequam se purificet* ("After he receives the cup, if there are any to communicate, he communicates them, before purifying himself"). Another formula follows and then the ablutions of his fingers and the chalice and paten. The priest then says the variable prayer after communion.

When one compares the solemn service described by *OR I* and *OM* of the medieval church reflected in *MR1962*, one can easily observe the difference between the public and external ceremony of the former and the intricate but private ritual of the priest in the latter. *MR1970*, as will be seen in the brief historical commentary that follows, greatly simplified and "rationalized" the ritual for the communion and postcommunion rites at the same time as providing for the active participation of the assembled faithful.

Lord's Prayer, Embolism, and Doxology (*OM2008*, nos. 124–25)

The first mention we have of the Lord's Prayer in the course of the eucharistic liturgy and immediately following the EP is in the late fourth-century mystagogical catecheses of Cyril of Jerusalem.[8] Theories differ as to the motivation for including this prayer in the Eucharist. Was it to remind the communicants of the "daily bread" that they were about to receive? Or was it to act as a kind of penitential ("forgive us our trespasses") preparation for Holy Communion? After a thorough review of the early evidence, Robert Taft has argued that the original inspiration for the inclusion of the Lord's Prayer in the Eucharist was related to the increased vocabulary of fear, awe, and unworthiness that became characteristic of Christian liturgy in the course of the fourth century.[9]

In the Roman Rite we have evidence that Gregory the Great (d. 604) placed the Lord's Prayer immediately after the Canon.[10] This prayer seems to have been considered a continuation of the Canon and was said by the priest alone at the altar—at least up to the phrase *Et ne nos inducas in tentationem* ("And lead us not into temptation"), to which *Sed libera nos a malo* ("But deliver us from evil") became the response. Despite the lack of balance, Josef Jungmann refers to the whole as "the people's Communion prayer."[11]

[8] Cyril of Jerusalem, *Mystagogical Catechesis* V:11, in Edward Yarnold, ed., *The Awe-Inspiring Rites of Initiation*, 2nd ed. (Collegeville, MN: Liturgical Press, 1994), 94.

[9] Robert Taft, *The Precommunion Rites: A History of the Liturgy of St. John Chrysostom, Volume V*, Orientalia Christiana Analecta 261 (Rome: Pontificio Istituto Orientale, 2000), 140–51.

[10] Gregory the Great, *Ep.* IX:12 = *PL* 77:956; see Jungmann MRR, 2:278.

[11] Jungmann MRR, 2:288; also Raffa, *Liturgia Eucaristica*, 519–28.

The prologue to the Lord's Prayer, taken over from *MR1570* is *Oremus, praeceptis salutaris moniti et divina institutione formati, audemus dicere* ("Let us pray. At the Savior's command and formed by divine teaching, we dare to say"). As Vincenzo Raffa notes, this introduction echoes Cyprian of Carthage's *Commentary on the Lord's Prayer* written in 258.[12] It is contained in the early sacramentaries and therefore dates in the Roman liturgy to at least the seventh century.

The embolism (or expansion) of the Lord's Prayer is mentioned in *OR I* (no. 94) and is present in the early sacramentaries as well. *MR2002* has edited the text significantly but kept its main theme as the expansion of the idea of delivering us from evil. It ends with a new idea: the joyful expectation of the coming of the Lord. This idea, in turn, prepares for an innovative element in *MR1970*, i.e., the doxology by the people: "For the kingdom, the power and the glory are yours now and for ever." This doxology can be found in several ancient manuscripts of the Gospel of Matthew as well as the late first- and early second-century catechetical manual and protochurch order, the *Didache*.[13] Since this doxology is found in the Byzantine, Anglican, and most Protestant rites of the Eucharist, its addition to the Roman Rite can also be understood as an ecumenical gesture.

The Rite of Peace (*OM2008*, no. 127)

To say the least, the rite of peace is confusing in both *OR I* and *MR1570*. *MR1970* places it between the Lord's Prayer and the fraction rite.[14] We know that the rite of peace has taken place in the Roman Rite after the EP at least since the time of Pope Innocent I in his famous letter written in 416 to Bishop Decentius of Gubbio (416).[15]

Fraction, Commingling, and *Agnus Dei* (*OM2008*, nos. 129–30)

Once again both our eighth-century and late medieval examples of the Roman Mass have an elaborate ritual for the fraction and commingling.

[12] Raffa, *Liturgia Eucaristica*, 529; see *Sancti Cypriani Episcopi Opera*, ed. Manlio Simonetti, *CCL* 3A (1976), 2:91ff.

[13] See Raffa, *Liturgia Eucaristica*, 530.

[14] Other traditional rites place the peace somewhere between the gospel and the beginning of the EP.

[15] See Martin Connell, *Church and Worship in Fifth Century Rome: The Letter of Innocent I to Decentius of Gubbio*, Alcuin/GROW Joint Liturgical Studies 52 (Cambridge: Grove Books, 2002), 23–25.

The fraction is clearly an aspect of the Eucharist from our very earliest NT sources in which the Eucharist is called "the breaking of bread" (Luke 24:35; Acts 2:46; 20:7; 1 Cor 10:17). In time this action took on symbolic meaning as well. At times it signified the passion of Christ as is clear from the accompanying chant, *Agnus Dei*.[16] That chant was borrowed from the Christian East and, according to the *Liber Pontificalis*, was imported into the Roman Eucharist by Pope Sergius I (d. 701).[17] As we have seen in *OR I*, the chant originally accompanied the fraction of leavened bread, which took some time. The phrase, *Agnus Dei, qui tollis peccata mundi* or some troped form of this text[18]—possibly with the people joining the schola in the constantly repeated *miserere nobis*[19]—was repeated for as long as necessary. Once the communion of the people declined severely and the bread for communion was unleavened the chant lost its original function and eventually became a communion song, especially in the era of polyphony.

The commingling of the Host with the contents of the chalice has a fascinating history. In Rome its remote origins can be found in the sending of the consecrated bread from the papal liturgy to the presbyters in the churches within the city, the so-called *fermentum*.[20] The origins of the practice might lie even further back in history in the sending of the eucharistic bread to various ethnic house-church communities in Rome in the second century.[21] Eighth- and ninth-century sources inform us that the presbyters placed a portion of the consecrated bread into the chalice at their own eucharistic celebrations in order to symbolize the unity of the celebration throughout the city. In *OR I*, the pope places a portion of the bread he had consecrated at the previous stational Eucharist into the chalice, probably to symbolize continuity as well as unity.[22] As the accompanying prayer in

[16] See Raffa, *Liturgia Eucaristica*, 548–49. Amalarius of Metz interpreted the three portions of the Host as the "threefold Body of Christ": resurrected, ecclesial, and in the grave. For this text and an extended commentary, see Henri de Lubac, *Corpus Mysticum: The Eucharist and the Church in the Middle Ages*, ed. Laurence Hemming and Susan Parsons, trans. Gemma Simmonds (Notre Dame, IN: University of Notre Dame Press, 2006), 263–301.

[17] See Raymond Davis, *The Book of Pontiffs (Liber Pontificalis): The Ancient Biographies of the First Ninety Roman Bishops to AD 715* (Liverpool: Liverpool University Press, 1989), 86–97; also, Jungmann MRR, 2:332–40.

[18] See Charles Atkinson, "The Earliest *Agnus Dei* Melody and Its Tropes," *Journal of the American Musicological Society* 30 (1977): 1–19.

[19] Edward Foley, "The Song of the Assembly in Medieval Eucharist," in *Medieval Liturgy*, ed. Lizette Larson-Miller (New York and London: Garland Publications, 1997), 209–10.

[20] For a review of the evidence, John Baldovin, "The *Fermentum* at Rome in the Fifth Century: A Reconsideration," *Worship* 79 (2005): 38–53; see also Taft, *Precommunion Rites*, 413–21.

[21] See Eusebius, *Ecclesiastical History*, V:24.14.

[22] See Jungmann MRR, 2:311–12.

the late medieval Mass (*Fiat commixtio*) attests, this commingling was also understood as symbolizing the life-giving unity of the Body and Blood of Christ. This symbolism was known in the East from the time of Theodore of Mopsuestia (late fourth century).[23]

Communion (*OM2008*, nos. 131–37)

MR1970 includes the two medieval priestly preparatory prayers (*Domine, Jesu Christe* and *Perceptio Corporis*) but allows the priest to choose between them.[24] What had been presumed to be ordinarily the communion of the priest alone has been transformed into a rite for the people. Jungmann traces the response to the communion invitation *Domine, non sum dignus* to the tenth century. This response became universal in the Roman Rite only with *MR1570*. Jungmann further notes that the rite for communion of the people was adapted from the rite of communion for the sick![25]

The priest's prayer during the purification of the vessels (*Quod ore sumpsimus*) can be found as early as the *Veronense* (nos. 531 and 1378).[26]

Postcommunion Prayer (*OM2008*, no. 139)

As with the other two action-points of the liturgy (entrance and presentation of the gifts) in the Roman Rite from as early as the sixth century, the procession and accompanying chant are concluded with a variable prayer.

[23] See Theodore of Mopsuestia, *Baptismal Homily* V:15–17, in Yarnold, ed., *Awe-Inspiring Rites*, 235–36.

[24] The first prayer is found in the ninth-century Sacramentary of Amiens and the second in two tenth-century sources: The Sacramentary of Fulda and the Sacramentary of Ratoldus of Corbie, see Jungmann MRR, 2:345.

[25] Jungmann MRR, 2:355–58.

[26] Jungmann MRR, 2:400–401.

Theology of the Latin Text and Rite

David Power

It is possible to enunciate an attractive theology of the communion rite, based on biblical, liturgical, and patristic sources, without any guarantee that this is what is expressed in the prescribed ritual.[1] In light of this, this essay has two parts, commenting first on the act of communion itself and then on the preliminary rites that prepare for it. The two together show us what *OM2008* offers by way of a possible interpretation through the performance of the rite.

The Act of Communion

Though one might expect the significance of the Eucharist to be clearly expressed at the moment of communion in the Body and Blood of Christ and in his sacrifice of obedience, the communion rite as prescribed in *OM2008* leaves some factors rather open-ended. To implement the rite requires that local churches or particular assemblies adopt their own way of commingling the words, ritual actions, song, music, and images found in the rite. This is an act of interpretation that necessarily differs from place to place and even from celebration to celebration. The elements in *OM2008* that leave room for variety in the meaning highlighted are the amount of singing and the kind of singing that is done by priest, by choir or cantor, and by the congregation as a whole; the form of exchange of peace that is adopted; the elements of bread and wine used; the manner of distributing Holy Communion; the location of the sacred silence that is suggested or prescribed.

Since this section of *OM2008* is titled *ritus communionis*, it is natural to begin with what is prescribed for the particular act of giving and of receiving communion. GIRM2003, no. 281, gives an ideal and highly theological explanation of the meaning of communion, an explanation it notes is better realized when the communicants receive both the Body and the Blood of

[1] See, for example, Patricia A. Gallagher, "The Communion Rite," *Worship* 63 (1989): 316–27.

Christ.[2] Subsequently, however, it suspends this explanation by appealing to the teaching of the Council of Trent on the presence of the whole Christ under one kind alone and in its declaration that in receiving under one kind the communicant is deprived of no grace "necessary for salvation."[3] The ritual of *OM2008* conforms more to the priority of communion under one kind alone, with a very significant *si adsint* (no. 135) to speak of the possibility of having communion under two kinds for some congregants and limiting the occasions for this to what are the provisions of existing law. If the theology enunciated in GIRM2002, no. 281, were followed, this would mean that communion under both kinds is normative, that is, the usual and most appropriate way of acting. The actual approach of *OM2008* implies that symbols have no great impact on what is offered and given, even if they cannot in action express the full significance of the offering and giving. This violates both the rules of linguistic expression and the liturgical adage, *lex orandi lex credendi.*[4]

Directly connected with the giving and taking of the sacrament are the invitation to communion, the order of communion, the communion of the priest, the words said at the moment of each congregant's communion, the communion chant, and a space of sacred silence.

To express a spirit of adoration even in receiving the sacrament, the priest genuflects before showing the Host raised over the paten to the faithful (no. 132). He then says the words *Ecce Agnus Dei*, etc., and joins with the people in the response, *Domine, non sum dignus*. Showing the sacrament as the Lamb of God or *Agnus Dei* harkens back to the words of John the Baptist in John 1:29. It highlights the paschal meaning of the sacrament and the acclamation of Jesus as the Lamb sent by God into the world for the forgiveness of sins. The response, adopted from the story of the centurion in Matthew 8:8 to express a sense of unworthiness, also highlights the nature of the sacrament as a sacrament of forgiveness and the humble trust with which a sinner should approach the sacrament. Forgiveness, however, is more than a remission of sin in any purely spiritual sense, for it is a healing, an action that restores people to their full spiritual and human reality: this

[2] GIRM2003, no. 281, locates the significance of communion in bread and cup in its reference to the paschal banquet and the eschatological banquet in the Father's kingdom and in the ratification of the covenant in the Blood of Christ.

[3] Ibid., 282.

[4] It is in writing of such an approach as it is found in practice that Margaret Kelleher notes a collective ecclesial amnesia, "evident in the impoverishment of the bread symbol, the forgetfulness regarding the wine and cup, and the domination of a single meaning for the Body of Christ." See Margaret Kelleher, "A Communion Rite: A Study of Roman Catholic Liturgical Performance," *Journal of Ritual Studies* 5, no. 2 (Summer 1991): 117.

is indicated by the word *sanabitur*, which, as a biblical term taken from the Latin translation of the Scriptures and used in the Roman liturgy, connotes a restorative action affecting the sinful person, undone by sin at the core of one's being.[5] The invocation *custodiat me in vitam aeternam* (no. 133)[6] says that the forgiving and sanctifying action of sacramental communion is a safeguard in this life against all that is sinful and the protection of a life given first sacramentally but to reach its completion in eternal life with God. In this it harks back to the intercessions for the dead in the EPs of *MR2002*.[7]

A clergy/laity distinction is introduced into the rite by the fact that the priest takes communion first and under both kinds, speaking *secreto*, before giving communion to the congregants, who will regularly receive under only one kind.[8] On the other hand, the communitarian significance of the action is suggested by the term *communicandos* (no. 134) and by the expectation that the entire communion rite be accompanied by chant (*cantus*, no. 136).[9] What is missed here is the equality of all before God when receiving the gift of sacramental communion.[10]

Preparation in the Rite of Communion

The rite with the title *ritus communionis* composes a single liturgical unit, beginning with the *Pater Noster* and closing with the postcommunion prayer (*OM2008*, nos. 124–39). Leading up to communion, it includes an embolism to the Lord's Prayer, a prayer for peace connected with the exchange of peace, the fraction rite and the mingling together of bread and wine in the cup, followed by the singing or saying of the *Agnus Dei*, and some private

[5] E.g., Sodi, nos. 1167, 1771, 2176, 2421, 2440, 2679.

[6] In English, "may it keep me unto eternal life."

[7] On these intercessions, see my commentary in regard to EP III and EP IV, 373 and 414 above.

[8] For a decidedly priestly interpretation of the Communion Rite, see Paul Gunter, "The Priest in the Communion Rite," http://www.ewtn.com/library/PRIESTS/zpriestcom.HTM (accessed 27 February 2011); this article was circulated by the Office for Liturgical Celebrations of the Sovereign Pontiff.

[9] On the chant itself there are no indications in *OM2008*, so one would have to consult the *Graduale Romanum* and the *Graduale Simplex* for the possibilities offered. On the history and meaning of the communion chant in the Roman liturgy, see Michel Huglo, "Communion Antiphon," *New Catholic Encyclopedia*, 2nd ed. (Detroit, MI: Gale, 2003), 4:32–34.

[10] On what it means to say Amen to *Corpus Christi*, see Robert Cabié, *The Eucharist*, ed. Aimé Georges Martimort, trans. Matthew O'Connell, The Church at Prayer 2 (Collegeville, MN: Liturgical Press, 1986), 118.

prayers for the priest. Each of these elements accentuates or modifies meanings given to communion.

The rite opens with the Lord's Prayer said by all at the invitation of the priest (always called *sacerdos*). The recitation of this prayer as a link between the anaphora and the communion in the Body and Blood of Christ is quite ancient. In fact, there is even evidence that the elevation of the sacramental bread and wine as a showing to the people was done during the *Pater Noster*.[11]

The bread and wine have been transformed, they are reverently shown as what is to be consumed, and for this consumption the most appropriate prelude is the prayer that the Lord himself gave the church. The phrase *praceptis salutaribus moniti et divina institutione formati* (no. 124) is not repeated anywhere else in *OM2008*.[12] It refers to an instruction given by Jesus pertaining to salvation. In context, the term *divina institutione* harks back to the institution of the Supper recalled in the EP and attaches a comparable origin and sacred character to the *Pater*. It is as though the Lord who instituted the sacrament also gave his church the prayer that best accompanies communion in the sacrament. Liturgical tradition has highlighted the petitions for daily bread and for the forgiveness of sin.

Thus, in proceeding to communion, the congregation addresses the Father in the way instructed by the Savior whose sacrament they are about to partake; it acclaims the kingdom and the glory to which its members aspire, and all act together in concert. The grace and glory asked in the EP carry over into this prayer and into what is hoped for in sacramental communion. This is a way of participating in the paschal mystery and the banquet of the kingdom. Since the entire communion rite omits mention of the action of the Spirit, however, the reference back to the EP is incomplete and takes no account of what has been said in the epiclesis. Since *OM2008* is developed on the basis of the Roman liturgy, this is not surprising, but it does mean that what was corrected, as it were, in the EP tradition is not taken into account in the modifications made in the communion rite.

The desire to be endowed with peace in approaching the table is first mentioned in the embolism, *Libera* (no. 125), and then in the prayer addressed to the Lord Jesus (no. 126) and in the greeting of peace (no. 127). What is sought is that peace that originated with Christ and that he left his

[11] On the *Agnus Dei*, see Jungmann MRR, 2:332–40.

[12] Though sometimes the saints are remembered as having given both *monitum* and *exemplum* to the church (e.g., Sodi, nos. 1435, 1687, 1694).

church after his resurrection from the dead (as said in *Domine Jesu*).[13] What is brought to the fore in the embolism is that this peace cannot exist in the church unless it is safeguarded against sin and a variety of ills. The petition to be freed from all *perturbatio* means the request for the freedom from all kinds of worldly onslaughts that militate against living in charity and against the tranquility needed for true worship. Without this, the pursuit even now of eternal life with God in glory is impossible. Without this, the people would not be able to live truly in the hope of the kingdom and of the coming of the Lord, as expressed in the doxology by which the congregants complete the priest's prayer (*populus orationem concludit*).

The exchange of peace (or mutual offering of peace) is allowed to be done according to local custom (*iuxta locorum consuetudines*, no. 128), and this, of course, is a key moment of cultural interpretative performance. The rubric spells out that this ritual signifies peace, communion, and charity. In other words, the needs to be one in peace, to be a true ecclesial communion, and to forge a life lived in charity are the prerequisites for approaching the Lord's table; there are bound to be cultural differences in the way that this is expressed in accordance with local custom.

On the fraction of the bread and the mingling of wine and bread in the cup (no. 129), not much need be added to what has been narrated by John Baldovin.[14] Of the breaking of the bread, *OM2008* simply says that while it is done the *Agnus Dei* is sung (no. 130). The commingling prescribed in *OM2008* also presupposes a breaking of the *hostia*, or of the consecrated bread. The use of the word *hostia* and mention of the Body and Blood in the prayer for the mixing of bread with wine shows that it is to the breaking of the Body of Christ that attention is drawn and then to the resurrection by which the union of Body and Blood is restored. On the other hand, concerning the fraction or breaking of bread, the term *fractio panis* is intended, no doubt, to recall the breaking of the one loaf to which GIRM2003 (nos. 72.3, 83, and 321) has drawn attention, recalling the breaking of bread by Christ mentioned in the supper narrative of the EP and also the one loaf mentioned by Paul in 1 Corinthians 10:17. While GIRM2003, no. 321, allows for the use of many small Hosts or particles of bread for consecration, and even accentuates the pastoral reasons involved, if the fraction is to have true meaning, the celebration of the rite needs to give priority to having one loaf that is shared by all and has to be broken for the sake of distribution.

[13] On the meaning of *pax*, see my comments above, 372.

[14] See Baldovin, 598–600.

The sacred and even contemplative nature of the action is brought out by the suggestion of a space of time for a *sacrum silentium* after communion and before the postcommunion prayer. Observing silence offers the desirability of quiet prayer at this awesome moment; that the silence is seen as "sacred" connects it with the mystery of the Lord's gift of his Body and Blood and with the mystery of the eucharistic action as memorial.[15]

OM2008 gives no hint of the content of the postcommunion prayer, but this would have to be found by examining the texts in *MR2002*. The prayers will have much to say to the meaning of the rite of communion as it is enacted, but that is not the subject matter of this commentary on the Order of the Mass.

Conclusion

This examination of *OM2008* shows that it is possible to give a theology of eucharistic communion drawing on scriptural, liturgical, and patristic sources, without being able to say that this is the meaning conveyed by the actual *lex orandi* in vogue. It is further necessary to note that the rite of the prescribed liturgical books may be given an interpretation in the way that it is performed, which is not identical in all places and celebrations. Looking at the text, it was seen that the nature of the sacrament as a communal act is brought forward but that it is also attenuated by some prescriptions, for example, on the rite of taking communion and on the fraction of the bread. One can also say that the aspect of eucharistic communion that is most to the fore is that communion is for the forgiveness of sins. This, however, is given a slant that brings out what God's forgiving mercy—mediated through the sacrament of the Supper—does by way of a restoration of the person and of the community and how it serves to protect the church and its people against the evils and the onslaughts that it suffers in its earthly history.

[15] E.g., see Sodi, nos. 1822 and 2682.

The ICEL2010 Translation

Tom Elich

The communion rite is comprised of the Lord's Prayer and its embolism, the rite of peace, the fraction, and communion itself. There are many issues relating to the worthy celebration of this part of the eucharistic liturgy, but this essay focuses on ICEL2010, mainly the translation of the spoken texts but also to some extent the translation of the private prayers and rubrics. There are no structural changes to the communion rite in *MR2002*, although the CDWDS has canvassed bishops' conferences concerning the possibility of moving the sign of peace to the beginning of the Liturgy of the Eucharist.[1]

Lord's Prayer (ICEL2010, no. 124)

The Lord's Prayer sits awkwardly in the English liturgy as the only text to employ the archaic second-person singular pronoun ("thy"). This traditional version was included in ICEL1973 and is retained in ICEL2010. It is substantially the version from the sixteenth-century *Book of Common Prayer* with only slight modernizations.[2] There does not appear to have been substantial discussion of alternatives to this translation of the Lord's Prayer within ICEL or in bishops' conferences in preparing ICEL2010.

There are two versions in modern English that have been considered seriously in recent decades and that are actually in use by Catholics in some English-speaking countries. They are the product of international ecumenical cooperation in liturgy. ICET was established in 1969 and produced *Prayers*

[1] This idea stems from the 2005 synod of bishops (proposition 23), which was taken up by Pope Benedict XVI in his post-synodal exhortation *SacCar* (nos. 49 and 150) where he specifically asked the curial offices to study the possibility of moving the sign of peace to another place. A letter consulting the bishops' conferences was sent by the CDWDS on 13 May 2008 (Prot. N. 318/07/L).

[2] The *Book of Common Prayer* translation was virtually unchanged since the first edition until the twentieth century: see F. E. Brightman, *The English Rite*, 2 vols. (London: Rivingtons, 1915), 2:641, 696, 705 *et passim*. Three variations were introduced with the 1928 revision: *which art* becomes *who art*; *in earth* becomes *on earth*; and *them that trespass* becomes *those who trespass*. The third of these changes only became common in the unofficial Catholic hand missals employed by the laity in the mid-twentieth century.

We Have in Common in 1970, revised in 1975.[3] A decade later ELLC was formed and produced a further revision in 1988, titled *Praying Together*.[4] ICEL played a leading role in both these groups until *LitAuth* excluded such ecumenical cooperation from its mandate in 2001.[5] The ICET Lord's Prayer was revised in 1975 but virtually unaltered in 1988.

ICET: 1970	ICET: 1975 = ELLC: 1988
Our Father in heaven, holy be your Name, your kingdom come, your will be done on earth as in heaven. Give us today our daily bread. Forgive us our sins as we forgive those who sin against us. Do not bring us to the test but deliver us from evil.	Our Father in heaven, hallowed be your name, your kingdom come, your will be done, on earth as in heaven. Give us today our daily bread. Forgive us our sins as we forgive those who sin against us. Save us from the time of trial[6] and deliver us from evil.

The ICET 1970 text was adopted by Roman Catholics very quickly in the Philippines,[7] India, and Pakistan, as well as Singapore, Hong Kong, and other English-speaking communities in Asia. ICEL's advisory committee agreed in 1991 to recommend that the Episcopal Board adopt the ELLC Lord's Prayer in the revised Sacramentary; it was printed with a commentary in the *Third Progress Report* of 1992[8] and was included with the white book Order of Mass segment sent to bishops' conferences for formal vote in 1994.[9] Meanwhile, the ELLC text had been introduced in the Catholic

[3] International Consultation on English Texts, *Prayers We Have in Common* (London: Geoffrey Chapman, 1970); 2nd ed. (Philadelphia: Fortress Press, 1975).

[4] English Language Liturgical Consultation, *Praying Together: A Revision of* Prayers We Have in Common (Norwich: Canterbury Press, 1988).

[5] "The 'mixed' commissions are to limit themselves to the translation of the *editiones typicae*, leaving aside all theoretical questions not directly related to this work, and not involving themselves either in relations with other 'mixed' commissions or in the composition of original texts" (no. 98).

[6] The removal of the negative in this line (i.e., "Do not bring us to the test" changed to "Save us from the time of trial") has been criticized. ELLC judged that "Save us from" adequately preserves the sense of the line (*Praying Together*, 4).

[7] In correspondence dated 23 April 2010, Anscar Chupungco indicated that it was adopted in 1976 in the Philippines, although a proposal to adopt the ELLC version in 1990 did not prosper.

[8] ICEL, *Third Progress Report on the Revision of the Roman Missal* (Washington, DC: ICEL, 1992).

[9] ICEL, *The Sacramentary. Segment Three: Order of Mass I*, White Book, August 1994.

Church in New Zealand in the early 1990s. Persuaded by the possibility of achieving ecumenical consensus in Australia and a harmony with the Catholic Church in Asia and the Pacific, the Australian Catholic Bishops Conference approved the use of the ELLC Lord's Prayer in 1994, but the Holy See replied that it was not opportune to confirm this text in view of ICEL's work on the Sacramentary, which would decide on a single version to be agreed upon by all the bishops' conferences of the English-speaking world.[10] When the time came for the USCC to vote on the white book segment, the Bishops' Committee on the Liturgy decided to withdraw the ELLC Lord's Prayer from consideration because it would not have garnered the required majority. At this point, several conferences were hoping to print both versions in the new Sacramentary. ICEL1998 included only the ELLC version, leaving it to individual bishops' conferences to add or substitute the traditional version. For a little while, it seemed possible to achieve a translation in contemporary English that would be used across the English-speaking world by all the main Christian Churches. That moment has passed.[11]

The Lord's Prayer is preceded by an invitation. The single Latin text—identical to that found in *OM2008*, no. 124—was supplemented with four invitations in ICEL1973 and five in ICEL1998; each set of invitations included a translation of the singular Latin text.[12] ICEL2006 adopted the first two lines of ICEL1998 and the third line from ICEL1973, providing a well-balanced and accurate translation: "Taught by the Savior's command and formed by the word of God we have the courage to say." Each line is changed in ICEL2010. Unfortunately spoiling the balance between *moniti-formati*, the first line now simply reads, "At the Savior's command"; the second line is dutifully literal ("divine teaching"); the third line happily reverts to the strong ICEL1998 rendering, "we dare."

[10] Prot. N. 1273/94/L, dated 11 August 1994. This was reiterated in a subsequent letter from the congregation (Prot. 1273/94/L, dated 31 January 1997), which also adduced a number of arguments in favor of the traditional text. Incidentally, both these letters insist that no confirmation had ever been given to any episcopal conference for an alternative English version of the Lord's Prayer.

[11] At the time of this writing, it is unclear whether bishops' conferences of countries already using an ecumenical version of the Lord's Prayer will request permission to continue using it and whether such a request would be confirmed by the Holy See.

[12] The Holy See encouraged individual presiders to adapt this and similar introductions in their instruction *EuchPar*: "By their very nature such introductions do not require that they be given verbatim in the form they have in the Missal; consequently it may well be helpful, at least in certain cases, to adapt them to the actual situation of a community. But the way any of these introductions is presented must respect the character proper to each and not turn into a sermon or homily" (no. 14 = DOL 1988).

Embolism (ICEL2010, no. 125)

The embolism is an elaboration of the Lord's Prayer, especially its last lines. ICEL1998 related the text explicitly to the ELLC Lord's Prayer: the former's "protect us in time of trial" amplified the latter's final petition "Save us from the time of trial," although this connection is not in the Latin. ICEL1973's "all anxiety" could be regarded as an example of the psychologizing tendency that is to be avoided,[13] so ICEL2010 uses "all distress," which can be external as well as internal. ICEL2010 recognizes the deferential nature of the text (*quaesumus . . . propitius*, rendered "we pray . . . graciously) and links the elements into a single sentence with the conjunction "that." Despite its length it reads well. The first two petitions, "deliver" and "grant," are set in apposition; ICEL2006 adopted the same strategy for the last two lines, allowing "the coming of our Savior" to explain "the blessed hope" and avoiding the sense that they were two different realities. ICEL2010 introduced "and" between them (line 8), which could leave the hearer somewhat mystified about the nature of the "blessed hope."[14] This final version also omits translating *adiuti*, meaning "sustained," rendering *ope misericordiae tuae adiuti* as "by the help of your mercy"; more accurate was ICEL2006's "sustained by the help of your mercy." The people's doxological acclamation, well known and memorable, remains unchanged.

Rite of Peace (ICEL2010, nos. 126–28)

The peace prayer is the first of a suite of communion prayers addressed to Christ.[15] The first five lines will sound very familiar: many listeners will not hear the change from the previous "you" to the current "who" (no. 126, line 3), which grammatically unifies the prayer into a single sentence. The Lord's greeting is given greater emphasis by beginning with the word "peace" (line 4).[16] Line 7 is disappointing and redundant: "graciously grant" is used in the embolism (no. 125, line 3), the feminine pronoun for the church sits uneasily in the contemporary ear, and the reduction of verbs (*pacificare* and *coadunare*) to nouns ("peace" and "unity") is uninspired.

[13] *LitAuth*, no. 54; *Ratio Translationis*, no. 80.

[14] An ICEL draft text from 1991 sorted this out nicely: "as we await the blessed hope and coming of our Savior, Jesus Christ."

[15] See also "Lamb of God," the two private communion prayers of the priest, and the people's response "Lord, I am not worthy" (ICEL2010, nos. 130, 131, 132, respectively).

[16] This is also the most common way of translating into English the biblical text John 14:27.

The line *secundum voluntatem tuam*, missing from ICEL1973, has been rightfully restored as "in accordance with your will" (line 8). Problematic is introducing a period at the end this line, followed by the relative pronoun "Who" in the second-person singular. This renders the Latin into English words but is not English. In English, a relative pronoun after "your will" would have to refer to "will" not "your." Inserting the relative pronoun "Who" is therefore confusing, since it ordinarily introduces a question and the verbs "live and reign" can be heard as plural (i.e., "who are they who live and reign") rather than second person. More effective would be the removal of the period and the addition of "you," i.e., "in accordance with your will, You who live and reign for ever and ever." At the very least, the proclaimed text will have to ignore the full stop.

The priest's greeting of peace (no. 127) directly takes up the theme of the prayer. It is unchanged, although the people's response is now uniformly, "And with your spirit." Also unchanged is the invitation to exchange the sign of peace if appropriate (no. 128). The explanatory rubric enriches the description of the sign given according to local custom: it is one "that expresses peace, communion, and charity." *MR2002* added the word *communionem* into this rubric, justifying the place of the sign of peace in the communion rite and articulating the rapport between the sacramental and ecclesial Body of Christ. This rubric provides useful catechesis.[17]

Fraction Rite (ICEL2010, nos. 129–30)

The rubric for the breaking of the bread presumes that the priest breaks a single Host over the paten and places a fragment into the chalice. The only rubrical indication of a fuller expression of this rite occurs after the Lamb of God, i.e., "The invocation may even be repeated several times if the fraction is prolonged" (no. 130, lines 9–10). Explanations of the breaking of the bread as a sign of the unity of all in the one bread are available in the *IGMR2002* and will shape the way this part of the rite unfolds.[18]

The text of the Lamb of God repeats a line from the Glory to God (ICEL2010, no. 8, line 13) where the grammatical structure is more complex.

[17] See also GIRM2003, no. 82.

[18] GIRM2003, no. 321, describes the bread for Eucharist and the meaning of the breaking; no. 83 describes the rite in which the priest may be assisted by the deacon or a concelebrant. "The supplication *Lamb of God* is, as a rule, sung by the choir or cantor with the congregation responding; or it is at least recited aloud. This invocation accompanies the fraction and for this reason may be repeated as many times as necessary until the rite has reached its conclusion" (no. 83).

Perhaps this is why the translators have chosen to translate *qui* as "you," instead of "who," which is the more usual solution adopted in ICEL2010; this leaves the text unchanged. It continues the themes of absolving sins, having mercy, and granting peace, which are the *leitmotifs* of the communion rite. ICEL1998 offered three alternative sets of invocations to Jesus, which were to have provided elaborations of the Lamb of God for occasions when a longer text was required to cover the preparation of the consecrated elements for Communion.

The fraction is also the occasion for the first of a series of private prayers of the priest, which are said *secreto*, rendered as "inaudibly" by ICEL1973, now "quietly" (no. 129, line 2). A prayer is said by the priest to himself as he drops the particle of bread into the chalice (no. 129), one of two longer prayers is said in silent preparation for communion (no. 131), the priest makes a brief prayer as he receives the Body and the Blood of Christ (no. 133), and finally he prays as he purifies the communion vessels (no. 137). These prayers establish that the priest performs all these ritual actions with a spirit of recollection, praying for the assembly and himself[19] that the communion will be fruitful.

Communion (ICEL2010, nos. 131–37)

Communion begins with a moment of silent prayer (no. 131, line 1). The ICEL1973 versions of these prayers were widely known by heart. Here, ICEL2010 follows the structure of the Latin more closely, and consequently the sequence of thought is more complex. Time will tell if these become as familiar and well loved as the texts of ICEL1973.

The invitation to communion (no. 132) takes up the vocabulary of the Lamb of God sung at the fraction. ICEL2010 affirms the choice of translating *Ecce* as "Behold" and *beati* as "Blessed," both proposed in ICEL1998. This version further uncovers from the Latin (*ecce . . . ecce*) the rhetorical force of a repeated "behold." It is a strong and compelling invitation. Translating *ad cenam Agni* as "supper of the Lamb" (line 5) should lay to rest the common misunderstanding, often vocalized by the priest, that the people are invited to "this supper," i.e., just to communion here and now. Rather, by this communion, we are called to the banquet of heaven where the Lamb of God is enthroned. The text refers to Revelation 19:9. The multitude cries out in joy that the marriage of the Lamb has come and his bride is ready: "Blessed are those who have been called to the wedding feast of the Lamb." ICEL1998

[19] The first and last of these prayers use the plural (*us*); the others are in the singular (*me*).

and ICEL2006 translated *cena* as "banquet," thinking the ICEL1973 choice of "supper" was too pedestrian. Scripture translations also use "feast." ICEL2010 reverts to "supper" with its clear reference to the Lord's Supper. Holy Communion is clearly cast in a joyful ecclesial and eschatological context.

The people respond (no. 132) with the words of the centurion from Luke 7:6-7. The Latin largely quotes the gospel quite literally and so now does the English. While the Scripture citation here is explicit, it is doubtful that anyone familiar with the gospel story of the centurion's sick servant would have missed the reference in ICEL1973. One danger with the phrase "enter under my roof" is that people may take it at face value and think "the roof of my mouth." This is not just a quaint misunderstanding but could lead to an unhelpful theology, limiting and localizing the real presence of the living risen Christ in the blessed Sacrament.[20] Catechesis, scriptural and sacramental, is necessary with this text. The language here of "my soul" is rich enough to evoke the depth of healing enjoyed when the sins of the world are taken away.

After the priest receives communion, communion is given to the people with the simple formula "The Body of Christ," "The Blood of Christ" (no. 134). The effectiveness of this simple affirmation, to which the communicant answers, "Amen," has led to a similar formula being adopted in English at the end of each reading ("The Word of the Lord" and "The Gospel of the Lord") and at the second acclamation in the EPs ("The mystery of faith"). Since 1973, users of the English Sacramentary have been accustomed to seeing "The Blood of Christ" included in the text. Now, in following the model of *MR2002*, the whole of Communion from the chalice is reduced to a rubric (no. 135).[21] This should not be interpreted as lessening the importance of communion under both kinds, for the unchanged rubric refers to the description of the rite that is found in GIRM2003.[22] It should be noted in passing that there is no mention of the tabernacle, since as far as possible the faithful receive the consecrated elements from what has been consecrated at that same Mass.[23] Singing at communion begins as the priest receives communion (no. 136). The *cantus ad communionem* is translated as

[20] "The body of Christ is present in the Eucharist not in the usual, natural, visible, local ways bodies are normally present, but rather in a spiritual, non-visible, substantial, and sacramental manner" (Nathan Mitchell, *Real Presence: The Work of Eucharist* [Chicago: Liturgy Training Publications, 1998], 112).

[21] Cf. Zimmerman, 619–20 below.

[22] The rite is described in GIRM2003, nos. 286–87. The rationale for offering communion from the chalice and provisions surrounding the rite are found in GIRM2003, nos. 85, 160–62, 281–85. Some of this material had been inserted in place in ICEL1973.

[23] GIRM2003, no. 85.

"communion chant," but this does not suggest a particular musical form because *cantus* is a generic word meaning "song." The whole assembly is expected to sing.[24]

As the priest purifies the communion vessels, he makes a private prayer. The new translation is something of an elaboration of the Latin text but is well balanced and memorable. A rubric enjoins a sacred silence be observed or a psalm, canticle of praise, or hymn be sung. The priest stands at the altar or chair and proclaims the prayer after communion, which concludes the communion rite.

Conclusion

The choice of the traditional Lord's Prayer in the communion rite will no doubt be a relief to some and will prove to be an important element of continuity for the great number of Catholics who participate in the liturgy only rarely. For others it will be a lost opportunity for evangelization by expressing a key gospel text in contemporary and unambiguous language. The choice will present significant issues for those countries that have used new versions for several decades. It will be a disappointment for those who dreamed that the dominical prayer at least could be prayed together by all Christian people in a common form of words.

Some of the texts of the communion rite remain unchanged; some have been enriched in their new translation. With the exception of one or two phrases, priest and assembly should be able to adopt these texts easily as a heartfelt expression of their worship at communion time.

It should be noted, however, that a commentary on ICEL2010 by necessity bypasses a large number of important issues and leaves unspecified many questions in relation to the celebration of the rite. This might include, for example, the way in which the sign of peace is carried out, the form of the eucharistic bread and its breaking, communion from the cup, the use and movements of lay communion ministers, the role of the tabernacle during the communion rite, and the form of the communion vessels and their purification. These issues, however, are addressed in GIRM2003 and the appropriate commentaries on that text.[25]

[24] The term "chant" is also used in GIRM2003 where the meaning of singing is explained: "its purpose is to express the communicants' union in spirit by means of the unity of their voices, to show joy of heart, and to highlight more clearly the 'communitarian' nature of the procession to receive communion" (GIRM2003, no. 86).

[25] See *A Commentary on the General Instruction of the Roman Missal*, ed. Edward Foley, Nathan Mitchell, Joanne Pierce (Collegeville, MN: Liturgical Press, 2007), 180–92, 253–61, 333–50, 385–96.

The Mystagogical Implications

Joyce Ann Zimmerman

In the earliest celebrations of the Mass, the communion rite was the conclusion of this action in memory of Jesus. The clear intent was that, after being nourished on the heavenly Bread, the participants then went forth to live what they had received. It did not take long, however, for the church to sense that there was a need for a more formal closing to Mass, giving birth to the concluding rite. As we shall see, the communion rite still has an impulse to send us forward, not only to go forth to live what we have received, but to live by looking forward in such a way as to be always journeying toward our eternal presence at the messianic table of the Lord. The communion rite leads us to the messianic banquet and the everlasting life promised those who faithfully follow Jesus Christ through his death to risen life.

For many people, receiving Holy Communion is the high point of the whole Mass, so much so that even receiving Holy Communion outside of Mass is a spiritual joy for them. The communion rite, nevertheless, is best interpreted less as a high point of the Mass and more as an affirmation of the transformation that has been taking place from the very beginning of Mass. Our "Amen" as we receive the Host and the Precious Blood from the chalice is a faith affirmation of the Body and Blood of Christ being received as well as a faith affirmation of who we are and are becoming: more perfect members of the Body of Christ. It is as members of the Body of Christ that we are sent forth to live as Jesus lived, to serve as he did, to continue the saving ministry that makes present God's reign in the here and now. The very brevity of the concluding rites underscores their connection to and meaning derived from the communion rite.

Furthermore, receiving Holy Communion is but one element of the whole communion rite. The 1975 English edition of the Sacramentary inserted a series of subtitles in the communion rite: Lord's Prayer, doxology, sign of peace, breaking of the bread, communion, communion song, period of silence or song of praise, prayer after communion.[1] While all those

[1] These subtitles were never a part of any of the Latin versions of the *MR* after Vatican II.

elements are still part of *MR2002*, this third edition of the Missal does not contain these subtitles. This accentuates a unity in the rite, with the differing elements each adding meaning to this concluding rite of the Liturgy of the Eucharist. Indeed, the title is "The Communion Rite," in the singular. This is one act in which we share.

A number of motifs are evident as we move from the Lord's Prayer to the concluding prayer, but they all converge on the single act of communion with the Lord and each other here, "communion" understood in a much broader sense than "Holy Communion." A perusal of these motifs helps us grasp not only the dynamic flow of this important rite but also its integrity as a unit.

Forgiveness, Unity, Peace

The qualifying petition for God to forgive us in the Lord's Prayer ought to leave us a bit uncomfortable and lead us to a broad examination of our relationships with others. We ask God to forgive us "as we forgive those" who have offended us. The verb tense in the Greek (better translated "as we *have forgiven*") indicates a relationship between our forgiveness of one another and God's forgiveness of us (cf. Sir 28:2, "Forgive your neighbor's injustice; / then when you pray, your own sins will be forgiven"). Yet, God's forgiveness is infinitely beyond our own; the entire history of salvation has been a record of God's utter fidelity and forgiveness in the face of humankind's repeated transgressions. And so we beg God to "deliver us from evil," the phrase picked up in the embolism (an insertion of text into the prayer, ICEL2010, no. 125): "Deliver us, Lord, we pray, from every evil." We acknowledge that it is by God's mercy that we "may be always free from sin and safe from all distress." No wonder at the end of the embolism the assembly breaks into a doxology: "For the kingdom, the power and the glory are yours now and for ever"!

There is no break between the Our Father, its embolism, and the assembly's doxological conclusion and the sign of peace. The prayer for peace links peace and forgiveness ("look not on our sins," no. 126, line 5) and strongly suggests Jesus' postresurrection appearance to the disciples in the Upper Room (see John 20:19, 21, 23). The risen Lord's peace is not simply the absence of strife but also the positive embrace of unity ("grant her peace and unity," no. 126, line 7). After the invitation to extend a sign of peace to one another, the rubric describes the meaning of the action: it "expresses peace, *communion*, and charity" (no. 128; emphasis added).

Most members of the assembly generally delight in this gesture. Yet there is much confusion about its deepest meaning (especially with regard to the whole communion rite); certainly, the prayer texts surrounding it serve to move us beyond understanding it as simply a gesture of human friendship and caring. Following the 2005 Synod of Bishops on the Eucharist, Pope Benedict XVI issued the apostolic exhortation *SacCar*. The Holy Father notes that "during the Synod of Bishops there was discussion about the appropriateness of greater restraint in this gesture [the sign of peace], which can be exaggerated and cause a certain distraction in the assembly just before the reception of Communion" (no. 49).

Two pastoral issues come to light here. First, exaggeration in terms of the length of time given to the kiss of peace and the emotive exuberance of some can easily distort the essential, liturgical meaning of this communion rite element. Second, while the Holy Father does endorse use of the sign of peace, he is concerned about what we convey to each other at this particularly sacred time of the Mass. To put it another way, is the sign of peace focused on ourselves or on something (Someone) else? The sign of peace at Mass is a celebration of our identity as the Body of Christ and a joyful expression of the risen life that Jesus already shares with us. We dare to approach the sacrament because we are united with Christ and each other in the close bond of divine Life. The peace we wish for each other is that which celebrates the presence of the risen Christ within and among us and is wholly dependent on that divine presence.

Placing the sign of peace before Holy Communion is not without its ethical demands, similar to how we previously noted that the Lord's Prayer ought to leave us a bit uncomfortable. It is unthinkable to celebrate the kind of unity that communion enacts if we are not at peace with one another, if we have not forgiven each other wrongdoing, if we are not striving to live out of our identity as the presence of the risen Christ. Giving each other a sign of peace, then, is a pledge to do all we can to bring forgiveness and reconciliation wherever it is needed: within families, cities, nations, our whole world. It is a pledge to make visible the risen life of Christ, a life that assures our unity in the one Body. The journey to life-giving unity is through forgiveness and peace.

Exchanging a sign of peace during the communion rite ought not to be a somber act. It is a joyful act. But perhaps the Holy Father's desire for greater restraint would take care of itself if our mystagogical catechesis on the sign of peace would be more adequate. The first challenge is to help people grasp beyond an intellectual assent that they are, indeed, the Body of Christ. If we internalized better our baptismal identity and dignity, then the joy appropriate to the sign of peace would not be an exuberant, emotive celebration of ourselves as a human community but rather an expression of our embrace of the shared identity we are given in Christ. It is Christ's peace we give to each other, emanating from the risen Christ and his Spirit who dwell within each of us.

The sign of peace is a paschal act. It is a sign of our baptismal entry into Jesus' paschal mystery. It is a promise that the community we share is more than a human community; it is the unity of Christ's Body made visible in reaching out to another. The exchange is a holy sign made possible by the Holy Spirit who is breathed into us at baptism, strengthened at confirmation, and affirmed every time we celebrate Eucharist. At the sign of peace we share the Life of the Spirit given us freely by our loving God.

For Eternal Life

The ultimate expression of our unity with God and each other, of course, is the actual act of receiving Holy Communion. This unity not only is marked by bonds that unite us to Christ and each other in his Body but also brings us to yearn for the ultimate peace that we will one day share when we have passed over into eternal glory. Woven throughout the communion rite text are points of reference that give expression to eschatological yearning: we are made for eternal life. The Our Father embolism ends with such an eschatological yearning: "we await the blessed hope and the coming of our Savior, Jesus Christ" (no. 125). On that day of second coming, for those who remain faithful, every tear will be wiped away and everlasting joy will be ours.

The fraction rite is a reminder that all new life comes through dying. The one Bread is fractured, broken, divided so that all might partake. A small piece of the Host (with roots in the historical practice of the *fermentum*)[2] is broken off and dropped into the Precious Blood. Originally signaling the unity of the local church under the bishop, the prayer the priest silently prays during this commingling now strongly indicates an eschatological thrust: "May this mingling of the Body and Blood of our Lord Jesus Christ *bring eternal life to us* who receive it" (no. 129; emphasis added). As the Host is mingled with the Precious Blood, so in Holy Communion are we mingled with that same Body and Blood of Christ. Our identity—commingling, if you will—with Christ assures us of eternal life.

Another eschatological text is strongly indicated by the new translation of *MR2002*. At the invitation to Holy Communion, the priest concludes with, "Blessed are those called to the supper of the Lamb" (no. 132). The phrase evokes Revelation 19:9: "Blessed are those who are invited to the

[2] On his history, see Baldovin, 599 above.

marriage supper of the Lamb" (NRSV; the NABRE has "wedding feast"). Who is the bride? The church, of course. Thus, our partaking in Holy Communion is our intimate, loving, everlasting union with Christ our Bridegroom. We are one with the Lamb of God in his risen glory.

Our response to this invitation can be interpreted also to be eschatological. We pray that our "soul shall be healed" (no. 132). Christ's healing ministry is a concrete sign of his saving ministry. The Hebrew word for "salvation" ultimately means wholeness and healing. Thus, our prayer to be healed is truly a prayer for salvation: the healing is not physical as in the gospel account (Matt 8:8) but is a healing of soul, of self for salvation, for eternal life. Indeed, St. Ignatius of Antioch spoke of Eucharist as a "medicine of immortality" in his Letter to the Ephesians (20:42), a medicine that "yields continuous life in union with Jesus Christ."

A marvelous gesture that captures our desire for eternal union with the Lamb of God is the communion procession. Far more than merely getting from one place to another, ideally (if the logistics of the sacred space and size of the assembly permit it), the communion procession moves forward toward the altar of sacrifice, the messianic banquet table. Processions always symbolize a willingness to be transformed from here to there, from this to that. The communion procession expresses our journey in this life toward the eternal messianic banquet. It expresses our surrender from clinging to our own human pleasures and desires to embracing God's will and the necessary self-emptying that leads us through dying to self to risen life. This communion procession in a tangible way makes visible the whole movement in the communion rite toward greater forgiveness, unity, peace, and desire for eternal life. This procession dramatizes our "blessed hope" (no. 125) that this life is not all there is. It reminds us that while here on earth we already share in communion with God at the same time we are on pilgrimage toward that in which we do not yet share fully. This is why standing is a good posture for receiving Holy Communion: we are ready, willing, eager to stand in the presence of the Lord for all eternity.

Some Pastoral Considerations

MR2002 includes no rubric in the communion rite for receiving the Precious Blood from the chalice; a rubric note directs that if anyone is to receive the Precious Blood, "the rite described in the proper place is to be followed" (no. 135).[3] This omission is unfortunate since the more complete sign of

[3] Cf. Elich, 613 above.

Holy Communion is to receive both the Body and Blood of Christ (see GIRM2003, no. 14). Jesus' body was broken for us; his blood was poured out for us. Receiving under both kinds emphasizes our entry into Jesus' death (one aspect of the paschal mystery). Wine also signifies joy, celebration, life; Jesus' Precious Blood, when drunk, warmly courses through our veins and brings us to new appreciation for the risen life of Christ (the other aspect of the paschal mystery) in which we already share by God's gracious gift.

Another rubrical note (no. 138) reminds us that the communion chant or song begins when the priest receives Holy Communion. While there is sometimes a logistical problem about when musicians and choir receive communion, the music beginning with the priest's communion is a good indication that his communion begins the communion procession and he himself is part of the procession of the assembly toward the messianic table. He leads where each member of the assembly is invited to follow.

A third issue concerns the proper reverence for receiving Holy Communion. Rather than limiting our focus to bowing and the appropriate extension of our hands as a throne to receive our King, it is good to remember that reverence begins already at home and in the streets with each other;[4] continues in the manner in which we actively, consciously, and fully participate in the liturgy; and is expressed through deliberate and aesthetic postures and gestures throughout Mass.

While purifying the vessels, the priest quietly prays, "What has passed our lips as food, O Lord, may we possess in purity of heart, that what has been given to us in time may be our healing for eternity" (no. 137). To that we can clearly answer "Amen" as we adore, praise, and thank in the silence of our hearts. Concluding with the prayer after communion, we are reminded in it to live and become what we have eaten and drunk, to come to eternal life in forgiveness, unity, and peace.

[4] See Serra, 125 above.

The Concluding Rites

The Latin Text

Ritus conclusionis

140. Sequuntur, si necessariae sint, breves annuntiationes ad populum.

141. Deinde fit dimissio. Sacerdos, versus ad populum, extendens manus, dicit:

Dóminus vobíscum.

Populus respondet:

Et cum spíritu tuo.

Sacerdos benedicit populum, dicens:

Benedícat vos omnípotens Deus,
Pater, et Fílius, ✠ et Spíritus Sanctus.

Populus respondet:

Amen.

---

142. Quibusdam diebus vel occasionibus, huic formulae benedictionis praemittitur, iuxta rubricas, alia formula benedictionis sollemnior, vel oratio super populum.

---

143. In Missa pontificali celebrans accipit mitram et, extendens manus, dicit:

Dóminus vobíscum.

Omnes respondent:

Et cum spíritu tuo.

Celebrans dicit:

Sit nomen Dómini benedíctum.

Omnes respondent:

Ex hoc nunc et usque in saéculum.

Celebrans dicit:

Adiutórium nostrum in nómine Dómini,

Omnes respondent:

Qui fecit caelum et terram.

Tunc celebrans, accepto, si eo utitur, baculo, dicit:

The English Text

The Concluding Rites

140. If they are necessary, any brief announcements to the people follow here.

141. Then the dismissal takes place. The Priest, facing the people and extending his hands, says:

The Lord be with you.

The people reply:

And with your spirit.

The Priest blesses the people, saying:

May almighty God bless you,
the Father, and the Son, ✠ and the Holy Spirit.

The people reply:

Amen.

---

142. On certain days or occasions, this formula of blessing is preceded, in accordance with the rubrics, by another more solemn formula of blessing or by a prayer over the people.

---

143. In a Pontifical Mass, the celebrant receives the miter and, extending his hands, says:

The Lord be with you.

All reply:

And with your spirit.

The celebrant says:

Blessed be the name of the Lord.

All reply:

Now and for ever.

The celebrant says:

Our help is in the name of the Lord.

All reply:

Who made heaven and earth.

Then the celebrant receives the pastoral staff, if he uses it, and says:

Benedícat vos omnípotens Deus,

ter signum crucis super populum faciens, addit:

Pater, ✠ et Fílius, ✠ et Spíritus ✠ Sanctus.

Omnes:

Amen.

---

144. Deinde diaconus, vel ipse sacerdos, manibus iunctis, versus ad populum dicit:

Ite, missa est.

Populus respondet:

Deo grátias.

145. Deinde sacerdos altare osculo de more veneratur, ut initio. Facta denique profunda inclinatione cum ministris, recedit.

146. Si qua actio liturgica immediate sequatur, ritus dimissionis omittuntur.

May almighty God bless you,

making the Sign of the Cross over the people three times, he adds:

the Father, ✠ and the Son, ✠ and the Holy ✠ Spirit.

All:

Amen.

---

144. Then the Deacon, or the Priest himself, with hands joined and facing the people, says:

Go forth, the Mass is ended.

Or:

Go and announce the Gospel of the Lord.

Or:

Go in peace, glorifying the Lord by your life.

Or:

Go in peace.

The people reply:

Thanks be to God.

145. Then the Priest venerates the altar as usual with a kiss, as at the beginning. After making a profound bow with the ministers, he withdraws.

146. If any liturgical action follows immediately, the rites of dismissal are omitted.

History of the Latin Text and Rite

Michael Witczak

The Concluding Rites

The use of a title for the concluding section of Mass (*Ritus conclusionis*) began with *MR1970*. A description of this part of the Mass can be found in *IGMR2002*, no. 90.

The concluding rites of the Mass are simple and functional: the liturgy concludes and the people and ministers depart. Yet the concluding rites have had a complex set of prayers and actions associated with them over the centuries.[1] The end of a service can be messy and even chaotic as the action winds down and ministers and people move to leave. Some would consider this a "soft moment" point in the liturgy.[2]

The earliest stratum of liturgical history describes a straightforward (though still complex) movement. Justin Martyr describes that after those present had received communion, the deacons took it to those who were absent. Then he adds that the president of the assembly (*proestes*) took the gifts that the wealthy had brought and distributed them among the needy of the community. It is not clear whether the wealthy brought their gifts at

[1] For an overview of the history of the concluding rites, see Jungmann MRR, 2:427–64; Mario Righetti, *La Messa: Commento storico-liturgico alla luce del Concilio Vaticano II*, vol. 3 of *Manuale di storia liturgica*, 3rd ed. (Milano: Ancora, 1998 [1966]), 534–42; Frederick McManus, "The Genius of the Roman Rite Revisited," *Worship* 54 (1980): 360–78, esp. 374–75; Adrien Nocent, "Storia della celebrazione dell'eucaristia," in *La liturgia eucaristia: Teologia e storia della celebrazione*, ed. Salvatore Marsili, Anamnesis 3:2 (Casale Monferrato: Marietti, 1983), 269–70; Robert Cabié, *The Eucharist*, ed. Aimé Georges Martimort, trans. Matthew O'Connell, The Church at Prayer 2 (Collegeville, MN: Liturgical Press, 1986), 121–23, 168–70, 219–20; Bugnini, 337–92, esp. 345 and 380–81; Mark Searle, "*Semper Reformanda*: The Opening and Closing Rites of the Mass," in *Shaping English Liturgy: Studies in Honor of Archbishop Denis Hurley*, ed. Peter Finn and James Schellman (Washington, DC: Pastoral Press, 1990), 53–92, esp. 85–89; Vincenzo Raffa, *Liturgia Eucaristica: Mistagogia della Messa: dalla storia e dalla teologia alla pastorale pratica*, Bibliotheca 'Ephemerides liturgicae' Subsidia 100 (Rome: CLV, 2003), 487–93.

[2] For reflection on "soft moments" in the liturgy, see Robert Taft, "The Structural Analysis of Liturgical Units," in *Beyond East and West: Essays in Liturgical Understanding*, 2nd ed. (Rome: Pontificium Institutum Orientale, 1997), 187–202, esp. 201–2; also Baldovin, 115 above.

this moment or whether the deacons taking communion to those who were absent sparked Justin's association with other things being taken to the needy.[3] ApTrad gives no hint of how the celebration of the ordinations concludes, but at the end of its description of initiation we learn that "everyone hastens to do good works."[4]

The late fourth century provides some instances of how this "simple" conclusion developed. The Apostolic Constitutions (*ca.* 380) tell us that, following a lengthy prayer of thanksgiving after communion, the deacon said, "Bow down before God through his Christ, and receive the blessing." The bishop then prayed a long blessing, at the end of which the deacon said, "Depart in peace."[5] The pilgrim Egeria (*ca.* 386) describes numerous services in Jerusalem and the nearby holy places. She describes the end of one service: "Then, after he has said a prayer and blessed the faithful, the bishop comes out from the grotto sanctuary, whereupon all present come forth to kiss his hand, and he blesses each of them in turn as he goes out. And so the dismissal is given, and by now it is daylight."[6] She has several descriptions of this sort for various services at various places.

According to the description found in *OR I*, following the prayer after communion, the archdeacon, after a nod by the pontiff, said *Ite, missa est*, with the response, *Deo gratias*. A procession including seven candlesticks and incense led the procession out. As the pontiff passed various groups, they said to him *Iube, domne, benedicere*, and he responded to each group *Benedicat nos dominus*, to which they said, *Amen*. Then those in the procession entered the sacristy (*secretarium*).[7]

The Frankish *OM* began to include private prayers to accompany the rubrics of the celebration. At the end of the celebration, we find the dismissal *Ite, missa est*, the kissing of the altar, the prayer *Placeat tibi sancta trinitas* and a second prayer, *Meritis et intercessionibus*. After all this was done, the min-

[3] I Apology 67, 5–6 = *Prex Eucharistica*, 1:70–73.

[4] ApTrad 21 = Paul Bradshaw, Maxwell Johnson, and L. Edward Phillips, *The Apostolic Tradition: A Commentary*, ed. Harold W. Attridge, *Hermeneia* series (Minneapolis: Fortress Press, 2002), 122–23.

[5] VIII, 15, 6–10; English translation in W. Jardine Grisbrooke, *The Liturgical Portions of the Apostolic Constitutions: A Text for Students*, Alcuin/GROW Liturgical Study 13–14 (Bramcote, Nottingham: Grove Books, 1990), 44-45; also, Raffa, *Liturgia Eucaristica*, 488–89.

[6] Egeria, *Itinerarium* 24, 2, translation in George E. Gingras, *Egeria: Diary of a Pilgrimage*, Ancient Christian Writers 38 (New York: Newman Press, 1970), 89; also, Raffa, *Liturgia Eucaristica*, 488; Cabié, *The Eucharist*, 123.

[7] *OR I*, nos. 125–26 = Andrieu, 2:107–8.

isters went to the sacristy where they prayed a series of verses and prayers.[8] Blessings at the end of Mass seem to have been associated with celebrations with bishops.

The desire to receive a blessing at the end of each Mass, no matter who the presider, evolved slowly during the Middle Ages. At first, it became a custom in some places to bless the people with the Host or with a relic. During the thirteenth century, recommendations were made to bless the people using the chalice or the paten or the corporal. The form that is codified in the *MR1570* is found already in the *OM* of Burchard of Worms, the papal master of ceremonies.[9] The order that was included in the *MR1570* and repeated in *MR1962* was:

- *V. Dominus vobiscum. R. Et cum spiritu tuo*
- *Ite Missa est* or *Benedicamus Domino* (the latter said when there was no *Gloria* in the Mass), *R. Deo gratias*
- Prayer to the Trinity: *Placeat tibi sancta Trinitas*, said bowing at the center of the altar, followed by kissing the altar
- Blessing of the people: *Benedicat vos omnipotens Deus . . . R. Amen*
- Reading of the Prologue to the Gospel of St. John (1:1-14), preceded by the greeting *Dominus vobiscum* with its response, and including the signing with the cross on the book, the forehead, mouth, and breast with the text *Initium sancti Evangelii secundum Ioannem*
- In some Masses, additional prayers were added at the end of Mass, according to the specification of the pope (e.g., the so-called Leonine prayers, promulgated by Pope Leo XIII in 1884 to pray for protection against enemies of the Holy See in the turbulent days of the dissolution of the Papal States and the establishment of the Italian State; and then modified by Pius XI in 1929, after the Lateran Treaty settled the relationship between the Vatican and the Italian government, for the peace of the Russian people)

[8] For example, see the *OM* text in Michael G. Witczak, "St. Gall Mass Orders (I): MS. Sangallensis 338: Searching for the Origins of the 'Rheinish Mass Order,'" *Ecclesia orans* 16 (1999): 407–8.

[9] Raffa, *Liturgia Eucaristica*, 487–90. He cites a synod in Albi in 1230 (Peter Browe, "Der Segen mit Reliquien, der Patene und Eucharistie," *Ephemerides liturgicae* 45 [1931]: 381); Guillaume Durand, *Instructiones et Constitutiones de Guillaume Durand*, ed. Joseph Berthelé and M. Valmary (Montpellier: Ricard, 1905), 77. Burchard's *ordo* is to be found in J. Wickham Legg, *Tracts on the Mass*, Henry Bradshaw Society, 27 (London: Harrison and Sons, 1904), 120–78; here 166.

- Once returned to the sacristy, the priest was given several antiphons and prayers of thanksgiving to recite[10]

The reforms after the Second Vatican Council sought to simplify and clarify this moment of the Mass.

Announcements (*OM2008*, no. 140)

This short rubric reads: *Sequuntur, si necessariae sint, breves annuntiationes ad populum.*[11]

While admonitions and diaconal directives have been a part of liturgies from the beginning of liturgical evidence (e.g., Apostolic Constitutions and *OR I*), the reform of the *OM* after Vatican II first included a specific mention of announcements. The custom had grown up in some places during the Middle Ages, with the disappearance of the general intercessions, to insert a service known as the *prône* (from Latin *praeconium*, "announcement"), which eventually involved announcements, the announcement of prayer intentions after each of which the people would say the Lord's Prayer, and then an instruction in the vernacular.[12] In the United States, the practice developed that after the gospel reading in Latin the priest would make various announcements, read the gospel in English, and then offer a sermon.[13]

The experimental *Missa normativa* after Vatican II included announcements at this point.[14] That decision was maintained in the subsequent editions.

[10] See Triacca-Sodi, nos. 1550–55; the prayers were given in the *OM* and included the antiphon *Trium puerorum* with the canticle from Daniel, *Benedicite omnia opera domini domino* (Dan 3:57ff); then Ps 150, with the repetition of the antiphon, *Trium puerorum*; then *Kyrie eleison, Christe eleison, Kyrie eleison* and the Lord's Prayer, followed by several responsories; and finally three orations: *Deus, qui tribus pueris mitigasti flammas ignium*; *Da nobis quaesumus, domine, vitiorum nostrorum flammas extinguere*; and *Actiones nostras quaesumus domine*.

In *MR* ed. Sodi-Toniolo, nos. 1589–1608, we find the antiphons and prayers have moved to the front matter (nos. 156*–73*), after the *Ritus servandus* and the prayers for preparing for Mass. They are listed as *pro opportunitate* (optional) and have numerous indulgences attached to them. After the antiphon, canticle, psalm, Lord's Prayer, and orations already found in *MR1570*, eleven other prayers are given, with appropriate indulgences granted by various pontiffs.

[11] In place of *si necessariae sint*, *MR1975* reads *si habendae sint*.

[12] See description and bibliography in Cabié, *The Eucharist*, 155–57.

[13] Bishop John Carroll of Baltimore included these regulations in his 1791 pastoral letter: "At the end of the Gospel, the prayer for the civil authorities of our country was to be read, the Gospel in the vernacular was to follow, the banns to be published, notices to be made of fasts and feasts, and then a short sermon was to be given of an exhortatory nature in order that all present should strive for higher Christian perfection" (Peter Guilday, *A History of the Councils of Baltimore* [New York: Macmillan, 1932], 68).

[14] See McManus, "The Genius of the Roman Rite Revisited," 374.

Blessing (*OM2008*, no. 141)[15]

The experimental *Missa normativa* had offered some simplifications of the rite found in the *MR1570* and *MR1972*. The apology *Placeat* has been omitted. The greeting and response were followed by the dismissal and the final blessing. *MR1970* revised the order further. The greeting is followed first by the blessing and then by the words of dismissal. It seemed incongruous that after the people had been dismissed more actions would follow. This current order is deemed more logical.[16]

Solemn Blessing and Prayer over the People (*OM2008*, no. 142)

The Gallican liturgy had included an episcopal blessing before the prayer after communion.[17] These prayers were in three moments, each with an Amen, followed by a final blessing formula mentioning the three persons of the Trinity but including no indication of the tracing of the sign of the cross over the people.

The Roman tradition included a prayer over the people (*super populum* or *ad populum*). In the *Veronense* (*ca*. 650) there is a prayer for almost every celebration.[18] By the time of the *Gelasianum* (*ca*. 750) and the *Hadrianum* (*ca*. 810), the prayer is limited to certain days, especially Lent.[19]

The solemn blessing did not enter the mainstream of the Roman Rite in the course of the Middle Ages, but the prayers over the people formed part of the Lenten liturgy, following the postcommunion prayer. The use of both the solemn blessing and the prayer over the people was included as an option in the post–Vatican II *Missa normativa*.[20] *MR1970* and *MR1975* made

[15] *MR1975* does not include the musical notation found in *MR2002*.

[16] See McManus, "The Genius of the Roman Rite Revisited," 374–75.

[17] A series of examples are found in the Supplement to the *Hadrianum*, nos. 1738–89, covering the great liturgical feasts and various feasts of saints. See the discussion of the document in Cyrille Vogel, *Medieval Liturgy: An Introduction to the Sources*, trans. and rev. William G. Storey and Niels Krogh Rasmussen (Washington, DC: Pastoral Press, 1986), 79–92; also, Eric Palazzo, *A History of Liturgical Books from the Beginning to the Thirteenth Century*, trans. Madeleine Beaumont (Collegeville, MN: Liturgical Press, 1993), 48–54; Raffa, *Liturgia Eucaristica*, 489; Cabié, *The Eucharist*, 123.

[18] See the background in Vogel, *Medieval Liturgy*, 38–46; and Palazzo, *A History of Liturgical Books*, 38–42.

[19] For the *Gelasianum* see Vogel, *Medieval Liturgy*, 64–70; and Palazzo, *A History of Liturgical Books*, 42–46; for the *Hadrianum* see Vogel, *Medieval Liturgy*, 80–85; and Palazzo, *A History of Liturgical Books*, 48–54.

[20] See McManus, "The Genius of the Roman Rite Revisited," 375.

provision for the use of either of these forms, with the addition of the trinitarian blessing and the sign of the cross made by the priest added to the end of the whole unit of prayer. These prayer texts were placed in an appendix found after the *OM* and a series of alternatives texts for various moments of the celebration.[21]

The *MR2002* places these texts immediately after the *OM*. In addition, a prayer over the people is given for each day of Lent for optional use.[22]

Pontifical Blessing (*OM2008*, no. 143)[23]

The texts for bishops had not been included in the *MR* tradition from 1570 until *MR2002*. It is taken from *CaerEp*, no. 169.

Dismissal (*OM2008*, no. 144)[24]

This is the traditional dismissal, found as early as *OR I* and continuously since. It is now placed after the blessing to conclude the action of the celebration.[25]

Reverencing the Altar (*OM2008*, no. 145)[26]

The kissing of the altar at the end of Mass does not appear in *OR I*. It does appear in the Frankish tradition as early as the Sacramentary of Amiens (*ca.* 750), where it is accompanied by the apology *Placeat*.[27] The *Missa Normativa*, the *MR1970*, and subsequent *MR*'s have omitted the apol-

[21] *MR1975*: *Ordo Missae sine populo*, 479–86; various texts of greeting, etc., 487–92; *Benedictiones in fine Missae et orationes super populum*, twenty solemn blessings, 495–506, and twenty-six prayers over the people, 507–11.

[22] *MR2002*, twenty solemn blessings, 532–41; twenty-eight prayers over the people, 542–46; the prayers for Lent constitute a new set of prayers.

[23] *MR1975* omits the pontifical blessing and the accompanying musical notation.

[24] The current *versus ad populum dicit* is a slight change from *MR1975*'s *ad populum versus dicit*.

[25] See McManus, "The Genius of the Roman Rite Revisited," 375; also, Raffa, *Liturgia Eucaristica*, 490–92.

[26] *MR1975* reads *debita reverentia* in place of *MR2002*'s *profunda inclinatione*; cf. Edward Foley, "The Structure of the Mass, Its Elements and Its Parts," in *A Commentary on the General Instruction of the Roman Missael*, ed. Edward Foley, Nathan Mitchell, Joanne Pierce (Collegeville, MN: Liturgical Press, 2007), 139 and 193.

[27] See Victor Leroquais, "L'*ordo missae* du sacramentaire d'Amiens, B.N. lat. 9432," *Ephemerides liturgicae* 41 (1927): 444. See also Ms. Sangallensis 338, nos. 78–79, in Witczak, "St. Gall Mass Orders (1)," 407–8.

ogy and placed the veneration of the altar and the profound bow at the end of the ritual to match the bowing and kissing of the altar at the beginning of Mass.[28]

Omitting the Rites of Dismissal (*OM2008*, no. 146)

While altering the end of the ritual was done as a matter of course throughout the history of liturgical books,[29] there was no rubric making this particular point until *MR1970.*

[28] *OM2008*, no. 1.

[29] See, for instance, the description of the Holy Week ceremonies in the various Roman Pontifical edited by Michel Andrieu, *Le Pontifical romain au moyen-âge*, 4 vols., Studi e Testi 86–88 and 99 (Vatican City: Biblioteca Apostolica Vaticana, 1938–41), *passim*.

Theology of the Latin Text and Rite

Susan K. Roll

Apart from the three new options in the dismissal formula itself and the fact that the tripartite dialogue that introduces the final blessing of a pontifical Mass (*OM2008*, no. 143) has been helpfully placed in the sequence of concluding rites, there has been little change in *MR2002*. A one-word change in a rubric concerning announcements (from *si habendae* in *MR1970*, to *si necessariae*, *OM2008*, no. 140) makes a minimal difference.

In spite of their relative brevity and their starkly functional character, the concluding rites conceal a rich variety of associations with the nature of what it means to live one's Christian faith outside the walls of the church building. The operative theology of these rites involves nothing less than the commission given in baptism to all Christians to live and preach the Good News in every aspect of their lives.

Dominus vobiscum and its response *Et cum spiritu tuo* is the last of four identical tripartite call-and-response formulations that mark pivotal points in the structure of the liturgy: the greeting of the gathered people (*OM2008*, no. 2), immediately before the proclamation of the gospel (*OM2008*, no. 15), and at the start of the eucharistic prayer (*OM2008*, no. 83). A fifth, roughly similar formulation introduces the rite of peace, *Pax Domini sit semper vobiscum. Et cum spiritu tuo* (*OM2008*, no. 127).[1] This dialogue includes a wish containing an invitation to respond, and the response contains a wish in return. The implied subjunctive in *Dominus vobiscum* shows up explicitly in its altered form, *Pax Domini sit semper vobiscum*, indicating that it is not within human power to make God present to another or to declare that God *is* (indicative mood) present, as if God might not be present without this declaration. The presider's next line, *Benedicat vos omnipotens Deus* (*OM2008*, no. 141, line 7), repeats the subjunctive mood in wishing a blessing upon the assembly. In a certain sense, we humans cannot compel God to be present or to act; we can only offer benevolent wishes to each other,

[1] This would not, however, constitute a particularly significant turning point in the structure of the liturgy.

in the trust-filled expectation that God's presence, whether felt or not, is indeed active in the worship event and never far from us.

Since the presider takes the initiative to issue the invitation and the people in turn respond, this interaction delineates the respective roles of presider and assembly. In each of the previous three instances, this dialogue indicates that something new is about to begin, and indeed at the concluding rites its use signals that the assembly is about to begin a new phase in its worship—the shift from one context to another, from worship within the church to living out one's Christian commitment in all other aspects of one's life.

In a second characteristic signal that the ending is in fact another beginning, the assembly signs themselves with the sign of the cross as at the start of the celebration. Its theological content lies not only in the trinitarian formulation but in the physical gesture that accompanies it—the act of tracing the cross, a silhouette of an instrument of death, upon our own bodies such that the crossing-point lies over our heart.[2] The cross represents our identity as the baptized people of God who have died and risen with Christ and are now, personally and communally, configured to Christ. While at the beginning this expression of our identity marked the depth of our common call to be *ekklesia*, at the conclusion of the liturgy we carry this identity, as problematic as it might become in the concrete and challenging circumstances of our lives, into the larger domains in which we live. The assembly accepts this task—simultaneously a blessing and a task—by responding with "Amen."

The pontifical blessing in its second dialogic exchange (*OM2008*, no. 143) employs the subjunctive to mirror the language implied in the bishop's first line here: *Dominus [sit] vobiscum.* The bishop calls out *Sit nomen Domini benedictum*, to which the people respond with an expansion of that wish: *Ex hoc nunc et usque in saeculum.* The following exchange reverts to the indicative although this is implied in the "call": *Adiutorium nostrum in nomine Domini* (*est*), to which the assembly responds with an affirmation that at the same time takes the form of a simple factual statement, *Qui fecit caelum et terram.* Furthermore, this assembly response implicitly acknowledges that the baptized can only accept this blessing, and the task of being themselves a blessing in the world, through God's sustaining help.

Ite is the common theme of the four options for the deacon's or the priest's commission to the assembly (no. 144). The imperative command is simply to "go" or, more specifically, "go forth." The first, traditional for-

[2] Also see Vincie, 145–46 above.

mulation *Ite, missa est*, simply urges the assembly forth by marking the conclusion of the liturgy. The fourth formulation, *Ite in pace*, conveys less urgency but more depth when linked by association to the idea of Christ as our peace, or the source of peace that passes all understanding (Phil 4:7).

The second and third options present a more specific mission reminiscent of that found in John 15:16, "It was not you who chose me, but I who chose you and appointed you to go and bear fruit that will remain." The third option, *Ite in pace, glorificando vita vestra Dominum*, references the peace of Christ like the fourth. The expansive element here introduces a commission to give glory to God by one's manner of life, both an explicit act of evangelization and a more subtle exhortation to live in such a way that one's life presents a model and an invitation to Christian faith. The second option, *Ite, ad Evangelium Domini annuntiandum* is more forceful and obvious in its specific mission and challenge. The purpose of the dismissal is to enable the people of God to serve as missioners and preachers of the Word of God, in a certain sense, empowered by their own participation in the living presence of God in Word and sacrament. The formulation of this second option may suggest to the well-informed churchgoer that the new evangelization toward contemporary secularized cultures as well as to the unchurched is interlaced here into the mission of the laity.

Whether the action to be undertaken upon departing is specified or left unspecified, the celebration and indeed the grace of the liturgy do not remain inert when the liturgical event draws to a close. Only those who are willing to let themselves become transparent to the Holy Spirit can fulfill the commission entailed in their sending. One might almost say that this being-sent constitutes a *kenosis*, a self-emptying in imitation of that ascribed to Christ in Philippians 2:7-8.[3] This charge is part of the task of "'a chosen race, a royal priesthood, a holy nation, a people of his own, so that you may announce the praises' of him who called you out of darkness into his wonderful light."

[3] Jeremy Driscoll, *What Happens at Mass?* (Chicago: Liturgy Training Publications, 2005), 133–34.

The ICEL2010 Translation

Tom Elich

The English texts for the concluding rites are extremely brief,[1] yet their function is crucial. They form a bridge between liturgy and life, sending forth the gathered church so that Christ present in the celebration of Word and sacrament may continue the work of the Gospel in the world. "The word 'dismissal' has come to imply a 'mission.' These few words succinctly express the missionary nature of the Church."[2]

The assembly is already standing for the prayer after communion and normally would remain standing for any necessary brief announcements allowed under the first rubric in this section (no. 140). The people's posture seems to demand that they be brief. The word *necessariae* ("necessary") is an addition to *MR2002*.[3] Such announcements, which ordinarily refer to events outside the liturgy, already orient people's attention to the transition taking place as they are sent from the Mass to their everyday lives.

In the title of this section, *Ritus* could be singular or plural. ICEL1973 translated it as "Concluding Rite," now changed to "The Concluding Rites," presumably so that it will correspond with "The Introductory Rites." The texts comprise a greeting, blessing, and dismissal,[4] although the rubrics call the ensemble of these concluding rites both "the dismissal" and "the rites of dismissal" (nos. 141 and 146). The texts are given with musical notation,[5] which invite the presider and assembly to sing the dialogue of the concluding rites. The Latin *dicit*, translated in the rubric as "says" (no. 141), can mean says or sings.

[1] *MR1975* had just twenty-two spoken Latin words for the entire section.

[2] Benedict XVI, *SacCar*, no. 51.

[3] *MR1975* had *si habendae sint*, "If there are."

[4] See GIRM2003, no. 90, which also mentions the brief announcements at the beginning and reverencing the altar at the end of the concluding rites. There are no subheadings in the rite itself, although they existed in the ICEL1973; cf. Witzcak, 630 above.

[5] On the absence of these in *MR1975*, see Witczak, 631, n. 15, above.

Greeting (ICEL2010, no. 141, lines 3–5)

The greeting takes the simplest form: "The Lord be with you," followed by the usual response. As at the beginning of Mass (no. 2), the gospel (no. 15), and the dialogue introducing the EP (no. 81), the greeting at this point acknowledges that the assembly is constituted as the Body of Christ (technically the greeting has no verb and is literally rendered "The Lord with you"). The dismissal thus becomes not just a dispersal of individuals but also an ecclesial act, sending forth the church as the Body of Christ to proclaim the kingdom of God in the world.

The rubric "facing the people," repeated at the words of dismissal (no. 144), is a relic of Mass celebrated with the priest facing *ad orientem*;[6] it makes it clear that the concluding rites are directly addressed to the assembly.

Blessing (ICEL2010, no. 141, lines 7–10, and no. 142)

The liturgy of the Mass ends as it began with the invocation of the Trinity. The unchanged translation of this blessing uses the traditional biblical names of Father, Son, and Holy Spirit.[7] The trinitarian formula is more than a dry creedal statement. It expresses the mystery of the Eucharist in which we participate: united in the communion of the Holy Spirit, the church is drawn into the saving event of the death and resurrection of the Son and joins the risen Christ in the eternal praise of the heavenly kingdom by which the Father is adored, praised, and thanked.[8] This trinitarian theology centered on the cross of Christ is reinforced by the sign of the cross that the priest makes over the people. At the beginning of the Mass, priest and people sign themselves with the cross (no. 1); now the cross is offered as a sign of God's blessing invoked on the people.[9]

[6] There may be occasions when the Mass is still celebrated with the priest facing *ad orientem*, in which case the rubric is taken literally, though the GIRM2003 specifies that Mass celebrated "facing the people . . . is desirable whenever possible" (no. 299).

[7] Attempts to reformulate the naming of the Trinity to avoid masculine bias have been firmly rejected by the CDF in relation to the baptismal formula. Baptism in the name of the Creator, Redeemer, and Sanctifier or in the name of the Creator, Liberator, and Sustainer was declared invalid. See *Responses to Questions Proposed on the Validity of Baptism* (1 February 2008), online at http://www.vatican.va/roman_curia/congregations/cfaith/documents/rc_con_cfaith_doc_20080201_validity-baptism_en.html (accessed 22 January 2010).

[8] For a concise statement of the liturgy as the work of the Holy Trinity, see CCC, nos. 1077–1112.

[9] The gesture is not specified in the rubric but is indicated in the text by a ✠. The bishop's blessing includes a threefold cross. The gesture is described in GIRM2003, no. 167.

ICEL1998 had proposed a blessing alternative text for regular use:

> May the blessing of almighty God,
> the Father, and the Son, + and the Holy Spirit,
> come upon you and remain with you for ever.

This text is found in a number of rites and blessings in the liturgical books.[10] In *MR2002* it is generally used as a conclusion for the solemn blessings and prayers over the people. In these places, the last line is now more literally translated, "descend upon you and remain for ever."

A rubric refers to these solemn blessings or prayers over the people that may be used on certain days or occasions (no. 142). The blessing is introduced by the deacon or, in his absence, by the priest.[11] ICEL2008 translated *Inclinate vos ad benedictionem* with the rather abrupt and unhelpful "Bow for the blessing." ICEL2010 improved the text, with "Bow down for the blessing." On the other hand, ICEL1973 had elaborated the instruction unnecessarily—no doubt because the solemn blessing was unfamiliar at the time—with "Bow your heads and pray for God's blessing." ICEL1998 provided an intermediate solution: "Bow your heads for God's blessing."

The collection of twenty solemn blessings is found in *MR2002* after the Order of Mass; there are blessings for the seasons and seasonal feasts, for Ordinary Time, for the celebration of the saints, for the dedication of a church, and Masses for the dead. It is followed by a collection of twenty-eight prayers over the people, mostly for general use.[12] Other solemn blessings are found with the formularies for ritual Masses. The solemn blessings are mostly structured in three parts, each calling for the people's response, "Amen," and then concluding with a trinitarian formula. A detailed examination of these texts lies outside the scope of a commentary on the Order of Mass. The principal difficulty in using these evocative texts has been that there is no verbal cue in the Latin or English texts to facilitate the people's "Amen." It is entirely left to the pace and cadence of the priest's voice. This has not changed in *MR2002* or in ICEL2010.

[10] For example, in the rites of ordination, the rites of anointing and viaticum, and the *Book of Blessings*.

[11] This rubric occurs in the unnumbered section of the Order of Mass titled "Blessings at the End of Mass and Prayers over the People," which follows no. 146.

[12] Only thirteen of the twenty-eight prayers over the people are found in *MR1970*'s collection of twenty-six texts. The Latin texts of the solemn blessings appear to be unchanged from the previous *MR*s.

Episcopal Blessing (ICEL2010, no. 143)

Next, a special form of the blessing is given for the bishop. At a stational Mass, one of the solemn blessings is recommended for the bishop.[13] At other Masses or for more general use, the *CaerEp* gives two forms for a bishop's blessing.[14] The first corresponds to the second Solemn Blessing for Ordinary Time; the second is a particular form of the blessing, which is now included here in *MR2002*. The latter includes the standard greeting, two psalm verses (113:2 and 124:8)—each divided into an invitation and response—and a concluding trinitarian formula.

This episcopal blessing adds an important dimension to the corpus of blessing prayers. All the other blessings take the form of an invocation of God's saving grace upon the assembly. Thus blessed by God, we are enabled to "bless the name of the Lord"; our praise of God is rendered possible by grace. The double movement of this blessing is a recapitulation of the twofold dynamic of the entire eucharistic liturgy. The text of this blessing dialogue with the bishop—only now introduced into the *MR*—is familiar in this 1989 ICEL translation of *CaerEp*, taken over into *MR2002* and, before that (at least in part), from the English-Latin rituals dating back to the 1940s in which virtually every blessing began with the verse from Psalm 124.[15]

Dismissal (ICEL2010, no. 144)

English-speaking worshipers have been accustomed to hearing a number of formulas for the dismissal, even though—until *MR2002*—the only Latin text was *Ite, missa est.*[16] This was because the dismissal was one of the places where ICEL1973 supplied alternative texts in accordance with the provisions of the original charter for liturgical translation, *CLP*.[17] These have disappeared from ICEL2010 and, no doubt, will be missed, especially the very commonly used, "Go in peace to love and serve the Lord."

The 2005 synod of bishops, keen to make more explicit the rapport between Eucharist and mission, recommended new formulas for the dismissal that would underline the mission to the world of those who had partici-

[13] *CaerEp*, no. 169.

[14] Ibid., 1120–21.

[15] A standard example in the United States was *The Roman Ritual in Latin and English*, trans. and ed. Philip Weller, vol. 3: *The Blessings* (Milwaukee, WI: Bruce Publishing, 1946).

[16] To which a double Alleluia is added in Latin and English for Easter, Easter week, and Pentecost.

[17] "Texts translated from another language are clearly not sufficient for the celebration of a fully renewed liturgy. The creation of new texts will be necessary" (*CLP*, no. 43 = DOL 880).

pated in the Eucharist.[18] This recommendation was taken up by Benedict XVI in his post-synodal exhortation *SacCar*:

> The people of God might be helped to understand more clearly this essential [missionary] dimension of the Church's life, taking the dismissal as a starting point. In this context it might also be helpful to provide new texts, duly approved, for the prayer over the people and the final blessing, in order to make this connection clear.[19]

The following year in October 2008, three new formulas for the dismissal were added to the emended version of *MR2002* and are now part of ICEL2010.

In the first alternative, the missionary sense of *ite* is strongly expressed in the phrase, "Go forth." It is more weakly expressed in the second alternative where the directional sense of *ad* is simply rendered by a juxtaposition, "Go and announce the Gospel of the Lord," rather than the more felicitous "Go out to announce the Gospel of the Lord." The third and fourth alternatives use the familiar, "Go in peace," to which the third adds, "glorifying the Lord by your life." The formulas are suitably concise and employ crisp alliterations: "Go . . . Gospel" in the second, and "Go . . . glorifying," "Lord . . . life" in the third. The translation of the people's response, "Thanks be to God," is unchanged. Thus, the final spoken words of the Mass, voiced by the assembly, express the eucharistic motif of thanksgiving, and the two common names "Mass" and "Eucharist" are both referenced in the words of the dismissal.

This dismissal is given to the deacon, if one is present, as also are the brief announcements and the invitation before the solemn blessing or prayer over the people. In these ways he exercises his ministry of guiding the people.[20]

Conclusion (ICEL2010, nos. 145–46)

The final rubrics indicate that the priest kisses the altar as at the beginning of Mass, makes a "profound bow,"[21] and withdraws. There is no mention either in the rubrics or GIRM2003 of a formal procession at the end of Mass or of any singing by the people. If any liturgical action is to

[18] Proposition no. 24.

[19] *SacCar*, no. 51.

[20] See GIRM2003, nos. 171 and 184–86.

[21] The "profound bow" ICEL2010 specifies what ICEL1973 rendered as the "customary reverence."

follow (for example, the final commendation at a funeral Mass), all of the concluding rites (ICEL2010, nos. 140–45) are omitted.

ICEL2010's rendering of the concluding rites is simple and straightforward. It serves well the purpose of the dismissal "that each may go out to do good works, praising and blessing God."[22] It highlights the essential lay vocation to take the Gospel out into the world. "The characteristic of the lay state being a life led in the midst of the world and of secular affairs, lay people are called by God to make of their apostolate, through the vigour of their Christian spirit, a leaven in the world."[23]

[22] GIRM 90.3.

[23] Vatican II, *Apostolicam Actuositatem*, 2.

The Mystagogical Implications

Joyce Ann Zimmerman

Perhaps nothing has been emphasized more strongly since the promulgation of *SC* than its call for full, conscious, and active participation by all during the liturgy (no. 14). This participation includes singing and praying, making earnest responses, changing postures, doing beautiful gestures, and engaging with symbols. Even things as nebulous as attitude, dress, and preparation for worship could be considered part of the participation the council fathers envisioned. No longer can we come to liturgy to pray our own private prayers or to stand in the back on the fringes of what is taking place or to let others do the responding and singing and praying for us.

At first glance it would seem that full, conscious, and active participation in the concluding rites is the easiest of any part of the Mass. There are only three short responses to say: "And with your spirit," "Amen," "Thanks be to God." There is only one gesture, to make the sign of the cross, followed by the action to which everyone wholeheartedly gives themselves over: *leaving*. Yet, to limit our understanding of the concluding rites only to these few words and this leave-taking action is to miss the whole point. Full, conscious, and active participation during Mass engages the whole person: mind, body, spirit. At the concluding rites full, conscious, and active participation engages the whole person as well as all of his or her life. Rather than a mere ending, the concluding rites are an open-ended beginning. And a challenge. And a promise.

We ought not to be fooled by the brevity of the concluding rites. Far more is going on than meets the eye. A careful look at how we experience these rites, how we receive them, and how we appropriate them into our very being is crucial if Mass itself is to be fruitful as the church intends.

Beginning

How can an ending be a beginning? This question opens up our exploration of the meaning of this final part of the Mass. An important point to make clearly is that what is concluding is the Mass, i.e., a ritual action that obviously has a beginning and an ending, each unfolding at a specific time and in a specific sacred space. One of the four formulae for dismissal makes this point clear: "Go forth, the Mass [the ritual event] is ended" (no. 144). So, although we conclude the ritual, our being dismissed does not at all imply that what we have celebrated is not to be continued into how we are to live. Several textual elements hint that this is so.

First, we conclude Mass with two gestures with which we also begin Mass, i.e., the priest (and deacon, if present) venerates the altar with a kiss and the whole assembly makes the sign of the cross. The first gesture is a reminder that the altar is a symbol of Christ in our midst. It was consecrated with Holy Chrism, the same oil used to consecrate all of us in Christ at baptism and confirmation and the priest at his ordination. At the beginning and end of Mass we acknowledge Christ's presence in our midst and express deep affection for Christ and his paschal mystery, which we celebrate.

The other gesture at the beginning and ending of Mass is so common that we can sometimes forget what we are really doing. By signing ourselves with the cross, we are reminded that we have been plunged into Christ's mystery of dying and rising. By naming God Father, Son, and Holy Spirit we remind ourselves that we pray to the Father, through the Son, and in the Holy Spirit.

These two gestures together form what in text interpretation is called an *inclusio*. This means that when words or gestures are repeated in a text, everything in between is considered one unit. Kissing the altar and making the sign of the cross are practical ways to remind us that all the many words, symbols, and gestures of the Mass form one action—that of making present Christ's paschal mystery. Participation in Mass means that we are drawn into Christ's self-giving. But being drawn into Christ's self-giving at Eucharist is only a *beginning*—the self-giving we embrace at Mass becomes a way of daily living that continues after the formal conclusion of the ritual.

Second, the concluding rites may begin with "brief" announcements. This is obviously not a time to read to everyone the weekly bulletin or tell everyone what is already posted on the website. Rather, it is a time to inform the community of important things that concern them, e.g., a newly scheduled funeral or impending parish forum addressing a serious parochial issue. These announcements remind us that our obligation to each other as a Christian community extends beyond the time together at Mass. Already at the announcements we are being reminded of our relationships to each other in Christ, our obligations to have care for each other. Such announcements reinforce that we have been nourished to emulate in our daily living the self-giving that Jesus has once again shown us during this celebration of Mass.

A third element indicating that the ending is really a beginning is that the text of the rite itself indicates that the priest "withdraws" (no. 145), i.e., leaves. Although most parishes and worshiping communities include a recessional hymn, the concluding rites themselves do not prescribe this. It is a practical addition; by singing, the people join with the priest as he withdraws. Of course, after the final hymn (if there is one) the people themselves leave, but they do not "withdraw." While not explicit in the rite, explicit in the ritual's spirituality is the fact that while we physically leave the church building, we actually never *spiritually* leave the Mass. The Eucharist is a life to be lived. Our leave-taking is truly a beginning: by our own reverence of the altar—the table of self-giving—and turning to go, we symbolize our own commitment to live the challenge of the Eucharist.

Challenge

Having been nourished with Christ's Body and Blood and transformed more perfectly into being members of his Body, we are dismissed at the end of the Mass to live what we have celebrated. As Christ continually gives himself and in this glorifies his Father, so are we continually to give of ourselves to others and in this we glorify our Father. The challenge of the concluding rites is to live the Word we have heard and the sacrament we have received.

MR2002 (no. 144) now has four choices for the dismissal. The deacon (or priest in the absence of a deacon), in dialogue with their communities, ought to choose wisely. Each says something quite different in terms of a challenge to us. The first option, "Go forth, the Mass is ended," sends us from church with the reminder that Mass is ended but implies by the "Go forth" that the "work of the people" continues wherever our everyday living leads us. The operative word in this option is "forth."[1] There is no limit to how far and how wide we bring Christ's presence. This would be a good option to choose especially during Ordinary Time, when we walk through one of the Synoptic Gospels Sunday after Sunday, hearing Jesus' teaching, striving to conform our lives to his, knowing full well that our paschal journey takes us with him to Jerusalem and the cross. The "Thanks be to God" is an affirmation that we have grasped that Mass transforms us to be Christ's self-giving presence for others.

[1] Cf. Elich, 643 above.

The second option, "Go and announce the Gospel of the Lord," challenges us to cooperate in the church's evangelizing mission not so much by verbal preaching as through virtuous living. The operative word in this option is "announce." Having celebrated Christ's paschal giving during Mass, our whole being is caught up in his dying and rising such that our every breath announces God's saving deeds. This would be a good option to choose during the manifestation cycle of Advent-Christmas-Epiphany, when we celebrate Jesus coming to dwell among us and his manifestation—now, through us—to all the nations. The "Thanks be to God" is an affirmation that we are willing to show forth for others that Christ now dwells within us.

The next option, "Go in peace, glorifying the Lord by your life," invites us to live out of the peace the risen Lord breathes on us his followers. The operative word here is "peace." Peace always implies right relationships, secured by the loving and caring ways we relate to all those who come into our lives every day, and our right relationship with the earth itself. God is glorified when we live the risen life given to us and bring the peace that embracing Jesus' way of living gives. This would be an effective option to choose during Easter, when we hear so often of Jesus' desire for his followers to share in the peace of his risen life. The "Thanks be to God" is an affirmation that we rejoice in the risen life given us by God and commit ourselves to bring about the justice and peace in our families, workplaces, nations, world that is indicative of Jesus having overcome death to bring us new life.

The fourth and final option is simply "Go in peace." Although this is the shortest and simplest of the four dismissal formulae, we ought not to let its brevity deceive us. In fact, perhaps precisely because of its brevity—only three one-syllable English words!—we ought to be alerted to its power and possibilities. Unlike option three, which shapes what we are to do ("glorifying the Lord by your life"), this last option challenges us to *be* persons of peace. In all we are and do, we ought to exude the silence of the heart that comes from being at one with God. In some respects this dismissal is the most challenging, as well as the one that would take the most catechesis to help the people begin to realize what they are saying in "Thanks be to God." This would be an appropriate option to choose during Lent. Its simplicity is in keeping with the season, but its impulse to be people of peace is also a reminder of what our Lenten conversion is about: turning away from all that takes us from God and turning toward the righteousness and goodness that bring salvation and peace. The "Thanks be to God" is an affirmation that we are committed to be serious peacemakers in a world all too fraught with selfishness and sin.

Promise

With the challenges inherent in being sent forth, we might be discouraged. After all, is not Mass supposed to feed and strengthen us, to comfort and encourage us, to leave us with hope and joy? Yes, Mass does all this, but for a purpose: to unite us with the risen Christ so that we can continue his ministry of bringing goodness and wholeness to others. The good feelings with which we personally might be graced at Mass prompt us to share that joy with others. The experience of community we experience as we sing and pray, respond and gesture together urges us to reach out to the broader communities in which we find ourselves sharing life, sharing a planet. Even on the days when the eucharistic liturgy does not seem to inspire us individually, we still know that God works within us to transform us by divine grace, and this prompts us to reach out to others who seem alone or frightened or overburdened. And when we respond to this gracious eucharistic gift, we are also given a most extraordinary promise.

The sign of the cross we make at the end of Mass is a blessing; it is a promise of God's favor upon us to accomplish that which we are sent forth to live. Sometimes this blessing is preceded by an invitation to "Bow [our] heads for God's blessing," which we do in all humility and expectation. Then we are blessed with a triple form of solemn blessing, asking for God's many gifts to come upon us, to which we respond to each invocation with "Amen." At other times the final blessing is preceded by a prayer over the people, which also asks for God's help to live worthy lives to which each of us responds "Amen." In any of these forms—even in the most simple blessing—the liturgical promise consists of an assurance that we are never left alone, that God is always with us to accompany us on our journey of living the gospel, and that all we are able to accomplish is because God is ready with the grace for us to persevere. As we reflect on such a promise, we ought to raise our voices in a full-throated "Amen."

Because the final blessing promises God's abiding presence and help, another promise is inherent in it. The celebration of Mass is but one graced moment in the lifelong journey of followers of Jesus. The journey of the liturgical year and of our whole Christian life is one toward eschatological fulfillment. One day we will stand at the Messianic table in heaven and forever sing God's praises, forever be filled to overflowing with God's eternal presence. The dismissal and blessing concluding Mass are poignant reminders that we are sent forth to travel persistently and in goodness and love toward our final destination.

Conclusion

The final words (excluding the closing hymn) we say as a community at the end of the concluding rites are "Thanks be to God." How resounding ought that sentiment be! Our thanksgiving includes not only the many gifts we have experienced during this Mass but also a heartfelt eagerness to live what we have celebrated. Our hearts are raised in thanksgiving because we are invited to share in Jesus' saving mission to all those we meet in our daily living.

The concluding rites are short and sweet, filled with challenge and promise. As each of us begins to appreciate all that happens in these few minutes, we are also called to help others experience more deeply what takes place as we are blessed and dismissed. Each of us is to be a catechist—even a missionary—helping our family and friends, those members of the Body of Christ with whom we worship, come to a deeper appreciation of the privilege it is to share in Jesus' saving mission. We ask God to bless us as we are sent forth with a strong command: an unambiguous "Go"! Let us respond with purpose and conviction. Let us respond with eagerness and joy. Let us go into the world equipped to bring God's saving presence to all those we meet.

Contributors

John Baldovin, SJ, is professor of historical and liturgical theology at the Boston College School of Theology and Ministry.

Anscar J. Chupungco, OSB, is former professor of liturgy and president of the Pontifical Liturgical Institute in Rome, consultor to the Sacred Congregations of Divine Worship and the Sacraments, and currently on the staff of the Paul VI Institute of Liturgy in Manila, which he helped found.

Mary Collins, OSB, is professor emerita at The Catholic University of America School of Theology and Religious Studies, Washington DC.

Tom Elich, the director of The Liturgical Commission and a parish priest in Brisbane, Australia, is an honorary fellow at Australian Catholic University.

Edward Foley, Capuchin, is the Duns Scotus Professor of Spirituality and professor of liturgy and music at Catholic Theological Union in Chicago.

Richard E. McCarron is associate professor of liturgy at Catholic Theological Union in Chicago.

Nathan D. Mitchell is professor of theology at the University of Notre Dame.

Gilbert Ostdiek, OFM, is professor of liturgy at Catholic Theological Union in Chicago.

Keith F. Pecklers, SJ, is professor of liturgy at the Pontifical Gregorian University in Rome and professor of liturgical history at the Pontifical Liturgical Institute in Rome.

Joanne M. Pierce is associate professor in the Department of Religious Studies at the College of the Holy Cross in Worcester, Massachusetts.

David N. Power, OMI, is professor emeritus at The Catholic University of America, currently working in an Oblate formation community in Lusaka, Zambia.

Patrick Regan, OSB, is a Benedictine from Saint Joseph Abbey in Louisiana and professor emeritus at the Pontifical Athenaeum of Saint Anselm in Rome.

Susan K. Roll is associate professor in the Faculty of Theology, Saint Paul University in Ottawa, Canada.

John F. Romano is assistant professor of history at Benedictine College in Atchison, Kansas.

Dominic Serra is associate professor and director of the graduate program in liturgical studies and sacramental theology at the Catholic University of America, Washington DC.

Catherine Vincie is professor of liturgical and sacramental theology at the Aquinas Institute of Theology in St. Louis, Missouri.

Mark E. Wedig, OP, is professor and chair in the Department of Theology and Philosophy and associate dean for graduate studies in the College of Arts and Sciences at Barry University in Miami Shores, Florida.

Michael Witczak is an assistant professor of liturgical studies at the Catholic University of America in Washington DC, and a priest of the Archdiocese of Milwaukee.

Demetrio S. Yocum is an affiliate scholar at the Department of Theology of the University of Notre Dame.

Joyce Ann Zimmerman, CPPS, is the director of the Institute for Liturgical Ministry in Dayton, Ohio.

Scriptural Index

Index of Proper Names

General Index